THE THIRD REICH FROM ORIGINAL SOURCES

THE NUREMBERG TRIALS

THE COMPLETE PROCEEDINGS

Vol 5 : The Concentration Camps

21st January-1st February 1946

Edited and introduced by Bob Carruthers

BOOKS LTD

This edition published in Great Britain in 2012 by
Coda Books Ltd, Office Suite 2, Shrieves Walk, 39 Sheep Street,
Stratford upon Avon, Warwickshire CV37 6GJ
www.codabooks.com

Copyright © 2012 Coda Books Ltd

All rights reserved. No part of this publication may be reproduced or transmitted in any form or by any means, electronic or mechanical, including photocopy, recording, or any information storage and retrieval system, without permission in writing from the publisher.

A CIP catalogue record for this book is available from the British Library

ISBN 978 1 78158 030 1

Originally published as
"The Trial of German Major War Criminals
Proceedings of the International Military Tribunal
Sitting at Nuremberg, Germany"
under the authority of
H.M. Attorney-General by His Majesty's Stationery Office
London : 1946

CONTENTS

Introduction 4

Thirty-ninth day: Monday, 21st January, 1946 7

Fortieth day: Tuesday, 22nd January, 1946 48

Forty-first day: Wednesday, 23rd January, 1946 86

Forty-second day: Thursday, 24th January, 1946 127

Forty-third day: Friday, 25th January, 1946 162

Forty-fourth day: Monday, 28th January, 1946 194

Forty-fifth day: Tuesday, 29th January, 1946 239

Forty-sixth day: Wednesday, 30th January, 1946 284

Forty-seventh day: Thursday, 31st January, 1946 315

Forty-eighth day: Friday, 1st February, 1946 353

About Coda Books 395

Introduction

The trial of the German major war criminals is better known to posterity as the Nuremberg Trials. This was a revolutionary new form of justice which was without parallel in the history of warfare.

In the wake of six years of savagery, inhumanity and turmoil it was sensed that a series of summary executions would not bring closure to the years of violence which had seen unheralded scenes of brutality as civilian populations were targeted for bombardment on a scale never before witnessed.

In 1945, faced with the stark evidence of the appalling crimes against humanity committed by the Nazi regime, there was an understandable clamour, particularly from the Soviet camp, for a series of quick summary executions to draw the line under the past and allow the world to get back to civilised behaviour. Given the scale of the crimes and the gruesome evidence emerging from Dachau, Auschwitz and Bergen-Belsen, it was certainly difficult to argue against making a rapid example of men like Hermann Göring, the father of the Gestapo.

Fortunately clearer heads prevailed and it was felt necessary to create some form of judicial process which would mark the transition back from barbarism to the rule of law. However there was then no such thing as an international court and there was no precedent for the legal trial of defeated belligerents. The plan for the "Trial of European War Criminals" was therefore drafted by Secretary of War Henry L. Stimson and the War Department. Following Roosevelt's death in April 1945, the new president, Harry S. Truman, gave strong approval for a judicial process. After a series of negotiations between Britain, the US, the Soviet Union and France, details of the trial were finally agreed. The trials were to commence on 20th November 1945, in the Bavarian city of Nuremberg.

At the meetings in Potsdam (1945), the three major wartime powers, the United Kingdom, the United States, and the Union of Soviet Socialist Republics finally agreed on the principles of punishment for 4those responsible for war crimes during World War II. France was also awarded a place on the tribunal.

The legal basis for the trial was established by the London Charter, issued on August 8th, 1945, which restricted the trial to "punishment of the major war criminals of the European Axis countries". Some 200 German war crimes defendants were ultimately tried at Nuremberg, and 1,600 others were tried under the traditional channels of military justice. The legal basis for the jurisdiction of the court was that defined by the Instrument of Surrender of Germany. Political authority for Germany had been transferred to the Allied Control Council which, having sovereign power over Germany, could choose to punish violations of international law and the laws of war. Because the court was limited to violations of the laws of war, it did not have jurisdiction over crimes that took place before the outbreak of war on September 3rd, 1939.

Leipzig, Munich and Luxembourg were briefly considered as the location for the trial. The Soviet Union had wanted the trials to take place in Berlin, as the capital city of the 'fascist conspirators', but Nuremberg was chosen as the site for the trials for two specific reasons: firstly because the Palace of Justice was spacious and largely undamaged (one of the few civic buildings that had remained largely intact through extensive Allied bombing), and secondly that a large prison was also part of the complex.

Nuremberg was also considered the ceremonial birthplace of the Nazi Party, and hosted annual rallies. It was thus considered a fitting place to mark the Party's symbolic demise.

As a compromise with the Soviet Union, it was agreed that while the location of the trial would be Nuremberg, Berlin would be the official home of the Tribunal authorities. It was also agreed that France would become the permanent seat of the IMT and that the first trial (several were planned) would take place in Nuremberg.

Each of the four countries provided one judge and an alternate, as well as a prosecutor.
- Major General Iona Nikitchenko (Soviet main)
- Lieutenant Colonel Alexander Volchkov (Soviet alternate)
- Colonel Sir Geoffrey Lawrence (British main and president)
- Sir Norman Birkett (British alternate)
- Francis Biddle (American main)
- John J. Parker (American alternate)
- Professor Henri Donnedieu de Vabres (French main)
- Robert Falco (French alternate)
- The chief prosecutors were as follows
- Attorney General Sir Hartley Shawcross (United Kingdom)
- Supreme Court Justice Robert H. Jackson (United States)
- Lieutenant-General Roman Andreyevich Rudenko (Soviet Union)
- François de Menthon (France)

Assisting Jackson was the lawyer Telford Taylor, Thomas J. Dodd and a young US Army interpreter named Richard Sonnenfeldt. Assisting Shawcross were Major Sir David Maxwell-Fyfe and Sir John Wheeler-Bennett. Mervyn Griffith-Jones, later to become famous as the chief prosecutor in the Lady Chatterley's Lover obscenity trial, was also on Shawcross's team. Shawcross also recruited a young barrister, Anthony Marreco, who was the son of a friend of his, to help the British team with the heavy workload. Assisting de Menthon was Auguste Champetier de Ribes.

The International Military Tribunal was opened on October 18th, 1945, in the Palace of Justice in Nuremberg. The first session was presided over by the Soviet judge, Nikitchenko. The prosecution entered indictments against 24 major war criminals and six criminal organizations – the leadership of the Nazi party, the Schutzstaffel (SS) and Sicherheitsdienst (SD), the Gestapo, the Sturmabteilung (SA) and the "General Staff and High Command," comprising several categories of senior military officers.

The indictments were for:
- Participation in a common plan or conspiracy for the accomplishment of a crime against peace
- Planning, initiating and waging wars of aggression and other crimes against peace
- War crimes
- Crimes against humanity

Under the circumstances the Proceedings of the International Military Tribunal just about passes muster as an exercise in establishing a platform from which to dispense a reasonably balanced form of justice. There was, of course, the questionable involvement of Stalin's legal team and it was ironic that his crimes against peace and humanity matched, if not surpassed those of Adolf Hitler. Ribbentrop and Molotov between them had secretly carved up Poland and in so doing had certainly been guilty of crimes against peace, planning war. Stalin had also waged an aggressive was against Finland and had annexed the Baltic States. Had

Stalin been on trial his own actions would have condemned him to a guilty verdict on all four counts, but history is always written by the victors, and Stalin's crimes were airbrushed out of history in order that his team could sit in judgement as if nothing untoward had ever happened.

It has been asked many times were the trials fair. In strict legal terms they certainly were not. Declaring the instruments of the Nazi state to be illegal was illogical and unreasonable, but this was certainly no Stalinist show trial with a guilty verdict and a hangman's noose already awaiting the defendants. Under the circumstances the court was incredibly well balanced as was evidenced by the fact that three of the Defendants were acquitted and others received comparatively light sentences. Of the twenty-four accused only twelve received death sentences.

Ultimately the process had its flaws but it did provide a civilised alternative to Stalin's suggestion that 50,000 to 100,000 German officers should be executed without trial, and it was to serve as a forerunner for the International Court now located at the Hague.

This is the fifth volume in the complete proceedings of the Nuremberg trial of the German major war criminals before the International Military Tribunal sitting at Nuremberg, Germany.

Taken from the original court transcript this volume covers the proceedings from 21st January to 1st February 1946 and represents an essential primary source for scholars and general readers alike. The transcripts are complete and contain the whole of the proceedings as taken from the original court documents.

This volume finalises the evidence of systematic economic looting and its effect on national wealth and public health by the Germans in the occupied countries of Denmark, Norway, the Netherlands, Belgium, Luxembourg and France.

It then presents the case of the individual responsibility of the Defendants Hans Fritsche, Franz von Papen and Constantin von Neurath, and their complicity in aggressive action against sovereign states, War Crimes and Crimes against Humanity. It also includes evidence and testimony of the torture and summary execution of French hostages as reprisals against resistance, and the uniform use of extreme cruelty to gain confessions. It proceeds to show the written evidence of the official Nazi policy of inhuman treatment of prisoners of war, including internment in concentration camps, massacres of captives and lynching of Allied airmen.

This volume includes, among others, the harrowing oral evidence of Maurice Lampe who was incarcerated in Mauthausen Concentration Camp and was tortured by the SS and Gestapo and Mme Claude Vaillant Courturier, a member of the French Resistance who was sent to Auschwitz and Ravenbruck. Dr Alfred Balachowsky gives his evidence on the medical experiments at Buchenwald.

This volume concludes with the policy of Germanization of annexed territories, including the elimination of sovereign law, language, the imposition of German nationality and the expulsion of undesirables and seizure of their property.

Bob Carruthers

Thirty-ninth day:
Monday, 21st January, 1946

M. GERTHOFFER: Mr. President, Your Honours: At the end of the last session I had the honour of beginning the account of the French prosecution on the economic pillage. In the first chapter I had indicated to you succinctly, how the Germans had become masters of the means of payment in the occupied countries, by imposing war tributes under the pretext of maintaining their Army of Occupation, and by imposing so-called clearing accords, functioning to their benefit almost exclusively.

In a second chapter, entitled "Subjection of Productivity in the Occupied Territories," I had the honour of expounding to you that, after the invasion, the factories were under military guard and that German technicians proceeded to transfer the best machinery to the Reich; that the working population, having come to the end of their resources, grouped themselves around the factories to ask for subsidies; and, finally, that the Germans had ordered the resumption of work and had reserved for themselves the right to designate provisional administrators to direct the enterprises.

At the same time, the Germans exercised pressure over the rulers of the occupied countries and over the industrialists, to bring the factories back to productivity.

In certain cases they themselves placed provisional German administrators in charge, and insinuated that the factories would be utilised for the needs of the occupied populations.

On the whole, to avoid unemployment and to maintain their means of production, the industrialists, little by little, resumed their work; trying to specialise in the manufacture of objects destined for the civilian population.

Resorting to various means of pressure, the Germans imposed the manufacture of defensive and then, progressively, of offensive armaments. They requisitioned certain enterprises, shut down those which they did not consider essential, themselves distributed raw materials and placed controllers in the factories.

The German control and seizure continually expanded in conformity with secret directives given by the defendant Goering himself, as can be seen in a document dated 2 August 1940, discovered by the Army of the United States, which bears the number EC-137 and which I place before the Tribunal under Exhibit RF 105. This is the essential passage of the document:

> "The extension of the German influence over foreign enterprises is an objective of German political economy. It is not yet possible to determine whether and to what extent the, Peace Treaty will effect the yielding of shares. It is essential, however, to exploit at once every opportunity to allow German economy, in time of war, to obtain access to interesting objectives of the economy of occupied territories, and to prevent any movement of capital which might hinder the realisation of the above-mentioned objective."

After becoming acquainted with such a document, no further doubt is possible as to the intentions of the German rulers. The proof of the putting into execution of such a plan is clear from a German document, which will be read when the particular case of France is called upon in the course of this expose.

The Tribunal will be able to study Michel, the Chief of the Administrative General Staff on Economic Questions, connected with the German military command in

France, who exposes the extent of the dictatorship of the Reich over the occupied countries in economic matters. The control of the enterprises in occupied countries was assured by civil or military officials who were on the spot, and also, later, by similar German enterprises which had become their Paten- Firma or home establishment.

To give an example of this economic domination here are the orders received by an important French company. This is the Thomson-Houston house, and I present a letter to the Tribunal under Number 106 in the French documentation, which is addressed to this establishment. It is dated Paris, 8 October 1943, to Societe des Procedes Thomson-Houston, 173 Boulevard Haussmann:

> "You are fully responsible for the punctual execution and carrying out of the German orders which are passed to you, as well as towards the person giving the orders in my office, which is the establishment responsible for all orders given to France.
>
> To facilitate for you the execution of your obligations, the firm: Allgemeine Elektricitaets Gesellschaft, Berlin, NW40, Friederich Karl Ufer 2-4, is designated by me as the Paten-Firma. I attach the greatest importance to your working in a close comradeship on the technical level with the above-mentioned firm. The Paten-Firma will have the following functions:
>
>> 1. To cooperate in the establishment of your production plan, and to utilise your capacities.
>>
>> 2. To keep itself at your disposal for all technical advice which you might need, and to exchange information with you.
>>
>> 3. To serve as an intermediary when there is a case for negotiations with German services.
>>
>> 4. To keep me informed as to anything that might occur that might prevent or limit the accomplishment of your obligations.
>
> In order to ensure these tasks, the Paten-Firma is authorised to delegate a Firmenbeauftragter to your firm and, when necessary, technical engineers from other German firms who may have handed you important orders.
>
> In order to permit the Paten-Firma to accomplish its task it will be necessary to give the firm, or its Firmenbeauftragter, the necessary authorisation on everything that relates to the German orders and to their execution:
>
>> 1. By placing at its disposal your correspondence with your supply houses and with your subcontractors;
>>
>> 2. By informing it of the manner in which the capacities of your factories are being utilised, and permitting it to check on the production;
>>
>> 3. By informing it of your connections and communicating to it your correspondence with the German services.
>
> It is your duty to inform the Paten-Firma or their Firmenbeauftragter to any orders which you may receive."

This is the end of the quotation.

Almost all the important enterprises were thus placed under the control of German firms in the occupied territories, with the double aim of favouring the Reich war effort and of achieving by progressive absorption an economic preponderance in Europe, even in case of a peace by compromise.

In the agricultural domain the Germans used similar means of pressure. They made wholesale requisitions of produce, leaving the population only grossly insufficient quantities to assure their subsistence.

I now take up the third chapter, devoted to individual purchases by the German military or civilian forces in the occupied countries.

If this presentation cannot take up individual acts of pillage or the numerous thefts committed in the occupied countries, it is important nevertheless to mention the individual purchases, these having been organised methodically by the German rulers to the benefit of their own nationals.

At the beginning of the occupation the soldiers or civilians effected purchases by means of vouchers of doubtful authenticity which had been handed to them by their superiors; but presently the Germans had at their disposal a quantity of money sufficient to allow them to purchase without any kind of rationing or by means of special vouchers considerable quantities of agricultural produce or of goods of all kinds, notably textiles, shoes, furs, leather goods, etc. It was thus, for instance, that certain shoe establishments were obliged every week to sell, in exchange for special German vouchers, 300 pairs of shoes for city use, for men, women and children.

This is indicated in an important report of the French economic control, which I will have occasion to refer to several times in the course of this presentation and which I submit to the Tribunal under Number 197.

The individual purchases which constitute a form of economic pillage were, I repeat, not only authorised but organised by the German rulers. In fact, when the Germans returned to their country they were encumbered by voluminous baggage. A package-sending postal service had been created by the Germans for the benefit of Germans living in the occupied countries. The objects were wrapped in a special kind of paper and provided with seals that granted them a customs franchise, before their entry into Germany.

In order to get an idea of the volume of the individual purchases, it is important to refer to the declaration of one Murdrel, ex-director of the Reichskreditkasse actually detained in Paris, who was heard before an examining Magistrate of the Court de Justice de la Seine on the 29th of October, 1945. This is the declaration made by Murdrel on the subject of individual purchases. The Judge asked him the following questions:

> "What were the needs of the army of occupation? What purchases did you have to make on its account?"

This will be Exhibit RF 108, Mr. President, the testimony of Murdel.

THE PRESIDENT: What are you doing about 107? Are you quoting from 107?

M. GERTHOFFER: Exhibit 107 is a report of the Economic Control -

THE PRESIDENT: You are asking the Tribunal to take judicial notice of that, are you?

M. GERTHOFFER: I submit it to the Tribunal, and I shall make readings from it from time to time in the course of my declaration.

THE PRESIDENT: And now you are going to read 108?

M. GERTHOFFER: Yes, I shall make readings from 108, on Page 9.

The judge asked Murdel the following questions:

> "What were the needs of the Army of occupation? What purchases did you have to make on its account?"

The answer: "It is impossible for me to answer the first part of the question. I had tried during the occupation to inform myself on this point, but it was objected that this was a military secret which I had no right to know. What I can tell you is that we settled the pay of the troops, and that a private earned from 50 to 60 Marks, a non-commissioned officer 50 per cent more, and an officer considerably more. Naturally, I have no idea of the forces that the occupation army may have included, as these forces were extremely variable."

I omit a few lines to make this shorter. Murdel adds:

"Aside from this, every soldier on leave returning from Germany had the right to bring back with him a certain number of marks-50. The same held good for any German soldier who was stationed for the first time in France. We made the exchange of marks for French francs. I calculate that the total amount that we paid over each month in this way was 5 billion francs.

That is the end of the quotation.

One may thus calculate that a sum of about 250 billion francs, at least, was spent individually in France by the Germans, of which the greater portion was employed for the purchase of products and objects sent to Germany, to the detriment of the French population.

To assess the importance of this amount, I would say that about 5 billion francs a month, in other words 60 billion francs a year, is greater than the budgetary receipts of the French budget in 1938, since this was only 54 billion francs per year.

After having studied the individual purchases, I shall launch upon a fourth chapter, devoted to the organisation of the black market by the Germans in the occupied territories. The population of the occupied countries had been subjected to a severe rationing of products of all kinds. They had been left only grossly insufficient quantities for their own vital needs. This left free a large quantity of the stock and of the production which the Germans seized by means of operations that were, to all appearances, regular, (requisitions, purchases by official services, individual purchases or in exchange for vouchers of German priority). We have just seen that these purchases represented, for France only, an average of five billion francs per month.

But such a regulation had, as its corollary, a concealment of merchandise and of products, the purpose being to keep them from the Germans. This state of things gave birth, in the occupied countries, to what was called the "black market," that is to say, secret purchases made in violation of rationing regulations.

The Germans themselves were not slow in buying in the black market, to an even greater extent, usually through agents and sub-agents, recruited amongst the most doubtful elements of the population, who were charged with finding where these products could be picked up.

These agents, compromised by reason of their violations of the rationing legislation, benefited by a total immunity; but they were constantly under the threat of denunciations on the part of their German employers in case they should slow up or stop their activity. Often these agents also fulfilled functions for the Gestapo and were paid for the services by commissions, which they obtained on the black market.

The different German organisations in the occupied countries got into the habit of making secret purchases that became increasingly important in volume. Indeed they began to compete amongst themselves for this merchandise, and the chief result of this competition was a rise in prices, which threatened to bring about inflation. The Germans, of course, while they continued to profit by the secret purchases, were anxious that the money which they utilised should maintain as high a value as possible.

To obviate such a situation, the rulers of the Reich decided in June 1942 to organise purchases on the black market methodically. Thus the defendant Goering, the "Plenipotentiary of the Four-Year Plan," on the 13th June, 1942, gave Colonel J. Veltjens, the task of centralising the structure of the black market in the occupied countries.

This fact is proved from a document discovered by the Army of the United States, which I submit to you as Exhibit RF 109. This includes three documents, one of them being the nomination of Colonel Veltjens signed by the defendant Goering. I do not want to waste the time of the Tribunal by giving a complete reading of these documents. I do not think they can be contested, but should they be so, later, I should reserve for myself the privilege of reading them then, unless the Tribunal would prefer I do so now.

THE PRESIDENT: I am afraid we must adhere to our ruling that those documents of which we cannot take judicial notice must be read if they are to be put in evidence. You need only read the portions of the document which you require to put in evidence, not necessarily the formal parts, but the substantial parts which you require for the purpose of your proof.

M. GERTHOFFER: This is the letter of the 13th of June, 1942, signed by the defendant Goering:

> "The purchases of merchandise affected simultaneously by the different organisations of the Wehrmacht and by other organisations have, in some of the occupied territories, created on the so-called black market, a situation which disturbs the methodical exploitation of these countries for the needs of the German war economy and is also harmful to the prestige indispensable to any military or civilian administration. This deplorable state of things can no longer be tolerated. I therefore charge you to regularise these commercial transactions in accordance with the services that are involved and, particularly, with the Chiefs of the Administration of the occupied territories. In principle, commercial transactions in the occupied territories that are affected outside the framework of the normal provisioning, or constitute a violation of price regulations, must be limited to special cases, and carried out only if your assent has been given. I approve your proposal to use the units controlled by the Reich and, above all, among these, the R.O.G.E.S., for the removal of merchandise.
>
> I beg you to submit, at the earliest possible date, a plan of work for putting into effect your activity in Holland, in Belgium, in France and Serbia. (In Serbia it is Consul General Neuhausen who is to be in charge). This plan must involve, in addition to the seizure of port installations, the utilisation of enterprises whose closing may be envisaged in occupied territories. As to the results of your activity, I beg you to submit a report to me every month, through my representative. The first of such reports is to be submitted to me on July 1st, 1942.
>
> If necessary, it will be the "Central Service of the Plan" to make decisions concerning the distribution of merchandise thus purchased.
>
> (Signed) Goering."

Thereupon, on September 4th, 1942, the defendant Goering gave orders for the complete gathering together of all the merchandise that could be utilised, even if this should result in signs of inflation in the occupied territories. This is brought out by a report signed "Wiehl," referring to the utilisation of funds derived from occupation expenses. I submit this to the Tribunal, as Exhibit RF 110.

Shortly after, on 4 October, 1942, the defendant Goering made a speech on the occasion of the Harvest Festival - a speech that is reported in "Das Archiv" of October 1942, Number 103, Page 645. In this speech he clearly showed that he meant purchases on the black market in the occupied countries to continue for the benefit of the German population. I submit a copy of this article as Exhibit RF 111 and I quote from the following passage:

> "I have examined with very special attention the situation in the occupied countries. I have seen how the people lived in Holland, in Belgium, in France, in Norway, in Poland and in every place where we have become settled. I have noticed that although very often their propaganda spoke officially of their food situation being difficult, in point of fact this was far from being the case. No doubt everywhere, even in France, the system of ration cards has been introduced, but what one is able to obtain in exchange for these ration cards is but a supplement, and people live normally on illegal commerce.
>
> This state of things has caused me to make a firm decision, a principle which I shall relinquish under no pretext. The task which must come before all others is to ensure to the German people the first place in the battle against hunger and in the problem of food supply. This is why I have decided that, in territories which have been conquered and placed under our protection, the population shall no longer suffer from hunger. But if the enemy should get the idea of opposing our policy of food supply, it is then necessary that all should know that if there is to be famine anywhere it shall in no case be in Germany."

The United States Army has discovered a secret report, made on the 15th of January, 1943 by Col. Veltjens, in which he gives to the defendant Goering an account of his activity over a period of six months. This is Document 1765-PS, which I submit now to the Tribunal as Exhibit RF 112. It is not possible for me to give a complete reading of this report, so I shall read only certain passages from it.

In the first part of his report Veltjens explains the reasons for the rise of the black market in these terms:

> "(a) The reduction in merchandise as a result of the regulations and rationing.
> (b) The impossibility of making an effective blocking of our maintenance of prices.
> (c) The impossibility of making an adequate survey of prices, on the German model, by reason of the lack of personnel in the surveillance organisations.
> (d) The neglect in the appliance of counter-measures on the part of the local administrative authorities, especially in France.
> (e) The imperfect penal justice of the local judiciary authorities.
> (f) The lack of discipline amongst the civilian population."

Then under the same number (f), a little further, Veltjens indicates:

> "The activity of the German services on the black market assumed little by little such dimensions that it created more and more unendurable situations. It was known that the black market operators offered their merchandise to several Bureaus at the same time and that it was one which offered the highest price who obtained it. Thus, the different German formations not only vied with each other in obtaining the merchandise, but also caused the prices to rise."

Further on in his report, Veltjens indicates that he has assumed the leadership of the service created for the "Four-Year-Plan" Office in these terms:

> "Finally, in June 1942, in accord with all the central services, the delegates

for the Special Missions, (B.F.S.), were charged with taking in hand the seizure and the direction of the black market. Thus, for the first time, was fulfilled the first necessary condition for effectively dealing with the problem of the black market."

In the second part of his report, Veltjens expounds the advantages of the organisation in charge of which he was placed and he writes, among other things:

"It has been claimed that purchases on the black market in their present volume and at the existing prices, became in the long run too much for the budget of the Reich. One could answer that by saying that the greater part of the purchases effected took place in France, and were financed by occupation costs. Thus, for purchases to the total amount of Rm 1.107.792.819, an amount of Rm 929,100,000 were charged to the French for occupation costs, and in no way were put on the account of the Reich budget."

After having indicated the conveniences of the black market, Veltjens concluded:

"In recapitulating, it must be recognised that the food situation of the Reich no longer makes it possible to do without purchases in the black market, even though this has nearly been exhausted, as long as there are hidden stocks to be utilised for the conduct of the war. To this vital interest all other considerations must be subordinated."

In a third part of this same report, Veltjens deals with the technical organisation of his bureaus. Here are some interesting passages:

"The General Directorate of the supervision specially organised for this purpose, i.e.:
  (a) supervisory service in France, with headquarters in Paris.
  (b) supervisory service in Belgium and North of France, headquarters in Bruxelles.
  (c) supervisory service in Belgium and in North of France, auxiliary service Lille, with headquarters in Lille.
  (d) supervisory service in Holland with headquarters in the Hague.
  (e) supervisory service in Serbia with headquarters in Belgrade.

Then Veltjens tells us that the purchases were carried out by a restricted number of licensed purchasing organisations, i.e. 11 for France, 6 for Belgium, 6 for Holland, 3 for Serbia.

"It is thus (he writes) that all the purchases are subject to the central surveillance of the delegate for the "Special Missions."

Further on Veltjens adds:

"The financing of the purchases and the transport of merchandise are effected by the R.O.G.E.S. of the Reich. The merchandise is then distributed in the Reich by the R.O.G.E.S. in conformity with the instructions of the Central Plan, or by departments designated to the Central Plan, and each time in order of the emergency of the needs of the different qualified services."

In the fourth section of his report Veltjens mentions the volume of the operations affected up to November 30, 1942, that is to say in less than five months, since his organisation had not begun its activity earlier than July 1st, 1942. Here are the figures that Veltjens gives:

"The volume of purchases made:
  (a) Since the inauguration of the purchases directed by the German commander or the Reich Commissar, and of the directed distribution of

merchandise in the Reich, there has been purchased a total of 1,107,792,818, 64 Reichsmark. In France, total amount of 929,100,000, Reichsmark; in Belgium 103,880,929, Reichsmark: in Holland 73,685,162, 64 Reichsmark; and in Serbia 1, 125,727, Reichsmark."

Veltjens adds:

"The regulation has been carried out in France on the basis of the occupation costs and in the other countries by means of the clearing device."

Then Veltjens gives a table of merchandise purchased in this way over the period of these five months. I shall give merely a summary to the Tribunal.

(1) Metals - 66,202 tons for a value of 273,078,287 Reichsmark

(2) Textiles, for a total value of 439,040,000, Reichsmark

(3) Leather, skins and hides to a total value of 120,754,000, Reichsmark.

Veltjens adds:

Besides these purchases there have been the following: Oils and industrial fats, oils and fats for consumers, wool, household articles, mess articles, wines and spirits, engineering equipment, sanitary articles, bags etc.

He then gives a table of the increase in prices during the five months. Then he states the principle that the black market must be used solely for the benefit of Germany, and must be severely repressed when it is used by the populations of the occupied countries. On this subject he actually writes:

"1. Develop the control of prices. Inasmuch as reinforcement of a control personnel, of a German control personnel is not possible, or is possible only to a limited extent, it will be necessary to obtain from the local administration authorities a greater activity, greater zeal, in this realm.

2. Apply severe penalties, according to the German methods, for violations of regulations. This is, indeed, the only means of finding a remedy for the lack of discipline of the populations, a lack of discipline which can be traced to their individualistic and liberal ideas and ways. A control of the sentences that have been passed by the local tribunals seems to be indicated.

3. The promise of a reward in case of denunciation of the violations. The amounts of these rewards should be sufficiently high, in relation to the value of the goods which are involved in the denunciation, and which have lead to their seizure.

4. The hiring of spies and of agents provocateurs.

5. Arrest or stoppage of all businesses that are not working for the war industry.

6. Stoppage or fusion of businesses whose capacity or production is only being partly exploited.

7. Increased control of the productivity of plants.

8. Close examination of the quantity of raw materials to be distributed at the moment of transfer of the market.

9. Policy of prices which affords the businesses sufficient benefits and are of a nature to guarantee an adequate price level."

Examining the demands of the rulers of the occupied countries with relation to the German purchases on the black market, Veltjens writes:

"In the recent period, the French and Belgian economic governmental circles, among others the chief of the French Government himself, have complained about purchases methodically carried out by the Germans. In response to protests of this kind, it should be observed, without prejudice to other arguments that, on the part of the Germans too, there is naturally the greatest interest in the disappearance of the black market, but that the chief responsibility for its persistence falls upon the governmental authorities themselves by reason of the incapacity which they show in controlling prices, and the weakness which they show in judiciary punishment of violations, whereby they encourage the spirit of rebellion, and lack of discipline of the population."

The Tribunal will allow me to stress the value of the argument developed by Veltjens by reminding it that the Germans were the principal purchasers on the black market, and that their agents benefited from it by complete immunity.

Finally, speaking of the machines in the factories, Veltjens writes in his report:

"The delegate to the special missions has moreover the duty of arranging for the recuperation of machines in inactive factories. Machines which thus are not in use, in particular tool machines, of which Germany has an urgent need for its war production, are extremely numerous. After an agreement among the delegates of special missions, the military commander and the plenipotentiary of machine production, there has been created in France, at the armament inspection service, a service for the for the distribution of machines (Maschinenausgleichstelle).

The creation of a distribution service of machines which is comparable to this is provided for Belgium and Holland. One must expect to meet a serious resistance in this direction, on the part of the owners of factories as well as on the part of the local governmental authorities.

The occupation authorities will have to use every means to break this resistance."

In conclusion, Veltjens alludes in his report to the R.O.G.E.S., which was a specialised organisation for the transport to Germany of the booty captured in occupied countries, and, more particularly, of produce obtained by operations in the black market.

Ranis, one of the directors of this service, was interrogated on the 1st of November, 1945, and declared in substance "that the R.O.G.E.S. had begun its activity in February 1941, succeeding another organisation."

On the whole he confirms the facts that are reported in Veltjens' report. I shall therefore simply submit his interrogatories before the Tribunal as Exhibit RF 113.

The scope of the operations on the black market -

THE PRESIDENT: Are you asking us to take notice of this interrogation?

M. GERTHOFFER: The interrogation was made in Nuremberg.

THE PRESIDENT: Yes; but unless you read all the parts of it that you wish, now, in court, it will not be in evidence.

M. GERTHOFFER: I think that it is not necessary, because Mr. Ranis only repeats the indications given by Mr. Veltjens. It seems to me superfluous.

THE PRESIDENT: Very well.

M. GERTHOFFER: The scope of the operations on the black market is thus established by German documents which cannot be contested by the opposition. I allow myself to remind you that these documents establish that in five months, in three countries, these operations amount to the sum of 1,107,792,818 Reichsmark. We shall come back to certain details in examining the special missions in certain countries, but it is necessary to indicate the reasons why the defendant Goering, in the end, decided that the black market operations should be suspended.

Indeed, on 15 March 1943, under the pretext of avoiding the risk of inflation in the occupied countries, Goering decided that the black market purchases be suspended. We have just seen that the defendant Goering worried little what became of the population of the occupied countries since he had decided that the black market purchases were to continue, even at the risk of inflation.

The real reason is the following: as the officials of the German services bought at prices which were strictly fixed by their services, the black market organisations accepted, at the same time, much higher prices. The merchandise was therefore always gravitating to the black market, to the detriment of the official market, and clandestine production in the end absorbed the normal production.

Finally, it must be added, that the corruption resulting from such practices in certain circles of the German Armed Forces became disquieting to the German leaders. The black market was suppressed officially on 15th March 1943, but certain purchasing bureaus continued their clandestine activities until the time of Liberation, though on a much smaller scale than before.

I cite a passage of the report of the French Economic Control which I have just put into evidence as Exhibit RF 107 and which gives an idea of the disorder that was created by the German actions and which shows the reasons why the Reich authorities officially suspended the black market (page 21 of the French text):

> "There was the period when the champagne, the cognac and the benedictine were handled by lots of 10 to 50,000 bottles and the pate de fois gras by the ton.
>
> From the beginning the general corruption had gained the support of a great number of Wehrmacht officers, who were tempted by the good life which surrounded them. Indeed it so thoroughly extended to the German military groups that, from mess sergeants to high ranking officers, all had dealings with the worst types of operators, and expected commissions from every market. A clandestine sale of wool thread took place, at one time, in the presence of a general of the Air Force.
>
> Around them congregated all the bad elements of France, the industrial adventurers and others who had already served their terms. Then came a horde of commercial operators, dressmakers, unofficial agents without special employment, general intermediaries or associates of slight consequence." (Page 22 of the French Document 107).
>
> "We understand that in such an environment, composed of unknown people and those one cannot lay one's hands on, black market business, which was transacted in cash, and without bills or receipts, except those of the German offices, can today no longer be appraised or evaluated.
>
> Originating in the course of the year 1941, the commercial activity of these Parisian purchasing bureaus continued in this manner for about twenty months. But after having reached its zenith at the end of 1942, this activity had to come to an abrupt end in March 1943; a victim of its own excesses.
>
> In effect, during the entire occupation, production prices were strictly limited by the French services, and even more so by the German economic services, which were systematically opposed to any rise in critical prices, anxious above all to maintain large purchasing power in the French capital at their disposal.
>
> But, since the stipulated merchandise for the enemy's uses was being paid

for at prices hardly better than the legal prices, the clandestine purchasing agencies accepted at the same time rates several times higher for the same products.

In production, the slipping of the merchandise toward the German black market thus occurred more frequently while, at the same time, the secret production increased. The disorder grew so rapidly that in certain branches of industry, deliveries according to contract could not be assured, except with great delay, in spite of the menacing protests of the Germans.

Completely swamped, the French Ministry of Industrial Production had to inform the German authorities that the national production would soon no longer be able to meet its obligations.

This irremediable situation, together with the necessity of putting an end to the incredible corruption provoked by the black market in the Wehrmacht, led the Reich Government, if not to suppress the black market altogether, at least to envisage a closing of the Paris purchasing bureaus.

This measure was made effective on the 13th March 1943, following the agreement Bichelonne-General Michel.

However - and this is very significant - the German economic services did not fail to request in compensation a considerable rise in quotas according to the agreements. Thus, for the Kehrl Plan alone, this rise amounted to 60,000 tons of textiles.

Only few bureaus were able to retain some of their activities until the Liberation, either by trying to deal with the R.O.G.E.S. (d'Humieres, Economic Union, etc.) or with military services buying quartermaster supplies or with the bureaus of the German Air Force or Navy."

THE PRESIDENT: We will adjourn for ten minutes.

(A recess was taken).

M. GERTHOFFER: In the course of my explanations I shall come back to the case of every particular country, in connection with black market operations, so as to be able to give a measure of their extent. But I think that it is established by the Veltjens report as well as by the passages from the French Economic Control Report, which I had the honour to read to the Tribunal, that the black market was organised by the leaders of the Reich, and notably by the defendant Goering.

To finish the general observation concerning the economic looting, I shall ask the Tribunal's permission to give a few explanations from the judicial point of view. They are treated in chapter five of the first part.

From a juridical point of view, it is not contestable that organised looting of the countries invaded by Germany is prohibited by the International Hague Convention, signed by Germany but deliberately violated by her, even though her leaders never failed to invoke this Convention every time they tried to benefit by it.

Section three of the Hague Convention - "The Military Authority over the Territory of the Enemy Government" - relates to the economic questions. These clauses are very clear and do not have to be discussed; if the Tribunal will allow me to recall them. Here is section three of the Hague Convention, which I put into the book of documents as Number 114, and which is called "The Military Authority over the Territory of the Enemy Government.":

Article 42: The territory is considered as being occupied when it is placed in effect under the authority of the hostile army. This occupation extends only to territory where such authority has been established and can be exercised.

Article 43: The authority of the legitimate power having in fact passed into the hands of the occupant, the latter ...

THE PRESIDENT: I think we can take judicial notice of these articles from the Convention.

M. GERTHOFFER: I shall, then, not read this article, since the Tribunal knows the Convention, and shall simply limit myself to certain juridical remarks. These articles of the Hague Convention show in a very clear way that the Germans could commandeer in occupied territories only what was necessary for the maintenance of such troops as were indispensable. All items which were levied beyond these limits were so levied in violation of the articles which you know, and consequently, were "looted" items.

Counsel for the defence may contend that all these prohibitions must be put aside, because Germany had given herself the aim of concluding the war against Britain and then against the USSR and the United States of America. Defence may pretend that, because of this, Germany was in a very needy state which had to checkmate the prohibitions of the Hague Convention and try to incorporate Article 23-G, which allows one to destroy or to seize even private property.

I shall immediately answer that this article does not lay down rules relating to the conduct of the occupant in enemy territory - these last rules are contained, I repeat, in Articles 42 to 56-they are relevant to the conduct which the belligerents must maintain in the course of the war.

The word "seizure" in the expression "No seizure of enemy property except in cases where these seizures are absolutely ordered by military necessity" - and no discussion as to translation can be referred to because actually the French text is binding - the word "seizure" means, not to appropriate a thing, but to put it under the protection of justice with a view to leaving it unused, in the same condition, and to keep it for its true owner or for any person who can show a right to it.

Such a seizure permits the military authority, during hostilities, to prevent the owner from using the property against the troops, but it does not authorise the military authority, under any circumstances, to appropriate it for itself.

The facts of economic looting are all contrary to the principle of International Law and are formally provided for by Article 68 of the Charter of the United Nations of the 8th of August 1945.

These constant violations of the Hague Convention did, as a consequence, enrich Germany and permitted her to continue the war against Britain, the Soviet Union, and the United States, while they ruined the invaded countries, the populations of which, subjected to a regime of slow famine, were actually physically weakened and, without the victory of the Allies, would be on the road to progressive extermination.

This inhuman conduct constitutes, therefore, War Crimes which come within the competency of this International Military Tribunal, as far as the leaders of the Reich are concerned.

Before finishing this rapid summary of juridical questions, the Tribunal will permit me to refute in advance an argument which will certainly be presented by the defence, notably so far as economic plundering is concerned. They will pretend that juridical jurisdiction did not exist, that the International Penal Law had not yet been formulated in any text at the time when the defendants perpetrated the acts which they were actually charged with, and that therefore by virtue of the principle of non-retroactivity of penal laws, they could not be condemned to any sentence whatsoever.

Why, gentlemen, is this principle adopted by modern legislation? It is indisputably in order that any person whatsoever, who is conscious of never having violated any prescribed law, could not be condemned because of acts which were committed in such conditions. For example, somebody issues a check without funds before his country had adopted a penalty against such an offence.

In this case the facts are quite different. The defendants cannot pretend that they were not conscious of having violated legislation of any kind. First of all, they violated international conventions: the Hague Convention of 1907, and the Briand-Kellogg Pact of the 27th of August 1938; then they violated the penal laws of all the invaded countries.

How shall, in this legislation, the economic looting be qualified - theft, swindling, blackmail, and even, I will add, murder - since, in order to attain their aims, the Germans have premeditated and committed numerous murders which enabled them to intimidate the population in order better to plunder them?

According to domestic law, these acts. certainly fall under the application of Article 295 and the following articles of the French Penal Law, and notably of Article 303, which stipulates as guilty of murder all offenders, of whatever category, who, to execute crimes, resorted to torture or perpetrated barbarous acts. I will add that the defendants violated even the German Penal Law, notably Articles 249 and following.

Counsel for the defence will certainly stress that certain of the leaders of the invaded countries were in agreement with the Reich Government as to the economic collaboration, and that consequently these governments cannot be charged with acts which derive from these agreements.

Such arguments must be refuted:

I. If, in all the invaded countries, patriots resisted with more or less courage, it is certain that some of them out of inertia, fear, or disinterest turned traitor to their country. They have been or will be condemned. But the crimes committed by certain of them cannot be exonerating or even extenuating circumstances in favour of the defendants, especially since the latter had very often put these traitors in to manage the occupied countries. On the contrary, the fact of having brought people to turn traitor to their country only aggravates the heavy charges against the defendants.

II. These so-called agreements had all been obtained by pressure or by threat. The concluding contracts show that these contracts are solely in favour of Germany, who also, as a matter of fact, never brought any compensation, but merely illusory benefits. More often the burdensome contract resulted from the mere reading of these contracts, as I will have the honour to show in certain particular cases.

With these explanations my general observations on the economic pillaging are concluded, and if the Tribunal is willing we can examine the particular case of Denmark.

When the Germans, contrary to all the precepts of the Law of Nations and to their engagements, invaded Denmark they were not certain of rapidly dominating Western Europe. At first they laid down the principle of not taking anything from the country. After their success of May 1940, their attitude changed. As a matter of fact, little by little they treated Denmark more or less like the other occupied countries.

Nevertheless, they sought to arrive at an annexation pure and simple, and took rigorous measures against the population only in the course of 1942, when they saw that they would not be able to win Denmark over. From the economic point of view, and to assure their domination, they tried to obtain control of most of the Danish means of payment, and they used, to this effect, two methods which to a great extent were used by them in other countries:

1. The levying of a veritable tribute of war, under the pretext of maintaining their army of occupation.

2. The functioning of the so-called clearing agreement to their almost exclusive benefit. These two methods should be studied in chapter one of this statement.

FIRST CHAPTER: GERMAN SEIZURE OF THE MEANS OF PAYMENT

1. Expenses of occupation.

Article 49 of the Hague Convention stipulated that, if the occupant levies a contribution, this money will only be for the army of occupation or for the administration of the country.

The occupant can therefore levy a contribution for the maintenance of the army, but this contribution must not exceed the sum strictly necessary for the needs of the army of occupation without expense to armament and equipment, that is: merely the expenses for board and lodging and the pay of the soldiers - I mean normal expenses, from which, of course, luxury expenses are excluded.

Article 52 authorises the occupying power to exact requisitions in, kind and service from the communes of the inhabitants for the needs of the army, with the express condition that they should be proportionate to the resources of the country, and it amounts to this: that they should not force the population to take part in operations against their own country.

The same Article 52 stipulates that levies in kind shall be paid so far as possible in cash; otherwise they will have to be established in receipts and the paying in of sums as soon as possible.

In other words, the Hague Convention allows the occupying army to levy in occupied territories, as much as is necessary for the maintenance of the troops, but under two conditions, apart from contributions in kind.

(a) That the levies and the service should be proportionate to the resources of the country, that is to say, that cash should be left over for the inhabitants, at least enough to enable them to live.

(b) That the levies be paid as soon as possible.

This does not mean a fictitious payment made with the funds extorted from occupied countries, but real payments, which imply furnishing of effective compensation.

Article 53 of the Convention of the Hague permits the occupying powers to seize everything which could be used against them - and, in particular, cash, funds, securities of all kinds belonging to the State of the occupied country - but does not authorise the occupying power to appropriate them.

According to information furnished by the Danish Government, when the Germans entered Denmark they declared that they would not demand anything from the country, but that the German Army would be supplied by convoys coming from the Reich.

Nevertheless, instead of buying Danish crowns to permit their troops to spend money in Denmark, as early as 9 May 1940 they imposed the circulation of notes of the Reichskreditkasse - which is shown in Number 26 of the Vobid, which I have already submitted as Exhibit RF 93.

Upon the protest of the National Danish Bank against the issuing of foreign paper money, the Germans withdrew those notes from circulation, but demanded the opening of an account at the National Bank, promising to draw upon it solely for sums which were indispensable for the maintenance of the Army in Denmark and for these sums only.

But the Germans did not lose time in violating their promises and in levying, on their account, in spite of the Danish protest, sums infinitely greater than the needs of the army of occupation.

According to the information given by the Danish Government, the Germans levied, per month,

    43 million crowns in 1940;
    37 million crowns in 1941;
    39 million crowns in 1942;
    83 million crowns in 1943;
    157 million crowns in 1944;
    187 million crowns in 1945.

The total of these levies amounts, according to the Danish Government, to 4,830,000,000 crowns.

I submit, as Exhibit RF 115, the financial report of the Danish Government concerning this, a report to which I shall refer in the course of this statement.

The information given by the Danish Government is corroborated by a German document discovered by the United States Army, EC-96, Page 11, which I submit to the Tribunal as Exhibit RF 116.

This is a secret report of the 10th of October 1944, written by the labour staff for foreign countries, and which concerns the conscription of funds in occupied territories.

On Page 11 it is said that "Denmark is not considered as occupied territory, and therefore does not pay occupation expenses. The means of payments necessary to the German troops are put at the disposal of the high administration of the Reichskreditkasse by the Central Danish Bank, by the channels of ordinary credit. Anyway, total levies are assured by Denmark."

The writer of this report says that the levies to the 31st of March 1944, for occupation expenses, amount to:

    1940-1941, 531 million crowns;
    1941-1942, 437 million crowns;
    1942-1943, 612 million crowns;
    1943-1944, 1,391 million crowns;

this represents, up to the 31st of March 1944, 2,971 million crowns. This corresponds to the information given by the Danish Government for approximately the same period, 2,723,000,000 crowns.

The same German report shows that the rate of exchange for the mark, as compared to the rate of exchange for the crown, had been fixed by the occupying powers from 47.7 to 53.1 marks per hundred crowns.

Even though the Germans pretended, against all evidence, that Denmark was not an occupied territory, they levied in this country the total sum of 4,830,000,000 crowns, an enormous sum, seeing the number of inhabitants and the resources of the country. In reality, this was nothing other than a war tribute which the Germans imposed under the pretext of furnishing means of payment to her army, which was stationed in Denmark.

The maintenance of the army necessary to the occupying of Denmark did not necessitate such heavy expenses. It is evident that the Germans used, as in other countries, the majority of the funds extorted in this manner from Denmark to finance their war effort.

SECOND CHAPTER: CLEARING:

In 1931 Germany was up against financial difficulties, which she used as a pretext to declare a general moratorium on all her foreign obligations.

Nevertheless, to be able to continue, to a certain extent, her commercial operations with foreign countries, she concluded, with a majority of the other nations, agreements permitting the payment of her commercial debts, and even of certain financial debts, on the basis of a system of compensation called "clearing."

Ever since the beginning of the occupation - the 9th of April 1940 - and for its duration, the Danish authorities did everything they could but to counteract the German activity in this domain, but in vain, Under the pressure of occupying forces Denmark could not prevent her credit for the clearing balance from constantly increasing, owing to the German purchases being made without the furnishing of any compensating counterpart.

According to the Danish Government, the credit balance of the account progressed in the following way:

    31 December 1940, 388,800,000 crowns;

    31 December 1941, 784,400,000 crowns;

    31 December 1942, 1,062,200,000 crowns;

    31 December 1943, 1,915,800,000 crowns;

    31 December 1944, 2,694,000,000 crowns;

    30 April 1945, 2,900,000,000 crowns;

These data are corroborated by the German report which I submitted a few minutes ago as Exhibit RF 116, and according to which, on the 31st of March, 1944, the Germans had procured for themselves means of payment, through clearing, amounting to a total sum of 2,243,000,000 crowns.

It has not been possible to establish the use which the occupants made of the sum of 7,730,000,000 crowns, which they procured fraudulently and to the detriment of Denmark, with the help of the indemnity of occupation and of clearing.

The information which we have up to now does not enable us to estimate the extent of the operations carried out by the Germans on the black market. Nevertheless, the writer of the report of the 10th of October 1944, which I have presented previously, indicates:

> "We must put aside all attempts to estimate the sums which were spent in the black market. Nevertheless, it must be admitted that members of the Wehrmacht used to buy, at top prices, butter and other products in Denmark. But it is impossible to fix these sums even approximately, for the black market seems to be less vast and less well co-ordinated than in the other occupied territories of the West, and is closer to the structure of the German black market, with its rather confused prices. Nevertheless, the prices of the Danish black market can generally be considered as much lower than the German prices. It is, therefore, not possible to speak of an average price, of an average high price, as in France, Belgium and Holland."

What should be remembered is that the Germans, and especially members of the Wehrmacht, used to operate on the black market in Denmark, and that the paying of expenses was done with funds extorted from Denmark.

Concerning the acquisitions, which seemed to be regular, we lack the necessary information to be able to give precise indications. Nevertheless, according to a report of the 9th of October 1944, addressed by the German office of the Economic Staff of Germany to their superiors in Frankfurt an der Oder - a document discovered by the United States Army, and which I submit as Exhibit RF 117 - the following goods were levied by his department:

    From January to July, 1943, 30,000 tons of turf.

    May 1944, 6,000 cubic metres of wood.

(The writer adds that they tried to push this production to 10,000 cubic metres per month).

September 1944, 5,785 cubic metres of cut timbers 1, 110 metres of uncut timber;

1,050 square metres of plywood;

119 tons of paint for ships; and special wood for the Navy.

Gentlemen, this is but an enumeration of the levies which just one German section happened to make within a short time.

Denmark had to furnish important quantities of cement. Germans furnished her, in exchange, with the coal necessary for this production.

According to this report which I have mentioned, in August 1944, the Germans spent, in Denmark, over 8,312,278 crowns on foodstuffs.

These numbers are below the truth. According to the last information we have received from the Danish Government, the levies of agricultural things alone amounted, on the average, to 70 million crowns per month; which represents, for 60 months of occupation, levies of a value of 4,700,000,000 crowns.

THIRD CHAPTER: LEVIES NOT FOLLOWED BY PAYMENT:

In addition to all that they managed to buy with the help of crowns which were deposited in their accounts under the pretext of the maintenance of the army of occupation and of clearing, the Germans appropriated an important quantity of goods without having paid for them in any regular manner.

It was in this way that they appropriated goods of the Danish Army and Navy; lorries, horses, means of transportation, furniture, clothes, which up to date have been estimated at about 850 million crowns.

Many requisitions and secret, and even apparent, purchases, have not yet been exactly estimated.

In this report the Danish Government estimates -

THE PRESIDENT: (interposing): Where do these figures come from?

M. GERTHOFFER: These figures come from the report of the Danish Government, Exhibit RF 115.

The same report, contains, on the part of the Danish Government, an estimate which is rather approximate and provisional, of the damages sustained by Denmark and of the German plundering, which is assessed as 11,600,000,000 crowns.

The information which we have to date does not permit me to give any more particulars concerning Denmark.

I will, therefore, if the Tribunal will permit me, begin with particulars in the case about Norway.

THE PRESIDENT: Are you submitting a document book with this?

(The document books were submitted).

M. GERTHOFFER: The Economic Plundering of Norway:

The German troops had only just arrived in Norway when Hitler declared, on the 18th of April, 1940, that they should proceed to the economic exploitation of this country which, for this reason, must be considered as an "enemy State."

The information which we have on the economic plundering of Norway is rather brief, but it is, nevertheless, sufficient to enable us to estimate the German activity in that country during the time of the occupation.

Norway was subjected to a regime of most severe rationing. As soon as they entered this country, the Germans tried - and this was contrary to the most elementary principles of International Law - to draw from Norway the maximum of resources possible.

In a document discovered by the United States Army, EC-384, and which I submit as Exhibit RF 116-a document which is made up by the Journal De Marche of Economic and Armament Service in Norway, written in May 1940-we have excerpts of the directives relative to the administration and to the economy in the occupied territories. Here are some of these excerpts

"Directive of Armament Economy:

The Norwegian industry, to the extent to which it does not directly supply the population, has, in its essential branches, a particular importance for the German war industry. That is why its production must be put, as soon as possible, at the disposal of the German armament industry, if this has not already been done. The industry consists, on the one hand, of 'intermediate products' which demand a certain amount of time to be transformed into finished, useful products; and, on the other hand, of raw materials - such as aluminium, for example - which can be used whilst we wait for our own factories, which are being built, to be in a position to produce.

In this connection we must, above all, take into consideration the following industries;

The production of copper, zinc, nickel, iron with a titanium base, wolfram, molybdenum, silver, and pyretic.

Metallurgical factories for the production of aluminium alumina, copper, nickel, zinc.

Chemical industries for the production of explosives, synthetic nitrogen, calcium nitrate, super-phosphate, carbonate of calcium and soda base products.

Armament industries, naval dockyards.

Industries for power supply; especially for supplying electric energy furnishing electric current, on which depend all the industrial branches enumerated above.

The production capacities of these industries must be maintained, for the duration of the occupation, at the highest possible levels.

Certain help coming from the Reich is, from time to time, necessary to surmount the difficulties of seizing English imports, or those coming from overseas.

It is most important to ensure this aid as far as the industries of raw materials are concerned, the production of which is based essentially on the imports coming from overseas.

We cannot for a moment overlook the question of the imports of bauxite coming from the German stocks and which can be used by the metallurgical factories of aluminium."

As soon as the troops entered Norway, Germany issued notes of the Reichskreditkasse which were legal only in Norway, and could not be used in Germany. As in the other occupied countries, this was a means of pressure to obtain financial advantages, which were supposedly freely accorded by these brutally enslaved countries.

The Germans did their best to become masters of the means of payment and of Norwegian credit by two classic methods; imposition of war tribute on the pretext of the maintenance of the occupational army, and also by the functioning of a clearing system which was to their profit.

GERMAN SEIZURE OF ALL THE MEANS OF PAYMENT
First: Indemnities for the maintenance of the army of occupation.

At the beginning of the occupation, the Germans used to purchase with notes of the Reichskreditkasse. The Norwegians who had this paper money used to change it at the Bank of Norway, but this financial institution could not obtain from the Reichskreditkasse any real counter-value.

In July 1940 the Bank of Norway had to absorb Rm 135,000,000 which came from the Reichskreditkasse.

To avoid losing control over the money calculation, the Bank of Norway was obliged to put the Norwegian notes at the disposal of the Germans. They used to draw cheques on the Reichskreditkasse which the Bank of Norway was obliged to endorse.

The debt account of the Bank of Norway, following the German levies, amounts to:

    1,450,000,000 crowns at the end of 1940;
    3,000,000,000 crowns at the end of 1941;
    6,300,000,000 crowns at the end of August 1942;
    8,700,000,000 crowns at the end of 1943;
    11,676,000,000 crowns at the liberation of this country.

All the Norwegian protestations were vain, in the face of German exigencies. The constant threat of the new issuing of notes of the Reichskreditkasse as instruments of obligatory payment next to the Norwegian currency, obliged the local financial authorities to accept the system of levies in account without actual counter value, which was less dangerous than the issuing of paper money, over the circulation of which the Norwegian administration had no power of control.

This is most clearly shown by the secret letter sent on 17th June 1941 by General von Falkenhorst, commander in Norway, to the commander of the Reich, Reichsleiter Terboven, a copy of which was found not so long ago in Norway and which I submit to the Tribunal as Exhibit RF 119.

In this document, after having stated that one could not reduce the expenses of the Wehrmacht in Norway, von Falkenhorst writes:

"I am nevertheless of the opinion that the problem cannot at all be solved in this manner. The only remedy is to abandon completely the actual monetary system; that is to say, to introduce Reich currency. But, of course, this does not belong to my domain. That is why I also regret not being able to offer you any other remedies, even though I am perfectly conscious of the seriousness of the situation in which you find yourself."

To the indemnities for the pretended maintenance of the army of occupation must be added a sum of 360,000,000 crowns paid by the Norwegian Treasury for the billeting of the German troops. This information comes to us from a report from the Norwegian Government, which I submit as Exhibit RF 120.

From the sum of approximately 12,000,000 crowns levied for the pretended maintenance of the occupation troops, a great part was used for other things; notably, for the expenses of the police and propaganda the occupant spent 900,000,000 crowns.

This comes from a second report of the Norwegian Government, which I submit as Exhibit RF 121.

Second: Clearing:

The clearing agreement of 1937 for the barter of goods between Norway and Germany remained in force during the occupation, but it was the Bank of Norway which had to advance the necessary funds for the Norwegian exporters.

The Germans also concluded clearing agreements in the name of Norway with other occupied countries, neutral countries, and with Italy.

At the liberation, the creditor balance of the Norwegian clearing amounted to 90,000,000 crowns, but this balance does not show up the actual situation, for:

1. The imports destined to the German military needs in Norway were handled through the clearing in a very abusive manner;

2. For certain goods-skins, furs, and fish, the Germans had decided that the exportation should be made into the Reich. Then they sold these products in other countries, especially Italy as far as the fish was concerned;

3. The Germans, who were the masters, and upon whom depended the fixing of prices, systematically raised the price of all raw products imported into Norway, and these were used for the great part for the military needs of the occupiers. On the other hand, they systematically drove down the prices of the products exported from Norway.

In spite of all their efforts and all of their sacrifices, and owing to the fraudulent operations of the occupiers, the Norwegian authorities could not hinder a very dangerous inflation.

From the report of the Norwegian Government, which I submitted as Exhibit RF 120 a few moments ago, it is seen that the fiscal circulation, which in April 1940 amounted to 712,000,000 crowns, rose progressively to reach, on 7th May 1945, 3,039,000,000 crowns. An inflation of this extent, which is the consequence of the activities of the occupiers, enables us to measure the impoverishment of this country.

The same report indicates that the Germans did not manage to seize the gold of the Norwegian Bank, as this had been hidden in good time.

Let us now, gentlemen, examine the levies in detail.

The Germans proceeded in Norway to numerous requisitions which were or were not followed by so-called regular payments.

According to the report of the Norwegian Government, here is the list of requisitioned goods

    Meat - 30,000 tons
    Milk, eggs, etc - 61,000 tons
    Fish - 26,000 tons
    Fruit and vegetables - 68,000 tons
    Potatoes - 500,000 tons
    Vinegar and allied products - 112,000 tons
    Fats - 10,000 tons
    Wheat, flour - 3,000 tons
    Other items - 5,000 tons
    Hay and straw - 30,000 tons
    Other articles of same nature - 13,000 tons
    Soap - 8,000 tons

But this statement which I have just read to the Tribunal only includes the official purchases which were made with Norwegian currency or which were paid for through clearing; it does not include the secret purchases. It is not yet possible to determine or to appreciate the total extent of these. We can, however say that the export of fish, which went to Germany, in the majority of cases, for one year only

(1942) came to about 202,400 tons, whereas the official requisitions during the whole occupation did not go beyond 26,000 tons.

As in other occupied territories, the Germans forced the continuance of work under threat of arrest.

The greatest part of the fleet was hidden from the Germans; nevertheless they requisitioned all ships which they could, notably, the majority of the fishing fleet.

If the occupier could not seize all railway rolling stock, tramways were transported to Germany, as well as about 30,000 motor cars.

If we refer to the report of 10th October 1944 of the German Economic Services, which I submitted as Exhibit RF 116, we will see that the writer of the report himself estimates that the effort demanded from Norway was above her possibilities, and he writes:

> "The Norwegian economy is seriously undermined by the exactions of the occupiers. It is for this reason that we had to limit the cost of occupation to part only of the expenses of the Wehrmacht."

After having mentioned that the cost of occupation which had been calculated to January 1943 amounted to 7,535,000,000 crowns, which corroborates the data given by the Norwegian Government, the writer of the German report says:

> "This sum of over Rm 5,000,000,000 is very high for Norway. Much richer countries, as for example, Belgium, pay expenses which are hardly higher, and Denmark does not furnish even half of this sum. These huge levies are only made possible through advances which were consented to by Germany. It is, therefore not surprising that the exterior German-Norwegian commerce should have a very active character for Germany. That is to say, that it consists of advances. Norway, owing to her very small population, can hardly put labour at the disposal of the German war economy. She is therefore one of the few countries which are our debtors in the clearing."

Further on the writer adds:

> "If we can deduct from these Rm 140,000,000 - the expenses of occupation and various credits calculated for after - we arrive at a very high figure for Norwegian levies; that is to say, approximately 4,900,000,00 Rm."

THE PRESIDENT: Perhaps that would be a good time to break off.

(A recess was taken).

M. GERTHOFFER: We continue with the expose of economic pillage in Norway. I had the honour, this morning, of relating to you how the occupants were able to exact great quantities of means of payment from Norway. We shall now see, from the first data which has been given us, the use to which the occupants put these payments. The Germans seized, as in the other occupied countries, considerable private property, on some pretext or other-that it was property belonging to Jews, Freemasons, Scout associations, et cetera. It has been impossible, thus far, to establish a very direct evaluation of these spoliations. We can give some indications of them, at this time, only from memory. According to the report of the Norwegian Government, in 1941 the Germans seized all the radio sets...

THE PRESIDENT: Have you any evidence to support the facts you are stating now?

M. GERTHOFFER: They are based on indications contained in the report of the Norwegian Government which I have submitted as Exhibit RF 121.

THE PRESIDENT: Yes.

M. GERTHOFFER: According to the same report, in 1941 the Germans seized almost all the radios belonging to private individuals. The value of these radio sets was approximately 120,000,000 kronen. The Germans imposed heavy fines on the Norwegian communities under the most varied pretexts, notably Allied bombing raids and acts of sabotage.

In their report the Norwegian Government gives two or three examples of these collective fines: On March 4th, 1941, after a raid on Lofoten, the population of the small community of Ostvagey had to pay 100,000 kronen. Communities also had to support German families and families of Quisling supporters.

On 25 September 1942, after a British raid on Oslo, one hundred citizens were obliged to pay 3,500,000 kronen.

In January 1941, Trondheim, Stavanger and Vest-Opland had to pay 60,000 50,000 and 100,000 kronen, respectively.

In September 1941, the municipality of Stavanger was obliged to pay 2 million kronen for an alleged sabotage of telegraph lines.

In August 1941, Rogaland had to pay 500,000 kronen, and Alesund 100,000 kronen.

It can thus be stated as a fact that, by various procedures which differed hardly from those employed in other countries, the Germans, during the occupation of Norway, not only exhausted all the financial resources of that country but placed it considerably in debt.

It has not been possible to furnish a detailed account of German exactions be they made after requisitions which were followed or not followed by indemnities, or be they made by purchase, apparently conducted by mutual agreement, fictitiously regulated by those very means of payments extorted from Norway.

In the report which I have submitted as Exhibit RF 121, the Norwegian Government tabulated the damages and losses suffered by its country. I shall give a summary of this report to the Tribunal.

The Norwegian Government estimates that the damage and losses undergone by industry and commerce amounted to a total of 440 million kronen, of which the Germans have made settlement, fictitiously to be sure, only up to 7 million kronen.

Other losses were:
- Merchant vessels, having a value of 1 billion 773 million kronen, for which the German Government has made no settlement;
- On ports and installations the sum is 74 million kronen, for which the German Government has fictitiously settled only to the extent of 1 million;
- On railroads, canals, airports, and other installations the spoliation can be represented by the sum of 947 million kronen, for which Germany has fictitiously settled with 490 million kronen;
- Roads and bridges, 199 million kronen, for which the settlement amounts to 67 million.
- Spoliation of agriculture reached 242 million kronen, for which settlement amounts to only 46 million;
- Personal property, 239 million for which no settlement has been made.
- Various requisitions, not included in the preceding categories, amount to 1 billion, 566 million kronen, for which the occupant, fictitiously, has settled to the amount of 1 billion, 154 million kronen.

The Norwegian Government estimates that the years of man-labour applied to the German war effort represent a sum of 226 million kronen. It estimates, on the other hand, that the years of man-labour lost to the national economy by deportation to Germany and forced labour on the order of Germany amounts to 3 billion, 122 million kronen.

Forced payments to German institutions amount to 11 billion, 54 million kronen, for which Germany has made no settlement whatsoever. The grand total, according to the Norwegian Government, is 21 billion kronen, which represents more than 4 billion 700 million dollars.

Norway suffered in particular during the German occupation. Indeed, though its resources are considerable, notably the timber of its forests, minerals, such as nickel, wolfram, molybdenum, zinc, copper and aluminium, nevertheless, it must import consumer goods of prime necessity for feeding its population.

As the Germans had absolute control over maritime traffic, nothing could come into Norway without their consent. They could therefore, by pressure, as they had to do in France by means of the line of demarcation between the two zones, impose their exactions more easily. The rations, as fixed by the occupiers, were insufficient to ensure the subsistence of the Norwegian population. The continued undernourishment over a period of years entailed the most malignant consequences: disease multiplied, mortality likewise increased, and the future of the population has been compromised by the physical deficiencies which its younger elements had to endure.

These are the few observations which I had to make on the subject of Norway. I shall, if the Tribunal will permit, now deal with the aspect of the subject which relates to the Netherlands.

Economic pillage of the Netherlands:

In invading the Netherlands in contravention of all the principles of the law of nations, the Germans installed themselves in a country abundantly provided with the most varied wealth, in a country in which the inhabitants were the best nourished of Europe, and which, in proportion to the population, was one of the wealthiest in the world. The gold reserve of Holland exceeded the amount of bills in circulation. Four years later, when the Allies liberated this country, they found the population afflicted by a veritable famine, and apart from the destructions consequent to military operations, a country almost entirely ruined by the spoliations of the occupants.

The dishonest intentions of Germany appear in a secret report by Seyss-Inquart on his governorship, a report, discovered by the U.S. Army, dated 29th May to 19th July 1940, which has been registered as Document 997-PS and which I submit before the Tribunal as Exhibit RF 122. These are the chief extracts from this report:

"It was clear that with the occupation of the Netherlands a large number of economic and police measures had to be taken, the first ones of which were to reduce the consumption of the population in order to get supplies for the Reich, on the one hand, and to secure a just distribution of the remaining supplies, on the other hand. In consideration of the assigned task, we had to try to see to it that all these measures carried the signature of Dutchmen. The Reich commissioner therefore authorised the Secretaries-General to take all the necessary measures by means of ordinances. As a matter of fact, up to today, almost all orders concerning the seizure of supplies and their distribution to the population, and decrees about restrictions in the formation of public opinion, which have been issued, as well as agreements concerning the transport of extraordinarily large supplies to the Reich which have been made, all bear the signatures of the Dutch Secretaries General or the competent economic leaders, so that all of these measures have the character of being voluntary. It should be mentioned in this connection that the Secretaries General were told in the first conversation, that loyal co-operation was expected of them, but that it would be their privilege to resign if something should be ordered which they felt they could not endorse. Up to date none of the Secretaries General has made use of this privilege, so that one may reasonably conclude that they have complied with all requests of their own free will.

Almost the entire seizure and distribution of food supplies and textiles has been carried out, at least all the respective orders have been issued and are being executed.

A series of instructions concerning the reorientation of agriculture have been issued and are being executed; essentially it is a question of seeing to it that the available fodder is used in such a way that as large a stock as possible of horned cattle is carried over into the next farming period, about 80 per cent, at the expense of the stock of chickens and hogs, which is too high. Rules and restrictions have been introduced in the organisation of traffic, and the principles for the regulation of gasoline, as in the Reich, were carried out here.

Restrictions of the right to quit jobs as well as to cancel leases have been issued, in order to check the liberal- capitalistic customs of the Dutch employers and to avoid unrest. In the same way the periods for repayment of debts have been extended under certain conditions.

Ordinances concerning news service, radio, etc., prohibit listening to foreign radio stations and introduce all other restrictions necessary in this field for defence reasons. The ordinance about registration and control of enemy property, as well as about confiscation of the property of persons who show hostility to the Reich and to Germans was, in this case, issued in the name of the Reich Commissioner. On the basis of this ordinance an administrator for the property of the Royal Family has already been appointed.

The supplies of raw materials have been seized and, with the consent of the General Field Marshal, distributed according to this system: the Dutch keep enough raw materials to maintain their economy for half a year, whereby they receive the same distribution quotas as in the Reich. The same principle of equal treatment is being used in the supply of food, etc. This enabled us to secure considerable supplies of raw materials for the Reich, as for instance 70,000 tons of industrial fats, which is about half the amount which the Reich lacks.

The bank moratorium could be cancelled; bank deposits are increasing the stock exchange has been reopened to a limited extent. Legislation concerning the control of foreign currencies has been introduced according to the standards in the Reich.

Finally it has been arranged that the Dutch Government shall make available, in sufficient quantities, all means needed by the Reich, including the German administration in the Netherlands, so that these expenses do not burden the Reich budget in any way.

Thus, a sum of guilders has been made available to redeem the occupation marks to the amount of about 36 million, an additional 100 million for the purpose of the occupation army, especially the extension of the airports; 50,000,000 for the production of raw materials to be shipped to the Reich, insofar as they are not booty; for unrestricted transfer to guarantee the remittance of the savings of the Dutch workers brought into the Reich to their families, etc. Finally, the rate of exchange of the occupation marks, set at first by the Army High Command as 1 guilder to 1.50 Reichsmark, has been correctly reduced to 1 guilder to 1.33 Reichsmark.

Above all, however, it was possible to get the consent of the President of the Bank of the Netherlands, Trip, to a measure suggested by Commissioner General Fischbock and approved by the General Field Marshal, namely the unrestricted mutual obligation of accepting each other's currencies; that means that the Bank of the Netherlands is bound to take over any amount of Reichsmark offered to it by the Reich Bank, and in return to make available Dutch guilders at the rate of 1,33, that is, 1 Reichsmark = 75 cents. Only the Reich Bank has control over this, not the Bank of the Netherlands, which will be notified only about the individual transactions. This ruling goes far beyond all pertinent rulings hitherto made with the political economies of neighbouring countries, including the Protectorate, and actually represents the first step toward a currency union.

In consideration of the significance of this agreement, which already touches the independence of the Dutch State, it is of special weight that the President of the Bank, Trip, who is unusually well-known in Western banking and financial circles, signed this agreement of his own free will in the above sense."

Here ends the quotation from the letter of Seyss-Inquart.

As you will see from the explanations which I shall have the honour of submitting to you, it was chiefly in the Netherlands that the Germans used all their ingenuity in extorting the means of payment. This spoliation will form the subject of the first chapter.

We shall next examine the use made by the occupants of these means of payment; in a second chapter we shall discuss the black market; in a third we shall consider the acquisition made in a manner only outwardly regular; a fourth chapter will be devoted to various kinds of spoliation. Finally, we shall touch upon the chief consequences to the Netherlands of this economic pillage.

FIRST CHAPTER: GERMAN SEIZURE OF MEANS OF PAYMENT
I. INDEMNITY FOR OCCUPATION COSTS

I have already had the privilege, gentlemen, of explaining under what conditions and within what limit, by virtue of the Hague Convention, the occupying power may raise contributions in money for the maintenance of its army of occupation.

I shall confine myself to reminding the Tribunal that these expenses which are charged to the occupied countries can include only costs of billeting, feeding, and eventually of paying those soldiers, strictly necessary to the occupation of territories.

The Germans knowingly ignored these principles by imposing upon the Netherlands the payment of an indemnity for the maintenance of their troops which was far out of proportion to their needs.

According to information furnished by the Netherlands Government, (which is contained in three reports: the reports of Trip, Hirchenfeld and the Minister of Finance, which I submit as Exhibit RF 123) the following sums were exacted on the pretext of being indemnity for the maintenance of occupation troops:

1940, (for the duration of seven months) - 477,000,000 guilders
1941 - 1,124,000,000 guilders
1942 - 1,181,000,000 guilders
1943 - 1,328,000,000 guilders

1944 - 1,757,000,000 guilders
1945 (for the duration of only 4 months) - 489,000,000 guilders
Total - 6,356,000,000 guilders

A sum as considerable as this constitutes a veritable war tribute raised on the pretext of the maintenance of an army of occupation.

Germany thus fraudulently circumvented the regulations of the Hague Convention to seize a considerable amount of means of payment.

II. CLEARING

In 1931 Germany, which faced economic and financial difficulties, declared a general moratorium on its previous commitments. Nevertheless, in order to be able to continue its foreign commercial operations, it had concluded with most of the other countries, notably with Holland, agreements making possible the regulation, the settling of commercial debts and, to a certain extent, of financial debts, on the basis of the compensation system called "clearing." Before the war there existed on the Netherlands "clearing" an excess of imports from Germany. But after the first months of occupation there was, on the contrary, a considerable excess of exports to Germany, whereas the receipts coming from that country dropped perceptibly.

From the month of June 1940 on, the Germans exacted from the Netherlands declarations of foreign currency, gold, precious metals, valuable papers, and foreign credits, as can be deduced from the Ordinance of 24th June 1940, hereby submitted as Exhibit RF 95. Moreover, the Dutch could, by virtue of the same ordinance, be obliged to sell their stocks to the Bank of the Netherlands. The German Commissar of the Reich, Seyss-Inquart, forced the Bank of the Netherlands to make advances in guilders to assure an equilibrium of the clearing, since Germany could furnish no equivalent in merchandise. On the other hand, it was decided that the clearing system should be utilised for the delivery of merchandise as well as for the payment of any debts.

In point of fact the Germans could, therefore, buy merchandise and titles to movable property in Holland without furnishing any equivalent. The credits, in marks, of the Dutch sellers were blocked in the Bank of the Netherlands which, on its part, had been obliged to make an equivalent advance on the clearing exchange.

To attempt to limit the falling of the Dutch account on the clearing exchange, and to avoid the transfer by this means of guilders or of transferable stock into Germany; on the 8th of October, 1940, the Secretary General of the Netherlands Finance imposed a sizeable tax on the marks that were blocked on the clearing exchange.

However, under date of the 31st of March, 1941, the credit of the Netherlands exceeded 400,000,000 guilders, which in fact had been advanced by the Netherlands Government. At this point the occupant's demanded:

(1) That a sum of 300,000,000 guilders be withdrawn from the balance of 400,000,000 and deposited in the German treasury under the heading of "Military Occupation Costs Incurred. 'Outside' The Netherlands," and this independently of payments already made for the occupation costs that had been paid by this country.

(2) By a decision of the Reich Commissar, under date of 31st March, 1941 (reported in the Verordnungsblatt in France, No. 14, which I submit to the Tribunal as Exhibit RF 124) the payment operations with the Reich were no longer to pass through the clearing exchange, but to be operated directly from bank to bank, which would create direct credits of the Netherlands banks on the German banks at the imposed exchange of 100 Reichsmark for 75.36 guilders.

(3) By a decree of the same date, 31st March 1941, (which I submit as Exhibit RF 125) the tax on blocked marks, created on the 8th of October, 1940, by the

Netherlands authorities, was abolished. Faced with this situation, particularly dangerous to the Netherlands treasury, M. Trip resigned his position as Secretary General for Finance and President of the Netherlands Bank. The Reich Commissar replaced him with Rost von Tonningen, a notorious collaborator who complied with all the demands of the occupying power.

As the private banks were unwilling to keep credits in marks at a rate very disadvantageous to the real parity of 100 Reichsmark to 75.36 guilders, they transferred their credits in marks to the Bank of the Netherlands. The credit account of the Institute of Exports to Germany, through the operations made with this country, rose considerably; while the credit balance as of 1st April 1941 amounted to 235,000,000 guilders, it was to rise by the 1st of May, 1945, to 4,488,000,000 guilders.

According to information given by the Netherlands Government this credit was accounted for by purchases of all kinds of merchandise made by the Germans in Holland, of transferable stock or other valuable papers, by payment of services imposed upon Dutch businesses, and of wages of workers deported to Germany, and by paying off the debts incurred by the occupant.

Aside from these two procedures, indemnities for the occupation troops, and clearing, the Germans were to procure resources for themselves by another method - by imposing collective fines - and this in violation of the provisions of Article 50 of the Hague Convention.

In the course of the occupation the Germans imposed, under every pretext, by way of reprisal or intimidation, considerable fines upon the municipalities. These fines were to be paid by the inhabitants, with the exception of persons of German nationality, members of pro-Nazi associations (NSV, Waffen SS, NSKK), of the technical aid services of the Dutch-German community, and of persons working for the Germans.

According to information which has been obtained up to the present of only 62 municipalities, the total fines thus imposed mounted to a minimum of 20,243,024 guilders. This is based on testimony of the Netherlands Government, which I submit as Exhibit RF 126.

From the same testimony, in the archives forgotten by the Germans at the Hague, there have been discovered two copies of letters relative to these collective fines.

According to the first of these copies, which is a letter of March 8th, 1941, collective fines amounting to 18,500,000 guilders had been raised at the beginning of the year 1941.

From the second, we learn that Hitler had given the order to employ this sum for National Socialist propaganda in the Netherlands.

The report of the Government of the Netherlands....

THE PRESIDENT: Where are these letters?

M. GERTHOFFER: These letters are in evidence, which I presented as Exhibit RF 126.

THE PRESIDENT: Will you read the passages which you consider material?

M. GERTHOFFER:

"Commissar of the Reich, The Hague, 1808, 8.3.1941.

To Liaison Headquarters, Berlin, 1720 hours.

For immediate transmission to Reichsleiter M. Bormann.

The sum of 18 1/2 million guilders representing the contribution exacted as reprisals from certain Dutch cities, will arrive in the next few days. The Commissar of the Reich asks whether the Fuehrer has earmarked this sum for a special purpose, or if it is to be used for the same purpose as the Fuehrer has previously ordered in the case of confiscation of enemy property. At that time the Fuehrer stipulated that these sums should be spent in the Netherlands for the needs of the community under the proper political considerations.

Heil Hitler
(Signed) Schmidt-Munster
General Commissar."

This, then, is the translation of the answer.

"Obersalzberg, 19.3.41; 1000 Nr/4
Reichsleiter M. Bormann."

THE PRESIDENT: One moment, some of the copies which you have just submitted to us do not seem to be accurate, and the passage which you have just been reading is omitted from some of them. (Another copy is presented to the President).

I now have another copy of the document which you have read out - two copies which have been handed up, and they appear to be wrongly copied in some way. I will hand them down again.

M. GERTHOFFER: The document has possibly been improperly numbered. There are two Exhibits RF 126; they should have been indicated as 126(I) and 126 (II). The representative of the Government of the Netherlands certifies the accuracy of the translation of the first copy; and in the second "126" document the same representative of the Netherlands Government certifies the existence of the copy of the answer from the Headquarters of the Fuehrer.

THE PRESIDENT: Just hand up the document again, the one I have handed down, will you? The first document is the one you have just read out. The second document begins with the words, "J'ai soumis aujourdhui." Is that the second document to which you are referring? Perhaps you had better look at it. Look at that and see whether that is it.

M. GERTHOFFER: It is the second document.

THE PRESIDENT: Could we see the originals? They are two different documents, are they? but they both begin in exactly the same way.

M. GERTHOFFER: The two documents have been submitted by the Netherlands Government. The representative of the Government of the Netherlands, who has delivered them, certifies that these two documents were found in the Netherlands among German papers.

THE PRESIDENT: Yes. Go on.

M. GERTHOFFER: The Dutch Government was obliged to make important payments to the German account and in, the reports submitted as Exhibit RF 123, there is clearly presented

First: The Germans required that a sum of 360,000,000 guilders, which was written to the credit of the Bank of the Netherlands, be used for the needs of its army of occupation outside the Netherlands and that a sum of 76,800,000 guilders in gold be deposited for the same use. The total which the Netherlands hid to pay under this pretext, namely, the maintenance of armies of occupation in other countries, was 376,800,000 guilders.

Second: From June 1941 on, the Netherlands was obliged to pay, as a contribution to the expenses of the war against Russia, a monthly sum of 37,500 guilders, of which a part was payable in gold. The total of the sum that Germany raised under this heading is 1,696,000,000 guilders.

Third: The Bank of the Netherlands was obliged to assume charge of redeeming occupation marks to the sum of 133,600,000 guilders.

Fourth: The expenses of the German civil government in Holland were charged to this country and amounted to 173,800,000 guilders.

Fifth: The Dutch Treasury was, moreover, obliged to pay 414,500,000 guilders to the account of the Reich, covering divers expenses, such as wages of Dutch workers deported to Germany, the costs of evacuation of certain regions, costs of the demolition of fortifications, so-called costs for guarding railroads, funds, placed at the disposal of the Reich Commissar, and for various industries utilised by the Germans.

Sixth: The Germans in July 1940, seized 816 bars of gold bullion belonging to the Bank of the Netherlands, which were in the wreck of a Dutch ship sunk in Rotterdam and which represented, including costs of recovery, 21,100,000 guilders.

Seventh: The Government of the Netherlands was obliged to bear annual expenses of 1,713,000,000 guilders to assure the financing of new administrative services imposed on Holland by the occupying power.

In this way, Holland lost a total of 8,565,000,000 guilders, including the raising of the gold from a ship sunk in the Meuse. The effective payments made to Germany amount to 11,380,800,000 guilders. If these costs are added to the costs of occupation and clearing, the total of the financial charges imposed on Holland during occupation, amounts to the sum of 22,224,800,000 guilders.

These operations had serious consequences for the economy of the Netherlands. Indeed, the gold supply which, on 1st April, 1940, amounted to 1,236,000,000 guilders, had, by the 1st April, 1945, fallen to 932,000,000 guilders.

The currency in circulation, on the contrary, had risen from 1,127,000,000 guilders on the 1st April, 1940, to 5,468,000,000 guilders on 1st April, 1945.

When the Germans occupied the Netherlands, a great portion of the gold of the Bank of the Netherlands had been evacuated abroad. However, the Germans under various pretexts seized all the gold that was found in the vaults of the bank. I recall that, under the heading of indemnity for occupation, they collected 75,000,000 gold guilders; and for the forced contribution of the Netherlands in the war against Russia, they demanded around 140,000,000 gold guilders.

Rost von Tonningen, Secretary-General of Finance and President of the Netherlands, appointed by the Germans, on 18th December 1943, wrote to the Reich Commissar that there had not been any gold in Holland since the preceding March.

The copy of this letter is submitted as Exhibit RF 127 and comes from a document discovered by the US Army, listed as ECR 174, which I submit as Exhibit RF 128, a document consisting of a report of the Commissar of the Bank of Belgium, of 12 June 1941, who also points out that the gold stock of the Bank of the Netherlands amounted on 12 June 1941, to 1,021,800,000 guilders, of which only 134,600,000 guilders were in Holland, the rest being either in England, South Africa or the United States.

The same report specifies that all the gold of Holland had been removed.

Not only did the Germans seize the gold of the Bank of the Netherlands, but they also placed a tax on the gold and other means of payment which were in foreign countries and owned by Netherlanders, The occupying power obliged private individuals to deposit gold which was in their possession with the Bank of the Netherlands, after which this gold was requisitioned and handed over to the Reichsbank. A sum of approximately 71,000,000 guilders was thus paid to the public in exchange for the requisitioned gold.

It was thus, also, that the Germans bought, from the public, various foreign stocks to a sum of 13,234,000 guilders and Swedish Government securities to a sum of

4,623,100 guilders.

With important financial means which they had at their disposal, the Germans proceeded to make important acquisitions in Holland. Such acquisitions, made through funds extorted from the Netherlands, cannot be considered as an exchange in a real equivalent, but as realised only by fictitious payments.

The Germans, in addition to numerous cases of requisitions which were followed by no kind of settlement, had clandestine dealings in the black market, and other dealings which only appeared to be regular. They thus procured a quantity of things of all kinds, leaving to the population only a minimum of products insufficient to ensure their vital needs.

In the second chapter of this presentation we shall examine the clandestine purchases on the black market; and in a third chapter, the acquisitions that were carried out in seemingly regular ways.

THE BLACK MARKET

In Holland, as in all other occupied countries, the Germans seized considerable quantities of merchandise on the black market, in violation of the legislation on rationing which they themselves had imposed.

It has not been possible, in view of the clandestine nature of the operations, to determine even approximately the quantities of all kinds of objects which the Germans seized by this dishonest means. However, the secret report of the German Colonel Veltjens, which I had the honour of submitting this morning as Exhibit RF 112, gives us for a period of five months, from July to the end of November, some indications of the scope of the German acquisitions. I quote a passage from the Veltjens report :

In the Netherlands, since the beginning of the 'action' the following purchases were made and paid for by ordinary bank remittances

    Non-ferrous metals - 6,706,744 Reichsmark
    Textiles - 55,285,568 Reichsmark
    Wool - 753,878 Reichsmark
    Leather skins and hides - 4,723,130 Reichsmark
    Casks - 254,928 Reichsmark
    Furniture - 272,990 Reichsmark
    Necessaries and luxuries - 590,859 Reichsmark
    Chemical and cosmetic products - 152,191 Reichsmark
    Various iron and steel wares - 3,792,166 Reichsmark
    Rags - 543,416 Reichsmark
    Motor oil - 52,284 Reichsmark
    Uncut diamonds - 25,064 Reichsmark
    Sundries - 531,890 Reichsmark
    <u>Total for a period of five month - 73,685,162 Reichsmark</u>

These purchases were paid for by bank cheques. A large quantity of other merchandise which has not been possible to determine was paid for by cash with guilders coming from the so-called occupation indemnity.

THE PRESIDENT: We will adjourn now for ten minutes.

(A recess was taken)

M. GERTHOFFER: As to Chapter 3 which deals with the economic plundering of the Netherlands, we will treat the question of dealings of outward regularity from information provided us by the Government of the Netherlands.

Industrial production: From testimony given by the Representative of the Government of the Netherlands, which I submit as Exhibit RF 129, it is clear that the Germans utilised to their own profit the largest part of the industrial potential of the Netherlands; all important stocks which were in the factories were thus absorbed. The value of those stocks was not less than 800,000,000 guilders; moreover, the occupants proceeded to large-scale removal of machinery. In certain cases these removals were not followed by even fictitious settlements. It has not yet been possible to establish a balance sheet of these spoliations, which often included all the machine equipment of an industry.

As an example, we may indicate that, on a requisition order of 4 March 1943, coming from the Reich Commissar, all the machinery and technical equipment, including the designs and blue prints of all the work shops and accessories of the blast furnaces of an important factory, were removed without any indemnity, and transported to the vicinity of Brunswick for the Hermann Goering Works. This is manifest in the document I submit as Exhibit RF 130.

The Germans had set up in all the occupied countries a certain number of organisations specially charged with the pillaging of machines. They had given them the name of "Machine Pool Office." These organisations, which were under the armament inspection, received demands of the German industry for means of production and had to fulfil these demands by requisitions on the occupied countries.

Moreover, gangs of technicians were charged with locating, dismantling and transporting the machines to Germany. The organisation of these official gangs of pillagers can be learned from German documents which are to be brought to your knowledge when the specific case of Belgium will be outlined to you.

We learned from the report of 1st March 1944, addressed to the military commandant, that the Machine Pool Office of the Hague could satisfy only a small proportion of the demands. Thus, under date of 1st January 1944, these demands totalled 677,000,000 Reichsmark, whereas in the month of January only 61,000,000 Reichsmark worth of machines had been delivered as against the new demands of 87,000,000, which made a total demand for machines amounting to 703,000,000 Reichsmark at the end of January.

This is Exhibit RF 131.

Before leaving the Netherlands the Germans effected large-scale destruction with, they said, a strategic purpose, but above all with the desire to do damage When they demolished factories, they removed beforehand and transported to Germany all the machinery which they could dismantle, as well as the raw materials. They acted in this manner, notably in the case of the Philipps Plants in Eindhoven, Hilversum and Bussum; the oil dumps of Amsterdam and Pernisse; and the armament factories of Breda, Tilburg, Berg-op-Zoom and Dordrecht. These facts are treated in the report of the economic officer attached to the German military commander in Holland, under date 9 October 1944, which I submit as Exhibit RF 132.

The same report gives some information on the organisations of German looters who were specialists in the removal of machines. I give here some extracts:

> "The Philipps Works at Eindhoven was the first and the most important military objective to be dealt with."

A little farther on the writer continues:

> "Before the arrival of the enemy we succeeded in destroying these important continental works for the fabrication of radio valves and lamps and the production of information apparatus, after the volunteer commando

(Fwi. Kdo 7) had previously sent off the most precious metals and all special machines.

Farther on he writes :

"As early as 7 September a Commando unit transported in trucks to the Reich, most important non-ferrous metals, (wolfram, manganese, copper) and very valuable apparatus from the Philipps Works. In addition, the Fwi-Kdo 7 took part in the transfer of finished and semi-finished products as well as machines from Philipps. Following the enemy's occupation of Eindhoven, the removal was stopped. They then proceeded to evacuate the branch factories of Philipps at Hilversum and Bussum. Here it was possible to remove completely all the stocks of non- ferrous metal products, finished and semi-finished goods, machinery and the blue prints and designs necessary for production.

At the same time removal commandos were detailed to the heads of various provincial branch offices under the representative of the Reich Ministry of Armaments and War Production in the Netherlands.

In agreement with the forementioned services and the competent civil offices, these commandos carried through the removal of important raw materials and products as well as machinery. Through the unswerving and commendable attitude of officers, officials, Sonderfuehrer, and enlisted men it was possible during the month of September to remove to the Reich considerable stocks of raw materials and products or to supply the troops with suitable material. This action was initiated and directed in the Western and Southern districts of the Netherlands by the Fwi-O-Netherland.

For the task of evacuation and for the preparation of the ARLZ measures within the area of the Army High Command 15, and at the same time as liaison with the staff quartermaster with the Army High Command 15, a squad under the command of Captain Rieder was detached by Fwi-Kd 7. Here, too, in close co-operation with the civil officers, and the Department IVa of the Army High Command 15, a valuable job was done concerning the removal of raw materials and rare goods as well as machinery. These actions commenced only at the end of the month covered by this report."

Along with the removal of machinery the Government of the Netherlands gives us exact figures on the stocks of raw materials and manufactured articles. Apart from the stocks located in the factories, the Germans acquired considerable quantities of raw materials and manufactured articles amounting to not less than one billion guilders.

This evaluation does not include the destruction resulting from military operations, which ranges around 300 million guilders.

The Germans proceeded to make requisitions and wholesale purchases of agricultural produce and livestock. A final estimate of these levies, amounting to a minimum of 300,000,000 Guilders is as yet impossible.

To give an idea of their magnitude we point out that, at the end of the year 1943, the Germans had seized 600,000 hogs, 275,000 cows and 30,000 tons of preserved meats.

The data is given in the testimony of the representative of the Netherlands Government, which I submit as Exhibit RF 133.

In passing I point out - although this question will be taken up again by my colleague in his presentation of War Crimes against persons - that on 17th April 1944, without any apparent strategic reason, twenty hectares of cultivated lands were flooded at Wieringermeer.

Transports and Communications:

The Germans made enormous levies on material, transport and communication. It is not yet possible to draw up an exact inventory of them. Nevertheless, the information given by the Netherlands Government makes it possible to form an idea of the magnitude of these spoliations.

I submit, as Exhibit RF 134, information given by the representative of the Netherlands Government concerning transport and communication. This is a summary:

(a) Railways

Of 890 locomotives 490 were requisitioned.

Of 30,000 railway cars 28,950 were requisitioned

Of 1,750 passenger cars 1,466 were requisitioned.

Of 300 electric trains 215 were requisitioned.

Of 37 Diesel engined trains 36 were requisitioned.

In general, the little material left by the Germans was badly damaged by wear and tear, by military operations and by sabotage.

In addition to rolling stock, the Germans sent to the Reich considerable quantities of rails, signals, cranes, turn-tables, repair cars, etc.

(b) The equipment was removed from the Hague and Rotterdam to German cities. Thus, for example, some 50 motor trams and 42 trailer cars were sent to Bremen and Hamburg.

A considerable amount of rails, cables and other accessories were removed and transported to Germany.

The motor buses of the street car companies were likewise taken by the occupying power.

(c) The Germans seized the greater part of the automobiles, motorcycles and about one million bicycles. They left the population only those machines which would not run.

(d) Navigation: The Germans seized a considerable number of barges and river boats, as well as a considerable part of the merchant fleet, totalling about 1,500,000 tons.

(e) Postal Equipment: The Germans seized a great number of telephone and telegraph apparatus, cables and other accessories, which has not yet been computed. 600,000 radio sets were confiscated.

I now come to Chapter 4: Miscellaneous spoliation:

Forced labour for the occupier: From information given by the Netherlands Government, which I submit as Exhibit RF 135, a great number of Dutch workers were obliged to work either in Holland or in Germany. About 550,000 were deported to the Reich, which represents a considerable number of man- hours lost to the national production of the Netherlands.

Plunder of the Royal Palaces:

The furniture, private archives, the stables and carriages and wine cellars of the royal house were plundered by the Germans. In particular, the Palace of Norrdeinde was completely looted of the movable contents, including furniture, linen, silverware, paintings, tapestries, art treasures and household utensils. A certain number of these were removed from the Palace of Het Loo and were to be used in a convalescent home for German generals.

The archives of the royal family likewise were stripped. This is manifest from a report given by the representative of the Netherlands Government, which I submit as Exhibit RF 136.

Pillage of the city of Arnhem.

Besides numerous cases of individual looting, which are not the matter of the present subject, there was systematically organised pillage of entire cities. In this manner the town of Arnhem was despoiled in October and November 1944.

The Germans brought miners in from Essen who, under military orders, proceeded, in specialised gangs, to dismantle all the removable furniture, and send it with goods of all kinds to Germany. This is manifest in the testimony given by the representative of the Netherlands Government, which I submit as Exhibit RF 137.

The consequences of economic plundering in the Netherlands are considerable. We shall just mention that the enormous decrease in the national capital will have, as corollary, a production inferior to the needs of the country, for many years yet to come.

But the gravest consequence is that affecting the public health, which is irreparable. The excessive rationing, over many years, of food, clothing, and fuel, ordered by the occupant to increase the amount of spoliation, had brought about a debilitation of the population.

The average calory consumption by the inhabitants, which varied between 2,800 and 3,000 dropped in large proportions to about 1,800 calories, finally to fall in April 1945 as low as 400.

Starting from the summer of 1944, the food situation became more and more serious. The commissar of the Reich, Seyss- Inquart, forbade the transport of food stuffs between the Southern and Northern zones of the country. This measure, which was not justified by any military operation, seems only to have been dictated by hatred for the population, only to oppress and intimidate them, weaken them, terrorise them.

Not until March 1945 was this inhuman measure lifted; but it was too late. The famine had already become general. The death rate in the cities of Amsterdam, The Hague, Leyden, Delft and Gouda increased considerably, rising from 19 to 60 per cent. Diseases which had almost been eliminated from these regions, reappeared. Such a situation will have irreparable consequences for the future of the population.

These facts are manifest in two reports which I submit as Exhibits RF139 and 140.

By ordering such severe rationing measures to get for themselves products indispensable to the existence of the Dutch, an act which was contrary to all principles of International Law, I may say that the German leaders committed one of their gravest crimes.

My explanations concerning Holland are concluded. My colleague, M. Delpech, will now state the case for Belgium.

M. DELPECH: Mr. President, gentlemen, I have the honour of presenting to the Tribunal a statement on the economic plundering of Belgium.

As early as 1940 the National Socialist leaders intended to invade Belgium, Holland and Northern France. They knew that they would find there raw materials, equipment, and the factories which would enable them to increase their war potential.

As soon as Belgium had been occupied, the German military administration did its best to reap the maximum benefit. To this end the German leaders took a series of measures to block all existing resources and to seize all means of payment. Important supplies built up during the years 1936 to 1938 were the object of enormous requisition. The machines and equipment of numerous factories were dismantled and sent to Germany, bringing about the closing down of many of them and in many sectors their forced consolidation.

Given the highly industrial character of this country, the occupying authorities imposed a very heavy tribute upon Belgian industries. Nor was agriculture spared.

The third part of the French economic expose deals with a study of all these measures. This will be the subject of four chapters. Chapter I deals with the German seizure of the means of payment. The second chapter will treat the clandestine purchases and an exposition of the black market. Chapter 3 will deal with the purchases of apparent regularity. The fourth chapter will concern impressment. In the fifth chapter the acquisition of Belgian investments in foreign concerns will be presented to the Tribunal, before concluding and emphasising the effect on the public health of the German intrusion. Finally, a few remarks will be presented concerning the conduct of the Germans after they had annexed the Grand Duchy of Luxembourg.

CHAPTER I: German seizure of means of payment. To enslave the country from an economic point of view, the most simple procedure was to secure the possession of the largest part of the means of payment and to make impossible the export of currency and valuables of all kinds.

There is an order of 17 June, 1940, which forbids the export of currency and valuables of all kinds. This order was published in the 'Verordnungsblatt' for Belgium, Northern France and Luxembourg and will hereafter be called by its usual abbreviated form 'V.O.B.E.L.' This order was published in 'V.O.B.E.L. No. 2' and is submitted as Exhibit RF 98. In the 'V.O.B.E.L.' of the same date appeared a notice dated 9 May, 1940, which regulated the issuing of occupation marks to provide the occupation troops with legal tender.

By this means the Germans could buy, without furnishing any compensating consideration, all they desired in a country which had products of all kinds, without the inhabitants being able to protect their possessions against the invader.

The occupants used, in addition, three other methods for obtaining the largest part of the means of payment. These three methods were; the creation of a bank of issue; the imposition of war tribute under the pretext of maintaining occupation troops; and a system of clearing, functioning to their own profit. These measures will be treated in three sections to be hereafter developed.

Section I: Establishment of a Bank of Issue. As soon as they arrived in Belgium the Germans established an office for supervising banks, entrusted at the same time with the control of the National Bank of Belgium. This was ordered on 14 June, 1940, (V.O.B.E.L. No. 2) which is submitted as Exhibit RF 141.

At this time the directorate of the National Bank of Belgium was outside the occupied territories. On the other hand, the amount of notes on hand would be insufficient to insure normal circulation, as a great number of Belgians had fled before the invasion, taking with them an important quantity of paper money.

These are, at any rate, the reasons which the Germans put forward for establishing the Bank of Issue, as of the ordinance of the 27th of June, 1940, published in 'V.O.B.E.L. No. 4 and 5', which I submit as Exhibit RF 142.

By virtue of this last ordinance, 21 June 1940, the new Bank of Issue with a capital of 150,000,000 Belgian francs, 20 per cent of which had been issued in cash, received the monopoly for issuing paper money in Belgian francs. As a matter of fact, the National Bank of Belgium no longer had the right to issue money. The issue of this bank was not backed by gold but:

1. By credits from discount operations and loans granted in conformity with article 8 of the new statutes.

2. By claims of the National Bank of Belgium as well as coin which was in circulation for the account of the public treasury.

3. Finally, by the third device: by circulation in foreign currency and francs particularly, German money which comprised occupation marks as well as assets of the Reichsbank at the Office of Compensation for the Reich and the Reich Credit Bank.

The German Commissar, who had been appointed by decree of 26 June, 1940, became the controller of the bank of issue. The decree of 26 June, 1940, was published in 'V.O.B.E.L.,' No. 3, Page 88, and is submitted as Exhibit RF 143.

After the return to Belgium of the directors of the National Bank on 10 July, 1940, an agreement between this bank and the new Bank of Issue was effected by the nomination of the head of the new issuing bank to the position of director of the National Bank of Belgium.

The Bank of Issue proceeded to put out a large amount of notes. On 8 May, 1940, the currency in circulation amounted to 29,800,000,000 Belgian francs. On 29 December, 1943, it amounted to 93,200,000,000 Belgian francs, and on 31 August, 1944, it was 100,200,000,000 Belgian francs, that is to say, an increase of 235 per cent.

The Bank of Issue worked, but not without certain difficulties, either with the military government, its own staff, or with the National Bank of Belgium. Actually, besides its function of issuing, the new bank had, as a principle function, the operations relating to postal checks and to currency; as well as the operations with German authorities, notably as concerned the indemnity for occupation and the clearing.

The National Bank of Belgium lost its right to issue paper money, but resumed its traditional operations of private as well as State accounts, notably transactions on the open market.

These data, gentlemen, are corroborated by the final report of the German military administration in Belgium, 9th part, treating of currency and finances. This final report of the German military administration in Belgium was discovered by the U.S. Army, and it is a document to which we shall refer many times. It is No. E.C.H. 5, and is submitted to the Tribunal as Exhibit RF 144.

The 9th part, which is of interest here, was written by three chiefs of the administration section of Brussels, Wetter, Hofrichter and Jost.

In spite of the establishment of the bank of issue, the occupation marks were valid in Belgium until August 1942, but it was the National Bank of Belgium that was obliged to absorb these notes in September 1944, and, owing to this, the Belgian economy underwent a loss of 3,567,000,000 Belgian francs. (This number is given by Wetter in the foregoing report, Page 112, excerpt of the report, which is submitted as Exhibit RF 145.)

Moreover, from information given by the Belgian Government, the issuing bank had in hand at the moment of liberation of the territory, a sum totalling 664,000,000 in occupation marks, drawn up in Reichsmark, and further, it had assets in a transfer account of 12 million Reichsmark on the books of the Reich Credit Bank, that is to say, a total loss of 656,000,000 Belgian francs. (This number is given in a report of the Belgian Government which is deposed in the archives of the Tribunal under Exhibit RF 146.)

Let us now treat the occupation costs. Article 49 of the Hague Convention stipulates that, if the occupant takes contributions in cash, it will only be for the needs of the army of occupation or for the administration of the territory. The occupant can, therefore, deduct a contribution for the maintenance of his army, but this must not exceed the sum strictly necessary. On the other hand, the words "needs of the army of occupation" do not mean the expenses of armament and equipment, but solely the normal costs of billeting, food, and pay, which exclude in all cases luxury expenses.

Moreover, Article 52 authorises the occupying authority to exact, for the use of its army, requisitions in kind and in service, on the express condition that they shall be proportionate to the resources of the country, and that they should not involve the population with the obligation to take part in military operations against their own country. The same Article 52 stipulates, moreover, that levies in kind will be, as far as possible, paid in cash.

THE PRESIDENT: Do you not think you might omit further references to these articles as we have already had them fully covered by your colleague?

M. DELPECH: As a consequence, the Germans exacted a monthly indemnity of 1,000,000,000 Belgian francs up to August 1941. On that date the indemnity was increased to 1,500,000,000 Belgian francs per month. By 20th August 1944, the payments under that designation totalled 67,000,000,000 Belgian francs. This number cannot be contested by the defence, seeing that in the report quoted, Pages 103 and following, M. Wetter wrote in June 1944: The total sum of Belgian francs paid for the army of occupation was 64,181,000,000. (This is deposed under Exhibit RF 147).

This sum of 64,000,000,000 was completely disproportionate to the needs of the occupying army. This is notably manifest in the report of Wetter, in a passage that I submit as Exhibit RF 148. On Page 245 of this report it is said that on 17 January 1941 the general who was commander in chief in Belgium had asked the High Command of the Army if the indemnity covered only the expenses of occupation. This point of view was not accepted by the commanding general, who, by decree of the 21 October 1941, specified that the indemnity of occupation was to be used not only for the needs of the occupying army but also for those of the operating armies. Moreover, on Page 11 of the original German text of the same report it is written - and I shall read to the Tribunal an excerpt which will be found in the book of documents, and will be Exhibit RF 149, the second paragraph :

"The increase in the expenses of the Wehrmacht made it clear that it would be impossible to make ends meet. The military administration demanded that the calculation of the occupation costs be straightened out by cancelling all expenses foreign to the occupation itself, from this account. This concerned especially the larger purchases of all kinds which the military services made in Belgium, such as horses, motor vehicles, equipment, all of which was designated for other territories, and were written off as occupation costs.

By decree of the Delegate of the Four Year Plan, dated the 11th of June 1941, the financing of the expenses other than occupation costs was to be met by the clearing. To comply with this decree, beginning in June 1941, the administration of the military commander ordered a monthly report to be rendered of all expenses other than those required for the occupation, but which had been paid under the account of occupation costs, in order to have these expenses refunded through the clearing.

Thanks to this, large sums could be recovered and put to the account of occupation costs."

Before concluding the examination of this point concerning war tribute, called "occupation costs," it is necessary to point out that the Germans had already demanded, by the order of 17 December, 1940, submitted as Exhibit RF 150, that the costs of billeting their troops should be charged to Belgium. Owing to this, the country had to meet expenses totalling 5,900,000,000 francs, which went for billeting German troops, costs of installation, and furniture.

In his report, Wetter writes an Page 104, - an excerpt submitted as Exhibit RF 147 - that at the end of June, 1944, the Belgian payments for billeting troops totalled 5,423,000,000 francs.

We now come to the third element of German plundering, the clearing. The issuance of occupation marks and the war tribute, called occupation costs, were not sufficient for Germany. Her leaders created a system of clearing which enabled them to procure improperly, the means of payment totalling 62,200,000,000 Belgian francs.

As soon as they arrived in Belgium, by the decrees of 10 July, 7 August and 7 December, 1940, which will be Exhibits RF 151, 152 and 153, the Germans promulgated:

(1) That all payments on debts of people living in Belgium to their creditors in Germany had to be paid into an account called the "Deutsche Verrechnungskasse, Berlin," an open account on the books of the National Bank of Belgium in Brussels, an account carried in belgas due to the prohibition re devices of 17 June 1940, the prohibition to which I have already referred concerning the blocking of the means of payment in the country.

By decision of 4 August 1940, it was moreover prescribed that the carrying out of the clearing would be henceforth entrusted no longer to the National Bank of Belgium but to the Bank of Issue in Brussels, which, as I have already had the honour of pointing out, had been established by, and was under the absolute control of, the occupant.

(2) The Germans laid down a second measure whereby all debtors living in the Reich should pay their Belgian creditors, by means of the open account in the Bank of Issue in Brussels, at the following rate of exchange, one hundred belgas to 40 marks, that is to say one mark for 12.50 Belgian francs.

These decrees moreover were extended to the countries occupied by Germany, with a view to facilitating their operations in these countries; they were even extended to certain neutral countries by various analogous decrees appearing in the Book of Ordinances.

The mission of the Bank of Issue in Brussels consisted, therefore, on the one hand of receiving payments from all persons or agencies established in Belgium, which carried on foreign transactions, and on the other hand, to pay those persons or agencies established in Belgium, which had foreign credit.

In other words, every time an exporter delivered goods to an importer of another country, a member of the clearing, it was the Bank of Issue which settled the invoice and which inscribed as equivalent, in the ledgers, a corresponding credit on the "Deutsche Verrechnungskasse in Berlin," the German Clearing Institute in Berlin. Imports were handled by the same procedures inversely.

In fact, under the German direction, this system functioned to the detriment of the Belgian community which, at the moment of the liberation, was creditor in the clearing to the extent of 62,665,000,000 Belgian francs.

It was the National Bank of Belgium which had been forced to make advances to the Bank of Issue to balance the account of the German Clearing Institute.

A large number of operations made through the clearing had no commercial character whatever, but were purely and simply military and political expenses.

From information given by the Belgian Government, the clearing operations could be resumed in the following manner - and I draw my conclusions from a report of the Belgian Government previously cited, which has been presented as Exhibit RF 146 - of the total transactions, 93 per cent. corresponds to Belgo-German clearing;

merchandise exchanges amounted to 93 per cent., and service 91 per cent.

If one considers the part taken respectively by merchandise, services or capital, one arrives at, as a balance, two quite significant tables: the entire clearing of Belgium with foreign countries, totalled on 2 September 1944, the sum of 61,636,000,000 Belgian francs of which 57,298,000,000 were for Belgo-German operations; 4 billion only with France; 1 billion with the Netherlands, and 929,000,000 with other countries.

It is only in the sector of goods and services that the unbalance is apparent, an unbalance due in large measure, to requisitions of property and services made by Germany for her own account.

It is known that the so-called exports affected especially metals and metal products, machines and textile products, nine tenths of which were seized by the Reich, which made itself, thereby, guilty of real spoliation.

Concerning the transfer of capital, which, during the first period of the occupation, was in an active state of flux, it is a question of the forced realisation of the participation of Belgian capital in foreign countries, as well as the forced cession to German groups of Belgian assets blocked in Germany. No effective compensation was given in exchange.

The transfer pertaining to services belonged primarily to the payments made for the use of the Belgian labour in foreign countries.

The creditors' balance of these services on 2 September 1944 is as follows: in millions of Belgian francs: Total clearing dealing with services - 20,016,000,000, that is to say, for paying labour, 73 per cent of the total; for Germany alone, 18,227,000,000, that is to say, 72 per cent of the total amount for France only 1,600,000 Belgian francs, that is to say, a very small part.

Not content with requisitioning workers for forced labour in Germany or in the occupied territories, the Germans compelled Belgium to bear the financial burden, and imposed it either through the liquidation of the transferred sums in the clearing, or by the remittance of Belgian notes to the Directorate of the Reich Bank in Berlin, for payment of workers in national currency.

THE PRESIDENT: Do you think it is necessary to go into these clearing operations again? In each case of the various countries which have been dealt with, the same clearing operations have taken place, have they not? Then perhaps it is really unnecessary to do it over again for Belgium.

M. DELPECH: Very well, I will continue without insisting on this.

At all events, the Germans recognised the fact, and the figures taken from the reports previously cited can only support the conclusions of our statement.

Before ending this chapter concerning the seizure of all the means of payment, it is fitting that the attention of the Tribunal be brought to the Germans' order of 22 July 1940, by which the rate of the Belgian franc was fixed at 8 Reichspfennig, that is to say, 12.50 francs per mark; and in the formentioned report, Wetter writes concerning this matter, on Pages 37 and 38 - a passage which I ask the Tribunal's permission to read, and which is in the document book as Exhibit RF 158.

> "The de facto maintenance of the pre-war parity was of considerable political importance, because a large group of the population would have had the impression that a sharp devaluation or a repeated change of parity was a manoeuvre of exploitation."

The following observation in connection with this conception must be made the occupants had no need in Belgium to decree, with the view of promoting their economic exploitation, that the Belgian franc should have a lesser value when, as a matter of fact, contrary to what occurred in France, they had, at the moment they entered Belgium, instituted new currency over which they had the control.

Lastly, let us just mention that Germany forced the Vichy Government to deliver 221,730 kilos of gold, amounting at the 1939 valuation to 9,500,000,000 francs; but as France had restored this gold to the Bank of Belgium, this question will be treated under the economic exploitation of France.

To sum up, the means of payment seized by the army of occupation, amounted to the following figures:

    Occupation marks - 3,567,000,000

    Various bills and accounts on the books of the Reich Credit Bank - 656,000,000

    War tribute under the pretext of occupation costs - 67,000,000,000

    To which may be added the credit balance of clearing - 62,665,000,000

    <u>Total (in Belgian francs) - 133,888,000,000</u>

The Germans seized no less than 130,000,000,000 Belgian francs, which they used for outwardly regular purchases, for payment of their requisitions, and to make clandestine purchases on the black market.

These so-called purchases and requisitions will be treated in the following chapters.

CHAPTER II: Clandestine Purchases, Black Market.

As in all the other occupied territories, the Germans organised a black market in Belgium as early as October 1941.

According to a secret report on the black market, called "Final Report of the Office of the Supervisor" of the military governor in Belgium and in the North of France, concerning the legal abolishment of the black market in Belgium and in the North of France, a report covering the period from the 13 March 1942 to the 31 May 1943, Exhibit RF 159 in the book of documents, the reasons given by the Germans for this organisation of the black market are three:

(1) To check competition on the black market between various German buyers.

(2) To make the best use of the Belgian resources for the economic goals of the German war.

(3) To do away with the pressure exercised on the general standard of prices, and by this to avoid all danger of inflation which would end up by endangering the German currency.

This same report tells us, Pages 3 and following, that an actual administrative organisation was set up by the Germans for carrying out this policy.

The bookkeeping was assured by the Clearing Institute of the Wehrmacht, which centralised all operations in its books.

The direction of the purchases was assured by a central organisation, the name of which changed in the course of the years, and which had a certain number of organisations subordinate to it, notably a whole series of purchasing offices.

The central organisation was set up in accordance with the decree of the Military Governor of Belgium, of 20 February 1942. It was formed on the 13th of the following March, and as soon as it was created it received special directives from the delegate of the Reich Marshal, defendant Goering. This delegate was Lt. Col. Veltjens, of whom we spoke this morning.

This organisation was only established to co-ordinate the legalisation and direction of the black market, as had been determined upon and planned, following conferences of the General Intendant and the Military Governor of Belgium with the chief of the Armament Inspection. According to the terms of that agreement under date of the 16th of February 1942, coming from the Reich Minister for Economics, the aim was to drain the black market, and to do so in accordance with directives, in a legal form; with the idea of complying with the supply requirements of the German Reich.

This organisation had its offices in Brussels. The purchases themselves were secured by a certain number of specialised offices, the list of which is given on Page 5 of the forementioned report.

These organisations received their orders from the 'Rohstoffhandelsgesellschaft,' which has been already mentioned in the beginning of the statement on the economic exploitation of Western Europe.

The role of the R O G E S was very important in the organisation of the black market. In effect it was fourfold:

(1) The purchasing directives, once the authorisation had been given by the central office in Brussels, were transmitted by the R O G E S to the proper purchasing office.

(2) The delivery of goods bought and marked for the Reich were made through the R O G E S, which took charge of their distribution in Germany.

(3) The R O G E S financed the operations.

(4) It was the R O G E S which was entrusted with paying the difference between the rate of purchase, generally very high because of the black market rate, and the fixed official rate of sale on the German domestic market. The difference was covered by an equalising fund, supplied from the occupation costs' account, on which the Reich Minister of Finance put sums at the disposal of the R O G E S through the channel of the Ministry of Economics.

The aforementioned report furnishes a complete series of interesting particulars on the functioning of even the central organisation. It is interesting to note that the central office in Brussels was instructed by order of the Military Governor of Belgium, dated 3 November 1942, to have a branch at Lille set up for the North of France. At the same time, the Brussels office was authorised to instruct its branch office at Lille. In the book of documents under Exhibit RF 160 is mentioned a final report of the Lille office. This report, made out 20 May, 1943, gives a whole series of interesting particulars on the functioning of this organisation.

THE PRESIDENT: It is 5 o'clock now. Perhaps, M. Delpech, I think it would be the wish of the Tribunal, if it were possible for you to omit any parts of this document which are on precisely the same principles with those which have already been submitted to us in connection with the other countries. If you could, I think that would be for the convenience of the Tribunal. Of course, if there are any essential differences in the treatment of Belgium then, no doubt, you would draw our attention to them.

M. DELPECH: Certainly, your Honour.

(The Tribunal adjourned until 22 January 1946, at 1000 hours).

Fortieth day:
Tuesday, 22nd January, 1946

M. MOUNTER: The representative of the French prosecution is here. He will appear before the Tribunal and take the floor.

M. HENRI DELPECH: Mr. President, Your Honours: I had the honour yesterday of beginning to explain before the Tribunal the methods of economic spoliation of Belgium by the Germans in the course of their occupation of the country.

Coming back to what was said in the course of the general considerations on economic pillage, and on the behaviour of the Germans in Norway and Denmark and in Holland, I have been able to show that in all places the determination to economic domination of National Socialism had manifested itself. The methods were the same everywhere, at least in their broad outlines. Therefore, in immediate response to the wish expressed yesterday by the Tribunal, and in order to fulfil the mission entrusted to the French prosecution by the Belgian Government to plead its case before your high jurisdiction, I shall confine myself to the main outlines of the development. and I shall take the liberty of referring for the details of the German seizure of Belgian productivity to the text of the report submitted to the Tribunal, and to the numerous documents which are quoted therein.

I have had the honour of calling your attention once before to the existence of the black market in Belgium, its organisation by the occupation troops, and their final decision to suppress this black market. One may, in this regard, conclude, as has already been indicated in the course of the general observations, that, in spite of their claims, it was not in order to avoid inflation in Belgium, that the German authorities led a campaign against the black market.

The day the Germans decided to suppress the black market, they loudly proclaimed their anxiety to spare the Belgian economy and the Belgian population the very serious consequences of the threatening inflation. In reality, the German authorities intervened against the black market, daily increasing in scope, in order to prevent it from further extension to the point where, in the end, it would absorb all the available merchandise and completely strangle the official market. In a word, the survival of the official market, with its lower prices, was finally much more profitable for the army of occupation.

I now come, gentlemen, to Page 46 of my presentation, to the third chapter; the acquisitions, which were regular in appearance, had only one aim, namely the subjugation of Belgian productive power.

Applying their programme of domination of the countries of Western Europe as it had been established even before 1939, the Germans, from the moment they entered Belgium in May 1940, took all the measures which seemed to them appropriate in order to assure the subjugation of Belgian productivity.

No sector of the Belgian economy was to be spared. If the pillaging seems more striking in the economic domain, this is only the consequence of the very marked industrial character of the Belgian economy.

The sectors of agriculture and of transportation were not to escape the German hold, and I propose to discuss first the levies in kind on industry.

The Belgian industry was the first to be attacked. Thus, the military commander in

Belgium, in agreement with the various offices of the Reich for raw materials, in agreement with the Office of the Four Year Plan and the Ministry of Economics, established a whole programme whose effect was to convert almost the entire Belgian productivity to the bellicose ends of the Reich.

As early as 13 December 1940 he could make known to the higher authorities a series of plans established for iron, coal, textiles, and copper. I submit Exhibit RF 162 in support of this statement.

Also a report by Lt. Col. Helder, entitled "Change in Economic Orientation" points out that from 14 September 1940 the Army Ordinance Branch was sending to its subordinate formations the following instructions to be found in the document book under Exhibit RF 163. I read the last paragraph of Page 41 of the German text:

> "I attach the greatest importance to the fact that the factories in the occupied territories, Holland, Belgium, and France, be as much as possible utilised to lighten the burden of the German armament production, and to increase the war potential. Enterprises located in Denmark are also to be employed to an increasing extent as sub-contractors. Hereby the regulations for the execution of the ordinance of the Reich Marshal, as well as the ordinances concerning the economy of raw materials in the occupied territories are to be strictly observed."

All these arrangements soon enabled the Germans to control and to direct Belgium's whole production and distribution facilities towards the German war effort.

The decree of 27 May 1940, V.O.B.E.L No. 2, submitted as Exhibit RF 164, established commodity control offices whose task was - and I quote from the third paragraph -

> "to issue, in accordance with Army Group directives, general regulations and special ordinances to enterprises producing, dealing with and consuming controlled commodities, in order to direct production and ensure a just distribution and rational utilisation, whereby working places should, as far as possible, be secured."

Article 4 of the same text indicated in detail the powers of these commodity control offices, and in particular they were given the right:

> "to force enterprises to sell their products to given purchasers; and to forbid or require the utilisation of certain raw materials. Every sale or purchase of commodities was subject to their approval."

To better conceal their real objective, the Germans gave these commodity control offices independence, and the status of a corporation. Thus, there were set up 11 commodity control offices which embraced the whole economy except coal, whose direction was left under the Belgian Office of Coal. Exhibit RF 165 gives proof of this.

The execution of the regulations was ensured by a series of texts promulgated by the Belgian authorities in Brussels. They issued in particular, a decree dated 3 September 1940, by virtue of which Belgian organisations took back the offices which the Germans had given up.

The functions of these offices were to have different fates: although originating from the Belgian Ministry of Economics they were closely controlled by the German military command. In this direction, the seizure of Belgian production was completed by the appointment of "Commissioners of Exploitation," under the ordinance of 29 April 1941, submitted as Exhibit RF 166. Article 2 of this text defines the powers of the Commissioners.

> " ... The duty of the Commissioner is to make or to keep going the

enterprise under his charge, to ensure the fulfilment of orders according to plan, and to take all measures which increase the output of the enterprise."

The decline of the commodity control offices began with an ordinance dated 6 August 1942, establishing the principle providing for the prohibition of manufacturing certain products, or for ordering the use of certain raw materials. This ordinance is to be found in the document book as Exhibit RF 167. Supervision of the commodity control offices was soon organised by the appointment to each of them of a German Commissioner, selected by the competent Reichs-stelle.

From the last months of 1943 on, the Rustungsobmann Office of the Armament Ministry, under Minister Speer, acquired the habit of passing its orders directly, without having recourse to the channel of the commodity control offices.

Even before this date measures had been taken to prevent any initiative that was not in accord with the German war aims. Furthermore, even before the above ordinance of 6 August 1942, it is proper to mention the ordinance of 30 March 1942, making the establishment or extension of commercial enterprises subject to previous authorisation by the military commander.

In the report of the military administration in Belgium that has already been cited, the Chief of the General Staff, Raeder, specifies that for the period of January to March 1943 alone, out of 2,000 iron mills, 400 were closed down for working irrationally or being useless to the war aims. The closing of these factories seems to have been caused less by the concern for a rationalised production than by the vicious desire to obtain cheaply, valuable tools and machines.

In this connection, it is appropriate to point to the establishment of Machine Pool Office. The above quoted report of the military administration in Belgium, in its 11th section, Pages 56 and following, is particularly significant in this respect. Here is an extract from the German text, the last paragraph of Page 56 in the French translation, the last lines of Page 56.

THE PRESIDENT: That passage you read about the defendant Raeder, was that from Exhibit RF 169 or 170?

M. DELPECH: Mr. President, I spoke yesterday of the chief of the administration section, Raeder. He was section chief in Brussels. He has no connection with the defendant here.

THE PRESIDENT: I see, very well.

M. DELPECH: Exhibit RF 171, second paragraph of the French text. The paragraph concerns: the Machine Pool transactions.

> "Proof is established by a rapid glance at the pool operations which have been considered and those which have been carried out. Five hundred and sixty-seven demands have been dealt with to a total value of 4.5 million Reichsmark."

Raeder furnished a number of figures.

I shall pass over these and I come to the end of the first paragraph, Page 57 in the German text.

> "The legal basis for the requisition of these machines was the Hague Convention of 1907, Articles 52 and 53. The wording of the Hague Convention, which provides for requisitions only for the benefit and the needs of the occupying power, applied to the circumstances of the year 1907, that is, to a time when war actions were contained within narrowly defined areas in practice, and the military front alone had to sustain war operations. In view of the special limitations of war, it was evident that the provisions of the Hague Convention stipulating that requisitions be made solely for the

needs of the occupying power were sufficient for the requirements of warfare. Modern war, however, which, by its expansion to total war, no longer has spacial limitations, but rather has become a war of peoples and economic spaces struggling against each other, requires that the regulations of the Hague Convention be maintained and its principles analogously interpreted according to the necessities of modern warfare."

I pass to the end of this quotation:

"Whenever, in requisitioning, reference was made to the ordinance of the military commander of 6th August 1942, this was done in order to make known to the Belgian population the necessary analogous interpretation of the regulations of the Hague Convention on which the requisition was based."

Such an interpretation may leave jurists wondering, if they have not been trained in the school of National Socialism. It may in any case justify the pillage of industry and the subjugation of Belgian production.

These few considerations show how subtle and varied were the methods employed by the Germans to attain their aims in the economic sphere. In the same way as the preceding statements on clearing operations and the utilisation of occupation costs, they make it possible to specify the methods employed for exacting heavy levies from the Belgian economy.

Whereas in certain sectors, as in agriculture and transportation, it has been possible to assess the extent of economic pillage with a certain exactitude, there are, on the other hand, numerous industrial sectors where assessments cannot yet be made. It is true that a considerable part of the industrial losses corresponds to the clearing operations, notably through requisition of supplies. It will therefore be necessary to confine ourselves to the directives of the policy practised by the Germans.

We may examine briefly the way in which the economic spoliation took place in three sectors: industry, agriculture, and transportation.

First the industrial sector: The statistics of the clearing in the first place furnish indications on the total obligations imposed upon the various industrial branches.

On its part, the report of the military administration in Belgium, to which I shall refer again and again, gives the following details, briefly summarised. From the very beginning of the occupation the Germans required an inventory of supplies on which they were to impose considerable levies, notably textiles and non-ferrous metals.

I shall confine myself to some brief remarks on textiles and non-ferrous metals. The example of the textiles industry is particularly revealing: On the eve of the invasion, the Belgian textile industry, with its 165,000 workers, was the second most important in the country after that of the metal industry. Under the pretext of avoiding the exhaustion of the very important supplies then still available, an ordinance of 27 July 1940 prohibited the textile industry to work at more than thirty percent of its 1938 capacity. For the period from May to December 1940 alone, requisitions were not less than one billion Belgian francs; particularly they notably affected nearly half of the wool stock available in the country on 10 May, 1940, and nearly one-third of the stock of raw cotton.

On the other hand, the forced closing down of factories constituted for the Germans an excellent excuse for taking away, under pretext of rental contracts, unused equipment; or else it was requisitioned at a low price. The ordinance of 7 September 1942, which is to be found in the document book and is Exhibit RF 174, laid down the manner in which factories were to be closed in execution of the right accorded to the occupation authorities; and it also gave the right to dissolve certain business and industrial groups and to order their liquidation. Consolidation of enterprises was the pretext given. In the month of January 1944 sixty-five per cent of the textile factories had been stopped.

I shall not go into the details of this operation, and I pass to Page 58 of the report. The report of the German military administration quoted above gives particularly significant figures as to production. Of a total output of the wool industry of 72,000 tons for the period May 1940 to the end of June 1944, representing a value of 397 million Reichsmark, the division of the deliveries between the German and Belgian markets is the following

The German market, 64,700 tons - 314 million Reichsmark.

Belgian market, 7,700 tons - 83 million Reichsmark.

The whole spoliation of the textile industry is contained in these figures.

The Belgian consumption obviously suffered a great deal from the German policy of directing the textile market. The same report of the military administration furnishes other details, stating that in 1938 the needs in textile products amounted in Belgium to a monthly average of 12 kilos. The respective figures for the occupation years are the following:

1940 to 1941 - 2.1 kilos per head
1941 to 1942 - 1.4
1942 to 1943 - 1.4
1943 to 1944 - 0.7

The exhaustion of Belgian consumption under the Germans is contained in these two figures: 12 kilos per head in 1938; 0.7 kilos at the end of the occupation.

From another angle the Belgian Government gives the following details on the pillage of this production. Compulsory deliveries to Germany during the occupation amounted to:

Cotton thread, about 40 per cent of the production.

Linen, 75 per cent.

Rayon, 15 per cent.

Finally, out of the textile stocks remaining in Belgium, a great percentage was still taken away by the Germans through purchases on the Belgian market, purchases of finished or manufactured products. The equivalent of these forced deliveries can generally be found in the clearing statistics, unless it corresponds to misrepresented occupation costs.

I have finished with textiles. As to the non-ferrous metal industry, Belgium was in 1939 the largest producer in Europe of non-ferrous metals, of copper, lead, zinc, and tin. The statistics included in the report of the military command, which are to be found in Exhibit RF 173, will furnish the evidence for the Tribunal.

On 18 February 1941, in connection with the Four Year Plan, the Reich Metal Office and the Supreme Command of the Army worked out a metal plan which provided for

Belgian consumption;

Carrying out of German orders;

Exports to the Reich.

These various measures did not satisfy the occupying authorities, so they ran a certain number of salvage campaigns which were called "special actions" (Sonderaktionen) in accordance with the method they applied in all the territories of Western Europe. I shall not go into the details of these actions, which are described on Page 63 and following of the report; that is the salvage campaign for bells, printing lead, lead and copper. According to the information given by the Belgian Government, - which will be Exhibit RF 146, Page 65 of the report, - in other fields, but without admitting it, the Germans pursued a policy intended to eliminate or to restrict Belgian competition, so that in case of a German victory the economic branches concerned would have had to restrict themselves to the Belgian market, which would then have remained wide open to German business. These attempts at immediate or future suppression of competition were clearly evident in certain industrial sectors casting and smelting, metal ware, textile construction work, car assembling, construction of material for narrow-gauge railroads, and especially the shoe-manufacturing industry, for which reconstruction of destroyed factories was systematically prohibited.

But in addition, in the textile industry as well as in numerous sectors, especially in the metal industry, the weakening of the economy cannot be measured only by the size of the compulsory deliveries, but is in relation to the policy practices by the occupier, Belgian industry, especially coal and iron, suffered considerable losses as a result of directives imposed to finance the war needs.

I shall pass over the question of prices of coal. The control of the coal industry was assured by the appointment of a plenipotentiary for coal, and by centralisation of all sales in the hands of a single organ, the "single seller," under Belgian direction but with a German commissioner, I am referring to the Belgian coal office, single seller for a single purchaser, Rheinisch Westphalisches Kohlensyndikat, which ordered deliveries to be made to the Reich, to Alsace- Lorraine and Luxembourg.

According to the same German report, Page 67 for the interpreters, in spite of the rise in the price of coal agreed to on the 20 August, 1940, 1 January 1941, and I January 1943, the coal industry showed in the course of the occupation years considerable losses. In February 1943, the coal office having agreed to an increase of the sales price, the price per ton was higher than on the German domestic market. The German commissioner for the mining industry forced the Belgian industry to pay the difference in rate when exporting to the Reich by means of compensating premiums.

From the figures indicated in Exhibits RF 176 and 178, Page 69, the Tribunal may gather information as to the financial losses caused by exploitation. The report of the military administration gives, in its eleventh section, details regarding the metal industry: it suffered as greatly as had the coal industry during the occupation. In the metal industry, the Thomas works in particular, the losses resulted from the increase in the cost price and from price fluctuations in respect to certain elements pertaining to the manufacture.

In this one sector, according to the memorandum of the Belgian Government, the respective losses may be assessed at three billion Belgian francs. Still according to the same report, out of a total production of 1,400,000 tons, 1,300,000 tons of various products were exported to Germany, not including the metal delivered to Belgian factories working exclusively for Germany.

According to information furnished by the Belgian Government, the Germans removed in bulk and transported to Germany material of very great value: the total industrial spoliation is estimated by the Belgian Government at a sum of two billion Belgian francs, at the 1940 rate, of course.

These removals constitute a real material loss, and from the fragmentary indications given to the Tribunal this sum of two billion francs is the figure of which I ask the Tribunal to take note.

In view of the information available at present it is not easy to estimate the extent of the levies made on industry; it is even more difficult to evaluate it in the agricultural sector, which I shall briefly present.

Apart from the admissible needs of the occupation troops, the German authorities made an effort to obtain a supplement to the food levies in Belgium, for the purpose of increasing the food of the Reich and other territories occupied by its troops. After having employed direct methods of levying, the Germans used the services of unscrupulous agents whose job it was to purchase at any price on the secret markets, and the black market in this field took on such proportions that the occupying authorities became concerned on several occasions and, in the course of 1943, had to suppress it.

Apart from the damage to livestock, the damage to the woods and forests - which play an important role in Belgium, - resulting from abnormal cutting in the forests, brought about an excess in deforestation, and reaching a figure of 2,000,000 tons, the damage to capital caused by this premature cutting can be estimated at about 200 million francs.

The military operations proper caused damage to an extent of one hundred million Belgian francs, and according to the memorandum of the Belgian Government the total damage caused to forestry reaches a figure of 460 million Belgian francs. Taking into account the damage caused by abnormal cutting in the forests and by the establishment of airfields, the Belgian Government estimates at approximately one billion Belgian francs the losses suffered by its agriculture during the occupation.

It must be noted, without going further into this subject, that these are net losses in capital, constituting a veritable exhaustion of substance, and a consequent reduction and real consumption of the nation's resources. With this I conclude my presentation of agriculture.

Transportation: The conduct of war led the Germans to utilise to the fullest the railroad network and the canal and river system of Belgium; the result was that the railroads and river fleet are included in those sectors of Belgian economy which suffered most from the occupation and the hostilities which took place on Belgian soil. German traffic was at the same time a traffic of personnel as demanded by military operations, and a traffic of merchandise, coal, minerals, woods, food stuffs, not to speak of the considerable quantities of construction material required for the fortification of the coast of the North Sea.

Railroads: The report of the Belgian Government shows that the damage suffered by the railroads consisted of losses in capital as well as in revenue. Losses in capital resulted first and principally from requisitions and removals, to which the Germans proceeded in a wholesale fashion from the moment of their entry into Belgium. Thus, in particular, they immediately drained the stock of locomotives under the pretext of recovering German locomotives surrendered to Belgium after the war of 1914-1918 as a means of reparation.

In addition to seizures of locomotives, the National Society of Railroads was subjected to numerous requisitions of material, sometimes under the form of rental; these requisitions are estimated at four and a half billion francs at the 1940 value.

As against the losses in capital, losses in revenue resulted principally from the free transportation service required by the Wehrmacht, also from the price policy pursued by the occupying power. These levies and these exceptional costs could be borne by the organisations concerned, only by making large drains on the treasury.

Regarding automobiles, I shall say almost nothing (Page 79). The losses amount to about 3,111 million Belgian francs, out of which individuals received as compensation for requisition approximately one billion only.

We come now to river transportation. The carrying out of the plan for economic spoliation of Belgium presented the occupying power with serious transportation problems, to which I have already called attention. In this sphere the German military administration imposed upon Belgian river shipping very heavy burdens.

According to the report of the Belgian Government, the losses suffered by the Belgian river fleet took three forms:

1. Requisitions and removals by the Germans;
2. Partial or total damage through military operations,
3. Excessive deterioration of material.

These three forms of damage amount to half a billion francs, of which only one hundred million are represented in the clearing. Damage to waterways (Page 81), rivers, streams and canals, can be evaluated at between one and a half and two billion francs of 1940 value, especially by reason of requisitions and removals of public or private port material.

Fishing boats were requisitioned for marking the river Scheldt, and then disappeared without leaving any trace. Others suffered damage through requisitions or rental for military manoeuvres.

Before closing this chapter, concerned with levies in kind, the question of removal of industrial material may briefly be mentioned. (Page 82).

It has already been pointed out that the policy of production and reorganisation in the industrial sphere, as pursued by the military administration, had as a result the closing of numerous enterprises; enabling the Germans, as a counter-measure, to seize a great number of machines under the pretext that they had become useless.

There were no branches of industry which were not despoiled in this way. The metal industry seems to be one of those that suffered most. Though we do not wish to try the patience of the Tribunal, it seems particularly pertinent to draw its attention briefly to the technique used in the organisation of the levies; details of which were decided upon even before the entry of German troops into the territories of Western Europe. There were organisations which introduced military detachments - organisations emanating from the economy bureau of the General Staff of the Army and under the defendant Keitel, as Chief of the OKW.

The existence of these military detachments, veritable pillaging detachments, is proved by various German documents. Under the name of economic detachments, "Wirtschaftstruppen," or special commandos, these pillaging crews carried out nefarious and illegal activities in all the countries of Western Europe.

The secret instructions for the "economic detachment J," stationed at Antwerp are found in the file as Exhibit RF 183. They constitute a very important document, irrefutable for the German intention to pillage and an additional proof of the contempt of the National Socialist leaders for the rules of International Law.

These instructions are dated from the last days of May 1940. I should like to read a few excerpts of these instructions to the Tribunal (Exhibit RF 183, Page 1).

> "The economic detachments are formed by the office for economic armament of the High Command of the Wehrmacht. They are placed at the disposal of the High Command of the Army for employment in the countries to be occupied."

I shall skip to the bottom of Page 1 of the German document.

> "It is their mission to reconnoitre quickly and completely in their districts the scarce and rationed goods (raw materials, semi-finished products, etc.) and machines of most vital importance for the purposes of national defence; and to make a correct inventory of these stocks.
>
> In the case of machines the requisition will be made effective by a label in the case of scarce and rationed goods, it will be secured both by labelling and

by guards.

Furthermore, the economic detachments have the mission to prepare and, by order of the Army Group, to carry out the removal of scarce and rationed goods, of mineral oils and the most important machines. These missions are the exclusive responsibility of the economic detachments.

The economic detachments are to begin their activities in newly occupied territories as early as the battle situation permits."

Machines and raw materials having thus been found and identified, the new organisations went into action to dismantle and to put these machines and raw materials to use in Germany.

The above quoted document, which is Exhibit RF 183, gives precise and very interesting information on the direction and the strength of detachment J at Antwerp. The eight officers are all reserve officers, engineers, wholesale dealers, directors of mines, importers of raw materials, engineering consultants. Their names and their professions are mentioned in the document. These men are, therefore, all specialists in commerce and industry. The choice of these technicians cannot be attributed to mere chance.

According to the above instructions, and more especially to the instructions found under date of May 10, 1940, coming from General Hannecke, which will be Exhibit RF 184, once the machines or the stocks have been identified, the offices go to work: the R.O.G.E.S. on the one hand, and the compensation bureaux on the other hand; to whose activities attention has already been called in connection with the pillage of non-ferrous metals of Holland and of the Belgian industry.

Another document, which is likewise presented as Exhibit RF 184, shows that the very composition of the economic detachments emanates from the High Command. Quoting from Page 6:

"The economic detachments already mentioned in Section 1, which are composed of experts in the branches of industry existent in the respective areas, shall reconnoitre and secure stocks of raw materials and special machinery for the production of ammunition and war equipment which are at present important."

THE PRESIDENT: Is that quotation set out in your dossier?

M. DELPECH: The quotation is on Page 84, bis.

THE PRESIDENT: Would this be a convenient time to break off?

(A recess was taken)

M. DELPECH: Besides the economic detachments to which I have just drawn the attention of the Tribunal, detailed to remove and re-distribute machinery, either to factories working in the occupied country on behalf of the occupier, or to factories in Germany, the Machine Pool Office also directed these operations. Such offices were set up in all the occupied territories of Western Europe during the last months of 1942, upon the order of the Minister for Armaments, i.e. the defendant Speer, and the Office of the Four Year Plan, i.e. the defendant Goering.

The Machine Pool Office for Belgium and Northern France was set up upon the decision of the Chief of the Military Economic Section in Brussels under date of February 18th, 1943. Its activity has already been outlined to the Tribunal in connection with the despoiling of non-ferrous metal industries. Its activity did not stop there, it is found in all branches of industry. Exhibit RF 185 can give figures on its activity. This activity continued to the very last days of the occupation. Levies on machinery and instruments were not limited to industry: Exhibits RF 193 and 194 show the extent of levies on scientific instruments.

I have finished with the levies on industrial material.

I shall present briefly in the fourth chapter the question of services, first of all billeting of troops.

1. By an ordinance dated the 17 December, 1940, Page 88, the Germans imposed the costs of billeting their troops upon Belgium. Having done this, the occupation authorities justified themselves by a rather liberal interpretation of Article 52 of the Hague Convention, according to the provisions of which the occupying power may require levies in kind and in services.

The Wetter report - Exhibit RF 186 - wrongly contends that the Convention does not specify by whom the settlement should be made; Article 49 gives the right to make the occupied country defray the expenses.

Therefore Belgium had to undergo expenses to the amount of 5,900,000,000 francs for billeting costs, equipment and furniture. The payments of the Belgian treasury for the billeting is estimated in the report of the Belgian Military Administration at 5,423,000,000 francs.

It is evident that under the pretext of billeting costs, other expenses were entered to the detriment of the Belgian economy, notably - as in other occupied countries - the purchases of furniture which was to be sent to Germany.

2. Transportation and Communications.

To insure transportation and communications, the Belgian treasury had to advance a total of 8,000,000,000 francs. As already pointed out to the Tribunal the seizure by the occupation authorities covered even the river fleet, to the same extent as the transportation plan restricted the use of rail to the operation troops.

According to Article 53 of the Hague Convention, the occupying army has the right to seize the means of transportation and communications, provided that it returns them and pays indemnity. This army, however, does not possess the right to make the occupied country pay the costs of transportation put at the army's disposal.

But that is what the German Army did in Belgium.

3. Labour.

The deportation of labour to Germany and forced labour in Belgium have already been presented to the Tribunal. It seems then unnecessary to stress this point. At the most, we should recall certain consequences unfavourable to the Belgian economy. The measures pertaining to the deportation of labour have caused an economic disorganisation and weakening without precedent.

Furthermore, the departure of workers, and particularly of specialists inadequately replaced by unskilled people, women, adolescents and pensioners, brought about a decrease in production at the same time as an increase in cost prices, which complicated the problem of the financial equilibrium of industrial enterprises.

The levy of labour was the cause of political and social discontent, by reason of the dispersion of families and the inequities consequent to the requisition of workers.

The workers were required to fill levies in spheres of work which were not necessarily their own, with a resultant loss of professional abilities. Personnel were divided and transferred. The closing of artisan workshops brought about changes more or less felt in certain branches of production. The losses thus suffered cannot be measured in terms of money, but are not less in need of submission to your jurisdiction.

I have finished with this subject and will turn to a last chapter, Chapter 5, the acquisition of Belgian investments in foreign industrial enterprises, Page 93.

Since 1940, according to their general policy in all occupied countries of Western Europe, the Germans were concerned with acquiring investments in Belgian financial enterprises abroad.

The official German point of view emerges clearly from a letter dated July 29, 1941, from the Minister of Finance to the Military Commander in Belgium. I have submitted it as Exhibit RF 187.

This conception of the right to acquire investments is certainly very far from the idea as laid down by the Hague Convention in respect to the right of requisition. It clearly shows the German leaders' will to enrichment at the expense of Belgium.

Thus, the Germans, since May 1940 sought to get influence in Belgian holding companies. Not being able to violate directly International Law, particularly Article 46 of the Hague Convention, they strove to influence the members of the executive boards through persuasion rather than by force.

In the course of a conference held on May 3, 1940, at the Reich Ministry of Economics, dealing with those parts of Belgian and Dutch capital which it would be still possible to acquire, it was decided that the Military Commander in Belgium should take all necessary measures to prevent, on the one hand, the destruction, transfer, sale and illegal holding of all bonds and stocks of these countries, and, on the other hand, to induce Belgian capitalists to hand over their foreign securities to the Germans. The minutes of this conference are found in the document book and will be submitted as Exhibit RF 187.

To prevent the flight of any capital, an ordinance of June 17, 1940, was promulgated, subjecting to authorisation any sending abroad of securities and any acquisition or disposal of foreign securities.

Since August 2, 1940, the German leaders and the defendant Goering himself took a definite stand on this point. In the course of the general remarks on economic exploitation I have read to you secret directives issued in this respect by the defendant Goering. It is Exhibit RF 105, Page 97.

In spite of the German assurances and in spite of the wish of the occupying power to preserve the appearance of legality, the German desire to absorb certain investments met with serious resistance. The occupation authorities several times had to resort to force to conclude sales, in spite of the rights which they had reserved for themselves in the above cited decree of August 27, 1940. This was particularly the case regarding the investments held by the Belgian Metal Trust, the electrical enterprise of Eastern Silesia, and, still more clearly regarding the stock of the Ostrovic Metal Company, which, at that time, were wanted by the Hermann Goering Werke.

The Belgian ill will increased as the German determination to pillage became more evident. In his report of December 1, 1942, Exhibit RF 191, the German Kommissar with the National Bank vehemently denounces this resistance on the part of the Belgian market. Almost all acquisitions which could have been realised by the Germans were regulated by means of clearing.

The balance of clearing capital credited to Belgium to the sum of 1 billion Belgian francs on August 31, 1944, represents the result of borrowing forced upon Belgium without any legal or logical relation to occupation costs except the Germans' will to hegemony.

Such a practice, contrary to the principles of International Law and to the rules of criminal laws of civilised nations, falls under Article 6B of the Charter of the International Military Tribunal, and constitutes an act of pillage of public or private property such as envisaged in the prementioned text.

Closely allied to the acquisition of investments, and always within the framework of legality, the levies made by the German authorities on foreign enemy property and Jewish property should be presented to the Tribunal.

As to foreign property seized by the Germans, it must be mentioned that this measure was applied to French capital in Belgium in spite of numerous protests by the French Government. As to Jewish property, for the years 1943 and 1944, the figures are presented in Exhibit RF 192.

With this I conclude the presentation of the economic spoliation of Belgium.

The damage caused to Belgian economy in its principal sectors has just been submitted to the Tribunal. The statistical data have been taken either from German reports or from reports of the Belgian Government. The available estimates and figures are not yet sufficiently exact to fix the costs of war, the occupation and the economic spoliation of Belgium; certain losses and certain damages cannot be expressed in money. Among them, first of an, we must mention the privations resulting from German commandeering of a large part of food supplies and from the particular situation of billeting and clothing. This purely material aspect of the question should not let us overlook the consequences of the occupation upon the public health. For lack of statistical data, it is difficult to show precisely the final state of public health resulting from the particular circumstances.

One fact, however, must be remembered: the considerable increase in the number of persons who were eligible for special invalid diets. This number rose from 2,000 a month in 1941 to more than 25,000 a month in 1944. It has therefore, increased more than ten times, in spite of rationing measures which became more and more severe.

This increase in nutritional aid given to sick persons deserves the attention of the Tribunal, less for its statistical interest, than because it is an indication of the rise of disease in Belgium. This is itself the result of the undernourishment of the population during the four years of occupation.

This deplorable state of affairs, however, had not escaped the attention of the occupation authorities, as appears from the letter of the Military Commander in Belgium already cited, which is found in the document book as Exhibit RF 187:

> "Regarding the food situation in Belgium, neither the minimum of existence for the civilian population is secured nor the minimum amount necessary for feeding heavy workers who are employed solely in the interest of the German war economy."

I shall not dwell on this. This undernourishment of the Belgian population has been the inescapable and the most serious result of the huge levies made by the occupation authorities, who wilfully disregarded the elementary requirements of an occupied country in order to pursue only the war aims of the Reich.

The lowering of the average standard of health and the rise in the death rate in Belgium from 1940 to 1945 may therefore be rightly considered the direct result of the spoliations committed by the Germans in Belgium in transgression of International Law.

I have concluded the presentation on Belgium.

I would like to make a few brief remarks on the economic pillaging of Luxembourg.

Supplementing my presentation on Belgium, it is proper to present to the Tribunal some details on the conduct of the Germans in Luxembourg.

The Government of the Grand Duchy has submitted a general summary of its charges, which has been lodged with the Tribunal as Exhibit UK 77, and in which an extract covering the crimes against property, is in the document book under No. 1.

The Germans shortly after their entry into the Grand Duchy proceeded to annex it in fact. This attitude, exactly similar to that adopted towards the inhabitants of the

Departments of Moselle, Bas-Rhin and Haut-Rhin, requires some remarks.

As was their wont, one of the first measures was in connection with the rate of exchange. This they fixed as ten Luxembourg francs to one mark. It was the subject of the ordinance of August 26, 1940, to be found in the document book under Exhibit RF 195. This rate of exchange did not correspond to the respective purchasing power of the two currencies. It constituted a considerable levy on the wealth of the nationals, and especially insured the Germans a complete seizure of monetary means of payment. It procured for them a way of seizing a considerable part of the reserves of raw materials and manufactured goods of the country. The acquisitions were settled in depreciated marks on the basis of controlled prices imposed by the Germans.

Finally, by the ordinance of January 29, 1941, the Reichsmark was introduced as the only legal tender (ordinance submitted under Exhibit RF 196); the Luxembourg francs and the occupation marks were taken out of circulation, as well as Belgian francs, up to then considered as currency of the Franco-Luxembourg monetary union; all of these became foreign currency, effective from February 5, 1941.

I should like to draw the attention of the Tribunal to the fact that, of all the countries occupied by Germany, Luxembourg, Alsace and Lorraine were the only ones totally deprived of their national currency.

Moreover, to procure for the Reich the financial means necessary for the prosecution of the war, the ordinance of August 27, 1940 (Exhibit RF 197) required the forced handing over of gold and foreign currency. In addition, the same ordinance laid down that foreign shares and bonds had to be offered for sale to the Reichsbank at rates and under conditions fixed by the occupying power.

As has already been pointed out, the Germans seized industrial stocks. In this respect, the report dated May 21, 1940, on the economic situation in Holland, Belgium and Luxembourg contains information on the stocks found in the country:

 1,600,000,000 tons of iron ore;

 125,000 tons of manganese;

 10,000 tons of crude iron;

 10,000 tons of ferro-manganese;

 36,000 tons of laminated products and finished products,

and I could continue this enumeration. The German seizure extended from these stocks to industrial production.

According to the memorandum presented by the Reparations Commission of the Luxembourg Government, Exhibit RF 198, the total economic damages amount to 5,800,000,000 Luxembourg francs at 1938 value.

This figure can be broken down as follows:

 Industry and commerce - 1,900,000,000

 Railroads - 207,000,000

 Roads and Highways - 100,000,000

 Agriculture - 11,600,000,000

 Damage to property in general - 1,900,000,000

From the same official source, the total loss in capital represents about 33 per cent of the national wealth of Luxembourg; before the war estimated at approximately 5,000,000,000 Luxembourg francs.

The effect on the financial and monetary situation of the country was a loss exceeding 6,000,000,000 Luxembourg francs.

These damages particularly figure the increase in circulation of money and the total amount of forced investments in Germany - more than 4,800,000,000 Luxembourg francs - as well as additional contributions imposed upon the taxpayers of the Grand Duchy following the introduction of the German fiscal system.

To these burdens must be added the skimming of profits, the fines and the allegedly voluntary gifts of every kind imposed upon Luxembourg.

Corresponding to what was done in other countries, the ordinance of February 21, 1941 (document 199 of the document book concerning Luxembourg) provided that German managers might be appointed in large enterprises, particularly enterprises which - and this is the text of the ordinance - "which refused to militate in favour of Germanism under any circumstances."

The mission of the Commissars was to ensure for the Reich, within the scope of the Four Year Plan, the direction and control of exploitation in the exclusive interest of the German war effort.

Thus, on August 2, 1940, the Reichskommissar for the "Administration of Enemy Property" appointed to the largest metal company in Luxembourg (Arbed), the United Steel Works of Burbach-Eich-Dudelange, three German Kommissars, who secured the total seizure of the company.

Neither did other large companies escape this domination, as can be seen from the documents submitted to the Tribunal under Exhibit RF 200.

The spoliation of Luxembourg and foreign interests in the insurance field, one of the most important sectors of Luxembourg business, was complete. With the exception of three Swiss companies and a German company, the Luxembourg companies, whose assets were transferred to German insurance companies - in an official way as regards the national companies and secretly as regards the foreign companies - were prohibited from carrying on any transactions.

The insurance companies of Luxembourg were deprived of the premiums from fire insurance by the introduction of compulsory fire insurance, for which the German companies were given the monopoly.

Introducing in Luxembourg their racial policy, the National Socialists seized and confiscated all Jewish property in the Grand Duchy to the profit of the Verwaltung fur Judenvermoogen (Administration for Jewish Property).

Also in regard to the Umsiedlungspolitik (resettlement policy), 1,500 Luxembourg families (that is, roughly, 7000 persons) were deported. The Germans took possession of their property. A German trust company, incorporated in the German Office for Colonisation and Germanisation was charged with the administration of this property, and, in fact, set about its liquidation. Important assets were thus confiscated and transferred to the Reich.

Tyrolian Germans were, as has already been pointed out, installed in the houses, and in the industrial, commercial and artisan enterprises of the deportees.

That is to say, your Honours, that the Grand Duchy of Luxembourg was the victim of economic pillage as systematically organised as that in Belgium.

THE PRESIDENT: M. Delpech, the Tribunal is grateful to you for the way in which you have performed the task which they asked you to perform last night, a task which is not altogether easy, of shortening the address which you had intended to make. As far as they are able to judge, no essential parts of your address have been omitted. It is of great importance that the trial should be conducted, as the Charter indicates, in an expeditious way, and it was for this reason that the Tribunal asked you, if you could, to shorten your address.

M. DELPECH: I thank you, your Honour, for your kindness. (M. Gerthoffer takes the floor)

THE PRESIDENT: Yes, M. Gerthoffer.

M. GERTHOFFER: Mr. President, your Honours, I come to the sixth section of this presentation, which deals with the economic pillage of France.

When the Germans invaded France, they found there considerable wealth. They set about with ingenuity to seize it and also to subjugate the national economy.

When they failed to attain their ends by mere requisitions, they resorted to devious methods, using simultaneously ruse and violence, striving to cloak their criminal actions with legality.

To accomplish this, they misused the conventions of the armistice. These, in fact, did not contain any economic clauses and did not include any secret provisions, but consisted only of regulations, which were published. Nevertheless, the Germans utilised two clauses to promote their undertakings. I submit to the Tribunal under Number 203 a copy of the Armistice Conventions, and I cite Article 18, which reads as follows:

> "The maintenance costs of German occupation troops in French territory will be charged to the French Government."

This clause was not contrary to the regulations of the Hague Conventions, but Germany imposed payment of enormous sums, far exceeding those necessary for the requirements of an occupation army. Thus they were enabled to dispose, without furnishing any compensation, of nearly all the money, which, in fact, they cleverly transferred into an instrument of pillage.

Article 17 of the Armistice Conventions reads as follows

> "The French Government is bound to prevent any transfer of economic values or stocks from the territory to be occupied by the German troops into the non-occupied area or into a foreign country. Those values and stocks in the occupied territory cannot be disposed of except by agreement with the Reich Government, it being understood that the German Government will take into account what is vitally necessary for the population of the non-occupied territories."

Apparently the purpose of this clause was to prevent things of any kind which might be utilised against Germany from being sent to England or any of the colonies. But the occupying power took advantage of this to get control of production and the distribution or raw materials throughout France, since the non-occupied zone could not live without the products of the occupied zone, and vice-versa.

The intention of the Germans is proved particularly by Document 1741-PS which was discovered by the American Army, and which I now submit to the Tribunal as Exhibit RF 204.

I do not want to trouble the Tribunal by reading this long document, I shall give only a short summary.

It is a secret report, dated 5 July 1940, addressed to the President of the Council ...

THE PRESIDENT: M. Gerthoffer, this is not a document of which we can take judicial notice, is it? I think you must read anything that you wish to put in evidence.

M. GERTHOFFER: I shall read a passage of the document to the Tribunal.

THE PRESIDENT: Very well.

M. GERTHOFFER: "Article 17 grants Germany the right to seize the economic values and reserves in occupied territory, and any arrangements of the French Government are subject to approval by Germany.

In compliance with the request of the French Government, Germany has agreed to take care equally of the vital requirements of the non-occupied zone by considering applications of the French Government regarding the disposal of values and reserves in the occupied zone."

I shall only cite this passage to shorten my explanatory remarks, and I now come to the following document, which is the reply to the German official who drew up this report, a document which I submit as Exhibit RF 205. This is a document found by the American Army. Here is the reply to the document from which I just quoted the passage:

> 2. Exploitation of occupied French territory.
>
> "It is the Fuehrer's opinion that in all negotiations with France the political and not the economic point of view should be dominant. The elimination of the demarcation line is now out of the question. Should thereby the economic life of France be prevented from resuscitation, this will be quite immaterial to us. The French lost the war, and now must pay the bill. To my remark that France would then soon become a centre of unrest, I got the reply that shots would fix that and the free zone be occupied. For all concessions we make, the French must pay dearly in deliveries from the unoccupied zone and the colonies. Every effort must be made that French economy shall no longer be uncoordinated.
>
> In the course of the negotiations regarding relaxation of the demarcation line, it has been suggested that the French Government take control of gold and foreign currency in the whole of France."

Further in this document:

> "The foreign currency reserves of occupied France would strengthen our war potential. This measure could, moreover, be used in negotiations with the French Government as a means of pressure in order to make it show a more conciliatory attitude in other respects."

This concludes the quotation.

A study of these documents shows the Germans' will, in disregard of all legal principles, to get all the wealth and economy of France under their control.

Through force the Germans succeeded, after one year of occupation, in putting all or nearly all the French economy under their domination. This is evident from an article, published by Dr. Michel, director of the Economic Office, attached to the Military Government in France, which appeared in the "Beliner Borsen Zeitung," of April 10, 1942. I submit it as Exhibit RF 207 and shall read one passage from it:

> "The timely task of the competent offices of the German military administration consisted in the 'Direction of Economic Directives,' i.e. in the issuance of directives and, at the same time, in the supervision of the actual execution of these directives."

Further, on Page 12 of the statement-

> "Now that the direction of raw materials and the placing of orders has been organised and is functioning efficiently, the matter of rigorous restrictions on consumption not important to war economy is a prime consideration in France. The restrictions imposed upon the French population in respect of food, clothing, footwear and fuel, have been for some time more severe than in the Reich."

I terminate here my quotation of Dr. Michel's article.

After having shown you, Mr. President, and members of the Court, in this brief introduction concerning the economic spoliation of France, the consequences of German domination upon this country, I will give you an account of the methods employed to arrive at such a result. This will be the purpose of the four following chapters:

I. German seizure of means of payment.
II. Clandestine purchases in the black market.
III. Outwardly legal acquisitions.
IV. Impressment of labour.

I. German seizure of means of payment.

This seizure was the result of

(a) paying occupation costs;
(b) the oneway clearing system;
(c) outright seizures and levies of gold, bank notes, and foreign currency and the imposition of collective fines.

I shall not recapitulate the legal principles of the matter, but shall merely confine myself to a few explanatory remarks, so that you may realise the pressure which was brought to bear on the leaders in order to obtain the payment of considerable sums.

As I have had the honour of pointing out to you, in the Armistice Conventions the principle of the maintenance of occupation troops is succinctly worded, with no stipulation as to the amount and the method of collection. The Germans took advantage of this to distort and amplify this commitment of France, which became nothing more than a pretext for the imposition of exorbitant tribute.

At the first conferences of the Armistice Commission the discussions bore on this point, whereas the French brought out the fact that they could only be forced to pay an indemnity representing the cost of maintaining an army strictly necessary for the occupation of the territory. The German General Wieth had to recognise the just foundation of this claim, and declared that troops which were to fight against England would not be maintained at the expense of France.

This is evident from an extract from minutes of the Armistice Commission, which I submit as Exhibit RF 208. But, later, General Wieth apparently was overruled by his superiors, as in the course of a subsequent conference, July 16, 1940, without expressly going back on his word, he declared that he could not say that this question would no longer be discussed and that, in short, everything necessary would be done to enable the French Government to draw up its budget. This appears from an extract of the minutes of the Armistice Commission, which I submit as Exhibit RF 209.

On 8 August 1940, Hemmen, Chief of the German Economic Delegation, at Wiesbaden, forwarded a memorandum to General Huntziger, President of the French Delegation, in which he stated:

"As at present it is impossible to assess the exact costs, daily instalments of at least 20 million Reichsmark are required until further notice, at a rate of exchange of 1 mark to 20 French francs," that is to say, 400 million francs daily. In this amount the costs for billeting troops were not included, but were to be paid separately."

This is found in Exhibit RF 210, which I submit to the Tribunal and which bears the signature of Hemmen.

These exorbitant requirements provoked the reply of 12 August 1940, in which it was emphasised that the amount of the daily payment did not permit the supposition that it had been fixed in consideration of the normal strength of an occupation army, and the normal cost of the maintenance of this army; that, moreover, such forces as corresponded to the notified figure would be out of proportion to anything that military precedent and the necessity of the moment might reasonably justify. This is the content of a note of 12 August, submitted as Exhibit RF 211.

On August 15, 1940, the German delegation took notice of the fact that the French

Government was ready to pay these accounts, but in a categorical manner refused to discuss either the amount of payment or the distinction between occupation and operation troops. This is found in Exhibit RF 212, which I submit to the Tribunal.

On August 18, the French Delegation took notice of the memorandum of 15 August and made the following reply.

"That France is to pay the costs for the maintenance of operation troops is a demand incontestably beyond the spirit and the provisions of the Armistice Convention.

That the required costs are converted into francs at a rate considerably in excess of the purchasing power of the mark and franc respectively; furthermore, that the purchases of the German army in France are a means of control over the life in that country and that they will, moreover, as the German Government admits, partly be replaced by deliveries in kind."

The memorandum terminates as follows:

"In these circumstances the onerous tribute required of the French Government appears arbitrary, and exceeds to a considerable extent what might legitimately be expected.

The French Government, always anxious to fulfil faithfully the clauses of the Armistice Convention, can only appeal to the Reich Government in the hope that it will take into account the arguments presented above."

THE PRESIDENT: The Court will adjourn now.

(A recess was taken)

M. GERTHOFFER: This morning I had the honour of presenting to the Tribunal the fact that the Germans demanded of France an indemnity of 400 million francs a day for the maintenance of their army of occupation. I had indicated that the French leaders of that time, though not failing to recognise the principle of their obligation, protested against the sum demanded. At the moment of their arrival in France the Germans had issued in France, as in the other occupied countries, for that matter, occupation marks and requisition vouchers over which the Bank of Issue had no control and which was legal tender only in France. This issuance represented a danger, for the circulation of this currency was liable to increase at the mere will of the occupying power.

At the same time, by a decree of 17 May 1940, published in the VOBIF of 17 May 1940, No. 7, which appears as Exhibit RF 214 in the document book, the occupying power fixed the rate of the Reichsmark at 20 French francs per Mark, whereas the real parity was approximately one Mark for 10 French francs.

The French Delegation, concerned over the increasing circulation of the occupation marks, and over the increased volume of German purchases, as well as over the rate of exchange of the Mark, was informed by the German Delegation, on 14 August 1940, of its refusal to withdraw these notes from circulation in France. This is to be found in a letter of 14 August, which I submit as Exhibit RF 215.

The occupying power thus unjustifiably created a means of pressure upon the French Government of that time, to make it yield to its exactions in the amount of the occupation costs as well as in the pegged rate of the Mark and the clearing agreements, which will be the subject of a later chapter.

In consequence, General Huntziger, President of the French Delegation, addressed several dramatic appeals to the German Delegation in which he asked that France be not hurled over the precipice. This is evidenced by a teletype report addressed by Hemmen on 18 August 1940 to the Minister of Foreign Affairs, a report discovered by the United States Army, (Document 1741-PS 5), which I submit to the Tribunal as Exhibit RF 216. Here is the interesting passage of this report:

> "These considerable payments would enable Germany to purchase the whole of France, including its foreign interests and investments, and this would mean the ruin of France."

In a letter and note of 20 August, the German Delegation put the French Delegation in a position to make partial payments, specifying that no distinction would be made about the German troops in France, and that the strength of the German occupation would have to be determined by the necessities of the conduct of war. In addition, the fixing of the rate of the mark would be inoperative as far as the payments were concerned, since they would constitute only payments on account.

I submit the note of 20 August of the German Government, which will be Exhibit RF 217.

The next day, 21 August, 1940, General Huntziger, in the course of an interview with Hemmen, made a last vain attempt to obtain a reduction in the German demands. According to the minutes of this interview, Germany was already considering close economic collaboration between herself and France through the creation of Kommissars of Control of Exchange and of Foreign Trade. At the same time Hemmen pledged elimination of the demarcation line between the two zones. But he refused to discuss the question of the amount of the occupation costs.

In a note of 26 August 1940 the French Government indicated that it considered itself obliged to yield under pressure and protested against the German demands; this note ended with the following passage:

> "The French nation fears neither work nor suffering, but it must be allowed to live. This is why the French Government would be unable in the future to continue along the road to which it is committed, if experience showed that the extent of the demands of the Reich government is incompatible with this right to live." This ends the quotation of this document which is submitted as Exhibit RF 219.

The Germans had the unquestionable intention of utilising the sums demanded as occupation costs, not only for the maintenance, the equipment, and the armament of their troops in France, or for operations based in France, but also for other purposes. This is shown in particular in a teletype from the Supreme Command of the Army, dated 2 September, 1940, discovered by the United States Army, which I submit as Exhibit RF 220. There is a passage from this teletype message which I shall read to the Tribunal: (Page 22).

> "To the extent to which the incoming amounts in francs are not utilised by the troops in France, the Supreme Command of the armed Forces reserves for itself the right to dispose further of the foreign currency. In particular, the allocation of foreign currency to other offices not belonging to the Armed Forces, requires the authorisation of the Supreme Command of the Armed Forces, in order to ensure definitely, first, that the entire amount of francs required by the Armed Forces shall be covered, and second that thereafter any possible surplus shall remain at the disposal of the Supreme Command of the Armed Forces for purposes important to the Four Year Plan."

From another teletype message, which was seized in the same manner and which I submit as Exhibit RF 221, I read the following:

> "It is clear that there was no agreement at all with the French as to what should be understood by 'costs for maintenance of occupation troops' in France. If among ourselves we are in agreement on the fact that at the

present moment we must, for practical reasons, avoid all discussion, then on the other hand, discussions with the French must leave no doubt that we have the right to interpret the term 'maintenance' in the broadest possible sense."

Further on in the same teletype, Page 24, paragraph 2 there is the following:
"In any case, the concessions demanded by the French on the question of specifying the amount of occupation costs and of the utilisation of the francs thus delivered must be rejected:

And finally the following paragraph:
"The utilisation of sums paid in francs:
Concerning the utilisation of the francs paid, and the fact that their use does not correspond to the costs really involved in the maintenance of occupation troops in France, this is a question that must be not discussed with the French authorities."

The French then attempted, in vain, to obtain a reduction in the occupation costs and also a modification in the rate of the Mark, but the Germans refused all discussion.

At the beginning of the year 1941 negotiations were resumed (Page 42). In view of the intransigence of the Germans, the French Government suspended payments in the month of May, 1941. Then, at the insistence of the occupying power they resumed it, but paid only 300 million francs a day. This is found in the document submitted as Exhibit RF 222.

On the 15 September, 1942, after the invasion of French territory, Germany demanded that the daily payment of 300 million francs be raised to 500 million.

The sums paid for the occupation troops increased to a total of 631 866,000,000 francs, or, on the imposed rate, 31,593,300,000 Mark. This amount can be calculated not only from the information given by the French administration but can also be verified by German documents, in particular the report of Hemmen.

Hemmen, director of the Ministry of Foreign Affairs in Berlin, had been designated President of the German economic delegation of the Armistice Commission, and he was acting, in fact, under the direct orders of his Minister, von Ribbentrop, as a veritable dictator in economic questions. His chief assistant in Paris was Doctor Michel, of whom we have already spoken.

While maintaining his functions as chief of the economic delegation of the Armistice Commission of Wiesbaden, the same Hemmen was to be appointed by a decision of Hitler, under date of 19 December 1942, delegate of the Government of the Reich for economic questions, attached to the French Government. This is verified in the Exhibit RF 223.

Hemmen periodically sent secret economic reports to his minister. These documents were discovered by the United States Army. They are of a fundamental importance in this part of the trial, since, as you will see, they contain Germany's admission of economic pillaging.

These voluminous reports are submitted under Exhibits RF 224, 225, 226, 227, 228, and 229 of the French documentation. It is not possible for me, important though they are, to read them in their entirety to the Tribunal. I shall confine myself to quoting a few brief extracts in the course of my presentation. As an example of their importance, here is the translation of the last volume of the Hemmen reports.

In this last report, printed in Salzburg on 15 December 1944, on Page 26, Hemmen recognises that France has paid by way of indemnity for the maintenance of occupation troops 31,593,300,000 Mark, that is ....

THE PRESIDENT: M. Gerthoffer, these documents are in German, are they not?

M. GERTHOFFER: Yes, Mr. President, they are in German. I have only been able to have the last one translated into French; because of their length it has not been possible for me to have all the translations made, but it is from the last volume, which is translated into French, that I will make certain very brief quotations.

THE PRESIDENT: Yes, well then are you confining yourself to the last document, and to certain passages in the last document?

M. GERTHOFFER: I shall limit myself to this.

THE PRESIDENT: And then, as these are not documents of which we can take judicial notice, only the parts which you read will be regarded as part of the record, and be treated as in evidence.

M. GERTHOFFER: This enormous sum imposed was much greater than that which Germany was entitled to demand. In spite of the enormous sums which the Germans may have spent in France during the first two years, they could not use even half of the amount of their credit.

This is brought out in the Hemmen report, where on Page 27, (Page 59 of the French translation) he gives a summary of the French payments made as occupational indemnity, and the German expenses in millions of Mark corresponding to these expenses. This summary is very short. I shall read it to the Tribunal. It will constitute a German proof in support of my presentation.

Year	French payment in millions of Marks	German expenditure in millions of Marks
1940	4,000	1,569
1941	6,075	5,205
1942	5,475	8,271
1943	9,698	9,524
1944	6,345	6,748

The figures contained in this table unquestionably constitute the German admission of the exorbitance of the indemnity for the maintenance of occupation troops, since Germany was not able to utilise the credit at its disposal, especially as most of this served to finance expenses relative to armament, operation troops, and feeding of Germany. This is shown by Document EC 232, which I submit as Exhibit RF 230 of the French documentation.

According to the calculation of the Economic Analysis Institute, the maximum sum of the indemnity which could be exacted amounted to 74,531,800,000 francs; taking as a basis the medium daily costs of upkeep per troop unit in the course of the entire Allied occupation of the Rhineland in 1919, namely the sum of seventeen francs increased to twenty- one francs, and taking into account the billeting, which was at that time provided by the German Government. According to the report of the average indices of living cost of 3.14, the sum of 21 francs should correspond to 66 francs at the 1939 value, when applying the co-efficient of depreciation of the franc during the occupation, that is 2.10 per cent, or a daily average cost of 199 francs per day.

Granting that the real costs of the occupation army were half of these calculated by Hemmen, that is to say, 27,032,079,120 Mark, this sum is still lower than the 74,531,800,000 calculated by the Economic Analysis Institute.

Even accepting the calculation most favourable to the accused, one can estimate that the indemnity imposed without justification amounted to 631, 866,000,000 less 74,531,800,000 or 557,334,200,000 francs.

In his final report, Page 19, at Page 22 of the French translation, Hemmen writes, -
"during the four years which have passed since conclusion of the Armistice, there has been paid in occupation and billeting costs, thirty-four million Reichsmark or six-hundred and eighty million francs."

France thus contributed approximately forty per cent of the total cost of occupation and war contributions raised in all the occupied and Allied countries. This represents a charge of eight hundred and thirty Reichsmark, or sixteen-thousand six hundred francs per head of the population.

In the second part of this chapter we shall examine briefly the question of Clearing. The Tribunal is acquainted with the function of the Clearing device; we shall not revert to this. I shall indicate under what conditions the French Government at the time was made to sign agreements which were imposed upon it.

Parallel to the discussions relative to the indemnity for the maintenance of occupation troops, discussions were entered into concerning the Clearing Agreement.

On 24 July 1940, the German Delegation announced that it would shortly submit a project. On 8 August 1940, Hemmen submitted to the French Delegation a project of Franco- German arrangement for payment of compensation. This project, which I submit as Exhibit RF 231 of the French documentation, contained drastic rules, which could not be voluntarily accepted.

First is provided financial transfers from France to Germany without any equivalent in financial transfers from Germany to France.

Then it fixed the rate of exchange of twenty francs for one Reichsmark by a unilateral and clearly arbitrary decision, whereas the rate on the Berlin exchange was approximately 17.65 and the real parity of the two currencies, taking into account their respective purchasing power on both markets, was approximately ten francs for one Mark.

I shall go on to Page 34. The French Delegation of the Armistice Commission submitted unsuccessfully on 20 August 1940, a counter project, and attempted to obtain a modification of the most unfavourable clauses. I submit this project as Exhibit RF 232 of the French documentation.

On 21 August 1940, at the Armistice Commission, the French Delegation brought up in detail the question of the Franc- Reichsmark parity, and it called attention to the fact of the prohibition of the financial transfer from Germany to France creating a gross inequality, whereas the transfer in the other direction was organised, and pointed out that this meant, that the French Government had to give its agreement to a veritable dispossession of French creditors. An extract from this report is presented and submitted as Exhibit RF 232.

In a letter of 31 August, General Huntziger again took up in vain the argument as to the Franc-Reichsmark rate of exchange. I submit this letter as Exhibit RF 234.

On 6 September 1940, the French Delegation made a new attempt to obtain a modification of the most unfavourable clauses of the Clearing Agreement, but it met with a flat refusal. The German Delegation meant to impose, under the cloak of a bilateral agreement, a project elaborated by it alone.

I quote a passage from the minutes of the Armistice Delegation. Herr Schone, the German delegate, stated:
"I cannot reopen the discussion on this question. I can make no concession."

Concerning the Franc-Reichsmark rate of exchange on 4 October 1940, Hemmen notified the French Delegation that the rate of twenty francs must be considered as definite and, according to his own words, "this is no longer to be discussed." He added that if the French for their part refused to conclude a payment agreement, that is to say the drastic contract imposed by Germany, he would advise the Fuehrer of this, and that all facilities with regard to the demarcation line would be stopped.

I submit this extract from the minutes as Exhibit RF 236.

Finally, in the course of the negotiations which followed on 10 October 1940, the French Delegation attempted for the last time to obtain an alleviation of the drastic conditions which were imposed upon it, but the Germans remained intransigent and Hemmen declared in particular...

THE PRESIDENT: M. Gerthoffer, do these negotiations lead up to a conclusion, because if they do, would it not be sufficient for your purpose to give us the conclusion without giving all the negotiations which lead up to it?

M. GERTHOFFER: Mr. President, I am just finishing the statement with the last quotation, in which the Tribunal may see what pressure - what threats were made upon the French, who were then in contact with the Germans. I shall have concluded the discussion of the Clearing with this quotation, if the Tribunal will allow it; it will be a short one and it will then be finished.

It was at the last meeting of 10 October 1940, in the course of which Hemmen declared the following: I submit this as Exhibit RF 237:

"You are attempting to make the rate of the Mark fictitious. I beg you to warn your government that we shall break off negotiations. I certainly foresaw that you would be unable to prevent the prices from rising, but now you are systematically causing them to rise for export purposes. We shall find other means of achieving our aims. We shall go and take the bauxite." This is the end of the quotation.

If the Tribunal will allow me a very brief comment. At the Armistice Commission all kinds of economic questions were discussed, and to the very end the French delegates resisted, for Germany wanted to seize immediately the bauxite resources, which were in the unoccupied zone. This last sentence is the threat: if you do not accept our Clearing Agreement, we shall seize the bauxite. That is to say, we shall occupy the free zone by force of arms.

The so-called compensation agreement worked only to Germany's advantage. The results of the agreement are the following (Page 116):

At the moment of liberation the total transfer from France to Germany amounted to 221,114,000,000 francs, while the total transfer from Germany to France amounted to 50,474,000,000 francs. The difference, that is, 170,640,000,000 francs credit balance on the French account, represents the means of payment which Germany improperly obtained through the functioning of the Clearing which it had imposed.

I now come to the third part of this chapter, which will be very brief. This is the seizure of goods and collective fines.

Besides the transactions which were outwardly legal, the Germans proceeded to make seizures and to impose collective fines, in violation of the principles of International Law.

Firstly: a contribution of one billion francs was imposed upon the French Jews on 17 December 1941, without any pretext. This is evidenced by the documents submitted as Exhibit RF 239, and cannot be contested.

Secondly: a certain number of collective fines were imposed. The amount made known by the Finance Ministry amounted to 412,636,550 francs.

Thirdly; the Germans proceeded to make immediate seizure of gold stocks, and even Hemmen admits in his last secret report, on Pages 33 and 34, Page 72 of the French translation, that on 24 September 1940, the Germans seized 257 kilograms of gold from the port of Bayonne, which represented at the 1939 rate 12,336,000 francs, and in July 1940 they seized a certain number of silver coins, amounting to 35 millions.

Still following the secret report of Hemmen for the period between January 1 and 30 June 1942, Germany had seized in France 221,730 kilograms of gold belonging to the Belgian National Bank, which represents, at the 1939 rate, the sum of nine billion five hundred million francs.

It is not possible for me to present in detail the conditions under which the Belgian gold was delivered to the Germans. This question in itself would involve me in an explanation which would take up several sessions. The fact is undeniable since it is admitted by Hemmen.

I shall simply indicate that, as early as the month of September 1940 in violation of International Law, Hemmen had insisted on the delivery of this gold, which had, in May 1940, been entrusted by the National Bank of Belgium to the Bank of France. Moreover these facts are part of the accusations made against the ex-minister of the Vichy Government before the High Court of Justice in Paris.

The sequels to this procedure were long and frequent discussions that took place at the Armistice Commission, and an agreement was concluded on 29 October 1940, but was not in fact carried out, because of difficulties raised by the French and Belgians.

According to the former Assistant Director of the Bank of France the German pressure became stronger and stronger. Laval, who was then determined to pay any price for the authorisation to go to Berlin, where he boasted that he would be able to achieve a large scale liberation of prisoners, the reduction of the occupation costs, as well as the elimination of the demarcation line, yielded to the German demands.

Thus, this gold was delivered to the Reichsbank and was requisitioned by order of the Plenipotentiary for the Four Year Plan. The documents relative to this question are submitted as Exhibit RF 240.

I shall simply add that after the liberation, the Provisional Government of the French Republic transferred to the National Bank of Belgium a quantity of gold equal to that which the Belgian Bank had entrusted to the Bank of France in the month of May 1940.

To conclude the gold question I shall indicate to the Tribunal that Germany was unable to obtain the gold resources of France, since these had been put in safe keeping in good time. Finally, still according to the last secret report of Hemmen, Page 29, and Page 49 of the French translation, at the moment of their retreat the Germans seized, without any right, the sum 6,899,000,000 francs from branches of the Bank of France in Nancy, Belfort and Epinal.

I note for the record that in the course of the occupation the Germans seized great quantities of gold which they arranged to be bought from private citizens by intermediaries. I cannot give figures for this. I simply touch on the question for the record.

If we summarise the question of the means of payment which Germany unduly raised in France, we shall reach - still taking the calculation most favourable to the defendants, and taking the maximum amount for the cost of maintaining occupation troops - a minimum total of 745,833,392,550 francs, in round figures 750,000,000,000 francs (Page 43).

M. GERTHOFFER: Gentlemen, I pass over the remarks in my written presentation in order not to take up the time of the Tribunal. I have quoted some passages from Hemmen's report, but I think it is superfluous, since the fact is known and indisputable.

I now come to Page 50, which refers to the use which the Germans made of these considerable sums, and first of all, to the black market organised by the occupying power. Here again I do not want to take advantage of your kind attention. I have had the honour of presenting to you the mechanism of the black market in all the occupied countries. I have indicated how it arose, how the Germans utilised it, how, under the orders of the defendant Goering, it was organised and exploited. I do not wish to revert to this, and I shall pass over the whole section of my written expose which was devoted to the black market in France.

I come to Page 69 of my written expose, Chapter 3: Ostensibly legal acquisitions appear.

Under the pressure of the Germans, the Vichy Government had to consent to reserve for them a very high quota of products of all kinds; in exchange the Germans undertook to furnish raw materials, the quantities of which were determined by them alone. But these raw materials, when they were delivered, which was not always the case, were for the most part absorbed by the industry which was forced to furnish them the finished products. In fact, there was no compensation, since the occupying power recovered, in the form of finished products, the raw materials delivered, and did not in reality give anything in return.

In the report of the Economic Control which has already been quoted, submitted as Exhibit RF 1075 the following example may be noted:

"An agreement permitted the purchase in the free zone of 5,000 trucks destined for the German G.B.K. whereby the Reich furnished five tons of steel per vehicle, or a total of 25,000 tons of steels destined for French industry. In view of the usual destination of the products of our metal industry at that time, this was obviously a one-sided bargain, indeed if our information is exact, the deliveries of steel to be made in return were never made, and they were partly used for the defence of the Mediterranean coast rails, anti-tank defences, etc."

It is appropriate to call attention to the fact that a considerable part of the levies in kind were the object of no regulation whatever, either because the Germans remained debtors in these transactions or because they considered, without justification, that these levies constituted war booty.

In regard to this there are no documents available; however, the United States Army has discovered a secret report of one Kraney representing the R.O.G.E.S., an organisation which was charged with collecting both war booty and acquisitions from the black market. It appears from this report that in September, 1944, the R.O.G.E.S. had resold to Germany for 10,858,499 Mark, or 217,169,980 francs, goods seized in the Southern zone as war booty. I submit this document as Exhibit RF 244.

As a result of the means of payment exacted by Germany and of requisitions, whether regulated or not, France was literally despoiled. Enormous quantities of articles of all kinds were removed by the occupying power. According to information given by the French statistical services preliminary estimates of the minimum of these levies have been made. These estimates do not include damage resulting from military operations, but solely the German spoliations computed, in cases of doubt, at a minimum figure; they will be summarised in the eight following sections.

1. Levies of agricultural produce.

I submit as Exhibit RF 245, the report of the Ministry of Agriculture, and a statistical table drawn up by the Institute for Statistics, summarising the official German levies, which included neither individual purchases nor black market purchases, both of which were considerable. It is not possible for me to read to the Tribunal a table of such length, so I will confine myself to giving a brief resume of it.

Here are some of the chief agricultural products which were seized, and their estimated value in millions of francs: (I am indicating the totals in round figures).

Cereals: 8,900,000 tons; estimate: 22,000,000 francs
Meat: 900,000 tons; estimate: 30,000,000 francs
Fish: 51,000 tons; estimate: 1,000,000 francs
Wines liquors: 13,413,000 hectolitres; estimate: 18,500,000 francs
Colonial products: 47,000 tons; estimate: 805,900 francs
Horses and mules: 690,000 heads;
Wood: 36,000,000 cubic metres
Sugar: 11,600,000 tons

I shall pass over the details. The Germans regulated by way of clearing and occupation costs 113,620,376,000 francs, the balance, that is 13 billions, was not subject to any regulation.

Naturally, these estimates do not include considerable damage caused to forests as a result of abnormal cutting, and the reduction of areas under cultivation. There is no mention, either, of the reduction in livestock or damage caused by soil exhaustion. This is a brief summary of the percentage of official German levies on agriculture in relation to the total French production

Wheat: 13%
Oats: 75%
Hay and straw: 80%
Meat: 21%
Poultry: 5%
Eggs: 60%
Butter: 20%
Preserved fish: 30%
Champagne: 56%
Wood for industrial uses: 50%
Forest fuels: 50%
Alcohol: 25%

These percentages, I repeat, do not include quantities of produce which the Germans bought up either by individual purchases or on the black market.

I have had the privilege of presenting to you the fact that these operations were of a considerable scope, and amounted for France approximately to several hundred billions of francs. The quantities of agricultural produce thus taken from French consumers are incalculable. I shall merely indicate that wines, champagne, liquors, meat, poultry, eggs, and butter were the object of a very considerable clandestine traffic to the benefit of the Germans, and that the French population, aside from certain privileged persons, was almost entirely deprived of these products.

In section 2 of this chapter I shall discuss the important question concerning levies of raw materials.

THE PRESIDENT: This would be a good time for us to adjourn for ten minutes.

(A recess was taken)

M. GERTHOFFER: The summary of the levies on raw materials, from the statistical point of view, is contained in charts which I shall not take the time to read to the Tribunal. I shall submit them as Exhibit RF 246 and point out that the total amount of these supplies reaches the sum of 83,804,145,000 francs.

On Pages 77 to 80 of the brief I had thought it necessary to make a summary of these charts, but I consider it impossible to read even the summary because the figures are too numerous.

According to information provided by the French administration, of that sum the Germans regulated by way of occupation costs and clearing only 59,254,639,000 francs, charging the difference of 19,506,109,000 francs to the French Treasury.

The percentage of the German levies in relation to the whole French production can be summarised in a chart which I have reproduced in my brief, and I shall ask the Tribunal for permission to read it. (Page 82.)

"The percentage of levies of raw materials in relation to French production,

Coal 29%
Electric power 22%
Petroleum and motor fuel 80%
Iron ore 74%
Steel products crude and half finished 51%
Copper 75%
Lead 43%
Zinc 38%
Tin 67%
Nickel 64%
Mercury 50%
Platinum 76%
Bauxite 40%
Aluminium 75%
Magnesium 100%
Sulphur Carbonate 80%
Industrial soap 67%
Vegetable oil 40%
Carbosol 100%
Rubber 38%
Paper and cardboard 16%
Wool 59%
Cotton 53%
Flax 65%
Leather 67%
Cement 55%
Lime 20%
Acetone 21%

This enumeration permits us to consider that officially about three quarters of the raw materials were seized by the occupying power, but these statistics must be qualified in two ways:

A great part of the quota of raw materials, which were theoretically left to the French economy, was in fact reserved for industries which had a priority on them; that is to say, those industries whose production was reserved for the occupying power.

These levies and percentages include only the figures of official deliveries. We have seen that the Germans acquired considerable quantities of raw materials from the black market, especially precious metals; - gold, platinum, silver, radium, - or rare metals, such as mercury, nickel, tin and copper.

In fact, one can say in general that the raw materials which were left for the needs of the population were insignificant.

Now, I come to Section 3. Levies of manufactured goods and products of the mining industry.

As I had the honour to point out to you in my general remarks, the Germans, using divers means of pressure, succeeded in utilising directly or indirectly the greater part of the French industrial production.

I shall not go over these facts again and I shall immediately pass to a summary of the products which were delivered. I submit as Exhibit RF 248 a chart which includes statistical data listed according to industries, of levies of manufactured goods during the course of the occupation by the occupying power.

I do not want to tax the patience of the Tribunal by reading this, I shall simply cite the summary of this chart, which is as follows:

Orders for products finished and invoiced from 25 June 1940 until liberation.

Mechanical and electrical industries 59,455,000,000

Chemical industry 11,744,000,000

Textiles and leather 15,802,000,000

Building and construction material 56,256,000,000

Mines, coal, aluminium and phosphates 4,160,000,000

Steel products 4,474,000,000

Motor fuel 568,000,000

Naval construction 6,104,000,000

Aeronautical construction 23,620,000,000

Miscellaneous industries 2,457,000,000

a total, then, of 184,640,000,000.

These statistics may be commented upon as follows:

(1) The information which is contained here, does not include the production of the very industrialised Departments of Nord and of Pas de Calais, attached to the German administration in Brussels, nor does it include the manufactures of the Haut-Rhin, Bas-Rhin and Moselle Departments, actually incorporated into the Reich.

(2) Out of the total sum of 184,640,000,000 francs worth of supplies, the information which we have up to date does not as yet permit us to fix the amount regulated by the Germans by way of either occupation costs or clearing, or the balance which was not made the subject of any final settlement.

(3) If one were to make, on the basis of contracts, an estimate of the industrial production levied by Germany in the Departments of Nord and Pas de Calais, [Page 68] one could obtain a figure for those two departments of 18,500,000,000, which would bring the approximate total up to more than 200,000,000,000 francs.

The extent of the German levies on manufactured products is summarised in the following chart, which I submit to the Tribunal and which I have summarised on Page 87.

I shall take the liberty of re-reading it to the Tribunal and it will show the proportion of the manufactured goods which were withdrawn from French consumption.

Automobile construction 70%

Electrical and radio construction 45%
Industrial precision parts 100%
Heavy castings 100%
Foundries 46%
Chemical industries 34%
Rubber industry 60%
Paint and varnish 60%
Perfume 33%
Wool industry 28%
Cotton weaving 15%
Flax and cotton weaving 12%
Industrial leather 20%
Buildings and public works 75%
Wood work and furniture 50%
Lime and cement 68%
Naval construction 79%
Aeronautic construction 90%

The scrutiny of this chart leads me to make the following remarks: The proportion of entirely finished products is very large, for instance:

Automobiles 70%
Precision instruments 100%
Heavy castings 100%

The proportion of the products in the process of manufacture, however, is not as large, for example:

Foundry 46%
Chemical industry 34% etc.

This state of affairs results from the fact that the Germans directed the products in the process of manufacture, in theory reserved for the French population, into finishing industries which had priority, that is to say, whose production was reserved for them.

Finally, through their purchases on the black market, the Germans procured an enormous quantity of textiles, machine tools, leather, perfume, and so forth. The French population was almost completely deprived of textiles during the occupation. That is also true for leather.

Now, I reach Section 4, the removal of industrial tools. I shall not impose on your time; this question has already been treated as far as the other occupied countries are concerned. I would merely point out that in France it was the object of statistical estimates which I submit to you as Exhibit RF 251. These statistical estimates show that the value of the material which was removed from the various French factories under private or public enterprise exceeds the sum of 9,000,000,000 francs.

It was observed that for many of the machines which were removed, the Germans merely indicated the inventory value after reduction due to depreciation, and not the replacement value of the machines.

I now come to Section 5: Securities and Foreign Investments, in document EC 57 which I submitted as Exhibit RF 105 at the beginning of my presentation, [Page 69] I had indicated that the defendant Goering himself had informed you of the aims of the German economic policy, and that he ventured to say that the extension of German influence over foreign enterprises was one of the purposes of that policy.

These directives were to be expressed much more precisely in the document of the 12 August, 1940, which I submit as Exhibit RF 252, and from which I shall read a short extract.

"Since "-as the document says-" the principal economic enterprises are in the form of stock companies, it is first of all indispensable to secure the ownership of securities in France."

Further on it says:

"the exertion of influence by way of directives..."

Then the document indicates all the means to be employed to achieve this, in particular this passage concerning International Law :

"According to Article 46 of the Hague Convention, concerning land warfare, private property cannot be confiscated. Therefore the confiscation of securities is to be avoided in so far as it does not concern securities belonging to the State. According to Article 42 and following of the Hague Convention concerning land warfare, the authority exercising power in the occupied enemy territory must restrict itself in principle to utilising measures which are necessary to re-establish or maintain order and public life; to conform to International Law it is forbidden in principle to eliminate the still existing boards of companies and to replace them by 'Kommissars.' Such a measure would, from the point of view of International Law, probably not be considered as efficacious. Consequently, we must strive to force the various boards of companies to work for the German economy, but not dismiss these persons..."

Further on :

"If these boards refuse to be directed, we must dissolve them and replace them by others of which we can make use."

We will briefly consider the three categories of seizure of financial investments, which were the purpose of German spoliation during the occupation, and first of all the seizure of financial investments in companies whose interests were abroad.

On the 14 August, 1940, an ordinance was published in V.O.B.I.F., Page 67, forbidding any negotiations regarding credits or foreign securities. But mere freezing of securities did not satisfy the occupying power; it was necessary for them to become outwardly the owners of the securities in order to be able if necessary, to negotiate with them in neutral countries.

They had some agents who purchased foreign securities from private citizens who needed money, but above all, they put pressure on the Vichy Government to hand over the principal French investments in foreign countries.

That is why, in particular, after long discussions, in the course of which the German pressure was very great, considerable surrenders of investments were made to the Germans.

It is not possible for me to submit to the Tribunal the numerous documents concerning the surrender of these investments, the minutes, the correspondence, the survey. They would, without exaggeration, take up several cubic metres. I shall merely quote several passages as examples.

Concerning the Bor Mines Company, the copper mines in Yugoslavia, of which the greatest part of the capital was in French hands, the Germans appointed on 26 July 1940, an administrative Commissar for these branches of the company situated in Yugoslavia. I submit this to the Tribunal as Exhibit RF 254. The administrative Commissar was Herr Neuhausen the German Consul General for Yugoslavia and Bulgaria.

In the course of the discussions of the Armistice Commission Hemmen declared - and this is found in an extract from the minutes of 27 September 1940 which I submit to the Tribunal as Exhibit RF 255:

> "Germany wishes to acquire the shares of the company, without concern for the juridical objections made by the French. Germany obeys, in fact, the imperative consideration of the economic order. She suspects that the Bor Mines are still delivering copper to England, and she has definitely decided to take possession of these mines... "

I now submit to the Tribunal, as Exhibit RF 256, an extract from the minutes of a meeting held on 4 October, 1940, which Hemmen faced with the refusal of the French delegates, stated,

> "I regret to have to transmit such a reply to my Government. See if the French Government cannot reconsider its attitude. If not, our relations will become very difficult. My Government is anxious to bring this matter to a close. If you refuse, the consequences will be extremely grave."

M. de Boisanger, the French Delegate, replied:

> "I will therefore put that question once more."

And Hemmen replied:

> "I shall expect your reply by to-morrow. If it does not come, I shall transmit the negative reply which you have just given."

Then, in the course of a meeting on 9 January 1941, Hemmen stated - and I submit again an extract from the minutes, which will be Exhibit RF 257:

> "I had, from the beginning, been entrusted with this affair at Wiesbaden. Then it was discussed by the Consul General Neuhausen, on behalf of a very high-ranking personage, (Marshal Goering) and it was handled directly in Paris with M. Laval and M. Abetz."

As far as French investments in petroleum companies in Roumania are concerned, the pressure was no less. In the course of the meeting of 10 October 1940, of the Armistice Commission, the same Hemmen stated - and I submit this as Exhibit RF 258, an extract from the minutes of the meeting:

> "Moreover, we shall be satisfied with the majority of the shares. We will leave in your hands anything which we do not need for this purpose. Can you accept on this point in principle? The matter is urgent. As for the Bor Mines, we want all."

On 29 of November 1940, Hemmen stated again - and I submit this extract of the minutes of the Armistice Commission meeting as Exhibit RF 259:

> "We are still at war and we must exert immediate influence over petroleum production in Roumania. Therefore we cannot wait for the peace treaty."

When the French Delegates asked that the surrender should at least be made in exchange for material compensation, Hemmen replied:

> "Impossible. The sums which you are to receive from us will be taken out of the occupation costs. This will save you from using the printing-press. This kind of participation will be generalised on the German side when the collaboration policy has been defined."

We might present quotations of this kind indefinitely, and many even much more serious from the point of view of the violation of the provisions of the Hague Convention.

All these concessions, apparently agreed to by the French, were only accepted under German pressure.

Scrutiny of the contracts agreed upon shows great losses to those who handed over their property, and enormous profits for those who acquired it, without the latter having furnished any real compensation.

The Germans thus obtained French investments in the Roumanian petroleum companies, in the enterprises of Central Europe, Norway and the Balkans, and especially those of the Bor Mines Company which I mentioned.

These surrenders, paid by francs coming from occupation costs, rose to rather more than 2 billion francs. The others were paid by the floating of French loans abroad, notably in Holland, and through clearing. Having given you a brief summary of the seizure of French business investments abroad, I shall examine rapidly the German seizure of the registered capital of French industrial companies.

Shortly after the Armistice, in conformity with the directives of the defendant Goering, a great number of French industries were the object of proposals on the part of German groups, anxious to acquire all or part of the assets of these companies.

Acquisition was facilitated by the fact that the Germans, as I have had the honour of pointing out to you, were, in reality, in control of industry, and had taken over the direction of production, particularly by the system of "Patenfirmen." Long discussions took place between the occupying power and the French Minister of Finance, whose department strove, without success, to limit to 30 per cent the maximum of German investments.

It is not possible for me to enter into details of the seizure of these investments. I shall point out, however, that the Finance Minister handed to us a list of the most important ones, which are reproduced in a chart appended to the French document book, and which will be Exhibit RF 260.

The result was that the seizure of investments, fictitiously paid through clearing, rose to the sum of 307,436,000 francs; through occupation costs to 160 millions, through foreign stocks, to a sum which we have not been able to determine; and finally, through various or unknown means to 28,718,000 francs.

We shall conclude the paragraph of this fifth section by quoting part of the Hemmen report relative to these questions, Page 63 of the original and 142 of the French translation. Here is what Hemmen writes, in Salzburg in January 1944, concerning this subject:

"The fifth report upon the activity of the delegation is devoted to the difficulty of future seizures of investments in France, in the face of the strongly accusing attitude of the French Government concerning the surrender of valuable domestic and foreign property. This opposition increased, during the period covered by the report, to such an extent that the French Government was no longer disposed to give any approval to the transfer of investments even if economic compensations were offered."

Further on, Page 104 in the second paragraph:

"During the four years of the occupation of France the Armistice Delegation transferred stocks representing altogether about RM 121 million from French to German ownership, among them investments in enterprises important to the war in other countries, as well as in Germany and France. Details of this are found in the earlier reports of the activities of the Delegation. For about half of these transfers, the Germans gave economic compensation by delivery of French foreign shares acquired in Holland and in Belgium, while the rest of the amount was paid by way of clearing or occupation costs. The fact of giving payment in French shares in foreign countries caused the differences, as far as the shares were concerned, between the German purchasing price and the French rates, and the result was that the Germans achieved gains of a sum of about seven million Reichsmark, which were delivered to the Reich."

One should emphasise that the profit derived by Germany, merely from the financial point of view, is not 7 million Reichsmark, or 140 million francs, according to Hemmen, but much greater. In fact, Germany paid principally for her acquisition by way of occupation costs, and by clearing and French loans issued in Holland or in Belgium, the appropriation of which by Germany amounted to spoliation of these countries and could not constitute a real compensation for France.

These surrenders of investments, carried out under the cloak of legality, moved the United Nations to lay down, in their declarations made in London, on 5 January 1943, the principle that such surrenders should be declared null and void, even when carried out with the apparent consent of those who made them.

I submit, as Exhibit RF 261, the solemn statement signed in London, on 5 January 1943, which was published in the French Official Journal on 15 August 1944 at the time of the liberation. I might add that all these surrenders are the subject of indictments before the French Courts of "high treason against Frenchman who surrendered their investments to the Germans," even though undeniable pressure was brought to bear upon them.

I shall conclude this chapter with one last observation: the German seizure of real estate in France. It is still difficult to give at this time a precise account of this subject, for these operations were nearly always made through an intermediary with an assumed name. The most striking is that of a certain Skolnikoff, who during the occupation was able to invest nearly 2 billion francs in the purchase of real estate.

It is true that this individual, of indeterminate nationality, who lived in poverty before the war, enriched himself in a scandalous fashion, thanks to his connection with the Gestapo and his operations on the black market in co-operation with the occupying power. But, whatever may have been the profits he derived from his dishonest activities, he could not personally have acquired almost 2 billions worth of real estate in France.

I submit, as Exhibit RF 262, a copy of a police report concerning him. It is not possible for me to read this to the Tribunal in its entirety, but it contains the list of the buildings and real estate companies acquired by him. These are without question choice buildings of great value. It is evident that Skolnikoff, an agent for the Gestapo, was an assumed name for certain Germans whose identity has not been discovered up to the present.

Now I shall take up Section 6 - the levy of transportation and communication material. A report from the French administration gives us statistics which are reproduced in a very complete chart, which I shall not read to the Tribunal. I shall merely point out to the Tribunal that most of the locomotives and rolling stock in good shape were removed, and that the total sum of the levies on transportation material reached the figure of 188,450,000,000 francs.

I shall now take up levies in the departments of Haut-Rhin, Bas-Rhin and Moselle. From the beginning of the invasion the Germans incorporated these departments into the Reich. This question will be presented subsequently by the French Prosecution when they discuss the question of Germanisation. From the point of view of economic spoliation it must be stressed that the Germans sought to derive a maximum from these three departments. Though they paid in marks for a certain number of products, they made no settlement whatever for the principal products, especially coal, iron, crude oil, potassium, industrial material, furniture, and agricultural machinery.

The information relating to this is given by the French administration in a chart which I shall summarise briefly, and which I submit as Exhibit RF 264.

The value of the levies in the three French departments of the East, levies not paid for by the Germans, reached the sum of 27,315,000,000 francs.

To conclude the question of the departments in the East, I should like to point out to the Tribunal that my colleague, who will discuss the question of Germanisation, will show how the firm, Herman Goering Werke, in which the defendant Goering had considerable interests, appropriated equipment from the mines of the large French company called the "Petits-Fils de Francois de Wendel et Cie."

I now come to the Eighth section, which concerns miscellaneous levies.

(1) Spoliations in Tunisia.

The Germans went into Tunisia on 10 November 1942, and were driven out by the Allied Armies in May 1943. During this period they indulged in numerous acts of spoliation.

THE PRESIDENT: Do you think that it is necessary to go into details of the seizures in this part of the country, if they are on the same sort of level as they were in other parts of the country?

M. GERTHOFFER: Mr. President, it is similar; there is only one detail, and that concerns the amount. I believe the principle cannot be contested by anyone; therefore I shall go on.

Gentlemen, I shall also pass over the question of compulsory labour. I shall conclude my summary, however, by pointing out to the Tribunal that French economy suffered losses from the deportation of workers, a subject which was discussed by my colleague. We have calculated the losses in working hours and we estimate - and this will be my only remark - that French economy lost 12,550,000,000 working hours through the deportation of workers, a figure which does not include the number of workers who were more or less forced to work for the Germans in companies in France.

If you will permit me, gentlemen, I shall conclude this presentation concerning France by giving you a general review of the situation, and I shall refer once more to Hemmen, the economic dictator who actually ruined my country upon the orders of his masters, the defendants.

In the first five reports submitted, despite their apparently technical nature, the author shows the assurance of the victor who can allow himself to do anything. In the last report, of 15 December 1944, at Salzburg - the only one I shall refer to - Hemmen sought visibly, while giving his work a technical quality, to plead the case of Germany, that of his Nazi masters and his own case, but he succeeded, unwittingly, only in bringing forth an implacable accusation against the nefarious work with which he was entrusted. Here are some short extracts, gentlemen, of Hemmen's final report.

On Page 1 of his report, Page 2 of the French text, he implied the co-responsibility of the German leaders, and of Goering particularly. He writes as follows:

> "According to the directive lines formulated on 5 July 1940 by the Reichsmarschall in charge of the Four-Year Plan, concerning the existing legal basis, the Armistice Convention does not give us rights in the economic domain in the part of France which is not occupied, not even when loosely interpreted."

A little farther on he admits blackmail in regard to the boundary lines, with these words, Page 3 of the translation:

"The Petain Government manifested from the beginning a strong desire, on the one hand, to rapidly re-establish the destroyed economy by means of German support, and on the other hand, to find work for the French workers in order to avoid the danger of unemployment, but above all the strong desire to see these two French zones, which were separated by this boundary line, once more joined together, to bring about an economic and administrative unity. It declared itself, at the same time, willing, to a great extent, to direct this unity under French management but in accordance with the German economic system, and to reorganise it completely according to the German model."

Then Hemmen adds:

"In order substantially to mitigate the demarcation line, the Armistice Delegation has come to an agreement with the French Government to introduce German law in monetary matters into French legislation."

Farther on, concerning pressure, on Page 4 and Page 7 of the translation Hemmen wrote:

"Thereby the prices, which rose automatically, together with an unhindered development of the black market, were felt all the more strongly, because the salaries remained fixed by force."

I pass over the passage in which Hemmen speaks of French resistance. However, I should like to point out to the Tribunal that, on Page 13 and Page 29 of the translation, Hemmen tries to show, through financial evaluations and most questionable arguments, that the cost of the war per head was heavier for the Germans than for the French. He himself destroys with one word the whole system of defence which he had built up, by writing at the end of his bold calculations that "from autumn, 1940, to February 1944, the cost of living increased 166 per cent in France while in Germany it increased only 7 per cent." Now, gentlemen, it is, I am quite sure, through the increase in the cost of living that one measures the impoverishment of a country.

Last of all, on Page 4, and this is my last quotation from the Hemmen report, he admits the German crime in these terms:

"Through the removal, for years, of considerable quantities of property of every kind without economic compensation, a perceptible decrease in substance had resulted, with a corresponding increase in monetary circulation, which had led evermore noticeably to the phenomena of inflation, and especially to a devaluation of money and a lowering of purchasing power."

These material losses, one may say, can be repaired. Through work and saving we can re-establish, in a more or less distant future, the economic situation of the country. That is true, but there is one thing which can never be repaired, the results of privations upon the physical state of the population.

If the other German crimes, such as deportations, murders, massacres, make one shudder with horror, the crime which consisted of deliberately starving whole populations is no less odious.

In the occupied countries, in France notably, many persons died solely because of undernourishment and because of lack of heat. It is estimated that people require from 3,000 to 3,500 calories a day, and manual labourers about 4,000. From the beginning of the rationing in September 1940 only 1,800 calories per person per day were distributed. Successively the ration decreased to 1,700 calories in 1942, then to 1,500, and finally fell to 1,200 and 900 calories a day for adults and to 1,380 and

1,300 for manual labourers; old persons were given only 850 calories a day.

But the true situation was still worse than the ration theoretically allotted through ration cards, for, in fact, frequently a certain number of coupons were not honoured.

The Germans could not fail to recognise the disastrous situation as far as public health was concerned, since they themselves estimated in the course of the war of 1914-1918 that the distribution of 1,700 calories a day was a regime of slow starvation, leading to death.

What aggravated the situation still more was the quality of the rations which were distributed. Bread was of the poorest quality; milk, when there was any, was skimmed to the point where the percentage of fat content amounted to only 3 per cent. The small amount of meat given to the population was of bad quality. Fish had disappeared from the market. If we add to that an almost total lack of clothing, shoes and fuel- frequently neither schools nor hospitals were heated-one may easily understand what the physical condition of the population was.

Incurable diseases such as tuberculosis developed, and will continue to extend their ravages for many years. The growth of children and adolescents is seriously impaired. The future of the race is a cause for the greatest concern.

The results of economic spoliation will be felt for an indefinite period.

THE PRESIDENT: Could you tell me what evidence you have for your figures of calories?

M. GERTHOFFER: I am going to show you this at the end of my presentation. It is a report of a professor at the Medical School of Paris who has been specially commissioned by the Dean of the University to make a report on the results of undernourishment. I am to quote it at the end of my statement. I am almost there.

THE PRESIDENT: Very well.

The results of this economic spoliation will be felt for an indefinite length of time. The exhaustion is such that, despite the generous aid brought by the United Nations, the situation of the occupied countries, taken as a whole, is still alarming. In fact, the complete absence of stocks, the insufficiency of the means of production and of transportation, the reduction of livestock and the economic disorganisation, do not permit the allotting of sufficient rations at this time. This poverty, which strikes all occupied countries, can disappear only gradually over a long period of time, the length of which no one can yet determine.

If, in certain rich agricultural regions, the producers were able, during occupation, to have, and still do have a privileged situation from the point of view of food supply, the same is not true in the poorer regions nor in urban centres.

If we consider that in France the urban population is rather more numerous than the rural population, we can state clearly that the great majority of the French population was, and still remains subject to a food regime definitely insufficient.

Professor Guy Laroche, delegated by the Dean of the Faculty of Medicine of Paris to study the consequences of undernourishment in France as a result of German levies, has just sent a report on this question.

I do not wish to prolong my explanation by reading the entire report. I shall ask the Tribunal's permission to quote the conclusion, which I submit as Exhibit RF 284-bis. I received the entire report only a few days ago. It is submitted in its entirety, but I have not been able to have 50 copies made of it. Two copies have been made and are being submitted. Here are Dr. Laroche's conclusions:

> "We see how great was the crime of rationing, which was imposed by the Germans upon the French during the occupation period from 1940 to 1944. It is difficult to give exact figures for the number of human lives lost due to

excessive rationing. We would need general statistics, and these we have been unable to establish.

Nevertheless, without overestimating, we may well believe that, including patients in institutions, the loss of human life from 1940 to 1944 amounted to at least 150,000 persons. We must add a great number of cases, which were not fatal, of physical and intellectual decline, often incurable, of underdevelopment of children, and so forth.

We think that we can draw from this presentation, which unfortunately is incomplete, three conclusions:

(1) The German occupation authorities deliberately sacrificed the lives of patients in public institutions and hospitals.

(2) Everything happened as if they had wished to organise, in a rational and scientific fashion, the weakening of the health of adolescents and adults.

(3) Unweaned children and young children received a normal ration it is probable that this privileged position can be explained by the fact that the Nazi leaders hoped to spread their doctrine more easily among beings who would not have known any other conditions of life and who would, because of a planned education, have accepted their doctrine, since they knew they could not expect to convince adolescents and adults through use of force."

The report is signed by Professor Guy Laroche.

This report, gentlemen, has attached to it a photograph, which you will find at the end of the document book. I permit myself to hand it to you. The unfortunate beings that you see in that picture are not the victims of a concentration or reprisal camp. They are simply the patients of an asylum in the outskirts of Paris who fell into this state of physical weakness as a result of undernourishment. If these men had had the diet of the asylum prior to rationing, they would have been as strong as normal people. Unfortunately for them they were reduced to the official rationing and were unable to obtain the slightest supplement.

Let not my adversaries say that the German people have reached any such degree of starvation.

I should reply that, in the first place, this is not correct. The German was not cold for four years; he was not undernourished. On the contrary, he was well fed, warmly clothed, warm, with products stolen from the occupied countries, at the expense of the minimum which was necessary for the existence of the peoples of these countries.

Remember, gentlemen, the words of Goering when he said "If famine is to reign, it will in any case not reign in Germany."

Secondly I should say to my adversaries, if they made such an objection that the Germans and their Nazi leaders wanted the war which they launched, but had no right to starve other peoples in order to carry out their attempt at world domination. If today they are in a difficult situation, it is the result of their conduct, and they seem to have no right to plead the famous sentence: "I did not want that."

I have concluded my explanatory remarks. If you will permit me, I will finish in two minutes the whole of this presentation, by reminding the Tribunal, in a few words, what the premeditated crime was, of which the German administrators have been accused from the economic point of view.

The application of racial theories and theories of living space was to engender an economic situation which could not be solved and which was to force the Nazi leaders to war.

In a modern society, because of the division of work, of its concentration and of its scientific organisation, the concept of national capital takes on more and more a primary importance, whatever may be the social principles of its distribution between nationals, or its possession in all or in part by States.

Now, national capital, public or private, is constituted by the joint effort of labour and of savings of successive generations.

Saving, or the putting in reserve of the products of labour as a result of privations which were freely consented to, must exist in proportion to the needs of the concentration of industrial enterprises of the country.

In Germany, a country highly industrialised, this equilibrium did not exist. In fact, the expenditures, private or public, of this country surpassed its means; saving was insufficient. The establishment of a system of compulsory savings was formulated only through the creation of new taxes, and has never replaced true savings.

As a result of the war of 1914-1918, after having freed herself of the burden of reparations, (and I shall point out that two-thirds of the sum remained charged to France as far as that country is concerned) Germany, who had established her gold reserve in 1926, began a policy of foreign borrowing, and spent without counting. Finding it impossible to keep her agreements, she could find no more creditors.

After Hitler's accession to power her policy became more definite. She isolated herself in a closed economic system, utilising all her resources for the preparation of a war which would permit her - or at least that is what she hoped - to take, through force, the property of her Western neighbours, and then to turn against the Soviet Union in the hope of exploiting, for her own profits, the immense wealth of that great country.

This is the application of the theories formulated in "Mein Kampf" which had as a corollary the enslavement and then the extermination of the populations of conquered countries.

In the course of the occupation, the invaded nations were systematically pillaged and brutally enslaved, and this would have permitted Germany to obtain her war aims, that is to say, to take the patrimony of the invaded countries, and to exterminate their populations gradually, had the valour of the United Nations not freed them.

Instead of becoming enriched from the looted property, Germany had to sink into a war, which she had provoked, until the very moment of her collapse.

Such actions, knowingly perpetrated and executed by the German leaders contrary to International Law, and clearly contrary to the Hague Conventions, as well as the general principles of penal law in force in all civilised nations, constituted War Crimes, for which they must answer before your High Jurisdiction.

Mr. President, I should like to add that the French Prosecution had intended to present a statement on the pillage of works of art in the occupied countries of Western Europe. But this question has already been discussed in two briefs of our American colleagues, briefs which seem to us to establish beyond any question the responsibility of the defendants. In order not to prolong the hearing, the French Prosecution feels that it is its duty to refrain from presenting this question again, but we remain respectfully at the disposal of the Tribunal in case in the course of the trial they feel they need further information on this question.

The presentation of the French Prosecution is concluded. I shall give the floor to Captain Sprecher of the American Delegation, who will give a statement on the responsibility of the defendant Fritzsche.

CAPTAIN SPRECHER: May it please the Tribunal, I notice that Dr. Fritz, the defendant's attorney, is not here, and, in view of the late hour, it would be agreeable if we hold it over until tomorrow.

THE PRESIDENT: It is five o'clock, so we shall adjourn in any event now.

(The Tribunal adjourned until 1000 hours on 23 January 1946)

Forty-first day:
Wednesday, 23rd January, 1946

CAPTAIN SPRECHER: May it please the Tribunal, it is my responsibility and my privilege to present today the case on the individual responsibility of the defendant Hans Fritzsche for Crimes against Peace, War Crimes, and Crimes against Humanity as they relate directly to the Common Plan or Conspiracy.

With the permission of the Tribunal, it is planned to make this presentation in three principal divisions:

First, a short listing of the various positions held by the defendant Fritzsche in the Nazi State.

Second, a discussion of Fritzsche's conspiratorial activities within the Propaganda Ministry from 1933 through the attack on the Soviet Union.

Third, a discussion of Fritzsche's connection, as a Nazi propagandist, with the atrocities and the ruthless occupation policy which formed a part of the Common Plan or Conspiracy.

In listing Fritzsche's positions, it is not intended, at first, to describe their functions. Later on, in describing some of Fritzsche's conspiratorial acts, I shall take up a discussion of some of these positions which he held.

Fritzsche's party membership and his various positions in the propaganda apparatus of the Nazi State are shown by two affidavits by Fritzsche himself, Document 2976-PS, which is already in evidence as Exhibit USA 20; and Document 3469-PS, which I offer in evidence as Exhibit USA 721. Both of these affidavits have been put into the four working languages of this Tribunal.

Fritzsche became a member of the Nazi Party on 1 May, 1933, and he continued to be a member until the collapse in 1945. He began his services with the staff of the Reich Ministry for People's Enlightenment and Propaganda - hereinafter referred to as the Propaganda Ministry - on the 1 May, 1933, and he remained within the Propaganda Ministry until the Nazi downfall.

Before the Nazis seized political power in Germany, and beginning in September 1932, Fritzsche was head of the Wireless News Service, Drahtloser Dienst, an agency of the Reich Government at that time under the defendant von Papen. After the Wireless News Service was incorporated into the Propaganda Ministry of Dr. Goebbels in May 1933, Fritzsche continued as its head until the year 1938. Upon entering the Propaganda Ministry in May 1933, Fritzsche also became head of the news section of the Press Division of the Propaganda Ministry. He continued in this position until 1937. In the summer of 1938, Fritzsche was appointed deputy to one Alfred Ingemar Berndt, who was then head of the German Press Division.

The German Press Division, in the indictment, is called the Home Press Division. Since "German Press Division " seems to be a more literal translation, we have called it the German Press Division throughout this presentation. It is sometimes otherwise known as the Domestic Press Division.

We shall show later that this Division was the major section of the Press Division of the Reich Cabinet.

Now, in December 1938, Fritzsche succeeded Berndt as the head of the German Press Division. Between 1938 and November 1942, Fritzsche was promoted three times. He advanced in title from Superior Government Counsel to Ministerial Counsel, then to Ministerial Assistant Director, and finally to Ministerial Director.

In November, 1942, Fritzsche was relieved of his position as head of the German Press Division by Dr. Goebbels, and accepted, from Dr. Goebbels, a newly created position in the Propaganda Ministry, that of Plenipotentiary for the Political Organisation of the Greater German Radio. At the same time he also became head of the Radio Division of the Propaganda Ministry. He held both these positions in radio until the Nazi downfall.

There are two allegations of the Indictment concerning Fritzsche's positions, for which we are unable to offer proof. These allegations appear at Page 34 of the English translation.

The first unsupported allegation states that Fritzsche was "Editor-in-Chief of the official German News Agency, Deutsche Nachrichten Buro." The second unsupported allegation states that Fritzsche was "head of the Radio Division of the Propaganda Department of the Nazi Party."

Fritzsche, in his affidavit, denies having held either of these positions, and therefore these two allegations must fall for want of proof.

Before discussing the documentation of the case, I wish, in passing, to state my appreciation of the assistance in research, analysis, and translation given to me by Mr. Norbert Halpern, Mr. Alfred Booth, and Lieutenant Niebergall, who sits at my right.

The Tribunal will note the relative shortness of this document book. It has been marked as document book MM. It contains only 32 pages, which have been numbered consecutively, I believe in red pencil, for your convenience. The shortness of the documentation on this particular case is possible only because of a long affidavit made by the defendant Fritzsche, which was signed by him on the 7 January 1946.

It seems appropriate to comment on this significant document before proceeding. It is before your Honours as Document 3469-PS, beginning at document book, Page 19.

As I said, it has been translated into the four working languages of this proceeding.

This affidavit contains materials which have been extracted from interrogations of Fritzsche, and many materials which Fritzsche volunteered to give himself, at my request, through his defence counsel, Dr. Fritz. Some of the portions of the final affidavit were originally typed or hand-written by the defendant Fritzsche himself, during this trial or during the holiday recess. All these materials were finally incorporated into one single affidavit.

This affidavit contains Fritzsche's account of the events which led to his entering the Propaganda Ministry and his account of his later connections with that Ministry. Before Fritzsche made some of the statements in the affidavit concerning the role of propaganda in relation to important foreign political events, he was shown illustrative headlines and articles from the German Press at that time, so that he could refresh his recollection and make more accurate statements.

It is believed that the Tribunal will desire to consider many portions of this affidavit, independent of this presentation, along with the proof on the conspirators' use of propaganda as a principal weapon in the conspiracy. Some of this proof, you will recall, was submitted by Major Wallis, in the first days of this trial, in connection with Brief E, entitled "Propaganda, Censorship and Supervision of the Cultural Activities," and the corresponding document book, to which I call the Tribunal's attention.

In the Fritzsche affidavit there are a number of statements which I would say were in the nature of defensive declarations. With respect to these, the prosecution requests only that the Tribunal consider them in the light of the whole conspiracy and the indisputable facts which appear throughout the record. The prosecution did not feel, either as a matter of expediency or of fairness, that it should request Fritzsche, through his defence Counsel, Dr. Fritz, to remove some of these defensive declarations at this time, and submit them later in connection with his defence.

Since I shall refer to this affidavit at numerous times throughout the presentation, perhaps the members of the Tribunal will wish to place a special marker in their document book.

By referring to paragraphs 4 and 5 of the affidavit, the Tribunal will note that Fritzsche first became a successful journalist in the service of the Hugenberg Press, the most important chain of newspaper enterprises in pre-Nazi Germany. The Hugenberg concern owned papers of its own, but was primarily important because it served newspapers which principally supported the so-called "national" parties of the Reich, including the NSDAP.

In paragraph 5 of the affidavit, Fritzsche relates that in September 1932, when the defendant von Papen was Reich Chancellor, he was made head of the Wireless News Service, replacing someone who was politically unbearable to the Papen regime. The Wireless News Service I might say, was a government agency for spreading news by radio.

Fritzsche began making radio broadcasts at about this time, with very great success, a success which Goebbels recognised, and was later to exploit very efficiently on behalf of these Nazi conspirators.

The Nazis seized power on 30 January 1933. From paragraph 10 of the Fritzsche affidavit we find that that very evening, 30 January 1933, two emissaries from Goebbels visited Fritzsche. One of them was Dressler-Andrees, head of the Radio Division of the NSDAP; the other was an assistant of Dressler-Andrees named Sadila-Mantau. These two emissaries notified Fritzsche that although Goebbels was angry with Fritzsche for writing a critical article concerning Hitler, still he recognised Fritzsche's public success on the radio since the previous autumn. They stated further that Goebbels desired to retain Fritzsche as head of the Wireless News Service on certain conditions: (1) That Fritzsche discharge all Jews; (2) that he discharge all other personnel who would not join the NSDAP; and (3) that he employ with the Wireless News Service Goebbels' second emissary, Sadila- Mantau.

Fritzsche refused all these conditions except the hiring of Sadila-Mantau. This was one of the first ostensible compromises, after the seizure of power, which Fritzsche made on his road to the Nazi camp.

Fritzsche continued to make radio broadcasts during this period, in which he supported the National-Socialist Coalition Government then still existing.

In early 1933 SA troops several times called at the Wireless News Service, and Fritzsche prevented them, with some difficulty, from making news broadcasts.

In April 1913 Goebbels called the young Fritzsche to him for a personal audience. At paragraph 9 of his affidavit, document 3469-PS, Fritzsche has volunteered the following concerning his prior relationships with Dr. Goebbels:

> "I had known Dr. Goebbels since 1928. Apparently he had taken a liking to me, besides the fact that in my Press activities I had always treated the National Socialists in a friendly way until 1931.
>
> Already before 1933, Goebbels, who was the editor of the 'Attack' in (Der Angriff) - a Nazi newspaper, had frequently made flattering remarks about the form and content of the work which I had done as contributor of many 'National' newspapers and periodicals, among which were also reactionary papers and periodicals."

At the first Goebbels-Fritzsche discussion in early April 1933, Goebbels informed Fritzsche of his decision to place the Wireless News Service within the Propaganda Ministry as from 1 May 1933. He suggested that Fritzsche make certain rearrangements in the personnel, which would remove Jews and other persons who did not support NSDAP. Fritzsche debated with Goebbels concerning some of these steps. It must be said that during this period Fritzsche made some effort to place Jews in other jobs.

In a second conference with Goebbels, shortly thereafter, Fritzsche informed him about the steps he had taken in reorganising the Wireless News Service. Goebbels thereupon informed Fritzsche that he would like him to reorganise and modernise the entire news service of Germany, within the controls of the Propaganda Ministry.

It will be recalled by the Tribunal that on 17 of March 1933, approximately two months before this time, the Propaganda Ministry had been formed by decree - 1933 Reichsgesetzblatt, Part 1, Page 104; our document 2029-PS.

Fritzsche was intrigued by the Goebbels offer. He proceeded to conclude the Goebbels-inspired reorganisation of the Wireless News Service and, on 1 May, 1933, together with the remaining members of his staff, he joined the Propaganda Ministry. On the same day he joined the NSDAP and took the customary oath of unconditional loyalty to the Fuehrer. From this time on, whatever reservations Fritzsche may have had, either then or later, to the course of events under the Nazis, he was completely within the Nazi camp. For the next 13 years he assisted in creating and in using the chief propaganda devices which the conspirators employed with such telling effect in each of the principal phases of this conspiracy.

From 1933 until 1942 Fritzsche held one or more positions within the German Press Division. For four years, indeed, he headed this Division, during those crucial years 1938 to 1942. That covers the period when the Nazis undertook actual military invasions of neighbouring countries. It is, therefore, believed appropriate to spell out in some detail, before this Tribunal, the functions of this German Press Division. These functions will show the important and unique position of the German Press Division as an instrument of the Nazi conspirators, not only in dominating the minds and the psychology of Germans through the German Press Division and through the radio, but also as an instrument of foreign policy and psychological warfare against other nations.

The already broad jurisdiction of the Propaganda Ministry was extended by a Hitler decree of 30 June, 1933, found in 1933 Reichsgesetzblatt, Part 1, Page 449. From that decree I wish to quote only one sentence. It is found in Document 2030-PS, Page 3 in your document book:

"The Reich Minister of Public Enlightenment and Propaganda has jurisdiction over the whole field of spiritual indoctrination of the nation, and the State, of cultural, and economic propaganda, and of enlightenment of the public at home and abroad. Furthermore, he is in charge of the administration of all institutions serving those purposes."

It is important to underline the stated propaganda objective of "enlightenment at home and abroad."

For a clear exposition of the general functions of the German Press Division of the Propaganda Ministry, the Tribunal is referred to Document 2434-PS, Document book Page 5. It is offered in evidence as Exhibit USA 722. This document is an appropriate excerpt from a book by George Wilhelm Muller, a Ministerial Director in the Propaganda Ministry, of which the Tribunal is asked to take judicial notice.

Fritzsche's affidavit, paragraphs 14, 15, and 16, beginning at Page 22 of your document book, contains an exposition of the functions of the German Press Division, a description which confirms and adds to the exposition in Muller's book.

Concerning the German Press Division, Fritzsche's affidavit states:

"During the whole period from 1933 to 1945 it was the task of the German Press Division to supervise the entire domestic Press, and to provide it with directives by which this division became an efficient instrument in the hands of the German State leadership. More than 2,300 German daily newspapers were subject to this control. The aim of this supervision and control, in the first years following 1933, was to change basically the conditions existing in the Press before the seizure of power. That meant the co-ordination into the New Order of those newspapers and periodicals which were in the service of capitalistic special interests or party politics. While the administrative functions, wherever possible, were exercised by the professional associations and the Reich Press Chamber, the political leadership of the German Press was entrusted to the German Press Division. The head if [sic] the German Press Division held daily Press conferences in the Ministry for the representatives of all German newspapers. Hereby all instructions were given to representatives of the Press. These instructions were transmitted daily, almost without exception, and mostly by telephone, from headquarters by Dr. Otto Dietrich, Reich Press Chief, in a fixed statement, the so-called "Daily Parole of the Reich Press Chief." Before the statement was fixed the head of the German Press Division submitted to him - Dietrich - the current Press wishes expressed by Dr. Goebbels and by other Ministries. This was the case especially with the wishes of the Foreign Office, about which Dr. Dietrich always wanted to make decisions personally or through his representatives at headquarters, Helmut Sundermann and chief editor Lorenz. The practical use of the general directions in detail was thus left entirely to the individual work of the individual editor. Therefore, it is by no means true that the newspapers and periodicals were a monopoly of the German Press Division, or that essays and leading articles through it had to be submitted to the Ministry. Even in war periods this happened in exceptional cases only. The less important newspapers and periodicals, which were not represented at the daily Press conferences, received their information in a different way by being provided either with ready-made articles and reports, or with a confidential printed instruction. The publications of all other official agencies were directed and co-ordinated likewise by the German Press Division. To enable the periodicals to get acquainted with the daily political problems of newspapers and to discuss these problems in greater detail, the "Informationskorrespondenz" was issued especially for periodicals. Later on it was taken over by the Periodical Press Division. The German Press Division was also in charge of pictorial reporting, insofar as it directed the employment of pictorial reporters at important events. In this way, and tempered by the current political situation, the entire German Press was made a permanent instrument of the Propaganda Ministry by the German Press Division.

Thereby, the entire German Press was subordinate to the political aims of the Government. This was exemplified by the timely measuring and the emphatic presentation of such Press polemics as appeared to be most useful, as shown for instance in the following themes: the class struggle of the system era; the leadership principle and the authoritarian State the party and interest politics of the system era; the Jewish problem the conspiracy of World Jewry; the Bolshevistic danger; the plutocratic Democracy abroad; the race problem generally; the church; the economic misery abroad; the foreign policy; the living space - "Lebensraum."

This description of Fritzsche establishes clearly - and in his own words that the German Press Division was the instrument for subordinating the entire German Press to the political aims of the Government.

We now pass to Fritzsche's first activities on behalf of the conspirators within the German Press Division. It is appropriate to read again from his affidavit - paragraph 17, your document book Page 23. Fritzsche begins by describing a conference with Goebbels in late April or early May of 1933:

"At this time Dr. Goebbels suggested to me, as a specialist on news technique, the establishment and direction of a section "News," within the Press Division of his Ministry, in order to organise fully and to modernise the German news agencies. In executing this assignment given to me by Dr. Goebbels I took for my field the entire news field for the German Press and the radio, in accordance with the directions given by the propaganda Ministry, at first with the exception of the D.N.B., German News Agency."

An obvious reason why the D.N.B. was excepted from Fritzsche's field at this time is that the D.N.B. did not come 4nto existence until the year 1934, as we shall see presently. Later on, in paragraph 17 of the Fritzsche affidavit, the Tribunal will note the tremendous funds put at the disposal of Fritzsche in building up the Nazi news services. Altogether, the German news agencies received a ten-fold increase in their budget from the Reich, an increase from 400,000 to 4,000,000 Mark. Fritzsche himself selected and employed the Chief Editor for the Transocean News Agency and also for the "Europa" Press. Fritzsche states that some of the "directions of the Propaganda Ministry which I had to follow were" . "increase of German news copy abroad at any cost" ... "spreading of favourable news on the internal construction and peaceful intentions of the National Socialist System."

About the summer of 1934, the defendant Funk, then Reich Press Chief, achieved the fusion of the two most important domestic news agencies, the Wolff Telegraph Agency and the Telegraph Union, and thus formed the official German news agency, ordinarily known as D.N.B. It has already been pointed out to the Tribunal that the indictment is in error in alleging that Fritzsche himself was Editor-in-Chief of the D.N.B. Fritzsche held no position whatsoever with the D.N.B. at any time. However, as head of the news section of the German Press Division, Fritzsche's duties gave him official jurisdiction over the D.N.B., which was the official domestic news agency of the German Reich after 1934. In the last part of paragraph 17 of the affidavit, Fritzsche states that he co-ordinated the work of the various foreign news agencies "within Europe and overseas with each other and in relationship to D.N.B."

The Wireless News Service was headed by Fritzsche from 1930 to 1937. After January, 1933, it was the official instrument of the Nazi government in spreading news over the radio. During the same time that Fritzsche headed it, he personally made radio broadcasts to the German people. These broadcasts were naturally subject to the controls of the Propaganda Ministry and reflected its purposes. The influence of Fritzsche's broadcasts upon the German people, during this period of consolidation of control by the Nazi conspirators, is all the more important since Fritzsche was concurrently head of the Wireless News Services, which controlled for the government the spreading of all news by radio.

It is by now well known to the world that the Nazi conspirators attempted to be -

and often were - very adept in psychological warfare. Before each major aggression, with some few exceptions based on the strategy of expediency, they initiated a Press campaign calculated to weaken their victims, and to prepare the German people psychologically for the impending Nazi madness. They used the Press, after their earlier conquests, as a means for further influencing foreign politics, and in manoeuvring for the next aggression.

By the time of the occupation of the Sudetenland on 1 October, 1938, Fritzsche had become deputy head of the entire German Press Division. Fritzsche states that the role of German propaganda before the Munich Agreement on the Sudetenland was directed by his immediate chief, Berndt, then head of the German Press Division. In paragraph 27 of the Fritzsche affidavit, Page 26 of your document book, Fritzsche describes this propaganda which Berndt directed. Speaking of Berndt, Fritzsche states:

"He exaggerated minor events very strongly, sometimes using old episodes as new - and there were complaints even from the Sudetenland itself, that much of the news reported by the German Press was untrustworthy. As a matter of fact, after the great foreign political success at Munich in September, 1938, there came a noticeable loss of confidence among the German people in the trustworthiness of their Press. This was one reason for the recalling of Berndt in December 1938, after the conclusion of the Sudeten action, and for my appointment as head of the German Press Division. In addition, Berndt, by his admittedly successful but still primitive military-like orders to the German Press, had lost the confidence of the German editors."

Now, what happened at that time? Fritzsche was made head of the German Press Division in place of Berndt. Between December 1938 and 1942, Fritzsche, as head of the German Press Division, personally gave to the representatives of the principal German newspapers the "daily parole of the Reich Press Chief." During this history-making period he was the principal conspirator directly concerned with the manipulations of the Press. The first important foreign aggression after Fritzsche became head of the German Press Division was the incorporation of Bohemia and Moravia. In paragraph 28, of the affidavit, your document book Page 26, Fritzsche gives his account of the propaganda action surrounding the incorporation of Bohemia and Moravia as follows:

"The action for the incorporation of Bohemia and Moravia, which took place on 15 March 1939, while I was head of the German Press Division, did not take so long to plan as the Sudeten action. According to my memory it was in February that I received the order from the Reich Press Chief, Dr. Dietrich, which was repeated as a request by the envoy Paul Schmidt of the Foreign Office, to bring the attention of the Press to the efforts for independence of Slovakia and to the continued anti- German coalition politics of the Prague Government. I did this. The daily paroles of the Reich Press Chief and the Press conference minutes at that time show the wording of the corresponding instructions. Typical headlines of leading newspapers and the emphatic leading articles of the German daily Press at that time were as follows: (1) the terrorising of Germans within the Czech territory by arrest, shooting of Germans by the State police, destruction and damaging of German homes by Czech gangsters; (2) the concentration of Czech forces on the Sudeten frontier; (3) the kidnapping, deporting and persecuting of Slovakian minorities by the Czechs; the Czechs must get out of Slovakia; (4)

secret meetings of Red functionaries in Prague. Some few days before the visit to Hacha, I received the instruction to publish in the Press very emphatically the incoming news on the unrest in Czechoslovakia. Such information came only in part from the German News Agency, D.N.B. Mostly it came from the Press Division of the Foreign Office, and some of it came from big newspapers with their own news services. Among the newspapers offering information was above all the Volkischer Beobachter which, as I learned later on, received its information from the S.S. Standartenfuehrer Gunter D'Alquen. He was at this time in Pressburg. I had forbidden all news agencies and newspapers to issue news on unrest in Czechoslovakia until I had seen it. I wanted to avoid a repetition of the very annoying results of the Sudeten action propaganda, and I did not want to suffer a loss of prestige caused by false news. Thus, all news checked by me was, though admittedly full of tendency, not invented news. After the visit of Hacha in Berlin and the beginning of the invasion of the German Army, which took place on 15 March 1939, the German Press had enough material for describing those events. Historically and politically the event was given justification by the indication that the declaration of independence of Slovakia demanded interference, and that Hacha by signing had avoided a war, and had reinstated a thousand-year union between Bohemia and the Reich."

The propaganda campaign of the Press preceding the invasion of Poland on 1 of September, 1939, and thus just preceding the precipitation of World War II, bears again the handiwork of Fritzsche and his German Press Division. In paragraph 30 of Fritzsche's affidavit, document book Page 27, Fritzsche speaks of the conspirators' treatment of this episode as follows:

"Very complicated and changing was the Press and propaganda treatment in the case of Poland. Under the influence of the German-Polish agreement, the German Press had, for many years, been generally forbidden to publish anything on the situation of the German minority in Poland. This remained the case too when, in the Spring of 1939, the German Press was asked to become somewhat more active about the problem of Danzig. Also, when the first Polish-English conversations took place, and when the German Press was instructed to use a sharper tone against Poland, the question of the German minority still remained in the background. But during the summer this problem was picked up again, and the result was an immediate and noticeable sharpening of the situation, for all the larger German newspapers had for some time quite an abundance of material on complaints of the Germans in Poland, without the editors having a chance to use it. The German papers, from the time of the minority discussion at Geneva, still had correspondents or free collaborators in Kattowitz, Bromberg, Posen, Thorn, etc. Their material now came forth with a rush. Concerning this, the leading German newspapers, as the result of directions given out in the so-called "daily parole," brought out the following headlines with great emphasis: (1) cruelty and terror against Germans, and their extermination in Poland; (2) forced labour of thousands of German men and women in Poland; (3) Poland, land of servitude and disorder; the desertion of Polish soldiers; the increased inflation in Poland; (4) provocation of frontier clashes upon direction of the Polish Government; the Polish lust to conquer; (5) persecution of Czechs and Ukrainians by Poles. The Polish Press replied particularly sharply."

The Press campaign preceding the invasion of Yugoslavia followed the conventional pattern. You will find the customary defamations, the lies, the incitement and the threats and the usual attempts to divide and to weaken the victim. Paragraph 32 of the Fritzsche affidavit, your document book Page 28, outlines this propaganda action as follows:

> "During the period immediately preceding the invasion of Yugoslavia, on 16 of April 1941, the German Press emphasised by headlines and leading articles the following topics: (1) the planned persecution of Germans in Yugoslavia, including the burning down of German villages by Serbian soldiers; the confining of Germans in concentration camps, and also the physical mishandling of German-speaking persons; (2) the arming of Serbian bandits by the Serbian Government; (3) the incitement of Yugoslavia by the plutocrats against Germany; (4) the increasing anti-Serbian feeling in Croatia; (5) the chaotic economic and social conditions in Yugoslavia."

Since Germany had a non-aggression pact with the Soviet Union and because these conspirators wanted the advantage of surprise, there was no special propaganda campaign immediately preceding the attack on the USSR. Fritzsche in paragraph 33 of his affidavit discusses what line the propaganda should take in order to justify this aggressive war to the German people.

> "During the night of 21-22 June 1941, Ribbentrop called me to a conference in the Foreign Office Building at about 5 o'clock in the morning, at which representatives of the domestic and foreign Press were present. Ribbentrop informed us that the war against the Soviet Union would start that same day, and asked the German Press to present the war against the Soviet Union as a preventative war for the defence of the Fatherland, a war which was forced upon us through the immediate danger of an attack by the Soviet Union against Germany. The claim that this was a preventative war was later repeated by the newspapers, which received their instructions from me during the usual daily parole of the Reich Press Chief, and I have, myself, in my regular broadcasts, given this presentation of the cause of the war."

Fritzsche, throughout his affidavit, constantly refers to his technical and expert assistance to the colossal apparatus of the Propaganda Ministry. In 1939 he apparently became dissatisfied with the efficiency of the existing facilities of the German Press Division in furnishing grist for the propaganda mill, and for its intrigues. He established a new instrument for improving the effectiveness of Nazi propaganda. In paragraph 19 of his affidavit, Page 24 of your document book, Fritzsche describes this new propaganda instrument as follows:

> "About the summer of 1939 I established within the German Press Division a section called 'Speed-Service.'" And then further on "At the start it had the task of checking the correctness of news from foreign countries. Later on, about the fall of 1939, this section also elaborated on collecting materials which were put at the disposal of the entire German Press. For instance, data from the British Colonial policy, from political statements of the British Prime Minister in former times, descriptions of social distress in hostile countries, etc. Almost al German newspapers used such material as a basis for their polemics. Hereby was achieved a great unification within the fighting front of the German Press. The title 'Speed Service' was chosen because materials for current comments were supplied with unusual speed."

Throughout the entire period preceding and including the launching of aggressive war, Fritzsche made regular radio broadcasts to the German people under the following titles: "Political Newspaper Review," "Political and Radio Show," and later "Hans Fritzsche Speaks." His broadcasts naturally reflected the polemics and the control of his Ministry and thus of the Common Plan or Conspiracy.

We of the prosecution contend that Fritzsche, one of the most eminent of Goebbels' propaganda team, helped substantially to bathe the world in the blood bath of aggressive war.

With the Tribunal's consent I will now pass to proof bearing on Fritzsche's incitement to atrocities, and his encouragement of a ruthless occupation policy. The results of propaganda as a weapon of the Nazi conspirators reach into every aspect of this conspiracy, including the abnormal and inhuman conduct involved in the atrocities, and the ruthless exploitation of occupied countries. Most of the ordinary members of the German nation would never have participated in or tolerated the atrocities committed throughout Europe, had they not been conditioned and goaded to barbarous convictions and misconceptions by the constant grinding of the Nazi propaganda machine. Indeed, the propagandists who tent themselves to this evil mission of instigation and incitement are more guilty than the credulous and callous minions who headed the firing squads, or operated the gas chambers, of which we have heard so much in these proceedings. For the very credulity and callousness of those minions was in large part due to the constant and evil propaganda of Fritzsche and his official associates.

With respect to Jews, the Department of Propaganda within the Propaganda Ministry had a special branch for the "Enlightenment of the German people and of the world as to the Jewish question, fighting with propagandistic weapons against enemies of the State and hostile ideologies." This quotation is taken from a book written in 1940 by Ministerial Director Muller, entitled "The Propaganda Ministry." It is found in Document 2434-A-PS, your document book, Page 10, offered in evidence as Exhibit USA 722. It is another excerpt from Ministerial Director Muller's book and I merely ask that you take judicial notice of it for that one sentence that I have read.

Fritzsche took a particularly active part in this "enlightenment" of the Jewish question, in his radio broadcasts. These broadcasts literally teemed with provocative libels, the only logical result of which was to inflame Germany to further atrocities against the helpless Jews who came within her physical power. Document 3064-PS contains a number of complete broadcasts by Fritzsche, which were monitored by the British Broadcasting Corporation and translated by BBC officials. For the convenience of the Tribunal I have had those excerpts upon which the prosecution relies to show illustrative types of Fritzsche's broadcasts, mimeographed and made into one document, which I offer into evidence as Exhibit USA 723. Even the defendant Streicher, the master Jew-baiter of all time, could scarcely outdo Fritzsche in some of his slanders against the Jews. All the excerpts in document 3064-PS are from speeches of Fritzsche given on the radio between 1941 and 1945, which we have already proved to have been a period of intensified anti-Jewish measures. With the permission of the Tribunal, I would like to read some of these excerpts:

Page 14 of our document book, Item 1. From a broadcast of 18 December 1941: It is found on Page 2122 of the translations from BBC:

> "The fate of Jewry in Europe has turned out to be as unpleasant as the Fuehrer predicted it would be in the event of a European war. After the extension of the war instigated by Jews, this unpleasant fate may also spread to the New World, for you can hardly assume that the nations of this New

World will pardon the Jews for causing this misery when the nations of the Old World did not do so."

From a radio broadcast of 18 March 1941, found at Page 2032 of the BBC translations:

"But the crown of all wrong-applied Rooseveltian logics is the sentence 'There never was a race and there never will be a race which can serve the rest of mankind as a master.' Here too we can only applaud Mr. Roosevelt. It is precisely because there exists no race which can be the master of the rest of mankind, that we Germans have taken the liberty to break the domination of Jewry and of its capital in Germany, of Jewry which believed itself to have inherited the Crown of secret world domination."

In passing, I would merely like to note that it seems to us that this is not only applause for persecution of Jews in the past, but an announcement that more was coming, and an encouragement of it.

I would like to read another excerpt from the broadcast of 9 October, 1941, translated at Page 2101 of the BBC translation:

"We know very well that these German victories have not yet stopped the source of hatred, which, for a long time, has fed the war-mongers and from which this war originated. The international Jewish-Democratic Bolshevistic campaign of incitement against Germany still finds cover in this or that fox's lair or rat-hole. We have seen only too frequently how the defeats suffered by the war-mongers only doubled their senseless and impotent fury."

Another broadcast of 8 January 1944. Your Honours, I have tried to pick out illustrative broadcasts from different periods here.

"It is revealed clearly once more that not a system of government, not a young nationalism, not a new and well applied Socialism brought about this war. The guilty ones are exclusively the Jews and the plutocrats. If discussion on the post-war problems should bring this to light so clearly, we welcome it as a contribution for such discussions, and also as a contribution to the fight we are waging now, for we refuse to believe that world history will confide its future developments to those powers which have brought about this war. This clique of Jews and plutocrats had invested their money in armaments, and they had to see to it that they got their interest and sinking funds; hence they unleashed this war."

Concerning the Jews, I had one last quotation from the year 1945. It is from a broadcast of 13 January, 1945, found on Pages 2258 and 2259 of the BBC translations:

"If Jewry provided a link between such divergent elements as plutocracy and Bolshevism, and if Jewry was first able to work successfully in the democratic countries in preparing this war against Germany, it has by now placed itself unreservedly on the side of Bolshevism which, with its entirely mistaken slogans of racial freedom against racial hatred, has created the very conditions the Jewish race requires in its struggle for domination over other races."

And then omitting a few lines in that quotation:

"Not the least result of German resistance in the field, so unexpected to the enemy, is the fruition of a development which began in the pre-war years, the subordination of British policy to far-reaching Jewish points of view. It began long before this, when Jewish emigrants from Germany started their warmongering against us from British and American soil."

And then omitting several sentences and going to the last sentence on that page.

"This whole attempt, aiming at the establishment of Jewish world domination, now increasingly recognisable, has come to a head at the very moment when the peoples' understanding of their racial origins has been far too much awakened to promise success to the undertaking."

Your Honours, we suggest that that is an invitation to further persecution of the Jews and, indeed, to their elimination.

Fritzsche also incited and encouraged ruthless measures against the peoples of the USSR. In his regular broadcasts Fritzsche's incitements against the peoples of the USSR were often linked to, and were certainly as inflammatory as, his slanders against the Jews. If these slanders were not so tragic in their relation to the murder of millions of people, they would be comical, indeed ludicrous. It is ironic that the propaganda libels against the peoples of the USSR, concerning atrocities, actually described some of the many atrocities committed, as we now well know, by the German invaders. The following quotations are again taken from the BBC intercepted broadcasts and their translations, beginning shortly after the invasion of the USSR in June 1941. The first one is taken again from Page 16 of our document book and I will read only the last half of item 7, beginning with the 3rd paragraph:

"The evidence of letters reaching us from the front, of P. K. reporters and may I interrupt my quotation there to say that "P.K" stands for "Propaganda Kompanien," propaganda companies were attached to the German Army wherever it went. - "P.K. reporters and soldiers on leave shows that, in this struggle in the East, not one political system is pitted against another, not one view of life is fighting another, but that culture, civilisation, and human decency make a stand against the diabolical principle of a sub-human world."

And then another quotation in the next paragraph

"It was only the Fuehrer's decision to strike in time that saved our homeland from the fate of being overrun by those sub-human creatures, and our men, women and children from the unspeakable horror of being their prey."

In the next broadcast I want to quote from, 10 July, 1941, in the first paragraph, Fritzsche speaks of the inhuman deeds committed in areas controlled by the Soviet Union, and he states that, on seeing the evidence of their commission, one is compelled - and here I quote "... at last to make the holy resolve to assist in the final destruction of those who are capable of such dastardly acts."

And then quoting again, the last paragraph:

"The Bolshevist agitators make no effort to deny that in towns, thousands, and in villages, hundreds, of corpses have been found of men, women and children who had been either killed or tortured to death. Yet the Bolshevik agitators allege that this was not done by Soviet Commissars but by German soldiers. Now we Germans know our soldiers. No German woman or parent requires proof that her husband or son cannot have committed such atrocious acts."

Evidence already in the record or shortly to be offered in this case by our Soviet colleagues will prove that representatives of these Nazi conspirators did not hesitate to exterminate Soviet soldiers and civilians by scientific mass methods. These inciting remarks by Fritzsche make him an accomplice in these crimes because his labelling of the Soviet peoples as members of a "subhuman world" seeking to "exterminate" the German people, and similar desperate talk, helped, by these propaganda diatribes, to fashion the psychological atmosphere of utter and complete unreason, and the hatred which instigated and made possible these atrocities in the East.

Although we cannot say that Fritzsche directed that ten thousand or one hundred thousand persons should be exterminated, it is enough to pause on this question. Without these incitements of Fritzsche, how much harder it would have been for these conspirators to have effected the conditions which made possible the extermination of millions of people in the East.

THE PRESIDENT: Would that be a convenient time to break off?

(A recess was taken)

CAPTAIN SPRECHER: Fritzsche encouraged and affirmed and glorified the policy of the Nazi conspirators in ruthlessly exploiting the occupied countries. Again I read an excerpt from his radio broadcast of 9 October 1941, found at Pages 2102 and 2103, of the BBC translation. I would like to shorten it, but it is one of those long German sentences that just cannot be broken down:

> "Today we can only say: Blitzkrieg or no - this German thunderstorm has cleansed the atmosphere of Europe. It is quite true that the dangers threatening us were eliminated one after the other with lightning speed; but in these lightning blows which shattered England's allies on the Continent, we saw not a proof of their weakness, but a proof of the strength and superiority of the Fuehrer's gift as a statesman and military leader; a proof of the German peoples' strength; we saw the proof that no opponent can stand up to the courage, discipline, and readiness for sacrifice displayed by the German soldier; and we are particularly grateful for these lightning, unmatched victories, because - as the Fuehrer emphasised last Friday - they give us the possibility of embarking on the organisation of Europe and on the lifting of the treasures" - I would like to repeat that - "lifting of the treasures of this old continent, already in the midst of war, without it being necessary for millions and millions of German soldiers to be on guard, fighting day and night along this or that threatened frontier; and the possibilities of this continent are so rich that they suffice for any of the needs of peace or war."

Concerning the exploitation of foreign countries, Fritzsche states himself, at paragraph thirty-nine of his affidavit

> "The utilisation of the productive capacity of the occupied countries for the strengthening of the war potential, I have openly and gloriously praised, chiefly because the competent authorities put at my disposal much material, especially on the voluntary placement of manpower."

Fritzsche was a credulous propagandist indeed if he gloriously praised the exploitation policy of the German Reich, chiefly or especially because the competent authorities gave him a sales talk on the voluntary placement of manpower.

I come now to Fritzsche as the high commander of the entire German radio system. Fritzsche continued as the head of the German Press Division until after the conspirators had begun the last of their aggressions. In November 1942 Goebbels created a new position, that of Plenipotentiary for the Political Organisation of the Greater German Radio, a position which Fritzsche was the first and the last to hold. In paragraph thirty-six, document 3469-PS - the Fritzsche affidavit - Fritzsche narrates how the entire German Radio and Television System was organised under his supervision. That is at Page 29 of your document book. He states:

> "My office practically represented the highest post of German radio."

As special Plenipotentiary for the Political Organisation of the Greater German Radio, Fritzsche issued orders to all the Reich propaganda offices by teletype. These were used first in conforming the entire radio apparatus of Germany to the desires of the conspirators.

Goebbels customarily held an eleven o'clock conference with his closest collaborators within the Propaganda Ministry. When both he and his undersecretary, Dr. Naumann, were absent, Goebbels after 1943, entrusted Fritzsche with the holding of this eleven o'clock Press conference.

In document 3255-PS the Court will find Goebbels' praise of Fritzsche's broadcasts. This praise was given in Goebbels' introduction to a book by Fritzsche called, "War to the War Mongers." I would like to offer the quotation in evidence as Exhibit USA 724, from the Rundfunk Archiv, at Page 18 of your Honours' document book. This is Goebbels speaking:

"Nobody knows better that I how much work is involved in those broadcasts, how many times they were dictated at the last minute, to find, some minutes later, the willing ear of the whole nation."

So we have it from Goebbels himself that the entire German nation was prepared to lend willing ears to Fritzsche, after he had made his reputation on the radio.

The rumour spread that Fritzsche was "His Master's Voice" (Die Stimme Seines Herrn). This is certainly borne out by Fritzsche's functions. When Fritzsche spoke on the radio it was indeed plain to the German people that they were listening to the high command of the conspirators in this field.

Fritzsche is not being presented by the prosecution as the type of conspirator who signed decrees, or as the type of conspirator who sat in the inner councils planning all of the overall grand strategy of these conspirators. The function of propaganda is, for the most part, distinct from the field of such planning. The function of a propaganda agency is somewhat more analogous to an advertising agency or public relations department, the job of which is to sell the product and to win the market for the enterprise in question. Here the enterprise, we submit, was the Nazi conspiracy. In a conspiracy to commit fraud, the gifted salesman of the conspiratorial group is quite as essential and quite as culpable as the master planners, even though he may not have contributed substantially to the formulation of all the basic strategy, but rather contributed to its artful execution.

In this case the prosecution most emphatically contends that propaganda was a weapon of tremendous importance to this conspiracy. We further contend that the leading propagandists were major accomplices in this conspiracy, and moreover, that Fritzsche was a major propagandist.

When Fritzsche entered the Propaganda Ministry, the most fabulous "lie factory" of all time, and thus attached himself to this conspiracy, he did this with a more open mind than most of these conspirators, who had committed themselves at an earlier date, before the seizure of power. He was in a particularly strategic position to observe the frauds committed upon the German people and upon the world by these conspirators.

The Tribunal will recall that in 1933, before Fritzsche took his party oath of unconditional obedience and subservience to the Fuehrer, and thus abdicated his moral responsibility to these conspirators, he had observed at first hand the operations of the Storm Troopers and the Nazi race pattern in action. When, notwithstanding this, Fritzsche undertook to bring the German news agencies in their entirety within Fascist control, he learned from the inside, from Goebbels' own lips, much of the cynical intrigue and many of the bold lies against opposition groups within and without Germany. He observed, for example, the opposition journalists, a profession to which he had previously been attached, being forced out of existence, crushed to earth - either absorbed or eliminated. He continued to support the conspiracy. He learned from day to day the art of intrigue and quackery in the process of perverting the German nation, and he grew in prestige and influence as he practised this art.

The Tribunal will also recall that Fritzsche had said that his predecessor Berndt lost the leadership of the German Press Division, partly because he over-played his hand by the successful but blunt and overdone manipulation of the Sudetenland propaganda. Fritzsche stepped into the gap which had been caused by the loss of confidence of both the editors and the German people, and Fritzsche did his job well.

No doubt Fritzsche was not as blunt as the man he succeeded, but his relative shrewdness and subtlety, his very ability to be more assuring and "to find," as Goebbels said, "the willing ears of the whole nation," these things made him the more useful accomplice of these conspirators.

Nazi Germany and its Press went into the actual phase of war operations with Fritzsche at the head of the particular propaganda instrument, controlling the German Press and German news. In 1942, when Fritzsche transferred from the field of the Press to the field of radio, he was not removed for bungling, but only because Goebbels then needed him most in the field of radio.

Fritzsche is not in the dock as a free journalist, But as an efficient controlled Nazi propagandist, a propagandist who helped substantially to tighten the Nazi stranglehold over the German people, a propagandist who made the excesses of these conspirators more palatable to the consciences of the German people themselves, a propagandist who cynically proclaimed the barbarous racialism which is at the very heart of this conspiracy, a propagandist who coldly goaded humble Germans to blind fury against people who were, he told them, sub-human and guilty of all the suffering of Germany; suffering which indeed these Nazis themselves had invited.

In conclusion, I wish to say only this. Without the propaganda apparatus of the Nazi State it is clear that the world, including Germany, would not have suffered the catastrophe of these years, and it is because of Fritzsche's able role on behalf of the Nazi conspirators, and their deceitful and barbarous practices in connection with the conspiracy, that he is called to account before this International Tribunal.

SIR DAVID MAXWELL FYFE: May it please the Tribunal. It was intended that the next presentation would be by Colonel Griffith-Jones in the case of the defendant Hess. I understand that the Tribunal has in mind that it might be better if that were left for the moment; if so, Major Harcourt Barrington is prepared to make the presentation with regard to the defendant von Papen.

THE PRESIDENT: Yes. We understood that the defendant Hess's counsel could not be present today, and therefore it was better to go on with one of the others.

SIR DAVID MAXWELL FYFE: If your Lordship please then, Major Harcourt Barrington will deal with the presentation against the defendant von Papen.

MAJOR J. HARCOURT BARRINGTON: My Lords, I understand that the court interpreters have not got the proper papers and document books up here yet, but they can get them in a very few minutes. Would your lordship prefer that I should go on or wait until they have got them?

THE PRESIDENT: Very well. Go on then.

MAJOR BARRINGTON: May it please the Tribunal. It is my duty to present the case against the defendant von Papen. Before I begin I would like to say that the documents in the document books are arranged numerically, and not in the order of presentation, and that the English document books are paged in red chalk at the bottom of the page.

THE PRESIDENT: Does that mean that the French and the Soviet are not?

MAJOR BARRINGTON: My Lord, we did not prepare French and Soviet document books.

The defendant von Papen is charged primarily, as are all the other defendants, with the guilt of the conspiracy itself. The proof of this charge of conspiracy will emerge automatically from the proof of the four allegations.

THE PRESIDENT: Major Barrington, the French members of the Tribunal have no document books at all.

MAJOR BARRINGTON: My Lord, there should be a German document book for the French members. I understand it is now being fetched. Should I wait until it arrives?

THE PRESIDENT: I think you can go on.

MAJOR BARRINGTON: The defendant Papen is charged primarily with the guilt of conspiracy, and the proof of this charge of conspiracy will emerge automatically from the proof of the four allegations specified in Appendix "A" of the Indictment. These are as follows:

(1) He promoted the accession of the Nazi conspirators to power.

(2) He participated in the consolidation of their control over Germany.

(3) He promoted the preparations for war.

(4) He participated in the political planning and preparation of the Nazi conspirators for Wars of aggression, etc.

Broadly speaking, the case against von Papen covers the period from 1 June 1932, to the conclusion of the Anschluss in March 1938.

So far in this trial, almost the only evidence specifically implicating von Papen has been evidence in regard to his activities in Austria. This evidence need only be summarised now. But if the case against von Papen rested on Austria alone, the prosecution would be in the position of relying on a period during which the essence of his task was studied plausibility, and in Which his whole purpose was to clothe his operations with a cloak of sincerity and innocent respectability. It is therefore desirable to put the evidence already given in its true perspective, by showing, in addition, the active and prominent part he played for the Nazis before he went to Austria.

Papen himself claims to have many times rejected Hitler's request that he should actually join the Nazi Party. Until 1938 this may indeed have been true, for he was shrewd enough to see the advantage of maintaining, at least outwardly, his personal independence. It will be my object to show that, despite his facade of independence, Papen was an ardent member of this conspiracy, and in spite of warnings and rebuffs was unable to resist its fascination.

In this submission of the prosecution, the key to von Papen's activities is that, although perhaps not a typical Nazi, he was an unscrupulous political opportunist, and ready to fall in with the Nazis when it suited him. He was not unpractised in duplicity, and viewed with an apparent indifference the contradictions and betrayals which his duplicity inevitably involved. One of his chief weapons was fraudulent assurance.

Before dealing with the specific charges, I will refer to document 2902-PS, which is on Page 38 of the English document book, and I put it in as Exhibit GB 233. This is von Papen's own signed statement showing his appointments. It is not in chronological order, but I will read the relevant parts as they come. I need not read the whole of it. The Tribunal will note that this statement is written by Dr. Kubuschok, counsel for von Papen, although it is signed by von Papen himself.

Paragraph 1:

"Von Papen many times rejected Hitler's request to join the NSDAP. Hitler simply sent him the golden Party badge. In my opinion, legally speaking, he did not thereby become a member of the Party."

Interposing there, my Lord, the fact that he was officially regarded as having become a member in 1938 will be shown by a document which I shall refer to later.

Going on to paragraph 2: "From 1933 to 1945 von Papen was a member of the Reichstag."

Paragraph 3: "Von Papen was Reich Chancellor from 1 June 1932, to 17 November 1932. He carried on the duties of Reich Chancellor until his successor took office 2 December 1932."

Paragraph 4: "On 30 January 1933, von Papen was appointed Vice-Chancellor. From 30 June 1934" - which was the date of the Blood Purge - "he ceased to exercise official duties. On that day he was placed under arrest. Immediately after his release on 3 July 1934, he went to the Reich Chancellery to hand in his resignation to Hitler."

The rest of the paragraph I need not read. It is an argument which concerns the authenticity or otherwise of his signature, as it appears in the Reichsgesetzblatt, to certain decrees of August 1934. I am prepared to agree with his contention that his signature on these decrees may not have been correct and may have been a mistake. He admits holding office only to 3 July 1934.

He was, as the Tribunal will also remember, in virtue of being Reich Chancellor, a member of the Reich Cabinet.

Going on to paragraph 5: "On 13 November 1933, von Papen became Plenipotentiary for the Saar. This office was terminated under the same circumstances as were described in paragraph 4."

The rest of the document I need not read. It concerns his appointments to Vienna and Ankara, appointments which are matters of history. He was appointed Minister to Vienna on 26 July 1934, and recalled on 4 February 1938, and he was ambassador in Ankara from April 1939 until August 1944.

The first allegation against the defendant von Papen is that he used his personal influence to promote the accession of the Nazi conspirators to power. From the outset von Papen was well aware of the Nazi programme and Nazi methods. There can be no question of his having encouraged the Nazis through ignorance of these facts. The official NSDAP programme was open and notorious; it had been published in "Mein Kampf" for many years; it had been published and republished in the Year-book of the NSDAP and elsewhere. The Nazis made no secret of their intention to make it a fundamental law of the State. This has been dealt with in full at an earlier stage of the trial.

During 1932 von Papen, as Reich Chancellor, was in a particularly good position to understand the Nazi purpose and methods, and, in fact, he publicly acknowledged the Nazi menace. Take, for instance, his Munster speech on 28 August 1932. This is document 3314-PS, on Page 49 of the English document book, and I now put it in as Exhibit GB 234, and I quote two extracts from the top of the page:

"The licentiousness emanating from the appeal of the leader of the National Socialist movement does not comply very well with his claims to governmental power.

I do not concede him the right to regard the mere minority following his banner solely as the German nation and to treat all other fellow countrymen as free game."

Take also his Munich speech of 13 October 1932. That is on Page 50 of the English document book, Document 3317-PS, which I now put in as Exhibit GB 235, and I will read only the last extract on the page:

"In the interest of the entire nation, we decline the claim to power by parties which want to own their followers body and soul, and which want to put themselves, as a party or a movement, over and above the whole nation."

I do not rely on these random extracts to show anything more than that he had, in 1932, clearly addressed his mind to the inherent lawlessness of the Nazi philosophy. Nevertheless, in his letter to Hitler of 13 November 1932, which I shall quote more fully later, he wrote of the Nazi movement as, I quote, "so great a national movement - "

THE PRESIDENT: Where is this?

MAJOR BARRINGTON: This is in a letter which I shall quote in a few minutes, my Lord, a letter to Hitler of 13 November 1932. He wrote:

"So great a national movement, the merits of which for people and country I have always recognised in spite of necessary criticisms."

So variable and so seemingly contradictory were von Papen's acts and utterances regarding the Nazis that it is not possible to present the picture of Papen's part in this infamous enterprise unless one first reviews the steps by which he entered upon it. It then becomes clear that he threw himself, if not wholeheartedly, yet with cool and deliberate calculation, into the Nazi conspiracy.

I shall enumerate some of the principal steps by which Papen fell in with the Nazi conspiracy.

As a result of his first personal contact with Hitler, von Papen as Chancellor rescinded, on 14 June 1932, the decree passed on 13 April 1932, for the dissolution of the Nazi para-military organisations, the SA and the SS. He thereby rendered the greatest possible service to the Nazi Party, inasmuch as it relied upon its para-military organisations to beat the German people into submission. The decree rescinding the dissolution of the SA and the SS is shown in Document D-631, on Page 64 of the document book, and I now put it in as Exhibit GB 236. It is an extract from the Reichsgesetzblatt, which was an omnibus decree. The relevant passage is in paragraph 29:

"This order comes into operation from the day of announcement. It takes the place of the Order of the Reich President for the Safeguarding of the State Authority of...." The date should be 13 April 1932.

THE PRESIDENT: Which page of the document book is it?

MAJOR BARRINGTON: I am sorry, my Lord; it is Page 64. And the date shown there should not be 3 May 1932; it should be 13 April 1932.

That was the decree which had previously dissolved the Nazi para-military organisations under the government of Chancellor Bruning. At the bottom of the page the Tribunal will see the relevant parts of the decree of 13 April reproduced. At the beginning of paragraph 1 of that decree it said:

"All organisations of a military nature of the German National Socialist Labour Party will be dissolved with immediate effect, particularly, the Storm Detachments (SA) and the Protective Detachments (SS)."

This rescission by von Papen was made in pursuance of a bargain with Hitler which is mentioned in a book called "Dates from the History of the NSDAP," by Dr. Hans Volts, a book published with the authority of the NSDAP. It is already an exhibit, USA 592. The extract I want to quote is on Page 59 of the document book, and it is Document 3463-PS. I quote an extract from Page 41 of this little book:

"28 May" - that was in 1932, of course. "In view of the imminent fall of Bruning, at a meeting between the former deputy of the Prussian Centre Party, Franz von Papen, and the Fuehrer in Berlin, (first personal contact in Spring, 1932), the Fuehrer agrees that a Papen cabinet should be tolerated by the NSDAP, provided that the prohibition imposed on the SA uniforms and demonstrations be lifted, and the Reichstag dissolved."

It is difficult to imagine a less astute opening gambit, for a man who was about to become Chancellor, than to reinstate this sinister organisation which had been suppressed by his predecessor. This action emphasises the characteristic duplicity and insincerity of his public condemnations of the Nazis, which I quoted a few minutes ago.

Eighteen months later he publicly boasted that at the time of taking over the chancellorship he had advocated paving the way to power for what he called the "young fighting liberation movement." That will be shown in Document 3375-PS, which I shall introduce in a few minutes.

Another important step was when, on the 20 July 1932, he accomplished his famous coup d'etat in Prussia, which removed the Braun-Severing Prussian Government, and united the ruling power of the Reich and Prussia in his own hands as Reichskommissar for Prussia. This is now a matter of history. It is mentioned in Document D 632, which I now introduce as Exhibit GB 237. It is on Page 65 of the document book. This document is, I think, a semi-official biography in a series on public men.

Papen regarded this step, his coup d'etat in Prussia, as a first step in the policy, later pursued by Hitler, of co-ordinating the States with the Reich, which will be shown in Document 3357, which I shall come to later.

The next step; if the Tribunal will look at Document D-632 on Page 65 of the document book, the last four or five lines at the bottom of the page; "The Reichstag elections of 31 July, which were the result of von Papen's disbandment of the Reichstag on 4 June," - which was made in pursuance of the bargain that I mentioned a few minutes ago - "strengthened enormously the NSDAP, so that von Papen offered to the leader of the now strongest party his participation in the government as Vice-Chancellor. Adolf Hitler rejected this offer on 13 August.

The new Reichstag, which assembled on 30 August, was disbanded by 12 September. The new elections brought about a considerable loss to the NSDAP, but did not strengthen the government parties, so that Papen's government retired on 17 November 1932 after unsuccessful negotiations with the party leaders."

My Lord, I shall wish to quote a few more extracts from that biography, but as it is a mere catalogue of events, perhaps Your Lordship would allow me to return to it at the appropriate time.

So far as those negotiations mentioned just now in the biography concern Hitler, they involved an exchange of letters in which von Papen wrote to Hitler, on 13 November 1932, and the latter replied on 16 November. Papen's letter to Hitler is Document D-633, on Page 68 of the English document book, and I now put it in as Exhibit GB 238. I propose to read a part of this letter, because it shows the positive efforts made by Papen to ally himself with the Nazis, even in face of further rebuffs from Hitler. I read the third paragraph. I should tell the Tribunal that there is some underlining in the English translation of that paragraph, which does not occur in the German text:

"A new situation has arisen through the elections of November 6, and at the same time a fresh opportunity for all nationalist elements to be concentrated anew. The Reich President has instructed me to find out, by conversations with the leaders of the individual parties concerned, whether and how far they will be prepared to support the carrying out of the political and economic programme on which the Reich Government has embarked. In spite of the National Socialist Press calling it a naive attempt for Reich Chancellor von Pa en to confer with the people concerned in the nationalist concentration and saying that there can only be one answer, viz.: "No negotiations with Papen," I should consider it a neglect of my duties, and I would be unable to justify it to my own conscience, if I did not approach you in this matter. I am quite aware, from the papers, that you are maintaining your demands to be entrusted with the Chancellor's office, and I am equally aware of the continued existence of the reasons for the decision of 13 August. I need not assure you again that I myself do not come into this matter at all. All the same, I feel that the leader of so great a national movement, the merits of which for the people and country I have always recognised, in spite of necessary criticisms, should not refuse to discuss with the German politician who at present bears the full responsibility, the situation and the decisions required. We must attempt to forget the bitterness of the elections, and to place the welfare of the country, which we, both of us, serve, above all other considerations."

Hitler replied on 16 November 1932 in a long letter, laying down terms which were evidently unacceptable to von Papen, since he resigned tile next day and was succeeded by von Schleicher. That document is D-634, put in as part of Exhibit GB 238, as it is part of the same correspondence. I need not read from the letter itself.

Then came the meetings between Papen and Hitler in January 1933, in the house of von Schroder and Ribbentrop, culminating in von Schleicher being succeeded by Hitler as Reich Chancellor on 30 January 1933. Referring again to the biography on Page 66 of the document book, second paragraph, there is an account of the meeting at Schroder's house:

"The meeting with Hitler, which took place in the beginning of January 1933, in the house of the banker Baron von Schroder, in Cologne, is due to his initiative" - that means, of course, Papen's initiative - "although von Schroder was the mediator." Both von Papen and Hitler later made public statements about this meeting (Press of 6 January 1933). After the rapid downfall of von Schleicher on 26 January 1933, the Hitler-von Papen-Hugenberg-Seldte Cabinet was formed on the 30th January 1933 as a government of national solidarity. In this cabinet von Papen held the office of Vice-Chancellor and Reich Commissar for Prussia."

The meetings at Ribbentrop's house, at which Papen was also present, have been mentioned by Sir David Maxwell Fyfe (Document D-472) which was Exhibit GB 130. I now wish to introduce into evidence an affidavit by von Schroder, but I understand that Doctor Kubuschok wishes to raise an objection to this. Perhaps before Doctor Kubuschok raises his objection it might help if I said, quite openly, that Schroder is now in custody, and according to my information he is at Frankfurt; so that physically he undoubtedly could be called. Perhaps I might also say at this moment that there would be no objection, from the prosecution's point of view, to interrogatories being administered to von Schroder on the subject matter of the affidavit.

DR. KUBUSCHOK (Counsel for defendant von Papen): I object to the reading of the affidavit of Schroder. I know that in individual cases the Tribunal has permitted the reading of affidavits. This occurred under Article 19 of the Charter, which is based on the proposition that the trial should be conducted as speedily as possible, and that for this reason the rules of ordinary court procedure should be modified to some extent. Of decisive importance, therefore, is the speediness of the trial. But in our case the reading of the affidavit cannot be approved for that reason.

Our case is quite analogous to the case that was decided on 14 December with regard to Schuschnigg's affidavit. Schroder is in the vicinity. Schroder was apparently brought to the neighbourhood of Nuremberg for the purposes of this trial. The affidavit was taken down on 5 December. He could be brought here at any time. The reading of the affidavit would result in my having to refer not only to him but also to several other witnesses. Schroder describes a series of facts in his affidavit, which in their entirety are not needed for the finding of a decision. However, once introduced into the trial, they must also be discussed by the defence in the pursuance of its duty.

The affidavit discusses internal political matters, using improper terms. For this reason misunderstandings would enter into the trial which could be obviated by the hearing of a witness. I believe, therefore, that the oral testimony of a witness is the only way in which Schroder's testimony should be submitted to the Tribunal, since otherwise a large number of witnesses will have to be called with the reading of Schroder's affidavit and his personal interrogation.

THE PRESIDENT: Have you finished?

DR. KUBUSCHOK: Yes.

THE PRESIDENT: Do you wish to make any observation?

MAJOR BARRINGTON: Yes, I do, my Lord.

The Tribunal has been asked to exclude this affidavit using as a precedent the decision on von Schuschnigg's affidavit. I think I am correct in saying that von Schuschnigg's affidavit was excluded as an exception to the general rule on affidavits, which the Tribunal laid down earlier the same day, when Mr. Messersmith's affidavit was accepted. Perhaps your Lordship will allow me to read from the transcript the Tribunal's decision on the affidavit of Messersmith.

THE PRESIDENT: Mr. Messersmith was in Mexico, was he not?

MAJOR BARRINGTON: That is so, my Lord, yes.

THE PRESIDENT: So that the difference between him and Schuschnigg in that regard was very considerable.

MAJOR BARRINGTON: In that regard, yes, but what I was going to say was this, my Lord: In ruling on Messersmiths affidavit your Lordship said:

"In view of those provisions" - that is Article 19 of the Charter - "the Tribunal holds that affidavits can be presented, and that in the present case it is a proper course. The question of the probative value of the affidavit as compared with the witness who has been cross-examined would, of course, be considered by the Tribunal, and if at a later stage the Tribunal thinks the presence of a witness is of extreme importance, the matter can be reconsidered."

And your Lordship added: "If the defence wish to put interrogatories to the witness, they will be at liberty to do so."

Now in the afternoon of that day, when Schuschnigg's affidavit came up

THE PRESIDENT: Which day was this?

MAJOR BARRINGTON: This was 28 November, my Lord. It is on Page 214 Pt. 1 of the transcript, the Messersmith affidavit, and Page 234 Pt. 1 is the Schuschnigg affidavit.

Now, when the objection was taken to the Schuschnigg affidavit, the objection was put in these words:

"Today when the resolution was announced in respect of the use to be made of the written affidavit of Mr. Messersmith, the Court was of the opinion that in a case of very great importance possibly it would take a different view of the matter"; and then defence counsel went on to say:

"As it is a case of such an important witness, the principle of direct evidence must be adhered to."

THE PRESIDENT: Have you a reference to a subsequent occasion on which we heard Mr. Justice Jackson upon this subject, when Mr. Justice Jackson submitted to us that on the strict interpretation of Article 19 we were bound to admit any evidence which we deemed to have probative value."

MAJOR BARRINGTON: My Lord, I have not that reference.

THE PRESIDENT: Why do you not call this witness?

MAJOR BARRINGTON: I say, quite frankly, - and I was coming to that - this witness is in a position of being an alleged co-conspirator, and I make no secret of the fact that for obvious reasons the prosecution would not desire to call him as a witness, and I put this affidavit forward as an admission by a co-conspirator. I admit that it is not an admission made in pursuance of the conspiracy, but I submit that, as the Tribunal is not bound by technical rules of evidence, this affidavit may be accepted in evidence as an admission by a co-conspirator; and, as I said before, there will be no objection to administering interrogatories on the subject matter of this affidavit, and indeed, the witness would be available to be called as a defence witness if required.

That is all I have to say on that, my Lord.

THE PRESIDENT: There would be no objection to bringing the witness here for the purpose of cross-examination upon the affidavit?

MAJOR BARRINGTON: I do not think there could be any objection if it were confined to the subject matter of the affidavit. I would not like ...

THE PRESIDENT: How could you object, for instance, to the defendant himself applying to call the witness?

MAJOR BARRINGTON: As I said, I do not think there could be any objection to that, my Lord.

THE PRESIDENT: The result would be the same, would it not? If the witness were called for the purpose of cross- examination, then he could be asked other questions which were not arising out of the matter in the affidavit. If the defendant can call him as his own witness, there can be no objection to the cross-examination going outside the matter of the affidavit.

MAJOR BARRINGTON: Of course he could not be cross-examined by the prosecution in that event, my Lord.

THE PRESIDENT: You mean you would ask him questions in re- examination, but they would not take the form of cross- examination?

MAJOR BARRINGTON: That is what I mean, my Lord.

THE PRESIDENT: You mean that you would prefer that he should be called for the defendants rather than be cross-examined outside the subject matter of the affidavit?

MAJOR BARRINGTON: Yes.

THE PRESIDENT: Is there anything you wish to add or not?

MAJOR BARRINGTON: There is nothing I wish to add.

THE PRESIDENT: It is time for us to adjourn. We will consider the matter.

(A recess was taken)

DR. HORN (Counsel for defendant Ribbentrop): In the place of Dr. von Rohrscheidt, defence counsel for Hess, I would like to make the following declaration.

Dr. von Rohrscheidt has been the victim of an accident. He has broken his ankle. The defendant Hess has asked me to notify the Tribunal that from now on until the end of the trial, he desires to make use of his right under the Charter to defend himself. The reason that he wants to do that for the whole length of the trial is to be found in the fact that due to his absence his counsel will not be informed of the proceedings of the Court.

THE PRESIDENT: The Tribunal will consider the oral application which has just been made to it on behalf of the defendant Hess.

As to the objection to the affidavit of von Schroder which was made this morning by counsel for the defendant von Papen, the Tribunal does not propose to lay down any general rule about the admission of affidavit evidence. But in the particular circumstances of this case, the Tribunal will admit the affidavit in question, but will direct that if the affidavit is put in evidence, the man who made the affidavit, von Schroder, must be presented, brought here immediately for cross-examination by the defendant's counsel. When I say immediately I mean as soon as possible.

MAJOR BARRINGTON: My Lord, I will not introduce this affidavit.

THE PRESIDENT: Yes, Major Barrington.

MAJOR BARRINGTON: My Lord, before coming on to that affidavit, I last read from the biography a passage about the meeting at von Schroder's house, and I ask the Tribunal to deduce from that extract from the biography that it was at that meeting that a discussion took place between von Papen and Hitler, which led up to the Hitler Government in which von Papen served as Vice Chancellor. So that now at that point the defendant von Papen was completely committed to joining the Nazi Party, and with his eyes open and on his own initiative, he had helped materially to bring them into power.

The second allegation against the defendant von Papen is that he participated in the consolidation of Nazi control over Germany.

In the first critical year and a half of the Nazi consolidation von Papen, as Vice Chancellor, was second only to Hitler in the Cabinet which carried out the Nazi programme.

The process of consolidating the Nazi control of Germany by legislation has been fully dealt with earlier in this trial. The high position of von Papen must have associated him closely with such legislation. In July 1934, Hitler expressly thanked him for all that he had done for the co-ordination of the Government of the National Revolution. That will appear in Document 2799-PS. In fact, although I shall read from that document in a minute, the document has been introduced to the Court by Mr. Alderman.

Two important decrees may be mentioned specially, as actually bearing the signature of von Papen. First, the decree relating to the formation of special courts, dated the 21st of March 1933, for the trial of all cases involving political matters. The Tribunal has already taken judicial notice of this decree. (see Part 1, p. 233).

This decree was the first step in the Nazification of the German judiciary. In all political cases it abolished fundamental rights, including the right of appeal, which had previously characterised the administration of German criminal justice.

On the same date, the 21 March 1933, von Papen personally signed the amnesty decree liberating all persons who had committed murder or any other crime between 30 January and 21 March 1933 in the National Revolution of the German people. That document is 2059-PS, and is on Page 30 of the English document book. I read

Section 1.

THE PRESIDENT: I do not think you need read the decrees if you will summarise them.

MAJOR BARRINGTON: If your Lordship pleases, I will ask you to take judicial notice of that decree.

THE PRESIDENT: Yes.

MAJOR BARRINGTON: As a member of the Reich Cabinet, von Papen was, in my submission, responsible for the legislation carried through even when the decrees did not actually bear his signature. But I shall mention as examples two categories of legislation in particular, in order to show by reference to his own previous and contemporaneous statements that they were not matters of which he could say that, as a respectable politician, he took no interest in them.

First, the civil service. As a public servant himself, von Papen must have had a hard but apparently successful struggle with his conscience when associating himself with the sweeping series of decrees for attaining Nazi control of the Civil Service. This has been dealt with in the afternoon session of 22 November. In this connection I refer the Tribunal to Document 351-PS, which is on Page 1 of the document book. It is Exhibit USA 389, and it is the minutes of Hitler's first cabinet meeting on 30 January 1933. I read from the last paragraph of the minutes, on Page 5 of the document book in the middle of the paragraph:

"The Deputy of the Reich Chancellor and the Reichskommissar for the State of Prussia suggested that the Reich Chancellor, in an interview, should state at the earliest opportunity that the rumours about the danger of inflation and the rumours about the danger to the rights of civil servants are untrue."

Even if this was not meant to suggest to Hitler the giving of a fraudulent assurance, at the best it emphasises the indifference with which von Papen later saw the civil servants betrayed.

Secondly, the decrees for the integration of the Federal States with the Reich. These again have been dealt with earlier in the trial. The substantial effect of these decrees was to abolish the States and to put an end to federalism, and any possible retarding influence which it might have upon the centralisation of power in the Reich Cabinet. The importance of this step, as well as the role played by Papen, is reflected in the exchange of letters between Hindenberg, von Papen - in his capacity as Reichskommissar for Prussia - and Hitler, in connection with the recall of the Reichskommissar and the appointment of Goering to the post of Prime Minister of Prussia. I refer to Document 3357-PS, which is on Page 52 of the English document book, and I now put it in as Exhibit GB 239.

In tendering his resignation on 7 April 1933, von Papen wrote to Hitler, and I read from the document:

"With the draft of the law for the co-ordination of the States with the Reich, passed today by the Reich Chancellor, legislative work has begun which will be of historical significance for the political development of the German State. The step taken by the Reich Government, which I headed at the time, is now crowned by this new interlocking of the Reich. You, Herr Reich Chancellor, will now, as once Bismarck was, be able to co-ordinate in all points the policy of the greatest of German States with that of the Reich. Now that the new law enables you to appoint a Prussian Prime Minister, I ask you to inform the Reich President that I return to his hands my post of Reichskommissar for Prussia."

I would like to read also the letter which Hitler wrote to Hindenburg in transmitting this resignation. Hitler wrote:

> "Vice-Chancellor von Papen has sent a letter to me which I enclose for your information. Herr von Papen had already informed me, within the last few days, that he agreed with Minister Goering to resign on his own volition, as soon as the unified conduct of the governmental affairs in the Reich and in Prussia were assured by the new law on the co-ordination of policy in the Reich and the States.
>
> On the eve of the day when the new law on the institution of Reich governors was adopted, Herr von Papen considered this aim as having been attained; and he requested me to undertake the appointment of the Prussian Prime Minister, when at the same time he would offer his full-time services in the Reich Government.
>
> Herr von Papen, in accepting the post of Kommissar for the Government of Prussia, in these difficult times since 30 January, has rendered a very meritorious service to the realisation of the idea of co-ordinating the policy in the Reich and the States. His collaboration in the Reich Cabinet, for which he now offers all his strength, is infinitely valuable; my relationship to him is such a heartily friendly one, that I sincerely rejoice at the great help I shall thus receive."

Yet it was only five weeks before this that on 3 March, 1933, von Papen had warned the electorate at Stuttgart against abolishing federalism. I will now read from Document 3313-PS, which is on Page 48 of the English document book, and which I now introduce as Exhibit GB 240, about the middle of the third paragraph. This is an extract from von Papen's speech at Stuttgart. He said:

> "Federalism will protect us from centralism, that organisational form which focuses all the living strength of a nation, like a burning mirror, on one point. No nation is less adaptable to being governed centrally than the German nation."

Earlier, at the time of the elections in the autumn of 1932, von Papen, as Chancellor, had visited Munich. The Frankfurter Zeitung of 12 October, 1932, commented on his policy. I refer to Document 3318-PS on Page 51 of the English document book, which I introduce as Exhibit GB 241. The Frankfurter Zeitung commented:

> "Von Papen claimed that it had been his aim from the very beginning of his tenure of office to build a new Reich for, and with, the various States. The Reich Government is taking a definite federalist attitude. Its slogan is not a dreary centralism or unitarianism."

That was in October 1932. All that was now thrown overboard in deference to his new master.

I now come to the Jews. In March, 1933, the entire Cabinet approved a systematic State policy of persecution of the Jews. This has already been described to the Tribunal.

Only four days before the boycott was timed to begin, "with all ferocity" - to borrow the words of Dr. Goebbels - von Papen wrote a radiogram of reassurance to the Board of Trade for German-American Commerce in New York, which had expressed its anxiety to the German Government about the situation. His assurance - which I now put in as Document D- 635, and it will be Exhibit GB 242, on Page 73 of the English document book - his assurance was published in the "New York Times" on 28 March, 1933, and it contained the following sentence, which I read from about the middle of the page. This document is the last but one in the German document book.

"Reports circulated in America and received here with indignation about alleged tortures of political prisoners and mistreatment of Jews, deserve strongest repudiation. Hundreds of thousands of Jews, irrespective of nationality, who have not taken part in political activities, are living here entirely unmolested."

This is a characteristic -

DR. KUBUSCHOK (Counsel for von Papen): The article in the "New York Times" goes back to a telegram of the accused von Papen, which is contained in the document book one page ahead. The English translation has the date of 27 March. This date is an error. The German text which I received shows that it is a question of a week-end letter, which, according to the figures on the German document, was sent on 25 March. This difference in time is of particular importance for the following reason

In effect, on 25 March nothing was yet known concerning the Jewish boycott, which Goebbels then announced for 1 April. The accused von Papen could, therefore, on 25 March, point to these then comparatively few smaller incidents, as he does in the telegram. In any case, the conclusion of the Indictment, that the contents of the telegram were a lie, thereby fails.

THE PRESIDENT: Major Barrington, have you the original of that?

MAJOR BARRINGTON: The original is here, my Lord, yes. It is quite correct that there are some figures at the top, which, though I had not recognised it, might indicate that it was dispatched on the 25th.

THE PRESIDENT: And when was the meeting of the cabinet which approved the policy of persecution of the Jews?

MAJOR BARRINGTON: Well, my Lord, I cannot say. It was sometime within the last few days of March, but it might have been on the 26th. I can have that checked up.

THE PRESIDENT: Very well.

DR. KUBUSCHOK: May I clarify that matter by saying that the cabinet meeting in which the Jewish question was discussed took place at a much later date, and that in this cabinet meeting, cabinet members, among others the accused von Papen, condemned the Jewish boycott. I shall submit the minutes of the meeting as soon as my motion has been granted.

THE PRESIDENT: I do not know what you mean by your motion being granted. Does counsel for the prosecution say whether he persists in his allegation or whether he withdraws it?

MAJOR BARRINGTON: I will say this. Subject to checking the date when the cabinet meeting took place

THE PRESIDENT: Well, you can do that at the adjournment and let us know in the morning.

MAJOR BARRINGTON: If your Lordship pleases.

At this point I will just say this: That it was, as the Tribunal has already heard, common knowledge at the time that the Nazi policy was anti-Jewish, and Jews were already in concentration camps. So I will leave it to the Tribunal to infer that at the time when that radiogram was sent, which I am prepared to accept as being 25 March, von Papen did not know of this policy of boycotting.

I will go further now that I am on this point, and I will say that von Papen was indeed himself a supporter of the anti-Jewish policy, and as evidence of this I will put in Document 2830-PS, which is on Page 37A of the document book, and which I now introduce as Exhibit GB 243.

This is a letter, my Lord, written by von Papen from Vienna on 12 May, 1936 to Hitler on the subject of the Freiheitsbund. Paragraph 4 of the English text is as follows:

> "The following incident is interesting. The Czech Legation secretary Dohalsky has made to Mr. Staud, leader of the Freedom Union, an offer to make available to the Freedom Union every desired amount from the Czech Government which he would need for the strengthening of his fight against the Heimwehr. His only condition is that the Freedom Union should guarantee to take a stand directed against Germany. Mr. Staud has simply refused this offer. It is shown by that how, even in the enemy's camp, there is one who already evaluates the new grouping of forces. From that arises the further necessity for us to support, as before, this movement financially, and especially in reference to the continuation of its fight against Jewry."

DR. KUBUSCHOK: I must point out here a difficulty which has apparently been caused by the translation. In the original German text the word "in reference" are used in regard to the transmittal in the following way:

> "In reference to the continuation of its fight against Jewry." These words "in reference" mean here that under this heading the money must be transmitted, although this was not the real purpose, for the Austrian Freiheitsbund (Freedom Union) was not an anti-Semitic movement but a legal trade union, to which Chancellor Dollfuss also belonged. This expression "in reference" means only that the transmittal of the money demanded a covering designation, because it was not permissible to transmit money from abroad to a party recognised by the State, for any party purposes, as is shown by the rejected offer of the Czechoslovaks. I only wanted to point out here that the words "in reference" perhaps give a wrong impression and should rather be translated "referring". In any case, I should like to point out that this "in reference" was a kind of camouflage for the transmittal of the money.

THE PRESIDENT: I do not know to which word you are referring, but as I understand it the only purpose of referring to this letter was to prove that in it von Papen was suggesting that a certain organisation should be financially assisted in its fight against Jewry. That is the only purpose of referring to the letter. I do not know what you mean about some word being wrongly translated.

DR. KUBUSCHOK: That is exactly how the error originated. The money was not transmitted to fight Jewry, for that was not at all the purpose of this Christian Trade Union in Austria, but a certain designation for the transmittal of the money had to be devised, so this continuation of its fight against Jewry was used. The purpose therefore was not the fight against Jewry, but the elimination, through financial support, of another foreign influence, namely that of Czechoslovakia.

THE PRESIDENT: I should have thought myself that the point which might have been taken against the prosecution was that the letter was dated nearly 3 years after the time with which you were then dealing.

MAJOR BARRINGTON: That is so, my Lord; it was not at the time of the previous one.

THE PRESIDENT: No, the previous one was marked 1933, and this was 1936.

MAJOR BARRINGTON: Yes. I only put it in, My Lord, to show what von Papen's position was by then, at any rate. If your Lordship has any doubt as to the translation I would suggest that it might now be translated by the interpreter. We have the German text, a photostat.

THE PRESIDENT: I think you can have it translated again tomorrow; if necessary, you can have it gone into again then.

MAJOR BARRINGTON: Yes, my Lord.

I come now to the Catholic Church. The Nazi treatment of the Church has been fully dealt with by the United States Prosecution. In this particular field von Papen, a prominent lay Catholic, helped to consolidate the Nazi position both at home and abroad, as perhaps no one else could have done.

In dealing with the persecution of the Church, Colonel Wheeler read to the Tribunal Hitler's assurance given to the Church on 23 March 1933 in Hitler's speech on the Enabling Act, an assurance which resulted in the well-known Fulda Declaration of the German Bishops, also quoted by Colonel Wheeler. That was Document 3387-PS, which was Exhibit USA 566. This deceitful assurance of Hitler's appears to have been made at the suggestion of von Papen eight days earlier at the Reich Cabinet meeting at which the Enabling Act was discussed, on 15 March, 1933. I refer to Document 2962-PS, which is exhibit USA 578, and it is on Page 40 of the English document book. I read from Page 44, that is at the bottom of Page 6 of the German text. The minutes say:

"The Deputy of the Reich Chancellor and Reich Kommissar for Prussia stated that it was of decisive importance to co-ordinate into the new State the masses standing behind the parties. The question of the incorporation of political Catholicism into the new State was of particular importance."

That was a statement made by von Papen at the meeting at which the Enabling Act was discussed, prior to Hitler's speech on the Enabling Act in which he gave his assurance to the Church.

On 20 July 1933 Papen signed the Reich Concordat negotiated by him with the Vatican. The Tribunal has already taken judicial notice of this as Document 3280-A-PS. The signing of the Concordat, like Hitler's Papen-inspired speech on the Enabling Act, was only an interlude in the church policy of the Nazi conspirators. Their policy of assurances was followed by a long series of violations which eventually resulted in Papal denunciation in the Encyclical "Mit brennender Sorge," which is Document 3476-PS, Exhibit USA 567.

Papen maintains that his actions regarding the Church were sincere, and he has asserted, during interrogations, that it was Hitler who sabotaged the Concordat. If von Papen really believed in the very solemn undertakings given by him on behalf of the Reich to the Vatican, I submit it is strange that he, himself a Catholic, should have continued to serve Hitler after all those violations and even after the Papal Encyclical itself. I will go further. I will say that Papen was himself involved in what was virtually, if not technically, a violation of the Concordat. The Tribunal will recollect the Allocution of the Pope, dated 2 June 1945, which is Document 3268-PS, Exhibit USA 356, from which, on Page 1647 of the transcript Colonel Storey read the Pope's own summary of the Nazis' bitter struggle against the Church. (Part 3, p. 50). The very first item the Pope mentioned was the dissolution of Catholic organisations and, if the Tribunal will look at Document 3376-PS on Page 56 of the English document book, which I now put in as Exhibit GB 244 and which is an extract from "Das Archiv," they will see that in September, 1934 von Papen ordered - and I say "ordered" advisedly - the dissolution of the Union of Catholic Germans, of which he was at the time the leader. The text of "Das Archiv" reads as follows:

"The Reich Directorate of the Party announces the self-dissolution of the

Union of Catholic Germans.

Since the Reich Directorate of the Party, through its Department for Cultural Peace, directly, and to an increasing extent, administers all cultural problems and those concerning the relationship of State and Churches, the tasks at first delegated in the Union of Catholic Germans are now included in those of the Reich Directorate of the Party in the interest of a stronger co-ordination.

Former Vice-Chancellor von Papen, up to now the Leader of the Union of Catholic Germans, declared, about the dissolution of this organisation, that it was done upon his suggestion, since the attitude of the National Socialist State toward the Christian and Catholic Church had been explained often and unequivocally through the Leader and Chancellor himself."

I said that von Papen "ordered" the dissolution, although the announcement said it was self-dissolution on his suggestion, but I submit that such a suggestion from one in Papen's position was equivalent to an order, since by that date it was common knowledge that the Nazis were dropping all pretence that rival organisations might be permitted to exist.

After nine months' service under Hitler, spent in consolidating the Nazi control, von Papen was evidently well content with his choice. I refer to Document 3375-PS, Page 54 of the English document book, which I put in as Exhibit GB 245. On 2 November 1933, speaking at Essen from the same platform as Hitler and Gauleiter Terboven, in the course of the campaign for the Reichstag election and the referendum concerning Germany's leaving the League of Nations, von Papen declared:

"Ever since Providence called upon me to become the pioneer of national resurrection and the rebirth of our homeland, I have tried to support with all my strength the work of the National Socialist Movement and its leader; and just as I at the time of taking over the Chancellorship" - that was in 1932 - "advocated paving the way to power for the young fighting liberation movement, just as I on 30 January was selected by a gracious fate to put the hands of our Chancellor and Fuehrer into the hand of our beloved Field Marshal, so do I today again feel the obligation to say to the German people and all those who have kept confidence in me:

The good Lord has blessed Germany by giving it in times of deep distress a leader who will lead it through all distresses and weaknesses, through all crises and moments of danger, with the sure instinct of the statesman, into a happy future."

And then the last sentence of the whole text on Page 55;

"Let us in this hour say to the Fuehrer of the new Germany that we believe in him and his work."

By this time the cabinet of which von Papen was a member, and to which he had given all his strength, had abolished civil liberties; had sanctioned political murder committed in aid of Nazism's seizure of power; had destroyed all rival political parties; had enacted the basic laws for abolition of the political influence of the Federal States ; had provided the legislative basis for purging the Civil Service and judiciary of anti-Nazi elements; and had embarked upon a State policy of persecution of the Jews.

Papen's words are words of hollow mockery: "The good Lord has blessed Germany ."

The third allegation against the defendant Papen is that he promoted preparations for war. Knowing as he did the basic programme of the Nazi Party, it is inconceivable that, as Vice-Chancellor for a year and a half, he could have been dissociated from the conspirators' warlike preparations; he, of whom Hitler wrote to Hindenberg on 10 April 1933 that "his collaboration in the Reich Cabinet for which he now offers all his strength is infinitely valuable."

The fourth allegation against Papen is that he participated in the political planning and preparations for wars of aggression and wars in violation of international treaties. In Papen's case this allegation is really the story of the Anschluss. His part in that was a preparation for wars of aggression in two senses: first, that the Anschluss was the necessary preliminary step to all the subsequent armed aggressions; second, that, even if it can be contended that the Anschluss was in fact achieved without aggression, it was planned in such a way that it would have been achieved by aggression if that had been necessary.

I need do no more than summarise Papen's Austrian activities, since the whole story of the Anschluss has been described to the Tribunal already, though, with the Tribunal's permission I would like to read again two short passages of a particularly personal nature regarding Papen. But, before I deal with Papen's activities in Austria, there is one matter that I feel I ought not to omit to mention to the Tribunal.

On 18 June 1934 Papen made his remarkable speech at Marburg University. I do not propose to put it in evidence, nor is it in the document book, because it is a matter of history, and in what I say I do not intend to commit myself in regard to the motives and consequences of his speech, which are not free from mystery, but I will say this : that as far as concerns the subject matter of Papen's Marburg speech, it was an outspoken criticism of the Nazis. One must imagine that the Nazis were furiously angry and, although he escaped death in the Blood Purge twelve days later, he was put under arrest for three days. Whether this arrest was originally intended to end in execution or whether it was to protect him from the Purge as one too valuable to be lost, I do not now inquire. After his release from arrest he not unnaturally, resigned his Vice-Chancellorship. Now the question that arises - and this is why I mention the matter at this point - is: why after these barbaric events did he ever go back into the service of the Nazis again? What an opportunity missed! If he had stopped then, he might have saved the world much suffering. Suppose that Hitler's own Vice-Chancellor, just released from arrest, had defied the Nazis and told the world the truth. There might never have been a reoccupation of the Rhineland; there might never have been a war. But I must not speculate. The lamentable fact is that he slipped back, he succumbed again to the fascination of Hitler.

After the murder of Chancellor Dollfuss only three weeks later, on 25 July 1934, the situation was such as to call for the removal of the German Minister Rieth, and for the prompt substitution of a man who was an enthusiast for the Anschluss with Germany, who could be tolerant of Nazi objectives and methods, but who could lend an aura of respectability to official German representation in Vienna. Hitler's reaction to the murder of Dollfuss was immediate. He chose his man as soon as he heard the news. The very next day, 26 July, he sent von Papen a letter of appointment. This is on Page 37 of the English document book; it is Document 2799-PS and it has already been judicially noticed by the Tribunal. Mr. Alderman read the letter, and I wish to refer only to the personal remarks toward the end. Hitler in this letter, after reciting his version of the Dollfuss affair, and expressing his desire that Austrian-German relations should be brought again into normal and friendly channels, says in the third paragraph "For this reason I request you, dear Herr von Papen, to take over this important task, just because you have possessed and continue to possess my most complete and unlimited confidence, ever since we have worked together in the Cabinet."

And the last paragraph of the letter

"Thanking you once more for all that you once did for the co-ordination of the Government of the National Revolution and, since then, together with us, for Germany."

THE PRESIDENT: This might be a good time to break off for ten minutes.

(A recess was taken)

MAJOR BARRINGTON: My Lord, I had just read from the letter of appointment as Minister in Vienna which Hitler sent to von Papen on 26 July 1934. This letter, which, of course, was made public, naturally did not disclose the real intention of von Papen's appointment. The actual mission of von Papen was frankly stated shortly after his arrival in Vienna in the course of a private conversation he had with the American Minister, Mr. Messersmith. I quote from Mr. Messersmith's affidavit, which is Document 1760-PS, Exhibit USA 57, and it is on Page 22 of the document book, just about half way through the second paragraph: Mr. Messersmith said:

"When I did call on von Papen in the German Legation, he greeted me with: ' Now you are in my Legation and I can control the conversation.' In the baldest and most cynical manner he then proceeded to tell me that all of South-eastern Europe, to the borders of Turkey, was Germany's natural hinterland, and that he had been charged with the mission of facilitating German economic and political control over all this region for Germany. He blandly and directly said that getting control of Austria was to be the first step. He definitely stated that he was in Austria to undermine and weaken the Austrian Government and, from Vienna, to work towards weakening the governments in the other States to the South and South-east. He said that he intended to use his reputation as a good Catholic to gain influence with certain Austrians, such as Cardinal Innitzer, toward, that end."

Throughout the earlier period of his mission to Austria, von Papen's activity was characterised by the assiduous avoidance of any appearance of intervention. His true mission was re-affirmed with clarity several months after it began, when he was instructed by Berlin that "during the next two years nothing can be undertaken which will give Germany external political difficulties" and that every appearance of German intervention in Austrian affairs must be avoided; and, von Papen himself stated to Berger- Waldenegg, an Austrian Foreign Minister: "Yes, you have your French and English friends now, and you can have your independence a little longer." All of that was told in detail by Mr. Alderman, again quoting from Mr. Messersmith's affidavit.

Throughout this earlier-period, the Nazi movement was gaining strength in Austria without openly admitted German intervention, and Germany needed more time to consolidate her diplomatic position. These reasons for German policy were frankly expressed by the German Foreign Minister von Neurath, in conversation with the American Ambassador to France. This was read into the transcript at Page 520 by Mr. Alderman from Document L- 150, Exhibit USA 65. (Part 1, p. 233).

The defendant von Papen accordingly restricted his activities to the normal ambassadorial function of cultivating all respectable elements in Austria, and ingratiating himself in these circles. Despite his facade of strict non-intervention, von Papen remained in contact with subversive elements in Austria. Thus, in his report to Hitler, dated 17 May 1935, he gave advice about Austrian-Nazi strategy as proposed by Captain Leopold, Leader of the illegal Austrian Nazis, the object of which was to trick Dr. Schuschnigg into establishing an Austrian coalition government with the Nazi Party. This is Document 2247-PS, Exhibit USA 64. (Part 1, pp. 231, 232). It is on Page 34 of the English document book. I do not want to read this letter again, but I would like to call the attention of the Tribunal to the first line of what appears as the second paragraph in the English text, where von Papen, talking about this strategy of Captain Leopold, says, "I suggest that we take an active part in this game."

I mention also in connection with the illegal organisations in Austria, Document 812-PS, Exhibit USA 61, which the Tribunal will remember was a report from Rainer to Nickel.

Eventually the agreement of 11 July 1936 between Germany and Austria was negotiated by von Papen. This is already in evidence as TC-22, Exhibit GB 20. The public form of this agreement provides that, while Austria in her policy should regard herself as a German State, yet Germany would recognise her full sovereignty, and would not exercise direct or indirect influence on her inner political order. More interesting was the secret part of the agreement, revealed by Mr. Messersmith, which ensured the Nazis an influence in the Austrian cabinet and participation in her political life.

After the Agreement the defendant von Papen continued to pursue his policy by maintaining contact with the illegal Nazis, by trying to influence appointments to strategic cabinet positions, and by attempting to secure official recognition of Nazi front organisations. Reporting to Hitler on 1 September 1936, he summarised his programme for normalising Austrian-German relations in pursuance of the agreement of 11 July. This is Document 2246-PS, Exhibit USA 67, on Page 33 of the English document book.

The Tribunal will recall that he recommended "as a guiding principle, continued, patient, psychological manipulations with slowly intensified pressure directed at changing the regime." Then he mentions his discussion with the illegal party and says that he is aiming at "corporative representation of the movement in the Fatherland Front, but nevertheless refraining from putting National-Socialists in important positions for the time being.

There is no need to go over again the events that led up to the meeting of Schuschnigg with Hitler in February 1938, which von Papen arranged and which he attended, and to the final invasion of Austria in March 1938. It is enough if I quote from the Biography again on Page 66 of the document book. It is about two-thirds of the way down the page:

"After the events of March 1938, which caused Austria's incorporation into the German Reich, von Papen had the satisfaction of being present at the Fuehrer's side when the entry into Vienna took place, having just been admitted on 14 February 1938 into the Party in recognition of his valuable collaboration, and having received the Golden Party Badge from the Fuehrer."

And the Biography continues:

"At first von Papen retired to his estate Wallerfargen in the Saar district, but soon the Fuehrer required his services again, and on 18 April 1939 appointed von Papen German Ambassador in Ankara."

Thus the fascination of serving Hitler triumphed once again, and this time it was at a date when the seizure of Czechoslovakia could have left no shadow of doubt in Papen's mind that Hitler was determined to pursue his programme of aggression.

One further quotation from the Biography, on Page 66, the last sentence of the last paragraph but one:

"After his return to the Reich" - that was in 1944 - "von Papen was awarded the Knight's Cross of the War Merit Order with Swords."

In conclusion, I draw the Tribunal's attention again to the fulsome praises which Hitler publicly bestowed upon von Papen for his services, especially in the earlier days. I have given two instances, where Hitler said "his collaboration is infinitely valuable," and again "You possess my most complete and unlimited confidence."

Papen, the ex-Chancellor, the soldier, the respected Catholic, Papen the diplomat, Papen the man of breeding and culture - there was the man who could overcome the hostility and antipathy of those respectable elements who barred Hitler's way. Papen was - to repeat the words of Sir Hartley Shawcross in his opening speech - "One of the men whose co- operation and support made the Nazi Government of Germany possible."

That concludes my case. Sir David Maxwell Fyfe will now follow with the case of von Neurath.

SIR DAVID MAXWELL FYFE: May it please the Tribunal, the presentation against the defendant von Neurath falls into five parts, and the first of these is concerned with the following positions and honours which he held.

He was a member of the Nazi Party from 30 January 1937 until 1945, and he was awarded the Golden Party Badge on 30 January 1937.

He was General in the SS. He was personally appointed Gruppenfuehrer by Hitler in September 1937 and promoted to Obergruppenfuehrer on 21 June 1943.

He was Reich Minister of Foreign Affairs under the Chancellorship of the defendant von Papen from 2 June 1932, and under the Chancellorship of Hitler from 30 January 1933 until he was replaced by the defendant von Ribbentrop on 4 February 1938.

He was Reich Minister from 4 February 1938 until May 1945.

He was President of the Secret Cabinet Council, to which he was appointed on 4 February 1938, and he was a member of the Reich Defence Council.

He was appointed Reich Protector for Bohemia and Moravia from 18 March 1939 until he was replaced by the defendant Frick on 25 August 1943.

He was awarded the Adler-orden by Hitler at the time of his appointment as Reich Protector. The defendant Ribbentrop was the only other German to receive this decoration.

If the Tribunal please, these facts are collected in Document 2972-PS, which is Exhibit USA 19, and in that document, which is signed by the defendant and his counsel, the defendant makes comments on certain of these matters with which I should like to deal.

He says that the award of the Golden Party Badge was made on 30 January 1937 against his will and without his being asked.

I point out that this defendant not only refrained from repudiating the allegedly unwanted honour, but, after receiving it, attended meetings at which wars of aggression were planned, actively participated in the rape of Austria, and tyrannised over Bohemia and Moravia.

The second point is that his appointment as Gruppenfuehrer was also against his will and without his being asked.

On that point, the prosecution submits that the wearing of the uniform, the receipt of the further promotion to Obergruppenfuehrer, and the actions against Bohemia and Moravia must be considered when the defendant's submission is examined.

He then says that his appointment as Foreign Minister was by Reichs-president von Hindenburg.

We submit we need not do more than draw attention to the personalities of the defendant von Papen and Hitler and to the fact that President von Hindenburg died in 1934. This defendant continued as Foreign Minister until 1938.

He then says that he was an inactive Minister from the 4 February 1938 until May 1945.

At that point attention is drawn to the activities which will be mentioned below and to the terrible evidence as to Bohemia and Moravia which will be forthcoming from our friend the Soviet prosecutor.

This defendant's next point is that the Secret Cabinet Council never sat nor conferred.

I point out to the Tribunal that that was described as a select committee of the Cabinet for the deliberation of foreign affairs, and the Tribunal will find that description in Document 1774-PS, which I now put in as Exhibit GB; 246. This is an extract from a book by a well-known author, and on Page 2 of the document book the first page of that document, in about the seventh line from the bottom of the page, they will see that among the bureaus subordinated to the Fuehrer for direct counsel and assistance, number four is the Secret Cabinet Council; President: Reich Minister Baron von Neurath.

And if the Tribunal will be kind enough to turn over to Page 3, about ten lines from the top, they will see the paragraph beginning:

"A Secret Cabinet Council to advise the Fuehrer in the basic problems of foreign policy has been created by the decree of 4 February 1938," and a reference is given. "This Secret Cabinet Council is under the direction of Reich Minister von Neurath, and includes the Foreign Minister, the Air Minister, the Deputy Commander to the Fuehrer, the Propaganda Minister, the Chief of the Reich Chancellery, the Commanders-in-Chief of the Army and Navy and the Chief of the Supreme Command of the Armed Forces. The Secret Cabinet Council constitutes a select staff of collaborators of the Fuehrer which consists exclusively of members of the Government of the Reich; thus, it represents a select committee of the Reich Government for the deliberation on foreign affairs."

In order to have the formal composition of the body, that is shown in document 2031-PS, which is Exhibit GB 217. I believe it has been put in. I need not read it again.

The next point that the defendant makes as to his offices is that he was not a member of the Reich Defence Council.

If I may very shortly take that point by stages, I remind the Tribunal that the Reich Defence Council was set up soon after Hitler's accession to power on 4 April 1933, and the Tribunal will find a note of that point in Document 2261-PS, Exhibit USA 24, and they will find that on the. top of Page 12 of the document book there is a reference to the date of the establishment of the Reich Defence Council.

The Reich Defence Council is also dealt with in Document 2986-PS, Exhibit USA 409, which is the affidavit of the defendant Frick, which the Tribunal will find on Page 14. In the middle of that short affidavit, defendant Frick says:

"We were also members of the Reich Defence Council, which was supposed to plan preparations in case of war, which later on were published by the Ministerial Council for the Defence of the Reich."

Now, that the membership of this Council included the Minister for Foreign Affairs, who was then the defendant von Neurath, is shown by Document EC-177, Exhibit USA 390. If the Tribunal will turn to Page 16 of the document book, they will find that document, and at the foot of the page, the composition of the Reich Defence Council, the permanent members including the Minister for Foreign Affairs. That document is dated "Berlin, 22 May 1933," which was during this defendant's tenure of that office. That is the first stage.

The functioning of this Council, with a representative of this defendant's department, von Bulow, present, is shown by the minutes of the 12th meeting on 14 May 1936. That is Document EC-407, which I put in as Exhibit GB 247. The Tribunal will find at Page 21 that the minutes are for 14 May 1936, and the actual reference to an intervention of von Bulow is in the middle of Page 22.

Then, the next period was after the Secret Law of 4 September 1938. This defendant was, under the terms of that law, a member of the Reich Defence Council by virtue of his office as President of the Secret Cabinet Council. That is shown by the Document 2194-PS, Exhibit USA 36, which the Tribunal will find at Page 24. You will see that the actual copy which is put in evidence was enclosed in a letter addressed to the Reich Protector in Bohemia and Moravia on 6 September 1939. It is rather curious that the Reich Protector for Bohemia and Moravia is now denying his membership in the Council, when the letter enclosing the law is addressed to him.

But if the Tribunal will be good enough to turn on to Page 28, which is still that document, the last words on that page describe the tasks of that Council and say, "The task of the Reich Defence Council consists, during peacetime, in deciding all measures for the preparation of Reich defence, and the gathering together of all forces and means of the nation according to the directions of the Leaders and Reich Chancellor. The tasks of the Council in wartime will be especially determined by the Leader and Reich Chancellor."

If the Tribunal will turn to the next page, they will see that the permanent members of the Council are listed, and that the seventh one is the President of the Secret Cabinet Council, who was, again, this defendant.

I submit that this deals, for every relevant period, with this defendant's statement that he was not a member of the Reich Defence Council.

The second broad point that the prosecution makes against this defendant is that, in assuming the position of Minister of Foreign Affairs in Hitler's Cabinet, this defendant assumed charge of a foreign policy committed to breach of treaties.

We say first that the Nazi Party had repeatedly and for many years made known its intention to overthrow Germany's international commitments, even at the risk of war. We refer to Sections 1 and 2 of the Party Programme, which, as the Tribunal has heard, was published year after year. That is on Page 32 of the document book. It is Document 1708-PS, Exhibit USA 255.

I just remind the Tribunal of these points 1 and 2:

" 1. We demand the unification of all Germans in Greater Germany on the basis of the right of self-determination of peoples.

2. We demand equality of rights for the German people in respect to other nations; abrogation of the peace treaties of Versailles and St. Germain."

But probably clearer than that is the statement contained in Hitler's speech at Munich on 15 March, 1939; and the Tribunal will find one of the references to that on Page 40, at the middle of the page. It begins:

"My foreign policy had identical aims. My programme was to abolish the Treaty of Versailles. It is futile nonsense for the rest of the world to pretend today that I did not reveal this programme until 1933 or 1935 or 1937. Instead of listening to the foolish chatter of emigrees, these gentlemen would have been wiser to read what I have written thousands of times."

It is futile nonsense for foreigners to raise that point. It would be still more futile for Hitler's Foreign Minister to suggest that he was ignorant of the aggressive designs of the policy. But I remind the Tribunal that the acceptance of force, as a means of solving international problems and achieving the objective's of Hitler's foreign policy, must have been known to anyone as closely in touch with Hitler as the defendant von Neurath; and I remind the Tribunal, simply by reference to the passages from "Mein Kampf," which were quoted by my friend Major Elwyn Jones, especially those toward the end of the book, Pages 552, 553, and 554.

So the prosecution say that, by the acceptance of this foreign policy, the defendant von Neurath assisted and promoted the accession to power of the Nazi Party.

The third broad point is that in his capacity as Minister of Foreign Affairs this defendant directed the international aspects of the first phase of the Nazi conspiracy, the consolidation of control in preparation for war.

As I have already indicated, from his close connection with Hitler this defendant must have known the cardinal points of Hitler's policy leading up to the outbreak of the World War, as outlined in retrospect by Hitler in his speech to his military leaders on 23 November, 1939.

This policy had two facets: internally, the establishment of rigid control externally, the programme to release Germany from its international ties.

The external programme had four points:

1. Secession from the Disarmament Conference;
2. The order to re-arm Germany;
3. The introduction of compulsory military services; and
4. The remilitarisation of the Rhineland.

If the Tribunal will look at Page 35 - in the document book, at the end of the first paragraph they will find these points very briefly set out, and perhaps I might just read that passage. It is Document 789-PS, Exhibit USA 23 - about ten lines before the break

"I had to reorganise everything, first the masses of the people and then the Armed Forces. First, reorganisation of the interior, abolishment of appearance of decay and defeatist ideas, education to heroism. While reorganising the interior I undertook the second task, to release Germany from its international ties. Two particular characteristics are to be pointed out: secession from the League of Nations and denunciation of the Disarmament Conference. It was a hard decision. The number of prophets who predicted that it would lead to the occupation of the Rhineland was large; the number of believers was very small. I was supported by the nation, which stood firmly behind me, when I carried out my intentions. After that, the order for rearmament. Here again there were numerous prophets who predicted misfortunes, and only a few believers. In 1935 the introduction of compulsory armed service. After that, militarisation of the Rhineland-again a process believed to be impossible at that time. The number of people who placed trust in me was very small. Then the beginning of the fortification of the whole country, especially in the West."

Now, these are summarised in four points. The defendant von Neurath participated directly and personally in accomplishing each of these four aspects of Hitler's foreign policy, at the same time officially proclaiming that these measures did not constitute steps toward aggression.

The first is a matter of history. When Germany left the Disarmament Conference this defendant sent telegrams dated 14 October, 1933, to the President of the conference - and that will be found in 'Dokumente der Deutschen Politik,' on page 94 of the first volume for that year. Similarly this defendant made the announcement of Germany's withdrawal from the League of Nations on 21 October, 1933. That again will be found in the official documents. (Part 1, pp. 183-203) and I remind the Tribunal of the complementary documents of military preparation, which of course were read and which are Documents C-140, Exhibit USA 51, 25 October 1933, and C- 153, Exhibit USA 43, 12 May, 1934. These have already been read, and I merely collect them for the memory and assistance of the Tribunal.

The second point the rearmament of Germany: When this defendant was Foreign Minister, on 10 March, 1935, the German Government officially announced the establishment of the German Air Force. That is Document TC-44 Exhibit GB 11, already referred to. On 21 May, 1935, Hitler announced a purported unilateral repudiation of the Naval, Military and Air Clauses of the Treaty of Versailles which, of course, involved a similar purported unilateral repudiation of the same clauses of the Treaty for the Restoration of Friendly Relations with the United States, and that will be found in Document 2288-PS, Exhibit USA 38, which again has already been read. On the same day the Reich Cabinet, of which this defendant was a member, enacted the secret "Reich Defence Law " creating the office of Plenipotentiary General for War Economy, afterwards described by the Wehrmacht armament expert as "the cornerstone of German rearmament." The reference to the law is Document 2261-PS, Exhibit USA 24, a letter of von Blomberg dated 24 June 1935, enclosing this law, which is already before the Tribunal; and the reference to the comment on the importance of the law is Document 2353- PS, Exhibit USA 35. Some of that has already been read, but if the Tribunal will be good enough to turn to Page 52 where that appears, they will find an extract, and I might just give the Tribunal the last sentence:

"The last orders were decreed in the Reich Defence Law of 21 May, 1935, supposed to be published only in case of war, and already declared valid for carrying out war preparations. As this law fixed the duties of the Armed Forces and the other Reich authorities in case of war, it was also the fundamental ruling for the development and activity of the war economy organisation."

The third point is the introduction of compulsory military service. On 16 March, 1935, this defendant signed the law for the organisation of the armed forces, which provided for universal military service and anticipated a vastly expanded German army. This was described by the defendant Keitel as the real start of the large-scale rearmament programme which followed. I will give the official reference in the Reichsgesetzblatt, year 1935, volume 1, Part 1, p. 369; (Part 1, pp. 187, 205).

The fourth point was the re-militarisation of the Rhineland. The Rhineland was reoccupied on 7 March, 1936. I remind the Tribunal of the two complementary documents, 2289-PS, Exhibit USA 56, the announcement of this action by Hitler; and C-139, Exhibit USA 53, which is the "Operation Schulung," giving the military action which was to be taken if necessary. These were the acts for which the defendant shared responsibility because of his position and because of the steps which he took; but a little later he summed up his views on the actions detailed above in a speech before Germans abroad made on 29 August, 1937, of which I ask the Tribunal to take judicial notice, as it appears in "Das Archiv," 1937, at Page 650. I quote only a short portion of it that appears on Page 72 of the document book.

"The unity of the racial and national will, created through Nazism with unprecedented elan, has made possible a foreign policy through which the bonds of the Versailles Treaty were slashed, the freedom to arm regained and the sovereignty of the whole nation re- established. We have again become master in our own home, and we have produced the means of power to remain so for all times. The world should notice from Hitler's deeds and words that his aims are not aggressive war."

The world, of course, had not the advantage of seeing these various complementary documents of military preparation which I have had the opportunity of putting before the Tribunal.

The next section - and the next point against this defendant - is that both as Minister of Foreign Affairs and as one of the inner circle of the Fuehrer's advisers on foreign political matters, this defendant participated in the political planning and preparation for acts of aggression against Austria, Czechoslovakia and other nations.

If I might first put the defendant's policy in a sentence, I would say that it can be summarised as breaking one treaty only at a time. He himself put it - if I may say so - slightly more pompously, but to the same effect, in a speech before the Academy of German Law on 30 October, 1937, which appears in " Das Archiv," October 1937, Page 921, and which the Tribunal will find in the document book on Page 73. The underlining is mine:

> "In recognition of these elementary facts the Reich Cabinet has always interceded in favour of treating every concrete international problem within the scope of methods especially suited to it; not to complicate it unnecessarily by involvement with other problems; and, as long as problems between only two powers are concerned, to choose the direct way for an immediate understanding between these two powers. We are in a position to state that this method has fully proved itself good not only in the German interest, but also in the general interest."

The only country whose interests are not mentioned are the other parties to the various treaties that were dealt with in that way; and the working out of that policy can readily be shown by looking at the tabulated form of the actions of this defendant when he was Foreign Minister, or during the term of his immediate successor when the defendant still was purported to have influence.

In 1935 the action was directed against the Western Powers. That action was the rearmament of Germany. When that was going on another country had to be reassured. At that time it was Austria, with the support of Italy - which Austria still had up to 1935. And so you get the fraudulent assurance, the essence of the technique, in that case given by Hitler, on 21 May, 1935. And that is clearly shown to be false, by the documents which Mr. Alderman put in. Then, in 1936, you have still the action necessary against the Western Powers, in the occupation of the Rhineland. You still have a fraudulent assurance to Austria in the treaty of 11 July of that year and that is shown to be fraudulent by the letters from the defendant von Papen, Exhibits USA 64 and 67, one of which my friend Major Barrington has just referred to.

Then in 1937 and 1938 you move on a step, and the action is directed against Austria. We know what that action was. It was absorption, planned, at any rate finally, at the meeting on 5 November, 1937 ; and action taken on 11 March 1938.

Reassurance had to be given to the Western Powers, so you have the assurance to Belgium on 13 October, 1937, which was dealt with by my friend Mr. Roberts. (See Part 2, pp. 198- 211).

We move forward a year and the object of the aggressive action becomes Czechoslovakia. Or I should say we move forward six months to a year. There you have the Sudetenland obtained in September; the absorption of the whole of Bohemia and Moravia on 15 March 1939.

Then it was necessary to reassure Poland; so an assurance to Poland is given by Hitler on 20 February, 1938, and repeated up to 26 September, 1938. The falsity of that assurance was shown over and over again in Colonel Griffith-Jones's presentation on Poland. (Part 2, pp. 125-176).

Then finally, when they want the action as directed against Poland in the next year for its conquest, assurance must be given to Russia, and so a non aggression pact is entered into on 23 August 1939, as shown by Mr. Alderman, at Pages 1160 to 1216 (see Part 2, pp. 229- 259).

With regard to that tabular presentation, one might quote the Latin tag, res ipsa loquitur. But quite a frank statement from this defendant, with regard to the earlier part of that, can be found in the account of his conversation with the United States Ambassador, Mr. Bullitt, on 18 May, 1936, which is on Page 74 of the document book, Document L-150, Exhibit USA 65, and if I might read the first paragraph after the introduction, which says that they called on this defendant, Mr. Bullitt remarks:

"Von Neurath said that it was the policy of the German Government to do nothing active in foreign affairs until 'the Rhineland had been digested.' He explained that he meant that, until the German fortifications had been constructed on the French and Belgian frontiers, the German Government would do everything possible to prevent rather than encourage an outbreak by the Nazis in Austria, and would pursue a quiet line with regard to Czechoslovakia. 'As soon as our fortifications are constructed and the countries of Central Europe realise that France cannot enter German territory at will, all those countries will begin to feel very differently about their foreign policies, and a new constellation will develop,' he said."

I remind the Tribunal, without citing it, of the conversation referred to by my friend, Major Barrington, a short time ago, between the defendant von Papen, as Ambassador, and Mr. Messersmith, which is very much to the same effect.

Then I come to the actual aggression against Austria, and I remind the Tribunal that this defendant was Foreign Minister.

First: During the early Nazi plottings against Austria in 1934.

The Tribunal will find these in the transcript (Part 1, pp. 214-220), and I remind them generally that it was the murder of Chancellor Dollfuss and the ancillary acts which were afterwards so strongly approved.

Second: When the false assurance was given to Austria on 21 May, 1935, and the fraudulent treaty made on 11 July, 1936.

References to these are Document TC-26, which is Exhibit GB 19, and Document TC-22, which is Exhibit GB 20 (see Part 1, p. 243).

Third: When the defendant von Papen was carrying on his subterranean intrigues in the period from 1935 to 1937.

I again give the references so that the Tribunal will have it in mind: Document 2247-PS, Exhibit USA 64 - letter dated 17 May 1935 - and Exhibit USA 67, Document 2246-PS - 1 September 1936. (Part 1, pp. 231, 232).

This defendant von Neurath was present when Hitler declared, at the Hoszbach interview on 5 November, 1937, that the German question could only be solved by force, and that his plans were to conquer Austria and Czechoslovakia. That is Document 386-PS, Exhibit USA 25, which the Tribunal will find at Page 82. If you will look at the sixth line of Page 82, after the heading, you will see that one of the persons in attendance at this highly confidential meeting was the Reich Minister for

Foreign Affairs, Freiherr von Neurath.

Without reading a document which the Tribunal have had referred to them more than once, may I remind the Tribunal that it is on Page 86 that the passage about the conquest of Austria occurs, and the next sentence is:

> "For the improvement of our military political position, it must be our first aim in every case of entanglement by war to conquer Czechoslovakia and Austria simultaneously, in order to remove any threat from the flanks in case of a possible advance Westwards."

That is developed on the succeeding page. The important point is that this defendant was present at that meeting; and it is impossible for him after that meeting to say that he was not acting except with his eyes completely open, and with complete comprehension as to what was intended.

Then the next point. During the actual Anschluss he received a note from the British Ambassador dated 11 March, 1938. That is Document 3045-PS, Exhibit USA 127. He sent the reply contained in Document 3287-PS, Exhibit USA 128. If I might very briefly remind the Tribunal of the reply, I think all that is necessary - and of course the Tribunal have had this document referred to them before - is the at top of Page 93. I wish to call attention to two obvious untruths.

The defendant von Neurath states in the sixth line: "It is untrue that the Reich used forceful pressure to bring about this development, especially the assertion, which was spread later by the former Chancellor Schuschnigg, that the German Government had presented the Federal President with a conditional ultimatum. It is a pure invention."

According to the ultimatum, he had to appoint a proposed candidate as Chancellor to form a Cabinet conforming to the proposals of the German Government. Otherwise the invasion of Austria by German troops was held in prospect.

> "The truth of the matter is that the question of sending military or police forces from the Reich was only brought up when the newly formed Austrian Cabinet addressed a telegram, already published by the Press, to the German Government, urgently asking for the dispatch of German troops as soon as possible, in order to restore peace and order and to avoid bloodshed. Faced with the immediate threat of the danger of a bloody civil war in Austria, the German Government then decided to comply with the appeal addressed to it."

Well, as I said, My Lord, these are the two most obvious untruths, and all one can say is that it must have, at any rate, given this defendant a certain macabre sort of humour to write that, when the truth was as the Tribunal know it from the report of Gauleiter Rainer to Burckel, which has been put in before the Tribunal as Document 812-PS, Exhibit USA 6 1, and when they have heard, as they have done at length, the transcripts of the defendant Goering's telephone conversation with Austria on that day, which is Document 2949-PS, Exhibit USA 76, and the entries of the defendant's Jodl's diary for 11, 13 and 14 February, which is Document 1780-PS, Exhibit USA 72.

In this abundance of proof of the untruthfulness of these statements, the Tribunal may probably think that the most clear and obvious correction is in the transcription of the defendant Goering's telephone conversations, which are so amply corroborated by the other documents.

The prosecution submits that it is inconceivable that this defendant who, according to the defendant Jodl's diary - may I ask the Tribunal just to look at Page 116 of the document book, the entry in the defendant Jodl's diary for 10 March so that they have this point clear? It is the third paragraph, and it says

> "At 1300 hours General Keitel informs Chief of Operational Staff and Admiral Canaris. Ribbentrop is being detained in London. Neurath takes over the Foreign Office."

I submit that it is inconceivable, when this defendant had taken over the of Foreign Office, was dealing with the matter and, as I shall show the Tribunal in a moment, co- operating with the defendant Goering to suit the susceptibilities of the Czechs, that he should have been so ignorant of the truth of events, and what really was happening, as to write that letter in honour and good faith.

His position can be shown equally clearly by the account which is given of him in the affidavit of Mr. Messersmith, Document 2385-PS, Exhibit USA 68. If the Tribunal will look at Page 107 of the document book, I remind them of that entry, which exactly describes the action and style of activity of this defendant at this crisis. Two-thirds of the way down the page the paragraph begins:

> "I should emphasise here in this statement that the men who made these promises were not only the dyed-in-the-wool Nazis, but more conservative Germans who already had begun willingly to lend themselves to the Nazi programme.
>
> In an official dispatch to the Department of State from Vienna, dated October 10, 1935, I wrote as follows :
>
> 'Europe will not get away from the myth that Neurath, Papen and Mackensen are not dangerous people, and that they are diplomats of the old school. They are in fact servile instruments of the regime, and, just because the outside world looks upon them as harmless, they are able to work more effectively. They are able to sow discord just because they propagate the myth that they are not in sympathy with the regime.'"

THE PRESIDENT: The Tribunal will adjourn now.

(The Tribunal adjourned until 24th January 1946 at 1000 hours)

Forty-second day: Thursday, 24th January, 1946

CAPTAIN PRICEMAN: May it please your Honour, the defendant Streicher and the defendant Kaltenbrunner are absent this morning on account of illness.

SIR DAVID MAXWELL FYFE: May it please the Tribunal, before the Tribunal adjourned, I was dealing with the share of the defendant Neurath in the aggression against Austria. Before I proceed with the next stage, I should like the Tribunal, if it will be so kind, to look at the original exhibit from which I will read, Document 3287-PS, and I would like to state it is Exhibit GB 128, which is the letter from this defendant to Sir Neville Henderson, who was then the British Ambassador. The only point on which I would be grateful, is if the Tribunal would note Page 92 of the document book. When I say original, I mean a certified copy certified by the British Foreign Office, but the Tribunal will see that the heading is from the President of the Secret Cabinet Council. That is the point that the Tribunal will remember. The question was raised as to the existence or activity of that body, and the letterhead is from the defendant in that capacity.

The next stage in the aggression is that at the time of the occupation of Austria, this defendant gave the assurance to M. Mastny, the Ambassador of Czechoslovakia to Berlin, regarding the continued independence of Czechoslovakia. On Page 123 of Document TC 27, which I have already put in as Exhibit GB 21, is a letter to Lord Halifax, who was then Foreign Secretary; and if I may read the second paragraph just to remind the Tribunal of the circumstances in which it was written M. Masaryk says:

> "I have in consequence been instructed by my Government to bring to the official knowledge of His Majesty's Government the following facts: Yesterday evening (11 March) Field-Marshal Goering made two separate, statements to M. Mastny, the Czechoslovak Minister in Berlin, assuring him that the developments in Austria will in no way have any detrimental influence on the relations between the German Reich and Czechoslovakia, and emphasising the continued earnest endeavour on the part of Germany to improve those mutual relations."

And then there are the particulars of the way in which it was put to defendant Goering, which have been brought to the Tribunal's attention, and I shall not repeat them. The 6th paragraph begins: "M. Mastny was in a position to give him definite and binding assurances on this subject" - that is, to the defendant Goering, on the Czech mobilisation - and then it continues:

> "and today spoke with Baron von Neurath, who, among other things, assured him on behalf of Herr Hitler that Germany still considers herself bound by the German- Czechoslovak Arbitration Convention, concluded at Locarno in October 1925."

In view of the fact that the defendant von Neurath had been present at the meeting on 5 November, four months previously, he had heard Hitler's views on Czechoslovakia, yet it was only six months before the Munich Agreement was disregarded forthwith. That paragraph is, in my opinion, an excellent example of the technique of which this defendant was the first professor.

I now come to the aggression against Czechoslovakia. On 28th May 1938, Hitler held a conference of important leaders, including Beck, von Brauchitsch, Raeder, Keitel, Goering and Ribbentrop, at which Hitler affirmed that preparations should be made for military action against Czechoslovakia by October, and it is believed though not - I say frankly - confirmed that the defendant von Neurath attended. The reference of that meeting is in the transcript. (Part 2, p. 6).

THE PRESIDENT: Sir David, is there any evidence?

SIR DAVID MAXWELL FYFE: No. Your Lordship will remember the documents, a long series of them, and it does not state who was present? therefore, I express that and put it with reserve.

On 4 September 1938, the Government of which von Neurath was a member, enacted a new Secret Reich Defence Law which denied various official responsibilities, in clear anticipation of war. This law provided, as did the previous Secret Reich Defence Law, for a Reich Defence Council as a supreme policy board for war preparations. If the Tribunal will remember, I have already referred them to Document 2194- PS, Exhibit USA 36, showing these facts. Then there came the Munich Agreement of 30 September 1938, but in spite of that, on 15 March 1939, German troops marched into Czechoslovakia? and the Proclamation to the German people and the Order to the Wehrmacht is Document TC 50, Exhibit GB 7, which the Tribunal will find at Page 124, which has already been referred to, and I shall not read it again.

On 16 March 1939, the German Government, of which von Neurath was still a member, promulgated the "Decree of the Fuehrer and Reich Chancellor on the Establishment of the Protectorate 'Bohemia and Moravia'." That date is 16 March. It is on Page 126 of the document book, Document TC 51, Exhibit GB 8.

If I may leave that for the moment, I will come back to it in dealing with the setting up of the Protectorate. In a moment I will read Article 5; but taking the events in the order of time, in the following week the defendant von Ribbentrop signed a Treaty with Slovakia, which is on Page 129, and the Tribunal may remember Article 2 of that Treaty, which is:

"For the purpose of making effective the protection undertaken by the German Reich, the German Armed Forces shall have the right at all times to construct military installations and to keep them garrisoned in the strength they deem necessary, in an area delimited on its Western side by the frontiers of the State of Slovakia, and on its Eastern side by a line formed by the Eastern rims of the Lower Carpathians, the White Carpathians, and the Javornik Mountains.

The Government of Slovakia will take the necessary steps to ensure that the land required for these installations is handed over to the German Armed Forces. Furthermore, the Government of Slovakia will agree to grant exemption from custom duties for imports from the Reich for the maintenance of the German troops and the supply of military installations."

The Tribunal will appreciate that the ultimate objective of Hitler's policies, disclosed at the meeting at which this defendant was present on 5 November, 1937, was the resumption of the "Drang nach Osten." It was obvious from the terms of this Treaty, as it had been explicit in Hitler's statement.

Then we come to the pith of this criminality. By accepting and occupying the position of Reich Protector of Bohemia and Moravia, the defendant von Neurath personally adhered to the aggression against Czechoslovakia and the world. Further, he actively participated in the conspiracy of world aggression, and he assumed a position of leadership in the execution of policies involving violation of the laws of war, and the commission of Crimes Against Humanity.

The Tribunal will appreciate that I am not going to trespass on the ground covered by my colleagues, and go into the crimes. I want to show quite clearly to the Tribunal the basis for these crimes, which was laid by the legal position which this defendant assumed.

The first point. The defendant von Neurath assumed the position of Protector under a sweeping grant of powers. The act creating the Protectorate provided, - if the Tribunal would be good enough to turn back to Page 126 in the document book and look at Article V of the Act, it reads as follows:

> "1. As trustee of Reich interests, the Leader and Chancellor of the Reich shall nominate a 'Reich Protector in Bohemia and Moravia.' His seat of office will be Prague.
> 2. The Reich Protector, as representative of the Leader and Chancellor of the Reich, and as Commissioner of the Reich Government, is charged with the duty of seeing to the observance of the political principles laid down by the Leader and Chancellor of the Reich.
> 3. The members of the Government of the Protectorate shall be confirmed by the Reich Protector. The confirmation may be withdrawn.
> 4. The Reich Protector is entitled to inform himself of all measures taken by the Government of the Protectorate and to give advice. He can object to measures calculated to harm the Reich and, in case of danger, issue ordinances required for the common interest.
> 5. The promulgation of laws, ordinances and other legal announcements, and the execution of administrative measures and legal judgments, shall be annulled if the Reich Protector enters an objection."

At the very outset of the Protectorate, the defendant von Neurath's supreme authority - was implemented by a series of basic decrees, of which I ask the Tribunal to take judicial notice. They established the alleged legal foundation for the policy and programme which resulted, all aimed towards the systematic destruction of the national integrity of the Czechs.

> 1. By granting the "racial Germans" in Czechoslovakia citizenship of the first class on 16 March 1939. I have already given the official reference to the Decree of the Fuehrer and Reich Chancellor concerning the Protectorate, to which decree I have just referred; and then,
> 2. An Act concerning the representation, in the Reichstag of Greater Germany, of German nationals resident in the Protectorate: 13 April 1939.
> 3. An Order concerning the acquisition of German citizenship by former Czechoslovakian citizens of German origin, 20 April 1939.

Then there was a series of decrees that granted "racial Germans" in Czechoslovakia a preferred status at law and in the courts.

> 1. An Order concerning the Administration of Justice in Criminal Proceedings, Protectorate of Bohemia and Moravia, 14 April 1939.
> 2. An order concerning the Administration of Justice in Civil Proceedings, 14 April 1939.

3. An Order concerning the Administration of Justice under Military Law, 8 May 1939.

Then the orders also granted to the Protector broad powers to change by decree the autonomous law of the Protectorate. That is contained in the Ordinance on Legislation in the Protectorate, 7 June 1939.

Finally, the Protector was authorised to act with the Reich Leader SS and the Chief of the German Police "to take if necessary, (police) measures which go beyond the limits usually valid for police measures."

May the Tribunal take judicial notice of this order, which we inserted in the document book at Page 131. It rather staggers the imagination to think what can be police measures even beyond the limits usually valid for police measures," when one has seen police measures in Germany between 1933 and 1939; but if such increase was possible, and presumably it was believed to be possible, then an increase was given by the defendant von Neurath, and used by him for coercion of the Czechs.

The declared basic policy of the Protectorate was concentrated upon the central objective of destroying the identity of the Czechs as a nation, and absorbing their territory into the Reich, and, if the Tribunal will be good enough to turn to Page 132, they will find evidence of this in Document 862-PS, Exhibit USA 313, which I think has been read to the Tribunal; still, the Tribunal might bear with me so that I might indicate the nature of that document to them.

This memorandum is signed by Lt. General of Infantry Friderici. It is headed "The Deputy General of the Armed Forces with the Reich Protector in Bohemia and Moravia." It is marked "Top Secret," dated 15 October 1940. That is practically a year before this defendant von Neurath went on leave, as he puts it, on 27 September 1941, and, it is called the "Basic Political Principles in the Protectorate." There are four copies. It also had gone to the defendant Keitel and the defendant Jodl, and it begins On 9 October of this year - " that is 1940:

"On 9 October of this year the Office of the Reich Protector held an official conference in which State Secretary Lt. General K. H. Frank" - that is not the defendant Frank, it is the other K. H. Frank - "spoke about the following:

Since the creation of the Protectorate of Bohemia and Moravia, party agencies, industrial circles, as well as agencies of the central authorities of Berlin have had difficulty in the solution of the Czech problem.

After ample deliberation, the Reich Protector expressed his view about the various plans in a memorandum. In this, three ways of solution were indicated:

(a) German infiltration of Moravia and reduction of the Czech nationality to be residual Bohemia.

This solution is considered as unsatisfactory, because the Czech problem even in a diminished form, will continue to exist.

(b) Many arguments can be brought up against the most radical solution namely, the deportation of all Czechs. Therefore the memorandum comes to the conclusion that it cannot be carried within a reasonable space of time.

(c) Assimilation of the Czechs, i.e. absorption of about half of the Czech nationality by the Germans, insofar as it is of importance by being valuable from a radical or other standpoint. This will be effected amongst other things, by increasing the Arbeitseinsatz of the Czechs in the Reich territory, with the exception of the Sudeten German border district, in other words by dispersing the closed Czech nationality. The other half of the Czech nationality must be deprived of its power, eliminated and shipped out of the country by every means. This applies particularly to the racially Mongoloid part, and to the major part of the intellectual class. The latter can scarcely be converted ideologically, and would make themselves a burden by constantly claiming leadership over the other Czech classes, thus interfering with a rapid assimilation.

Elements which counteract the planned Germanization are to be handled roughly and should be eliminated.

The above development naturally presupposes an increased influx of Germans from the Reich territory into the Protectorate.

After a discussion, the Fuehrer has chosen Solution C (assimilation) as a directive for the solution of the Czech problem, and decided that, while keeping up the autonomy of the Protectorate on the surface, the Germanization will have to be carried out in a centralized manner by the Office of the Reich Protector, for years to come.

From the above no particular conclusions are drawn by the Armed Forces. This is the direction which has always been sponsored from here. In this connection, I refer to my memorandum which was sent to the Chief of the Supreme Command of the Armed Forces, dated 12 July 1939, entitled 'The Czech Problem'; and that is signed, as I said, by the Deputy Lt.-General of the Armed Forces.

That view of the Reich Protector was accepted, and formed a basis of his policy. The result was a programme of consolidating German control over Bohemia and Moravia by the systematic oppression of the Czechs through the abolition of civil liberties, and the systematic undermining of the native political, economic, and cultural structure by a regime of terror, which will be dealt with by my Soviet Union colleagues. They will show clearly, I submit, that the only protection given by this defendant was protection to the perpetrators of innumerable crimes.

I have already drawn attention of the Tribunal to the many honours and rewards which this defendant received as his reward, and it might well be said that Hitler showered more honours on von Neurath than on some of the leading Nazis who had been with the party since the very beginning. His appointment as President of the newly created Secret Cabinet Council in 1938 was in itself a new and singular distinction. On September 22 1940, Hitler awarded him the War Merit Cross 1st Class as Reich Protector for Bohemia and Moravia. That is in the Deutsches Nachrichten-Buero, 22 September 1940.

He was also awarded the Golden Badge of the Party, and was promoted, by Hitler personally, from the rank of Gruppenfuehrer to Obergruppenfuehrer in the SS, on June 21st, 1943. I would also inform the Tribunal that he and Ribbentrop were the only two Germans to be awarded the Adlerorden, a distinction normally reserved for foreigners. His seventieth birthday, February 2 1943, was made an occasion for most of the German newspapers to praise his many years of service to the Nazi regime. This service, as submitted by the prosecution, may be summed up in two ways:

(1) He was an internal Fifth Columnist amongst Conservative political circles in Germany. They had been anti-Nazi but were converted in part by seeing one of themselves, in the person of this defendant, wholeheartedly with the Nazis.

(2) His previous reputation as a diplomat made public opinion abroad slow to believe that he would be a member of a cabinet which did not stand by its words and assurances. It was most important for Hitler that his own readiness to break every treaty or commitment should be

concealed as long as possible, and for this purpose he found in the defendant von Neurath his handiest tool.

That concludes the presentation against the defendant von Neurath.

THE PRESIDENT: In view of the motion which was made yesterday by Counsel for the defendant Hess, the Tribunal will postpone the presentation of the individual case against Hess, and will proceed with the presentation of the case by counsel for France.

M. DUBOST (Counsel for France): When exposing the charges which now weigh upon the defendants, my British and American colleagues put forward the evidence that these man conceived and executed a plan and plot for the domination of Europe. They have shown you the Crimes against Peace of which these men became guilty by launching unjust wars. They have shown you that, as leaders of Nazi Germany, they had all premeditated unjust wars, and had participated in the Conspiracy.

Then my friends and colleagues of the French Delegation, M. Herzog, M. Faure and M. Gerthoffer submitted documents establishing that the defendants who, in various positions all counted among the leaders of Nazi Germany, are responsible for the repeated violations of the laws and customs of war committed by the representatives of the Reich in the course of military operations. However, it still remains for us to show the atrocities of which men, women and children of the occupied countries of the West were victims.

We intend at this point to prove that the defendants, in their capacity as leaders of Hitlerite Germany, systematically pursued a policy of extermination the cruelty of which increased from day to day until the final defeat of Germany that the defendants conceived and prescribed these atrocities as part and parcel of a system which was to enable them to achieve a political aim. This political aim is the net which closely binds all the facts we intend to present to you. The crimes perpetrated against people and property, as presented so far by my colleagues of the French Prosecution, were in close connection with the war. Therefore they clearly featured as war crimes stricte sensu. Those which I shall present to you surpass them both in meaning and scope. They form part of the plans of a policy of domination, of expansion beyond war itself. It is Hitler himself who gave the best definition of this policy in one of his speeches in Munich on 16 May 1927. He was deceiving his listeners about the danger that France, an agricultural country of only 40 million inhabitants, might represent for Germany, which was already a highly-industrialised country with a population of nearly 70 millions.

That day Hitler said "There is only one way for Germany to escape encirclement, and it is by the destruction of the Country, which, by the natural order of things, will always be her mortal enemy: France. When a nation is aware that its whole existence is endangered by an enemy it must aim at one thing only: the annihilation of that enemy."

During the first months that followed their victory, the Germans seemed to have abandoned their plan of annihilation, but this was only a tactical pretence. They hoped to draw into their war against England and the Union of the Soviet Socialist Republics the Western nations they had enslaved. By doses of treachery and violence, they attempted to make these Western nations go the way of collaboration. The latter resisted, and the defendants then abandoned their tactics and came back to their big game, the annihilation of conquered peoples, in order to secure in Europe the space necessary for the 250 million Germans whom they hoped to settle there in generations to come.

This destruction, this annihilation - I repeat the very words used by Hitler in his speech - was undertaken under various pretences: the elimination of inferior, or negroid races, the extermination of Bolshevism, and the destruction of Judeo-Masonic influences hostile to the founding of the pseudo "New European Order."

In fact, this extermination, this elimination, tended to the assassination of the elite and vital forces opposed to Nazism; it also tended to the reduction of the means of livelihood of the enslaved nations.

All of this was done, as I shall prove to you, in execution of a deliberate plan, the existence of which is confirmed among other things by the repetition and the constancy of the same facts in all the occupied countries.

Faced with this repetition and this constancy, it is no longer possible to claim that only the one who committed the crime was guilty. This repetition and this constancy prove that the same criminal will united all the members of the German Government, all the leaders of the German Reich.

It is from this common will that the official policy of terrorism and extermination which directed the strokes of the executioners, was born and it is for having participated in the creation of this common will that each of the defendants here present has been placed in the ranks of major war criminals.

I shall come back to this point when, having finished my presentation of the facts, I shall have to qualify the crime, in accordance with the legal tradition of my country.

Allow me to give you now some indications as to how, with your kind permission, I intend to make my presentation.

The facts I am to prove here are the results of many testimonies. We could have called innumerable witnesses to this stand. Their statements have been collected by the French Office for Research on War Crimes. It seemed to us that it would simplify and shorten the procedure if we were to give you extracts only from the testimony that we have received in writing.

With your permission, therefore, I shall limit myself to reading excerpts from the written testimonies collected in France by official organisations qualified to investigate War Crimes. However, if in the course of this presentation it appears necessary to call certain witnesses, we shall proceed to do so, but with constant care not to slow down the sessions in any way and to bring them speedily to the only possible conclusion; the one our people expect.

The whole question of atrocities is ruled by the German terrorist policy. Under this aspect it is not without precedent in the Germanic practice of war. We all remember the execution of hostages at Dinand during the war of 1914, the execution of hostages in the citadel of Laon and of hostages at Senlis. But Nazism perfected this terrorist policy; for Nazism, terror is a means of subjugating. We all remember the propaganda picture about the war in Poland, shown in Oslo on the eve of the invasion of Norway.

For Nazism, terror is a means of subjugating all enslaved people, in order to submit them to the aims of its policy.

The first signs of this terrorist policy during the occupation are fresh in the memory of all Frenchmen. Only a few months after the signing of the armistice they saw red posters edged with black appear on the walls of Paris' as well as in the smallest villages of France, proclaiming the execution of hostages. We know mothers who were first informed of the execution of their sons in this way. These executions were carried out by the occupant after anti- German incidents. These incidents were the answer of the French people to the official policy of collaboration. Resistance to this policy stiffened, became organised, and with it the repressive measures increased in intensity until 1944, the climax of German terrorism in France and in the countries of the West. At that time, the Army and the SS Police no longer spoke of the execution of hostages; they organised real reprisal expeditions during which whole villages were set on fire, and thousands of civilians killed, arrested and deported; but before reaching this stage, the Germans attempted to justify their criminal actions in the eyes of a susceptible public opinion. They published, as we shall prove, a real code of hostages, and merely pretended to comply with law every time they proceeded to carry out reprisal executions.

The taking of hostages, as you know, is prohibited by Article 50 of the Hague Convention. I shall read this text to you. It is to be found in the Fourth Convention: Article 50.

> "No collective penalty, pecuniary or other, can be decreed against populations for individual acts for which they cannot be held jointly and severally responsible."

And yet, supreme perfidy! The German General Staff, the German Government, will endeavour to turn this regulation into a dead letter, and to set up as law the systematic violation of the Hague Convention.

I shall describe to you how the General Staff formed its pseudo-law on hostages, a pseudo-law, which in France found its final expression in the hostage code of Stulpnagel. I shall show you, in passing, which of these defendants are the most guilty of this crime.

On 15 February 1940, in a secret report, addressed to the defendant Goering, the OKW justifies the taking of hostages, as proved by the excerpt from Document 1585-PS, which I propose to read to you. This document is dated Berlin, 15 February 1940. It bears the heading: "Supreme Command of the Armed Forces. Secret." To the Reich Minister for Aviation; Supreme Command of the Air Force.

> Subject: Arrest of Hostages.
>
> "According to the opinion of the OKW, the arrest of hostages is justified in all cases in which the security of the troops and the carrying out of their orders demands it. In most cases it will be necessary to have recourse to it in case of resistance or an uncertain attitude on the part of the population of an occupied territory, should the troops be engaged in fighting or that a situation exists which renders other means of restoring security insufficient."
>
> Further, paragraph 4: In selecting hostages, it must be borne in mind that their arrest should take place only if the refractory sections of the population are anxious that they should not be executed. The hostages shall therefore be chosen from sections of the population from which a hostile attitude may be expected. The arrest of hostages shall be carried out among persons whose fate, we may suppose, will influence the insurgents."

This document is filed by the French Delegation as Exhibit RF 267.

To my knowledge, Goering never opposed any objection to this thesis. Here is one more paragraph from an order, Document 508-F, from the Commander-in-Chief of the Ground Forces in France, administrative section, signed "Stroccius," 12 September 1940, three months after the beginning of the occupation. The hostages are defined therein as follows. I quote from Page two,:

> "Hostages are inhabitants of a country who guarantee with their lives the faultless attitude of the population. The responsibility for their fate is thus placed in the hands of their compatriots. Therefore, the population must be publicly threatened that the hostages will be held responsible for the unfriendly acts of individuals. Only French citizens may be taken as hostages. The hostages can be held responsible only for actions committed after their

arrest and after the public proclamation."

This order cancels 5 directives prior to 12 September 1940. This question was the subject of numerous texts, and two General Staff orders, dated, as indicated at the head of Document 510F, 2 November and 13 February, Page two:

"If acts of violence are committed by the inhabitants of the country against members of the occupation forces, if offices and installations of the Armed Forces are damaged or destroyed, or if any other attacks are directed against the security of German units and service establishments, and if, under the circumstances, the population of the place of the crime or the immediate neighbourhood can be considered as co-responsible for those acts of sabotage, measures of prevention and expiation may be ordered, by which the civil population is to be deterred in future from committing, encouraging or tolerating acts of that kind. The population is to be treated as co-responsible for individual acts of sabotage if, by its attitude, in general, towards the German Armed Forces it has favoured hostile or unfriendly acts of individuals; if, by its passive resistance against the investigation of previous acts of sabotage, it has encouraged hostile elements to similar acts, or otherwise created a favourable atmosphere for opposition to the German occupation. All plans must be made in such a way that it is possible to carry them out. Threats without execution give the impression of weakness."

These last two lines are at the top of Page three of the French text. I submit these two documents as Exhibits RF 268 and 269.

Until now we have not found any trace in these German texts of an affirmation which might lead one to think that the taking of hostages and their execution constitutes a right of the occupying power; but here is a German text which explicitly formulates this idea. It is quoted in your document book as 507-F, dated Brussels, 18 April 1944. It is issued by the Chief Judge to the military Commander-in-Chief in Belgium and the North of France, and it is addressed to the German Armistice Commission in Wiesbaden. It reads in the margin: "Most Secret." Subject: Execution of 8 terrorists in Lille on 22 December 1943. Reference: Your letter of 16 March 1944." You will read in the middle of paragraph 2 of the text:

"Moreover, I maintain my point of view that the legal foundations for the measures taken by the Oberfeldkommandantur of Lille in compliance with the letter of my police group of 2 March, 1943, are, regardless of the opinion of the Armistice Commission, sufficiently justified, and further explanations are superfluous. The Armistice Commission is in a position to declare to the French if it wishes to go into the question in detail, that the executions have been carried out in conformity with the general principles of the law concerning hostages."

It is, therefore, quite obviously a State doctrine which is involved. Innocent people become forfeit. They answer with their lives for the attitude of their fellow-citizens towards the German Army. If an offence is committed of which they are completely ignorant, they are the object of a collective penalty, possibly entailing death. This is the official German thesis imposed by the German Armistice Commission in Wiesbaden. I repeat, it is a thesis imposed by the German High Command, and I will produce the evidence.

Keitel, on 16 September 1941, signed a general order which has already been read, and filed by my American colleagues under Document 389-PS, and on which I shall begin my comments. This order concerns all the occupied territories of the East and the West, as established by the list of addressees which includes all the military commanders of the countries then occupied by Germany: France, Belgium, Norway, Denmark, Eastern Territories, Ukraine, Serbia, Salonica, Southern Greece, Crete. This order was in effect for the duration of the war. We have a text of 1944 which refers to it. This order of Keitel, Chief of the OKW, is dictated in a violent spirit of anti-Communist repression. It aims at all kinds of repression of the civilian population.

This order, which concerns even the commanders whose troops are stationed in the West, points out to them that in all cases in which attacks are made against the German Army it is necessary to establish - I read the second paragraph of the text -

"that we are dealing with a mass movement uniformly controlled by Moscow, to which may also be imputed the seemingly unimportant sporadic incidents which may occur in regions which otherwise have remained quiet until now."

Consequently Keitel orders, among other things, that fifty to a hundred Communists are to be put to death for each German soldier killed. This is a political conception which we constantly meet in all manifestations of German terrorism; as far as Hitlerite propaganda is concerned, all resistance to Germany is of Communist inspiration, if not in essence Communist. The Germans thereby hoped to eliminate from the resistance the nationalists whom they thought hostile to Communism. But the Nazis also pursued another aim: they still hoped above all to divide France and the other conquered countries of the West into two hostile factions, and to put one of these factions at their service under the pretext of anti-Communism.

(A recess was taken)

M. DUBOST: We had stopped at this order of 16 September 1941, signed by the defendant Keitel, which governs, as I explained to you, the whole question of hostages. Keitel confirmed this order on 24 September 1941. We submit it as Exhibit RF 271 and you will find it in your document book as RF-554. I shall read you the first paragraph:

"Following directives of the Fuehrer, the Supreme Command of the Armed Forces issued on 16th September 1941, an order concerning the Communist revolutionary movement in the occupied territories. The order was addressed to the Ministry for Foreign Affairs, for the attention of Ambassador Ritter. It also deals with the question of capital punishment in military tribunals.

According to the order, in future, most stringent measures must be taken in the occupied territories."

The choice of hostages is also indicated thus in Document 877-PS, which has already been read to you and which is previous to the aggression of Germany against Russia. It is necessary to remind the Tribunal of this document because it shows the premeditation of the German Command and the Nazi Government to divide the occupied countries, to take away from the partisan resistance all its patriotic character, and to substitute a political character which it never had. You will find on Page 2, paragraph 4 of Document 877-PS filed under Exhibit RF 273, the following sentence:

"In this connection it must be borne in mind that, apart from other adversaries with whom our troops have to contend, a particularly dangerous element of the civilian population, destructive of all order, the propagator of Judeo-Bolshevist philosophy, opposes them. There is no doubt that, wherever he possibly can, he uses this weapon of disintegration maliciously and in ambush against the German Armed Forces, whether in combat or liberating the country."

This document is an official document issued by the General Staff of the High Command of the Army. It expresses the general doctrine of all the German Staffs. Now, it is Keitel who presides over the formation of this doctrine. He is therefore not only a soldier under the orders of his government; besides being a general he is also a Nazi politician whose acts are, at the same time, those of a war leader and of a politician serving the Nazi policy. You have proof of it in the document which I have just read to you: a general who is also a politician, in whom both politics and conduct of the war are combined in one occupation. This is not surprising for those who know the German line of thought, which has never separated war and politics. Was it not Klausewitz who said that war was only politics continued by other means?

This is doubly important. This constitutes a direct and crushing charge against Keitel; but Keitel is the German General Staff. Now this organisation is indicted and you see by this document that this indictment is justified, as the German General Staff dabbled in the criminal policy of the German Cabinet.

In the case of France, the general orders of Keitel were adopted by Stulpnagel in his order of September 30th, 1941, better known in France under the name of "Code of Hostages," which repeats and specifies in detail the previous orders, namely that of 23 August, 1941. This order of 30 September 1941, is of major importance to anyone who wishes to prove under what circumstances French hostages were shot. This is why I shall be obliged to read large extracts. It defines, in paragraph 3, the categories of Frenchmen who are to be considered as hostages. I shall read this document, which I submit to the Tribunal as Exhibit RF 274.

THE PRESIDENT: What is the number of this document?

M. DUBOST: 1588-PS. Paragraph 1 concerns the seizure of hostages. I read:

"22 August 1941, I issued the following announcement:

On the morning of 21 August 1941, a member of the German Armed Forces was killed in Paris, as a result of a murderous attack.

I therefore order that:

1. All Frenchmen held in custody of whatever kind by the German authorities, or on behalf of German authorities in France, are to be considered as hostages as from 23 August.

2. If any further incident occurs, a number of these hostages, to be determined according to the gravity of the attempt, are, to be shot.

On 19 September 1941 by an announcement to the Plenipotentiary of the French Government, I ordered the Military Commander in France, that, as from 19 September 1941, all the male French who are under arrest of any kind by the French authorities, or who are taken into custody because of communist or anarchist agitation, are to be kept under arrest by the French authorities also, on behalf of the Military Commander in France.

On the basis of my notification of 22 August 1941 and of my order of 19 September 1941 the following groups of persons are therefore hostages:

(a) All Frenchmen who are kept in detention of any kind whatsoever by the German authorities, such as police detention, imprisonment on remand or penal detention.

(b) All Frenchmen who are kept in detention of any kind whatsoever by the French authority on behalf of the German Authorities. This group includes:

(aa) All Frenchmen who are kept in detention of any kind whatsoever by the French authorities because of communist or anarchist activities;

(bb) All Frenchmen on whom the French penal authorities impose terms of imprisonment at the request of the German military courts;

(cc) All Frenchmen who are arrested and kept in custody by the French authorities on behalf of the German authorities or who are being handed over by the Germans to French authorities with the demand to keep them under arrest.

(c) Stateless inhabitants who have already been living for some time in France are to be considered as Frenchmen within the meaning of my notification of 22 August 1941.

3. Release from detention: Persons who were not yet in detention on 22nd August 1941 or on 19th September 1941, but who were arrested later on or are still being arrested, are hostages as from the date of detention if the other conditions apply to them.

The release of arrested persons, authorised on account of expiration of sentences, lifting of the order for arrest, or for other reasons, will not be affected by my announcement of 22 August 1941. Those released are no longer hostages.

In as far as persons are in detention of any kind with the French authorities for communist or anarchist activity, their release is possible, as I have informed the French Government, only with my approval."

At the end of this paragraph you will read this sentence:

"Among those Frenchmen who may be drawn on by the German military command, a list can be made out of the hostages to be executed immediately in the event of an incident."

THE PRESIDENT: Which paragraph are you reading?

M. DUBOST: It is a summary of paragraph 6. I will read you all the text, if you will bear with me for a moment. It is a text of capital importance and cannot very well be summarised. Paragraph 6, Page 4

"If an incident occurs which, according to my announcement of 22 August 1941 necessitates the shooting of hostages, the execution must immediately follow the order.

The district commanders, therefore must make a selection for their own districts from the total number of people in detention (hostages) who from a practical point of view may be considered for execution, and who are to entered on a list of hostages. These lists of hostages serve as a basis for the proposals to be submitted to me in the case of an execution.

1. According to the observations made so far, the perpetrators originate from communist or anarchist terror-gangs. The district commanders are therefore to select from those in detention (hostages), persons who, because of their communist or anarchist views in the past, or their positions in such organisations, or their former attitude in other ways are most suitable for execution. One must take into consideration when making a selection, that the intimidating effect of the shooting of hostages is all the greater, on the perpetrators themselves, and on those persons who, in France or abroad bear the spiritual responsibility - as instigators or by their propaganda - for acts of terror and sabotage, the more the persons shot are widely known. Experience shows that the instigators and the political circles interested in these attacks,

are not concerned about the lives of obscure followers, but are more likely to be concerned about the lives of their own former officials. Consequently, we must place at the head of these lists:

(a) Former deputies and officials of communist or anarchist organisations.

(Allow me to comment, gentlemen. There never were any anarchist organisations represented in Parliament, in either of our chambers, and this paragraph (a) could only refer to former deputies and officials of the communist organisations of whom we know, moreover, that some were executed by the Germans as hostages).

(b) Persons who have supported the spreading of communist ideas by word of mouth or writing (preparing of leaflets) - Intellectuals.

(c) Persons who have proved by their attitude that they are particularly dangerous (for example: attacks on members of the Armed Forces, acts of sabotage, possession of arms).

(d) Persons who collaborated in the distribution of leaflets."

One idea is dominant in this selection: "We must punish the elite."

In conformity with paragraph (b) of this article, we shall see that the Germans shot a number of intellectuals, including Solomon and Politzer, in 1941 and 1942, in Paris and the provincial towns.

I shall come back to these executions later, when I give you examples of German atrocities committed in relation to the policy of hostages in France.

2. Following the same directives, a list of hostages is to be prepared from amongst the prisoners of de Gaullist sympathies.

3. Racial Germans of French nationality, who are imprisoned for communist or anarchist activity may be included in the list. Special attention must be drawn to their German origin on the attached form.

Persons who have been condemned to death but who have been pardoned, can also be included in the lists.

5. The lists have to record for each district about 150 persons, that of the Command of Greater Paris about 300 to 400 persons. The district chiefs should always record on their lists those persons who had their last residence or permanent domicile in their districts, because those to be executed should as far as possible be taken from the district where the act was committed."

Last sentence of paragraph 5:

"The lists are to be kept up to date. Particular attention is to be paid to new arrests and releases."

7. In the French text:

Proposals for execution:

"In case of an incident which necessitates the shooting of hostages, within the meaning of my announcement of 22 August 1941, the district chief in whose territory the incident happened is to select from the list of hostages persons whose execution he wishes to propose to me. In making the selection he must, from the personal as well as local point of view, draw from persons belonging to a circle which is presumed to include the guilty."

I omit a paragraph.

"For execution, only those persons who were already under arrest at the time of the crime may be proposed for execution.

The proposal must contain the names and number of the persons proposed for execution, i.e. in the order in which the choice is recommended."

And, at the very end of Paragraph VIII we read:

> "When the bodies are buried, the communal burial of a large number in the same cemetery is to be avoided, in order not to create centres which, now or later, might form nuclei for anti-German propaganda. Therefore, if necessary, the burials must be carried out in different places."

Parallel to this document, concerning France, there exists in Belgium an order of Falkenhausen of 19 September 1941, which you will find on Page 6 of the official report on Belgium, Document F 643, which I shall submit as Exhibit RF 275.

I beg your Lordship's pardon. I have sent for the German text to be handed over to the interpreters. If you will allow me, I shall read you the translation in French. If you consider it necessary, we shall subsequently give time for the German interpreters to read the text in German.

THE PRESIDENT: Is the Belgian document worded in substantially the same terms as the document you have just read?

M. DUBOST: Exactly.

THE PRESIDENT: Then I do not think you need to read that.

M. DUBOST: As you wish. Then it will not be necessary, either, to read in its entirety the warning of Seyss-Inquart concerning Holland.

I think that by referring to these exhibits in your document book, you will extract some pieces of evidence which will only confirm what I read to you of Stulpnagel's order.

For Norway and Denmark there is a teletyped letter from Keitel to the Supreme Command of the Navy, dated 30 December 1944, which you will find in the document book as Exhibit 48- C, I read the end of paragraph 1:

> "Every ship-yard worker must know that any act of sabotage occurring within his sphere of activity entails for him personally, or for his relatives, if he disappears, the most serious consequences."

Page 2 of Document 870-PS:

> "4. 1 have just received a teletype from Field Marshal Keitel requesting the publication of an order according to which the personnel or, if need be, their, near relatives (liability of next of kin) will be held collectively responsible for the acts of sabotage occurring in their factories."

And Terboven, who wrote this sentence, added: (and it is he who condemns Marshal Keitel)

> "This request only makes sense and will only be successful if I am actually allowed to perform executions by firing squad."

All these documents will be submitted.

THE PRESIDENT: M. Dubost, do I understand that in Belgium, Holland, in Norway, and in Denmark there were similar orders or decrees with reference to hostages?

M. DUBOST: I mean to read those concerning Belgium, Holland and Norway. For Belgium, for instance, you will find at Page 6 of the French text, document 683-F, which is the official document of the Belgian Ministry of Justice, headed,

> "Brussels, 29 November 1941, 1 rue de Turin" .... "Decree of Falkenhausen of 17 September, 1941." It is from Paragraph 5, in the middle of Page 6.
>
> "In the future, the population must expect that, if attacks are made on members of the German Army or the German Police, and the culprits are not arrested, a number of hostages proportionate to the gravity of the

offence, five at a minimum, will be shot if the attack causes death. All political prisoners in Belgium are with immediate effect to be considered as hostages."

THE PRESIDENT: M. Dubost, I did not want you to read these documents if they are substantially in the same form as the document you have already read.

M. DUBOST: They are more or less in the same form, Mr. President. I shall submit them because they constitute the proof of the systematic repetition of the same methods to obtain the same results, that is, to cause terror to reign in all the occupied countries of the West. But if the Tribunal considers it constant and established that these methods were systematically used in all the Western regions, naturally I shall spare you the reading of documents which are monotonous, and which repeat in substance what was said in the document relating to France.

THE PRESIDENT: Perhaps you had better give us references to the documents which concern Belgium, Holland, Norway and Denmark.

M. DUBOST: Yes, Mr. President. So I repeat: for Belgium -
Document 683-F, Page 6, decree of Falkenhausen of 19 September 1941, submitted as Exhibit RF 275, as constituting the official report of the Kingdom of Belgium against the principal war criminals.

The second document is 46-C, corresponding to UK-42 (24 November 1942) submitted under Exhibit RF 276.

For Holland, a warning by Seyss-Inquart, which you may feel it necessary for me to read, since Seyss-Inquart is one of the defendants.

For Holland, Document 224-F, warning of Seyss-Inquart.

"For the destruction or the damaging of railway installations, telephone cables, and post offices, I shall make responsible all the inhabitants of the community in the area which the act is committed.

The population of these communities must expect that reprisals will be taken against private property, and that houses or whole blocks will be destroyed."

THE PRESIDENT: I am afraid I do not know where you are reading. Which paragraph are you reading?

M. DUBOST: I am told, Mr. President, that this document has not been bound with the Dutch report. I shall file it at the end of the hearing, if I may.

THE PRESIDENT: Very well.

M. DUBOST: "The population of these communities must expect that reprisals will be taken against private property, and that houses or whole blocks will be destroyed."

THE PRESIDENT: M. Dubost, are you reading from C-46?

M. DUBOST: I have only submitted it.

THE PRESIDENT: Are you reading from some other document?

M. DUBOST: I quote now from another document, the warning of Seyss-Inquart to Holland.

THE PRESIDENT: What number is that?

M. DUBOST: Exhibit RF 152, in your document book concerning German justice, which will be submitted for the hearing tomorrow.

THE PRESIDENT: M. Dubost, are you now proposing to read from some document which is not in our document book?

M. DUBOST: I shall postpone it until tomorrow, Mr. President.

THE PRESIDENT: Very well, you will read it tomorrow.

M. DUBOST: For Norway and Denmark we have several documents which establish that the same policy of execution of hostages was followed. We have, notably, Document C-48, from which I read a short time ago.

All those special orders for each of the occupied regions of the West are the result of the general order of Keitel, which my American colleagues have already read, and on which I merely commented this morning. The responsibility of Keitel in the development of the policy of execution of hostages is total. He was given warning: German generals even told him that this policy went beyond the aim pursued and might become dangerous.

On 16 September 1942, General Falkenhausen addressed a letter to him, from which I extract the following passage: it is Document 1594-PS, which I submit as Exhibit RF 281:

I quote:

"In the Appendix is forwarded a table of the shootings of hostages which have taken place until now in my area, and the occurrences on account of which these shootings took place.

In a great number of cases, particularly the most serious, the perpetrators were apprehended and sentenced.

This result is doubtless unsatisfactory to a great degree. It acts not so much as a deterrent, as an instrument for inciting the feelings of the population under communist influence with the rest of the population. All circles become joined with a common feeling of hatred toward the occupying forces, and effective inciting material is given to enemy propaganda. Thereby military dangers and general political reactions of an entirely unwanted nature follow. Signed: Falkenhausen."

Further there is Document 1587-PS, a further letter from the same German General, and he seems to make himself quite clear-third paragraph of the fourth sheet.

"In several cases the authors of aggression or acts of sabotage were discovered when the hostages had already been shot, shortly after the criminal acts had been committed according to instructions. Moreover, the real culprits often did not belong to the same circles as the hostages. There is no doubt that in such cases the execution of hostages does not inspire terror in the population, but indifference to repressive measures, and even resentment on the part of some sections of the population, who until then had displayed a passive attitude. The result for the occupying power is therefore negative, as planned and intended by the English agents, who were often the instigators of these acts. It will therefore be necessary to prolong the delays in cases where there is hope that we may arrest the culprits. I therefore request that you leave to me the responsibility for fixing such delays, in order that the greatest possible success in the fight against terrorist acts may be obtained."

THE PRESIDENT: Is the date of that document known?

M. DUBOST: It is after 16 September 1941. We do not know the exact date. The document is appended to another, the date of which is illegible, but it is after Keitel's order, since it accounts for the executions of hostages, carried out in compliance with that order. It points out that after the execution of the hostages the culprits were found, and that the effect was deplorable and aroused the resentment of some of the population.

You will find also in this Document 1587-PS, on Page 2 - but this time it is an extract from the monthly report of the Commander of the Wehrmacht in the

Netherlands, the report for the month of August, 1942,- a new warning to Keitel:

"B. Special events and the political situation:

On the occasion of an attempt against a leave train, due to arrive in Rotterdam, a Dutch rail guard was seriously wounded by touching a wire connected with an explosive charge, thus causing an explosion. The following repressive measures were announced in the Dutch Press:

The expiration of the time appointed for the arrest of the perpetrators, with the help of the population, is fixed at 14 August, midnight. A reward of 100,000 florins is offered for a denunciation, which will remain confidential. If the culprits are not arrested within the time appointed, arrests of hostages are threatened; railway lines will be guarded by Dutchmen.

Since, despite this summons, the perpetrator did not report and was not otherwise discovered, the following persons, among whom some had already been in custody for several weeks as hostages, were shot on the order of the Higher SS and Police Fuehrer ... "

I will pass over the enumeration of the names. I omit the next paragraph.

"Public opinion was particularly impressed - "

THE PRESIDENT: Could you read the names and the titles?

M. DUBOST: "Ruys, Willem, Director General, Rotterdam; Count E.O. G. van Limburg-Stirum, Arnheim; Baelde, Robert, Doctor of Law, Rotterdam Bennekers, Christoffel, former Inspector General of the Police at Rotterdam Baron Alexander Schimmelpennink van der Oye-Noordgouwe, Zeeland."

One paragraph further on:

"Public opinion was particularly impressed by the execution of these hostages. The enclosed reports express the opinion that, from the beginning of the occupation, no stroke inflicted by the Germans was more deeply felt. Many anonymous letters, and even some signed letters, were sent to the Commander of the Wehrmacht, who was considered as responsible for this 'unheard-of event,' an opinion which certainly prevailed among the mass of the Dutch people. From the bitterest insults to pious petitions and prayers - not to resort to the extreme, no nuance was lacking which did not, in one way or another, indicate, to say the least, complete disapproval and misunderstanding, both of the threat, and of the actual execution of the hostages. Reproaches of the most severe infractions of law (which were based on a serious argument and must have been carefully considered) and also expressions of disappointment on the part of idealists, who, in spite of all that had occurred in the political sphere, still believed in an understanding between Germans and Dutch - all this was found in the correspondence. In addition, the reproach was voiced that such methods were only doing the work of the communists who must have been jubilant at their achievement as the real instigators and saboteurs, in adding to the success of their sabotage the pleasure of seeing 'such hostages' disposed of.

In short: such disapproval even in the ranks of the very few really pro-German Dutch had never been seen, so much hatred at one time had never been felt.

Signed : Schneider, Captain."

Despite these warnings proffered by conscientious subordinates, neither the General Staff nor Keitel ever gave any order to the contrary. The order of 16 September 1941, always remained in force. When I have shown you examples of executions of hostages in France you will see that a number of facts which I shall refer to are dated 1942, 1943 and even 1944.

(A recess was taken)

COURT OFFICER: May it please your Honour, the defendants Kaltenbrunner and Streicher will continue to be absent during this afternoon's session.

M. DUBOST: This morning I had finished presenting the general rules which prevailed during the five years of occupation, in the matter of the execution of numerous hostages in the occupied countries of the West. I bring the evidence before you by reading a series of official German documents, proving that the highest authorities of the Army, of the Party and of the Nazi Government, had deliberately chosen to practise a terroristic policy through the seizure of hostages.

Before passing to the examination of a few particular cases, it seems to me to be necessary to say exactly whereof this policy consisted, in the light of the texts which I have quoted.

According to the circumstances, people belonging by choice or ethnically to the vanquished nations were apprehended, and held as a guarantee for the maintenance of order in a given sector, or after a given incident of which the enemy army had been the victim. They were apprehended and held with a view to forcing the vanquished population to carry out acts determined by the occupying authority, such as: denunciation, payment of collective fines, the handing over of perpetrators of assaults committed against the German Army, and the handing over of political adversaries. The persons thus arrested were very often massacred subsequently by way of reprisal.

From such methods the following appears: Any human being is subject, at the will of the enemy, to seizure as a hostage, and so becomes a private guarantor for the conduct of his fellows.

How contrary is this to the rights of individual liberty, of human dignity?

All the members of the German Government are jointly responsible for this iniquitous concept and for its application in our vanquished countries. No member of the German Government can throw this responsibility on to subordinates by claiming that they merely executed clearly determined orders with an excess of zeal.

I have shown you that upon many occasions, on the contrary, the persons who carried out the orders reported to the Chiefs the moral consequences resulting from the application of the terroristic policy of hostages. And we know that in no case were contrary orders given. We know that the original orders were always maintained.

I shall not endeavour to enumerate fully all the cases of executions of hostages for our country. In France alone, there were 29,660 executions. This is proved in Document RF 420 dated Paris, 21 December 1945, the original of which will be submitted as Exhibit RF 266.

It is at the beginning of the document book, the second document. You see there in detail, region by region, the number of the hostages who were executed.

For the region of:
- Lille - 1143
- Laon - 222
- Rouen - 658
- Anger - 863
- Orleans - 501
- Reims - 353
- Dijon - 1691

Poitiers - 82
Strasbourg - 211
Rennes - 974
Limoges - 2863
Clermont Ferrand - 441
Lyon - 3674
Marseille - 1513
Montpellier - 785
Toulouse - 765
Bordeaux - 806
Nancy - 571
Metz - 220
Paris - 11000
Nice - 342
Total - 29,660

I shall limit my presentation to a few typical cases of executions which unveil the political plan of the General Staff which prescribed these executions - plans of terror, plans that were intended to create and accentuate the division between Frenchmen, or, more generally, between citizens of the occupied countries.

You will find in your document book a brief quoted 133-F, which I submit as Exhibit RF 288. This is called "Posters of the Paris Region," Document 133-F. At the head of the page you will read, "Pariser-Zeitung." This document reproduces a few of the very numerous posters and bills, and some of the numerous notices inserted in the Press from 1940 to 1945, announcing the arrest of hostages in Paris, in the Region of Paris and in France. I shall read only one of these documents, which you will find on the second page. It is the one entitled No. 6, 19 September 1941. You will see in it an appeal to inform, an appeal to treason, you will see means of corruption, means which systematically applied to all the countries of the West for years, all tended to demoralize them to an equal extent:

"21 August. Appeal to the population of occupied territories. On 21 August a German soldier was shot in an attack by cowardly murderers. In consequence, I ordered, on 23 August, that hostages be taken, and threatened to have a certain number of them shot, in the case of such an assault being repeated. New crimes have obliged me to put this threat into effect.

In spite of this, new assaults have taken place.

I recognise that the great majority of the population is conscious of its duty, which is to help the authorities in their unremitting effort to maintain calm and order in the country, in the very interest of this population."

And here is the appeal to denunciation.

"But among you there are agents paid by powers hostile to Germany, Communist criminal elements who have only one aim, which is to sow discord between the occupying power and the French population. These elements are completely indifferent to the consequences for the entire population which result from their activity.

I will no longer allow the lives of German soldiers to be threatened by these assassins. I shall stop at no measure in order to fulfil my duty, however stringent it may be.

But it is likewise my duty to make the whole population responsible for the fact that, up to the present, it has not yet been possible to lay hands on the cowardly murderers, and to impose upon them the penalty which they deserve.

That is why I have found it necessary - first of all for Paris - to take measures, which - unfortunately - will hinder the everyday life of the entire population. Frenchmen, it depends on you whether I am obliged to increase the severity of these measures, or whether they can again be suspended.

I appeal to you all, to your administration and to your police, to cooperate, through your extreme vigilance and your active personal intervention, in the arrest of the guilty. It is necessary, by anticipating and denouncing the criminal activities, to avoid the creation of a critical situation which would plunge the country into misfortune.

He who fires in ambush on German soldiers who are only doing their duty here, and who are safeguarding the maintenance of a normal life, is not a patriot, but a cowardly assassin and the enemy of all decent people.

Frenchmen! I count on you to understand these measures which I am taking, which are only in your own interests. Signed von Stulpnagel."

Numerous notices follow which all have to do with executions.

Under No. 8 on the following page you will find a list of twelve names, among which are three of the best known lawyers of the Paris Bar, who are characterised as militant Communists : Pitard, Hajje and Rolnikas.

In file 21, submitted by my colleague M. Gerthoffer, in the course of his economic presentation, you will find a few notices which are similar, published in the official German newspaper "VOBIF."

You will observe, in connection with this notice of 16 September, announcing the execution, or rather the assassination of M. Pitard and his companions, that the murderers had neither the courage nor the honesty to say that they were all Parisian lawyers. Was it by mistake? I think that it was a calculated lie, for at this time it was necessary to handle the elite gently. The occupying power still hoped to separate them from the people of France.

I shall describe to you in detail two cases which spread grief in the hearts of the French in the course of the month of October 1941, and which have remained present in the memory of all my compatriots.

They are known as the "executions of Chateaubriant and of Bordeaux." They are related in Document 415 in your document book, which I submit to the Tribunal as Exhibit RF 285.

After the attack on two German officers at Nantes on 20 October 1941, and another in Bordeaux a few days later, the German Army decided to make an example. You will find, on Page 22 of Document 415, a copy of the notice in the newspaper "Le Phare," on 21 October, 1941. It is the last page of the document:

"Notice. Cowardly criminals in the pay of England and of Moscow have killed, by shooting in the back, the Feldkommandant of Nantes on the morning of 20 October 1941. Up to now the assassins have not been arrested.

As expiation for this crime I have ordered that 50 hostages be shot, to begin with. Because of the gravity of the crime, 50 more hostages will be shot in the case of the guilty not being arrested between now and midnight of 23 October 1941."

The conditions under which these reprisals were executed are worth describing in detail:

Stulpnagel, who was commanding the German troops in France, ordered the Ministry of the Interior to select prisoners. These prisoners were to be selected from among the Communists who were considered the most dangerous (these are the terms of Stulpnagel's order). A list of 60 Frenchmen was furnished by the Minister of the Interior. This was Pucheu. He has since been tried by my compatriots, sentenced to death and executed.

On the first page you will find a copy of the letter from the Sub-prefect ofChateaubriant to the Kommandantur of Chateaubriant, in reply to the order which he received from the Minister of the Interior:

> "Following our conversation of today, I have the honour of confirming to you that the Minister of the Interior has communicated today with General Stulpnagel, in order to point out to him the most dangerous Communist prisoners among those who are now held at Chateaubriant. You will find enclosed herewith the list of 60 individuals who have been handed over this day."

On the following page is the German order

> "Because of the assassination of the Feldkommandant of Nantes, Lt. Col. Hotz on 20 October 1941, the following Frenchmen, who are already imprisoned as hostages in accordance with my publication of 22 August 1941, and of my decree to the legal representative of the French Government of 19 September 1941, are to be shot."

In the following pages you will find a list, which I shall not read, of all the men who were shot on that day. I leave out the reading of the list in order not to lengthen the proceedings unduly.

On Page 16 you will find a list of 48 names. On Page 13 you will find the list of those who were shot in Nantes. On Page 12 you will find the list of those who were shot in Chateaubriant. From these lists you will observe that the bodies were sent out for burial to all the surrounding communes.

I shall read to you the testimony of eyewitnesses as to how they were buried after having been shot. On Page 3 of this document you will find that note of M. Dumesnil, concerning the executions of 21 October 1941, which was drawn up the day after these executions. The second paragraph reads:

> "The priest was called at 11.30 to the prison of La Fayette. An officer, probably of the G.F.P., told him that he was charged with announcing to certain prisoners that they were going to be shot. The priest was then locked up in a room with the 13 hostages who were in the prison. The other three, who were at Les Rochettes, were attended by Abbe Theon, professor at the College Stanislas.
>
> The Abbe Fontaine said to the condemned: 'Gentlemen, you must understand, alas, what my presence means.' He then spoke with the prisoners collectively and individually for the two hours which the officers had said would be granted to arrange the personal affairs of the condemned, and to write their last wills to their families.
>
> The execution had been fixed for 2 o'clock in the afternoon, half an hour having been allowed for the journey. But the two hours passed by, another hour passed, and still another hour before the condemned were sent for. There were some, like M. Fourny, who were optimistic by nature, and hoped that a countermanding order would be given. The priest himself did not at all believe this.
>
> The condemned were all very brave. It was two of the youngest, Gloux

and Grolleau, who were students, who constantly encouraged the others, saying that it was better to die in this way than to perish uselessly in an accident.

When they left, the priest, for reasons which were not explained to him, was not authorised to accompany the hostages to the place of execution. He went down the stairs of the prison with them as far as the truck. They were chained together in twos. The thirteenth had on handcuffs. Once they were in the truck, Gloux and Grolleau made another gesture of farewell to him, smiling and waving their chained hands.

Signed: Dumesnil (Counsellor attached to the Cabinet)."

Sixteen were shot in Nantes. Twenty-seven were shot in Chateaubriant. Five were shot outside the Department. As to those who were shot in Chateaubriant, we know what their last moments were like. The Abbe Moyon, who was present, wrote on 22 October 1941, Page 17 of your document, the account of this execution. This is the third paragraph, Page 17:

"It was a beautiful autumn day. The temperature was mild. There had been lovely sunshine since morning. Everyone in town was going about his usual business. There was great animation in the town since it was Wednesday, which was market day. The population knew from the newspapers, and from the information it had received from Nantes, that a superior officer had been killed in a street in Nantes, but they refused to believe that such savage and extensive reprisals would be applied.

At Choisel Camp the German authorities had, for some days, put into special quarters a certain number of men who were to serve as hostages in case of special difficulties. It was from among these men that those who were to be shot on this evening of 22 October 1941 were chosen.

The Cure of Bere was finishing his lunch when M. Moreau presented himself. M. Moreau was Chief of Choisel Camp. In a few words the latter explained to him the object of his visit; that, having been delegated by M. Lecornu, the Sub-prefect of Chateaubriant, he had come to inform him that 27 men selected from among the political prisoners of Choisel, were to be executed that afternoon, and he asked Monsieur Le Cure to go immediately to attend them.

The priest said he was ready to accomplish this mission, and he went to the prisoners without delay. When the priest appeared to carry out his mission, the Sub- prefect was already with the condemned. He had come to announce the horrible fate which was awaiting them, asking them to write letters of farewell to their families without delay. It was under these circumstances that the priest arrived at the entrance to the quarters."

You will find on Page 19 the "departure for the execution," paragraph 4:

"Suddenly there was the sound of car engines. The door, which I had shut at the beginning so that we might be more private, opened. A German officer appeared. He was actually a chaplain. He said to me: 'Monsieur le Cure, your mission has been accomplished and you must withdraw immediately.'"

At the bottom of the page, the last paragraph:

"Access to the quarry where the execution took place being absolutely forbidden to all Frenchmen, I only know that the condemned were executed in three groups of nine men, that all the men who were shot refused to have their eyes bound, that young Mocquet fainted and fell, and that the last cry that sprang from the lips of all of them was an ardent 'Vive la France.'"

On Page 21 of the same document you will find the declaration of Police Officer Roussel. It also is worth reading:

"22 October 1941, at about 3.30 in the afternoon, I happened to be in the Rue du 11 Novembre in Chateaubriant, and I saw coming from Choisel Camp four or five German trucks, I could not say definitely how many, preceded by a sedan, in which was a German officer. Several civilians in handcuffs were in the trucks and were singing patriotic songs; the 'Marseillaise,' the 'Chant du Depart' and so forth. One of the trucks was filled with armed German soldiers.

I learned subsequently that these were hostages who had just been taken from Choisel Camp, to be led to the quarry of Sabliere on the Soudan Road, to be shot in reprisal for the murder in Nantes of the German Colonel Hotz.

About two hours later these same trucks came back from the quarry and drove into the court of the Chateau of Chateaubriant, where the bodies of the men who had been shot were deposited in a cellar until coffins could be made.

On coming back from the quarry the trucks were covered and no noise was heard, but a stream of blood escaped from them and left a mark on the road from the quarry to the castle.

The following day, 23 October, the bodies of the men who had been shot were put into coffins, without any French persons being present, the entrances to the chateau having been guarded by German sentinels, and were taken to the cemeteries of the surrounding communes, three coffins per commune. The Germans were careful to choose communes to which there was no regular transport service, presumably to avoid the population's going en masse to the graves of these martyrs.

I was not present at the departure of the hostages from the camp nor at the shooting in the quarry of Sabliere, as the approaches to it were guarded by German soldiers armed with machine guns."

Almost at the same time, in addition to these 48 hostages who were shot, there were others: those of Bordeaux. You will find in your document book, under Document 400-F, documents which have been communicated to us by the Prefecture of the Gironde, which we submit to the Tribunal as Exhibit RF 286.

You will find the first document issued by the Section of Political Affairs, dated 22 October 1941, marked 400-F (C), at the bottom of which you will read:

"In the course of the conference which took place last night at the Feldkommandantur of Bordeaux, the German authorities asked me to proceed immediately with the arrest of 100 individuals known for their sympathy with the Communist Party or the de Gaullist movement, who will be considered as hostages, and to make a great number of house searches.

These operations have been in progress since this morning. So far no result of interest has been brought to my attention. In addition, this morning at 11 o'clock the German authorities informed me of the reprisal measures which they had decided to take against the population."

These reprisal measures you will find set forth on Page "A" of the same document, in a letter addressed by General von Faber Du Faur, Chief of the Regional Administration of Bordeaux, to the Prefect of the Gironde. I quote:

"Bordeaux, 23 October 1941.

To the Prefect of the Gironde

As expiation for the cowardly murder of the Councillor of War, Reimers, the military Commander in France has ordered fifty hostages to be executed. The execution will take place to-morrow.

In the case of the murderers not being arrested in the very near future, other measures will be taken, as in the case of Nantes.

I have the honour of making known this decision to you.

Chief of the Military Regional Administration

Signed : von Faber du Faur."

All of these men were executed.

There is a famous place in the suburbs of Paris, which has become a place of pilgrimage for the French since our liberation. It is the Fort of Romainville. During the occupation the Germans converted this fort into a hostage depot, from which they selected victims when they wanted to take revenge after some patriotic demonstration. It is from Romainville that Professors Jacques Solomon, Decourtemanche, Georges Politzer, Dr. Boer and six other Frenchmen went forth. They were arrested in March 1942, tortured by the Gestapo, then executed without trial in the month of May 1942.

On 19 August, 1942, 96 hostages left this fort, among them Monsieur Le Gall, a municipal councillor of Paris. They left the fort of Romainville, were transferred to Mont-Valerien, and executed.

In September 1942, an attack had been made against some German soldiers at the Rex Cinema in Paris. General von Stulpnagel issued a proclamation announcing that, because of this attack, he had ordered 116 hostages to be shot and that extensive measures of deportation were to be taken. You will find an extract from this newspaper in Document 402 under letter "B."

The notice was worded as follows:

"As a result of attacks committed by communist agents and terrorists in the pay of England, German soldiers and French civilians have been killed or wounded.

As reprisal for these attacks I have had 116 communist terrorists shot, whose participation or implication in terroristic acts has been proved by confessions.

In addition, severe measures of repression have been taken to prevent incidents on the occasion of demonstrations planned by the communists for 20 September 1942. I ordered the following:

From Saturday, 19 September 1942, at 3 o'clock in the afternoon, until Sunday, 20 September 1942, at midnight, all theatres, cinemas, cafes and other places of amusement shall remain closed to the French population in the Departments of the Seine, Seine-et-Oise and Seine- et-Marne; all public demonstrations, including sport activities, are forbidden.

From Sunday, 20 September 1942, from 3 o'clock in the afternoon until midnight, it is forbidden to non-German civilians to move about in the streets and on public squares in the Departments of the Seine, the Seine-et-Oise and the Seine-et-Marne. The only exceptions are persons representing official services, etc."

In fact, it was only on the day of 20 September that 46 of these hostages were chosen from the list of 116. The Germans handed newspapers of 20 September to the prisoners of Romainville, announcing the decision of the High Military Command. It was, therefore, through the newspapers, that the prisoners of Romainville learned that a certain number of them would be chosen at the end of the afternoon to be led before the firing squad.

All lived during that day in expectation of the call that would be made that evening. Those who were called knew their fate beforehand. All died innocent of the crimes for which they were being executed, for those who were responsible for the attack in the Rex Cinema were arrested a few days later.

It was in Bordeaux that the 70 other hostages, of the total of 116 announced by General von Stulpnagel, were executed. In reprisal for the murder of Ritter, the German official of the Labour Front, 50 other hostages were shot at the end of September 1943, in Paris. You will find in this same file 402 (C), a reproduction of the newspaper article which announced these executions to the French people as reprisal against terroristic acts, saying that the attacks and acts of sabotage had multiplied in France in recent days, and for this reason 50 terrorists, convicted of having participated in acts of sabotage and of terrorism, had been shot on 2 October 1943, on the order of the Higher SS and Polizeifuehrer.

All these facts concerning the hostages of Romainville have been related to us by one of the survivors, one of the hundreds of Frenchmen imprisoned in this fort, Monsieur Rabate, a mechanic living at 69, Rue de la Ton beIssiore, Paris, whose testimony was taken by one of our collaborators.

You will find this testimony under letter "A" in Document 402 RF, which has already been submitted as Exhibit RF 287? at the bottom of Page 1 you will read:

"There were 70 of us, including Professors Jacques Solomon, Decourtemanche and Georges Politzer, Dr. Boer and MM. Engros, Dudach, Cadras, Dalidet, Golue, Pican, who were shot in the month of May, 1942, and an approximately equal number of women.

Some of us were transferred to the German quarter of the Sante (a prison in Paris), but the majority of us were taken to the military prison of Cherche-Midi (in Paris). We were questioned in turn by a Gestapo officer, in the offices of the Rue des Saussaies. Certain of us, in particular Politzer and Solomon, were tortured to the point of having their limbs broken, according to the testimony of their wives.

Moreover, while questioning me, the Gestapo officer confirmed this to me:

I repeat his words:

'Rabate, here you will have to speak. Professor Langevin's son-in-law came in here arrogant. He went out crawling.'

After a short stay of five months in the prison of Cherche-Midi, in the course of which we learned of the execution, as hostages of the 10 prisoners already mentioned, we were transferred, on the 24 August 1942, to the Fort of Romainville.

It is to be noted that from the day of our arrest we were forbidden to write or to receive mail, or to inform our families where we were. On the doors of our cells was written: 'Alles verboten' (Everything is forbidden). We received only the strict prison ration, namely, three- fourths of a litre of vegetable soup and two hundred grams of black bread per day. The biscuits sent to the prison for political prisoners by the Red Cross or by the Quakers' Association were not given to us because of this prohibition.

In the fort of Romainville we were interned as 'isolated prisoners,' an expression corresponding to the 'NN' (Nacht und Nebel), of which we have heard in Germany."

THE PRESIDENT: M. Dubost, the Tribunal thinks that, unless there is anything very special that you wish to read in any of these documents, they have already heard the number of the hostages who were put to death and they think that they really do not add to it - the actual details of these documents.

M. DUBOST: I thought, Mr. President, that I had not spoken to you of the regime to which men were subjected when they were prisoners of the German Army. I thought that it was my duty to enlighten the Tribunal on the condition of these men in the German prisons.

I thought that it was also my duty to enlighten the Tribunal on the ill-treatment inflicted by the Gestapo, who left the son-in-law of Professor Langevin with his limbs broken.

THE PRESIDENT: Certainly, if there are matters of that sort which you think it right to go into, you must do so, but the actual details of individual shooting of hostages we think you might, at any rate, summarise. But if there are particular atrocities to which you wish to draw our attention, by all means do so.

M. DUBOST: Mr. President, I have only given you two examples of executions out of the multiple executions which caused 29,660 deaths in my country.

THE PRESIDENT: Go on.

M. DUBOST: In the region of the North of France, which was administratively attached to Belgium and subjected to the authority of General Falkenhausen, the same policy of execution was practised. You will find in Document 123 RF, submitted as Exhibit RF 288, the reproduction of a great number of placards announcing either arrests, executions or deportations. Certain of these placards include, moreover, an appeal to denunciation; and they are analogous to those which I read to you in connection with France. Perhaps it would be well, nevertheless, to point out the one that you will find on Page 3 concerning the execution of 20 Frenchmen, ordered as the result of a theft; that on Page 4 which concerns the execution of 15 Frenchmen prescribed as a result of an attack against a railroad installation; and finally, particularly this last, the one that you will find on Pages 8 and 9, which announces that executions will be carried out, and invites the civilian population to hand over the guilty ones, if they know them, to the German Army.

As particularly concerns those countries of the West other than France, we have a very great number of cases. You will find in your document book, as No. 680, a copy of a placard by the Military Commander-in-Chief for Belgium and the North of France, which announces the arrest in Tournai, on 18 September 1941, of 25 inhabitants as hostages, on which it specifies the condition on which certain of them will be shot if the guilty are not discovered. But you will find, as Document 680, a document particularly remarkable since it comes from the German authorities themselves; it is the secret report of the German Chief of Police in Belgium dated 13 September 1944, that is to say, when Belgium was totally liberated, and this German official wished to summarise for his Chiefs his service during the occupation of Belgium.

This document will be submitted as Exhibit RF 290: on the first page you will find the following passage.

> "The growing incitement of the population by the radio and the Press of the enemy which urge them to acts of terrorism and sabotage" - this is applied to Belgium - "the passive attitude of the population, in particular of the Belgian administration, the complete failure of the public prosecutors, the examining judges and of the judicial police, in disclosing and preventing terrorist acts, have at last led to preventive and repressive measures of the most rigorous kind, that is to say, to the execution of persons closely related to the group of the culprits themselves.
>
> As early as 19 October 1941, on the occasion of the murder of two police

officials in Tournai, the Military Commander-in-Chief declared, by an announcement appearing in the Press, that all the political prisoners in Belgium would be considered as hostages, with immediate effect. In the provinces of the North of France, subject to the jurisdiction of the same Military Commander-in-Chief, this ordinance was already in force as from 26 August 1941. Through repeated notices appearing in the Press the civilian population has been informed that political prisoners taken as hostages will be executed if the murders continue to be committed.

As a result of the assassination of Teughels, Rexist Mayor of Charleroi, and other attempts at assassination against public officials, the Military Commander-in-Chief has been obliged to order, for the first time in Belgium, the execution of 8 terrorists. The date of the execution is 27 November 1942."

On the following page of this same document, 680 (B), you will find another order dated 22 April 1944, marked "Secret," also issued by the Military Commander in Belgium and the North of France, concerning measures of expiation for the murder of two Walloon SS, who had fought at Tcherkassy; 5 hostages were shot on that day.

On the following page 9 hostages are added to these 5, and still a 10th on the following page. Then 5 others on the following page.

You will find, finally, on the penultimate page of the document, a projected list of persons to be shot in expiation of the murder of the SS men. Compare the dates, and judge of the ferocity with which the assassination of these two Walloon traitors, SS volunteers, was revenged.

Finally, under No. 7, you will see the names of the 20 Belgian patriots who were thus murdered.

THE PRESIDENT: Which page did you say?

M. DUBOST: The last page, Mr. President, Page 6, the last document reproduced on the last page. I have not read it in order not to lengthen the case, but I will read it, if you wish.

"Brusseler Zeitung-25 April 1944.

Measures of expiation for the murder of men who fought at Tcherkassy. The German authority announces: the perpetrators of the assassination on 6 April of the members of the SS Sturmbrigade Wallonie, Hubert Stassen and Francois Musch, who fought at Tcherkassy, have so far not been apprehended. Therefore, in accordance with the communication dated 10 April 1944, the 20 terrorists whose names follow have been executed :

Renatus Diericks of Louvain; Francois Boets of Louvain; Antoine Smets of Louvain; Jacques Van Tilt of Holsbeek; Emiliens Van Tilt of Holsbeek; Franciskus Aerts of Herent; Jean Van der Elst of Herent; Gustave Morren of Louvain; Eugene Hupin of Chapelle-lez-Herlaimont; Pierre Leroy of Boussois; Leon Hermann of Montigny-sur- Sambre; Felix Trousson of Chaudfontaine; Joseph Grab of Tirlemont; Octave Wintgens of Baelen-Hontem; Stanislaw Mrozowski of Grace- Berleur; Marcel Boeur of Athus; Marcel Dehon of Ghlin; Andre Croquelois of Pont des Briques, near Boulogne; Gustave Hos of Mons; and the Stateless Jew, Walter Kriss of Herent."

THE PRESIDENT: We will adjourn now for ten minutes.

(A recess was taken)

M. DUBOST: As far as the other Western Countries, Holland and Norway are concerned, we have received documents which we submit as Document 224 RF, Exhibit RF 291. Page 2 of Document 224 RF.

In the French text you will find a long list of civilians who were executed. Also on Pages 4 and 5 you will find a report of the Chief of the Criminal Police, Munt, in connection with these executions, and you will observe that Munt tries to prove his own innocence, in my opinion without success.

On Page 6 you will find the account of an investigation concerning mass executions which the Germans carried out in Holland. I do not think it is necessary to read this investigation. It brings no new factual element and simply illustrates the thesis that I have been presenting since this morning: that in all the Western countries the German military authorities systematically carried out executions of hostages, as reprisals.

On Page 8, second paragraph, you will see that on 7 March 1945 an order was given to shoot 80 prisoners, and the authority who gave this order said : "I do not care where you get the prisoners" - execution without any designation of age or profession or origin.

On Page 9 the Tribunal will see that there was a total of 2080 executions - that is on lines 6 and 7. In paragraph one, on Page 9, the Tribunal will note that as a reprisal for a murder committed against an SS soldier, a house was destroyed and 10 Dutchmen were executed and, in addition, two other houses were destroyed - under No. 1, in the middle of the page. Under No. 2, 10 Dutchmen were executed, and under No. 3, 14. Altogether, 3,000 Dutchmen were thus executed according to the testimony of this document, which was established by the War Crimes Commission, and signed by the Chief of the Dutch Delegation to the International Military Tribunal, Colonel Baron Van Tuyll van Serooskerken.

Pages 33 and 34 of this document give the approximate number of victims, region by region. The Tribunal will excuse me if I do not read these pages: it seems unnecessary, and they are before you.

I do not wish to conclude the statement about hostages, concerning Holland without drawing the attention of the Tribunal to section (B) of Document 224, which gives a long list of hostages, prisoners or deceased, arrested by the Germans in Holland. The Tribunal will observe that most of these hostages were intellectuals or very highly placed personages in Holland. We note therein, the names of members of parliament, lawyers, senators, Protestant clergymen, and judges, and amongst them we find a former Minister of Justice. The arrests were made systematically from amongst the intellectual elite of the country.

As far as Norway is concerned, the Tribunal will find in Document 240, submitted as Exhibit RF 292, a short report of the executions which the Germans carried out in that country. On 26 April, 1942, two German policemen who tried to arrest two Norwegian patriots were killed on an island on the West coast of Norway. In order to avenge them, four days later 18 young men were shot without trial. All these 18 Norwegians had been in prison since 22 February of the same year, and therefore had nothing to do with this affair.

In the first paragraph of the French translation in the French document book, which is Page 22 of the Norwegian original, it states that:

"On 6 October, 1942, 10 Norwegian citizens were executed in reprisal for attempts at sabotage.

On 20 July, 1944, an unspecified number of Norwegians were shot without trial. They had all been taken from a concentration camp. The reason for this arrest and execution is unknown."

Finally after the German capitulation the bodies of 44 Norwegian citizens were found in graves. All had been shot and we do not know the reason for their execution; it has never been published, and we do not believe they were tried. The executions were effected by a shot through the back of the neck or a revolver bullet through the ear, the hands of the victims being tied behind their backs. This information is given by the Norwegian Government for this Tribunal.

I draw the attention of the Tribunal to the final document, 54-R, signed by Terboven, which concerns the execution of eighteen Norwegians who were taken prisoner for having made an illegal attempt to reach England.

It is by thousands and tens of thousands that in all the Western countries citizens were executed without trial, in reprisal for acts in which they never participated. It does not seem necessary to me to multiply these examples. Each of these examples involves individual responsibility which is not within the competency of this Tribunal. The examples are only of interest in so far as they show that the orders of the defendants were carried out, and notably the orders of Keitel.

I believe that I have amply proved this. It is incontestable that in every case the German Army was concerned with these executions, which were not solely carried out by the police or the SS.

Moreover, they did not achieve the results expected. Far from reducing the number of attacks, it increased them. Each attack was followed by an execution of hostages, and every shooting of hostages occasioned more attempts on lives. In a general way, new executions of hostages plunged the countries into a stupour and forced every citizen to become conscious of the fate of his country, despite the efforts of the German propaganda. Faced with the failure of this terroristic policy, one might have thought that the defendants would modify their methods. Far from modifying them, they intensified them. I shall endeavour to show what was the activity of the police and the law from the time when, the policy of hostages having failed, it was necessary to appeal to the German police in order to keep the occupied countries in servitude. The German authorities made arbitrary arrests at all times, and from the very beginning of the occupation; but with the failure of the policy of the execution of hostages, which was, as you remember, commented upon by General Falkenhausen in the case of Belgium, arbitrary arrests increased to the point of becoming a constant practice, substituted for that of arresting hostages.

We submit to the Tribunal Document 715-PS, as Exhibit RF 294.

The document concerns the arrest of high-ranking officers, who were to be transferred to Germany in honourable custody.

"Subject: Measures to be taken against French Officers.

In agreement with the German Embassy in Paris, and with the Chief of the Security Police and the SD, the Supreme Commander in the West has made the following proposals:

First: The senior officers enumerated below will be arrested and transferred to Germany in honourable custody:

The Generals of the Army, Frere - who died subsequently in Germany after his deportation - "Gerodias, Cartier, Revers, de Lattre de Tassigny, Fornel de la Laurencie, Robert de Saint-Vincent, Laure, Doyen, Pisquendar, Mittelhauser, Paquin; Generals of the Air Force, Bouscat, Carayon, de Greffrier, d'Harcourt, Mouchard, Mendigal, Rozoy; Colonels Loriot and Fonck."

I continue on Page 2:

"It affects generals whose names have a propaganda value in France and in foreign countries, or whose attitude or abilities represent a danger."

I pass over paragraph two.

"Moreover, we have chosen from the index of officers of the 'Arbeitsstab' in France, about 120 officers who have distinguished themselves by their anti-German attitude during the last two years. The SD has also made a list of about 130 officers who have previously been under suspicion. After the compilation of these two lists, the arrest of these officers is to be arranged at a later date, depending on the situation."

The sixth paragraph at the bottom of the page:

"In the case of all officers of the French Army at the time of the Armistice, the Chief of the Security Police, in collaboration with the Supreme Commander of the West, will fix the same day for the whole territory, for a check by the police of their domiciles and of occupation."

Page 3, paragraphs 7 and 8:

"As a measure of reprisal, families of suspected persons having already shown themselves recalcitrant, or who might become such in the future, will be transferred as internees to Germany or to the territory of Eastern France. For these the question of billeting and supervision must first of all be solved. Afterwards we can contemplate, as a later measure, the withdrawal of their French nationality and the confiscation of property, already carried out in other cases by Laval."

The police and the army were involved in all of these arrests. A telegram in cipher shows that the Minister of Foreign Affairs himself was concerned in the matter. Document 723-PS, which becomes Exhibit RF 295, will be read in this session. It is the third document of the document book. It is addressed to the Minister of Foreign Affairs and is dated Paris, 5 June, 1943:

"In the course of a conference which took place yesterday with the representatives of the High Command of the Western Front and the SD, the following agreement was made concerning measures to be taken: The aim of these measures must be to make impossible, through preventive action, the escape from France of any more well-known soldiers and at the same time to prevent these personages from organising a resistance movement in France itself, in the event of an attempted landing by the Anglo-Saxon powers.

The circle of officers here concerned comprises all who by their rank and experience, or by their names, would considerably strengthen the military command or the political credit of the resisters should they decide to join them. In the event of military operations in France, we must consider them as being of the same importance."

Page 2, fourth paragraph:

"The list has been compiled in agreement with the High Command of the West, the Chief of the Security Police, and the General of the Air Force in Paris."

I will not read the names of the additional high-ranking French officers who were to be arrested, but I will ask you to turn on to Page 4, where the Tribunal will see, in the second paragraph, that the German authorities contemplated causing officers already arrested by the French Government, and under the supervision of the French authorities, to suffer the same fate as, for example, de Lattre de Tassigny, Laure, and Fornel de la Laurencie.

These generals were destined to be literally torn away from the French authorities for deportation.

Paragraph 3:

"Considering the general situation at present and the security measures which are envisaged, all officers present consider it inopportune to keep these generals in French custody, for they might, either through negligence or with the voluntary aid of the guard personnel, escape and recover their freedom."

Page 7, under Roman Numeral IX, concerning reprisals against their families:

"General Warlimont had asked the Commander in Chief of the Western Front to raise the question of reprisal measures to be taken against the families of persons who had become resisters, and to make certain proposals concerning their eventual fate."

President Laval declared himself ready, not long ago, to take measures of this kind on behalf of the French Government, but would limit himself to the families of several outstanding personalities.

I refer to the penultimate paragraph of the telegram No. 3,486 of 29 May 1943: 'We must wait and see whether Laval is really willing to apply reprisal measures in a practical way.'

"All those present at the meetings were in agreement that such measures should be taken in any event, as rapidly as possible, against families of well-known personages who had become resisters, for example, members of the families of Generals Giraud, Juin, Georges, the former Minister of the Interior, Pucheu, and of the Inspectors of Finance Couvre de Murville, le Roy-Beaulieu and others.

The measures may also be carried out by the German authorities, since the persons who have become resisters may be considered as foreigners belonging to an enemy power, and the members of their families are also to be considered as such.

In the opinion of those present, the members of these families should be interned; the practical carrying out of this measure and its technical possibilities must be carefully examined."

I omit one paragraph:

"We might also study the question of whether these families should be interned in regions particularly exposed to air attacks, for instance, in the region of dams or in industrial regions which are often bombed.

A list of families who are to be interned is to be drawn up in collaboration with the Embassy."

In this premeditation of criminal arrests we find involved the defendant Ribbentrop, the defendant Goering and the defendant Keitel; for it is their departments which made these proposals, and we know that these proposals were agreed to.

Document 720-PS, submitted as Exhibit RF 296, is the second in your document book -

In conclusion we must point out the participation of the Ministry for Foreign Affairs through the intermediary of the OKW. It is a fact that these arrests were carried out. Members of the family of General Giraud were deported. General Frere was deported and died in a concentration camp. Thus the orders were carried out. They were approved before being carried out, and the approval incriminates the defendants whose names I have mentioned. The arrests affected not only high-ranking officers, but were much more extensive, and a great number of Frenchmen were arrested. We have no exact statistics.

THE PRESIDENT: M. Dubost, did you produce any evidence for your last statement?

M. DUBOST: I shall bring you the proof of the arrest of General Frere, and his death in a concentration camp, when I deal with concentration camps; with regard to the arrest and death of several French generals in the concentration camp in Dachau, the Tribunal must still remember the testimony of Blaha; so far as the family of General Giraud is concerned, I shall endeavour to bring proofs, but I did not think it was necessary, as it is a well-known fact that the daughter of General Giraud was deported.

THE PRESIDENT: I am not sure that we can take judicial notice of all facts which may be public knowledge in France?

M. DUBOST: I shall submit to the Tribunal the supplementary proof concerning the generals who died on deportation when I deal with the question of the camps. General Frere died in Struthof Camp, and we shall explain the circumstances under which he was assassinated. In addition, there exists in your document book a document numbered 417-F, Exhibit RF 297, which was captured from the archives of the German Armistice Commission, which establishes that the German authorities refused to free French generals who were prisoners of war and whose state of health and age made it imperative that they should be released. Paragraph 2:

"So far as this question is concerned, the Fuehrer has always taken a negative line, not only towards their release, but also towards their hospitalisation in neutral countries."

THE PRESIDENT: Are you reading 720 now?

M. DUBOST: That is 417-F, the fourth in your document book.

THE PRESIDENT: Yes, I have it.

M. DUBOST: "Today there is less question of release and hospitalisation than ever, since the Fuehrer has only recently ordered the transfer to Germany of all French generals living in France."

It is signed by Warlimont, and in the manuscript it is noted, "no reply to be given to the French."

Please bear in mind this last sentence - since the Fuehrer has only recently ordered a transfer to Germany of all French generals living in France." But, as I explained, these arrests went far beyond the comparatively small number of generals or the families of well-known persons as envisaged by the document which I have just read to the Tribunal. Many Frenchmen were arrested. We have no statistics, but we have an idea of the number, which is considerable, according to the figures given of Frenchmen who died in French prisons alone, prisons which had been placed under German command and were supervised by German personnel during the occupation.

We know that forty thousand Frenchmen died in French prisons alone in France. This is shown in a document which will be submitted in the case about atrocities, to be dealt with at the end of my statement, a document which originates from the Ministry of Prisoners of War and Deportees. These are the official figures produced by this Ministry. In the prison registry is written "Protective Custody." My American colleagues have explained to the Tribunal what this protective custody meant, when they read Document 1723-PS, submitted as Exhibit USA 266. It is useless to return to this document. It is sufficient to remind the Tribunal, that imprisonment and protective custody were considered by the German authorities as the strongest measure calculated to educate in a forceful manner any foreigners who would deliberately neglect their duty towards the German community, or compromise the security of the German State; they must act in accordance with the general interests and submit to the discipline of the State.

This protective custody was, as the Tribunal will remember, a purely arbitrary detention. Those who were interned in protective custody enjoyed no rights and could not defend themselves. There were no tribunals before which they could plead their cause.

Now, we know through official documents which were submitted to us, notably by Luxembourg, that protective custody was carried out on a very large scale. The Tribunal will read in Document 229-F, already submitted as Exhibit USA 243, No. 215, a list of twenty-five persons arrested and placed in different concentration camps under protective custody.

The Tribunal will recall that our colleagues drew its attention to the case of the arrest of Ludwig (bottom of the page), because he was strongly suspected of having aided deserters.

A testimony of the application of protective custody in France is given in Document 278-F, submitted as Exhibit RF 300, which is the next in your document book:

"Copy of VAA 7236 - Secret - Ministry for Foreign Affairs, Berlin, 18 September 1941." There is a typing error here. The date is not clear, but we know it is 1941.

"Subject: Report of 30 August, 1941.

The explanations of the Military Commander in France of 1 August 1941 are considered in general to be satisfactory as a reply to the French note.

Here, also, we consider there is every reason to avoid any further discussion with the French concerning preventive arrest, for this would only lead to a limitation of its application by the occupying power, which would not be desirable or in the interests of the freedom of action of the military authorities. By order (signed)."

The signature cannot be read; and below: "the representative of the Ministry for Foreign Affairs at the German Armistice Commission at Wiesbaden. - The Ministry for Foreign Affairs - VAA P 7236, SECRET, dated Wiesbaden, 23 September 1941, copy:

"The representative of the Ministry requests to be informed, when convenient, of the reply made to the French note."

The Ministry for Foreign Affairs was still involved in this question of protective custody.

The justification for this custody was as the Ministry for Foreign Affairs admits, and according to the testimony of this document, very weak; nevertheless, the Ministry for Foreign Affairs does not forbid it.

The arrests were carried out under manifold pretexts, but all these pretexts may be summarised under two general conceptions. Arrests were carried out either for political or for racial reasons. The arrests were individual or collective, in both cases.

Pretexts of a political nature:

From 1941, the French observed that there was a certain synchronism between the evolution of political events and the rhythm of arrests. Exhibit RF 301, which is at the end of your document book, will show this. Pages 3 to 6.

The Tribunal will be able to follow, Pages 3 to 6. On Page 3, a description is given by the Ministry of Prisoners of war and Deportees of the conditons under which these arrests took place, beginning in 1941; it was a critical period in the German history of the war, since it was from 1941 that Germany was at war with the Soviet

Union.

Page 7 of the German translation:

"The synchronism between the evolution of political events and the rhythm of arrests is evident. The suppression of the line of demarcation between the occupied and non-occupied zones, the establishment of resistance groups, the formation of the Maquis - which was the result of forced labour - the landings in North Africa and in Normandy, all had immediate repercussions on the figures for arrests, of which the maximum curve is reached for the period of May to August 1944, especially in the Southern zone and particularly in the region of Lyons.

We repeat that these arrests were carried out by members of all the categories of the German repressive system: the Gestapo in uniform or in civilian clothes, the SD, the Gendarmerie, particularly at the demarcation line, the Wehrmacht and the SS."

Page 4, second paragraph :

"The arrests took on the characteristics of collective operations. In Paris, as a result of an attempted assassination, the 18th Arrondissement was surrounded by the Feldgendarmerie. Its inhabitants, men, women, and children, could not return to their homes and spent the night where they could find shelter. A round-up was carried out in the Arrondissement."

I do not think that it is necessary to read the following paragraph, which deals with the arrests at the University of Clermont-Ferrand, which the Tribunal will certainly remember, and also the arrests in Brittany in 1944, at the time of the invasion. The last paragraph, at the bottom of Page 11:

"I cannot enumerate the cities and villages where, on the pretext of conspiracy or attempted assassinations, whole families were made to suffer. The Germans resorted to round-ups when compulsory labour recruitment no longer furnished them with sufficient workers.

Round-up in Grenoble, the 24th of December 1943, Christmas Eve

Round-up in Cluny, Saone-et-Loire, in March 1944.

Round-up in Figeac in May 1944.

Most Frenchmen who were rounded up in this way were, in reality, not used for work in Germany, but were deported to be interned in concentration camps."

We might multiply the examples of these arbitrary arrests by delving into official documents which have been submitted by Luxembourg, Denmark, Norway, Holland, and Belgium. These round-ups were never legally justified, they were never even represented as an action taken in accordance with the pseudo- law of hostages to which we have already referred. They were always arbitrary and carried out without any apparent reason, for no apparent reason, or at any rate, without its being possible to motivate them even as a reprisal for the act of any Frenchman, Other collective arrests were made for racial reasons. They were of the same odious nature as those made for political reasons.

On Page 5 of the official document of the Ministry of Prisoners of War and Deportees, the Tribunal may read a few odious details connected with these racial arrests; the third line at the bottom of the page.

"Certain German policemen were especially entrusted to seek out Jewish persons, according to their physiognomy. They called this group 'The Brigade of Physiognomists'. This verification sometimes took place in a public way as far as men were concerned. (At the railway-station at Nice, some were stripped with a revolver pointed at them).

The Parisians remember these roundups in their quarters. The big police buses transported old men, women and children and brought them en masse to the Velodrome D'Hiver, under dreadful sanitary conditions, before taking them to Drancy, where they awaited deportation. The round-up of the month of August 1941, has become infamous for its sad associations. All the exits of the subway of the 11th Arrondissement were closed and all the Jews in that quarter were arrested and imprisoned. The round-up of December 1941 was particularly aimed at intellectual circles. Then there were the round-ups of July 1942.

All the cities in the southern zone, particularly Lyons, Grenoble, Cannes, and Nice, where many Jews had taken refuge, experienced these round-ups after the total occupation of France."

Then there is a revolting detail:

"The Germans sought out all Jewish children who had found refuge with private citizens or with institutions. In May, 1944, they proceeded to arrest the children of the Colony of Eyzieux, and to arrest children who had sought refuge in the Colonies of the U.G.I.F. in June and July 1944."

I do not believe that these children were enemies of the German people, nor that they represented a danger of any kind to the German army in France.

THE PRESIDENT: Perhaps we had better break off now.

(The Tribunal adjourned until 25th January 1946, at 1000 hours.)

Forty-third day:
Friday, 25th January, 1946

COURT OFFICER: Your Honours, Defendants Kaltenbrunner and Streicher will be absent from this morning's session.

M. DUBOST: Yesterday I was reading from an official French document, which appears in your document book. - permit me to remind you of it - under the title "Report of the Ministry of Prisoners of War and Deportees.". It concerned the seizure by the Germans of Jewish children in France, who were taken from private houses or public institutions where they had been placed.

With your permission I will come back to a statement which I had previously made, concerning the execution of orders given by the German General Staff with the approval of the Reich Minister for Foreign Affairs, to arrest all French generals and, in reprisal, to arrest as well all the families of these generals who might be dissentients, in other words who were on the side of our Allies.

In accordance with Article 21 of the Charter, the Tribunal will not require facts of public knowledge to be proved. In the enormous amount of facts which we submit to you there are many which are known but not of public knowledge. They are few, but there are certain facts, nevertheless, which are both known and also of public knowledge in all countries. There is the famous case of the deportation of the family of General Giraud, and I shall allow myself to recall to the Tribunal the six principal points concerning this deportation. First: we all remember having learned through the Allied radio that Madame Giraud, wife of General Giraud ...

THE PRESIDENT: What is it that you are going to ask us to take judicial notice of with reference to the deportation of General Giraud's family?.

M. DUBOST: I have to ask the Tribunal, Mr. President, to apply as far as these facts are concerned, to Article 21 of the Charter, namely, the provision specifying that the Tribunal will not require facts to be proved which are of public knowledge.

Second: I request the Tribunal to hear my statement of these facts which we consider to be of public knowledge, for they are known not only in France but in America, as the American Army learned something of these events.

THE PRESIDENT: The words of Article 21 are not "of public knowledge" but "of common knowledge". It is not quite the same thing.

M. DUBOST: I have before me the French translation of the Charter. I am interpreting according to the French translation: "The Tribunal will not require that facts of public knowledge ("notoriete publique") be proved."

We interpret these words thus: it is not necessary to bring documentary or testifying proof of facts universally known.

THE PRESIDENT: You say "universally known," but supposing, for instance, the members of the Tribunal did not know the facts? How could it then be taken that they were of common knowledge? The members of the Tribunal may be ignorant of the facts. It is difficult for them to take cognisance of the facts if they do not know them.

M. DUBOST: It is a question of fact which will be decided by the Tribunal. The Tribunal will say whether it does or does not know that these six points which I shall recall to it are correct.

THE PRESIDENT: The Tribunal will retire.

(A recess was taken)

THE PRESIDENT: The Tribunal is of the opinion that the facts with reference to General Giraud's deportation and the deportation of his family, although they are very probably matters of common knowledge or of public knowledge within France, cannot be said to be of common knowledge or of public knowledge within the meaning of Article 21, which applies generally to the world.

Of course, if the French Prosecution have governmental documents or reports from France which state the facts with reference to the deportation of General Giraud, the matter assumes a different aspect, and if there are such documents the Tribunal will, of course, consider them.

M. DUBOST: I must bring proof that the crimes committed individually by the leaders of the German police in each city and in each region of the occupied authorities, the will of the German Government, a fact which permits us to charge all the defendants one by one. I shall not be able to prove this by submitting documents alone. That you may consider it a fact, it is necessary that you accept as valid the evidence which I am about to read. This evidence was collected by the American and French Armies, and the French Service for Investigation of War Crimes. The Tribunal will excuse me if I am obliged to read numerous documents. This systematic will can only be proved by showing that everywhere and in every case the German police used the same methods concerning patriots whom they interned or detained.

Internment or imprisonment in France was in civilian prisons which the Germans had seized, or in certain sections of French prisons which the Germans had requisitioned, which they occupied, and which all French officials were forbidden to enter. The prisoners in all these penitentiaries were subject to the same regime. We shall prove this by reading to you depositions of prisoners from each of these German penal institutions in France or the Western occupied countries. This regime was absolutely inhuman. It allowed the prisoners to survive only under the most precarious conditions.

In Lyons, at Fort Montluc, the women received as their only food a cup of herb tea at 7 o'clock in the morning and a spoonful of soup with a small piece of bread at 5 o'clock in the evening. This is established by Document 555-F, which you will find the eleventh in your document book, which we submit as Exhibit RF 302.

THE PRESIDENT: One moment. I have not found the document.

M. DUBOST: The eleventh in the document book, Document 555- F, first page of the document.

THE PRESIDENT: Yes, M. Dubost, but you see, these document books are not paged or tabbed in any way. Yes, we have it now.

M. DUBOST: The first page of this document, second paragraph, is an analysis of the depositions which were received. It is sufficient to refer to this analysis. I shall take some lines from the following deposition. The witness declares that at their arrival at Fort Montluc,

> "the prisoners who were taken in the round-up by the Gestapo on 20 September 1943, were stripped of all their property.
>
> They were treated in a brutal fashion. The food rations were quite inadequate. The modesty of the women was not respected."

The same deposition, dated 9 October 1944, at Saint Gingolph: This deposition refers to the arrests made at Saint Gingolph, which were carried out in the month of September 1943. The witness relates on page 2, fifth paragraph, at the top of the page:

> "After returning from the interrogation the young boys had their toes burned by means of cotton-wool which had been dipped in petrol; others had their calves burned by the flames of a blow-lamp ... others were bitten by police dogs..."

DR. MERKEL (Counsel for the Gestapo): The French Prosecution submits here documents which do not represent sworn affidavits, and confirmations which do not show who took them. As a matter of principle I have to protest against these mere depositions of persons who did not take an oath, and which do not represent sworn affidavits, being admitted as proof at this trial.

THE PRESIDENT: Is that all you have to say?

DR. MERKEL: Yes, Sir.

THE PRESIDENT: We will hear M. Dubost's answer.

M. DUBOST: Mr. President, the Charter, which goes so far as to admit evidence of public knowledge, has not fixed any rules as to the manner in which this evidence, which shall be submitted to you as proof, shall be presented. The Charter leaves the Tribunal free to decide whether this or that method of investigation is acceptable, or whether the way in which these investigations have been carried out is regular, if it conforms to the customs and usages of my country. As a matter of fact, it is certain that all official records of the police and gendarmerie may be accepted without the witnesses being under oath. Moreover, according to the provisions of the Charter, all investigations for the discovery of war crimes should be deemed to have probative value. Article 21 says:

> "The Tribunal shall not require proof of facts of common knowledge but shall take judicial notice thereof. It shall also take judicial notice of official governmental documents and reports of the United Nations, including the acts and documents of the committees set up in the various Allied countries for the investigation of war crimes, and the records and findings of military or other Tribunals of any of the United Nations."

THE PRESIDENT: M. Dubost, is the document that you are reading to us either an official government document or a report, or is it an act or document of a committee set up in France?

M. DUBOST: This report, Mr. President, comes from the Surete Nationale. You can establish that by examining the second sheet of the copy which you have in your hand, at the top to the left: Direction Generale de la Surete Nationale. Commissariat Special de Saint Gingolph. Record of witnesses' testimony.

THE PRESIDENT: May we see the original document?

M. DUBOST: Certainly. This document was submitted to the Secretary of the Tribunal. The Secretary has only to bring that document to you.

THE PRESIDENT: Very well. Is this a certified copy?

M. DUBOST: It is a copy certified by the Director of the Cabinet of the Ministry of Justice.

THE PRESIDENT: M. Dubost, I am told that the French prosecutors have all the original documents and are not depositing them in the way it is done by the other prosecutors. Is that so?

M. DUBOST: The French prosecutors submitted the originals of yesterday's session, and they were handed over this morning to M. Martin.

THE PRESIDENT: Well, we wish to see the original document. We understand it is in the hands of the French Secretary. We should like to see it.

(A document was submitted to the Tribunal)

M. DUBOST: I have sent for it, Mr. President. This document is a certified copy of the original, which is preserved in the archives of the Service for Inquiry into Enemy War Crimes. This certification was made, on the one hand, by the French Delegate of the Prosecution - you will see the signature of M. de Menthon on the document you have - on the other, by the Director of the Cabinet of the Minister of Justice, M. Zambeaux, with the official seal of the French Ministry of Justice.

THE PRESIDENT: It does appear to be a governmental document. It is the document of a committee set up by France for the investigation of war crimes, is it not?

M. DUBOST: Mr. President, it is a document which comes from the Office of National Security (Direction Generale de la Surete Nationale), which was set up in connection with an investigation of War Crimes, as prescribed by our French Office for the Investigation of War Crimes.

The original remained in Paris at the War Crimes Office but the certified copy which you have was signed by the Director of the Cabinet of the Ministry of Justice in Paris.

THE PRESIDENT: Yes, M. Dubost, I was not asking whether it was a true copy or not; the question I was asking was whether or not it was, within Article 21, either a governmental document or a report of the United Nations, or an act or a document of a committee set up in France for the investigation of war crimes and I was asking whether it is, and it appears to be so. It is, is it not?

M. DUBOST: Yes, Sir.

THE PRESIDENT: Do you wish to add anything to what you have said?

M. DUBOST: No, I have nothing to add.

THE PRESIDENT: (to Dr. Merkel) Now you may speak, Sir.

DR. MERKEL: I should only like to stress briefly that these reports which are presented here are not reports of an official government agency, and cannot be considered as governmental reports. Rather, they are only minutes which have been taken in police offices, and thus can in no way be authentic declarations of a government or of an investigating committee. I emphasise once more that these declarations, which have certainly been taken, partially at least, in petty police offices, have not been made under oath, and do not represent sworn statements, and I have to protest firmly against their being considered as evidence here.

THE PRESIDENT: Do you wish to add anything?

DR. MERKEL: No.

THE PRESIDENT: Who is M. Binaud? J. Binaud?

M. DUBOST: He is the Police Inspector of the Special Police, who was attached to the Special Commissariat of Saint Gingolph.

I must correct an error made by the defence counsel, who said this was a petty police office. This was a frontier post. The Special Commissariats at the frontier post are all important offices even though they are located in small towns. I think it is similar in all countries.

THE PRESIDENT: Well, M. Dubost, you understand what the problem is? It is a question of the interpretation of Article 21.

M. DUBOST: I understand.

THE PRESIDENT: The Tribunal requires your assistance upon that interpretation, as to whether this document does come under the terms of Article 21. If you have anything to say upon that subject we will be glad to hear it.

M. DUBOST: Mr. President, it seems to me impossible that the Tribunal should rule out this and similar documents which I am going to present, for all these documents bear, for authentication, not only the signature of the French representative at this Tribunal, but that of the Delegate of the Minister of Justice from the War Crimes Commission as well. Examine the imprint beside, the second signature. It is the seal.

THE PRESIDENT: Do not go too fast; tell us where the signatures are.

M. DUBOST: (Indicates on document) Here, your Honours, is a note of the release of this document to the French Prosecutor as an element of proof by the Service for Investigation of War Crimes, and below is the signature of the Director of the Cabinet of the French Minister of Justice, the Keeper of the Seals, and, in addition, over this signature, is the imprint of the Minister of Justice. You may read: Enemy War Crimes Commission.

THE PRESIDENT: Is this the substance of the matter, that this was an inquiry by the police into these facts, and that police inquiry was recorded, and then the Minister of Justice, for the purposes of this trial, adopted that police report? Is that the substance of it?

M. DUBOST: That is correct, Mr. President. I think that we agree. The Service for Investigation of War Crimes in France is directly attached to the Ministry of Justice. It carries out investigations. These investigations are made by the police authorities, such as M. Binaud, Inspector of Special Police, attached to the Special Commissariat of Saint Gingolph.

THE PRESIDENT: The Tribunal would like to know when the Service for Investigation of War Crimes was established.

M. DUBOST: I cannot give you the exact date from memory, but this Service was set up in France the day after the liberation. It began to function in October 1944.

THE PRESIDENT: Was it established after the police report was made?

M. DUBOST: In the month of September, about the same time.

THE PRESIDENT: September of what year?

M. DUBOST: In September, 1944, this Service for Investigation of War Crimes in France was established, and this Service it was which gave orders.

THE PRESIDENT: Then the police inquiry was held under the Service? You see, the police report is dated 9 October, and therefore the police report appears to have been made after the Service had been set up. Is that right?

M. DUBOST: You have the evidence, Mr. President. If you look at the top of the second page at the left, it shows the beginning of the record and you read: "Purpose: Investigation of atrocities committed by Germans against civilian population."

These investigations were prescribed by the Service for Investigation of War Crimes.

THE PRESIDENT: Yes. That would appear to be so if the Service was established in September, and this police investigation is dated 9 October.

The Tribunal will adjourn for consideration of this question.

(A recess was taken)

THE PRESIDENT: The Tribunal has considered the arguments which have been addressed to it, and is of the opinion that the document offered by counsel for France is a document of a committee set up for the investigation of war crimes within the meaning of Article 21 of the Charter. The fact that it is not upon oath does not prevent it being such a document within Article 21, of which the Tribunal is directed to take judicial notice. The question of its probative value would of course be considered under Article 19 of the Charter, and therefore in accordance with Article 19 and Article 21 of the Charter the document will be admitted in evidence, and the objection of counsel for the Gestapo is denied.

The Tribunal would wish that all original documents should be filed with the General Secretary of the Tribunal, and that when they are being discussed in Court the original documents should be present in Court at the time.

DR. BABEL (Counsel for the SS): I have been informed that General Giraud and his family were, in fact, deported to Germany upon the orders of Himmler, but that they were treated very well, were billeted in a villa, and were brought back to France in good health; also that things went well with them and that they are still well today. I do not see -

THE PRESIDENT: Counsel, forgive me for interrupting you. But the Tribunal is not now considering the case of General Giraud and his family. Are you unable to hear?

What I was saying was that you were making some application in connection with the deportation of General Giraud, and were stating to us what you allege to be facts, as to that deportation. The Tribunal is not considering that matter. The Tribunal has already ruled that it cannot take judicial notice of the facts as to General Giraud's deportation.

DR. BABEL: I was of the opinion that what I had to say might bring about an explanation by the prosecution, and might expedite the trial in that respect. That was the purpose of my inquiry.

THE PRESIDENT: Was that what you stated? ...I am merely pointing out to you that we are not now considering General Giraud's case.

DR. BABEL: Yes.

M. DUBOST: If the Tribunal will permit me to continue ? It seems to me necessary to come back to the proof which I propose to submit. I must show that through uniformity of methods, of torture used in each bureau of the German Police...

THE PRESIDENT: Have you finished the document we have just admitted?

M. DUBOST: Yes, Mr. President; I have completed this and I will now read from other documents. But first I would like to sum up the proofs which I have to submit this morning by reading these documents.

I said that I was going to demonstrate how, through the uniformity of ill-treatment inflicted by all branches of the German Police upon prisoners under interrogation, we are faced with a realisation of a common will, of which we cannot give you direct proof, as we did yesterday, regarding hostages, by bringing you papers signed by Keitel, but at which we shall arrive by a way just as certain; for this uniformity of methods implies a uniformity of will, which we can only attribute to the very head of the police, that is to say, the German Government itself, to which the defendants belonged.

This Document 555-F, from which I have just read, refers to the ill-treatment of prisoners at Fort Montluc in Lyons.

I pass to Document 556-F, which we shall submit as Exhibit RF 303, which relates to the prison regime at Marseilles, and which follows the Document 555-F, in the document book.

The Tribunal will note that this is an official record taken by the Military Security Service of Vaucluse, concerning the atrocities committed by Germans against political prisoners, and that this record includes the written deposition of M. Mousson, chief of an intelligence service who was arrested on 16 August 1943 and then transferred on 30 August 1943 to St. Pierre prison at Marseilles. In the last paragraph of the first page of this document we read:

"Transferred to Marseilles, St. Pierre prison on 30 August 1943, placed in room P, 25 metres long, 5 metres wide. We are crammed in, as many as 75 and often 80. Two straw mattresses for three. Repulsive hygienic conditions: lice, fleas, bed-bugs, tainted food. For no reason at all comrades are beaten and put in cells two or three days without food."

Following page, fourth paragraph

"Taken into custody again 15 May in a rather brutal way I was imprisoned in the prison of Ste. Anne and ..." 5th paragraph: "Living conditions in Ste. Anne: deplorable hygiene; food supplied by National Relief Society."

Next page, second paragraph:

"Living conditions in Petites Beaumettes: Food, just enough to keep one alive; no parcels Red Cross gives many, but we receive few.

The prison of Poitiers ." It concerns (I repeat) - prisons entirely under control of the Germans. The prison of Poitiers, Document 558-F, which we submit as Exhibit RF 304. Attached to the last page of this document is a report from the Press Section of the American Information Service in Paris, dated 18th October 1944. The Tribunal should know that all these reports were incorporated with the documents which were presented by the French Office for the Investigation of War Crimes. We read under number two:

"M. Claeys was arrested 14 December 1943, by the Gestapo and kept in custody in the "Pierre Levee" Prison until 26 August 1944. While in jail he asked for a mattress, as he had been wounded in the war. He was told that he would get it if he confessed. He had to sleep on straw of only one inch thickness. Seven men in one room 4m x 2m x 2.80m. use of WC twice a day only. Twenty days without leaving of cell. WC was a great discomfort to him because of wounds. The Germans refused to do anything about it."

Paragraph 4 (b).

"Another prisoner weighed 120 kilograms and lost 30 kilograms in a month. Was kept in isolation cell for a month. Was tortured there and died of gangrene of legs due to wounds caused by torture. Died after ten days of agony, alone and without help."

Under paragraph 5 (a), the methods of torture:

"Victim was kept bent up with his hands round his right leg. Was then thrown on the ground and beaten for twenty minutes. If he fainted, they would throw a pail of water in his face. This was to make him speak.

M. Francheteau was thus treated for four days out of six. In some cases, patient was not tied. If he fell they would pick him up by his hair, and go on."

Page two.

"At other times the victim was put naked in a special punishment cell, and his hands were tied to an iron grating above his head. He was then beaten until he talked.

(b) Beating as above was not usual, but M. Claeys has friends who have seen electric tortures. One electric wire was attached to the foot and another wire was placed in different parts of the body.

6. Torture was all the more horrible as the Germans, in many cases, had no clear ideas as to what information they wanted, and just tortured aimlessly."

And at the very end, the five last lines.

"One torture consisted in hanging up the victim by the hands, which were tied behind the back until the shoulders were completely dislocated. Afterwards the soles of the feet were cut with razor blades, and then the victim was made to walk on salt."

The Prisons of the North: This is Document 560-F, which follows in your document book and is submitted as Exhibit RF 305. It also comes from the American War Crimes Commission. On Page 1, under the letter "A" you will read:

"A general report of Professor Paucot on the atrocities committed by the Germans in Northern France and in Belgium. The report covers, the activities of the German police in France: in Arras, Bethune, Lille Valenciennes, Malo les Bains, La Madeleine, Quincy, Loos; in Belgium: Saint Gilles, Fort de Huy, and Camp de Belveroo. This report is accompanied by seventy-three depositions of victims. From examination of these testimonies the fact emerges that the brutal barbarity of methods used during the interrogations was the same as in the various places cited."

This synthesis which I have read to you is from the American report. It seems to me unnecessary to stress this as it is confirmed on the first page. The Tribunal can read further on Pages 4, 5, 6 and 7 a detailed description of the atrocities, systematic and all identical, which the German police inflicted to force confessions.

On Page 7, the fifth paragraph, you will find:

"A prisoner captured while trying to escape was left in his cell to the fury of police dogs who tore him to bits."

On Page 17, second paragraph of the German text there is reproduced the report of M. Prouille, which, as an exception, I shall read, because of the nature of the facts.

"Condemned by the German Tribunal to eighteen months of imprisonment for possessing arms and after having been in the prisons of Arras, Bethune and Loos, I was sent to Germany.

As a result of ill-treatment in Eastern Prussia I was obliged to have my eyes looked after. Having been taken to an infirmary, a German doctor put drops in my eyes. A few hours later, after painful suffering, I became blind. After spending several days in the prison of Fresnes I was sent to the clinic of Quize-Vingt in Paris. Professor Guillamat examined me, and certified that my eyes had been burned by a corrosive agent."

Under number 561-F, I shall read a document from the American War Crimes Commission, which we submit as Exhibit RF 306. The Tribunal will find on Page 2, proof in that M. Herrera was present at tortures inflicted on numerous persons, and saw a Pole, by the name of Riptz, have the soles of his feet burned. Then his head was split open with an axe. After the wound healed he was shot. Quoting again:

"Commander Grandier, who had had a leg fractured in the war, was threatened by those who conducted the interrogations that they would fracture his other leg. This was carried out. When he was half mad as a result of a hypodermic injection, the Germans did away with him."

We do not care to take more of your time than necessary, but it is quite proper that the Tribunal should know these American official documents in their entirety, as all of them show in a very exact way the tortures carried out by the various German police services in numerous regions of France, and give evidence as to the similarity of methods used.

Document 571-F, which we submit as Exhibit RF 307, of which we shall only read one four-line paragraph - page thirty- six, third paragraph from the bottom in the

German text, fourth paragraph of page twenty - runs as follows:

"M. Robert Vanessche, of Tourcoing, states:

I was arrested 22 February 1944 at Mouscron in Belgium by the Gestapo, who were dressed in civilian clothing. During the interrogation they wore military uniform."

I omit a paragraph.

"I was interrogated for the second time at Cand in the main German prison, where I remained thirty-one days. There I was shut up for two or three hours in a sort of wooden coffin where one could breathe only through three holes in the top."

Page 38 of the same document:

"M. Remy, residing at Armentieres, states:

Arrested May 2, 1944, at Armentieres I arrived at the Gestapo headquarters, 18 Rue Francois Debats, in La Madeleine, about three o'clock the same day. I was subjected to interrogation on two different occasions. The first time, for about an hour, I had to lie on my stomach, and received about 120 lashes with an oxhide whip. The second interrogation lasted a little longer. The same thing followed: I was laid on my stomach and lashed. As I would not talk, they stripped me and put me in the 'bathtub.'

On 5 May I was subjected to a new interrogation at Loos. That day they hung me by my feet and rained blows on my body. As I refused to speak, they untied me and laid me again on my stomach. As the suffering drew cries from me they kicked me in the face with their boots. As a result I lost seventeen lower teeth."

The names of two of the torturers follow, but are of no concern to us here. We are merely trying to show that the torturers everywhere used the same methods. This could only have been done in execution of orders given by their chiefs.

Page 48, the testimony of M. Guerin, first paragraph, eighth line.

"As I refused to admit anything, one of the interrogators put my scarf around my mouth to stifle my cries. Another German policeman took my head between his legs, and two others, one on each side of me, began to beat me with a club on my loins. Each beat me twenty-five times; each time I got up. This session lasted two hours. The next morning they began again, and it lasted as long as the day before. These tortures were inflicted upon me because on 11 November, I, with my comrades of the Resistance, had taken part in a manifestation, by placing a wreath on the memorial to those who fell in the war of 1914-18."

Page 48, page 29 of the German text. Report of M. Alfred Deudon. Paragraph three. Here is the ill-treatment which was inflicted upon him.

"18 August sensitive parts were struck with a hammer. 19 August was passed under water. 20 August my head was placed in a squeezing apparatus. 21 and 24 August I was chained day and night. 26 August I was chained day and night and hung by the arms."

Page 49; Page 30 of the German text. Report of M. Delltombe, arrested by the Gestapo 14 June 1944. Paragraph two:

"Thursday, 15 June, at eight o'clock in the morning, I was taken to the torture cellar. There they demanded that I confess the sabotage which I had carried out with my group, and denounce my comrades and disclose our hiding place. Because I did not, the torture commenced. They made me put my hands behind my back. They put on special handcuffs and hung me by my wrists. Then they beat me with an oxhide whip, principally on the loins and in the face. That day the torture lasted three hours.

Friday, 16 June, the same thing took place only for an hour and a half, for I could stand it no longer, and they took me back to my cell on a stretcher.

Saturday, the tortures began with even more severity. At last I was obliged to confess my sabotage, for the brutes stuck needles in my arms. After that they left me alone until 10 August; then they had me called to the office and told me I was condemned to death. I was put on a train of deportees going to Brussels, from which I was freed on 3 September by Brussels patriots.

Page 56:

Women were subjected to the same treatment as men, To the physical pain the sadism of the torturers added the moral anguish, especially mortifying for a woman or a young girl, of being stripped nude by her torturers. Pregnancy did not save them from lashes. When brutality brought about a miscarriage they were left without any care, exposed to all the hazards and complications of these criminal abortions."

This is the text of the summary drawn up by the American officer who carried out this investigation.

The Tribunal will find, on Page 58 - Page 36 in the German text - at the bottom of the French text, the report of Madame Sindemans, who was arrested in Paris on 24 February, 1944,"by four soldiers each armed with a submachine gun, and two other Germans in civilian clothes holding revolvers :

"Having looked into my handbag, they found three identification cards. Searching my room, they discovered the pads and stamp of the Kommandantur and German workman passes which I had succeeded in stealing from them the day before."

Immediately, they handcuffed me and took me to be interrogated. Getting no reply, they slapped me in the face with such force that I fell from my chair. Then they whipped me with a rubber hose, full in the face. This interrogation began at 10 o'clock in the morning and ended at 11 o'clock that night. I must tell you that I had been pregnant for three months."

We shall submit now Documents 563-F and 564-F as Exhibit RF 308. It is a report concerning the atrocities committed by the Gestapo in Bourges. We shall read from a part of this report, Page 6 of the French text, Page 5 of the German text.

THE PRESIDENT: M. Dubost, how do you establish what this document is? It appears to be the report of M. Marc Toledano.

M. DUBOST: That is correct, Mr. President. This report was incorporated with the rest of the documents in the same bundle, into the document presented by the French Commission for the Investigation of War Crimes, as is evident from the official signature of M. Zambeaux on the original, which is in the hands of the Secretary of the Court. I shall read from it, Page 5. This is the first page of the original:

"I, the undersigned, Madame Bondeux, supervisor of the Prison in Bourges, certify that nine men, mostly youths, were subjected to heinous treatment. With their hands bound behind their backs and chains on their feet for 15- 20 days, it was absolutely impossible for them to carry on the normal functions of life. They screamed with hunger. In the face of this situation several ordinary criminal prisoners showed their willingness to help these martyrs by making small packets from their own provisions, which I passed to them in the evening. A certain German supervisor, whom I knew under the first name of Michel, threw their bread in a corner of the cell and at night came to beat them. All these young men were shot on 20 November 1943.

Moreover, a woman named Hartwig of Chavannes, I believe - told me that she had remained for four days bound to a chair. At all events, I can testify that her body was completely bruised."

On Page 6, Page 5 of the German text, we shall read the statement of M. Labussiere, who is a captain on the reserve and teacher at Marseille-les-Aubigny. Eighth line from the bottom of the page:

"On the 11th I was twice beaten with an oxhide whip, being forced to bend over a bench. The muscles of my thighs and my calves were stretched out. At first I received some 30 blows from a heavy whip, then the session was continued with another instrument which had a buckle at the end, I then was struck on the anus, on the thighs, and on the calves. To do this my torturer got up on a bench and made me spread my legs. Then with a very thin oxhide thong he finished by giving me some 20 more biting lashes. When I picked myself up I was dizzy and I fell to the ground. I was always kicked up again. Needless to say, the handcuffs were never taken off my wrists."

I recoil from reading the remainder of this testimony. I pass on to the bottom of Page 7, third line from the end. The details which preceded are horrifying.

"At ten o'clock, on the 12th, after having beaten a woman, Paoli came to find me and said: 'Dog, you have no heart. It was your wife I have just beaten. I'll do it as long as you won't talk.' He wanted me to disclose the place of our hide-out and the names of my comrades.

From 2 o'clock to 6 o'clock I was again, in the torture chamber. I could hardly crawl. Before he let me come in Paoli said 'I give you five minutes to tell me all that you know. If after these five minutes you've said nothing you'll be shot at 3 o'clock. Your wife will be shot at six, and your boy will be sent to Germany.'"

Page 9:

"After signing the record of my interrogation the German said to me: 'Look at your face. See what we can make of a man in five days. You haven't seen the finish yet!' And he added: 'Now get out of here. You make me sick!'" And the witness concluded with: "I was, in fact, covered with ordure from head to foot. They put me in a cart and took me back to my cell. During these five days I certainly had received more than 700 blows with an oxhide whip."

A large hematosis (blood clot) appeared on both his buttocks. A doctor had to operate. His comrades in custody would not go near him because of the foul odour from the abscesses covering his body as a result of the ill-treatment. On 20 November, the date on which he was interrogated, he had not yet recovered from his wounds.

Page 10. His testimony concludes with a general statement of the methods of punishment:

"(1) An oxhide thong

(2) The bath: The victim was plunged headfirst into a tub of cold water until he was asphyxiated. Then they gave him artificial respiration. If he did not talk, they repeated the process several times. With soaking clothes he spent the night in a cold cell.

(3) Electric current: The terminals were placed on the hands, then on the feet, and in the ears, then one in the anus and another on the end of the penis.

(4) The crushing of the testicles in a press specially prepared for the purpose: Twisting of the testicles was frequent.

(5) Hanging: The victim's hands were handcuffed together behind his back. A hook was slipped through his handcuffs, and the victim was lifted by a pulley. At first they jerked him up and down. Later, they left him suspended for varying, fairly long, periods. Often, arms were dislocated. I saw in the camp Lt. Lefevre, who, having remained suspended for more than four hours, had lost the use of both arms.

(6) Burning with a soldering lamp or with matches.

On 2 July my comrade Laloue, a teacher from Cher, who had been subjected to most of these tortures at Bourges came to the camp. One arm had been put out of joint and he was unable to move the fingers of his right hand as a result of the hanging. He had been subjected to whipping and electricity. He had been burned by sharp-pointed matches which had been driven under all the nails of his hands and feet. His wrists and ankles had been wrapped with rolls of wadding, and this had been set on fire. While it was burning, a German plunged a pointed knife into the soles of his feet several times and another lashed him with an oxhide whip. The phosphorus burns had eaten away several fingers as far as the second joint. Abscesses which had developed had burst, and this saved him from blood poisoning."

Page 13 of the same document, Page 14 in the German text; we read, under the signature of one of the Chiefs of the General Staff of the French Forces of the Interior who freed the Department of Cher, M. Magnon - signature authenticated by the French official authorities whom you know - the following:

"Since the liberation of Bourges, 6 September, 1944, an inspection of the Gestapo cellars disclosed an instrument of torture, a ring composed of several balls of hardwood with steel spikes. There was a device for tightening the bracelet round the victim's wrist. This bracelet was seen by numerous soldiers and leaders of the Maquis of Menetou-Salon.

It was in the hands of Adjutant Neuilly, now in the first battalion of the 34th Brigade.

A drawing is attached to this declaration.

Commander Magnon, the undersigned, certifies having seen the instrument described above."

We now submit Document 565-F, from the Military Security Service of the Department of Vaucluse, which becomes Exhibit RF 309. It is a repetition of the same methods. We do not consider it necessary to dwell upon them.

We will now turn to Document 567-F, which we submit as Exhibit RF 310. It refers to the tortures practised by the German police in Besancon. Page 1 of our French text and of the German text is a deposition of M. Dommergues, Professor at Besancon. This deposition was collected by the American War Crimes Commission - under Captain Miller. We shall read from the statement of M. Dommergues, Professor at Besancon:

"Arrested on 11 February 1944. Violently struck with an oxhide thong during the interrogation. While a woman who was being tortured cried out, they made him believe that it was his own wife. He saw a comrade hung with a weight of 50 kilograms on each foot. Another had his eyes pierced with pins. A child lost its voice completely."

This is from the American War Crimes. Commission, summing up M. Dommergues' deposition. This document includes a second part, 567 F (b). We shall read some excerpts from Pages 3, 4, 5, 6 and 7 of this document, Page 9 of the German text.

THE PRESIDENT: Whose statement is it?

M. DUBOST: Page 3, Mr. President.

THE PRESIDENT: Yes, but you see, one of the members has not got his document marked, and I want to know whose statement it is you are referring to Is it Dr. Gomet?

M. DUBOST: It is not a deposition, it is a letter sent by Dr. Gomet, Secretary of the Council of the Departmental College of Doubs and of the National Association of Physicians. This letter is addressed by him to the Chief Medical Officer of the Feldkommandantur in Besancon on 11 September, 1943. Here is it's text:

"Doctor-in-Chief and Honourable Colleague:

I have the honour to deliver to you the note which I have drafted at your request and addressed to our colleagues of the Department in our memorandum of 1 September.

In addition, my conscience compels me to take up another subject with you.

Quite recently I had to treat a Frenchman who had wounds and widespread ecchymosis on his face and body, as a result of the torture apparatus employed by the German security service. He is a man of good standing, holding an important appointment under the French Government, and he was arrested because they thought he could furnish certain information. They could make no accusation against him, as is proved by the fact that he was released in a few days, when the interrogation to which they wanted to subject him was finished.

He was subjected to torture, not as a penalty or as the result of a trial, but for the sole purpose of forcing him to speak under stress of violence and pain.

As for myself, as representative here of French Medical Corps, my conscience and a strict conception of my duty force me to inform you of what I have just observed in the exercise of my profession. I appeal to your conscience as a doctor, and, as we have accepted the task of protecting the physical health of our fellow human beings, which is the duty of every doctor, ask you if we should not intervene here."

Returning to Page 4. He must have had a reply from the German doctor, for Dr. Gomet writes him a second letter, and here is the text:

"Doctor-in-Chief and Honourable Colleague:

You were good enough to note the facts which I put before you in my letter of 11 September, 1943, regarding the torture apparatus used by the German Security Service during the interrogation of a French official for whom I had subsequently to prescribe treatment. You asked me, as was quite natural, if you could visit the person in question yourself. I replied, at our recent meeting, that the person concerned did not know of the step which I had taken ; and I did not know whether he would authorise me to give his name. I wish to emphasise, in fact, that I myself am solely responsible for this step. The person through whom I learned, by virtue of my profession, the facts which I have just related to you, had nothing to do with this report. The question is strictly professional. My conscience as a doctor has forced me to bring this matter to your attention. I reported only what I knew from absolutely reliable observation, and I guarantee the truth of my statement on my honour as a man, as a physician, and a Frenchman.

My patient was interrogated twice by the German Security Service about the end of August, 1943. I had to examine him on 8 September 1943, that is to say, about ten days after he left prison, where he had in vain asked for medical attention, He had a palpebral ecchymosis on the left side and abrasions in the region of his right temple, which he said were made with a sort of disc which they had placed upon his head and which they struck with small clubs. He had ecchymosis on the backs of his hands, these having been placed, according to what he told me, in a squeezing apparatus. On the front of his legs there were still scars with scabs and small surface wounds - the result, he told me, of blows administered with flexible rods studded with short spikes.

Obviously, I cannot swear to the means by which the ecchymosis and wounds were produced, but I note that their appearance is in complete agreement with the explanations given me.

It will be easy for you, Sir, to learn if an apparatus of the kind to which I allude is really being used by the German Security Service."

I pass over the rest.

THE PRESIDENT: It may be convenient for counsel and others to know that the Tribunal will not sit in open session tomorrow, as it has many administrative matters to consider. We will adjourn now until 2 o'clock.

(A recess was taken)

COURT CLERK (Captain Priceman): If your Honours please, the defendants Kaltenbrunner and Streicher will continue to be absent this afternoon.

M. DUBOST: We left off this morning at the enumeration of the tortures that had been inflicted habitually by the Gestapo in the various cities in France where inquiries had been conducted, and I was proving to you by reading numerous documents amongst them the last letter, that everywhere the accused, and frequently the witnesses themselves were questioned with brutality and subjected to tortures that were usually identical. This systematic repetition of the same methods of torture leads us to believe that there was a common plan, formulated by the heads of the police service themselves and by the German government.

We still have a great many testimonies, all extracted from the report of the American Services, which concern the prison at Dreux, the prison at Morlaix, and the prison in Metz. These testimonies are given in Documents 689-F, 690-F, and 691-F, which we are now presenting to you as Exhibits RF 311, 312, and 313. With your permission, your Honour, I will now abstain from further citing these documents. The same acts were systematically repeated; this is also true of the tortures inflicted in Metz, in Cahors, in Marseille and Quimperle. The subject is dealt with in Documents 692, 693, and 694-F, which we are presenting to you as Exhibits RF 314 and 315.

We now come to one of the most odious crimes committed by the Gestapo, and it is not possible for us to keep silent about it, in spite of our desire to shorten these proceedings. This is the murder of a French officer by the Gestapo at Clermont-Ferrand, in the Southern zone, and so in a zone which was considered to be free according to the terms of the Armistice - a murder which was committed under extremely shameful conditions in contempt of all common rights, since it was perpetrated in a region where, according to the terms of the Armistice, the Gestapo had nothing to do and had no right to be.

The name of this French officer was Major Henri Madeline. His case is given in Document S-575, which we submit as Exhibit RF 316. He was arrested on the 1st of October, 1943, at Vichy. The interrogation began in January 1944, and he was beaten in such a savage manner in the course of the first interrogatory that when he was brought back to his cell his hands were already slit. On 27 January he was subjected to two other interrogations. You will find, sir, this document in a bundle of papers contained in a pink file in your document book, No. S-575.

On 27 January this officer was questioned again on two occasions during which he was beaten so violently that when he returned to his cell it was impossible to see the manacles he had on, so swollen were his hands. The following day German police came back and seized him in his cell, where he had passed the whole night in agony. They took him while he was still alive and threw him down on a road a kilometre away from a small village in the Massif Central Peringant-Les-Sarlieves, so that it should be thought that he had been the victim of a road accident. His body was found later, and a post mortem, showed that the throat was completely crushed. He had multiple fractures of the ribs and perforation of the lungs. There was also dislocation of the spine, fracture of the lower jaw, and most of the tissues of the head were loose.

We all know that a few French traitors did assist in the arrests and in the misdeeds of the Gestapo in France under the orders of German officers. One of these traitors, who was arrested when our country was liberated, has described the ill-treatment inflicted on Major Madeline. The name of this traitor is Verniere, and we are going to read a passage from his statement.

> "He was beaten with an oxhide whip and a bludgeon. He was beaten on his fingernails, and his fingers were crushed. He was obliged to walk barefooted on tacks. He was burned with cigarette ends. Finally, he was beaten unmercifully and taken back to his cell in a dying condition."

Major Madeline was not the only victim of such evil treatment which several German officers of the Gestapo helped to inflict. This inquiry has shown that twelve known persons succumbed to the tortures inflicted by the Gestapo of Clermont-Ferrand, that some women were stripped naked and beaten before they were raped." I am anxious not to lengthen these proceedings by useless citations. I hope the Tribunal will consider the facts that I have presented as established. They are contained in the document that we are placing before you, and in it the Tribunal will find in full the written testimony taken on the day which followed the Liberation. This systematic repetition of the same criminal methods in order to achieve the same purpose, - to bring about a reign of terror - was not the isolated act only of a subordinate having authority in France, and not under the control of his government or of the Army General Staff. An examination of the methods of the German police in all countries of the West shows that the same horrors, the same atrocities, were repeated systematically everywhere. Whether in Denmark, Belgium, Holland or Norway, the interrogations were everywhere and at all times conducted by the Gestapo with the same savagery, the same contempt of legal rights, the same callousness towards human life.

In the case of Denmark, we cite from a document already placed before the Tribunal, under No. 317, which contains an official report of the Danish Government, dated October 1945. I merely cite a few lines from this document. You will find them in the small book of documents appended to the large book that was handed to you this morning. We think these few lines summarise the whole question. This is Document 666-F, which should be the sixth in your book of documents.

THE PRESIDENT: Does it come after 641-A?

M. DUBOST: Yes, Sir.

It is an extract from the Danish Memorandum of October, 1945, concerning the German Major War Criminals appearing before the International Military Tribunal. Page 5, under the title "Torture" we read, in a brief resume, everything that concerns the question with regard to Denmark:

"In numerous cases German police and their assistants used torture in order to force the prisoners to confess or to give information. This fact is supported by irrefutable evidence. In most cases the torture consisted in lashing or beating with sticks or with a rubber bludgeon.

But much more serious forms of torture were used, including some which will have lasting effects. Bovensiepen had stated that the order to use torture came, in certain cases, from the higher authorities, perhaps even from Goering as Chief of the Gestapo, but, in any event, from Heydrich. The instructions were to the effect that torture might be used in order to force the victims to give information that might serve to give away subversive organisations working against the German Reich, and not only to force the victim to confess his own acts."

A little further on: "The methods prescribed were, among other things, a specified number of blows with a stick. Bovensiepen does not remember whether the maximum was ten or twenty blows. An officer from the criminal police was there, and also, when circumstances so required, there was a medical officer present."

The above mentioned instructions were modified several times, and all members of the criminal police were notified.

The Danish Government points out, in conclusion, two particularly repugnant cases of torture inflicted on Danish patriots. They are the cases of Professor Mogens and the ill- treatment inflicted on Col. Einar Thiemroth. Finally, the Tribunal can read that Doctor Hoffman-Best states that his official prerogatives did not authorise him to prevent the use of torture.

In the case of Belgium we should recall first of all the tortures that were inflicted in the camp of Breendonck of tragic fame, where hundreds, even thousands of Belgium patriots, were confined. We shall revert to Breendonck when we deal with the question of concentration camps. We shall merely quote from the report of the Belgian War Crimes Commission a few definite facts in support of our original affirmation, that all acts of ill-treatment imputed to the Gestapo in France were reproduced in an identical manner in all the countries of Western Europe. The documents which we shall submit to you are to be found in the small book of documents as Exhibits RF 318 and 319. It is 942 (b) in your document book. It is the second document.

THE PRESIDENT: The second?

M. DUBOST: The second. You have a first document of 4 pages, it would be the 5th page of the small document book.

This report comprises minutes which I will not read, inasmuch as it contains testimonies which are analogous to, if not identical with those that were collected in France, However, on Pages 1 and 2 you will find the statement made by M. Auguste Ramael and also one made by M. Paul Desomer, which show that the most extreme cruelties were inflicted on these men, and that when they emerged from the offices of the Gestapo, they were completely disfigured and unable to stand.

And now I submit to you in regard to Belgium, Documents 611- F (a) and 641-F (b), which now become Exhibits RF320 and 321. I shall not read them. They, too, contain reports describing tortures similar to those I have already mentioned. If the Court will accept the cruelty of the methods of torture employed by the Gestapo as having been established, I will abstain from reading all the testimonies which have been collected.

In the case of Norway our information is taken from a document submitted by the Norwegian Government concerning the Punishment of the Major War Criminals. In the French translation of this Document UK 79, which we present as exhibit RF 323, on Page 2 you will find - and it is also to be found in the small document book - the confirmed statement that many Norwegians died. The Tribunal will find the statement of the Norwegian Government according to which numerous Norwegian citizens died as a result of the cruel treatment inflicted on them during their interrogation. The number of cases for the district of Oslo alone is known to be 52. The number in the various regions of Norway is undoubtedly much higher. The total number of Norwegian citizens who died during the occupation, as the result of tortures or ill-treatment or execution or suicide in prisons or concentration camps is approximately 2,100.

In paragraph (b), Page 2 of the document, there is a description of the methods employed by the Gestapo in Norway, and which were identical with those I have already described.

In the case of the Netherlands, we shall submit Document 224- S, which becomes Exhibit RF 324, and which is extracted from the statement of the Netherlands Government for the Prosecution and Punishment of the Major German War Criminals. This document bears the date 11 January, 1946. It has been distributed and should now be in your hands. The Tribunal will find in it a great number of testimonies which were collected by the Criminal Investigation Department, all of which describe the same ill-treatment and tortures as those already known to you, and which were committed by the Gestapo in Holland. In the Netherlands, as elsewhere, the accused were beaten with sticks. When their backs were completely raw from the beating they were sent back to their cells. Sometimes icy water was poured over them and sometimes they were exposed to electrical current. At Amersfoort a witness saw with his own eyes a prisoner, who was a priest, beaten to death with a rubber truncheon. The systematic character of such tortures has been definitely established. The document of the Danish Government is striking proof in support of my contention that these systematic tortures were the deliberate policy of the higher authorities of the Reich, and that the members of the German Government are responsible. In any case these systematic tortures were certainly known to them, because there were protests from all European countries against such methods, which plunged us again into the darkness of the Middle Ages. At no time was an order given to forbid such methods. At no time were those who used them disavowed by their superiors. The methods followed were devised to intensify the policy of terrorism pursued by Germany in the occupied countries - a policy of terrorism which I have already described to you when I dealt with the question of hostages.

It is now incumbent on me to give you the names of those among the accused whom France, as well as other countries in the West, considers to be especially guilty of having prepared and developed this criminal policy carried out by the Gestapo. We maintain they are Bormann and Kaltenbrunner who, because of their positions, must have known more than any others, about the acts of their subordinates. Although we are not in possession of any document signed by them in respect to the

Western countries, the uniformity of the acts we have described to you, and the fact that they were analogous and even identical in places far apart, enables us to assert that all these orders were dictated by a single will, and, among the accused, Bormann and Kaltenbrunner were the direct instruments of that single will.

Everything I described to you here concerned the procedure prior to trial, if any. We know with what ferocity this procedure was applied. We know that this ferocity was intentional. It was known to the populations of the invaded countries, and its purpose was to create an atmosphere of terror around the Gestapo and all the German police services.

After the examination came the judicial proceedings. These proceedings were, as we see them, only a parody of justice. The prosecution was based on a legal concept which we dismiss as being absolutely inhuman. That part will be dealt with by my colleague, M. Edgar Faure, in the second part of the report on the German atrocities in the Western countries: crimes against the spirit. It is sufficient for us to know that the German courts which dealt with crimes committed by the citizens of those occupied Western countries which did not accept defeat, applied only one penalty, and that was the death penalty, and this in execution of an inhuman order by one of these men, Keitel, an order which appears in Document 90-L, submitted to you as exhibit USA 503.

THE PRESIDENT: What is the number?

M. DUBOST: USA 503. It has already been submitted to the Tribunal by my United States colleagues, It is the penultimate document in your big document book. Line 5:

> "If these offences are punished with imprisonment, or even with hard labour for life, this will be looked upon as a sign of weakness. Efficient and lasting intimidation can only be achieved either by capital punishment, or measures by which the relatives of the culprit and the population are prevented from knowing the fate of the culprit ... "

Is it necessary to make any comment? Can we be surprised at this war leader giving orders to the judges? What we heard about him yesterday makes us doubt if he is merely a military leader. We have quoted you his own words: " Efficient and lasting intimidation can only be achieved by capital punishment." Such orders given to the judges - are these compatible with military honour? "If, in effect," Keitel goes on to say in Document 90-L, "the Court cannot arrive at a death sentence, then the man must be deported." I think you will share my opinion that, when such orders are given to a Court, one can no longer speak of justice.

In execution of this order, those of our compatriots who were not condemned to death and immediately executed, were deported to Germany. We now come to the third part of our expose which falls to me, namely, the deportations.

I should explain to you in what circumstances the deportations were carried out. If prior to that the Tribunal could adjourn for a very few minutes, I should be very grateful.

(A recess was taken)

DR. NELTE (Counsel for the defendant Keitel): The French Prosecutor just now read from Document 90-L, the so-called "Nacht und Nebel" decree. He referred to this decree and cited the words:

> "Efficient and lasting intimidation can only be achieved by capital punishment, or measures by which the relatives of the culprit and the population are prevented from knowing the fate of the culprit."

The French Prosecutor mentioned that these were the words of Keitel.

In connection with a previous case the president and the Tribunal have pointed out that it is not permissible to quote only a part of a document when by so doing a wrong impression might be created.

The French prosecutor will agree with me when I say that document 90-L makes it quite clear that these are not the words of the Chief of the OKW, but of Hitler. In this short decree it says that it is the carefully considered will of the Fuehrer that, when attacks are made in occupied countries against the Reich or against the occupying power, the culprits must be dealt with by other measures than those decreed heretofore. The Fuehrer is of the opinion that if these offences are punished with imprisonment, or even with hard labour for life, this will be looked upon as a sign of weakness. Efficient and enduring intimidation can only be achieved by capital punishment, etc."

The decree then goes on to say:

"The enclosed directives on how to deal with the offences comply with the Fuehrer's point of view. They have been examined and approved by him."

I take the liberty to point out this fact, especially as this decree, which is known as the notorious "Nacht und Nebel" decree, in its formulation and execution has been opposed by Keitel. That is why I am protesting.

M. DUBOST: I owe you an explanation. I did not read the decree in extenso because you know it. In line with the customary procedure of the Tribunal it has been read. It is not necessary to read it again. I did not know that the accused, Keitel, had signed it but that Hitler had conceived it. Therefore, I have made allusion to the military honour of this general, who was not afraid to become the lackey of Hitler.

THE PRESIDENT: The Tribunal understood that from your mentioning the fact that the document had already been submitted to the Tribunal, and does not think that there was anything misleading in what you did.

M. DUBOST: If the Tribunal accepts this, we shall proceed to the hearing of a witness, a Frenchman.

THE PRESIDENT: This is your witness, is it not? Is this the witness you wish to call?

M. DUBOST: Yes.

M. MAURICE LAMPE, a witness called by the French prosecution, takes the stand.

THE PRESIDENT: Will you stand up. What is your name?

THE WITNESS: Lampe, Maurice.

THE PRESIDENT: Will you repeat this oath after me: Do you swear to speak without hate or fear, to speak the truth, all the truth, only the truth.

(The witness repeats the oath in French)

THE PRESIDENT: Raise the right hand and say, I swear.

THE WITNESS: I swear.

THE PRESIDENT: Spell the name.

THE WITNESS: L-A-M-P-E.

THE PRESIDENT: Thank you.

(The witness M. Maurice Lampe was examined as follows by M. Dubost)

Q. You were born in Roubaix on 23 August, 1900; you were deported by the Germans?

A. Yes.

Q. You were interned in Mauthausen?
A. That is correct.
Q. Will you testify as to what you know concerning this internment camp?
A. Willingly.
Q. Say what you know.
A. I was arrested on 8 November, 1941. After two years and a half of internment in France, I was deported on the 22 March 1944 to Mauthausen in Germany.

The journey lasted three days and three nights under particularly vile conditions - 104 deportees in a cattle truck without air. I do not believe that it is necessary to give all the details of this journey, but one can well imagine the state in which we arrived at Mauthausen on the morning of 25 March 1944, in temperature 12 degrees below zero.

I mention, however, that from the French border we travelled in trucks, naked.

When we arrived at Mauthausen, the SS officer who received this convoy of about 1,200 Frenchmen informed us in the following words, which I shall quote from memory almost word for word: "Germany needs your arms. You are, therefore, going to work, but I want to tell you that never again will you see your families. Who enters this camp, will leave it only by the chimney of the crematorium."

I remained about three weeks in quarantine in an isolated block, and I was then selected to work in a working gang in a stone quarry. The quarry at Mauthausen was in a hollow about 800 metres from the camp proper. There were 186 steps leading down to it.

It was a particularly hard Calvary, because the steps were so rough-hewn that even to go up without a load was extremely tiring.

That day, 15 April, 1944, I was detailed to a team of 12 men, all of them French, under the orders of a German foreman, a common criminal, and of an SS man.

We started work at seven o'clock in the morning. By eight o'clock, one hour later, two of my comrades had already been murdered. They were an elderly man, M. Gregoir from Lyons, and quite a young man, Lefevre from Tours. They were murdered because they had not understood the order, given in German, detailing them for a task. We were frequently beaten because of our inability to understand the German language.

On the evening of that first day - 15 April 1944, we were told to carry the two corpses to the top, and the one that I with three of my comrades carried was that of M. Gregoir, a very heavy man, and we had to go up 186 steps with a corpse, and we all were beaten before we reached the top.

Life in Mauthausenn - and I shall state before this Tribunal only what I myself experienced - was one long cycle of torture and of suffering. However, I would like to recall a few scenes which were particularly horrible and have remained most firmly fixed in my memory.

During September - I think it was on 6 September 1944, there came to Mauthausen a small convoy of 47 British, American and Dutch officers. They were airmen who had come down by parachute. They had been arrested after they had tried to make their way back to their country. Because of this they were condemned to death by a German Court. They had been in prison about a year and were brought to Mauthausen for execution.

On their arrival they were transferred to the "bunker," the camp prison. They were made to undress and had only their pants and a shirt. They were barefooted.

The following morning they answered the roll-call at seven o'clock. The working gangs went to their tasks. The 47 officers were assembled in front of the office and were told by the commanding officer of the camp that they were all under sentence of death.

I must mention that one of the American officers asked the commander that he should be allowed to meet his death as a soldier. In reply, he was lashed with a whip and beaten. The 47 were led barefoot to the quarry.

For all the prisoners at Mauthausen the murder of these men has remained in their minds like a scene from Dante's Inferno. The procedure was: At the bottom of the steps they loaded stones on the backs of these poor wretches and they had to carry them to the top. The first ascent was made with stones weighing 25 to 30 kilos and was accompanied by blows. Then they were made to run down. For the second ascent the stones were still heavier, and whenever the poor wretches sank under their burden, they received kicks and blows with a bludgeon - even stones were hurled at them.

In the evening when I rejoined the gang with which I was then working, the road which led to the camp was a path of blood. I almost stepped on a lower jaw of a man. Twenty-one bodies were strewn along the road. Twenty-one had died on the first day. The twenty-six others died the following morning.

I have tried to make my account of this horrible episode as short as possible. We were not able, at least when we were in camp, to find out the names of these officers, but I think that by now they must have been established.

In September 1944 Himmler visited us. Nothing was changed in the camp routine. The work gangs went to their tasks as usual, and I had occasion - and it was a sad occasion - to see Himmler close by. If I mention Himmler's visit to the camp - after all it was not a great event - it is because that day they presented Himmler with the spectacle of the execution of fifty Soviet officers.

I must tell you that I was working in a Messerschmidt gang, and I was then on night shift. The blockhouse where I was lodged was just opposite the crematorium and the execution room. We saw - I saw - these Soviet officers lined up in rows of five in front of my block. They were called one by one. The way to the execution room was comparatively short. It was reached by a stairway. The execution room was under the crematorium.

The execution, which Himmler himself witnessed - at least the beginning of it, because it lasted throughout the afternoon - was another particularly horrible spectacle. I repeat: the Soviet Army officers were called one by one, and there was a sort of human chain between those who were awaiting their turn and the man who was standing in the stairway and heard the shot which killed his predecessor. They were all killed by a shot in the neck.

Q. You witnessed this personally?

A. I repeat that on that afternoon I was in Block 11, which was situated opposite the crematorium, and although we did not see the execution itself, we heard every shot, and we saw the condemned men who were waiting on the stairway opposite us embrace each other before they parted.

Q. Who were these men who were condemned?

A. The majority of them were Soviet officers, political Commissars, or members of the Bolshevik party. They came from Oflags.

Q. I beg your pardon, but were there officers among them?

A. Yes.

Q. Did you know where they came from?

A. It was very difficult to know from what camp they came because, as a general rule, they were locked up as they arrived in camp. Either they were taken directly to prison or else to Block No. 20, which was an annex of the prison, about which I shall have occasion...

Q. How did you know they were officers?

A. Because we were able to communicate with them.

Q. Did all of them come from prisoner of war camps?

A. Probably.

Q. You did not really know?

A. No, we really did not know. We were chiefly interested in finding out of what nationality they were, and did not ask other details.

Q. Do you know where the British, American and Dutch officers came from, about whom you have just spoken and who were executed on the steps leading to the quarry?

A. I believe they came from the Netherlands, especially the air force officers. They had probably baled out after having been shot down, and they had hidden themselves while trying to get back to their country.

Q. Did the Mauthausen prisoners know that prisoners of war, officers or non-commissioned officers, were executed?

A. That was a frequent occurrence.

Q. A frequent occurrence?

A. Yes, very frequent.

Q. Do you know about any mass executions of the men kept at Mauthausen?

A . I know of many instances.

Q. Could you cite a few?

A. Besides those I have already described, I feel I ought to mention what happened to a part of a convoy coming from Sachsenhausen which was executed by a special method. This was on the 17 February, 1945.

When the Allied armies were advancing, various camps were moved back toward Austria. Of a convoy of 2,500 internees which had left Sachsenhausen, only about 1,700 were left when they arrived at Mauthausen on the morning of the 17 February. 800 had died or had been killed in the course of the journey.

The Mauthausen camp was at that time, if I may use this expression, choked up. Therefore, when 1,700 survivors of this convoy arrived, Kommandant Dachmeier had 400 selected from among them. He encouraged the sick, the old and the weak prisoners to come forward with the idea that they might be taken to the infirmary. These 400 men, who had either come forward of their own free will, or had been arbitrarily selected, were stripped entirely naked. They were left for 18 hours in weather 18 degrees below zero between the laundry building and the wall of the camp.

Q. You saw that yourself?

A. I saw it personally.

Q. You are citing this as a direct witness?

A. Exactly.

Q. In what part of the camp were you at that time?

A. This scene lasted, as I said, 18 hours, and when we went in or came out of the camp we saw these unfortunate men.

Q. Very well. Will you please continue? You have spoken of the visit of Himmler and the execution of Soviet officers and People's Commissars. Did you frequently see prominent Germans in the camp?

A. Yes, but I cannot give you the names.

Q. You did not know them?

A. One could hardly mistake Himmler.

Q. But you did know they were prominent men?

A. We did indeed. First of all, they were always surrounded by a complete General Staff, who went through the prison itself as well as the adjoining blocks.

If you will allow me, I would like to go on with my description of the murder of these 400 people from Sachsenhausen. I said that after selecting the sick, the feeble and the older prisoners, Dachmeier, the camp commander, gave orders that these men should be stripped entirely naked in weather 18 degrees below zero. Several of them soon got congestion of the lungs, but it seemed that things were not going fast enough for the SS. Three times during the night these men were sent down to the showers; three times they were drenched for half an hour in freezing water, and then made to come out without having dried themselves.

In the morning when the gangs went to work the corpses were strewn over the ground. I must add that the last of them were finished off with blows from an axe.

I now bring the most direct testimony of a fact which can easily be verified. Among the 400 men I have mentioned was a Captain in the French cavalry, Captain Dodionne, who today is a Major in the Ministry of War. This Captain was among the 400. He owes his life to the fact that he hid among the corpses and thus escaped the blows of the axe. When the corpses were taken to the crematorium he managed to get away, but not without having received a blow on the shoulder which has left a mark for life.

He was caught again by the SS. What saved him was the fact that the SS considered it very amusing that a live man should manage to extricate himself from a heap of corpses. We took care of him, we helped him, and we brought him back to France.

Q. Do you know why these executions were carried out?

A. Because there were too many people in the camp; because the prisoners coming from all the camps that were falling back could not be drafted into working gangs at a quick enough pace. The blocks were overcrowded. That is the only explanation that was given.

Q. Do you know who gave the order to exterminate the British, American and Dutch officers whom you saw put to death in the quarry?

A. I believe I said that these officers had been condemned to death by German tribunals. Probably a few of them had been condemned many months before they were taken to Mauthausen for the sentence to be carried out. It is probable that the order came from Berlin.

Q. Did you know how the infirmary was built?

A. Here I must state quite clearly that the infirmary was built before my arrival at the camp.

Q. So you are giving us indirect testimony?

A. Yes, indirect testimony. But I heard it from all of the internees, also the SS themselves. The infirmary was built by the first Soviet prisoners who arrived in Mauthausen. Four thousand Soviet soldiers were massacred during the construction of these ten blocks of the infirmary. So deeply had these massacres remained impressed on the memory, that the infirmary was always referred to as the "Russian Camp." The SS themselves called the infirmary the "Russian Camp."

Q. How many Frenchmen were at Mauthausen?

A. There were in Mauthausen about 10,000 Frenchmen, including the outside detachments.

Q. How many of you came back?

A. Three thousand of us came back.

Q. There were some Spaniards with you also?

A. 8000 Spaniards arrived in Mauthausen in 1941 toward the end of the year. When we left at the end of April 1945, there were still about 1,600. All the rest had been exterminated.

Q. Where did these Spaniards come from?

A. These Spaniards came from labour companies which had been organised in 1939 and 1940 in France, or were delivered by the Vichy Government to the Germans.

Q. Is this all you have to tell us?

A. With the permission of the Tribunal, I would like to cite another example of an atrocity which remains clearly in my memory. This also took place during September 1944. I am sorry I cannot remember the exact date, but I do know it was a Saturday, because on Saturday at Mauthausen all the outside detachments had to answer evening roll call inside the camp. That took place only on Saturday night and on Sunday morning.

That evening the roll call took longer than usual. Someone was missing. After a long wait and searches carried out in the various blocks, they found a Russian, a Soviet prisoner, who perhaps had fallen asleep, and had forgotten to answer roll call; what the reason was we never knew, but at any rate he was not present at the roll call. Immediately the dogs and the SS went, seized the poor wretch, and before the whole camp - I was in the front row, not because I wanted to be, but because we were arranged like that - we witnessed the fury of the dogs let loose upon this unfortunate Soviet man. He was torn to bits in the presence of the whole camp.

I should add that this man, in spite of his sufferings, faced his death in a particularly brave manner.

Q. What were the living conditions of the prisoners? Were they all treated in the same way, or were they treated differently according to their origin and nationality, or, perhaps, their racial background, or because they belonged to any particular race?

A. As a general rule the camp regime was the same for all nationalities, with the exception of the quarantine blocks and the annexes of the prison. The kind of work we did, the particular detachment to which we were detailed, sometimes allowed us to get a little more food than usual, for instance, those who worked in the kitchens or in the stores certainly did get a little more.

Q. Were Jews permitted to work in the kitchen or the store rooms?

A. At Mauthausen the Jews had the hardest tasks of all. I must point out that, until December 1943, the Jews did not live more than three months at Mauthausen. There were very few of them at the end.

Q. What happened in that camp after the murder of Heydrich?

A. In this connection there was a particularly dramatic episode. At Mauthausen there were 3,000 Czechs, 600 of whom were intellectuals. After the murder of Heydrich, the Czech colony in the camp was exterminated with the exception of 300 out of 3,000, and six intellectuals out of the 600 that were in the camp.

Q. Did anyone speak to you of scientific experiments?

A. They were commonplace at Mauthausen, as they were in other camps. But we have evidence which I think has been found: the two skulls which Were used as paper weights by the chief SS medical officer. These were the skulls of two young Dutch Jews who had been selected from a convoy of 800 because they had fine teeth.

To make this selection the SS doctor had led these two young Dutch Jews to believe that they would not suffer the fate of their comrades of the convoy. He had said to them "Jews do not live here. I need two strong, healthy, young men for surgical experiments. You have your choice; either you offer yourselves for these experiments or else you will suffer the fate of the others."

These two Jews were taken to the hospital, one of them had his kidney removed, the other his stomach. Then they had benzine injected into the heart and were decapitated. As I said, these two skulls with fine sets of teeth were kept on the desk of the chief SS doctor until the liberation.

Q. At the time of Himmler's visit - I would like to come back to that question - are you certain that you recognised Himmler and saw him presiding over the executions?
A. Yes.

Q. Do you think that what was taking place in Mauthausen could not be known to all members of the German Government? The visits you had received, were they simply visits by the SS, or were they visits of other prominent people?
A. As regards your first question; we all knew Himmler, and if we did not, all the others in the camp did; also the SS told us a few days before, that his visit was expected. He was present at the beginning of the executions of the Soviet officers. But, as I said a little while ago, these executions lasted throughout the afternoon, and he did not remain until the end. With regard to ...

Q. Is it possible that only the SS knew what happened in the camp? Was the camp visited by others than the SS? Did you know the SS uniforms? The people you saw, the authorities you saw - did they all wear a uniform?
A. The people that we saw at the camp were, generally speaking, soldiers, officers. Some time afterwards, a few weeks before the liberation, we had a visit from the Gauleiter of the Gau Oberdonau. We also had frequent visits from members of the Gestapo in plain clothes. But the people, that is, the Austrian population, were perfectly aware of what was going on at Mauthausen. The foremen were nearly all from outside.

I said just now that I was working in a Messerschmidt gang. The foremen were mobilised German civilians who, in the evening, went home to their families. They knew quite well our sufferings and privations. They frequently saw men fetched from the shop to be executed, and they could bear witness to most of the massacres I mentioned a little while ago.

I should add that once we received - I am sorry I put it like that - once there arrived in Mauthausen 30 firemen from Vienna. They were imprisoned, I think, for having taken part in some sort of workers' action. The firemen from Vienna told us that when one wanted to frighten children in Vienna, one said to them: "If you are not good, I will send you to Mauthausen."

Another detail, a more concrete one: Mauthausen camp is built on a plateau and every night the chimneys of the crematorium would light up the whole district, and everyone knew what the crematorium was for.

Another detail: The town of Mauthausen was situated five kilometres from the camp. The convoys of deportees were brought to the station of the town. The whole population could see these convoys pass. The whole population knew in what state these convoys were brought into the camp.

M. DUBOST: Thank you very much.

THE PRESIDENT: Does the Soviet prosecutor wish to ask any questions?

GENERAL RUDENKO: I should like to ask a few questions.
BY GENERAL RUDENKO:

Q. Can you tell me, witness, why the execution of the 50 Soviet officers was ordered? Why were they executed?

A. As regards the specific case of these 50 officers, I do not know the reasons why they were condemned and executed but, as a general rule, all Soviet officers all Soviet Commissars, or members of the Bolshevist Party, were executed at Mauthausen. If a few among them succeeded in slipping through, it is because their identity was not known to the SS.

Q. You affirm, that Himmler was present at the execution of the 50 Soviet officers?

A. I testify to the fact, because I saw him with my own eyes.

Q. Can you give us more precise details about the execution of the 4,000 Soviet prisoners of war which you have just mentioned?

A. I cannot add much to what I have said, except that these men were assassinated at their work, probably because the task demanded of them was beyond their strength, and they were too underfed to perform it. They were murdered on the spot by blows with a cudgel, or struck down by the SS; they were driven by the SS to the wire fence and shot down by the sentinels in the watchtowers. I cannot give more details, because, as I said, I was not a witness, an eye witness.

Q. That is quite clear.

And now one more question: Can you give me a more detailed statement concerning the destruction of the Czech colony?

A. I speak with the same reservations as before. I was not in the camp at the time of the extermination of the 3,000 Czechs, but the survivors with whom I spoke in 1944 were unanimous in confirming the accuracy of these facts and probably, as far as their own country is concerned, have drawn up a list of the murdered men.

Q. This means, if I have understood you correctly, that in the camp where you were interned executions were carried out without trial or inquiry. Every member of the SS had the right to kill an internee. Have I understood your statement correctly?

A. Yes, that is so. The life of a man at Mauthausen counted for absolutely nothing.

THE PRESIDENT: Does any member of the defendants' counsel wish to ask any questions of this witness? Then the witness can retire. Witness, a moment.

BY THE TRIBUNAL (Mr. Biddle):

Q. Do you know how many guards there were at the camp?

A. The number of the guards varied but, as a general rule, there were 1,200 SS, and also soldiers of the Volkssturm. However, it should be stated that only 50 to 60 SS were authorised to come inside the camp.

Q. Those 50 or 60 SS men, were they SS men that were authorised to go into the camp?

A. Yes, they were.

Q. All SS men?

A. All of them were SS.

THE PRESIDENT: Then the witness can retire.

M. DUBOST: With your permission, gentlemen, we shall proceed with the presentation of our case on German atrocities in the Western countries of Europe from 1939 to 1945, by retaining from these testimonies the particular acts which, taken separately, all equally constitute common crimes. The general idea, around which we have grouped all our work and the presentation, is the German terrorism, intentionally conceived as an instrument for governing all enslaved peoples.

We shall remember the testimony brought by the French witness who said that in Vienna, when one wished to frighten a child, one told it about Mauthausen.

The people who were arrested in the Western countries were deported to Germany, where they were put into camps or into prisons. The information that we have concerning the prisons has been taken from the official report of the Prisoners of War Ministry, which we have already read; it is the bound volume which was in your hands this morning. In it you will find, namely on page 35, and page 36 to page 42, a detailed statement as to what the prisons were like in Germany.

THE PRESIDENT: 274-F?

M. DUBOST: It was 274-F, on page 35. The Tribunal can read that the prison at Cologne, where many Frenchmen were interned, was situated between the goods station and the main station, so that the Prosecutor in Cologne wrote, in a report which was used by the Ministry of Deportees and Prisoners of War when compiling the book which is before you, that the situation of that prison was so dangerous that no concern engaged in war work would undertake to furnish its precious materials to a factory in that area. The internees could not seek shelter during air attacks. They remained locked in their cells, even if fire broke out.

The victims of air attacks in the prisons were numerous. The May 1944 raid claimed 200 victims in the prison at Alexander Platz in Berlin.

The buildings were always dirty and damp, and were very small. In Aix-la-Chapelle the prisoners numbered three or four times as many as the facilities permitted. In Munster the women who were there in November 1943 lived underground without any air. In Frankfurt the prisoners had as cells a sort of iron cage, 2 x 1.50 metres. It was impossible to keep clean. At Aix-la-Chapelle, as in many other prisons, the prisoners had only one bucket in the middle of the room, and it was forbidden to empty it during the day.

The food ration was extremely small. As a rule, ersatz coffee in the morning with a thin slice of bread; soup at noon; a thin slice of bread at night with a little margarine or sausage or jam.

The internees were forced to do extremely heavy work, war industry, procuring of food products, weaving and plaiting. No matter what kind of work it was, at least twelve hours were required at Cologne in particular, from 7 o'clock in the morning to 9 or 10 o'clock in the evening, that is to say, 14 or 15 consecutive hours. I am still quoting from the file of the Public Prosecutor of Cologne, document 87, sent to us by the Ministry of Prisoners. A shoe factory gave work to the inmates of 18 German prisons. I quote the last 2 lines of this page:

> "Most of the Frenchmen flatly refused to work in war industries, for example, the manufacture of gas masks, filing of cast iron plates, slidings for shells, radio or telephone apparatus intended for the Army."

In such cases Berlin gave orders to send recalcitrants to reprisal camps, for example, they sent women from Kottbus to Ravensbruck on 13 November 1944. The Geneva Convention was, of course, not applied. The political prisoners frequently had to retrieve unexploded bombs.

This is from the official German text of the Public Prosecutor of Cologne.

There was no medical supervision. Either there were no prophylactic measures taken in these prisons in the event of epidemics, or the SS doctor intentionally gave the wrong instructions.

At the prison of Dietz or Lahn, under the direction of Director Gammradt, a former major in the German Army, the SS or SA guards struck the prisoners. Dysentery, diphtheria, pulmonary lesions, pleurisy, were not considered to be reasons for stoppage of work, and those who were dangerously ill were forced to work to the very limit of their strength, and were only admitted to the hospital in exceptional cases.

In Aix-la-Chapelle the presence of a Jewish prisoner in the cell caused the other prisoners to lose half of their ration. At Amrasch they could go to toilets only when ordered. At Magdeburg the recalcitrants had to make one hundred genuflexions before the guards. The interrogations were carried out in the same manner as in France, that is, the victims were brutally treated and were given practically no food.

At Asperg the doctor gave the internees injections in the heart so that they died. At Cologne those condemned to death were perpetually kept in chains. At Sonnenburg those who were dying were given a greenish liquor to drink which hastened their death. In Hamburg sick Jews were forced to dig their own graves until, exhausted, they fell into them. We are speaking of Frenchmen, Dutchmen, Luxembourgers, Danes and Norwegians interned in German prisons. These descriptions apply only to citizens of those countries. In the prison of Boers in Berlin, Jewish babies were massacred before the eyes of their mothers. The sterilisation of men is confirmed by German documents in the file of the Prosecutor of Cologne, which contains a ruling to the effect that the victims cannot be reinstated in their military rights. These files also contain documents which show the role played by children who were in prison. They had to work inside the prison. A German functionary belonging to the penitentiary service inquired as to the decision to be taken with regard to a four months old baby, which was brought to the prison at the same time as its father and mother.

Page 39, last paragraph, shows what kind of people the prison staff consisted of: "They were recruited from the NSKK (National Socialist Motor Corps) and the SA because of their political views and because they were above any suspicion and would submit to a harsh discipline." This is also to be found in the file of the Public Prosecutor at Cologne.

At Rheinbach those condemned to death and destined to be executed in Cologne, were beaten to death for any break of this discipline. We can easily imagine the brutality of the men who were in charge of the prisoners. The German official text will furnish us with details regarding the executions. The condemned were guillotined. Nearly all the condemned showed surprise, say the German documents which we are analysing, and expressed their dissatisfaction at being guillotined, instead of being shot, for patriotic deeds of which they were declared guilty. They thought they deserved to be treated as soldiers.

Among those executed in Cologne were some young people of eighteen and nineteen years of age, and one woman. Some French women, who were political prisoners, were taken from the Lubeck prison in order to be executed in Hamburg. They were nearly always charged with the same thing, "helping the enemy." The files are incomplete, but we have those of the Prosecutor of Cologne; in every case the offences committed were of the same nature. Keitel systematically rejected all appeals for mercy which were submitted to him.

Although the lot of those who were held in the prisons was very hard, and sometimes terrible, it was infinitely less cruel than the fate of those Frenchmen who had the misfortune to be interned in the concentration camps. The Tribunal is well informed about these camps; my colleagues of the United Nations have presented a long statement on this matter. The Tribunal will remember that it has already been shown a map indicating the exact location of every camp which existed in Germany and in the occupied countries. We shall not, therefore, revert to the geographical distribution of the camps.

With the permission of the Tribunal I should now like to deal with the conditions under which Frenchmen and nationals of the Western Occupied Countries were taken to these camps. Before their departure, the internees, who were victims of arbitrary arrest, such as I described to you this morning, were brought together in prisons or in assembly camps in France.

The main assembly camp in France was at Compiegne. It is from there that most of the deportees left who were to be sent to Germany. There were two other assembly camps, Beaume La Rolande and Pithiviers, reserved especially for Jews, and Drancy. The conditions under which people were interned in those camps were rather similar to those under which internees in the German prisons lived. With your permission I shall not dwell any longer on this. The Tribunal will have taken judicial notice of the declarations made by Monsieur Blechmall and Monsieur Jacob in Document 457, which I am now submitting as Exhibit RF 328.

THE PRESIDENT: Which book is this in?

M. DUBOST: That is in the eleventh group of papers in the new file.

THE PRESIDENT: Is it the book which is described as "deporation?"

M. DUBOST: That is correct. It is entitled "Deporation" and it is the eleventh document in the book.

THE PRESIDENT: The index, M. Dubost, does not include that. 457 is it?

M. DUBOST: 457.

THE PRESIDENT: Yes, we have it.

M. DUBOST: To avoid making these discussions too long and too ponderous with long quotations and testimonies which, after all, are very similar, we shall confine ourselves to reading to the Tribunal a passage from the testimony of Monsieur Jacob concerning the conduct of the German Red Cross. This passage is to be found on page 4 at the very bottom of the French document:

> "We received a visit from several prominent Germans, such as Stulpnagel, Du Paty de Clem, Commissioner for Jewish Questions, and Colonel Baron von Berg, Vice President of the German Red Cross. This von Berg was very formal and very spectacular. He always wore the small insignia of the Red Cross, which did not prevent his being inhuman and a thief."

And on page 6, the penultimate paragraph, Colonel von Berg was, as we have already said earlier, very spectacular.

I omit two lines.

THE PRESIDENT: Which paragraph now?

M. DUBOST: Page 6, last three lines.

> "In spite of his title of Vice President of the German Red Cross, of which he dared to wear the insignia, he selected at random a number of our comrades for deportation."

Concerning the assembly centre of Compiegne, the Tribunal will find in document 174-F, pages 14 and 15, some details about the fate of the internees. I do not think it is necessary to read them.

In Norway, Holland and Belgium there were, as in France, assembly camps The most typical of these camps, and certainly the best known, is the Breendonck Camp in Belgium, about which it is necessary to give the Tribunal a few details because a great many Belgians were interned there and died of privations, hardships and tortures of all kinds, or were executed either by shooting or by hanging.

This camp was established in the Fortress of Breendonck in 1940, and we are now extracting from a document which we have already deposited as 231-F and which is also known as UK-76, a few details about the conditions prevailing in that camp. It is the fourth document in your new document book. It is marked 231-F, and is entitled, "Report on the Concentration Camp of Breendonck."

THE PRESIDENT: What did you say the name of the camp is?

M. DUBOST: Breendonck, B-r-e-e-n-d-o-n-c-k.

We will ask the Tribunal to be good enough to grant us a few minutes. Our duty is to expose in rather more detail the conditions at this camp because a considerable number of Belgians were interned there and their internment took a rather special form. I will read a few pages:

> "The Germans occupied this fort in August 1940, and they brought the internees there in September. They were Jews. The Belgian Government has not been able to find out how many people were interned from September 1940 to August 1944, when the camp was evacuated and Belgium liberated. Nevertheless, it is thought that about 3,000 to 3,600 internees passed through the camp of Breendonck. About 250 died of privation; 450 were shot and 12 were hanged.
>
> But we must bear in mind the fact that the majority of the prisoners in Breendonck were transferred at various times to camps in Germany. Most of those transferred prisoners did not return. There should, therefore, be added to those who died in Breendonck, all those who did not survive their captivity in Germany.
>
> Various categories of prisoners were received into the camp: Jews - for whom the regime was more severe than for the others: Communists and Marxists, of which there were a good many, in spite of the fact that those who interrogated them had nothing definite against them: persons who belonged to the Resistance: people who had been denounced to the Germans: hostages, among them -'

THE PRESIDENT (Interposing): M. Dubost, where have you got to now?

M. DUBOST: The fourth paragraph of the second page.

> "... hostages, among them Monsieur Fougery, a former minister, and Monsieur van Kesbeek, who was a liberal deputy, were interned there for ten weeks as expiation for the throwing of a grenade on the main square of Malines. Both of them died after their liberation as a result of the ill-treatment which they suffered in that camp.
>
> There were also in that camp some black market operators, and the Belgian Government said of them that they were not ill-treated, and were even given preferential treatment." That is in paragraph (b) of page 2.
>
> "The prisoners were compelled to work. The most repugnant collective punishments were inflicted on the slightest pretext. One of these punishments consisted in forcing the internees to crawl under the beds and to stand up at command; this was done to the accompaniment of whipping."

You will find that at the top of page 3 of the first paragraph.

In the second paragraph of the same page is a description of the conditions of the prisoners who were isolated from the others, and kept in solitary confinement. They were forced to wear a hood every time they had to leave their cells or when they had to come in contact with other prisoners.

THE PRESIDENT: This is a long report, is it not?

M. DUBOST: That is why I am summarising it rather than reading it, and I do not think I can make it any shorter, because it was given to me by the Belgian

Government, which attaches much importance to the brutalities, excesses and atrocities that were committed by the Germans in the Camp of Breendonck, and suffered by the whole of the population, especially the Belgian elite.

THE PRESIDENT: Very well. I understand you are summarising it?

M. DUBOST: I am now summarising it, Mr. President.

THE PRESIDENT: Very well.

M. DUBOST: I had reached, in my summary, the description of the life of these prisoners who had been put into cells and who sometimes wore handcuffs and had their feet shackled. They could not leave their cells without being forced to wear a hood.

One of these prisoners, M. Paquet, states that he spent eight months under such a regime, and when one day he tried to lift the hood so as to find his way, he received a violent blow with the butt of a gun which broke three vertebrae in his neck.

On page 8 are the following: discipline, labour, acts of brutality, murders. We are told that the work of the prisoners consisted of removing the earth covering the fort, and carrying it outside the moat. This work was done by hand. It was very painful and dangerous, and caused the loss of a great many human lives.

Small wagons were used. The wagons were hurled along the rails by the SS and they often broke the legs of the prisoners who were not warned of their approach. The SS made a game of this, and at the slightest stoppage they would rush at the internees and beat them.

One page further, in paragraph 5, in the middle of the page, we are told that frequently, for no reason at all, the prisoners were thrown into the moat surrounding the fort. According to the report of the Belgian Government, dozens of prisoners were drowned. Some prisoners were killed after they had been buried up to their necks, and the SS finished them off by kicking them or beating them with a stick. Food, clothing, correspondence, medical care, all this information is given in this report, as in all the other similar reports which I have already read to you.

The conclusion is important and should be read in part, - second paragraph:

> "The former internees of Breendonck, many of whom have experienced the concentration camps in Germany, Buchenwald, Neuengamme, Oranienburg, state that, generally speaking, the conditions prevailing at Breendonck as regards discipline and food, were worse. They add that, in the camps in Germany which were more crowded, they felt less under the domination of their guards, and had the feeling that their lives were less in danger."

The figures given in this report are only minimum figures. To quote but one example, in the last paragraph of the last page: M. Verheirstraeten declares that he put 120 people in their coffins during the two months, December 1942 to January 1943. If one bears in mind the executions of the 6 and 13 of January, which accounted for the lives of 20 persons, respectively, we see that during that time, that is to say, over a period of two months, 80 persons died of disease or ill-treatment. From these camps the internees were transported to Germany in convoys, and a description of these should be given to the Tribunal.

The Tribunal should know, first of all, that from France alone, excluding the three departments of the Haut-Rhine, Bas-Rhine, and Moselle, 326 convoys left between 1 January 1944 and 25 August of the same year, that is to say, an average of ten convoys per week. Each convoy transported from 1,000 to 2,000 persons, and we know now, from what our witness has just said, that each truck carried from 60 to 120 individuals. It appears that there left from France, excluding the above mentioned three Northern departments, three convoys in 1940, 19 convoys in 1941, 104 convoys in 1942, 257 convoys in 1943. These are figures given in document 274, page 14 of the book which we submitted to the Tribunal this morning.

These convoys nearly always left from the Compiegne camp where more than 50,000 internees were registered and from there 78 convoys left in 1943 and 95 convoys in 1944.

The purpose of these deportations was to terrorise the population. The Tribunal will remember the text I read; that the families, not knowing what became of the internees, were seized with terror, and advantage was taken of this to round up more workers to replace German labour resources which had become depleted, owing to the war with Russia.

The manner in which these deportations were carried out not only made it possible more or less to select this labour, but also it constituted the first stage of a new German policy which we now see appearing; that is purely and simply the extermination of all racial or intellectual categories whose political activity appeared a menace to the Nazi leaders.

These deportees, who were locked up 80 or 120 in each truck in any season, who could neither sit nor crouch down, were given nothing whatsover to eat or drink during their journey. In this connection we would particularly like to put forward Dr. Steinberg's testimony, taken by Lt. Col. Badin, from the Committee for the Investigation of Enemy War Crimes in Paris, Document 392-F, which we submit as Exhibit RF 330, which is the 12th in your document book. We will read only a few paragraphs on page 2. Paragraph 3 - third from the bottom:

> "We were crowded into cattle trucks, about 70 in each. Sanitary conditions were frightful. Our journey lasted two days. We reached Auschwitz on the 24 June 1942. It should be noted that we had been given no food at all when we left and that we had to live during those two days on what little food we had taken with us from Drancy."

The deportees were at times refused water by the German Red Cross. Evidence was taken by the Ministry of Prisoners and Deportees, and this appears in document 274-F, the bound book, page 12, paragraph 3, 4th and 5th lines.

It is about a convoy of Jewish women which left Bobigny station on 19 June 1942. "They travelled for three days and three nights, dying of thirst. At Breslau they begged the nurses of the German Red Cross to give them a little water, but in vain."

Moreover, Lt. Geneste and Dr. Bloch have testified to the same facts and other different facts, which are set out in the printed document, Exhibit RF 321, entitled "Concentration Camps," which we have been able to submit to you in three languages: French, Russian, and German, the English version having been exhausted. Page 21, at the top of the page:

"In the station of Bremen water was refused to us by the German Red Cross, who said that there was no water." This is the testimony of Lt. Geneste of O.R.C.G. Concerning this conduct of the German Red Cross, and to conclude the subject, there is one more word to be said. This same document gives you - on page 162, paragraph 3 - the proof that it was an ambulance car bearing a red cross which carried gas in iron containers, destined for the gas chambers of Auschwitz camp.

(The Tribunal was adjourned until 28th January 1946 at 1000 hours.)

Forty-fourth day:
Monday, 28th January, 1946

DUBOST (Counsel for France): With the authorisation of the Court, I should like to proceed with this part of the presentation of the French case by hearing a witness who, for nearly three years, lived in German concentration camps.

THE PRESIDENT: Would you stand up, please? Do you wish to swear the French oath? Will you tell me your name?

MADAME CLAUDE VAILLANT COUTURIER

THE WITNESS: Claude Vaillant Couturier.

THE PRESIDENT: Will you repeat after me: I swear to speak without hate or fear, to state the truth, all the truth.

(The witness repeated the oath after the President).

THE PRESIDENT: Raise the right hand and say "I swear."

THE WITNESS: I swear.

Direct Examination

QUESTIONS BY M. DUBOST:

Q. Is your name Madame Vaillant Couturier?
A. Yes.

Q. You are the widow of M. Vaillant Couturier?
A. Yes.

Q. Were you born in Paris on 3 November 1912?
A. Yes.

Q. And you are of French nationality, French born and of parents who were of French nationality?
A. Yes.

Q. You are a Deputy in the Constituent Assembly?
A. Yes.

Q. You are a Knight of the Legion of Honour?
A. Yes.

Q. You have just been decorated by General Leugentilhomme at the Invalides?
A. Yes.

Q. Were you arrested and deported? Will you please give your testimony?

A. I was arrested on 9 February 1942 by Petain's French police, who handed me over to the German authorities after six weeks. I arrived on 20 March at the "Sante" prison in the German quarter. I was questioned on 9 June 1942. At the end of my interrogation they wanted me to sign a statement, which was not consistent with what I had said. I refused to sign it. The officer who had questioned me threatened me, and when I told him that I was not afraid of death or of being shot, he said, "But we have at our disposal means for killing that are far worse than merely shooting." And the interpreter said to me," You do not know what you have just done. You are going to leave for a concentration camp in Germany. One never comes back from there."

Q. You were then taken to prison?

A. I was taken back to the Sante prison where I was placed in solitary confinement.

However, I was able to communicate with my neighbours through the piping and the windows. I was in a cell next to that of George Politzer, the philosopher, and Jacques Solomon, physicist. M. Solomon is the son-in-law of Professor Langevin, a pupil of Curie, one of the first to study atomic disintegration.

George Politzer told me through the piping that during his interrogation, after having been tortured, he was asked whether he would write theoretical pamphlets for National Socialism. When he refused, he was told he would be in the first train of hostages to be shot.

As for Jacques Solomon, he also was horribly tortured, and then thrown into a cell and only came out on the day of his execution to say goodbye to his wife, who also was under arrest at the Sante. Helen Solomon Langevin told me in Romainville, where I found her when I left the Sante, that when she went to her husband he moaned and said: "I cannot take you in my arms, because I can no longer move them."

Every time that the internees came back from their questioning one could hear moaning through the windows, and they all said that they could not make any movement.

Several times during the five months I spent at the Sante, hostages were taken to be shot. When I left the Sante on the 20 of August, 1942, I was taken to the Fortress of Romainville, which was a camp for hostages. There I was present on two occasions when they took hostages, on the 21 of August and the 22 of September. Among the hostages who were taken away were the husbands of the women who were with me and who left for Auschwitz. Most of them died there. These women, for the most part, had been arrested only because of the activity of their husbands. They themselves had done nothing.

Q. When did you leave for Auschwitz?

A. I left for Auschwitz on the 23 of January 1943, and I arrived there on the 27.

Q. Were you with a convoy?

A. I was with a convoy of 230 French women; among us were Danielle Casanova who died in Auschwitz, Mai Politzer who died in Auschwitz and Helene Solomon. There were some elderly women -

Q. What was their social position?

A. They were intellectuals and school teachers; they came from all walks of life. Mai Politzer was a doctor, and the wife of the philosopher George Politzer. Helene Solomon is the wife of the physicist Solomon; she is the daughter of Professor Langevin. Danielle Casanova was a dental surgeon and she was very active among the women. It is she who organised a resistance movement among the wives of prisoners.

Q. How many of you came back out of 230?

A. 49. In the convoy there were some elderly women. I remember one who was 67, and had been arrested because she had in her kitchen her husband's shotgun, which she kept as a souvenir and had not declared, because she did not want it to be taken from her. She died after a fortnight at Auschwitz.

THE PRESIDENT: When you said only 49 came back, do you mean only 49 arrived at Auschwitz?

THE WITNESS: No. Only 49 came back to France.

There were also cripples, among them a singer who had only one leg. She was taken out and gassed at Auschwitz.

There was also a young girl of sixteen, a high school pupil, Claudine Guerin she also died at Auschwitz. There also were two women who had been acquitted by the

German Military Tribunal, Marie Alonzo and Marie-Therese Fleuri; they died at Auschwitz.

It was a terrible journey. We were 60 in a wagon and we were given no food or drink during the journey. At the various stopping places we asked the Lorraine soldiers of the Wehrmacht who were guarding us, whether we would arrive soon, and they replied: "If you knew where you are going you would not be in a hurry to get there."

We arrived at Auschwitz at dawn. The seals on our wagons were broken, and we were driven out by blows with the butt end of a rifle, and taken to the Birkenau camp, a section of the Auschwitz camp. It is situated in the middle of a great plain, which was frozen in the month of January. During this part of the journey we had to drag our luggage. As we passed through the door, we knew only too well how slender were our chances of coming out again. For we had already met columns of living skeletons going to work, and as we entered we sang the Marseillaise to keep up our courage.

We were led to a large shed, then to the disinfecting station. There our heads were shaven and our registration numbers were tattooed on the left forearm. Then we were taken into a large room for a steam bath and a cold shower.

In spite of the fact that we were naked all this took place in the presence of SS men and women. We were then given clothing which was soiled and torn: a cotton dress and jacket of the same material.

As all this had taken several hours, we saw from the windows of the block where we were, the camp of the men, and toward the evening an orchestra came in. It was snowing and we wondered why they were playing music. We then saw that the camp foremen were returning to the camp. Each foreman was followed by men who were carrying the dead. As they could hardly drag themselves along every time they stumbled they were put on their feet again by blows with the butt end of a rifle.

After that we were taken to the block where we were to live. There were no beds but only bunks, measuring 2 x 2 metres, and there nine of us had to sleep without any mattress, and the first night without any blanket. We remained in blocks of this kind for several months. We could not sleep all night, because every time one of the nine moved - this happened unceasingly because we were all ill - she disturbed the whole row.

At 3 in the morning the shouting of the guards woke us up and with cudgel blows we were driven from our bunks to go to roll call. Nothing in the world could release us from going to the roll call; even those who were dying had to be dragged there. We had to stand there in rows of five until dawn - i.e. until seven or eight o'clock in the morning in winter, and when there was a fog, sometimes until noon. Then the kommandos would start on their way to work.

M. DUBOST:

Q. Excuse me - can you describe the roll call?

A. For roll call we were lined up in rows of five, and we waited until daybreak, until the "Aufseherinnen," the German women guards in uniform, came to count us. They had cudgels and they beat us more or less at random.

We had a comrade, Germaine Renaud, a school-teacher from Azay-Le-Rideau, in France, who had her skull broken before my eyes, from a blow with a cudgel during the roll call.

The work at Auschwitz consisted of clearing demolished houses and especially draining of marsh land. This was by far the hardest work, for all day long we had our feet in the water and there was the danger of sinking. It frequently happened that we had to pull out a comrade who had sunk in up to the waist. During the work the SS men and women who stood guard over us would beat us with cudgels, and set their dogs on us. Many of our friends had their legs torn by the dogs. I even saw a woman torn to pieces and die under my very eyes when Tauber, a member of the SS, encouraged his dog to attack her and grinned at the sight.

The causes of death were extremely numerous. First of all, there was the complete lack of washing facilities. When we arrived at Auschwitz, for 12,000 internees there was only one tap of water, unfit for drinking and it was not always flowing. As this tap was in the German wash-house we could reach it only by passing through the guards, who were German women prisoners, and they beat us horribly as we went by. It was therefore almost impossible to wash ourselves or our clothes. For more than three months we remained without changing our clothes. When there was snow, we melted some to wash in. Later, in the spring, when we went to work, we would drink from a puddle by the road side and then wash our underclothes in it. We took it in turns to wash our hands in this dirty water. Our companions died of thirst, because we got only half a cup of some herbal tea twice a day.

Q. Please describe in detail one of the roll calls at the beginning of February.

A. On the 5 of February there was what is called a general roll call.

Q. In what year was that?

A. In 1943; at 3.30 the whole camp -

Q. 3.30 in the morning?

A. In the morning at 3.30 the whole camp was awakened and sent out on the plain, whereas normally the roll call was at the same time, but inside the camp. We remained out in front of the camp in the snow until five in the afternoon without any food. Then when the signal was given we had to go through the door one by one, and we were struck in the back with a cudgel, each one of us, in order to make us run. Those who could not run, either because they were too old or too ill, were caught by a hook and taken to Block 25, "waiting block," for the gas chamber.

On that day 10 of the French women of our convoy were thus caught and taken to the waiting block.

When all the internees were back in the camp, a party to which I belonged was organised to go and pick up the bodies of the dead which were scattered over the plain as on a battlefield. We carried to the yard of Block 25 the dead and the dying without distinction, and they remained there stacked in the courtyard.

This block 25, which was the anteroom of the gas chamber, if one may so call it, is well known to me because at that time we had been transferred to Block 26 and our windows opened on the yard of Block 25. One saw stacks of corpses piled up in the courtyard, and from time to time a hand or a head would stir amongst the bodies, trying to free itself; it was a dying woman attempting to get free and live.

The rate of mortality in that block was even more terrible than elsewhere because, having been condemned to death, they received food or drink only if there was something left in the cans in the kitchen; which means that very often they went for several days without a drop of water.

One of our companions, Annette Epaux, a fine young woman of thirty, passing the block one day, was overcome with pity for those women who moaned from morning till night in all languages, "drink, drink, water!" She came back to our block to get a little herbal tea, but as she was passing it through the bars of the window she was seen by the Aufseherin, who took her by the neck and threw her into Block 25.

All my life I will remember Annette Epaux. Two days later I saw her on the truck which was taking the internees to the gas chamber. She had her arms round another French woman, old Clina Forcher, and when the truck started moving, she cried, "think of my little boy, if you ever get back to France," Then they started singing the Marseillaise.

In Block 25, in the courtyard, there were rats as big as cats running about and gnawing the corpses and even attacking the dying, who had not enough strength left to chase them away.

Another cause of mortality and epidemics was the fact that we were given food in large red mess tins, which were merely rinsed in cold water after each meal. As all the women were ill, and had not the strength during the night to go to the trench which was used as a lavatory, and the access to which was beyond description, they used these containers for a purpose for which they were not meant. The next day the mess tins were collected and taken to a refuse heap. During the day another team would come and collect them, wash them in cold water, and put them in use again.

Another cause of death was the problem of shoes. In the snow and mud of Poland, leather shoes were completely worn out at the end of a week or two. Therefore our feet were frozen and covered with sores. We had to sleep in our muddy shoes, lest they be stolen, and when the time came to get up for roll call cries of anguish could be heard: "My shoes have been stolen." Then one had to wait until the whole block had been emptied to look under the bunks for odd shoes. Sometimes one found two shoes for the same foot, or one shoe and one sabot. One could go to roll call like that but it was an additional torture for work, because sores formed on our feet, which quickly became infected for lack of care. Many of our companions went to the "Revier" for sores on their feet and legs and never came back.

Q. What did they do to the internees who came to roll call without shoes?

A. The Jewish internees who came without shoes were immediately taken to Block 25.

Q. They were gassed then?

A. They were gassed for any reason whatsoever. Their conditions were moreover absolutely appalling. While we were crowded eight hundred in a block and could scarcely move, they were fifteen hundred to a block of similar dimensions, so that many of them could not sleep during the whole night or even lie down.

Q. Can you tell me about the "Revier?"

A. To reach the "Revier " one had to go first to the roll call. What ever the state was...

Q. Would you please explain what the "Revier" was in the camp?

A. The "Revier" was the block where the sick were put. This place could not be given the name of hospital, because it did not correspond in any way to our idea of a hospital.

To go there one had first to obtain authorisation from the block Chief, who seldom gave it. When it was finally granted we were led in columns to the Revier where, no matter what weather, whether it snowed or rained, even if one had a temperature of 40 degrees one had to wait for several hours standing in a queue to be admitted. It frequently happened that patients died outside, before they could get in. Moreover, lining up in front of the Revier was dangerous because, if the queue was too long the SS came along, picked up all the women who were waiting, and took them straight to Block 25.

Q. That is to say, to the gas chamber?

A. That is to say to the gas chamber. That is why very often the women preferred not to go to the Revier, and they died at their work or at roll call. Every day, after the evening roll call in winter time, dead were picked up who had fallen into the ditches.

The only advantage of the "Revier" was that as one was in bed, one had not to go to roll call, but conditions were appalling, four in a bed of less than one metre in width, each suffering from a different disease, so that anyone who came for sores on their legs would catch typhus or dysentery from their neighbours. The straw mattresses were dirty and they were changed only when absolutely rotten. The bedding was so full of lice that one could see them swarming like ants. One of my companions, Marguerite Corringer, told me that when she had typhus, she could not sleep all night because of the lice. She spent the night shaking her blanket over a piece of paper and emptying the lice into a receptacle by the bed, and this went on for hours.

There were practically no medicines. Consequently the patients were left in their beds without any attention, without hygiene and unwashed. The dead lay in the bed with the sick for several hours, and finally, when they were noticed, they were simply tipped out of bed and taken outside the block. There the women porters would come and carry the dead away on small stretchers, with heads and legs dangling over the sides. From morning till night the carriers of the dead went from the "Revier" to the mortuary.

During the big epidemics, in the winters of 1943 and 1944, the stretchers were replaced by carts, as there were too many dead bodies. During those periods of epidemics from 200 to 350 died each day.

Q. How many people died at that time?

A. During the big epidemics of typhus in the winters of 1943 and 1944, from 200 to 350, it depended on the days.

Q. Was the "Revier" open to all the internees?

A. No. When we arrived Jewish women had not the right to be admitted. They were taken straight to the gas chamber. At Auschwitz there were experimental blocks -

Q. Would you please tell us about the disinfection of the blocks, before that?

A. From time to time, owing to the filth which caused the lice and gave rise to so many epidemics, they disinfected the blocks with gas, but these disinfections were also the cause of many deaths because, while the block were being disinfected with gas, the prisoners were taken to the shower-baths, and their clothes taken away from them to be steamed. Meanwhile they were left naked outside, waiting for their clothing to come back from the steaming, and then they were given back to them all wet. Even those who were sick, who could barely stand on their feet, were sent to the showers. It is quite obvious that a great many of them died in the course of these proceedings. Those who could not move were washed all in the same bath during the disinfection.

Q. How were you fed?

A. We had 200 grams of bread, three-quarters or half a litre - it varied - of swede soup, and a few grams of margarine or a slice of sausage in the evening. This daily.

Q. Regardless of the work that was exacted from the internee?

A. Regardless of the work that was exacted from the internee. Some who had to work in the factory of the "Union," an ammunition factory where they made grenades and shells, received what was called a "Zulage" that is a supplementary ration, when the amount of their production was satisfactory. Those internees had to go to roll call morning and night as we did, and they were at work twelve hours in the factory. They came back to the camp after the day's work making the journey both ways on foot.

Q. What was this "Union" factory?

A. It was an ammunition factory. I do not know to what company it belonged. It was called the "Union."

Q. Was it the only factory?

A. No. There was also a large factory at Buna, but as I did not work there I do not know what was made there. The internees who were taken to Buna never came back to our camp.

Q. Will you tell us about experiments, if you witnessed any?

A. As to the experiments, I have seen in the "Revier" - because I was employed there - the queue of young Jewesses from Salonica who stood waiting in front of the X-ray room for sterilisation. I also know that they performed castration operations in the men's camp. Concerning the experiments performed on women I am well informed, because my friend, Doctor Hade Hautvat, of Montbeliard, who has returned to France, worked for several months in that block, nursing the patients, but she always refused to participate in those experiments. They sterilised women either by injections or by operations; or also with rays. I saw and knew several women who had been sterilised. There was a very high mortality rate among those experimented upon. Fourteen Jewesses from France who refused to be sterilised were sent to a "Strafarbeit" commando, that is to hard labour.

Q. Did they come back from those commandos?

A. Very seldom. Quite exceptionally.

Q. What was the aim of the SS?

A. Sterilisation - they did not conceal it - They said that they were trying to find the best method for sterilising, so as to replace the native population in the occupied countries by Germans after one generation, once they had made use of the inhabitants as slaves to work for them.

Q. In the "Revier" did you see any pregnant women?

A. Yes. The Jewish women, when they arrived in the first months of pregnancy, were subjected to abortion. When their pregnancy was near the end, after confinement, the babies were drowned in a bucket of water. I know that because I worked in the "Revier" and the woman who was in charge of that task was a German mid-wife, who was imprisoned for having performed illegal operations. After a while another doctor arrived and for two months they did not kill the Jewish babies. But one day an order came from Berlin saying that they had again to be done away with. Then the mothers and their babies were called to the infirmary, they were put in a lorry and taken away to the gas chamber.

Q. Why did you say that an order came from Berlin?

A. Because I knew the internees who worked in the secretariat of the SS and in particular a Slovakian woman by the name of Hertha Rotk, who is now working with UNRRA at Bratislava.

Q. Is it she who told you that?

A. Yes. And moreover, I also knew the men who worked in the gas commando.

Q. You have told us about the Jewish mothers. Were there other mothers in your camp?

A. Yes, in principle non-Jewish mothers were allowed to have their babies, and the babies were not taken away from them, but conditions in the camp, being so horrible, the babies rarely lived for more than four or five weeks.

There was one block where the Polish and Russian mothers were. One day the Russian mothers, having being accused of making too much noise, had to stand for roll call all day in front of the block, naked, with their babies in their arms.

Q. What was the disciplinary system of the camp? Who kept order and discipline? What were the punishments?

A. Generally speaking, the SS economised on many of their own personnel by employing internees for supervising the camp. They only supervised. These internees were chosen from criminals and German prostitutes and sometimes those of other nationalities; but most of them were Germans. By corruption, accusation and terror, they succeeded in making veritable human beasts of them and the internees had as much cause to complain about them as about the SS themselves. They beat us just as hard as the SS, and as to the SS, the men behaved like the women and the women were as savage as the men. There was no difference.

The system employed by the SS of degrading human beings to the utmost by terrorising them and causing them through fear to commit acts which made them ashamed of themselves, resulted in their being no longer human. This was what they wanted - it took a great deal of courage to resist this atmosphere of terror and corruption.

Q. Who meted out punishments?

A. The SS leaders, men and women.

Q. What was the nature of the punishments?

A. Bodily ill-treatment in particular; one of the most usual punishments was fifty blows with a stick, on the loins, They were administered with a machine which I saw, a swinging apparatus manipulated by an SS. There were also endless roll calls day and night, or gymnastics; flat on the belly, get up, lie down, up, down for hours, and anyone who fell was beaten unmercifully and taken to Block 25.

Q. How did the SS behave towards the women? And the women SS?

A. At Auschwitz there was a brothel for the SS and also one for the male internees of the staff, which were called "Kapo."

Moreover, when the SS needed servants they came accompanied by the Oberaufseherin, that is, the woman commandant of the camp, to make a choice during the process of disinfection. They would point to a young girl, whom the Oberaufseherin would take out of the ranks. They would look her over and make jokes about her physique, and if she was pretty and they liked her, they would hire her as a maid, with the consent of the Oberaufseherin, who would tell her that she was to obey them absolutely, no matter what they asked of her.

Q. Why did they go during disinfection?

A. Because during the disinfection the women were naked.

Q. The system of demoralisation and corruption - was it exceptional?

A. No. The system was identical in all the camps where I have been and I have spoken to internees coming from camps where I myself had never been; it was the same thing everywhere. The system was identical no matter what the camp was. There were, however, certain variations. I believe that Auschwitz was one of the harshest, but later I went to Ravensbruck, where there also was a house of ill fame, and where recruiting was also carried out among the internees.

Q. Then, according to you, everything was done to degrade those women in their own sight?

A. Yes.

Q. What do you know about the convoy of Jews which arrived from Romainville about the same time as yourself?

A. When we left Romainville the Jewesses who were there at the same time as ourselves were left behind. They were sent to Drancy, and subsequently arrived at Auschwitz, where we found them again three weeks later, three weeks after our arrival. Of the original 1,200 only 125 actually came to the camp; the others were immediately sent to the gas chambers. Of these 125 not one was left alive at the end of one month.

The transports operated as follows:

When we first arrived, whenever a convoy of Jews came, a selection was made; first the old men and women, then the mothers and the children, were put into lorries, together with the sick or those whose constitution appeared to be delicate. They only took in the young women and girls, as well as the young men who were sent to the men's camp.

Generally speaking, of a convoy or about 1,000 to 1,500, seldom more than 250 - and this figure really was the maximum - actually reached the camp. The rest were immediately sent to the gas chamber.

At this selection also, they picked out women in good health between the ages of 20 and 30, who were sent to the experimental block, and young girls and slightly older women, or those who had not been selected for that purpose, were sent to the camp where, like ourselves, they were tattooed and shaved.

There was also, in the spring of 1944, a special block for twins. It was during the time when large convoys of Hungarian Jews - about 700,000 - arrived. Dr. Mengele, who was carrying out the experiments, kept back from each convoy twin children and twins in general, regardless of their age, so long as both were present. So we had both babies and adults on the floor of that block. Apart from blood tests and measuring I do not know what was done to them.

Q. Were you an eye witness of the selections on the arrival of the convoys?

A. Yes, because when we worked at the sewing block in 1944, the block where we lived directly faced the stopping place of the trains. The system had been improved. Instead of making the selection at the place where they arrived, a side line now took the train practically right up to the gas chamber, and the stopping place - about 100 metres from the gas chamber - was right opposite our block though, of course, separated from us by two rows of barbed wire. Consequently, we saw the unsealing of the coaches and the soldiers letting men, women and children out of them. We then witnessed heartrending scenes, old couples forced to part from each other, mothers made to abandon their young daughters, since the latter were sent to the camp whereas mothers and children were sent to the gas chambers. All these people were unaware of the fate awaiting them. They were merely upset at being separated but they did not know that they were going to their death. To render their welcome more pleasant at this time - June, July 1944 - an orchestra composed of internees - all young and pretty girls, dressed in little white blouses and navy blue skirts - played, during the selection on the arrival of the trains, gay tunes such as "The Merry Widow," the "Barcarolle" from the "Tales of Hoffman," etc. They were then informed that this was a labour camp, and since they were not brought into the camp they only saw the small platform surrounded by flowering plants. Naturally, they could not realise what was in store for them.

Those selected for the gas chamber, i.e., the old people, mothers and children, were escorted to a red-brick building.

Q. These were not given an identification number?

A . No.

Q. They were not tattooed?

A. No. They were not even counted.

Q. You were tattooed?

A. Yes. They were taken to a red-brick building, which bore the letters "B-a-d," that is to say "bath." There, to begin with, they were made to undress and given a towel before they went into the so-called shower room. Later on, at the time of the large convoys, they had no more time left to playact or to pretend; they were brutally undressed, and I know these details as I knew a little Jewess from France who lived with her family at the "Republique."

Q. In Paris.

A. In Paris. She was called "little Marie" and she was the only one ...

Q. Slow down please. The interpreters have difficulty in following you.

A. Little Marie was the sole survivor of a family of nine. Her mother and her seven brothers and sisters had been gassed on arrival. When I met her she was employed to undress the babies before they were taken into the gas chamber. Once the people were undressed they took them into a room which was somewhat like a shower room, and gas capsules were thrown through an opening in the ceiling. An SS man would watch the effect produced, through a porthole. At the end of five or seven minutes, when the gas had completed its work, he gave the signal to open the doors, and men with gas masks - they too were internees - went into the room and removed the corpses. They told us that the internees must have suffered before dying, because they were closely clinging to each other and it was very difficult to separate them.

After that a special squad would come to pull out gold teeth and dentures and again, when the bodies had been reduced to ashes, they would sift them in an attempt to recover the gold.

At Auschwitz there were eight crematoriums, but as from 1944 these proved insufficient. The SS had large pits dug by the internees, where they put branches, sprinkled with gasoline, which they set on fire. Then they threw the corpses into the pits. From our block we could see after about three quarters of an hour or one hour after the arrival of a convoy, large flames coming from the crematorium and the sky was carmined by the burning pits.

One night we were awakened by terrifying cries, and we discovered, on the following day ...

THE PRESIDENT: You go too quickly.

A. Forgive me. One night we were awakened by terrifying cries. And we discovered, on the following day, from the men working in the "Sonderkommando" (the "Gas Kommando") that on the preceding day, the gas supply having run out, they had thrown the children into the furnaces alive.

Q. Can you tell us about the selections that were made at the beginning of winter?

A. Every year, towards the end of the autumn, they proceeded to make selections on a large scale in the infirmary (Revier). The system appeared to work as follows: I say this because I noticed the fact for myself during the time I spent in Auschwitz. Others, who had stayed there even longer than myself, had observed the same phenomenon:

In the spring, all through Europe, they rounded up men and women whom they sent to Auschwitz. They kept only those who were strong enough to work all through the summer. Very naturally some died every day, but even the strongest, those who had succeeded in holding out for six months, were so exhausted that they too had to go to the "Revier." It was then that the large scale selections were made, so as not to feed too many useless mouths during the winter. All the women who were too thin were sent to the gas chamber, as well as those who had long, drawn-out illnesses; but the Jewesses were gassed for practically no reason at all. For instance, they gassed everybody in the Scabies Block, whereas everybody knows that with a little care, scabies can be cured in three days. I remember the Typhus Convalescent Block whence 450 out of 500 patients were sent to the gas chamber.

During Christmas 1944 - no, 1943, Christmas 1943, when we were in quarantine, we saw, since we lived opposite it, women brought to Block 25, stripped naked. Uncovered trucks were then driven up and on them the naked women were piled, as many as the trucks could hold. Each time a truck started, the famous Hessler - he was one of the criminals condemned to death at the Luneberg trials - ran after the truck and with his bludgeon repeatedly struck the naked women going to their death. They knew they were going to the gas chamber and tried to escape. They were massacred. They attempted to jump from the truck and we, from our own block, watched the trucks pass by and heard the grievous wailing of all those women who knew they were going to be gassed. Many of them could very well have lived on, since they were only suffering from scabies and were, perhaps, a little too undernourished.

Q. You told us, Madame, a little while ago, that the deportees, from the moment they stepped off the train and without even being counted, were sent to the gas chamber. What happened to their clothing and their luggage?

A. The non Jews had to carry their own luggage and were billeted in separate blocks, but when the Jews arrived they had to leave all their belongings on the platform. They were stripped before entering the gas chamber and all their clothes, as well as all their belongings, were taken over to large barracks and there sorted out by a Kommando named "Canada." Then everything was shipped to Germany: jewellery, fur coats, etc.

Since the Jewesses were sent to Auschwitz with their entire families, and since they had been told that this was a sort of Ghetto and were advised to bring all their goods and chattels along, they consequently brought considerable riches with them. As for the Jewesses from Salonica, I remember that on their arrival they were given picture post- cards, bearing the post office address of "Waldsee," a place which did not exist, and a printed text to be sent to their families, stating, " We are doing very well here; we have work and we are well treated. We await your arrival." I myself saw the cards in question and the "Schreiberinnen," i.e., the secretaries of the Block, were instructed to distribute them among the internees. I know that whole families arrived as a result of these post-cards.

I myself know that the following occurred in Greece. I do not know whether it happened in any other country, but in any case it did occur in Greece (as well as in Czechoslovakia) that whole families went to the Recruiting Office at Salonica in order to rejoin their families. I remember one Professor of Literature from Salonica, who, to his horror, saw his own father arrive.

Q. Will you tell us about the Gypsy camps?

A. Right next to our camp, on the other side of the barbed wires, three metres apart, there were two camps; one for Gypsies, which towards August 1944 was completely gassed. These Gypsies came from all parts of Europe including Germany. Likewise on the other side there was the so-called "family-camp." These were Jews from the Ghetto of Theresienstadt, who had been brought there and, unlike ourselves, they had neither been tattooed nor shaved. Their clothes were not taken from them and they did not have to work. They lived like this for six months and at the end of six months the entire "family-camp" amounting to some 6,000 or 7,000 Jews, were gassed. A few days later other large convoys again arrived from Theresienstadt with their families and six months later they too were gassed, like the first inmates of the "family-camp."

Q. Would you, Madame, please give us some details as to what you saw when you were about to leave the camp and under what circumstances you left it?

A. We were in quarantine before leaving Auschwitz.

Q. When was that?

A. We were in quarantine for ten months, from the 15th July 1943, yes - until May 1944. And after that we returned to the camp for two months. Then we went to Ravensbruck.

Q. These were all Frenchwomen from your convoy, who had survived?

A. Yes. All the surviving Frenchwomen of our convoy. We had heard from Jewesses who had arrived from France, in July 1944, that an intensive campaign had been carried out by the British Broadcasting Corporation in London, in connection with our convoy and quoting Mai Politzer, Danielle Casanova, Helene Solomon-Langevin and myself. As a result of this broadcast we knew that orders had been issued from Berlin to the effect that Frenchwomen should be, transported under better conditions.

So we were placed in quarantine. This was a block situated opposite the camp and outside the barbed wire. I must say that it is to this quarantine that the forty-nine survivors owed their lives because, at the end of four months, there were only fifty-two of us. Therefore it is certain that we could not have survived eighteen months of this regime had we not had these ten months of quarantine. It was imposed because exanthematic typhus was raging at Auschwitz. One could only leave the camp to be freed or to be transferred to another camp, or to be summoned before the Court after spending fifteen days in quarantine, these fifteen days being the incubation period for exanthematic typhus. Consequently, as soon as the papers arrived announcing that the internee would probably be liberated, she was placed in quarantine until the order for her liberation was signed. This sometimes took several months, and fifteen days was the minimum.

Now a policy existed for freeing common-law criminals and German anti-social elements in order to employ them as workers in the German factories. It is therefore impossible to imagine that the whole of Germany was unaware of the existence of the concentration camps and of what was going on there, since these women had been released from the camps and it is difficult to believe that they never mentioned them. Besides, in the factories where the former internees were employed, the "Vorarbeiterinnen," i.e., the forewomen - were German civilians in contact with the internees and able to speak to them. The forewomen from Auschwitz, who subsequently came to Siemens at Ravensbruck as "Aufseherinnen," had been former workers at Siemens in Berlin - they met forewomen they had known in Berlin and, in our presence, they told them what they had seen at Auschwitz. It is therefore incredible that this was not known in Germany.

We could not believe our eyes when we left Auschwitz and our hearts were sore when we saw the small group of 49 women - all that was left of the 250 who had entered the camp 18 months earlier. But to us it seemed that we were leaving hell itself, and for the first time hopes of survival, of seeing the world again, were vouchsafed to us.

Q. Where were you sent then, Madame?

A. On leaving Auschwitz we were sent to Ravensbruck. There we were escorted to the NN Block - meaning "Nacht und Nebel," that is, "The Secret Block." With us, in that block, were Polish women with the identification number 7,000. Some were called "rabbits" because they had been used as experimental guinea pigs. They selected from the convoys girls with very straight legs who were in very good health, and they submitted them to various operations. Some of the girls had parts of the bone removed from their legs, others received injections, but what was injected, I do not know. The mortality rate was very high among the women operated upon. So when they came to fetch the others to operate on them, they refused to go to the

"Revier." They were forcibly dragged to the cells where the Professor, who had arrived from Berlin, operated in his uniform, without taking any aseptic precautions, without wearing a theatre coat and without washing his hands. There are some survivors of these "rabbits." They still suffer a great deal. They suffer periodically from suppurations and, since nobody knows to what treatment they had been subjected, it is extremely difficult to cure them.

Q. These internees, were they tattooed on their arrival?

A. No. People were not tattooed at Ravensbruck but, on the other hand, we had to go up for a gynaecological examination and, since no precautions were ever taken and the same instruments were frequently used in all cases, infections spread, partly because criminal prisoners and political internees were all herded together.

In Block 32, where we were billeted, there were also some Russian women prisoners of war, who had refused to work voluntarily in the ammunition factories. For that reason they had been sent to Ravensbruck. Since they persisted in their refusal, they were subjected to every form of petty indignity. They were, for instance, forced to stand in front of the block a whole day long without any food. Some of them were sent in convoys to Barthe. Others were employed to carry lavatory receptacles in the camp. The "Strafblock" (penitentiary block) and the Bunker also housed internees who had refused to work in the war factories.

Q. You are now speaking about the prisons in the camp?

A. About the prisons in the camp. As a matter of fact I have visited the camp prison. It was a civilian prison - a real one.

Q. How many French were there in that camp?

A. From eight to ten thousand.

Q. How many women all told?

A. At the time of liberation the identification numbers represented 105,000 and possibly more.

There were also executions in the camps. The numbers were called at roll call in the morning, and the victims then left for the "Kommandantur" and were never seen again. A few days later the clothes were sent down to the "Effektenkammer," where the clothes of the internees were kept. After a certain time their cards would vanish from the filing cabinets in the camp.

Q. The system of detention was the same as at Auschwitz?

A. No it was quite obvious that extermination was the sole aim and object of Auschwitz. Nobody was at all interested in the output. We were beaten for no reason whatsoever. It was sufficient to stand from morning till evening but whether we carried one brick or ten was of no importance at all. We were quite aware that the human element was employed as slave labour in order to kill, that this was the ultimate purpose, whereas at Ravensbruck the output was of great importance. It was a selection camp. When the convoys arrived at Ravensbruck, they were rapidly dispatched either to the munition or to the powder factories, either to work at the airfields or, latterly, to dig trenches.

The following procedure was adopted for going to the munition factories the manufacturers or their foremen or else their representatives came down themselves to pick and choose their workers, accompanied by SS men; the effect was that of a slave market. They felt the muscles, examined the faces to see if the person looked healthy - and then made their choice. Finally, they made them walk naked past the doctor and he eventually decided if a woman was fit or not to leave for work in the factories. Latterly, the doctor's visit became a mere formality as they ended by employing anybody who came along. The work was exhausting, principally because of lack of food and steep, since in addition to twelve solid hours of work one had to attend roll-call in the morning and in the evening. In Ravensbruck there was the Siemens factory, where telephone equipment was manufactured as well as wireless sets for aircraft. Then there were workshops in the camp for camouflage material and uniforms and for various utensils used by soldiers. One of these I know best.

THE PRESIDENT: I think we had better break off now for ten minutes.

(A recess was taken)

Q. Madame, did you see any SS chiefs and members of the Wehrmacht visit the camp of Ravensbruck and Auschwitz when you were there?
A. Yes.
Do you know if any German government officials came to visit these camps?
A. I know it only as far as Himmler is concerned. Apart from Himmler I do not know.
Q. Who were the guards in these camps?
A. At the beginning there were the SS guards exclusively.
Q. Will you please speak more slowly so that the interpreters can follow you?
A. At the beginning they were only SS men but from the spring of 1944, as the young SS men in many companies were replaced by elder men of the Wehrmacht both at Auschwitz and also at Ravensbruck, we were guarded by soldiers of the Wehrmacht as from 1944.
Q. You can therefore testify that, on the order of the Greater German General Staff, the German Army was implicated in the atrocities which you have described?
A. Obviously, since we were guarded by the Wehrmacht as well, and this could not have occurred without orders.
Q. Your testimony is formal and involves both the SS and the Army.
A. Absolutely.
Q. Will you tell us about the arrival at Ravensbruck in the winter of 1944 of Hungarian Jewesses who had been arrested "en masse?" You were in Ravensbruck, this is a fact about which you can testify?
A. Yes, naturally. There was no longer any room left in the blocks, and the prisoners already slept four in a bed, so there was raised, in the middle of the camp, a large tent. Straw was spread in the tent and the Hungarian women were brought to this tent. Their condition was deplorable. There were a great many cases of frozen feet because they had been evacuated from Budapest and had walked a good part of the way in the snow. A great many of them had died en route. Those who arrived at Auschwitz were led to this tent and there an enormous number of them died. Every day a squad came to remove the corpses in the tent. One day, on returning to my block, which was next to this tent, during the cleaning up -

THE PRESIDENT: Madam, are you speaking of Ravensbruck or of Auschwitz?

THE WITNESS: Now I am speaking of Ravensbruck. It was in the winter of 1944, about November or December, I believe, though I cannot say for certain which month it was. It is so difficult to give a precise date about events in concentration camps since one day of torture was followed by another day of similar torment, and the prevailing monotony made it very hard to keep track of time.

One day therefore, as I was saying, I passed the tent while it was being cleaned, and I saw a pile of smoking manure in front of it. I suddenly realised that this manure was human excrement, since the unfortunate women no longer had the strength to drag themselves to the lavatories.

Q. What were the conditions in the workshops where the jackets were manufactured?

A. At the workshop where the uniforms were manufactured ...

Q. Was it the camp workshop?

A. It was the camp workshop, known as "Schneiderei I." 200 jackets or pairs of trousers were manufactured per day. There were two shifts; a day and a night shift, both working twelve hours at a stretch. The night shift, when starting work at midnight, after the standard amount of work had been reached, but only then, received a thin slice of bread. Later on this practice was discontinued. Work was carried on at a furious pace; the internees could not even take time off to go to the lavatories. Both day and night they were terribly beaten up, both by the women of the SS and by the men, if a needle broke, owing to the poor quality of the thread, if the machine stopped, or if these ladies and gentlemen did not like one's looks. Towards the end of the night one could see that the workers were so exhausted that every movement was an effort to them. Beads of sweat stood out on their foreheads. They could not see clearly. When the standard amount of work was not reached the foreman, Binder, rushed up and beat up, with all his might, one woman after another, all along the line, with the result that the last in the row waited their turn petrified with terror. If one wished to go to the "Revier " one had to receive the authorisation of the SS - who granted it very rarely - and even then, if the doctor did give a woman a permit authorising her to stay away from work for a few days, the SS guards would often come round and fetch her out of bed in order to put her back at her machine. The atmosphere was frightful since, by reason of the "black-out," one could not open the windows at night. Six hundred women therefore worked for twelve hours without any ventilation. All those who worked at the "Schneiderei" became like living skeletons after a few months, they began to cough, their eyesight failed, and they developed a nervous twitching of the face for fear of beatings to come.

I well knew the conditions of this workshop since my little friend, Marie Rubiano, a little French girl who had just passed three years in the prison of Kottbus, was sent, on her arrival at Ravensbruck, to the "Schneiderei I," and every evening she would tell me about her martyrdom. One day, when she was quite exhausted, she obtained permission to go to the "Revier" and as on that day the German nursing sister, Erica, was less evil tempered than usual, she was X- rayed. Both lungs were severely affected and she was sent to the horrible Block 10, the block for consumptives. This block was particularly terrifying, since tubercular patients were not considered as "recuperable material"; they received no treatment and, because of shortage of staff, they were not even washed. We might even say that there were no medical supplies at all.

Little Marie was placed in the ward which housed patients with bacillary infections, in other words such patients who were considered incurable. She spent some weeks there and had no courage left to put up a fight for her life. I must say that the atmosphere of this room was particularly depressing. There were very many patients, several to one bed, as well as in three-tier bunks, in an overheated atmosphere, lying between internees of various nationalities, so that they could not even speak to each other. Then, too, the silence in this antechamber of death was only broken by the yells of the German personnel on duty, and from time to time by the muffled sobs of a little French girl thinking of her mother and of her country which she would never see again.

And yet, Marie Rubino did not die fast enough to please the SS, so one day Dr. Winkelmann - selection specialist at Ravensbruck entered her name in the black-list, and on the 9 February 1945, together with 72 other consumptive women, 6 of whom were French, she was shoved on the truck for the gas chamber.

During this period, in all the "Revieren," selections were made, and all patients considered unfit for work were sent to the gas chamber. The Ravensbruck gas chamber was situated just behind the wall of the camp, next to the crematorium. When the trucks came to fetch the patients we heard the sound of the motor across the camp, and the noise ceased right by the crematorium whose chimney rose above the high wall of the camp.

At the time of the liberation I returned to these places. I visited the gas chamber, which was a hermetically sealed building made of boards, and inside it one could still smell the disagreeable odour of gas. I know that at Auschwitz the gases were the same as those which were used against the lice, and the only traces they left were small, pale green crystals which were swept out when the windows were opened. I know these details, since the men employed in delousing the blocks were in contact with the personnel who gassed the victims, and they told them that one and the same gas was used in both cases.

Q. Was this the only way used to exterminate the internees in Ravensbruck?

A. In Block 10 they also experimented with a white powder. One day the German nursing sister, Martha, arrived in the block and distributed a powder to some twenty patients. The patients subsequently fell into a deep sleep. Four or five of them were seized with violent fits of vomiting and this saved their lives. During the night the snores gradually ceased and the patients died. This I know because I went every day to visit the French women in the block. Two of the nurses were French, and Dr. Louise Leporz, a native of Bordeaux, can likewise testify to this fact.

Q. Was this a frequent occurrence?

A. During my stay this was the only case of its kind within the "Revier" but the system was also applied at the "Jugendlager," so called because it was a former reform school for German juvenile delinquents.

Towards the beginning of 1945 Dr. Winkelmann, no longer satisfied with making selections from the Revier, proceeded to make his selections from the blocks. All the prisoners had to answer roll-call in their bare feet and expose their breasts and legs. All those who were sick, too old, too thin or whose legs were swollen with oedemata, were set aside and then sent to this Jugendlager, a quarter of an hour away from the camp at Ravensbruck. I visited it at the Liberation.

In the blocks an order had been circulated to the effect that the old women and the patients who could no longer work should apply in writing for admission to the Jugendlager, where they would be far better off, where they would not have to work and where there would be no roll-call. We learned about this later, through some of the people who worked at the Jugendlager - the chief of the camp was an Austrian woman, Betty Wenz, whom I knew from Auschwitz - and from a few of the survivors, one of whom is Irene Otteland, a French woman living in Drancy, 17, Rue de la Liberte, who was repatriated at the same time as myself and whom I nursed after the liberation. Through her we discovered the details about Jugendlager.

Q. Can you tell us, Madame, if you can answer this question? The SS doctors who made the selection, were they acting on their own accord or were they merely obeying orders?

A. They were acting on orders received, since one of them, Dr. Lukas refused to participate in the selections and was withdrawn from the camp, and Dr. Winkelmann was sent from Berlin to replace him.

Q. Did you personally witness these facts?

A. It was he himself who told the Chief of the Block and Dr. Louise Leporz, when he left.

Q. Could you give us some information as to the conditions in which the men at the neighbouring camp at Ravensbruck lived on the day after the Liberation, when you were able to see them?

A. I think it advisable to speak of the "Jugendlager" first since, chronologically speaking, it comes first.

Q. If you wish it.

A. At the "Jugendlager" the old women and the patients who had left our camp were placed in blocks, which had no water and no conveniences; they lay on straw-mattresses on the ground, so closely pressed together that one was quite unable to pass between them. At night one could not sleep because of the continuous coming and going and the internees trod on each other when passing. The straw-mattresses were rotten and teemed with lice; those who were able to stand remained for hours on end for roll call until they collapsed.

By way of nourishment they only received one thin slice of bread and half a quart of turnip soup, and all the drink they got in 24 hours was half a quart of herbal infusion (tisone). They had no water to drink, none to wash in and none to wash their mess tins.

In the "Jugendlager" there was also a "Revier" for those who could no longer stand. Periodically, during the roll-calls, the "Aufseherin" would choose some internees, who would be undressed and left in nothing but their chemises. Their coats were then returned to them - they were hoisted on to a truck and were driven off to the gas chamber. A few days later the coats were returned to the "Kammer," i.e., the clothing warehouse and the labels were marked "Mitwerda." The internees working on the labels told us that the word "Mitwerda" did not exist and that it was a special term for the gases.

At the "Revier" white powder was periodically distributed, and the sick died as in Block 10, which I mentioned a short time ago. They made ...

THE PRESIDENT: The details of the witness' evidence as to Ravensbruck seem to be very much alike, if not the same, as at Auschwitz. Would it not be possible now after hearing this amount of detail, to deal with the matter more generally, unless there is some substantial difference between Ravensbruck and Auschwitz.

M. DUBOST: I think there is a difference which the witness has pointed out to us: namely that in Auschwitz the prisoners were purely and simply exterminated. It was merely an extermination camp, whereas at Ravensbruck they were interned in order to work, and were weakened by work until they died of it.

THE PRESIDENT: If there are any other distinctions between the two, no doubt you will lead the witness, I mean ask the witness about those other distinctions.

M. DUBOST: I shall not fail to do so.

BY M. DUBOST:

Q. Could you tell the Tribunal in what condition the men's camp was found at the time of the Liberation and how many survivors remained?

A. When the Germans went away they left two thousand sick women and a certain number of volunteers, myself included, to take care of them. They left us without water and without light. Fortunately the Russians arrived on the following day. We therefore were able to go to the men's camp and there we found a perfectly indescribable sight. They had been for five days without water. There were eight hundred serious cases, three doctors and seven nurses, who were unable to separate the dead from the sick. Thanks to the Red Army, we were able to take these sick persons over into clean blocks and to give them food and care; but unfortunately I can only give the figures for the French:

There were four hundred of them when we came to the camp and only one hundred and fifty were able to return to France; for the others it was too late, in spite of all our care ...

Q. Were you present at any of the executions and do you know how they were carried out in the camp?

A. I was not present at any of the executions. I only know that the last one took place on the 22 April, 8 days before the arrival of the Red Army. The prisoners were sent, as I said, to the Kommandantur; then their clothes were returned and their cards were removed from the files.

Q. Was the situation in these camps of an exceptional nature or do you consider it was part of a system?

A. It is difficult to convey an exact idea of the concentration camps to anybody, unless one has been in the camp oneself, since one can only quote examples of horror, but it is quite impossible to convey any impression of that deadly monotony. If asked, what was the worst of all, it is impossible to answer, since everything was atrocious: It is atrocious to die of hunger, to die of thirst, to be ill, to see all one's companions dying round one and be unable to help them; it is atrocious to think of one's children, of one's country which one will never see again, and there were times when we asked if our life were not a living nightmare, so unreal did this life appear in all its horror.

For months, for years we had one wish only: the wish that some of us would escape alive, in order to tell the world what the fascist convict prisons were like: everywhere, at Auschwitz as at Ravensbruck - and the comrades from the other camps told the same tale-there was the systematic and implacable urge to use human beings as slaves and to kill them when they could work no more.

Q. Have you anything further to relate?

A. No.

M. DUBOST: If the Tribunal wishes to question the witness, I have finished.

GENERAL RUDENKO: I have no questions to ask.

DR. MARX (acting for Dr. Babel, counsel for the SS, absent): Attorney Babel was prevented from coming this morning as he has to attend a conference with General Mitchell.

My Lords, I should like to take the liberty of asking the witness a few questions to elucidate the matter.

Q. Madame Couturier, you declared that you were arrested by the French police?

A. Yes.

Q. For what reason were you arrested?

A. Resistance. I belonged to a resistance movement.

Q. I did not ...

A. Activity in a resistance movement.

Q. Your statement leads to an important ... and to a further question. Your statement shows much skill in ... yes, wait until I finish my question. What education did you receive and what post did you ever occupy?

A. What was what?

Q. I mean what kind of post did you ever hold? Have you ever held a post?

A. Where?

Q. For example as a teacher or a lecturer?

A. Before the war?

Q. Before the war.

A. I do not quite see what this question has to do with the matter. I was a journalist.

Q. Yes. The fact of the matter is that you, in your statement, showed great skill in style and expression, and I should like to know whether you held any position such as teacher or lecturer.

A. No. I was a newspaper photographer.

Q. How do you explain that you yourself came through these experiences so well and are now in so good a state of health?

A. First of all, I was liberated a year ago, and in a year one has time to recover. Secondly, I was ten months in quarantine for typhus and I had the great luck not to die of exanthematic typhus, although I had it and was ill for three months and a half.

Also, in the last months at Ravensbruck, as I knew German, I worked on the "Revier" roll-call, which explains why I did not have to work quite so hard or to suffer from the inclemencies of the weather. On the other hand, out of 230 of us only 49 from my convoy returned alive, and we were only 54 at the end of four months. I had the great fortune to return.

Q. Yes. Does your statement contain what you yourself observed or is it concerned with information from other sources as well?

A . Whenever such was the case I mentioned it in my declaration. I have never quoted anything which had not previously been verified at the source and by several persons, but the major part of my evidence is based on personal experience.

Q. How can you explain your very precise statistical knowledge, for instance, that 700,000 Jews arrived from Hungary?

A. I told you that I have worked in the offices and, where Auschwitz was concerned, I was a friend of the secretary, the "Oberaufseherin," whose name and address I gave to the Tribunal.

Q. It has been stated that only 350,000 Jews came from Hungary, according to the testimony of the Chief of the Gestapo, Eichmann.

A. I am not going to argue with the Gestapo. I have good reason to know that what the Gestapo states is not always true.

Q. How were you treated personally? Were you treated well?

A. Like the others.

Q. Like the others? You said before that the German people must have known of the happenings in Auschwitz. What are your grounds for this statement?

A. I have already told you: to begin with there was the fact that, when we left, the Lothingrian soldiers of the Wehrmacht had said to us in the train: "if you only knew where you are going, you would not be in such a hurry."

THE PRESIDENT: Madame, you are going too fast.

A. - the Lothingrian soldiers who were taking us to Auschwitz said to us: "If you knew where you are going, you would not be in such a hurry to get there." Then there was the fact that the German women who came out of quarantine to go to work in German factories knew of these events, and they all said that they would speak about them outside.

Further, the fact that in all the factories where the prisoners worked they were in contact with the German civilians, as also were the "Aufseherinnen" who were in touch with their friends and families and often told them what they had seen.

Q. One more question. Up to 1942 you were able to observe the behaviour of he German soldiers in Paris. Did not these German soldiers behave well throughout and did they not pay for what they took?

A. I have not the least idea whether they paid or not for what they requisitioned. As for their good behaviour, too many of my friends were shot or massacred for me not to differ with you.

DR. MARX: I have no further question to put to this witness. I would only like to be allowed to ...

THE PRESIDENT: If you have no further questions there is nothing more to be said.

DR. MARX: Thank you, yes.

THE PRESIDENT: There is too much laughter in the Court I have already spoken about that.

I thought you had said you had no further question?

DR. MARX: Yes. Please excuse me. - I only want to make a proviso for Attorney Babel that he might cross-examine the witness himself at a later date, if that is possible, either in addition -

THE PRESIDENT: Babel, did you say?

DR. MARX: Yes.

THE PRESIDENT: I beg your pardon; yes, certainly. When will Dr. Babel be back in his place?

DR. MARX: I presume that he will be back in the afternoon. He is in the building. However, he must first read the minutes.

THE PRESIDENT: We will consider the question. If Dr. Babel is here this afternoon we will consider the matter, if Dr. Babel makes a further application.

Does any other of the defendant's counsel wish to ask any questions of the witness?

(No response)

M. Dubost, have you any questions you wish to ask on re-examination?

M. DUBOST: I have no further questions to ask.

THE PRESIDENT: Then the witness may retire.

M. DUBOST: If the Tribunal will kindly allow it, we shall now hear another witness, M. Veith.

JEAN FREDERIC VEITH takes the stand.

THE PRESIDENT: Are you calling this witness on the treatment of prisoners in concentration camps?

M. DUBOST: Yes, Mr. President, and also because this witness can give us particulars of the ill-treatment to which certain prisoners had been exposed in the camp of internees. This is no longer a question of concentration camps only, but of soldiers who had been brought to the concentration camps and subjected to the same cruelty as the civilian prisoners.

THE PRESIDENT: Well, you will not lose sight of the fact that there has been practically no cross-examination of the witness you have already called about the treatment in concentration camps? The Tribunal, I think, feels that you could deal with the treatment in concentration camps somewhat more generally than the last witness.

Are you not hearing what I say?

M. DUBOST: Yes, I hear it very well.

THE PRESIDENT: The Tribunal thinks that you could deal with the question of treatment in concentration camps rather more generally now, after we have heard the details from the witnesses whom you have already called.

M. DUBOST: Is the Tribunal willing to hear this witness?

BY THE PRESIDENT:
Q. What is your name?
A. Jean Frederic Veith.
Q. Will you repeat this oath?
I swear to speak without hate or fear,
To say the truth, all the truth, and only the truth.
(The witness repeated the oath after the President)

THE PRESIDENT: Raise your right hand.
THE WITNESS: swear it.
THE PRESIDENT: Would you like to sit down?
THE WITNESS: Thank you.
BY M. DUBOST:
Will you please spell your name and surname?
A. Jean Frederic Veith. I was born on 28 April 1903 in Moscow.
Q. You are of French nationality?
A. I am of French nationality, born of French parents.
Q. In which camp were you interned?
A. At Mauthausen; from the 22 April 1943 until the 22 April 1945.
Q. You knew about the work carried out in the factories supplying material to the Luftwaffe. Who controlled these factories?
A. I was in the "Arbeitseinsatz" at Mauthausen as from June 1943, and I was therefore well acquainted with all questions dealing with work.
Q. Who controlled the factories working for the Luftwaffe?
A. There were outside camps at Mauthausen where workers were employed by Heinkel, Messerschmidt, Alfa-Vienne and the Saurer-Werke, and there was, moreover, the construction work on the Leibl Pass Tunnel by Alpine Montana.
Q. Who controlled this work, supervisors or engineers?
A. There was only an SS inspection. The work itself was controlled by the engineers and the firms themselves.
Did these engineers belong to the Luftwaffe?
A. On certain days I saw Luftwaffe officers who came to visit the Messerschmidt workshops in the quarry.
Q. Were they able to see for themselves the conditions under which the prisoners lived?
A. Yes, certainly.
Q. Did you see any high-ranking fascist officials visiting the camp?
A. I saw a great many high-ranking officials, among them Himmler, Kaltenbrunner, Pohl, Maurer, the Chief of the Labour Office D II, of the Reich, and many other visitors whose names I do not know.
Who told you that Kaltenbrunner had come?
A. Our offices faced the parade ground overlooking the Kommandantur we therefore saw the high-ranking officials arriving, and the SS men themselves would tell us: "There goes so and so."
Q. Could the civilian population know, and did it know of the plight of the internees?
A. Yes, the population could know, since at Mauthausen there was a road near the quarry and those who passed by that road could see all that was happening.

Moreover, the internees worked in the factories. They were separated from the other workers, but they had certain contacts with them and it was quite easy for the other workers to realise their plight.

Q. Can you tell us what you know about a journey to an unknown castle, of a bus carrying prisoners who were never seen again?

A. At one time a method for the elimination of sick persons by injections was adopted at Mauthausen. It was particularly used by Dr. Krebsbach, nicknamed Dr. Spritzbach by the prisoners, since it was he who had inaugurated the system of injections. There came a time when the injections were discontinued and then persons who were too sick or too weak were sent to a castle which, we learned later, was called Harthein, but was officially known as "Genesunglager" (convalescent camp); of those who went there, none ever returned. We received the death certificates directly from the political section of the camp; these certificates were secret. Everybody who went to Harthein died. The number of dead amounted to about 5,000.

Q. Did you see prisoners of war arrive at Mauthausen Camp?

A. Certainly I saw prisoners of war. Their arrival at Mauthausen Camp took place, first of all, in front of the political section. Since I was working at the Hollerith I could watch the arrivals, for the offices looked on to the parade ground in front of the political section where the convoys arrived. The convoys, were immediately sorted out. One part was sent to the camp for registration and very often some of the uniformed prisoners were set aside; these had already been subjected to special violence in the political section, were handed straight over to the prison guards and then sent to the prisons, and never heard of again. They were not registered in the camp. The only registration was, made in the political section by Muller who was in charge of these prisoners.

Q. They were prisoners of war?

A. They were prisoners of war, they were very often in uniform.

THE PRESIDENT: Do not go so fast, please.

A. (continuing): They were generally men in uniform.

BY M. DUBOST:

Q. Of what nationality?

A. Mostly Russians and Poles.

Q. They were brought to your camp to be killed there?

A. They were brought to our camp for "action K."

Q. What do you know about action K and how do you know it?

A. My knowledge of "action K" is due to the fact that I was head of the Hollerith service in Mauthausen, and consequently received all the transfer forms from the various camps. And when prisoners were erroneously transferred to us as ordinary prisoners, we would put on the transfer form which we had to send to the Central Office in Berlin - or rather, we would not put any number at all, as we were unable to give any. The "Political Section" gave us no indications at all and even destroyed the list of names if, by chance, it ever reached us.

In conversations with my comrades of the "Political Section" I discovered that this "action K" was originally applied to prisoners of war who had been captured while attempting to escape. Later this action was extended further still, but always to soldiers and especially to officers who had succeeded in escaping, but who had been recaptured in countries under German control.

Moreover, any person engaged in activities which might be interpreted as not corresponding to the wishes of the fascist chiefs could also be subjected to "action K." These prisoners arrived at Mauthausen and disappeared, i.e., they were taken to the prison, where one part would be executed on the spot and another sent to the annexe of the prison - to the famous Block 20 of Mauthausen.

Q. You definitely state that these were prisoners of war?

A. Yes, they were prisoners of war, or most of them, at any rate.

Q. Do you know of an execution of officers, prisoners of war, who had been brought to the camp at Mauthausen?

A. I cannot give you any names, but there were some.

Q. Did you witness the execution of Allied officers who were murdered within 48 hours of their arrival in camp?

A. I saw the arrival of the convoy of the 6th September. I believe that is the one you are thinking of; I saw the arrival of this convoy and the very same afternoon these 47 went down to the quarry dressed in nothing but their shirts and drawers. Shortly after we heard the sound of machine gunfire. I then left the office and passed at the back, pretending I was carrying documents to another office, and with my own eyes I saw these unfortunate people shot down. 19 were executed on the very same afternoon and the remainder on the following morning; later on all the death certificates were marked: "Killed while attempting to escape."

(A recess was taken)

MARSHAL OF THE COURT: If the Court please, it is desired to announce that the defendant Kaltenbrunner will be absent from this afternoon's session on account of illness.

THE PRESIDENT: You may go on, M. Dubost.

M. DUBOST: We are going to complete hearing of the witness Veith, to whom, however, I have only one more question to put.

THE PRESIDENT: Have him brought in.

(Whereupon the witness again took the stand and was questioned further by M. Dubost as follows):

Q. You continue, to testify under the oath that you already made this morning. Will you give some additional information concerning the execution of the 47 Allied Officers whom you saw shot within 48 hours at camp Mauthausen where they had been brought?

A. Those officers, those parachutists, were shot in accordance with the usual system used whenever prisoners had to be done away with. That is to say, they were forced to work to excess, to carry heavy stones. Then they were beaten, until they took heavier ones; and so on and so forth, until, finally driven to extremity, they turned towards the barbed wire. If they did not do it of their own accord, they were pushed there, or they were beaten until they did so, and the moment they approached it and were perhaps about one metre away from it, they were mown down by machine guns fired by the SS patrols in the miradors. This was the usual system for the "killing for attempted escape" as they afterwards called it.

These 47 men were killed on the afternoon of the 6th and morning of the 7th of September.

Q. How did you know their names?

A. Their names came to me with the official list, because they had all been entered in the camp registers and I had to report to Berlin all the changes in the actual strength of the Hollerith Section. I saw all the rosters of the dead and of the new arrivals.

Q. Did you communicate this list to an official authority?

A. This list was taken by the American official authorities when I was at Mauthausen. I immediately went back to Mauthausen after my liberation, because I knew where the documents were, and the American authorities then had all the lists which we were able to find.

M. DUBOST: Mr. President, I have no further questions to ask the witness.

THE PRESIDENT: Does the British prosecutor want to ask any questions?

BRITISH PROSECUTOR: No.

THE PRESIDENT: Does the United States prosecutor?

UNITED STATES PROSECUTOR: No.

THE PRESIDENT: Do any members of the defence counsel wish to ask any questions?

DR. BABEL (defence counsel for SS and SD): Mr. President, I was in the Dachau camp on Saturday and at the Augsburg-Gottingen camp yesterday. I found out various things there which now enable me to question individual witnesses. I could not do this before as I was not acquainted with local conditions. I should like to put one question. When the witness was questioned this morning ...

THE PRESIDENT: Will you try to go a little more slowly?

DR. BABEL: Yes. I was unable to attend here this morning on account of a conference to which I was called by General Mitchell. Consequently I did not conduct the cross-examination of the witness this morning. I have only one question to put to the witness now - I should like to ask if I may cross-examine the witness further later, or if it is better to reserve the question?

THE PRESIDENT: You can cross-examine this witness now, but the Tribunal is informed that you left General Mitchell at 15 minutes past ten.

DR. BABEL: In consequence of the conference I had to send a telegram and dispatch some other pressing business so that it was impossible for me to attend the session.

THE PRESIDENT: You can certainly cross-examine the witness now.

DR. BABEL: I had only one more question in the meantime, namely:

(Cross-examination by Dr. Babel)

Q. The witness stated that the officers in question were driven toward the wire fence. By whom were they so driven?

A. They were driven to the barbed wire by the SS guards who accompanied them, and the entire Mauthausen staff was present. They were beaten as well by the SS and by one or two "green" prisoners, who were with them and who were the "Kapo." In the camps these green prisoners were often worse than the SS themselves.

Q. In the Dachau camp, inside the camp itself, within the wire enclosure, there were almost no SS guards, and that was probably also the case in Mauthausen?

A. Inside the camp there was only a certain number of SS, but they changed, and none of those who belonged to the troops guarding the camp could fail to be aware of what went on in it, as even if they did not enter the camp, they watched it from the miradors or from outside, and they saw absolutely everything.

Q. Were the guards who shot at the prisoners inside or outside the wire enclosure?

A. They were in the miradors in the same line as the barbed wire.

Q. Could they see from there that the officers were driven to the barbed wire by anyone by means of blows?

A. They could see it so well that once or twice some of the guards refused to shoot, saying that it was not an attempt to escape and they would not shoot. They were immediately relieved of their posts, and disappeared.

Q. Did you see that yourself?

A. I did not see it myself, but I heard about it; it was told me by my Kommandofuehrer among others, who said: "There is a watchguard who refused to shoot."

Q. Who was this Kommandofuehrer? The chief of the group?

A. The Kommandofuehrer was Wieleman. I do not remember his rank. He was not Unterscharfuehrer, but the rank immediately below Unterscharfuehrer and he was in charge of the Hollerith section in Mauthausen.

DR. BABEL: I have no more questions to ask just now. I shall, however, make application to call the witness again, and I shall then take the opportunity to ask the rest ... to put such further questions to him as I consider necessary and to retain him for this purpose, here, in Nuremberg. I am not in a position to cross-examine the witness this afternoon, as I did not bear his statements this morning, and I would request that the witness ...

THE PRESIDENT: You ought to have been here. If you were released from an interview with General Mitchell at 10.15, there seems to the Tribunal - to me at any rate - to be no reason why you should not have been here whilst this witness was being examined.

THE PRESIDENT: The Tribunal thinks that you could deal with the question of treatment in concentration camps rather more generally now, after we have heard the details from the witnesses whom you have already called.

M. DUBOST: Is the Tribunal willing to hear this witness?

BY THE PRESIDENT:

Q. What is your name?

A. Jean Frederic Veith.

Q. Will you repeat this oath?

I swear to speak without hate or fear,

To say the truth, all the truth, and only the truth.

(The witness repeated the oath after the President)

THE PRESIDENT: Raise your right hand.

THE WITNESS: swear it.

THE PRESIDENT: Would you like to sit down?

THE WITNESS: Thank you.

BY M. DUBOST:

Will you please spell your name and surname?

A. Jean Frederic Veith. I was born on 28 April 1903 in Moscow.

Q. You are of French nationality?

A. I am of French nationality, born of French parents.

Q. In which camp were you interned?

A. At Mauthausen; from the 22 April 1943 until the 22 April 1945.

Q. You knew about the work carried out in the factories supplying material to the Luftwaffe. Who controlled these factories?

A. I was in the "Arbeitseinsatz" at Mauthausen as from June 1943, and I was therefore well acquainted with all questions dealing with work.

Q. Who controlled the factories working for the Luftwaffe?

A. There were outside camps at Mauthausen where workers were employed by

Heinkel, Messerschmidt, Alfa-Vienne and the Saurer-Werke, and there was, moreover, the construction work on the Leibl Pass Tunnel by Alpine Montana.

Q. Who controlled this work, supervisors or engineers?

A. There was only an SS inspection. The work itself was controlled by the engineers and the firms themselves.

Q. Did these engineers belong to the Luftwaffe?

A. On certain days I saw Luftwaffe officers who came to visit the Messerschmidt workshops in the quarry.

Q. Were they able to see for themselves the conditions under which the prisoners lived?

A. Yes, certainly.

Q. Did you see any high-ranking fascist officials visiting the camp?

A. I saw a great many high-ranking officials, among them Himmler, Kaltenbrunner, Pohl, Maurer, the Chief of the Labour Office D II, of the Reich, and many other visitors whose names I do not know.

Who told you that Kaltenbrunner had come?

A. Our offices faced the parade ground overlooking the Kommandantur we therefore saw the high-ranking officials arriving, and the SS men themselves would tell us: "There goes so and so."

Q. Could the civilian population know, and did it know of the plight of the internees?

A. Yes, the population could know, since at Mauthausen there was a road near the quarry and those who passed by that road could see all that was happening. Moreover, the internees worked in the factories. They were separated from the other workers, but they had certain contacts with them and it was quite easy for the other workers to realise their plight.

Q. Can you tell us what you know about a journey to an unknown castle, of a bus carrying prisoners who were never seen again?

A. At one time a method for the elimination of sick persons by injections was adopted at Mauthausen. It was particularly used by Dr. Krebsbach, nicknamed Dr. Spritzbach by the prisoners, since it was he who had inaugurated the system of injections. There came a time when the injections were discontinued and then persons who were too sick or too weak were sent to a castle which, we learned later, was called Harthein, but was officially known as "Genesungslager" (convalescent camp); of those who went there, none ever returned. We received the death certificates directly from the political section of the camp; these certificates were secret. Everybody who went to Harthein died. The number of dead amounted to about 5,000.

Q. Did you see prisoners of war arrive at Mauthausen Camp?

A. Certainly I saw prisoners of war. Their arrival at Mauthausen Camp took place, first of all, in front of the political section. Since I was working at the Hollerith I could watch the arrivals, for the offices looked on to the parade ground in front of the political section where the convoys arrived. The convoys, were immediately sorted out. One part was sent to the camp for registration and very often some of the uniformed prisoners were set aside; these had already been subjected to special violence in the political section, were handed straight over to the prison guards and then sent to the prisons, and never heard of again. They were not registered in the camp. The only registration was, made in the political section by Muller who was in charge of these prisoners.

Q. They were prisoners of war?

A. They were prisoners of war, they were very often in uniform.

THE PRESIDENT: Do not go so fast, please.

A. (continuing): They were generally men in uniform.

BY M. DUBOST:

Q. Of what nationality?

A. Mostly Russians and Poles.

Q. They were brought to your camp to be killed there?

A. They were brought to our camp for "action K."

Q. What do you know about action K and how do you know it?

A. My knowledge of "action K" is due to the fact that I was head of the Hollerith service in Mauthausen, and consequently received all the transfer forms from the various camps. And when prisoners were erroneously transferred to us as ordinary prisoners, we would put on the transfer form which we had to send to the Central Office in Berlin - or rather, we would not put any number at all, as we were unable to give any. The "Political Section" gave us no indications at all and even destroyed the list of names if, by chance, it ever reached us.

In conversations with my comrades of the "Political Section" I discovered that this "action K" was originally applied to prisoners of war who had been captured while attempting to escape. Later this action was extended further still, but always to soldiers and especially to officers who had succeeded in escaping, but who had been recaptured in countries under German control.

Moreover, any person engaged in activities which might be interpreted as not corresponding to the wishes of the fascist chiefs could also be subjected to "action K." These prisoners arrived at Mauthausen and disappeared, i.e., they were taken to the prison, where one part would be executed on the spot and another sent to the annexe of the prison - to the famous Block 20 of Mauthausen.

Q. You definitely state that these were prisoners of war?

A. Yes, they were prisoners of war, or most of them, at any rate.

Q. Do you know of an execution of officers, prisoners of war, who had been brought to the camp at Mauthausen?

A. I cannot give you any names, but there were some.

Q. Did you witness the execution of Allied officers who were murdered within 48 hours of their arrival in camp?

A. I saw the arrival of the convoy of the 6th September. I believe that is the one you are thinking of; I saw the arrival of this convoy and the very same afternoon these 47 went down to the quarry dressed in nothing but their shirts and drawers. Shortly after we heard the sound of machine gunfire. I then left the office and passed at the back, pretending I was carrying documents to another office, and with my own eyes I saw these unfortunate people shot down. 19 were executed on the very same afternoon and the remainder on the following morning; later on all the death certificates were marked: "Killed while attempting to escape."

(A recess was taken)

MARSHAL OF THE COURT: If the Court please, it is desired to announce that the defendant Kaltenbrunner will be absent from this afternoon's session on account of illness.

THE PRESIDENT: You may go on, M. Dubost.

M. DUBOST: We are going to complete hearing of the witness Veith, to whom, however, I have only one more question to put.

THE PRESIDENT: Have him brought in.

(Whereupon the witness again took the stand and was questioned further by M. Dubost as follows):

Q. You continue, to testify under the oath that you already made this morning. Will you give some additional information concerning the execution of the 47 Allied Officers whom you saw shot within 48 hours at camp Mauthausen where they had been brought?

A. Those officers, those parachutists, were shot in accordance with the usual system used whenever prisoners had to be done away with. That is to say, they were forced to work to excess, to carry heavy stones. Then they were beaten, until they took heavier ones; and so on and so forth, until, finally driven to extremity, they turned towards the barbed wire. If they did not do it of their own accord, they were pushed there, or they were beaten until they did so, and the moment they approached it and were perhaps about one metre away from it, they were mown down by machine guns fired by the SS patrols in the miradors. This was the usual system for the "killing for attempted escape" as they afterwards called it.

These 47 men were killed on the afternoon of the 6th and morning of the 7th of September.

Q. How did you know their names?

A. Their names came to me with the official list, because they had all been entered in the camp registers and I had to report to Berlin all the changes in the actual strength of the Hollerith Section. I saw all the rosters of the dead and of the new arrivals.

Q. Did you communicate this list to an official authority?

A. This list was taken by the American official authorities when I was at Mauthausen. I immediately went back to Mauthausen after my liberation, because I knew where the documents were, and the American authorities then had all the lists which we were able to find.

M. DUBOST: Mr. President, I have no further questions to ask the witness.

THE PRESIDENT: Does the British prosecutor want to ask any questions?

BRITISH PROSECUTOR: No.

THE PRESIDENT: Does the United States prosecutor?

UNITED STATES PROSECUTOR: No.

THE PRESIDENT: Do any members of the defence counsel wish to ask any questions?

DR. BABEL (defence counsel for SS and SD): Mr. President, I was in the Dachau camp on Saturday and at the Augsburg- Gottingen camp yesterday. I found out various things there which now enable me to question individual witnesses. I could not do this before as I was not acquainted with local conditions. I should like to put one question. When the witness was questioned this morning ...

THE PRESIDENT: Will you try to go a little more slowly?

DR. BABEL: Yes. I was unable to attend here this morning on account of a conference to which I was called by General Mitchell. Consequently I did not conduct the cross- examination of the witness this morning. I have only one question to put to the witness now - I should like to ask if I may cross-examine the witness further later, or if it is better to reserve the question?

THE PRESIDENT: You can cross-examine this witness now, but the Tribunal is informed that you left General Mitchell at 15 minutes past ten.

DR. BABEL: In consequence of the conference I had to send a telegram and dispatch some other pressing business so that it was impossible for me to attend the session.

THE PRESIDENT: You can certainly cross-examine the witness now.

DR. BABEL: I had only one more question in the meantime, namely:

(Cross-examination by Dr. Babel)

Q. The witness stated that the officers in question were driven toward the wire fence. By whom were they so driven?

A. They were driven to the barbed wire by the SS guards who accompanied them, and the entire Mauthausen staff was present. They were beaten as well by the SS and by one or two "green" prisoners, who were with them and who were the "Kapo." In the camps these green prisoners were often worse than the SS themselves.

Q. In the Dachau camp, inside the camp itself, within the wire enclosure, there were almost no SS guards, and that was probably also the case in Mauthausen?

A. Inside the camp there was only a certain number of SS, but they changed, and none of those who belonged to the troops guarding the camp could fail to be aware of what went on in it, as even if they did not enter the camp, they watched it from the miradors or from outside, and they saw absolutely everything.

Q. Were the guards who shot at the prisoners inside or outside the wire enclosure?

A. They were in the miradors in the same line as the barbed wire.

Q. Could they see from there that the officers were driven to the barbed wire by anyone by means of blows?

A. They could see it so well that once or twice some of the guards refused to shoot, saying that it was not an attempt to escape and they would not shoot. They were immediately relieved of their posts, and disappeared.

Q. Did you see that yourself?

A. I did not see it myself, but I heard about it; it was told me by my Kommandofuehrer among others, who said: "There is a watchguard who refused to shoot."

Q. Who was this Kommandofuehrer? The chief of the group?

A. The Kommandofuehrer was Wieleman. I do not remember his rank. He was not Unterscharfuehrer, but the rank immediately below Unterscharfuehrer and he was in charge of the Hollerith section in Mauthausen.

DR. BABEL: I have no more questions to ask just now. I shall, however, make application to call the witness again, and I shall then take the opportunity to ask the rest ... to put such further questions to him as I consider necessary and to retain him for this purpose, here, in Nuremberg. I am not in a position to cross-examine the witness this afternoon, as I did not bear his statements this morning, and I would request that the witness ...

THE PRESIDENT: You ought to have been here. If you were released from an interview with General Mitchell at 10.15, there seems to the Tribunal - to me at any rate - to be no reason why you should not have been here whilst this witness was being examined.

Q. What about those who were left?

A. Those who were left when the last convoy went out? That is a complicated story. We were deeply grieved about them. About the 1st of April - though I cannot guarantee the exact date, the Commander of the Camp, Pister, assembled a large number of prisoners, and addressed them as follows: "The Allied advance has already reached the immediate neighbourhood of Buchenwald. I wish to hand over to the Allies the keys of the camp. I do not want any atrocities. I wish the camp as a whole to be handed over." As a matter of actual fact, the Allied advance was held up - more than we wanted, at least - and evacuation was begun. A delegation of prisoners went to see the commander, reminding him of his promise, for he had given his word emphasising that it was his "word of honour as a soldier." He seemed acutely embarrassed and explained that Sauckel, the Governor of Thuringia, had given orders that no prisoner should remain in Buchenwald, for that constituted a danger to the province.

Furthermore, we knew that all who knew the secrets of the administration of Buchenwald camp would be put out of the way. A few days before we were liberated forty-three of our comrades belonging to different nationalities were called out to be done away with; then an unusual phenomenon occurred - the camp revolted; the men were hidden and never given up. We also knew that under no circumstances would anyone who had been employed either in the extermination block, or in the hospital be allowed to leave the camp. That is all I have to say about the last few days.

Q. This officer in command of the camp, whom you have just said gave his word of honour as a soldier, was he a soldier?
A. His attitude towards the prisoners was ruthless; but he had his orders. Frankly, he was a special type of soldier; but he was not acting on his own initiative in treating the prisoners in this way.
Q. To what branch of the service did he belong?
A. He belonged to the SS Totenkopf Division.
Q. Was he an SS man?
A. Yes, he was an SS man.
Q. He was acting on orders, you say?
A. He was certainly acting on orders.
Q. For what purpose were the prisoners used?
A. They were used in such a way that no attention was paid to the fact that they were human beings. They were used for experimental purposes.

At Buchenwald the experiments were made in Block 46. The men who were to be employed there were always selected by means of a medical examination. On those occasions when I was present it was performed by Dr. Schidlowsky, of whom I have already spoken.

Q. Was he a doctor?
A. Yes, he was a doctor. They were used for the hardest labour; in the Laura mines; working in the salt mines as, for instance, in the Mansleben am See detachment - clearing up bomb debris. It must be remembered that the more difficult the labour conditions were, the harsher was the supervision by the guards.

They were used in Buchenwald for any kind of labour; earth works, quarries, in factories - and so forth. To quote a particular case: There were two factories attached to Buchenwald - the Gustloff works and Mibao works. They were munition factories under technical and non-military management. In this particular case there was some sort of rivalry between the SS and the technical management of the factory. The technical management, concerned with its output, took the part of the prisoners to the extent of occasionally obtaining supplementary rations for them. Internee-labour had certain advantages. The cost was negligible, and from a security point of view the maximum of secrecy was ensured, as the prisoners had no contact with the outside world and therefore no leakage was possible.

Q. You mean - leakage of military information?

A. I mean leakage of military information.

Q. Could outsiders see that the prisoners were ill-treated and wretched?

A. That is another question.

Q. Will you answer it later?

A. I shall answer it later. I have omitted one detail. The internees were also used to a certain extent after death. The ashes resulting from the cremations were thrown into the excrement pit and served to fertilise the fields around Buchenwald. I add this detail because it struck me vividly at the time.

Finally, as I said, work - whatever it might be - was the prisoners' only chance of survival. As soon as they were no longer of any possible use, they were done for.

Q. Were not internees used as "blood donors," involuntary - of course?

A. I forgot that point. Prisoners assigned to light work, whose output was poor, were used as blood donors. Members of the Wehrmacht came several times. I saw them twice at Buchenwald, taking blood from these men. The blood was taken in a ward known as CP-2, i.e. operations ward 2.

Q. This was done on orders from higher quarters?

A. I do not see how it could have been done otherwise.

Q. On their own initiative?

A. Not on the initiative of anyone in the camp. These elements had nothing to do with the camp administration or the guards. I must make it clear that those whom I saw belonged to the Wehrmacht, whereas we were guarded by SS, all of them from the Totenkopf Division. Towards the end, a special use was made of them.

In the early months of 1945, members of the Gestapo came to Buchenwald and took away all the papers of those who had died, in order to re-establish their identity and to make out forged papers. One Jew was specially employed to take photographs to adapt the papers which had belonged to the dead for the use of persons whom, of course, we did not know. The Jew disappeared, and I do not know what became of him. We never saw him again.

But this utilisation of identification papers was not confined to the dead. Several hundred French prisoners were summoned to the "Fliegerverwaltung" and there subjected to a very precise interrogation on their identity, their convictions and their background. They were then told that they would on no account be allowed to receive any correspondence, or even parcels - those of them who ever had received any. From an administrative point of view all traces of them were effaced, and contact with the outside world was rendered even more impossible for them than it had been under ordinary circumstances. We were deeply concerned about the fate of our comrades. We were liberated very soon after that, and I can only say that prisoners were used in this way - i.e., that their identification papers were used for manufacturing forged documents.

Q. What was the effect of this kind of life?

A. The effect of this kind of life on the human organism?

Q. On the human organism.

A. As to the human organism, there was only one effect: the degradation of the human being. The living conditions which I have just described were enough in themselves to produce such degradation. It was a systematic process; an unrelenting will seemed to be at work to reduce those men to one level - the lowest possible level of human degradation.

To begin with, the first degrading factor was the indiscriminate way in which they were mixed. It was permissible to mix nationalities, but not to mix indiscriminately every possible type of prisoner-political, military - for the members of the French resistance movement were soldiers - racial elements and common criminals.

Criminals of all nationalities were herded together with their compatriots, and prisoners of every nationality lived side by side.

In addition, there were overcrowding, insanitary conditions and compulsory labour. I shall quote a few examples to show that prisoners were mixed quite indiscriminately.

In March 1945, I saw the French General Duval die. He had been working on the "terrasse" with me all day. When we came back, he was covered with mud and completely exhausted. He died a few hours later.

The French General Vernaud died on a straw mattress, filthy with excrement, in room No. 6, where those on the verge of death were taken, surrounded by dying men.

I saw M. de Tessan die ...

Q. Will you explain to the Tribunal who M. de Tessan was?

A. M. de Tessan was a former French Minister, married to an American. He also died on a straw mattress, covered with pus, from a disease known as septicopyohemia.

I also witnessed the death of Count de Lipokowski, who had done brilliant service in this war. He had been granted the Honours of war by the German Army and had, for one thing, been invited to Paris by Rommel, who desired to show the admiration he felt for his military brilliance. He died miserably in the winter of 1944.

One further instance. The Belgian Minister Janson was in the camp living under the conditions which I have already described, and of which you must have already heard, very often. He died miserably, a physical and mental wreck. His intellect had gone and he had partially lost his reason.

I quote only extreme cases and especially those of generals, as they were said to be granted, special conditions. I saw no sign of that.

The last stage in this process of the degradation of human beings was the setting of prisoner against prisoner.

Q. Before dealing with this point, will you describe the conditions in which you found your former professor, Leon Kindberg, Professor of Medicine?

A. I studied medicine under Professor Leon Kindberg at the Beaujon Hospital.

Q. In Paris?

A. Yes, in Paris, He was a very highly cultured and brilliantly intelligent man.

In January 1945 I learned that be had just arrived from Monovitz. I found him in Block 58, a block which in normal circumstances would hold three hundred men, and into which twelve hundred had been crowded - Hungarians, Poles, Russians, Czechs, with a large proportion of Jews. I did not recognise Leon Kindberg because there was nothing to distinguish him from the usual type of prisoner to be found in these blocks. There was no longer any sign of intellect in him and it was hard to find anything of the man that I had formerly known. We managed to get him out of that block but his health was unfortunately too much impaired and he died shortly after his liberation.

Q. Can you tell the Tribunal, as far as you know, what crimes were committed by these men?

A. After the Armistice Leon Kindberg had settled in Toulouse to practice "physiology". I know from an absolutely reliable source that he had taken no part whatsoever in resistance activities directed against the German occupation authorities in France. They found out that he was a Jew and as such he was arrested and deported. He drifted into Buchenwald by way of Auschwitz and Monovitz.

Q. What crime had General Duval committed that he should be imprisoned along with pimps, moral degenerates and murderers? What had General Vernaud done?

A. I know nothing about the activities of General Duval and General Vernaud during the occupation. All I can say is that they were certainly not anti-social.

Q. What about Count de Lipokowski and M. de Tessan?

A. Neither Count de Lipokowski nor M. de Tessan had committed any of the faults usually attributed to asocial elements or common criminals.

Q. You may proceed.

A. The means used to achieve the final degradation of the prisoners as a whole was the torture of prisoners by their fellow prisoners. Let me give a particularly brutal instance. In Kommando A.S.6, which was situated at Mansleben am See, 40 miles from Buchenwald, there were prisoners of every nationality, including a large proportion of Frenchmen. I had two friends there: Antoine d'Aimery, a son of General d'Aimery, and Thibani, who was studying to become a missionary.

Q. Catholic?

A. Catholic.

At Mansleben am See prisoners were hanged in public in the hall of a factory connected with the salt-mine. The SS were present at these hangings in full dress uniform, wearing their decorations.

The prisoners were forced to be present at these hangings under threats of the most cruel beatings. When they hanged the poor wretches, the prisoners had to give the Hitler salute.

Worse still, one prisoner was chosen to pull away the stool on which the victim stood. He could not evade the order, as the consequences to himself would have been too grave. When the execution had been carried out, the were prisoners had to file in front of the victims between 2 SS men. They were made to touch the body and look the dead man in the eyes.

I believe that men who had been forced to go through such rites must inevitably lose the sense of their dignity as human beings.

In Buchenwald itself all the administrative work was entrusted to the prisoners - i.e., the hangings were carried out by a German prisoner, assisted by other prisoners. The camp was policed by prisoners. When someone in the camp was sentenced to death, it was their duty to find him and take him to the place of execution.

Selection for the labour-squads, with which we were well acquainted, especially for Dora, Lora and S III - extermination detachments - was carried out by prisoners, who decided which of us were to go there.

In this way the prisoners were forced down to the worst possible level of degradation, inasmuch as every man was forced to become the executioner of his fellow.

I have already referred to Block 61, where the extermination of the physically unfit and those otherwise unsuited for labour was carried out. These executions were also carried out by prisoners under SS supervision and control. From the point of view of humanity in general, this was perhaps the worst crime of all, for these men who were forced to torture their fellow-beings were indeed, allowed to live, but became profoundly changed.

Q. Who was responsible for these crimes, as far as your personal knowledge goes?

A. One thing which strikes me as being particularly significant is that the methods which I observed in Buchenwald now appear to have been the same, or almost the same, as those prevailing in all the other camps. The degree of uniformity in the way in which the camps were run is clear evidence of orders from higher quarters. In the case of Buchenwald in particular, the personnel, no matter how rough they might be, would not have done such things on their own initiative. Moreover, they - the camp chief and the SS doctor himself - frequently pleaded superior orders. The name most frequently invoked was that of Himmler. Other names also came up. The chief medical officer for all the camps - Lolling - was mentioned on numerous occasions in connection with Block 61 - the extermination block, especially by an SS doctor in the camp, named Bender. In regard to the selection of physically unfit prisoners and Jews to be sent to Auschwitz or Bergen-Belsen, to be gassed, I heard the name of Pohl mentioned.

Q. What were the functions of Pohl?

A. He was chief of the SS administration in Berlin, Div. D 2.

Q. Could the German people as a whole have been in ignorance of these atrocities, or were they bound to know of them?

A. As these camps had been in existence for years, it is impossible for them not to have known of them. Our transport stopped at Treves on its way in. The prisoners in some vans were completely naked while in others they were clothed. There was a crowd of people around the station and they all saw the transport. Some of them annoyed the SS men patrolling the platform. But there were other channels through which information could reach the population. To begin with, there were squads working outside the camps. Labour squads went out from Buchenwald to Weimar, Erfurt and Jena. They left in the morning and came back at night; and during the day they were among the civilian population. In the factories, too, the supervisors were not members of the armed forces. The "Meister" was not an SS man. They went home every night after supervising the work of the prisoners all day. Certain factories - the Gustloff works in Weimar, for instance - even employed civilian labour.

The civil authorities were responsible for victualling the camps and were allowed to enter them, and I have seen civilian lorries coming into the camp.

The railway authorities were necessarily informed on those matters. Numerous trains carried prisoners daily from one camp to another, or from France to Germany, and these trains were driven by railway-men. Moreover, there was a regular daily train to Buchenwald. Buchenwald station was the terminus. The railway administrative authorities must, therefore, have been well informed.

Orders were also given in the factories, and industrialists could not fail to be informed regarding the personnel they employed in their factories. I may add that visits took place; the German prisoners were sometimes visited. I knew certain German internees, and I know that on the occasion of those visits they talked to their relatives, who could hardly fail to inform their home circle of what was going on. It would seem impossible to deny that the German people knew of the camps.

Q. The Army?

A. The Army knew of the camps. At least, so far as I could observe

Every week so-called commissions came to Buchenwald - a group of officers who came to visit the camp. There were SS officers among them; but I very often saw members of the Wehrmacht - Air Force officers - who came on these visits. Sometimes we were able to identify those who visited the camp, though not often so far as I was concerned. On 22 March 1945, General Bougrowski came to visit the camp. He spent a long time in Block 61 in particular. He was accompanied on this visit by an SS General and the Chief Medical Officer of the camp, Dr. Schidlowsky.

Another point, during the last few months, the Buchenwald guard, plus SS-men -

Q. Excuse me for interrupting you. Could you tell us about Block 61?

A. Block 61 was the extermination block for those suffering from cachaxia - in other words, those who arrived in such a state of exhaustion that they were totally unfit for work.

Q. Can you tell us about this visit to Block 61 from your own personal observation?

A. This is from my own personal observation.

Q. Whom does it concern?

A. Dr. Bougrowski.

Q. In the Army?

A. No. A doctor and an SS-General.

Q. Were University circles aware of the work done in the camps?

A. At the Pathological Institute in Buchenwald, pathological preparations were made, and naturally some of them were out of the ordinary, - since - I am speaking as a doctor - we encountered cases that can no longer be observed, cases such as have been described in the books of the last century. Some excellent pieces of work were prepared and sent to Universities, especially the University of Jena. On the other hand there were also some exhibits which could not properly be described as anatomical: some prepared tattoo marks were sent to Universities.

Q. Did you personally see that?

A. I saw these tattoo marks prepared.

Q. Then how did they obtain the anatomic exhibits, how did they get these tattoo marks? They waited for a natural death, of course.

A. The cases I observed were natural deaths or executions. Before our arrival, and I can name witnesses who can testify to this - they killed a man to get these tattoo marks. It happened, I must emphasise, when I was not at Buchenwald. I am repeating what was told me by witnesses whose names I will give. During the period when the camp was commanded by Koch, people who had particularly artistic tattoo marks were killed. The witness I can refer to is Nicolas Simon, who lives in Luxembourg. He spent six years in Buchenwald in exceptional conditions, where he had unprecedented opportunities of observation.

Q. But I am told that Koch was sentenced to death and executed because of those very excesses.

A. As far as I know, Koch was mixed up with some sort of swindling affair. He quarrelled with the SS administration. He was undoubtedly arrested and imprisoned.

THE PRESIDENT: We had better have an adjournment now.

(A recess was taken)

BY M. DUBOST:

Q. We stopped at the end of the Koch story, and the witness was telling the Tribunal that Koch had been executed not for the crimes that he had committed with regard to the internees in his charge, but because of the numerous indiscretions of which he had been guilty during his period of service.

Did I understand the witness's explanation correctly?

A. I said explicitly that he had been accused of indiscretions. I cannot give precise details of all the charges. I cannot say definitely that he was accused only of minor misdemeanours in his administration; I know that such charges were made against him, but I have no further information.

Q. Have you nothing to add?

A. I can say that this information came from Dr. Owen, who had been arrested at the same time and released again, and who returned to Buchenwald towards the end, that is, early in 1945.

Q. What was the nationality of this doctor?

A. German. He was in detention. He was an SS-man, and Koch and he were arrested at the same time. Owen was released and came back to Buchenwald restored to his rank and his functions at the beginning of 1945. He was quite willing to talk to the prisoners and the information that I have given comes from him.

M. DUBOST: I have no further questions to ask the witness, Mr. President.

THE PRESIDENT: Are there any further questions?

MEMBERS OF THE BRITISH PROSECUTION: No.

THE PRESIDENT: Does any member of the defence counsel wish to ask any questions?

BY DR. MERKEL: I am the defence counsel for the Gestapo.

Q. Witness, you previously stated that the methods of treatment in Buchenwald were not peculiar to the Buchenwald camp but must be ascribed to a general order. The reasons you gave for this statement was that you had seen these things in all the other camps too. How am I to understand this expression "in all other camps?"

A. I am speaking of concentration camps; to be precise, a certain number of them, Mauthausen, Dachau, Sachsenhausen, and labour squads such as Dora, Lora, Mansleben, Ebensee, to mention these only.

Q. Were you yourself in these camps?

A. I myself went to Buchenwald. I collected exact testimony about the other camps from friends who were there. In any case, the number of friends of mine who died is a sufficiently eloquent proof that extermination was carried out in the same way in all the camps.

BY DOCTOR BABEL: (Counsel for the SS and SD)

Q. I should like to know to what block you belonged. Perhaps you can tell the Tribunal - you have already mentioned the point - how the prisoners were distributed? Did they not also bear certain external markings - red patches on the clothing of some and green on that of others?

A. There were in fact a number of badges, all of which were found in the same commandos. To give an example, where I was- in the "Terrassekommando" known as "Entwasserung" (drainage) - I worked alongside German common law criminals wearing the green badge. Regarding the nationalities in this commando, there were Russians, Czechs, Belgians and French among us. Our badges were different; our treatment was identical, and in this particular case we were even under the orders of common law criminals.

Q. I did not quite hear the beginning of your answer. I asked whether the prisoners were divided into specific categories identifiable externally by means of stars or some kind of distinguishing mark: green, blue, etc ...?

A. I said that there were various badges in the camp, triangular badges which applied in principle to different categories, but all the men were mixed up together, and subjected to the same treatment.

Q. I did not ask you about their treatment, but about their distinctive badges.

A. For the French it was a badge in the form of a shield.

Q. (interpolating): For all the prisoners, not only the French.

A. I am answering you: in the case of the French, who were those I knew best, the red, political, badge was given to everyone without discrimination, including the prisoners brought over from Fort Barrault, who were common criminals. I saw the same thing among the Czechs and the Russians. It is true that the use of different badges had been intended, but that was never put into practice in any reasonable way.

To come back to what I have already stated. Even if there were different badges, the people were all mixed up together, nevertheless, subjected to the same treatment and the same conditions.

Q. We have already heard several times that prisoners of various nationalities were mixed up together. That is not what I asked you.

THE PRESIDENT: You are speaking too fast.

DR. BABEL: Yes. Thank you.

BY DR. BABEL:

Q. You were in the camp for a sufficiently long period to be able to answer my question. How were the prisoners divided? As far as I know, they were divided into criminal, political and other groups, and each group was distinguished by a special sign worn on the clothing - green, blue, red or some other colour.

A. The use of different badges for different categories had been planned. But these categories were mixed up together. Criminals were side by side with prisoners classed as political. There were, however, blocks in which one or other of those elements predominated; certain specific groups were distributed, but they were not divided up into specific groups distinguished by the particular badge they wore.

Q. I have been told, for instance, that political prisoners wore blue badges and the criminals wore red ones. We have already had a witness who confirmed this to a certain extent, by stating that criminals wore a green badge and antisocial offenders a different badge, and that the category to which a particular prisoner belonged could be seen at a glance.

A. It is true that different badges existed. It is true that the use of these badges for different categories was foreseen, but if I am to confine myself to the truth, I must emphasise the fact that the full use was not made of the badges. For the French in particular, there were only political badges, and this increased the confusion still more since notorious criminals from the ordinary civil prisons came to be regarded everywhere as political prisoners. The badges were intended to identify the different categories, but they were not employed systematically. They were not employed at all for the French prisoners.

Q. If I understand you correctly, you say that all French prisoners were classified as political prisoners

A. That is correct.

Q. Now, among these French prisoners, as you said yourself, is it not true to say that there were not only political prisoners but also a large proportion of criminals?

A. There were some among

Q. At least, I took your previous statement to mean that. You said that quite definitely.

A. I did say so. I said that there were criminals from special prisons who were not given the green badge with an F, which they should have received, but the political badge.

Q. What was your employment in the camp? You are a doctor, are you not?

A. I arrived in January. For three months I was assigned first to the quarry, and then to the "terrasse". After that I was assigned to the Revier, that is to say the camp infirmary.

Q. What were your duties there?

A. I was assigned to the ambulance service for internal diseases.

Q. Were you able to act on your own initiative? What sort of instructions did you receive regarding the treatment of patients in the Revier?

A. We acted under the control of an SS doctor. We had a certain number of beds for certain patients, in the proportion of one bed to twenty patients We had practically no medical supplies. I worked in the infirmary up to the liberation.

Q. Did you receive instructions regarding the treatment of patients? Were you told to look after them properly or were you given instructions to administer treatment which would cause death?

A. As regards that, I was ordered to select the incurables for extermination. I never carried out this order.

Q. Were you told to select them for extermination? I did not quite hear your reply. Will you please repeat it?

A. I was ordered to select those who were dangerously ill so that they might be sent to Block 61 where they were to be exterminated. That was the only order I received concerning the patients.

Q. "where they were to be exterminated." but I asked if you were told that they were to be selected for extermination. Were you told - according to what you said - "They will be sent to Block 61." Were you also told what could happen to them in Block 61?

A. Block 61 was in charge of a non-commissioned officer called Wilhelm, who personally supervised the executions, and it was he who ordered what patients should be selected to be sent to that block. I think the situation is sufficiently clear.

Q. I beg your pardon. You received no express orders?

A. The order to send the incurables

Q. (interrupting): Witness, it strikes me that you are not giving a straightforward answer of "yes" or "no," but that you persist in evading the question.

A. It was said that these patients were to be sent to Block 61. Nothing more was added, but every patient sent to Block 61 was executed.

Q. That is not firsthand observation. You found out or you heard that those who were sent there did not come back.

A. That is not correct. I could see for myself, for I was the only doctor who could enter Block 61, which was under the command of a prisoner called Louis Cunish (Remisch?) I was able to get a few of the patients out; the others died.

Q. If such a thing was said to you, why did you not say that you would not do it?

A. If I understand the question correctly, I am being asked why - when I was told to send the most serious cases -

Q. (interrupting): When you received instructions to select patients for Block 61 why did you not say: "I know what will happen to those people, and therefore I will not do it."

A. Because it would have meant death.

Q. And what would it have meant if Germans had refused to carry out such an order?

A. What Germans are you talking about? German internees?

Q. A German doctor, if you like, or anyone else employed in the hospital. What would have happened to him if he had received such an order and refused to carry it out?

A. If a prisoner refused point-blank to execute such an order, it meant death. In point of fact, we sometimes could evade such orders. I emphasise the fact that I never sent any one to Block 61.

Q. I have one more general question to ask about conditions in the camp. For those who have never seen a camp it is difficult to imagine what conditions were actually like. Perhaps you could give the Tribunal a short description of how the camp was arranged.

A. I think I have already spoken at sufficient length on the organisation of the camp. I should like to ask the President whether it will serve any useful purpose to return to this subject.

THE PRESIDENT: If you want to put any particular cross-examination to him to show he is not telling the truth, you can, but not to ask him for a general description.

BY DR. BABEL:

Q. The camp consists of an inner camp surrounded and secured by barbed wire. The barracks in which the prisoners were housed were inside this camp. How was this inner camp guarded?

THE PRESIDENT: Will you kindly put one question at a time? The question you have just put involves three or four matters.

Q. How is the part of the camp in which the living-quarters are situated separated from the rest? What security measures are taken?

A. The camp was a unified whole, cut off from the rest of the world by an electrified barbed wire network.

Q. Where were the guards?

A. The guards of the camp were in towers situated all round the camp; they were stationed at the gate and they patrolled inside the camp itself.

Q. Inside the camp? Inside the barbed wire enclosure?

A. Inside the camp and inside the barracks of course. They had the right to go everywhere.

Q. I have been informed that each separate barrack was under the supervision of only one man - a German SS-man or a member of some other organisation, that there were no other guards, that these guards were not intended to act as guards but only to keep order, and that the so-called Kapos, who were chosen from the ranks of the prisoners, had the same authority as the guards and performed the duties of the guards. It may have been different in Buchenwald. My information comes from Dachau.

A. I have already answered all these questions in my statement by saying that the camps were run by the SS in a manner which is common knowledge, and that in addition the SS employed the internees as intermediaries in many instances. This was the case in Buchenwald and, I suppose, in all the other concentration camps.

Q. The answer to the question has again been highly evasive. I shall not, however, pursue the matter any further, as in any case I shall not receive a definite answer.

But I should like to put one further question.

You stated in connection with the facts you described that a professor, whose name I could not understand through the earphones and who was, I believe, a teacher of your own, was housed in Block 59. You stated in connection with the question of degradation - that at first 300 people - I think were housed there and later on 1200. Is that correct?

A. There were 1200 men in Block 58 when I found Dr. Kindberg there.

Q. Yes. And if I understood you correctly, you said that in this block there were not only Frenchmen, but also Russians, Poles, Czechs and Jews and that a state of degradation was caused not only through the herding together of 1200 people but also through the intermingling of so many different nationalities.

A. I want to make it clear that the intermingling of elements speaking different languages, men who are unable to understand each other - is not a crime, but it was a pre- disposing factor which furthered all the other measures employed to bring about a state of human degradation among the prisoners.

Q. So you consider that the intermingling of Frenchmen, Russians, Poles, Czechs and Jews is a degradation?

A. I do not see the point of this question - the fact of intermingling -

Q. There is no need for you to see the point; I know why I am asking the question.

The fact of putting men who speak different languages together is not degrading. I did not either think or say such a thing, but the herding together of elements which differ from each other in every respect, and especially in that of language, in itself made living conditions more difficult, and paved the way for the application of other measures which I have already described at length and whose final aim was the degradation of the human being.

Q. I cannot understand why the necessity of associating with people whose language one does not understand should be degrading.

THE PRESIDENT: Dr. Babel, he has given his answer, that he considers it tended to degradation. It does not matter whether you understand it or not.

DR. BABEL: Mr. President, the transmission through the earphones is sometimes so imperfect that I, at least, often cannot hear exactly what the witness says and for that reason I have unfortunately been compelled to have an answer repeated from time to time.

M. DUBOST: I should not like the Tribunal to mistake this interpolation for an interruption of the cross-examination; but I think I must say that some confusion was undoubtedly created in the mind of the defence counsel just now in consequence of an interpreter's error which has been brought to my notice.

He asked my witness an insidious question, namely, whether the French deportees were criminals for the most part, and the question was interpreted as follows: whether the French deportees were criminals. The witness answered the question as translated into French and not as asked in German. I therefore request that the question be put once more by defence counsel and correctly translated.

THE PRESIDENT: Do you understand what M. Dubost said, Dr. Babel?

DR. BABEL: I think I understand the substance. I think I understand that there was a mistake in the translation. I am not in a position to judge; I cannot follow both the French and German text. **THE PRESIDENT:** I think the best course is to continue your cross-examination, if you have any more questions to ask, and M. Dubost can clear up the difficulty in re-examination.

DR. BABEL: Surely the point is that as counsel for the defence we reserved the right -

(M. Dubost approached the lectern.)

THE PRESIDENT: What is the matter, M. Dubost? Why do you come forward again?

M. DUBOST: I repeat that the question was translated as follows -

THE PRESIDENT: I have said that Dr. Babel can continue his cross-examination. You may clear up this point about the translation in re-examination.

M. DUBOST: Thank you.

DR. BABEL: Mr. President, defence counsel for Kaltenbrunner has already explained to-day that it is very difficult for the defence to cross-examine a witness if they are not informed at least one day before as to the subjects on which the witness is to be heard. The testimony given by today's witnesses was so voluminous that it is impossible for us to follow it without previous preparation, and to prepare and conduct from brief notes the extensive cross-examinations which are necessary.

To, my knowledge, the President has already informed defence counsel for the Organisations that we shall have an opportunity of re-examining the witnesses later or of calling them on our own behalf.

THE PRESIDENT: I have already said what I have to say on behalf of the Tribunal on that point, but as counsel for the defence must have anticipated that witnesses would be called as to the conditions in the concentration camps, I should have thought they could have prepared their cross-examination during the forty or more days which the trial has taken.

DR. BABEL: Mr. President; I do not think that this is the proper time for me to argue the matter with the Tribunal, but I may perhaps be given the opportunity of doing so later in a closed session. I consider this necessary in the interests of the rapid and unhampered progress of the trial.

I have no desire whatsoever to delay the proceedings. I have the greatest interest in expediting them as far as possible, but I am anxious not to do so at the cost of prejudicing the defence of the Organisations.

THE PRESIDENT: Dr. Babel, I have already pointed out to you that you must have anticipated that the witnesses might be called to state the conditions in concentration camps. You must therefore have had full opportunity during the days the trial has taken for making up your mind on what points you would cross-examine, and I see no reason to discuss the matter with you.

DR. BABEL: Thank you for this information. But naturally I cannot - I do not agree with you. I cannot know in advance exactly what the witness is going to say, and I cannot cross-examine him until I have heard him. I know, of course, that a witness is going to make a statement about concentration camps but I cannot know in advance which particular points he will discuss.

M. DUBOST: I would ask the Tribunal to note that in questioning the French witness the defence used certain words, the literal translation of which is "for the most part." This applied to the character of the French deportees. The question was: "Were they criminals for the most part?" The witness understood it to be as I did: "Did you say that they were criminals?" and not "that the convoys were for the most part composed of criminals." His reply was the natural one. The Tribunal will allow me to ask the witness to give details. What was the proportion of criminals and patriots respectively among the deportees? Was he himself a criminal or a patriot? Were the generals and other personages whose names he had given us criminals or patriots, speaking generally?

A. The proportion of French criminals was very small. The criminals came from Fort Barreau in a convoy. I cannot give the exact figure, but there were only a few hundred out of all the internees. In other incoming convoys the proportion of criminals included was only two or three per thousand.

M. DUBOST: Thank you.

THE PRESIDENT: The witness can retire.

M. Dubost, are you proposing or asking to call other witnesses on concentration camps? As I have already pointed out to you, the evidence, with the exception of Dr. Babel's recent cross-examination, has practically not been cross-examined, and it is supported by other film evidence. We are instructed by Article 18 of the Charter to conduct the trial in as expeditious a way as possible, and I will point out to you, as ordered under 24-E of the Charter, you have the opportunity of calling rebutting evidence, if it were necessary, and, therefore, if the evidence. which has been so fully gone into as to the condition in concentration camps. Is what I say not coming through to you?

M. DUBOST: The witness whom I propose to ask the Tribunal to hear will elucidate a point which has been pending for several weeks. The Tribunal will remember that when my colleagues were presenting their evidence, the question arose of ascertaining whether Kaltenbrunner had been in Mauthausen. In evidence of this, I am going to call M. Boix, who will prove to the Tribunal that Kaltenbrunner had been in Mauthausen. He took photographs, and the Tribunal will hear his statement and see the photographs which the witness has brought with him.

(FRANCOIS BOIX took the stand.)
BY THE PRESIDENT:
Q. Very well. What is your name?
A. Francois Boix.
Q. Are you French?
A. I am a Spanish refugee.
THE PRESIDENT: Will you repeat this oath after me. I swear to speak without hate or fear, to speak the truth, all the truth, only the truth.

(The witness repeated the oath.)

THE PRESIDENT: Raise your right hand and say, "I swear."
THE WITNESS: I swear.
THE PRESIDENT: You may sit down. M. Dubost, will you spell the name.
M. DUBOST: B-O-I-X.
BY M. DUBOST:
Q. You were born on 14 August 1920 in Barcelona?
A. Yes.
Q. You are a news photographer? and you were interned in the camp of Mauthausen, since ...?
A. Since the 27 January, 1941.
Q. You handed over to the commission of inquiry a certain number of photographs?
A. Yes.
Q. They are going to be projected on the screen and you will state under oath under what circumstances and where these pictures were taken?
A. Yes.
Q. How did you obtain these pictures?
A. Owing to my professional knowledge I was sent to Mauthausen to work in the identification branch of the camp. There was a photographic branch, and pictures of everything happening in the camp could be taken and sent to the High Command in Berlin.

(Projection of the pictures.)

This is the general view of the quarry.
Is this where the internees worked?
A. Most of them.
Q. Where is the stairway?
A. In the rear.
Q, How many steps were there?
A. 160 steps at first; later on there were 186.
Q. We can proceed to the next picture.

A. This was taken in the quarry during a visit from Reichsfuehrer Himmler, Kaltenbrunner, the Governor of Linz, and some other leaders whose names I do not know. What you see below is the dead body of a man who had fallen from the top of the quarry, as some did every day.

Q. We can proceed to the next picture.

A. This was taken in April 1941. My Spanish comrades who had sought refuge in France are dragging a waggon loaded with earth. That was the work we had to do.

Q. By whom was this picture taken?

A. At that time by Paul Ricker, a professor from Essen.

Q. We may proceed to the next one.

A. This is a picture of an Austrian who had escaped. He was a carpenter in the garage and he managed to make a box, a box in which he could hide and so get out of the camp. But after a while he was recaptured. They put him on the wheelbarrow in which corpses were carried to the crematorium. There were some placards saying in German: "All the birds are back again." He was sentenced, and then paraded in front of 10,000 deportees to the music of a gipsy band. When he was hanged, his body swung to and from in the wind while they played the "Beer Barrel Polka."

Q. The next one. In this picture the Spaniards are on the left; they are smaller.

A. The man in the front with the beret is a criminal from Berlin by the name of Schulz, who was employed on these occasions. In the background you can see the man who is about to be hanged.

Q. Next one. Who took these pictures?

A. The SS Oberscharfuehrer Fritz Kornac. He was killed by American troops in Holland in 1944.

This man got a bullet in the head. They hanged him to make us think he was a suicide and had tried to hurl himself against the barbed wire. The other picture shows some Dutch Jews. That was taken at the quarantine barracks. The Jews were driven to hurl themselves against the barbed wire on the very day of their arrival because they realised that there was no hope of escape for them.

Q. By whom were these pictures taken?

A. At this time by the SS Oberscharfuehrer Paul Ricker, a professor from Essen, assistant SS leader.

Q. Next one.

A. These are two Dutch Jews. You can see the red star they wore. That was an alleged attempt to escape "Fluchtversuch."

Q. What was it in reality?

A. The SS sent them to pick up stones near the barbed wire, and the SS guards at the second barbed wire fence fired on them, because they received a reward for every man they stopped.

The other picture shows a Jew in 1941, during the construction of the Russian camp, which later became the sanitary camp. He hanged himself with the cord which he used to keep up his trousers.

Q. Was it suicide?

A. It was alleged to be. It was a man who no longer had any hope of escape. He was driven to desperation by forced labour and torture.

Q. What is this picture?

A. A Jew whose nationality I do not know. He was put in a barrel of water until he could not stand it any longer. He was beaten to the point of death and then given ten minutes in which to hang himself. He used his own belt to do it, for he knew what would happen to him otherwise.

Q. Who took that picture?

A. The SS Oberscharfuehrer Paul Ricker.

Q. And what is this picture?

A. Here you see the Viennese police visiting the quarry. This was in June or July 1941. The two deportees whom you see here are two of my Spanish comrades.

Q. What are they doing?

A. They are showing the police how they had to raise the stones, because there were no other appliances for doing so.

Q. Did you know any of the policemen who came?

A. No, because they only came once. We just had time to glance at them.

The date of this picture is September, 1943, on the birthday of SS Obersturmbannfuehrer Franz Ziereis. He is surrounded by the whole staff of Mauthausen camp. I can give you the names of all the people in the picture.

Q. Pass the next photo.

A. This is a picture taken on the same day as Obersturmbannfuehrer Franz Ziereis's birthday. The other man was his adjutant - I forget his name. It must be remembered that this adjutant was a member of the Wehrmacht and put on SS uniform as soon as he came to the camp.

Q. What is this picture?

A. That is the same visit to Mauthausen by police officials in June or July 1941. This is the kitchen door. The prisoners standing there had been sent to the disciplinary company. They used that little appliance on their backs for carrying stones up to a weight of 80 kilos, until they were exhausted. Very few men ever came back from the disciplinary company.

This particular picture shows Himmler's visit to the Fuehrerheim at Camp Mauthausen in April 1941. It shows Himmler with the Governor of Linz in the background and Obersturmbannfuehrer Ziereis, the commanding officer of Camp Mauthausen, on his left.

Here is another picture which was taken in the quarry. In the rear to the left you see a group of deportees at work. In the foreground are Franz Ziereis, Himmler and Obergruppenfuehrer Kaltenbrunner. He is wearing the gold Party emblem.

Q. This picture was taken in the quarry? By whom?

A. By the SS Oberscharfuehrer Paul Ricker again. This was in April or May 1941. This gentleman frequently visited the camp at that period to see how similar camps could be organised throughout Germany and in the occupied countries.

Q. I have finished. You give us your assurance that it is really Kaltenbrunner?

A. I give you my assurance.

Q. And that this picture was taken in the camp?

A. I give you my assurance.

Q. Were you taken to Mauthausen as a prisoner of war or as a political prisoner?

A . As a prisoner of war.

Q. You had fought as a volunteer in the French Army?

A. In Infantry battalions, in the Foreign Legion, in the pioneer regiments attached to the Army to which I belonged. I was in the Vosges with the 5th Army. We were taken prisoner. We retreated as far as Belfort where I was taken prisoner in the night of 20 to 21 June 1940. I was put with some fellow Spaniards and transferred to Mauthausen. Knowing us to be former Spanish Republicans and anti-fascists, they put us in among the Jews as members of a lower order of humanity. We were prisoners of war for six months, and then we learned that the Minister for Foreign Affairs had had an interview with Hitler to discuss the question of foreigners and other matters. We knew that our status had been among the questions raised. We heard that the Germans had asked what was to be done with Spanish prisoners of war who had served in the French Army - those of them who were Republicans and ex-members of the Republican Army. The answer ...

Q. Never mind that. So although you were a prisoner of war you were sent to a camp not under Army control?

A. Exactly. We were prisoners of war. We were told that we were being transferred to a subordinate command like all the other Frenchmen. Then we were transferred to Mauthausen, where, for the first time, we saw ...

THE PRESIDENT: Speak more slowly.

A. ... we saw that there were no Wehrmacht soldiers, and we realised that we were in an extermination camp.

Q. How many of you arrived there?

A. There were 1500 of us, and 8,000 Spaniards altogether.

Q. How many of you were liberated?

A. Approximately 1,600.

Q. I have no more questions to ask.

THE PRESIDENT: Do you want to ask any questions?

GENERAL RUDENKO: I shall have some questions. If the President will permit me I shall present them in tomorrow's session.

THE PRESIDENT: We will adjourn now.

(The Tribunal adjourned until 29th January 1946 at 1000 hours.)

Forty-fifth day: Tuesday, 29th January, 1946

COURT OFFICER: May it please the Court, I desire now to say that the defendant Kaltenbrunner will be absent from this morning's session on account of illness.

M. DUBOST: In my capacity as representative of the French Prosecution, I wish to ask the Tribunal to consider this request: The witnesses that were interrogated yesterday are to be cross-examined by the defence. The conditions under which they are here are rather precarious, for it takes 30 hours to return to Paris. We would like to know whether we are to keep them here, and, if the defence really intends to cross-question them, we should like to proceed with that as quickly as possible, in order to ensure their return to France.

THE PRESIDENT: In view of what you said yesterday, M. Dubost, I said on behalf of the Tribunal that Dr. Babel might have the opportunity of cross-examining one of your witnesses within the next two days. Is Dr. Babel ready to cross-examine that witness now?

DR. BABEL (Counsel for SS and SD): No, Mr. President, I have not yet received a copy of his interrogation and consequently have not been able to, prepare my cross- examination. The time from yesterday to today is, naturally, also too short. Therefore, I cannot yet make a definite statement as to whether or not I shall want to cross-examine the witness. If I were given an opportunity during the course of the day to get the record ...

THE PRESIDENT: (interposing): Well, that witness must stay until tomorrow afternoon, M. Dubost, but the other witnesses can go.

M. Dubost, will you see, if you can, that a copy of the shorthand notes is furnished to Dr. Babel as soon as possible; the shorthand notes of that witness' evidence?

M. DUBOST: Yes, Mr. President.

FRANCOIS BOIX returned to the stand.

M. DUBOST: I shall see that it is done, My Lord. To continue; the Tribunal will remember that yesterday afternoon we projected six photographs of Mauthausen, which were brought to us by the witness who is now before you, and on which he offered his comments. This witness specifically stated under what conditions the photograph representing Kaltenbrunner in the quarry of Mauthausen had been taken. We offer these photographs as Exhibit RF 332.

Will you allow me to formulate one more question to the witness? Then I shall have finished with him, at least concerning the important part of this testimony. Does the witness recognise among the defendants anyone who visited the camp of Mauthausen?

A. Herr Speer.

Q. When did you see him?

A. He came to the Gusen camp in 1943 to arrange for some constructions, and also to the quarry at Mauthausen. I did not see him myself as I was in the identification service of the camp and could not leave, but during these visits Paul Ricker, head of the identification department, took a roll of film with his Leica which I developed. On this film I recognised Speer and with him other leaders of the SS. Speer wore a light-coloured suit.

Q. You saw that on the pictures that you developed?

A. Yes. I recognised him on the photos and afterward he had to sign his name and the date because there were always many SS who wanted to have collections of all the photos of visits to the camp.

THE PRESIDENT: I think the witness was going a little too fast. I think he had better repeat that.

BY M. DUBOST:

Q. Will you please repeat that you recognised Speer on pictures that you developed.

A. I recognised Speer on 36 photographs which were taken by SS Oberscharfuehrer Paul Ricker in 1943, during Speer's visit to the Gusen camp and the quarry of Mauthausen. He always looked extremely pleased on these pictures. There are even pictures which show him congratulating Obersturmbannfuehrer Franz Ziereis, then commander of the Mauthausen camp, with a cordial handshake.

Q. One last question. Were there any officiating chaplains in your camp? How did the internees die who wanted religious consolation?

A. I do not understand.

Q. Were there any chaplains in your camp?

A. Yes, so far as I could see, there were several. There was an order of German Catholics, known as "Bibelforscher." But officially ...

Q. But officially did the administration of the camp grant the internees the right to practice their religion?

A. No, they could do nothing, it was absolutely forbidden, even to live.

Q. Even to live?

A. Even to live.

Q. Were there any Catholic chaplains or any Protestant pastors?

A. The members of "Bibelforscher " were almost all Protestants. I do not know much about this matter.

Q. How were monks, priests and pastors treated?

A. There was not the slightest difference between them and ourselves. They died in the same way as we did. Sometimes they were sent to the gas chamber, at times they were shot, or plunged in freezing water, any way was good enough. The SS had a particular harsh method of handling these people, because they knew that they were not able to work as normal labourers. They treated all intellectuals of all countries in this manner.

Q. They were not allowed to practice their ministration?

A. No, not at all.

Q. Did the men who died have a chaplain before being executed?

A. No, not at all. On the contrary, at times, instead of being consoled, as you say, by anyone of their faith, they received, just before being shot, 25 or 75 lashes with a leather thong, sometimes from even an SS Obersturmbahnfuehrer personally. I noticed that especially in the case of a few officers, Political Commissars, Russian prisoners of war.

M. DUBOST: I have no further questions to ask of the witness.

THE PRESIDENT: General Rudenko.

BY GENERAL RUDENKO:

Q. Witness, will you be so kind as to tell us what you know about the extermination of Soviet prisoners.

A. I cannot possibly tell you all I know about it; I know so much that one month would not suffice to tell you all about it.

Q. I would like you to tell us concisely what you know about the extermination of Soviet prisoners of war in the camp of Mauthausen.

A. The arrival of the first prisoners of war took place in 1941. The arrival of 2000 Russian prisoners of war was announced. In regard to Russian prisoners of war they took the same precautions as in the case of the Republican Spanish prisoners of war. They put machine guns everywhere around the barracks and expected the worst. As soon as the Russian prisoners of war entered the camp one could see that they were in a very bad state, they could not even understand anything. They were human scarecrows. They were then put in barracks, 1600 to a barrack. You must bear in mind these barracks were 7 metres wide by 50 long. They were divested of their clothes, of the very little they had on. They could keep only one pair of drawers and one shirt. One has to remember, that this was in November, and in Mauthausen it was more than 10 degrees below zero.

Upon their arrival 24 died just from walking the short distance of 4 kilometres from the station to the camp of Mauthausen. At first the same system was applied to them as to us Republican Spanish prisoners. At first they left us, with nothing to do, with no work.

THE PRESIDENT: You go too fast. Speak more slowly.

A. They applied the same system to the Russians. They were left to themselves, but with scarcely anything to eat. At the end of a few days they were already at the end of their endurance. Then began the process of elimination. They were made to work under the most horrible conditions, they were beaten up, hit, kicked, insulted; and out of the 7,000 Russian prisoners of war who came from almost everywhere, only 30 survivors were left at the end of three months. Of these 30 survivors photographs were taken by Paul Ricker's department, as a photo-document. I have these pictures and I can show them if the Tribunal so wishes.

Q. You do have these pictures?

A. M. Dubost knows about that, yes. M. Dubost has them.

Q. Thank you. Can you show these pictures?

A. M. Dubost has them.

Q. Thank you. What do you know about the Yugoslavs and the Poles?

A. The first Poles came to the camp in 1939, at the time of the defeat of Poland. They received the same treatment as everybody else. At that time there were only ordinary German criminals there. Then the work of the extermination was begun. There were tens of thousands of Poles who died under frightful conditions.

The position of the Yugoslavs should be brought to notice. They began to arrive in convoys, wearing civilian clothes, and they were shot in a formal way, so to speak. The SS wore even their steel helmets for these executions. Yugoslavs were shot two at a time, 165 came with the first transport, 180 with the second, after that they came in small groups of 15, 50, 60, 30 ; even women came then.

It is necessary to note that among these, four women were shot - and that was the only time in the camp of deportees. Some of them spat in the face of the camp Fuehrer before dying. The Yugoslavs suffered as few people have suffered. Their position is comparable only to that of the Russians. Until the very end they were massacred by every means imaginable. I would like to say more about the Russians, because they have gone through so much ...

Q. Do I understand correctly from your testimony that the concentration camp was really an extermination camp?

A. The camp was placed in the last category, grade 3. That is, it was a camp from which no one came out.

GENERAL RUDENKO: I have no further questions.

THE PRESIDENT: Does counsel for Great Britain desire to cross-examine?

COLONEL PHILLIMORE: No questions.

THE PRESIDENT: Counsel for the United States?

MR. DODD: No questions.

THE PRESIDENT: Do any counsel for the defendants wish to cross-examine?

BY DR. BABEL (Counsel for SS and SD):

Q. Witness, how were you, marked in the camp?

A. The number? What, if you please? What kind of brand?

Q. No. The prisoners were marked by variously coloured stars, red, green, yellow, and so forth. Was this so in Mauthausen also? What did you wear?

A. Everybody wore insignia. They were not stars; they were triangles, and letters to show the nationality. Yellow and red stars were for the Jews, stars with six red and yellow points, two triangles, one over the other.

Q. What colour did you wear?

A. A blue triangle with an "S" in it, that is to say "Spanish."

Q. Were you a "Kapo?"

A. I was an interpreter at first.

Q. What were your tasks and duties there?

A. I had to translate into Spanish all the barbaric things the Germans wished to tell the Spanish prisoners. Afterwards my work was on photography, developing the films which were taken all over the camp, showing the full story of what happened in the camp.

Q. What was the policy with regard to visitors? Did visitors go only into the inner camp and to places where work was being done?

A. They visited every camp. It was impossible for them not to know what was going on. Exception was made only when high officials or other important persons from Poland, Austria, or Slovakia, from all countries, came. Then they would show them only the best parts. Franz Ziereis would say: "See for yourselves." He looked out cooks, interned bandits, and common criminals, fat and well-fed. He would select these so as to be able to say and show that all internees looked like these.

Q. Were the prisoners forbidden to communicate with each other or with the outside?

A. It was so completely forbidden that, if anyone was caught doing so, it meant not only his death, but terrible reprisals for all those of his nationality.

Q. What observations did you make regarding the Kapos? How did they behave toward their fellow prisoners?

A. At times they were really worthy of being SS themselves. To be a Kapo, you had to be a pure Aryan. That meant that they had a martial bearing and, like the SS, full rights over us; they had the right to treat us like animals. The SS gave them carte blanche to do with us what they wished. That is why, at the Liberation, the prisoners and deportees executed all the Kapos on whom they could lay their hands. Shortly before the Liberation the Kapos asked to enlist voluntarily in the SS, and they left with the SS because they knew what was awaiting them. In spite of that we looked for them everywhere, and executed them on the spot.

Q. You said they behaved like wild beats. From what facts do you draw the conclusion that they were obliged to?

A. One would have to be blind not to see. One could see the way they behaved. It was better to die like a man than to live like a beast, but they preferred to live like beasts, like savages, like criminals. They were known as such.

Q. I understand nothing. Please repeat. I have not understood you.

A. One would have had to be blind in order not to see what was happening to them. I lived there four and a half years and I know very well what they did. There were many among us who could have become Kapos for their work, because they were specialists in some field or another in the camp. But they preferred to be beaten up, and massacred if necessary, rather than become a Kapo.

DR. BABEL: Thank you.

THE PRESIDENT: Does any other member of the defendants' counsel wish to ask questions of the witness? M. Dubost, do you wish to ask any questions?

M. DUBOST: I have no further questions, Mr. President.

GENERAL RUDENKO: My Lord, the witness informed us that he had at his disposal the documentary photograph of 30 Soviet prisoners of war, the sole survivors of several thousand internees in this camp. I would like to ask your permission, Mr. President, to present this documentary photograph to the witness so that he can confirm before the Tribunal that this is really a document about this group of Soviet prisoners of war.

THE PRESIDENT: Certainly you may show the photograph to the witness if you have it. You may put the photograph to the witness if it is available.

GENERAL RUDENKO: Yes.

BY GENERAL RUDENKO:

Q. Witness, can you see this picture?

A. What was it please? To whom?

BY THE PRESIDENT:

Q. Is this the photograph? *(Indicating)*

A. Yes, that is the same 30. I can assure you that these 30 survivors were still living in 1942. Since then, in view of the conditions of the camp, it is very difficult to know whether any one of them is still alive.

Q. Would you please give the date when this photograph was taken?

A. It was at the end of the winter of 1941-42. At that time, it was still 10 degrees below zero. You can see from the picture the appearance of the prisoners because of the cold.

THE PRESIDENT: Has this book been put in evidence yet?

M. DUBOST: This book has been submitted as evidence, as official evidence.

THE PRESIDENT: Have the defendants got copies of it?

M. DUBOST: It was submitted as Exhibit RF 331. It is an official document which has been submitted to the defence also.

THE PRESIDENT: The document has been submitted by the French as Exhibit RF 331?

M. DUBOST: The defence have also received a copy of this book in German, I am not certain whether the German text has the pictures as well. No, the pictures are not in the German version, your Honour.

THE PRESIDENT: Well then, let this photograph be marked. It had better be marked with a French exhibit number, I think. What will it be?

M. DUBOST: We shall give it number 333, RF 333.

THE PRESIDENT: Let it be marked in that way, and then hand it to Dr. Babel.

GENERAL RUDENKO: Thank you, Sir. I have no more questions.

(The document was handed to Dr. Babel.)

THE PRESIDENT: I think it should be handed about to the other defendants' counsel in case they wish to ask any question about it. M. Dubost, I think that an approved copy of this book, including the photographs, has been deposited in the defendants' Information Centre.

M. DUBOST: The whole book, except for the pictures.

THE PRESIDENT: Why not the pictures?

M. DUBOST: We did not have them at that moment to submit. In our exposition wehave not mentioned the photographs.

THE PRESIDENT: The German counsel ought to have the same documents as are submitted to the Tribunal. The photographs have been submitted to the Tribunal; therefore they should have been submitted to the Information Centre.

M. DUBOST: Mr. President, the French text, including the pictures, was deposited in the defendant's Information Centre, and, in addition, a certain number of texts in German, to which the pictures were not added because we had that translation prepared for the use of the defence. But there are French copies of the book that you have before you, which include the pictures.

THE PRESIDENT: Very well.

M. DUBOST: We have here four copies which we shall place before you, of the picture which was shown yesterday, which shows Kaltenbrunner and Himmler in the quarry of Mauthausen, in accordance with the testimony given by M. Boix. One of these pictures will also be delivered to the defence, that is, to the lawyer of the defendant Kaltenbrunner.

THE PRESIDENT: The photograph has now been handed around to the defendants' counsel. Do any members of the defendants' counsel wish to ask any questions of the witness upon this photograph? No question? The witness can then retire.

THE WITNESS: I would like to say something more. I would like to note that there were instances when Soviet officers were massacred. It is worth noting because it concerns prisoners of war. I would like the Tribunal to listen to me carefully.

BY THE PRESIDENT:

Q. What is it you wish to say about the massacre of the Soviet prisoners of war?

A. In 1943 there was a transport of officers. They were Russian officers. On the very day of their arrival in the camp their massacre began by every means. But it seems that an order from higher authority had been received concerning these officers, saying that something extraordinary had to be done.So they put them in the best block in the camp. They gave them new Russian prisoner's clothing; they even gave them cigarettes; they gave them beds with sheets ; they were given everything they wanted to eat. Sturmbannfuehrer Krebsbach examined them with a stethoscope.

They went down in the quarry, but they carried only small stones, and in fours. At that time Oberscharfuehrer Paul Ricker, chief of the identification service, was there with his Leica taking endless pictures. He took about 48 pictures. These I developed, and five copies of each, 13 x 18, with the negatives, were sent to Berlin. It is a pity I did not steal the negatives, as I did the others.When it was all over, the Russians were made to give up their clothing and everything else and were sent to the gas chamber. The comedy was ended. Everybody could see from the pictures that the Russian prisoners of war, the officers, and especially the political Commissars, were well treated, and well cared for, worked hardly at all, and were in good condition. That is one thing that should be noted because I think it is important.

And another thing. There was a barrack called No. 20. That barrack was inside the camp, and in spite of the electrified barbed wire around the camp, there was an additional wall with electrified barbed wire around it, and in that barrack there were prisoners of war - Russian officers and commissars, some Slavs, a few Frenchmen and, they said, even a few Englishmen. No one could enter that barrack except the two fuehrer who were of the SD, that is, the commandants of the inner and outer camps. These internees were dressed, as we were, like criminal prisoners, but without any tag or identification of their nationality. One could not tell their nationality from their dress. The service "Erkennungsdienst " took their pictures. A tag with a number was placed on their chest. These began with a number over 3,000. There were numbers looking like No. 11 (two blue darts). Numbers started at 3,000 and went up to 7,000. SS Unterscharfuehrer Hermann Schinbauer was then chief photographer. He was from the Berlin region, somewhere outside Berlin, I do not remember the name. He had orders to develop the films and to do all work personally, but like all the SS of the internal camp services, they were men who knew nothing. They always needed prisoners to get their work done.

That is why he needed me to develop these films. I made the enlargements, 5 x 7. These photos were sent to Obersturmfuehrer Karl Schultz, of Cologne, the Chief of the Polizeiabteilung. He told me not to tell anything to anybody about these pictures, and about the fact that we developed these films, and that if we did we would be liquidated at once. Without any fear of the consequences I told all my comrades about it. If one of us should succeed in getting out he could tell the world about it.

THE PRESIDENT: I think we have heard enough of this detail that you are giving us. But come back for a moment to the place you were speaking of where the Russian prisoners of war in 1943 - just a moment; I wish you would repeat the case of the Russian prisoners of war in 1943. You said that the officers were taken to the quarry to carry the heaviest stones.

THE WITNESS: No, just very small stones, weighing not even twenty kilos, and they carried them in fours to show on the pictures that the Russian officers did not do heavy work, on the contrary, very light work. That was only for the pictures, whereas in reality it was entirely different.

BY THE PRESIDENT: I thought you said they carried big, heavy stones.

THE WITNESS: No.

THE PRESIDENT: Were the photographs taken while they were in their uniforms carrying these light stones?

A. Yes, Sir ; they had to put on clean uniforms, neatly arranged, to show that the Russian prisoners were well and properly treated.

THE PRESIDENT: Very well. Is there any other particular incident you want to refer to?

A. Yes, about Block 20. Thanks to my knowledge of photography I was able to see it; I had to be there to handle the lights while my chief took photographs. In this way I could follow, detail by detail, everything that took place in this barrack. It was an inner camp. This barrack, like all the others, was 7 metres wide and 50 long. There were 1,800 there, with a food ration less than one quarter of what we would get for food. They had neither spoons, nor plates. Large kettles of spoiled food were emptied on the snow and left there until it began to freeze; then the Russians were ordered to get at it. The Russians were so hungry, they would fight for this food. The SS used these fights as a pretext to beat up some of prisoners with bludgeons.

BY THE PRESIDENT: Do you mean that the Russians were put directly into Block 20?

THE WITNESS (M. Boix): The Russians did not come to the camp directly. Those who were not sent to the gas chamber right away, were placed in Block 20. Nobody of the inner camp, not even the "Blockfuehrer" was allowed to enter this barrack. Small convoys of 50 or 60 came several times a week, and always one heard the noise of a fight going on inside. In January 1945, when the Russians learned that the Soviet Armies were approaching Yugoslavia, they took one last chance. They seized fire extinguishers and killed soldiers, posted under the watch tower. They seized machine-guns and everything possible as weapons. They took blankets with them and everything they could find. They were 700, but only 62 succeeded in passing into Yugoslavia with the partisans. That day, Franz Ziereis, camp commander, issued an order by radio to all civilians to cooperate, "to liquidate" the Russian criminals, who had escaped from the concentration camp. He stated that everyone who could produce evidence that he had killed one of these men, would receive a special reward in marks. This was why all the Nazi adherents in Mauthausen went to work and succeeded in killing more than 600 escaped prisoners. It was not hard because some of the Russians could not drag themselves for more than ten metres. After the Liberation one of the surviving Russians came to Mauthausen to see how everything was then. He told us all the details of his painful march.

THE PRESIDENT: I do not think the Tribunal wants to hear more details which you did not see yourself. Does any member of the defence counsel wish to ask any question of the witness upon the points which he has dealt with himself.

BY DR. BABEL (Counsel for SS and SD):

Q. One question only. In the course of your testimony you gave certain figures namely 105, 180 and just now 700. Were you, yourself, in a position to count them?

A. Nearly always, the convoys came into the camp in columns of five. It was easy to count them. These transports were always sent from the Wehrmacht prisons somewhere in Germany. They were sent from all prisons in Germany - from the Wehrmacht, the Luftwaffe, the SD or the SS.

THE PRESIDENT: Just answer the question and do not make a speech. You have said they were brought in in columns of five, and it was easy to count them.

THE WITNESS: Very easy to count them, particularly for those who wanted to be able to tell the story some day.

BY DOCTOR BABEL:

Q. Did you have so much time, that you were able to observe all these things?

A. The transports always came in the evening after the deportees had returned to the camp. At this time we always had two or three hours when we could wander about in the camp waiting for the bell that was the signal for us to go to bed.

THE PRESIDENT: The witness may now retire.

M. DUBOST: If the Tribunal permits, we shall now hear M. Cappelen, who is a Norwegian witness. The testimony of M. Cappelen will be limited to the conditions that were imposed on Norwegian internees in Norwegian camps and prisons.

THE PRESIDENT: Very well.

(HANS CAPPELEN, a witness on behalf of the French Prosecution, takes the stand.)

THE PRESIDENT: I understand that you speak English.

THE WITNESS: Yes, I speak English.

THE PRESIDENT: Will you take the English form of oath?

THE WITNESS: Yes, I prefer to speak in English.

THE PRESIDENT: What is your name?

THE WITNESS: My name is Hans Cappelen.

THE PRESIDENT: Will you repeat this oath after me. I swear that the evidence I shall give shall be the truth, the whole truth, and nothing but the truth, so help me God.

(Witness repeats oath in English)

THE PRESIDENT: M. Dubost, can you spell the name?

M. DUBOST: C-a-p-p-e-l-e-n.

BY M. DUBOST:

Q. M. Cappelen, you were born 18 December 1903?

A. Yes.

Q. In what town?

A. I was born in Kvietseid, in the province of Telemark, Norway.

Q. What is your profession?

A. I was a lawyer; but now I am a business man.

Q. Will you tell us what you know of the brutalities of the Gestapo in Norway?

A. Your Honour, I was arrested 29 November 1941 and taken to the Gestapo prison in Oslo, Moellergata 19. After ten days I was interrogated by two Norwegian N.S., or Nazi police agents. They started at once to beat me with bludgeons. How long this interrogation lasted I cannot exactly remember but it led to nothing. So after some days I was brought to 32 Victoria Terrace. That was the headquarters of the Gestapo in Norway. It was about eight o'clock at night. I was brought into a fairly big room and they asked me to undress. I had to undress until I was absolutely naked. I was a little bit swollen after the first treatment I had had by the Norwegian police agents, but it was not so bad.

There were present about six or eight Gestapo agents, and their leader was - Kriminalrat was his title - Femer. He was very angry and they started to bombard me with questions which I could not answer. So Herr Fermer ran at me and tore all the hair off my head ; hair and blood were all over the floor around me. Then, suddenly, they all started to run at me and beat me with rubber bludgeons and iron wires. It hurt me very badly and I fainted. But I was brought back to life again by their pouring ice-cold water over me. I vomited, naturally, because I was feeling very sick. But that only made them angry, and they said, "Clean up, you dirty dog" and I had to make an attempt to clean up with my bare hands.

In this way they carried on for a long, long time, but the interrogation led to nothing because they bombarded me with questions and asked me of persons whom I did not know or scarcely knew.

I suppose it must have been in the morning that I was brought back again to the prison. I was placed in my cell and was very sick and ill. During all the day I asked the guard if I could not have a doctor; that was the 19th. After some days - I suppose it must have been the day before Christmas Eve, 1941 - I was again brought in the night to the Victoria Terrace. The same things happened as last time, only this time it was very easy for me to undress because I had only a coat on me; I was swollen up from the last beating. As last time, six, seven, or eight Gestapo agents were present.

BY THE PRESIDENT:

Q. German Gestapo, do you mean?

A. Yes, German Gestapo, all of them, And Femer was present on that occasion as well, he held a rank in the SS and was Criminal Commissar. Then they started to beat me again, but it was useless to beat a man like me who was so swollen up and looking so bad. Then they started in another way: they started to screw and break my arms and legs. My right arm was dislocated. I felt that awful pain, and fainted again. Then the same happened as last time: They poured water on me and I recovered consciousness.

By now all the Germans there were absolutely mad. They roared like animals and bombarded me with questions again, but I was so tired I could not answer.

Then they placed a sort of home-made - it looked to me home- made - wooden thing, with a screw arrangement, on my left leg, and they started to screw so that all the flesh loosened from the bones. I felt an awful pain and fainted away, but I came back to consciousness again, and I have still big marks here on my leg from the screw arrangement, now, four years afterwards.

So that led to nothing, and then they placed something on my neck - I still have marks here (indicating) - and loosened the flesh here. But then I had a collapse, and all of a sudden I felt that I was paralysed in the right side. It has been proved since that I had a cerebral haemorrhage. And I got double vision; I saw two of each Gestapo agent, and everything was going round and round. That double vision I have had for four years, and when I am tired it still comes back again. But I am better now, so that I can move again in the right side, but my right side is still a little bit affected from that.

I cannot remember much more from that night, but the other prisoners who had to clean up the corridors in the prison saw them bring me back again in the morning. That must have been about six o'clock in the morning. They thought I was dead, because I had no irons on my hands. Whether I lay there for one day or two I can not tell, but one day I moved again and was slightly conscious, and then the guard came at once to my cell, where I was lying on a cot among my own vomiting and blood, and afterwards a doctor came to me.

He had, I suppose, quite a high rank; which rank I cannot exactly say. He told me that most probably I would die. I asked him, "Could you not take me to a hospital?" He said, "No. Such fools as you are not to be taken to any hospital before you do just what we say you shall do. Like all Norwegians, you are a fool."

They put my arm into joint again. That was very bad, but two soldiers held me and they drew it in, and I fainted away again. So the time passed and I rested a bit. I could not walk, because everything seemed to be going round. I was lying on the cot. It must have been at the end of February or in the middle of February 1942, when one night they came again. It must have been about ten o'clock at night, because the light in my cell had been out for quite a long time. They asked me to stand up, and I made an attempt and fell down again because of the paralysis. Then they kicked me, but I said, "Is it better not to put me to death, because I cannot move?"

Well, they dragged me out of the cell, and I was again brought to Victoria Terrace; that is the headquarters where they made their interrogations. This time the interrogation was led by an SS man called Stehr. I could not stand, so, naked as I was, I was lying on the floor. This Stehr had some assistants, four or five Gestapo agents, and they started to trample on me, and kick me. Then all of a sudden they brought me to my feet again and brought me to a table where Stehr was sitting. He took my left hand like this (indicating) and put some pins under my nails and started to break them up. It hurt me badly, and everything went round and round, the double vision came again but the pain was so intense that I drew my hand back. I should not have done that, because that made them absolutely furious. I fainted away, collapsed, I do not know for how long, but I came back to life again, to the smell of burned flesh or burned meat. One of the Gestapo agents was standing with a little lamp burning me under my feet. It did not hurt me too much, because I was so feeble that I did not care, and I was so paralysed that I could not speak, I only groaned a bit, crying, naturally, always.

I do not remember much more of that occasion, but this was one of the worst things I went through with respect to interrogations. I was brought back again to the prison and time passed and I attempted to eat a little bit. I vomited most of it up again, but little by little I recovered. I was still paralysed in the side, so I could not stand up.

But I was also taken to be interrogated again, and I was then confronted with other Norwegians, people I knew and people I did not know, and most of them were badly treated. They were swollen up, and I remember especially two of my friends, two very good persons. I was confronted with them, and they were looking very ill from torture, and when I came back again after my imprisonment, I learned that they were both dead; they had died from the treatment they had received.

Another incident of which I wish to tell - I hope your Honour will permit me concerned a person called Snerre Emil Halwuschen. One day - that must have been in the autumn, or in August or October, 1943, he was swollen and very distressed, and he said they had treated him badly, and that he and some of his friends had been in some sort of a court where they had been told that they were to be shot the next day. They had sentenced them, just to set an example.

Well, Halwuschen had, naturally, a headache and felt very ill, and I asked the guard to bring the head guard, who was a certain Herr Gotz. He came and asked what the devil I wanted. I said, "My comrade is very ill, could he not have some aspirins?" "Oh no," he said, "it would be a waste to give him aspirin, because he is to be shot in the morning."

Next morning he was brought out of the cell, and after the war they found him at Trondheim, together with other Norwegians in a grave there, with a bullet through his neck.

Well, the Moellergata 19, in Oslo, the prison where I was for about twenty-five months, was a house of horror. I heard people screaming and groaning nearly every night. One day, it must have been in December 1943, about the 8 December, they came into my cell and told me to dress. It was in the night. I put on what ragged clothes I had. Now I had recovered, practically. I was naturally lame on the one side, I could not walk so well, but I could walk, and I went down the corridor and there they placed me as usual against the wall, and I waited for them to take me away and shoot me. But they did not shoot me, they brought me to Germany together with many other Norwegians. I learned afterwards that we were called "Nacht und Nebel" prisoners, "Night and Mist" prisoners. We were brought to a camp called Natzweiler, in Alsace. It was a very bad camp.

We had to work taking stones out of the mountains. But I shall not bore you with my tales of Natzweiler, your Honour, I will only say that people of all other nations: French, Russians, Dutch and Belgians were there, and there are alive now about five hundred Norwegians who have been there. Between sixty and seventy per cent died, there or in other concentration camps. Two Danes also were there.

We saw many cruel things there, so cruel that they are well known. The camp had to be evacuated in September 1944. We were then brought to Dachau near Munich, but we did not stay there long; at least, I did not. I was sent to a Command called Aurich in East Friesland, that was an under-command of Neuengamme, near

Hamburg. There were about fifteen hundred prisoners there. We had to dig tank traps. We had to work about three or four hours every day, and go an hour's journey by train to the Panzer Grabon where we worked. The work was so hard, and the way they treated us so bad, that most of us died there. I suppose about half of the prisoners died of dysentery or of ill-treatment in the five or six weeks we were there. It was too much even for the SS, who had to take care of the camp, so they gave it up, I suppose, and I was sent via Neuengamme, Hamburg, to a camp called Gross Rosen, in Silesia, near Breslau. That was a very bad camp, too. There were about forty Norwegians there, and of those forty Norwegians there were about ten left after four to five weeks.

THE PRESIDENT: You will be some little time longer, so I think we had better adjourn now for ten minutes.

(A recess was taken)

THE PRESIDENT: Continue.
QUESTIONS BY M. DUBOST:

Q. Will you please continue to tell us of your passage through those camps, and mention specifically what you know of the camp of Natzweiler, and the role at Natzweiler of Dr. Hirtz of the German medical faculty at Strassbourg?

A. Well, in Natzweiler, experiments were conducted. Just beside the camp there was a farm called Struthof. It was practically a part of the camp, and some of the prisoners had to work there to clean up the rooms and, not so often, but sometimes, they were ordered out there. For instance, one day, I remember, all the gipsies were taken down to Struthof. They were very afraid of being taken down there.

One friend of mine, a Norwegian called Hridding, who had a job in the hospital, or so-called hospital, in the camp, told me the day after the gipsies were taken to Struthof, "I must tell you something. They have so far as I understand, tried some sort of gas upon them."

"How do you know that?" I asked.

"Well, come along with me."

And then, through the window of the hospital, I could see four of the gipsies lying on beds. They did not look well, and it was not easy to look through the glass, but they had some mucus, I suppose, around their mouths. Hridding told me that the gipsies could not say much because they were so ill, but so far as he had been able to understand, it was gas which they had used upon them. There had been twelve of them, and four were still living; the other eight, so far as Hridding understood, died down there at Struthof.

Hridding told me later, "You know that man who sometimes walks through the camp together with some others?"

"Yes, I have seen him," I said.

"That is Professor Hirtz from the German University in Strassbourg."

I am quite sure Hridding said that this man was Hirt or Hirtz. He came there nearly daily with a so called commission to see those who had come back from Struthof, to see the result. That is all I know about that.

Q. How many Norwegians died at Gross Rosen?

A. In Gross Rosen, it is not possible for me to say exactly, but I know about forty persons who went there, and I also know about ten who came back again. Gross Rosen was a bad camp. But nearly the worst thing about it was its evacuation. I suppose it must have been in the middle of February of that year. The Russians came nearer and nearer to Breslau.

THE PRESIDENT: You mean 1945?

MR. CAPPELEN: Yes, I meant 1945. One day we were placed upon a so-called "Appellplatz" (drill ground). We were very feeble, all of us. We had had hard work, little food, and all sorts of ill-treatment. We started to march in parties of about two to three thousand. The party I was with numbered about 2,500 to 2,800. We heard how many when they numbered them.

Well, we started to walk, and we had SS guards on each side. They were very nervous and almost like mad persons, Several were drunk. We could not walk fast enough, and they smashed in the heads of five who could not keep up. They said in German. "That is what happens to those who cannot walk." The others would have been treated in the same way if they had not been able to keep up. We walked as best we could. We attempted to help one another but we were all too exhausted. After walking for six to eight hours we came to a station, a railway station. It was very cold and we had only striped prison clothes on, and bad boots, but we said, "Oh, we are glad that we have come to a railway station. It is better to stand in a cow truck than to walk, in the middle of winter." It was very cold, 10 to 12 degrees below zero. It was a long train with open trucks. In Norway we call them sand trucks, and we were kicked on to those trucks, about 80 on each truck. We had to sit together and on these trucks we sat for about five days without food, and without water. When it was snowing we stood like this (indicating) just to get some water into our mouths, and, after a long, long time, it seemed to me years, we came to a place which I afterwards learned was Dora. That is in the neighbourhood of Buchenwald.

Well, we arrived there. They kicked us down from the trucks, but many were dead. The man who sat next to me was dead, but I had no chance to get away. I had to sit with a dead man for the last day. I did not see the figures myself, naturally, but about one third to a half of us were dead and stiffening. And they told us that one third - I heard the figure afterwards in Dora-that the dead on our train numbered 1447.

After Dora I do not remember much, because I was more or less dead. I have always been a man of good humour and high spirits, for my own sake and that of my friends, but I had nearly given up.

I do not remember much more, but then I bad good fortune, because Bernadottes' action came, and we were rescued and brought to Neuengamme, by Hamburg. When we arrived, there were some of my old friends, the student from Norway who had been deported to Germany, other prisoners who came from Sachsenhausen and other camps, and the few, comparatively few Norwegian "NN" prisoners who were still living, all in very bad health. Many of my friends are still in hospital in Norway. Some died after coming home.

That is what happened to me and my comrades in the three and three-quarter years I was in prison.

I am fully aware that it is impossible for me to give more details than I have done, but I have spoken of the parts of it which show, I hope, how the German SS behaved toward Norwegians, and in Norway.

QUESTIONS BY M. DUBOST:

Q. For what reason were you arrested?

A. I was arrested on the 29 November 1941, in a place then called Hoestboey. That is a sort of health resort where one goes skiing.

Q. What had you done? What was held against you?

A. We Norwegians mostly regarded ourselves as at war with Germany in one way or another, and naturally most of us were opposed to the Germans in sentiment, so when the Gestapo asked me, I remember, "What do you think of M. Quisling?" I only answered, "What would you have done if a German officer, even a major, when your country was at war, and your Government had given an order for mobilisation, came and said, 'Better forget the Mobilisation Order'? A man with any self-respect cannot do that."

Q. On the whole, did the German population know of, or were they unaware of, what went on in the camps?

A. That is, naturally, very difficult for me to answer. But in Norway at least, even at that time when I was arrested, we knew quite a lot about how the Germans treated their prisoners.

And there is one thing I remember when I was working in Munich - I was then in Dachau for a short time. I was with some others, brought to the town of Munich to go into the ruins to look for persons, and find bombs and things like that. I suppose that was the idea. They never told us anything, but we knew what was happening. There were about a hundred of us; prisoners. We were looking like corpses, all of us very bad. We went through the streets and people could see us, and they also could see what we were being sent to do - the kind of work which one would think was very dangerous and which should in some way help them, but they did not appreciate seeing us. Some of them shouted at us, "It is your fault that we are bombed."

Q. Were there any chaplains in your camp? Were you allowed to have prayers?

A. Well, we had among the "NN" prisoners in Natzweiler a priest from Norway. He was, I suppose, what you call in English a Dean. He was quite senior. In Norwegian we call it "Prost." He was from the West coast of Norway. He also was brought to Natzweiler as an "NN" prisoner, and some of my comrades asked him if they could not meet sometimes, so that he could preach to them. But he said, "No, I would rather not! I had a bible, but they have taken it from me, and they joked about it and said, 'You dirty churchmen.' If you showed the bible and things like that, you knew what to expect, so we did not do anything of that kind.

Q. Those who were dying among you, did they have the consolation of religion at the time of their death?

A. No.

Q. Were the dead treated with decency?

A. No.

Q. Was any religious service conducted?

A. No.

M. DUBOST: I have no further questions to ask.

GENERAL RUDENKO: I have no question, Mr. President.

THE PRESIDENT: Has the United States?

Then does any member of the defendants' counsel wish to ask the witness any questions?

CROSS EXAMINATION QUESTIONS BY DR. MERKEL (Counsel for the Gestapo):

Q. Witness, at your first interrogation, which as a rule took place about ten days after arrest, were you interrogated by German or by Norwegian Gestapo men?

A. It was done by two Norwegians who belonged, as I learned afterwards, to the so-called State Police. That was not the Norwegian police force. They were working together with the Gestapo; in fact, it was the same thing. But it was by them I was interrogated after the first ten days. But, as I heard afterwards, they usually did it in that way, because it was easier to interrogate in Norwegian, and some of the Germans could not speak Norwegian. Most of them could not. I think that is why they used the Norwegians and you could call them Gestapo, more or less. They let them handle the prisoners first.

Q. Then in the Victoria Terrace, which name I believe you used to designate the Gestapo headquarters in Oslo, were there Norwegian or German officials present during your interrogation?

A. I dare say there may have been one Norwegian as some kind of interpreter, but as I spoke in German I cannot say for certain whether or not there were one or two Norwegian policemen there. It is difficult. But as Victoria Terrace was the headquarters of the Gestapo, naturally they had some Norwegian Nazis there to help them. But most of them were German.

Q. Were the officials who interrogated you in uniform or in civilian clothes?

A. During my interrogations I sometimes saw them in uniform. But when they tortured me they mostly were in civilian clothes. So far as I can remember, there was only one person in uniform during one of the torture interrogations.

Q. You stated that you were then treated by a physician. Did this physician come of his own free will or was he asked to come?

A. The first time I asked for a doctor, but then I did not get one. But at the time when I recovered consciousness, when I was apparently presumed dead, the guard had possibly been looking at me, because he was then running away, and afterwards they came with a doctor.

Q. Did you know that in the German concentration camps talking was absolutely forbidden about the conditions in the camp, either among the prisoners or, of course, to outsiders, and that any violation of the order not to talk was subject to most severe penalties?

A. In the camps it was like this; it was of course more or less understood that it was pretty well forbidden to talk about the tortures we had gone through, but naturally in the camps, the "Nacht and Nebel" Camps where I was, the situation was so bad that even torture sometimes seemed to be better than dying slowly away like that; so almost the only thing we spoke about was: "when shall the war end; how can we help our comrades; and are we to get some food tonight or not?"

DR. MERKEL: Thank you.

THE PRESIDENT: Does any other defendants' counsel wish to ask any questions? M. Dubost, have you anything you wish to ask?

M. DUBOST: I have nothing further to ask, Mr. President.

THE PRESIDENT: Then the witness can retire.

M. DUBOST: If the Tribunal will permit, we will now hear a witness, Roser, who will give a few details of the conditions under which they kept French prisoners of war in reprisal camps.

THE PRESIDENT: (to the witness): What is your name?

THE WITNESS: Roser, Paul.

THE PRESIDENT: You swear to speak without hate or fear, to state the truth, all the truth, only the truth? Raise the right hand and say "I swear."

(The witness raises his right hand and repeats the oath in French.)

DIRECT EXAMINATION:
QUESTIONS BY M. DUBOST:

Q. Your name is Paul Roser, R-O-S-E-R?

A. R-O-S-E-R.

Q. You were born on the 8 of May 1903? You are of French nationality?

A. I am French.

Q. Were you born of French parents?

A. I was born of French parents.

Q. You were a prisoner of war?

A. Yes.

Q. You were taken prisoner in battle?

A. Yes, I was.

Q. In what year?

A. 14 June 1940.

Q. You sought to escape?

A. Yes, several times.

Q. How many times?

A. Five times.

Q. Five times. You were transferred finally to a disciplinary camp?

A. Yes.

Q. Will you indicate the regime of such a camp - will you indicate your rank, and the treatment to which you were exposed, the people of your rank in those disciplinary camps, and for what reasons?

A. Very well, I was an aspirant: that is between sergeant- major and second lieutenant. I was in several disciplinary camps. The first was a small camp which the Germans called Strafkommando in Linzburg, near Hanover. That was in 1941. There were thirty of us.

While I was in that camp, during the summer of 1941, we attempted to escape once again. We were recaptured by our guards at the very moment when we were leaving the camp. We were naturally unarmed. The first among us -

THE PRESIDENT: You are going much too fast for us to be able to follow you. Now continue more slowly, please.

A. (continuing): The Germans, our guards, having recaptured one of us, attempted to make him reveal who the others were who also had sought to escape. The man remained silent. The guards hurled themselves upon him, beating him with the butts of their pistols in the face, and with bayonets - with the butts of their rifles. At that moment, not wishing to let our comrade be killed, several of us stepped forward and revealed that we had been trying to escape. I then received a beating with bayonets on my head and fell into a swoon. When I recovered consciousness, one of the Germans was kneeling on my leg and was still striking me. Another one, raising his gun, was about to strike my head. I was saved on that occasion through the intervention of my comrades, who threw themselves between the Germans and myself. That night we were beaten for exactly three hours with rifle butts, with bayonet blows, and with pistol butts in the face. I lost consciousness three times.

The following morning we were taken to work, nevertheless. We were digging trenches for the draining of the marshes. It was very heavy work, which started at 6.30 in the morning and finished at 6 o'clock at night. We had two breaks, each of half an hour. We had nothing to eat during the day. Soup was given to us when we came back at night with a piece of bread and a small piece of sausage or two cubic centimetres of margarine and that was all.

Following our attempted escape, our guards withheld from us all the parcels which our families sent for a whole month. We could not write nor could we receive mail.

At the end of three and a half months, in September 1941, we were shipped to the regular Kommandos. I, personally, was quite ill at that time and I recovered in

Stalag10 B at Sandbostel.

Q. Why were you subjected to such a special regime, although you were an officer-cadet?

A. Definitely because of my attempted escape.

Q. Had you agreed to work?

A. No, not at all. Like all my comrades of the same rank and like most of the non-commissioned officers and like all aspirants, I had refused to work, invoking the provision of the Geneva Convention, which Germany had signed and which prescribed that non-commissioned officers who were prisoners cannot be forced to perform any labour without their own consent. The German Army, into whose hands we had fallen, never, practically speaking, respected that provision endorsed by Germany.

Q. Are you familiar with executions that took place in Stalag 11 B?

A. I was made familiar with the death of several French prisoners or Allied prisoners. Specifically at Oflag 11 in Grossborn in Pomerania, a French prisoner, Lieutenant Robin, who with some of his comrades had prepared an escape and for that purpose had dug a tunnel, was killed in the following manner. The Germans having had information that the tunnel had been prepared, Hauptmann Buchmann, who was a member of the officers' staff of the camp, watched with a few German guards for the exit of the would-be escapees. Lieutenant Robin, who was first to emerge, was killed with one shot while obviously he could in no manner attack anyone or defend himself.

Other cases of this type occurred. One of my friends, a French Lieutenant Ledoux, who was sent to Graudenz Fortress where he was subjected to a hard detention regime, saw his best friend, a British Lieutenant, Anthony Thomson, killed by Hauptfeldwebel Osterreich with one pistol shot in the neck, in their own cell. Lieutenant Thomson had just sought to escape and had been recaptured by the Germans on the airfield. Lieutenant Thomson belonged to the RAF.

I should like also to state that in the camp of Ravaruska in Galicia, where I spent five months, several of our comrades -

Q. Would you tell us why you were at Ravaruska?

A. In the course of the winter 1941-42, the Germans wanted to intimidate first, the non-commissioned officers who were refractory in labour; secondly, those who had sought to escape, and, thirdly, the men who were being employed in Kommandos (labour gangs) and who were caught in the act of performing sabotage. The Germans warned us that from 1st April 1942 onward all these escapees who were recaptured would be sent to a camp, a special camp called a "punishment camp" at Ravaruska in Poland.

It was following another attempt to escape that I, with about two thousand other Frenchmen, was taken to Poland. I was at Limburg an der Lahn, Stalag 12A, where we were regrouped and placed in cars, railways cars. We were stripped of our clothes, of our shoes, and of all the food which some of us had been able to keep. We were placed in cars, where the number varied from 53 to 56. The trip lasted six days. The cars were open generally for a few minutes in the course of a stop in the countryside. In six days we were given soup on two occasions only, once at Oppeln when the soup was not edible, and another time at Jaroslow. We remained for thirty-six hours without anything to drink in the course of that trip, as we had no receptacles with us and it was impossible to get a supply of water.

When we reached Ravaruska on 1st June 1942, we found other prisoners, most of them French, who had been there for several weeks, extremely discouraged, with a ration scale much inferior to anything that we had experienced until then, for no parcel for anyone had been delivered, from their families, or from the International Red Cross.

At that time there were about twelve to thirteen thousand in that camp. There was for that total number one single faucet which supplied, for several hours a day, undrinkable water. This situation lasted until the visit of two Swiss doctors, who came to the camp in, I think, September. The billets consisted of our barracks. The small rooms contained as many as six hundred men in one room. We were stacked in tiers along the walls, three rows of them, thirty to forty centimetres for each of us.

During our stay in Ravaruska there were many attempts at escape, more than five hundred in six months. Several of our comrades were killed. Some were killed as a guard noticed them. In spite of the sadness of such occurrences, no one of us contested the rights of our guards in such cases, but several were murdered. In particular, on the 12 of August 1942, in the Tarnopol Kommando, there is the case of soldier Lavesque. He was found bearing evidence of several shots and several large wounds caused by bayonets.

On the 14 of August in the Werciniec Kommando, ninety-three Frenchmen, having succeeded in digging a tunnel, escaped. The following morning three of them, Conan, Van den Boosch and Poutrelle, were caught by German soldiers, who were searching for them. Two of them were sleeping. The third, Poutrelle, was not. The Germans, a corporal and two enlisted men, verified the identity of the three Frenchmen. Very calmly they told them: "Now we are obliged to kill you." The three wretched men spoke of their families, begged for mercy. The German corporal gave the following reply, which we heard only too often: "An order is an order," and they shot down immediately two of the French prisoners, Van den Boosch and Conan. Poutrelle was left like a madman and by sheer luck was not caught again. But he was captured a few days later in the region of Kracow. He was then brought back to Ravaruska proper, where we saw him in a condition close to madness.

On the 14 of August, once again in the Stryj Kommando, a team of about twenty prisoners accompanied by several guards, were on their way to work.

Q. Excuse me - you are talking about French prisoners of war?

A. Yes, French prisoners of war, so far.

Going along a wood, the German non-commissioned officer, who for some time had been annoying two of them, Pierrel and Ondiviella, directed them into the woods. A few moments later the others heard shots. Pierrel and Ondiviella had just been killed.

On the 20 September 1942, at Stryj once again, a Kommando was at work under the supervision of German soldiers and German civilian foremen. One of the Frenchmen succeeded in escaping. Without waiting, the German non-commissioned officer selected two men - if my memory serves me - named Saladin and Duboeuf, and shot them on the spot. Incidents of this type occurred in other circumstances. The list of them would be long indeed.

Q. Can you speak concerning the conditions under which the refractory non-commissioned officers who were with you at camp at Ravaruska lived?

A. The non-commissioned officers who refused to work were grouped together in one section of the camp, in two of the large stables, which served as billets. They were subjected to a regime of most severe oppression: frequent roll-call for assembly, drills "lie down! " "stand up" - gymnastics which after one has performed them for a while leave one quite exhausted.

One day, Sergeant Corbihan, having refused Captain Fournier - a German captain with a French name - having refused to pick up a tool to work with, the German captain made a motion and one of the German soldiers with him ran Corbihan through with his bayonet, Corbihan by miracle escaped death.

Q. How many of you disappeared?

A. At Ravaruska, in the five months that I spent there, we buried sixty of our comrades who had died from disease or who had been killed in attempted escapes. But so far, 100 of those who were with us and sought to escape have not been found.

Q. Is this all that you have witnessed?

A. No. I should say that our sojourn at the punishment camp Ravaruska involved one thing more awful than anything we prisoners saw and endured. We were horrified by what we knew was taking place all about us. The Germans had transformed the area of Lemberg-Ravaruska into an immense ghetto. Into that area, where the Israelites were already quite numerous, had been brought the Jews from all the countries of Europe. Every day for five months, except for an interruption of about six weeks in August and September 1942, we saw passing about 150 metres from our camp, one, two and sometimes three trains, made up of freight cars in which there were crowded men, women and children. One day a voice, coming from one of these cars, shouted: "I am from Paris. We are on our way to be slaughtered." Quite frequently, comrades who went outside the camp to go to work found corpses along the railway track. We knew then in a vague sort of way that these trains stopped at Belcec, which was located about seventeen kilometres from our camp, and at that point they executed these wretched people, by what means I do not know.

One night, in July 1942, we heard machine gun fire throughout the entire night, and the moans of women and children. The following morning, bands of German soldiers were going through the rye fields on the very edge of our camp, their bayonets pointed downward, seeking people hiding in the fields. Those of our comrades who went out that day to go to their tasks told us that they saw corpses everywhere in the town, in the gutters, in the barns, in the houses. Later some of our guards, who had participated in this operation, quite good-humouredly explained to us that 2,000 Jews had been killed that night under the pretext that two SS had been murdered in the region.

Later on, in 1943, during the first week of June, there occurred a pogrom which in Lemberg caused the death of 30,000 Jews. I was not personally in Lemberg but several French military doctors, Major Guiguet of the French Medical Corps, Lieutenant Levin of the French Medical Corps, described this scene to me. The street-cars of the city ...

THE PRESIDENT: The witness appears not to be finishing and therefore I think we had better adjourn now until two o'clock.

(A recess was taken)

MARSHAL OF THE COURT: I desire to announce that the defendant Kaltenbrunner will be absent from this afternoon's session on account of illness.

M. DUBOST: With the permission of the Tribunal, we will continue examining the witness, M. Roser.

M. Roser, this morning you finished the description of the conditions under which you witnessed the pogrom of Ravaruska and you wanted to give us some details of another pogrom. You have told us that a soldier, who had taken part in it, talked about it in your presence, is that right?

M. PAUL ROSER: Yes.

Q. Did he tell you something you wanted to relate to us?

A. Yes.

Q. We are listening to you.

A. At the end of 1942 I was taken to Germany, and I, together with a French doctor, had the opportunity of meeting the chauffeur of the German physician who was head of the infirmary where I was at that time. This soldier, whose name I have forgotten, told us the following:

"In Poland" - in a city the name of which I have also forgotten - "a sergeant from our regiment went with a Jewess. A few hours later, he was found dead. Then," said the German soldier, "my battalion was called out. Half of it cordonned off the ghetto, and the other half, two companies, to one of which I belonged, forced its way into the houses and threw out of the windows pell-mell, the furniture and the inhabitants."

The German soldier finished his story by saying:

"Oh, it was terrible, inhuman." We asked him then "How could you do such a thing?" He gave us the fatalistic reply: "An order is an order."

This is the example which I previously mentioned.

Q. If I remember rightly, when speaking of Ravaruska you started describing the treatment of Russian prisoners, who were in this camp before you.

A. Yes. That is correct. The first French batch arriving in Ravaruska on the 14 or 15 April, 1942, followed a group of 400 Russian prisoners of war, who were the survivors of a detachment of 6,000 men decimated by typhus. The few medicines found by the French doctors upon arrival at Ravaruska came from the infirmary of the Russian prisoners. There were a few aspirin tablets and other drugs - absolutely nothing against typhus. The camp had not been disinfected after the sick Russians had left.

I cannot speak here of these wretched Russian survivors of Ravaruska, without asking the Tribunal for permission to describe the terrible picture we all - I mean all the French prisoners who were in the Stalags of Germany in the autumn or winter of 1941 - saw when the first batches of Russian prisoners arrived.

As for me, it was on a Sunday afternoon that I watched this spectacle which seemed like a nightmare. The Russians arrived in batches, five by five, holding each other by the arms, as none of them could walk by themselves. "Walking skeletons" was really the only fitting expression. Since then we have seen photographs of those camps of deportation and death. Our unfortunate Russian comrades had been in this very same condition since 1941. The colour of their faces was not even yellow; it was green. Almost all squinted, the eyes having become so weak. They fell by rows, five men at a time. The Germans rushed on them and beat them, with rifle butts and whips. As it was Sunday afternoon the prisoners were allowed a certain amount of liberty, inside the camp, of course. Seeing that, all the French started yelling and the Germans made us return to the barracks. The typhus spread immediately in the Russian camp, where, out of the 10,000 who had arrived in November, only 2,500 survived till the beginning of February.

These figures are accurate. I have them from two sources, first, from a semi-official source, which was the kitchen of the camp: there was in front of the kitchen a big chart posted where the Germans recorded the ridiculously small rations, and the number of men in the camp. This number decreased daily by 80 to 100.

Secondly, some French comrades employed in the camp's reception office called "Aufnahme," also knew the figures; and from them I got the figure of 2,500 survivors in February. Later, particularly at Ravaruska, I had the opportunity of seeing French prisoners from all parts of Germany. All those who were in Stalags, that is, in the central camps, at the time mentioned saw the same thing. Many of the Russian prisoners were thrown in common pits, even still alive. The dead and the dying were piled up between the barracks and thrown into carts. The first few days we saw the corpses in the carts, but as the German camp commandant did not like to see French soldiers salute their fallen Russian comrades he subsequently had them covered with canvas.

Q. Were your camps guarded by the German Army or by the SS?
A. By the Wehrmacht.
Q. Only by the German Army?
A. I was never guarded by anybody but the German Army and once by the Schutzpolizei, after I escaped.
Q. And were you recaptured?
A. Yes.
Q. One last question. You were kept in a number of prisoner of war camps in Germany, were you not?
A. Yes.
Q. In all those camps did you have the opportunity to practice your religion?
A. In the camps ...
Q. What is your religion?
A. I am a Protestant.
In the camps where I was kept, Protestants and Catholics were generally allowed to practice their religion. But I was detailed to different working groups, and in particular to one agricultural group in the Bremen district called "Marburg," I think, where there was a Catholic priest. There were about 60 of us in this group. This Catholic priest could not read mass, they would not let him.
Q. Who?
A. The sentries - " The Posten."
Q. Who were soldiers of the German Army?
A. Yes, always.
M. DUBOST: I have no further questions.
THE PRESIDENT: Does the British Prosecutor wish to ask any questions?
THE BRITISH PROSECUTOR: No.
THE PRESIDENT: Or the United States?
THE AMERICAN PROSECUTOR: No.
THE PRESIDENT: Do any of the defence counsel wish to ask any questions?
(Cross-examination by DR. NELTE (Counsel for the defendant Keitel.)
Q. Witness, when were you taken prisoner?
A. I was taken prisoner on the 14 of June 1940.
Q. In which camp for prisoners of war were you put?
A. I was immediately sent to the Oflag, 11 D, at Grossborn Westphalenhof in Pomerania.
Q. Oflag?
A. Yes.
Q. What regulations were made known to you in the prisoner of war camp regarding a possible attempt to escape?
A. We were warned that we would be shot at, and that we should not try to escape.
Q. Do you think that this warning was in agreement with the Geneva Convention?
A. This one certainly.

Q. You mentioned, if I heard correctly, the case of Robin from Oflag II D. You said that there was an officer who dug a tunnel in order to escape from the camp, and that as he was the first to emerge from the tunnel, he was shot.

A. Yes. So I said.

Q. Were you with those officers who tried to escape?

A. I said before that this was related to me by Lieutenant Ledoux who was still in Oflag II D when that happened.

Q. I only wanted to ascertain that this officer, Robin, met his death whilst trying to escape.

A. Yes, but here I should like to mention one thing, namely, all the prisoners of war who escaped knew that they risked their lives. Every one attempting to escape, knew that he risked a bullet, But it is one thing to be killed trying to cross the barbed wire, for instance, and it is another thing to be ambushed and murdered at the very moment when you are helpless, when you are without arms and at the mercy of anybody, as was the case with Lieutenant Robin, who was in a low tunnel, flat on his stomach, crawling along, when he was killed. This was no longer in accordance with international rules.

Q. I see what you mean, and you may rest assured that I respect every prisoner of war who tried to do his duty as a patriot. In this case, however, which you did not witness, I wanted to make the point that this first, courageous officer who left the tunnel might not have answered when challenged by the guards and was therefore shot. Though you have just given a vivid description of the incident, I think this was a product of your imagination because, according to your own testimony, you did not see it yourself; is this correct?

A. No. There are not 36 different ways of getting out of a tunnel. You lie flat on your stomach, you crawl, and if you are killed before you get out of the tunnel, I call that murder.

Q. And then you saw the officer -

THE PRESIDENT: Dr. Nelte!

DR. NELTE: Your Honour?

THE PRESIDENT: We do not want argument in cross examination. The witness has already stated that he was not there and did not see it, and he has explained the facts.

DR. NELTE: Thank you.

Q. The incident in respect to Lt. Thomson is not quite clear to me. In this case too, I believe you said you had no direct knowledge, but were informed by a friend. Is his correct?

A. I cannot but repeat what I said before. I related the story of a French Lieutenant, Ledoux, who told me that he was in the fortress of Graudezs together with Anthony Thomson, Lt. in the RAF. This British officer escaped from the fortress. He was recaptured on the airfield, taken back to the fortress, put into the same cell as Lt. Ledoux, and Ledoux saw him killed by a revolver shot in the back of the neck. Ledoux gave me the name of the murderer. I think I mentioned him, Sergeant-Major Osterreich. This is the story told me by a witness.

Q. Was Sergeant-Major Osterreich a guard at the camp, or to which formation did he belong?

A. I do not know.

Q. Do you know that you, as prisoner of war, had a right to complain?

A. Certainly; I know the Geneva Convention signed by Germany in 1934.

Q. Knowing those regulations you also knew, did you not, that you could complain to the camp commander? Did you avail yourself of this opportunity?

A. I tried to do so, but without success.

Q. May I ask you for the name of the camp commander who refused to hear you?

A. I do not know the name, but I will tell you when I tried to complain.

Q. Please do.

A. It happened when I was in the infamous Linzburg punitive squad in the province of Hanover. This squad was detached from Stalag 10C. In the morning following the night I have just described when, after an unsuccessful attempt at escape, we were beaten for three hours running, some of us were kept in the barracks. We then saw the immediate superiors of the commander of the squad; first, an Oberleutnant, whose name I do not know, saw that we were bruised, particularly on our heads, and he considered this to be all right. In the afternoon we went to work. When we returned at 7 o'clock we were visited by a major, a very distinguished looking man, who also found that, as we had tried to escape, it was quite in order that we be punished. As to our complaint, it did not get any further.

Q. Did you know that the German Government had made an agreement with the Vichy Government regarding prisoners of war?

A. Yes, I have heard of that, but they did not inspect squads of this kind.

Q. You mean to say that only the camps were inspected but not the labour squads?

A. There were inspections of the labour squads but not of the punitive squads. That is the difference.

Q. You were not always in a punitive squad, were you?

A. No.

Q. When were you put in a punitive squad?

A. In April 1941, for the first time. It was a squad to which only officer cadets and priests were sent, without any obvious reasons. This was the Linzburg punitive squad, which did not receive any visits. At Ravaruska we received the visit of two Swiss doctors, - I think it was in September 1942.

Q. In September 1942?

A. Yes, in September 1942.

Q. Did you complain to the Swiss doctors?

A. Not I personally, but our spokesman could talk to them.

Q. And were there any results?

A. Yes, certainly.

Q. Do you not think that a complaint made through the camp commander would have been likewise successful, if you had wished to resort to it?

A. We were not on very friendly terms with the German staff at Ravaruska.

Q. I did not quite understand you.

A. I said we were not on friendly terms with the German commander of the Ravaruska camp.

Q. It is not a question of good terms, but of a complaint which could be made in an official manner. Do you not think so?

When did you leave Ravaruska?

A. At the end of October 1942.

Q. If I remember rightly, you mentioned the number of victims counted or observed by you, did you not?

A. Yes.

Q. How many victims were there?'

A. It was a figure given to me by Dr. Lievin, a French doctor at Ravaruska. There were, as I said, about 60 deaths in the camp itself, to which approximately 100 must be added, who disappeared.

Q. The translation is not coming through.

THE PRESIDENT: Would you be kind enough to repeat the last few statements about the number of victims?

A. Yes. I said that there were about 60 deaths in the Ravaruska camp during the time I was there.

Q. Are you speaking of French victims or in general?

A. When I was at Ravaruska there were only Frenchmen there, a few Poles and a few Belgians.

Q. I am putting this question because the report dated 14 June, 1945, states that the victims were 14 Frenchmen and because we are now speaking of August and September: and in consequence we find that the number is a very high one for the period.

Thank you.

THE PRESIDENT: Does any other German counsel want to put any questions to this witness?

(No response)

THE PRESIDENT: M. Dubost?

M. DUBOST: I have finished with this witness, Mr. President. If the Tribunal will permit me, I will now call another witness, the last one.

THE PRESIDENT: One moment, M. Dubost. The witness can retire.

Could you tell the Tribunal whether the witness you are about to call is going to give us any evidence of a different nature from the evidence which has already been given? You will remember that we have in the French document, of which we shall take judicial notice - a very large French document - I forget the number - 321, I believe it is - 321 - we have a very large volume of evidence on the conditions in concentration camps. Is the witness you are going to call going to prove anything fresh?

M. DUBOST: The witness whom we are going to call is to testify to a certain number of experiments which he witnessed. He has even submitted certain documents.

THE PRESIDENT: Are these experiments about which the witness is going to speak all recorded in these, in the book 321?

M. DUBOST: They are referred to, but not reported in detail. Moreover, in view of the importance which, in the French presentation concerning the camps, is being attached to statements of witnesses, I shall curtail considerably the documentary evidence after these witnesses have been heard. On the other hand, Dr. Balachowsky...

THE PRESIDENT: You may call the witness, but try not to let him be too long.

M. DUBOST: I shall do my best, Mr. President.

(Witness takes the stand)

THE PRESIDENT: What is your name?

THE WITNESS: Alfred Balachowsky.

THE PRESIDENT: Are you French?

THE WITNESS: French.

THE PRESIDENT: Will you take this oath? Do you swear to speak without hate or fear, to say the truth, all the truth, only the truth? Raise your right hand and swear.
THE WITNESS: I swear.
THE PRESIDENT: You may sit if you wish.
EXAMINATION BY M. DUBOST:

Q. Your name is Balachowsky, Alfred B-a-l-a-c-h-o-w-s-k-y?
A. That is correct.

Q. You are head of the Pasteur Institute in Paris?
A. That is correct.

Q. Your residence is Viroflay? You were born 15 August 1909 at Korotcha in Russia?
A. That is correct.

Q. You are French?
A. Yes.

Q. By birth?
A. Russian by birth, French by naturalisation.

Q. When were you naturalised?
A. 1932.

Q. Were you deported on 16 January 1944 after being arrested on 2 July 1943, and after six months in prison first at Frenes then at Compiegne? Were you then transferred to the Dora camp?
A. That is correct.

Q. Can you rapidly tell us what you know about the Dora camp?
A. The Dora camp is situated five kilometres north of the town of Nordhausen, in southern Germany. This camp was considered by the Germans as a secret detachment, which prisoners who were kept there, could never leave.

This secret detachment had as its task the manufacture of V-1's and V-2's, the reprisal weapons which the Germans launched on England. That is why Dora was a secret detachment. This camp was divided into two parts: one outer part, which included one third of the total number of persons in the camp, and the remaining two-thirds were concentrated in the underground factory. Dora, then, was an underground factory for the manufacture of V-1's and V-2's. I arrived at Dora on the 10 February 1944, coming from Buchenwald.

Q. Please do not speak so fast. You arrived at Dora from Buchenwald on ....?
A. ... on the 10 February 1944 - that is, at a time when life in the Dora camp was particularly hard.

On the 10 February we were loaded, 76 men on a large German lorry. We were forced to crouch down, four SS guards occupying the seats at the front of the lorry. As we could not all crouch down being too many, whenever a man raised his head, he got a blow with a rifle butt, so that in the course of our 10 hours' journey several people were injured.

After our arrival at Dora, we spent a whole day and night without food, in the cold, in the snow, waiting for all the formalities of registration in the camp, completing forms, with surnames, first names, etc.

In comparison with Buchenwald, Dora was a considerable change as the management of the camp Dora was entrusted to a special category of prisoners who were criminals. These criminals were our block leaders, served out our soup, looked after us. Whereas the political prisoners wore red triangular badges, the criminals were marked by green triangular badges stamped with a black S. We called them the

"S" men (Sicherheitsverband)., They were people convicted of crimes by German courts before the war, who, instead of being sent home after having served their terms, were kept for life in concentration camps to supervise the other prisoners. Needless to say these criminals who supervised us ...

THE PRESIDENT: You are going too fast; please slow down.

A. (continuing): These criminals with the green triangles were asocial elements; sometimes they had served 5, 10, even 15 years in prison, and afterward, five or ten years in concentration camps. These social outcasts no longer had any hope of ever getting out of the concentration camps. These criminals, however, thanks to the support and Cupertino they were offered by the SS management of the camp, now had the chance of their lives. This meant stealing from and robbing the other prisoners, and obtaining from them the maximum output as demanded by the SS. They beat us from morning till night. We got up at 4 o'clock in the morning and had to be ready within five minutes in the underground dormitories where we were crammed, without ventilation, in foul air in blocks about as large as this room, into which 3,000 or 3,500 internees were crowded. There were five tiers of bunks with rotting straw mattresses. Fresh ones were never issued. We were given five minutes in which to get up, so we went to bed completely dressed. We were hardly able to sleep, for there was a continuous coming and going and all sorts of thefts took place among the prisoners. Furthermore, it was impossible to sleep because we were covered with lice; the whole Dora camp swarmed with vermin. It was virtually impossible to get rid of the lice. In five minutes we had to be in line in the tunnel and ready to march to a given place.

THE PRESIDENT: Just a minute, please.

M. Dubost, you said you were going to call this witness upon experiments. He is now giving us all the details of camp life which we have already heard on several occasions.

M. DUBOST: So far nobody has spoken about the Dora camp, Mr. President.

THE PRESIDENT: But every camp we have heard of has got the same sort of brutalities, has it not, according to the witnesses who have been called?

You were going to call this witness because he was going to deal with experiments.

M. DUBOST: If the Tribunal is convinced that all the camps had the same regime, then my point has been proved and the witness will now testify to the experiments at the Buchenwald camp. However, I wanted to show that in all German camps where people were interned the regime was the same. I think this has now been proved.

THE PRESIDENT: If you were going to prove that, you would have to call a witness from every camp, and there are hundreds of them.

M. DUBOST: This question has to be proved because it is the uniformity of the system which establishes the culpability of these defendants. In every camp there was one responsible person who was the camp commander. We are not trying the camp commander, but the defendants here in the dock and we are trying them for ...

THE PRESIDENT: I have already pointed out to you that there has been practically no cross-examination, and I have asked you to confine this witness, so far as possible, to the question of experiments.

M. DUBOST: The witness will then confine himself to experiments at Buchenwald as this is the Tribunal's wish. The Tribunal will consider the uniformity of treatment in all German internment camps as proved.

BY M. DUBOST:

Q. Will you now testify to the criminal practices of the SS Medical Corps in the camps, criminal practices in the form of scientific experiments?

A. I was recalled to Buchenwald on the 1st of May, 1944, and assigned to Block 50, which was, in fact, a factory for the manufacture of vaccines against typhus. I was recalled from Dora to Buchenwald, because, in the meantime the management of the camp had learned that I was a specialist in this sort of research, and consequently they wished to utilise my services in Block 50 for the manufacture of vaccines. However, I was unaware of it until the very last moment.

I came to Block 50 on the 1st of May, 1944, and I stayed there until the liberation of the camp on the 11 April, 1945.

Block 50 was the block where vaccines were manufactured under Sturmbannfuehrer Schuler, who was a doctor with the rank of Sturmbannfuehrer, equal to a Major. He was in charge of the block and was responsible for the manufacture of vaccines. This same SS Sturmbannfuehrer Schuler was also in charge of another block in the Buchenwald camp. This other block was Block 46, the infamous block for experiments, where the internees were utilised as guinea pigs.

Blocks 46 and 50 were both run by one office. There all archives, index cards pertaining to the experiments, all mail, all decisions concerning Block 46, the block for experiments, as well as Block 50, were kept.

The secretary of Block 50 was an Austrian political prisoner, my friend, Eugene Cogol. He and a few other comrades had, consequently, opportunities for looking through all the archives of which they had charge. Therefore they could know, day by day, exactly what went on either in Block 50, our block, or in Block 46. I myself was able to get hold of most of the archives of Block 46 and even the book in which the experiments were recorded has been saved. It is in our possession, and has been forwarded to the Psychological Department of the American Forces.

In this record book, all experiments were entered which were made in Block 46. Block 46 was established in October 1941 by a supreme committee set up by the Health Division of the Waffen SS, and we see as members of its Administrative Council, a certain number of names, as this Block 46 came under the Research Section No. 5 of Leipzig of the Supreme Command of the Waffen SS. Inspector Bougrowski, Obergruppenfuehrer of the Waffen SS, was in charge of this section. The Administrative Council which set up Block 46 was composed of the following members:

Dr. Genzken, Obergruppenfuehrer (the highest rank in the Waffen SS), Dr. Poppendieck, Gruppenfuehrer of the Waffen SS, and also Dr. Handlose of the Wehrmacht and of the Military Academy of Berlin, who was also associated with the establishment of experiments on human beings.

Thus, in the Administrative Council there were members of the SS, and also Dr. Handlose. The experiments proper were carried out by Sturmbannfuehrer Schuler, but all the orders and directives concerning the different types of experiments, which I shall speak about to you, were issued by Leipzig, i.e., by the Research Section of the Waffen SS. So there was no personal initiative on the part of Schuler or the management of the camp.

As to the experiments, all orders came directly from the Supreme Command in Berlin. Among these experiments, which we could follow closely (at least some of them) on the basis of the files, results, registration numbers of people admitted to and discharged from Block 46, were: First, numerous exanthematic typhus experiments. Second, experiments on phosphorus burns. Third, experiments on sexual hormones. Fourth, experiments on starvation oedema or avitaminosis. Fifth, experiments in the field of forensic medicine. So we have five different types of experiments.

Q. Were the people who were subjected to these experiments volunteers or not?

A. The people subjected to experiments were recruited, not only in the Buchenwald camp, but also from outside the camp. They were not volunteers; in most cases they did not know that they would be used for experiments until they entered Block 46. The recruitment took place among the criminals, in order to reduce their large numbers. But the recruitment was also carried out among Russian political prisoners, and I have to point out that among the political prisoners and prisoners of war who were used for experimental purposes in Block 46, the Russians were always in the majority, for the following reason: of all the prisoners kept in concentration camps it was the Russians who had the greatest physical resistance, which was obviously superior to that of the French or other people of Western Europe. They resisted hunger and ill- treatment, and, generally speaking, showed physical resistance in every respect. For this particular reason, the Russian political prisoners were recruited in greater numbers than others. However, there were people of other nationalities among them, notably French. I should now like to deal with details of the experiments.

Q. Do not go too much into detail, because we are not specialists. It will suffice us to know that these experiments were carried out without any regard to humanity and under compulsion. Will you please describe to us the atrocious methods of these experiments and their results.

A. The experiments carried out in Block 46 did, without doubt, serve a medical purpose, but not, for the greater part, a scientific one. Therefore, they can hardly be called experiments. The victims were used for checking the effects of drugs, poisons, bacterial cultures, etc. I take as an example the use of vaccine against exanthematic typhus. To manufacture this vaccine it is necessary to have bacterial cultures of typhus. For experiments such as are carried out at the Pasteur Institute and all other similar Institutes in the world, it is not necessary to create these "sources" of supply artificially, as typhus patients can always be found for samples of infected blood. Here it was quite different. From the records and the chart you have in hand, we could ascertain in Block 46 twelve different "sources" of typhus germs, designated by the letter BU, (meaning Buchenwald) and numbered Buchenwald 1 to Buchenwald 12. A constant supply of these twelve "sources" was kept in Block 46 through the contamination of healthy individuals by sick ones. This was achieved by artificial inoculation of typhus germs by means of intravenous injections of 0.5 to 1.00 cubic centimetres of virulent blood drawn from a patient at the height of the crisis. Now, it is well known that artificial inoculation of typhus by intravenous injection is invariably fatal. Therefore all these men, who served as living ground for bacterial cultures during the whole period when germs were required (from October 1942 to the liberation of the camp) died and we counted 600 victims sacrificed for the sole purpose of "supplying" typhus germs.

Q. They were literally murdered to keep typhus germs alive?

A. They were literally murdered to keep typhus germs alive. Apart from these, other experiments were made to the efficacy of vaccines.

Q. What is this document?

A. This document contains a record of the typhus cultures.

Q. This document was taken by you from the camp?

A. Yes, I took this document from the camp, and its contents were summarised by me in the experiment book of Block 46.

Q. Is this the document you handed to me?

A. We have actually made a more complete document - which is in the possession of the American Psychological Division - as we have the entire record, and this represents only one page of it.

M. DUBOST: I ask the Tribunal to take note that the French prosecution submits this document as Exhibit RF 334, as appendix to the testimony of Dr. Balachowsky.

A. (Dr. Balachowsky continuing): In August 1944 experiments were also made on the effects of vaccines. One hundred and fifty men lost their lives in these experiments. The vaccines used by the German Army were not only those manufactured in our Block 46, but also ones which came from Italy, Denmark and Poland, and the Germans wanted to ascertain the value of these different vaccines. Consequently, in August 1944 they began experiments on 150 people who were locked up in Block 46.

Here, I should like to tell you how this Block 46 was run. It was entirely isolated and surrounded by barbed wire. The internees had no roll call and no permission to go out. All the windows were kept closed, the panes were of frosted glass. No unauthorised person could enter the block. A German political prisoner was in charge of the block. This German political prisoner was Kapo Dietzsch, an asocial individual who had been in prisons and camps for 20 years and who worked for the SS. It was he who made the injections and the inoculations and who executed people upon order. Extraordinarily enough, there were arms in the block, automatic pistols, and hand grenades, to quell any possible uprisings whether from outside or inside the block. I can also tell you that the order slip submitted for Block 46 sent to the office at Block 50 in January 1945 mentioned three strait jackets to deal with those who refused to be inoculated.

Now I come back to the typhus and vaccine experiment. You can picture how they were carried out.

The 150 prisoners were divided into two groups: the "controls" and the subjects. Only the latter received (ordinary) injections of the different types of vaccines to be tested. The "controls" did not get any injections. After the vaccination of the subjects they inoculated (always by means of intravenous injections) everybody selected for this experiment, controls as well as subjects. The controls died about two weeks after the inoculation - as such is approximately the period required before the disease develops to its fatal issue. As for the others, who received different kinds of vaccines, their deaths were in proportion to the efficacy of the vaccine administered to them. Some vaccines had excellent results, with a very low death rate- such was the case with the Polish vaccines. Some others had a much higher death rate. After the conclusion of the experiments, no survivors were to be left alive, according to the custom prevailing in Block 46. All the survivors of the experiment were "liquidated" and murdered in Block 46, by the customary methods which some others of my comrades have already described to you, i.e. intracardiac injections of phenol. The intracardiac injection of 10 cubic centimetres of pure phenol was the usual system in Buchenwald.

THE PRESIDENT: The Russian translation is not coming through. Can you repeat what you said about the survivors being killed by intracardiac injections?

A. I repeat that those who did not die as a result of the experiments in Block 46 were not allowed to survive, according to the prevailing habits and customs. Once an experiment was concluded, the survivors were murdered. They were done away with by the methods customary at Buchenwald, as already described by some of my comrades.

BY M. DUBOST:

Q. Will you go more slowly, please? I think the interpreters are having difficulty.

A. In Buchenwald the liquidation was carried out by intracardiac injections of pure phenol in doses of ten cubic centimetres.

THE PRESIDENT: We are not really concerned here with the proportion of the particular injections.

THE WITNESS: Will you repeat that please?

THE PRESIDENT: As I have said, we are not concerned with the proportions in which these injections were given, and will you kindly not deal with these details? M. Dubost, you must try and confine the witness.

A. (continuing) Then I will speak of other details which may interest you. They are experiments of a psychotherapeutic nature, utilisation of chemical products to cure typhus, the conditions in Block 46 being always the same. The German industries co-operated in these experiments, notably the I.G. Farben Industrie which supplied a certain number of drugs to be used for experiments in Block 46. Among the professors who supplied the drugs knowing that they would be used in Block 46 for experimental purposes, was Professor Lautenschlager of Frankfurt.

So much for the typhus question. I now come to experiments with phosphorus, made particularly on internees of Russian origin. These phosphorus burns were inflicted in Block 46 on Russian internees for the following reason: certain bombs, dropped in Germany by the Allied aviators, caused burns on the civilians and soldiers, which were difficult to heal. Consequently, the Germans tried to find a whole series of suitable drugs to hasten the cicatrisation of the wounds and sores caused by these burns. Thus, experiments were carried out in Block 46, on Russian prisoners who were artificially burned with phosphorus products, and then treated with different drugs supplied by the German chemical industry.

Now as to experiments on sexual hormones.

BY M. DUBOST:

Q. What were the results of these experiments?

A. All these experiments resulted in death.

Q. Always in death? So each experiment is equivalent to a murder for which the SS are collectively responsible?

A. For which are responsible those who established this institution.

Q. That is the SS as a whole, and the German medical corps in particular?

A. Definitely so, as the orders came from the research Section No. 5. The SS were responsible, as the orders were issued by this section at Leipzig and, therefore, came from the Supreme Command of the Waffen SS.

Q. Thank you. What were the results of the experiments made on sexual hormones?

A. They were less serious. Besides, these were ridiculous experiments from the scientific point of view. There were, at Buchenwald, a number of homosexuals, that is to say, men who had been convicted by German tribunals for this vice. These homosexuals were sent to concentration camps, especially to Buchenwald, and were mixed with the other prisoners.

Q. Especially with so-called political prisoners, who in reality were patriots?

A. With all kinds of prisoners.

Q. All were in the company of these German inverts?

A. Yes. They were designated with a pink triangle.

Q. Was the wearing of this triangle a well-established custom, or on the contrary, was there much confusion in the classification?

A. At the very beginning, before my arrival, from what I heard, there was some order with respect to triangular badges, but when I arrived at Buchenwald, in January of 1944, there was the greatest confusion in the badges, and many prisoners wore no badge at all.

Q. Or did they wear badges of a category different from their own?

A. Yes, this was the case with many Frenchmen, who were sent to Buchenwald because they were ordinary criminals, and who finally wore the red triangle of political prisoners.

Q. What was the colour of the triangle worn by the ordinary German criminals?

A. They had a green triangle.

Q. Did they not wear eventually a red triangle?

A. No, because they were guarded more severely than the others and they distinctly wore the green triangle.

Q. And in the working groups?

THE PRESIDENT: We have heard that they were all mixed up.

M. DUBOST: The fact will not have escaped the Tribunal that these questions are put to counter other questions, which were asked this morning by the counsel for the defence, with the intent to confuse not the Tribunal but the witnesses.

THE WITNESS: I can repeat to you that we had a complete conglomeration of nationalities and categories of prisoners.

THE PRESIDENT: That is exactly what he said, that these triangles were completely mixed up.

M. DUBOST: I think, that the statement by this second witness, will definitely enlighten the Tribunal on this point, whatever the efforts of the defence might be to mislead us.

BY M. DUBOST:

Q. Do you know anything of tattooed people?

A. Yes indeed.

Q. Will you please tell us what you know about them?

A. Tattooed human skins were stored in Block 2, which was called at Buchenwald the Pathological Block.

Q. Were there many tattooed human skins in Block 2?

A. There were always tattooed human skins in Block 2. I cannot say whether there were many, as they were continually being received and passed on, but there were not only tattooed human skins. There were also tanned human skins - simply tanned, not tattooed.

Q. Did they skin people?

A. They removed the skin and then tanned it.

Q. Will you continue your testimony on that point?

A. I saw SS come out of Block 2, the Pathological Block, carrying tanned skins under their arms. I know, from my comrades who worked in Block 2, that there were orders for skins, and these tanned skins were given as gifts to certain guards, and to certain visiting officials, who used them to bind books.

Q. We were told that Koch, who was the Commander at that time, was sentenced for this practice.

A. I was not a witness of the Koch affair, which happened before I came to the camp.

Q. So that even after he left there were still tanned and tattooed skins?

A. Yes, there were constantly tanned and tattooed skins, and when the camp was liberated by the Americans, they found in the camp, in Block 2, tattooed and tanned skins, on the 11 of April, 1945.

Q. Where were these skins tanned?

THE PRESIDENT: I am afraid you are still going too fast.

A. These skins were tanned in Block 2, and perhaps also in the crematorium buildings, which were not far from Block 2.

Q. Then, according to your testimony, it was a customary practice which continued even after Koch's execution?

A. Yes, this practice continued, but I do not know to what extent.

Q. Did you witness any inspections made of the camp by German officials, and if so, who were these officials?

A. I can tell you something about Dora, concerning such visits.

Q. Excuse me, I have one more thing to ask you, about the skins. Do you know anything about Koch's conviction?

A. I heard rumours and remarks about Koch's conviction from old comrades, who were in the camp at that time. But personally, I did not witness the case.

Q. Never mind. It is enough for me to know that after his conviction, skins were still tanned and tattooed.

A. That is correct.

Q. You expressly state it?

A. Absolutely. Even after his conviction there were tanned and tattooed skins.

Q. Will you tell us now what visits were made to the camp by German officials, and who these officials were?

A. Contact between the outside, that is German civilians and even German soldiers, and the interior of the camp were made possible by departure or the leaves that some political prisoners were able to obtain from the SS in order to spend some time with their families, and, vice versa, there were visits to the camp by members of the Wehrmacht. In Block 50 we had the visit of Luftwaffe cadets. These Luftwaffe cadets, i.e. members of the regular German Armed Forces, passed through the camp and were able to see practically everything that went on there.

Q. What did they do in Block 50?

A. They just came to see the equipment, on the invitation of Sturmbannfuehrer Schuler. We received several visits.

Q. What was the equipment?

A. Equipment for the manufacture of vaccines, laboratory equipment.

Q. Thank you.

A. There were other visits also, and some Red Cross nurses visited this Block in October 1944.

Q. Do you, know the names of any German personalities who visited the camp?

A. Yes. Such a personality was the Crown Prince of Waldeck and Pyremont, who was an Obergruppenfuehrer of the Waffen SS, and Chief of Police of Hessen and Thuringia, who visited the camp on several occasions, including Block 46 as well as Block 50. He was greatly interested in the experiments.

Q. Do you know what the attitude of mind of the prisoners was shortly before their liberation by the American forces?

A. The internees of the camp expected the liberation to come at any moment. On the 11 April, in the morning, there was perfect order in the camp and exemplary discipline. We hid, with extreme difficulty and in the greatest secrecy, weapons, cases of hand grenades, and about 250 guns which were divided in two lots, one lot of a hundred guns for the hospital, and another lot of about 150 guns in my Block 50, and cases of hand grenades. As soon as the Americans began to appear below the camp of Buchenwald, at about 3 o'clock in the afternoon of the 11th of April, the political prisoners, assembled in line, seized the weapons and made prisoner most of the SS guards of the camp or shot all those who resisted. These guards had great difficulty in escaping as they had knapsacks filled with booty, i.e. objects they had stolen from the prisoners during the time they had guarded the camp.

M. DUBOST: Thank you. I have no further questions to put to the witness.

THE PRESIDENT: We will adjourn now for ten minutes.

(A recess was taken)

M. DUBOST: I had no more questions to ask the witness, your Honours.

THE PRESIDENT: Do any of the defendant's counsel want to ask any questions of this witness?

BY DR. KAUFFMANN (counsel for Kaltenbrunner):

Q. Are you a specialist in research concerning the manufacture of vaccines?

A. Yes, I am a specialist in research.

Q. According to your opinion, was there any sense in the treatment to which these people were subjected?

A. It had no scientific significance; it only had a practical purpose. It permitted the verification of the efficacy of certain products.

Q. You must have your own opinion since you were in contact with those men? Did you really see these people?

A. I saw these people at very close hand, since in Block 50 I was in charge of part of this manufacture of vaccine. Consequently, I was quite able to realise what kind of experiments were being made in Block 46 and the reasons for these experiments. Further, I also realised the almost complete inefficiency of the SS doctors and how easy it was for us to sabotage the vaccine for the Germany Army.

Q. Now, these people must have gone through much misery and suffering before they died.

A. These people certainly suffered terribly, especially in the case of certain experiments.

Q. Can you certify that through your own experience, or is that just hearsay?

A. I saw in Block 50, photographs, taken in Block 46, of phosphorus burns, and it was not necessary to be a specialist to realise that these patients, whose flesh was burned to the bones, must have suffered.

Q. Then your conscience certainly revolted at these things.

A. Absolutely.

Q. Now, I would like to ask you, how were you able to follow the dictates of your conscience, in order to help these people in some way?

A. That is quite simple. When I arrived at Buchenwald as a deportee, I simply specified that I was a "laborant." That is a man who is trained in laboratory work but has no special and definite qualifications. I was sent to Dora, where the SS regime made me lose 30 kilos in two months. I became anaemic ....

Q. Witness, I am just concerned with Buchenwald. I do not wish to know anything about Dora. I ask you ...

A. It was the prisoners at Buchenwald who, by their connections within the camp, were the causes of my return to the Buchenwald camp. It was M. Julien Cain, a Frenchman, the Director of the French National Library, who called my presence to the attention of a German political prisoner, Walter Kummilscheim, who was a secretary in Block 50, and it is he who drew attention to my presence without my knowing it and without my having spoken of being a specialist in Dora. That is the reason why the SS called me back from Dora to work in Block 50.

Q. Please pardon the interruption. We do not wish to elaborate too much on these matters. I believe everything that you have just said, your reason why you were sent to Dora and why you were sent back. My point is a completely different one. I would like to ask you once more: You knew that these people were being treated in an inhuman way. Is that correct? Please answer yes or no.

A. I knew it of course, but long after -

Q. (Interposing): Please answer yes or no.

A. I answer the question. When I arrived at Block 50 I knew nothing, either of the Block or of the experiments. It was only later when I was in Block 50, that little by little and through the acquaintances I was able to make in the block. I found out the details of the experiments.

Q. Very well. And after you learned about the details of the experiments, did you not have the deepest sympathy for these poor creatures?

A. My pity was very great, but it was not a question of having pity or not, one had to carry out to the letter the orders that were given or be killed.

Q. Very well. Then you are stating that if in any way you had not followed the orders that you had received you might have been killed? Is that right?

A. There is no doubt about that. On the other hand, my work consisted in manufacturing vaccine, and neither I nor any other prisoners in Block 50 could ever enter Block 46 and actually witness experiments.

We knew what went on concerning the experiments only through the index cards which were sent from Block 46, to be officially registered in Block 50.

Q. Very well, but I believe there is no difference in your conscience, whether you see the suffering with your own eyes, or whether you have direct knowledge that in the same camp people are being murdered in such a way. Now, I come to another question.

THE PRESIDENT: Was that a question you were putting there? Will you confine yourself to questions.

THE WITNESS: I beg your pardon. I should like to answer the last question.

DR. KAUFFMANN: That was not a question. I will put another question now.

THE WITNESS: I should like to reply to this remark then.

DR. KAUFFMANN: I am not interested in your answer.

THE WITNESS: I am anxious to give it.

THE PRESIDENT: Answer the question, please.

THE WITNESS: Suffering was everywhere in the camps, and not only in the experimental blocks. It was in the quarantine blocks, it was among all the men who died every day by the hundreds. Suffering reigned everywhere in the concentration camps.

BY DR. KAUFFMANN:

Q. Was there a decree or an announcement that there was to be no conversation about these experiments?

A. As a rule the experiments were meant to be kept absolutely secret. An indiscreet remark in regard to the experiments could entail immediate death. I must add that there were very few of us who knew the details of these experiments.

Q. You mentioned the visits to this camp, and you also mentioned that German Red Cross members, or nurses, and members of the Wehrmacht visited the camp, and that furloughs were granted to political prisoners. Were you ever present at one of these visits inside the camp?

A. Yes, I was present at the visits inside the camp of which I spoke.

Q. Did the visitors to this camp see that cardiac injections were being given? Or did the visitors see that human skin was tanned? Were those visitors present while internees were being ill-treated?

A. I cannot answer this question in the affirmative, and I can only say that visitors passed through my block. One had to pass almost through the entire camp. I do not know where the visitors went either before or after visiting my block.

Q. Did one of your own comrades perhaps tell you whether the visitors personally saw these excuses? Yes or no.

A. I do not understand the question. Would you mind repeating it?

Q. Did perhaps one of your comrades tell you that the visitors at the camp were present at these excesses?

A. I never heard that visitors were present at experiments or at excesses of this kind. The only thing I can say, is that concerning the tanned skins I saw with my own eyes SS, non-commissioned officers or officers - I cannot remember exactly whether they were officers or non-commissioned officers - come out of block 2, carrying tanned skins under their arms. But these were SS men; they were not visitors to the camp.

Q. Did these visitors, and in particular the Red Cross nurses, know that these experiments were medically completely worthless, or did they just wish to inspect the laboratories and the equipment?

A. I repeat again that these visitors came to my laboratory section, where they saw what was being done, that is, the sterilised filling of the vials or tubes. I cannot say what they saw before or after. I only know that these visitors of whom I am speaking, these Luftwaffe cadets or the Red Cross people, visited the whole installation of the block. They certainly knew, however, what was the basis of this culture, and that men might be used for experiments, as there were charts and graphs showing the stages of cultures starting with men; but it could have been blood initially taken from typhus patients and not necessarily from patients artificially inoculated with typhus.

I really think that these visitors did not generally know about the atrocities in the form of experiments that were being performed in Block 46, but it is impossible for visitors who went into the camp not to see the horrible conditions in which the internees were held.

Q. Do you know whether people who received leave, that is, inmates who temporarily were permitted to leave the camp, were allowed to speak about their experiences within the camp and relate these experiences to the outside world?

A. All the concentration camps were, after all, vast transit- camps. The inmates were constantly being exchanged and replaced, passing from one camp to another, coming and going. Consequently there were always new faces. But most of the time these prisoners were, apart from those whom we knew before or after our arrest, strangers, and generally we knew nothing about those who came and went.

Q. Perhaps I did not express myself clearly. I meant the following:

From time to time, as you said before, political inmates were permitted to leave the camp temporarily. Did these inmates know about these excesses, and if they did know were they permitted to speak about these experiments in the rest of Germany?

A. The political prisoners (very few and all of German nationality) who had obtained leave were prisoners whom the SS had entrusted with important posts in the camp and who had been imprisoned for at least ten years in the camp. This was the case, for instance, of Karl, the Kapo, the head of the canteen of the Buchenwald camp, the canteen of the Waffen SS, who had the responsibility for the canteen, and who was given a fortnight's leave to visit his family at home in the town of Zeitz. Consequently the "Kapo" was free for these two weeks and was able to tell of anything he wished, but I do not know, of course, whether he so did. Evidently he had to be careful. In any case, the prisoners who were allowed to leave the camp were old prisoners, as I have said, who knew approximately everything that was going on, including the experiments.

Q. Now I come to my last question. If I assume that the people whom you have just described told anything to members of their families, even on the pledge of secrecy, and the leadership of the camp was informed of these indiscretions, do you not believe that the death penalty might have been incurred?

A. If there were indiscretions of this kind on the part of the family (for such indiscretions may be repeated among one's circle of acquaintances) or at least, if these indiscretions came to the knowledge of the SS, it is obvious that these prisoners risked the death penalty.

DR. KAUFFMANN: Thank you very much.

THE PRESIDENT: Is there any other defence counsel who wants to ask any questions?

DR. BABEL (defence counsel for the SS and the SD): I protest against the declaration that I tried to confuse witnesses with my questions. I am not here to worry about the good opinion or otherwise of the press, but to do my duty as a defence attorney ...

THE PRESIDENT: You are going too fast.

DR. BABEL (Continuing) ... and I am of the opinion that things should not be complicated through the interference of any one here - not even the Press.

This war has brought me so much misfortune and sorrow that I have no reason to vindicate anyone who was responsible for our unhappy fate or the misfortune that fell on all our people ...

THE PRESIDENT: Will you kindly resume your seat?

DR. BABEL (Continuing): . . . anyone who is guilty in this respect, and I will not try to prevent any such person from receiving his proper punishment. I am only concerned with helping the Tribunal to determine the truth so that just sentences may be pronounced, and that innocent people may not be condemned.

THE PRESIDENT: I said kindly resume your seat. It is not fit for you to make a speech. You have been making a speech, as I understand it; this is not the occasion for it.

DR. BABEL: I find it necessary because I was not protected against the Prosecution's reproach.

(Dr. Babel starts to resume his seat.)

THE PRESIDENT: One moment; come back.

(Dr. Babel comes before the microphone again.)

I do not know what you mean about not being protected. Listen to me. I do not know what you mean by not being protected against the Prosecution. The Prosecution called this witness, and the defendants' counsel had the fullest opportunity to cross-examine, and we understood you came before the Tribunal for the purpose of cross-examining the witness. I do not understand your protest.

DR. BABEL: Your Honour, unfortunately I do not know the court procedure customary in England, America and other countries. According to the German penal code and the German trial regulations it is customary for unjustified and unfounded attacks of this kind made against a participant of the trial, to be rejected by the presiding Judge. I therefore expected that perhaps this would be done here too, but when it did not happen I was occasioned to ...

If by so doing, I violated the rules of court procedure, I ask to be excused.

THE PRESIDENT: What unjust accusations are you referring to?

DR. BABEL: The prosecuting Attorney implies that I put questions to the witnesses calculated to confuse them, in order to prevent the witnesses from testifying in a proper manner. This is an accusation against the defence which is an insult to us, at least to myself - I do not know what position other defence counsels will take.

THE PRESIDENT: I am afraid I do not understand what you mean.

DR. BABEL: Your Honour, I am sorry. But I think I cannot convince you, as you probably do not know this aspect of German mentality, for our German regulations are entirely different. I do not wish to reproach our President in any way. I merely wanted to point out that I consider this accusation unjust and that I reject it.

THE PRESIDENT: Dr Babel, I understand you are saying that the Prosecuting Attorney said something to you? Now, what is it you say the Prosecuting Attorney said to you?

DR. BABEL: The Prosecuting Attorney said that I wanted to confuse witnesses by my way of questioning, and, in my opinion that means that I am doing something improper. I am not here to confuse witnesses, but to assist the Court to find the truth, and this cannot be done by confusing the witnesses.

THE PRESIDENT: I understand now. I do not think that the Prosecuting Attorney meant to make accusations against your professional conduct at all. If that is only what you wish to say, I quite understood the point you wish to make. Do you want to ask this witness any questions?

DR. BABEL: Yes, I have one question.

Q. You testified that weapons, fifty guns, if I understood correctly, were brought into either Block 46 or 50. Who brought these weapons in?

A. We the prisoners, brought and hid them.

Q. For what purpose?

A. To save our skins.

Q. I did not understand you.

A. I said that we hid these guns because we meant to sell our lives dearly at the last moment - that is, to defend ourselves to the death rather than be exterminated as were most of our comrades in the camps, with flame-throwers and machine guns. In that case we would have defended ourselves with the guns we had hidden.

Q. You said "we prisoners"; who were these prisoners?

A. The internees inside the camp.

Q. What internees?

A. We, the political prisoners.

Q. In the main they were supposed to have been German?

A. They were of all nationalities. Unknown to the SS, there was an international secret defence organisation with shock battalions in the camp.

Q. There were German inmates who wanted to help you?

A. German prisoners also belonged to these shock battalions - German political prisoners, and in particular former German Communists who had been imprisoned for ten years, and who were of great help towards the end.

Q. Very well, that is what I wanted to know. Then with the exception of the criminals who wore the green triangle, you and the other inmates, even those of German origin, were on friendly terms and helped each other; is that right?

A. The question of the "greens" did not arise, because the SS evacuated the "greens" in the last few days before the liberation of the camps. They exterminated most of them; in any case they left the camp, and we do not know what became of them. No doubt some are still hiding among the German population.

Q. My question did not refer to the green-marked prisoners but to your relations with the German political prisoners.

A. The political prisoners, whether they were German, French, Russian, Dutch, Belgian or from Luxembourg, formed inside the camp secret shock battalions which took up arms at the last minute, and co-operated in the liberation of the camp. The arms that were hidden came from the Guslow armament factories which were located near the camp. These arms were stolen by the workers employed in this factory, who every day brought back with them either a butt hidden in their clothes, or a gun-barrel, or a breach. And, in secret, with much difficulty, the guns were assembled from the different pieces and hidden. These were the guns we used in the last days of the camp.

DR. BABEL: Thank you. I have no further questions.

THE PRESIDENT: Does any other German counsel wish to ask questions? Have you any questions, M. Dubost?

M. DUBOST: I have no further questions, Mr. President.

THE PRESIDENT: Then the witness can retire.

M. DUBOST: These two days of testimony will obviate my reading the documents any further, since it seems established in the eyes of the Tribunal, that the excesses, ill-treatment, and crimes which our witnesses described to you occurred repeatedly and were identical in all the camps; and therefore are evidence of a higher will originating in the Government itself, a systematic will of extermination and terror under which all occupied Europe had to suffer.

Therefore I shall only submit to you, without reading them, the documents we have gathered and confine myself to a brief analysis whenever they might give you ...

THE PRESIDENT: M. Dubost, you understand, of course, that the Tribunal is satisfied with the evidence which it has heard up to date, but, of course it is expecting to hear evidence or possibly may hear evidence from the defendants, and it naturally will suspend its judgement until it has heard the evidence and, as I pointed out to you, yesterday, I think, under Article 24E of the Charter you will have the opportunity of applying to the Tribunal, if you think it right, to call rebuttal evidence in answer to any evidence which the defendants may call. All I mean to indicate to you now is that the Tribunal is not making up its mind at the present moment. It will wait until it has heard the evidence for the defence.

M. DUBOST: I think that the evidence we submitted in the form of testimony during these two days constitutes an essential part of our accusation. It will allow us to shorten considerably the presentation of our documents, of which we shall simply submit an analysis or very brief extract.

We stopped at the description of the prisoner's transports and under what conditions they were transported, when we started calling our witnesses.

In order to establish who, among the defendants, are those particularly responsible for these transports, I present Document UK 56, signed by Jodl and ordering the deportation of Jews from Denmark. It will appear among the documents as Exhibit RF 335.

THE PRESIDENT: I think you had better put your earphones on, I have here two books before me, one of which ...

M. DUBOST: It is in the first book of documents.

THE PRESIDENT: On the deportation?

M. DUBOST: That is right, on deportation.

THE PRESIDENT: When were these books handed out? Because apparently the United States members of the Tribunal ....

M. DUBOST: They were handed to you on Saturday*[1] Mr. President.

I now continue presenting a question which was interrupted on Saturday*(see footnote below) when the session was suspended at 1700 hours. This Document UK 56 is a telegram transmitted "en clair" with the mention " Secret Document." It is the eighth in the first book. Its second paragraph reads as follows: "The deportation of Jews ..." It is the eighth in your first book.

THE PRESIDENT: What page?

M. DUBOST: If the Tribunal thinks that our secretary interpreter can be of help in finding the documents ...

THE PRESIDENT: Go on.

M. DUBOST: The second paragraph:

> "The deportation of Jews must be undertaken by the Reichsfuehrer SS, who will send two battalions to Denmark for this purpose.
>
> For authorisation:
>
> Signed: JODL."

Here we have the carrying out of a political act by a military organisation or at least by a leader belonging to a military organisation: The German General Staff. This charge therefore affects both Jodl and the German General Staff.

We have submitted as Exhibit RF 324 in the Saturday (*see above) afternoon session an extract from the report of the Dutch Government. The Tribunal will find in this report a passage concerning the transport of Dutch Jews detained in Westerbork - which I quote: On the first page, second paragraph ...

THE PRESIDENT: Is that in the same book?

M. DUBOST: In the same book, Mr. President.

THE PRESIDENT: What Number? 324?

M. DUBOST: 224-F which has become Exhibit RF 324 after having been filed. It is an extract from the report of the Dutch Government, Paragraphs 2 and 3....

> "All Dutch Jews seized by the Germans were assembled at the camp of Westerbork" - Paragraph 3 - "little by little all prisoners of Westerbork were deported to Poland."

Is it necessary to recall the consequences of these transports (carried out in the conditions described to you), when three witnesses have come to tell you that each time the cars were opened numerous corpses had first to be taken out before a few

---

[1] The French transcript reads "Saturday". As the Court did not sit on Saturday, M. Dubost must mean "Friday" since there was a recess from Friday 25 January 1700 hrs to Monday 28 January 1000 hrs.

survivors could be found?

The French Document 115 which is the report of Professor Charles Richest will also be found in your first document book No. 115, the thirteenth in your document book, Page 6. Professor Richest repeats what our witnesses have said, that the deportees were -

THE PRESIDENT: What paragraph?

M. DUBOST: Last paragraph, Page 6. - There were 75 to 120 deportees in a car. In every transport men died. Arriving in Buchenwald from Compiegne, after an average trip of 60 hours, at least 25 per cent of the men had succumbed. This testimony corroborates those of Blaha, Madame Vaillant Couturier and Professor Dupont.

Blaha's testimony appears in your document book as Document 3249-PS. It is the second statement of Blaha, the second document in your book. We have heard Blaha. I do not think it necessary to re-read what he has already stated to us.

THE PRESIDENT: No.

M. DUBOST: A horribly infamous transport was that to Dachau, during the months of August and September 1944, when numerous trains which had left France, generally from the camps in Brittany, arrived in that camp with four to five hundred dead out of about two thousand men per train. We have this information from Document 140-F, which is in your first document book. The first page of this document states - and I quote so as not to have to return to it again - in the fourth paragraph which deals with Auschwitz: "About seven million persons died in this camp." This is Page 5 of your document book, second to last paragraph, in the middle, Document 406, which it is not necessary to submit, after the testimony that was given; it only repeats the conditions under which the transports were made and which Madame Vaillant Couturier has described to you.

Document 174, Page 16, indicates that in the train of the 2 of July, 1944, which left from Compiegne, men went mad and fought with each other and that more than 600 of them died between Compiegne and Dachau. It is with this train that Document 83-F deals - I repeat 83-F, which we submit as Exhibit RF 337, and which reads in the minutes of Dr. Louviers: Rheims, 12 February 1945. - (Page 5 of Document 83- F, in the first document book) - which indicates that these prisoners - (it is the fourteenth document in your first document book) - by the time they reached Rheims -

THE PRESIDENT: What paragraph are you reading?

M. DUBOST: Fourth paragraph, Page 5 . . . these people were already half dead of thirst - seventh page of this document, second paragraph: - "8 dying men were taken out even in Rheims; one of them was a priest."

This train was headed for Dachau. A few kilometres past Compiegne there were already numerous dead in every car.

Exhibit RF 320, Page 21 - it is the book handed to you on Saturday (*see above) and submitted as an official document, as Exhibit RF 324, pages 21 to 24 - contains other examples of the atrocious conditions under which our compatriots were transported from France to Germany.

THE PRESIDENT: What paragraph?

M. DUBOST: Page 21 at the top of the page:

> "At the station of Rheims water was refused us by the German Red Cross."

Second paragraph:

> "We were dying of thirst. In Breslau the prisoners again begged nurses of the German Red Cross to give us a little water. They refused and remained unmoved by our appeals" etc.

To prevent escape, in disregard of the most natural and elementary feelings of modesty, the deportees were obliged in many trains to strip themselves of all their clothes, and thus they travelled for many hours entirely naked from France to Germany. A testimony to this effect is given by our official document already submitted as Exhibit RF 274, page 17 of the French text, second paragraph...

THE PRESIDENT: 274 did you say? or 214?

M. DUBOST: 274 - it is this stitched booklet-page 17, second paragraph:

> "One of the means used to prevent escape, or as reprisals for the same, was to unclothe the prisoners completely," and another report adds: "This was also aimed at the moral degradation of the individual."

The most restrained testimonies report that this crowding together of naked men barely having room to breathe, was a horrible sight. When escapes occurred in spite of the precautions, hostages were taken from the cars and shot. Testimony to this effect is provided by the same document, page 18, at the top of the page:

> "5 deportees were executed."

Thus near Montmorency five deportees from the train of the 5 August, 1944 were buried, and five others of the same train were executed by pistol shots by German Police and officers of the Wehrmacht at Domremy. Added to this quotation is that of another official document, Exhibit RF 321, which we have already submitted. On page 20 you will read. (page 11 of the German text, page 2 of Exhibit RF 321):

THE PRESIDENT: What document?

M. DUBOST: Page 20 of Exhibit RF 32 1, page 11 of the German text.

> "Several young men were rapidly chosen. The moment they reached the trench each policeman seized a prisoner, pushed him against the side of the trench, and fired a pistol into the nape of his neck."

The same rule prevailed in deportations from Denmark. The Danish Jews were particularly affected. A certain number warned in time had been able to escape to Sweden with the help of Danish patriots. Unfortunately eight to nine thousand persons were arrested by the Germans and deported. It is estimated that 475 of them were transported by boat and truck under inhuman conditions to Theresienstadt (Bohemia and Moravia). This is stated in the Danish document submitted as Document 666. The Tribunal will find it in the first volume of its document book, and the quotation which I have just made is on page two of this document. That is the sixteenth (second to last) document in the first document book.

In connection with this country it is necessary to inform the Tribunal of the deportation of the frontier guards - page 3, the third paragraph, excerpt from the last paragraph.

> "In most places the policemen were dismissed immediately after having been disarmed; only in Copenhagen and in the nearby provincial towns were they held back and sent partly by truck, partly by boat to Southern Germany."

And for the frontier guards the following paragraph:

THE PRESIDENT: Page five is that?

M. DUBOST: Page 3, Document 666.

THE PRESIDENT: Which paragraph?

M. DUBOST: Third paragraph now. Second for the police, and third for the frontier guards. (Fourth line, at the end of the line.)

> "The policemen were brought to Buchenwald. They were kept under indescribably insanitary conditions, and a very large proportion of them fell

ill. About one hundred policemen and frontier guards died, and several still bear signs of their stay."

When this deportation had been carried out all the citizens of the subjugated countries of the West and of Europe found themselves in the company of their Eastern comrades of misfortune in the concentration camps of Germany. These camps were mere means of realisation of the policy of extermination which Germany had pursued ever since the National Socialists seized power. This policy of extermination would lead, according to Hitler, to the installing of 225,000,000 Germans in Europe, in the territories adjoining Germany, which constitute her vital living space.

The police and the German Army no longer dared to shoot their hostages, but neither of the two had any mercy on them. Even more were transported after 1943 to German concentration camps, where all means were used to annihilate them - from exhausting labour to the gas chambers.

The census made in France enables us to affirm that there were more than 250,000 French deportees of which only 35,000 returned. Document 417 submitted as Exhibit 339, which is the third in the first document book, indicates that out of 600,000 arrests which the Germans made in France, 350,000 were carried out with a view to internment in France or in Germany. This document brings to the Tribunal ...

THE PRESIDENT: Where is this Document 417?

M. DUBOST: In the book you have before you, Mr. President, the third in this book.

THE PRESIDENT: It is 417.

M. DUBOST: First page of this document, fourth paragraph.

"The total number of deported: 250,000.

Number of returned: 35,000."

On the following page a few names of deported French officials:

Prefects M. Bussieres, M. Bonnefoy, disappeared.

Generals de Lestraing, executed at Dachau.

Job, executed at Auschwitz.

Frere, died at Struthof.

Bardi de Fourtou, died at Neuengamme.

Colonel Roger Masse, died at Auschwitz.

High officials: Marquis of Moustier, died at Neuengamme.

Boulloche, Inspector General of Roads and Bridges, died at Buchenwald, his wife died at Ravensbruck, one of his sons died during deportation, his other son alone returned to Flossenburg.

Jean Deveze, engineer of roads and bridges, disappeared at Nordhausen.

Pierre Block, engineer of roads and bridges, died at Auschwitz.

Mine, Getting, founder of the social service in France, disappeared at Auschwitz.

Among the university professors of great renown: Henri Maspero, Professor at the College de France, died at Buchenwald. Georges Bruhat, Director of the Ecole Normale Superieure, died at Oranienburg. Professor Vieille died at Buchenwald.

It is impossible to name each of the intellectuals exterminated by the German frenzy.

Among the doctors, we must mention the disappearance of the Director of the Rothschild Hospital and of Professor Florence, one murdered at Auschwitz, the other at Neuengamme.

As to Holland:

110,000 Dutch citizens of Jewish religion were arrested, five thousand only returned; sixteen thousand patriots were arrested, six thousand only returned. Out of a total of 126,000 deportees, 11,000 were repatriated after the liberation.

In Belgium, 197,150 deportees, not including the prisoners of war - including the prisoners of war, 250,000.

In Luxembourg, 7,000 deportees. More than 700 Jews, 4,000 Luxembourgers, out of these 4,000, 500 died.

It is Documents 681-F, 231-F, 659-F, which we submit as Exhibits RF 343, 341 and 342.

In Denmark (see Document 666-F already submitted, page three) 614 Danes were interned, 583 died.

There were camps within Germany and outside of Germany. Most of the latter were used only for the sorting out of prisoners. However, some of them functioned like those in Germany and among them, that of Westerbork in Holland must be mentioned. This camp is dealt with in Document 222-F already submitted as Exhibit RF 324, which is the official report of the government of the Netherlands. The camp of Amersfoort, also in Holland, is the subject of Document 677, which will be submitted as Exhibit RF 344, the eleventh document in the book.

What we already know, through direct testimony, of the regime of the Nazi internment camps makes it unnecessary for me to read the whole report, which is rather voluminous, and which does not bring any noticeably new facts on the regime of these camps.

There is also the camp of Vught in Holland; then in Norway the camp of Grini, Falstatt, that of Expetend and that of Sipsizen which are described in a document provided by the Norwegian Government, Document 240, which is the fifth in your first document book, and which we have already submitted. The Tribunal will excuse me for not reading this document, which does not give us any information that we have not heard already from the witnesses.

The camps in Germany, like all those outside of Germany which were not only transit camps, must be divided into three categories, according to the German instructions which fell into our hands. You will find these instructions in your second document book, Page 11. The pages follow in regular order. It is Document 1063-PS, which we submit as Exhibit RF 345, Page 11 of your second document book. We read :

> "The Reichsfuehrer SS, and Chief of the German Police has given his approval relative to the division of the concentration camps into various categories, which take into account the prisoner's character and the degree of danger he represents to the State. Accordingly, the concentration camps will be classified into the following categories.
>
> Category 1: For all prisoners accused of minor delinquencies and definitely qualified for reform.
>
> Category 1a: For aged prisoners and those whose health will not permit them to do much work.
>
> Category 2: (Page 12, second document book): For prisoners with more serious charges, but still qualified for re-education and correction.
>
> Category 3: For all prisoners charged with particularly serious crimes.

On 2 January 1941, the date of this document, the German Administration, in dividing the camps into three categories, made an enumeration of the principal German camps throughout Germany in each category. It seems unnecessary to me to come back to the geographical location of these camps within Germany, since my American colleagues, geographical maps in hand, have already exhausted this question. The organisation and the functioning of those camps were regulated so as to obtain . . .

THE PRESIDENT: Will your address take much longer, because we are going to adjourn unless you are going to close in a few moments?

M. DUBOST: It will be five more minutes, and I could finish then with details to which it will not be necessary to come back tomorrow morning. The organisation and functioning of these camps had a double purpose: The first one, according to Document 285, which is on Page 14 of the second document book, is to reduce the labour shortage, in obtaining a maximum output at a minimum cost.

This document will be submitted as Exhibit RF 346, but we shall not read it in extenso. However, on Page 14 of your second document book you will read in the first paragraph (this is at the date of the 17 December 1942 and coincides with the difficulties resulting from the Russian campaign) that because of great difficulties of a military nature not to be discussed here the Reichsfuehrer SS and Chief of the German Police has ordered on 14 December 1942 that, by the end of January 1943 at the latest, 35,000 internees fit for work shall be sent to concentration camps.

Paragraph 2: "To obtain this number the following is ordered:

"As from this date and until 1 November 1943, all workers from the Eastern countries, and those of foreign nationality, who escaped or broke their contracts, and who do not belong to allied, friendly or neutral states shall be sent back to concentration camps by the quickest means possible."

Arbitrary internments with a view to procuring at the least possible cost the maximum output from labour which had already been deported to Germany, but which had to be paid since it was under labour contracts.

It was further intended to exterminate all unproductive forces which could no longer be exploited by German industry, and which might hinder the Nazi expansion. Evidence for this is furnished by Document 91-R, Pages 20 and 21 of the second document book, submitted as Exhibit RF 347, which is a telegram from the Chief of Staff of the Reichsfuehrer SS, received at 0210 hours, 16 December 1942, from Berlin.

"In connection with the increased transfer of labour to concentration camps, to be completed by 30 January 1943, the following procedure may be applied regarding the Jews:

1. Total number: 45,000 Jews.

2. Start of transportation 11 January 1943.

End of transportation 31 January 1943.

3. (The most important part of the document). Composition: the 45,000 Jews are to consist of 30,000 Jews from the District of Bialystok. 10,000 Jews of the Ghetto Theresienstadt, of which 5,000 are capable of working and who until now were used for small tasks in the ghetto, and 5,000 generally incapable of working, including those over 60 years of age. In order to use this opportunity for reducing the number of inmates, now amounting to 48,000, which is too high for the ghetto, I ask that special powers be given to me."

At the very end of this paragraph:

"The number of 45,000 includes the invalids (appendix "old jews and children" included). Through rational means, the screening of the newly arrived Jews in Auschwitz should yield at least 10,000 to 15,000 people fit for work."

And now here is an official document which corroborates the testimony of Mme. Vaillant Couturier, among various other testimonies on the same question, according to which the systematic selections made in each shipment arriving at Auschwitz were not made by the mere will of the Chief of the camp of Auschwitz but ordered by members of the German Government itself.

If it please the Tribunal, my report will finish here this evening, and will be continued tomorrow, dealing with the utilisation of this manpower, which I shall endeavour to deal with as quickly as possible in the light of the testimonies we have already had.

(The Tribunal adjourned until 30th January 1946, at 1000 hours)

Forty-sixth day: Wednesday, 30th January, 1946

MARSHAL OF THE COURT: May it please the Court, I desire to announce that defendants Kaltenbrunner and Seyss-Inquart will be absent from this morning's session on account of illness.

THE PRESIDENT: Dr. Babel, I understand that you do not wish to cross-examine that French witness.

DR. BABEL: That is correct.

THE PRESIDENT: Then the French witness can go home.

M. DUBOST: Thank you, Mr. President.

THE PRESIDENT: M. Dubost, there is one reason why perhaps that French witness ought not to go. I think I saw her leaving the Court. Could you stop her, please? I am afraid that she must stay for today.

M. Dubost, are you going to deal with documents this morning?

M. DUBOST: Yes, Mr, President.

THE PRESIDENT: Would you be so good as to give us carefully and slowly the number of the documents first, because we have a good deal of difficulty in finding them.

M. DUBOST: Yes, Mr. President.

THE PRESIDENT: And specify, also, so far as you can, the book in which they are to be found.

M. DUBOST: With the permission of the Tribunal, I shall continue my description of the organisation of the camps and the way in which they functioned. We gave notice of it last night by submitting to the Tribunal Document R-91 which is cited in extracts-in order to attain a double end: to make up for the lack of labour and to eliminate vain effort...

After Document R-91, which I submitted yesterday and which the Tribunal will find on Pages 20 and 21 of the second document book, we shall read Document F-285, particularly Pages 14, 17, 18 and 19 of the second document book. This document has been submitted as Exhibit RF 346.

This document is dated 17 December 1942 and is a sequel to the document which we read to you yesterday. First paragraph:

"For important military reasons, which must not be specified, the Reichsfuehrer SS and Chief of the German Police -

THE PRESIDENT: You read that yesterday.

M. DUBOST: That is correct, Mr. President. Page 18, sixth paragraph, at the top of the page:

Poles qualifying for Germanisation and prisoners for whom special requests have been made will not be handed over."

Last paragraph, Page 19: "Other papers will not be required for workman who are nationals of Eastern Countries."

This shows that arrests were made without discrimination, in order to obtain labour, and that this labour was considered to be so important that it was sufficient to register it under serial numbers.

Now, we will show how this labour was utilised. Men were housed, as the witness Balachowsky said yesterday, near factories in Dora, in underground caves which they themselves dug, and where they lived under conditions which violated all the rules of hygiene. At Ohrdruf near Gotha, the prisoners constructed munition camps: Buchenwald supplied the labour for Hollerith and Dora and the salt mines of Neustasstfurt.

The Tribunal will read in Document 274, Page 45, at the bottom of the page:

"Ravensbruck supplied the Siemens factories, those of Czechoslovakia, and the workshops in Hanover."

This special labour, according to the witness, enabled the Germans to keep secret the manufacture of certain war weapons, such as the V-1 and V-2, about which M. Balachowsky told us: "The deportees had no contact with the outside world. The work of deportees enabled the Germans to obtain an output which they could not have obtained even from foreign workmen."

The French prosecution will now submit document R-129 as Exhibit RF 348, which the Tribunal will find at Page 22 of the second document book. The second paragraph of this document deals with the management of concentration camps: "The extent of the output of his organisation depends on the camp commandant."

Fifth paragraph: "The camp commandant is the only one responsible for the work carried out by the workmen. This work - I underline the word " work " - this work must, in the true sense of the word, be exhausting, so that we can attain the maximum labour output."

Two paragraphs lower on the page, "The duration of the work is not limited. The duration depends on the nature of the work to be done and is determined by the camp commandant alone."

Last paragraph, Page 23 of this book, the four last lines: "He", the camp commandant - "must combine a technical knowledge in the economic and military field with wise and shrewd management of groups of men, from whom he must obtain a high potential of output."

This document is signed by Pohl, It is dated Berlin, 30 April, 1942.

I should merely like to recall now for the record a document which we have already quoted in relation to the camp of Ohrdruf, and which was submitted as Exhibit RF-140.

I will now read from Document 1584-PS which is in the appendix of your second document book. It is the sixth document in the appendix. The document will become Exhibit RF 349.

The document is signed by Goering and is addressed to Himmler. The second paragraph definitely establishes the responsibility of Goering in the criminal utilisation of this deportee labour. I shall read the second paragraph of the second page.

"Dear Himmler:

I ask you to keep at my disposal for air armament the greatest possible number of KZ prisoners." (The initials KZ mean "concentration camp.") " The experiments made up to the present show that this labour can very well be used. The situation of the air war necessitates the transfer of this air industry to underground workshops. It is precisely in such workshops that "KZ" prisoners can be best kept together as far as work and housing is concerned."

We know then who was responsible for the frightful conditions which the deportees of Dora had to endure. The person responsible is in the defendants' dock.

THE PRESIDENT: You did not give us the date of that, did you?

M. DUBOST: I did not see it on the document.

THE PRESIDENT: Is it 19 February, 1944?

M. DUBOST: On the first page you see that on 19 February, 1944, a letter was addressed to Dr. Braut, referring to teletypes which are appended and which were sent by the Field Marshal.

THE PRESIDENT: Is it the second letter, the letter that you read? Is the date of that 19.2.44?

M. DUBOST: It is 15 April, 1944 on the original, of which this is a photostat.

THE PRESIDENT: And could you tell us what K.Z. means, the two letters, K.Z.?

M. DUBOST: 15.4.44 on the original of the teletype. That means concentration camp.

THE PRESIDENT: Yes, I am not talking about that now.

M. DUBOST: K.Z. refers to concentration camps.

THE PRESIDENT: For the accuracy of the record, it appears that the letter on the second page is not 15 April, 1944, but 14 February. Is that not so?

M. DUBOST: Yes. It is 14 February, 2030 hours. It is a teletype, which was registered 15 April, 1944. That was the cause of my error.

THE PRESIDENT: But, M. Dubost, were you submitting or suggesting that this letter showed that the defendant Goering was a party to the experiments which took place, or only to the fact that these prisoners were used for work?

M. DUBOST: I was not referring to experiments. I was referring to internment in underground camps, as in the Dora camp, of which the witness Balachowsky spoke yesterday in the first part of his testimony.

THE PRESIDENT: Very well.

M. DUBOST: With regard to this will to exterminate, of which I have been speaking from the beginning of my presentation this morning, I think it is proved first of all by the text of Document R-91, which I read yesterday afternoon at the end of the session, a letter which has not as yet been authenticated, and by statements made by the witnesses who brought you the proof that in all the camps in which they stayed, the same methods of extermination through work were carried out.

As far as the brutal extermination by gas is concerned, we have the bills for gases, intended for Oranienburg and Auschwitz, which we submit to the Tribunal as Exhibit RF- 350. The Tribunal will find translations on Page 27 of the second document book, Document 1553-PS.

Moreover, I wish to point out, Page 27 of the second document book, that the French translation of these invoices - and I do this in order to be quite honest - is not absolutely in agreement with the German text. Therefore, in the fifth line for "extermination" read "purification".

The testimony of Madame Vaillant Couturier informed us that these gases were used for the destruction of lice and other parasites, and were also used to destroy human beings. Besides, the quantity of gas which was sent and the frequency with which it was sent, as you can see from the great number of invoices, which we offer in evidence, prove that the gas was used for a double purpose.

We have invoices dated 14 February, 16 February, 8 March, 13 March 20 March, 11 April, 27 April, 12 May, 26 May, and 31 May, which are all submitted as Exhibit RF 350.

THE PRESIDENT: Are you putting in evidence the originals of these other bills to which you refer on this document?

M. DUBOST: I request the court clerk to hand them over to your Honour, and I take advantage of this to request the Tribunal to examine these invoices carefully. You will observe that the quantities of toxic crystals sent to Oranienburg and Auschwitz were considerable; from the invoice of 30 April 1944 the Tribunal will see that 832 kilograms of crystals were sent, giving a net weight of 555 kilograms.

THE PRESIDENT: What is this document that you have just put in?

M. DUBOST: 30 April, 1944, but I am taking them at random.

THE PRESIDENT: I am not asking the date. What I want to know is, what is the authority for this document? It comes, does it not, from one of the committees set up by the French Republic?

M. DUBOST: No. Mr. President. This is an American document which was in the American archives, under the number 1553- PS.

THE PRESIDENT: M. Dubost, this note at the bottom of Document 1553-PS was not on the original put in by the United States, was it?

M. DUBOST: No, Mr. President, but you have before you all the originals under the number which the clerk of the court has just handed you.

THE PRESIDENT: Unless you have an affidavit identifying these originals, the originals do not prove themselves. You have got to prove these documents which you have just handed up to us either by a witness or by an affidavit. The documents are documents, but they do not prove themselves.

M. DUBOST: These documents were found by the American Army and filed in the Archives of the Nuremberg trial. I took them from the archives of the American delegation, and I consider them to be as authentic as all the other documents which were filed by my American colleagues in their archives. They were probably captured by the American Army.

THE PRESIDENT: There are two points, M. Dubost. The first is, that in the case of the original Document 1553-PS, it was certified, we imagine, by an officer of the United States. These documents which you have now drawn our attention to are not so certified by anyone, as far as we have been able to see. Certainly we cannot take judicial notice of these documents, which are private documents, and therefore, unless they are read in court they cannot be put in evidence. That can all be rectified very simply by a certificate or by an affidavit to be affixed to these documents, showing that they are analogous to the document which is the United States exhibit.

M. DUBOST: They are all United States documents, and they are all filed in the Archives of the United States in the American Delegation under the number 1553-PS.

THE PRESIDENT: The American Document 1553-PS has not yet been submitted to the Tribunal and the Tribunal are of the opinion that they cannot take judicial notice of it without any further certification, and they think that some short affidavit identifying the document must be made.

M. DUBOST: I will request my colleagues of the American prosecution to furnish this affidavit. I did not think it possible that this document, which was classified in their archives, could be ruled out.

This will for extermination, moreover, does not need to be proved by this document. It is sufficiently established by the testimony which we have submitted to the Tribunal. The witness Lampe spoke these words: "No one is to leave this camp alive. There is only one exit, and that is the chimney of the crematorium."

Document F-321, Page 49, at the top of the page, Page 36 of the German text, relates that the only explanation which the SS men gave to the prisoners was that nobody would leave the place alive.

On Page 179, the second last paragraph of the French text, Page 152 of the German text: "The SS told us there was only one exit - the chimney."

On page 174, Page 148 of the German text, the last paragraph: "Gassing and Cremation."

The essential purpose of these camps was the extermination of the greatest possible number of men. They were known as extermination camps. This destruction, this extermination of the internees, assumed two different forms. One was progressive; the other was brutal.

In the second document book which is before the Tribunal, Pages 28, 29, and 30, we find the report of a delegation of British Members of Parliament dating from April, 1945, this will be Exhibit RF 351, from which we quote these words (the third paragraph on Page 29):

"Although the work of cleaning out the camp had gone on busily for over a week before our visit ... our immediate and lasting impression was of intense general squalor."

Page 30, below the dashes, next to the last paragraph, third line of this paragraph:

"We should conclude, however, by stating that it is our considered and unanimous opinion, on the evidence available to us, that a policy of steady starvation and inhuman brutality was carried out at Buchenwald for a long period of time; and that such camps as this mark the lowest point of degradation to which humanity has yet descended."

Likewise, there is the report of a committee including General Eisenhower on Pages 31, 32 and 33 of the same document book. We read the second paragraph of the French extract, Page 32 in your document book:

"The purpose of this camp was extermination."

In the first paragraph on the top of the page:

"The means of extermination were blows, torture, over- crowding of the dormitories, illness."

Page 32, at the top, in the second document book -

THE PRESIDENT: Will you go a little bit slower over these numbers. You said, first of all, 31, and then 32. It came to, us as 22. It is quite impossible to follow you unless we know the right page.

M. DUBOST: The document L 159 is on Pages 31, 32 and 33 of the second document book.

THE PRESIDENT: You have read 31 now, have you not? Have you read 31?

M. DUBOST: I said to the Tribunal that the document which we now submit and read (Document L 159, Exhibit RF 352) is in the second document book, Pages 31, 32 and 33.

Page 31: "Atrocities and other conditions in the concentration camps in Germany. Report of a committee set up by General Eisenhower under the auspices of the Chief of Staff, General George Marshall, to the Congress of the United States, concerning atrocities and other conditions in concentration camps in Germany."

THE PRESIDENT: I asked you whether you had read the part you wished to read on Page 31.

M. DUBOST: Yes, Mr. President, I read the title, and then, from Page 32.

THE PRESIDENT: Where are you going to read on page 32?

M. DUBOST: The second paragraph.

THE PRESIDENT: On Page 32?

M. DUBOST: Page 32, second paragraph.

"The purpose of this camp was extermination, and the means of extermination."

THE PRESIDENT: M. Dubost, that is Page 31.

M. DUBOST: I beg your pardon Mr. President. I have a sheet which is numbered in a different way from yours.

We find then on Page 31, the first paragraph:

"The purpose of this camp was extermination, and the means of extermination were blows, torture, overcrowding of the dormitories, and illness. The result of these measures was heightened by the fact that prisoners were obliged to work in an armament factory adjoining the camp which manufactured small firearms, rifles" - and so on.

The means which were used to carry out this progressive extermination are numerous. We are going to submit documents which have just been handed to us, which we have communicated to the defence, and which consist more or less of printed formulas from Auschwitz, concerning the number of blows which could be administered to the internees or prisoners.

These documents will be handed over to the defence for their criticism. They have just been given to us. I am not able to authenticate their origin today. They appear to me to be of a genuinely authentic character. Photostats of these documents have been given to the defence.

THE PRESIDENT: The Tribunal think that they cannot admit these documents at present. It may be that after you have had more time to examine the matter you may be able to offer some evidence which authenticates the documents, but we cannot admit the documents simply upon your statement that you believe them to be genuine.

M. DUBOST: Moreover, everything in the camps contributed to pave the way for the progressive extermination of the people who were interned there. Their situation was as follows: all suffered from the hard climate, and severe exposure. Some worked in subterranean caves. Their living conditions have been brought to light by the testimony which you have heard, including the conditions under which the internees were received, being compelled to remain naked for hours while they were being registered or waiting to be tattooed.

Everything combined to cause the rapid death of those who were interned in the camps. A good number of them were subjected to an even harder regime, the description of which was given to the Tribunal by the American Prosecution when they submitted Exhibit USA 243 and the following dealing with the "Nacht und Nebel" regime, the NN.

I do not think it is necessary to return to the description of this regime. I shall merely submit a new document which shows the rigour with which it was applied to our compatriots. This document is the second of the first document book. It is included under the number 278. It comes from the German Armistice Commission of Wiesbaden, and shows that no steps were ever taken in reply to repeated protests by the French population, and even by the de facto government of Vichy, against the silence which shrouded the internees of the NN camps (paragraphs 1 and 2).

I shall now read from paragraph 2, which explains why no reply could be given to families who had good reason to worry.

This was foreseen and desired by the Fuehrer His opinion was that effective intimidation of the population, which would put a stop to criminal activities against the occupation forces, would be achieved by the death sentence, or by measures which would leave the offender's next of kin, and the population generally, uncertain as to their fate.

This document becomes Exhibit RF 326.

We will not devote any more time to describing the blocks and the unhygienic conditions under which the internees in the blocks lived. Four witnesses who all came from different camps have pointed out to you that the hygienic conditions in different camps were identical. The blocks were equally overcrowded in all these camps. We know that in all cases the water supply was insufficient, and that deportees slept two or three in beds only 75 to 80 centimetres wide. We know that the linen was never renewed or was in very bad condition. We know likewise the conditions in which the medical services of the camp functioned. Several witnesses belonging to the medical profession have testified to this fact before the Tribunal. The Tribunal will find confirmation of their testimony in Document F-121, Exhibit RF 354, Page 98 of the second document book. We shall read the last line of Page 100 of your document book.

> "Because of lack of water the prisoners were obliged to satisfy their thirst by drinking the stagnant water in the water closets."

Page 119 of Document F-121, Page 103 in the German text, third paragraph:

> "The surgical work was done by a German who claimed to be a surgeon from Berlin, but who was an ordinary criminal. At each operation he killed the patient."

Two paragraphs lower:

> "The management of the block was carried out by two Germans, who acted as sick-bay attendants; unscrupulous men, who carried out surgical operations on the spot with the help of a certain H - who was a mason by trade."

After the statement by our witnesses, who in their capacity as doctors of medicine, were able to care for patients in the camp infirmaries, it seems superfluous to give further quotations from our documents.

When the workers had been worked to the point of exhaustion, when it seemed impossible that they could ever recover, selections were made to set apart those who were of no further use, with a view to exterminating them either in the gas-chambers, as related by our first witness, Madam Vaillant Couturier, or by intra-cardiac injections, as related by two other French witnesses, Dr. Dupont and Dr. Balachowsky.

This system of screening was carried out in all the camps, and was done in execution of general orders, proof of which we find in Document R-91.

In the first document book the Tribunal will find the testimony of Blaha, testimony which it will certainly recall and which was given here on 9 January - it is the 5th document of the first document book, the testimony of Blaha, Document 3249-PS -

THE PRESIDENT: You have already given this as evidence, have you not?

M. DUBOST: I am not going to read it. I merely wish to recall this for the record, because it enters into the body of proofs which I wish to submit.

THE PRESIDENT: We do not want affidavits by witnesses who have already given evidence. This affidavit, PS-3249, has not been put in, has it?

M. DUBOST: No, I am merely recalling the testimony which was given at the session. We shall not submit this document, Mr. President. We are merely using it to remind the Tribunal that during the session Blaha pointed out conditions existing in the infirmaries.

To all these wretched living conditions must be added work, exhausting work, for all the deportees were intended to carry out extremely hard work. We know that they worked in labour gangs and in factories, we know, according to the witnesses, that the duration of this work was a minimum of 12 hours, and that it was often prolonged to suit the whim of the camp commandant.

Document R-129, from which I have already read, which was issued by Pohl, and addressed to Himmler, Pages 22 and 23 of the second document book, suggests that the working hours should be limited to a certain extent.

This work was carried out, according to the witnesses, in water, and in mud, in underground factories in Dora, for instance, and in quarries in Mauthausen. In addition to the work, which was exhausting in itself, the deportees were subject to ill-treatment by the SS and the Kapo, such as blows, or being bitten by dogs.

Our Document F-274, Pages 74 and 75, brings official testimony to this effect. Is it necessary to read to the Tribunal from this document, which is an official one, to which we constantly refer, and which has been translated into German and into English?

THE PRESIDENT: I do not think you need read it. Give us the page.

M. DUBOST: Thank you, Mr. President.

This same document, Pages 77, 78, informs us that all the prisoners were forced to do the work assigned to them, even under the worst conditions of health and hygiene. There was no quarantine for them even in case of contagious diseases or during epidemics.

The French Document 392, which we have already submitted and which is in the first document book - the testimony of Doctor Steinberg - confirms that of Madame Vaillant-Couturier. It is the twelfth document of your first document book, third paragraph, Page 4.

> "We received half a litre of herb tea; this was when we were awakened. A supervisor, who was at the door, hastened our washing by giving us blows with a cudgel. The lack of hygiene led to an epidemic of typhus."

At the end of the third paragraph and the beginning of the fourth :

> "The conditions under which the prisoners were taken to the factories."

In the fifth paragraph: "Description of shoes.

> We had been provided with wooden shoes which in a few days caused us wounds. These wounds produced boils which brought death to many."

I shall now read Document R-129, Pages 22, 23 and 24 in the second document book, and which we submit under the number-

THE PRESIDENT: One moment; the Tribunal will adjourn now for fifteen minutes.

(A recess was taken)

THE PRESIDENT: M. Dubost, the Tribunal have been considering the question of the evidence which you have presented on the concentration camps, and they are of the opinion that you have proved the case for the present, subject, of course, to any evidence which may be produced on behalf of the defendants, and of course subject also to your right under Article 24(e) of the Charter to bring in rebutting evidence, should the Tribunal think it right to admit such evidence. They think, therefore, that it is not in the interests of the Trial, which the Charter directs should be an expeditious one, that further evidence should be presented at this stage on the question of concentration camps, unless there are any particular new points about the concentration camps to which you have not yet drawn our attention; and, if there are such points, we should like you to particularise them before you present any further evidence upon them.

M. DUBOST: I thank the Tribunal for this statement. I do not conceal from the Tribunal that I shall need a few moments to select the points which it seems necessary to stress. I did not expect this decision.

With the authorisation of the Tribunal, I shall pass to the examination of the situation of prisoners of war.

THE PRESIDENT: M. Dubost, possibly you could, during the adjournment, consider whether there are any particular points, new points, on concentration camps which you wish to draw our attention to, and present them after the adjournment, in the meantime proceeding with some other matter.

M. DUBOST: The 1 o'clock recess?

THE PRESIDENT: . Yes, that is what I meant.

M. DUBOST: I shall, therefore, consider as established provisionally the proof that Germany, in its internment camps and in its concentration camps, pursued a policy tending towards the annihilation and extermination of its enemies, while at the same time creating a system of terror, which it exploited to facilitate the realisation of its political aims.

Another aspect of this policy of terror and extermination appears when one studies the War Crimes committed by Germany against prisoners of war. These crimes, as I shall prove to you, had two motives among others: the first was to debase the prisoners as much as possible in order to sap their energy; to demoralise them, to make them lose faith in themselves and in the cause for which they fought, and despair of the future of their country. The second was to cause the disappearance of those of them who, by reason of their previous history or of indications which they had given since their capture, showed that they could not be adapted to the new order which the Nazis intended to set up.

With this aim, Germany multiplied the inhuman methods of treatment intended to debase the men in her hands, men who were soldiers and who had surrendered trusting in the military honour of the army to which they had surrendered.

The transfer of prisoners was carried out under the most inhuman conditions. The men were badly fed, and were obliged to make long marches on foot, exposed to every kind of punishment, and struck down when they were tired and could no longer follow the column. No shelter was provided at the halting places, and no food. Evidence of this is given in the report on the evacuation of the column that left Sagan on 8 February, 1945, at 12.30 p.m., a document which the Tribunal will find in the appendix to the document book on the prisoners. This document has been submitted by my colleague, M. Herzog, under No. 46.

THE PRESIDENT: Where shall we find it?

M. DUBOST: I shall read the second appendix, last line.

THE PRESIDENT: I have not got the document, I am afraid, M. Dubost. I have the document book.

M. DUBOST: The document has been submitted.

THE PRESIDENT: If you could tell us which book it is in - just hand it up.

M. DUBOST: It is in the document book submitted by M. Herzog. The French Secretariat was instructed to hand these documents to you. I am surprised that this has not yet been done.

Will the Tribunal excuse me? I shall not be able to read this document now. It was handed over at the time of M. Herzog's speech. The Tribunal will find it among M. Herzog's documents. It is the report on the evacuation of the column that left Sagan on 8th February, 1945. We have no other copies.

THE PRESIDENT: Can you identify the document book in which it is, so that we can find it thereafter, and then pass on to the next document?

M. DUBOST: It is the document book which was handed to the Tribunal by my colleague, M. Herzog, when he gave his presentation on the question of labour.

THE PRESIDENT: And how is it marked?

M. DUBOST: It is U.K. 78, submitted under No. 46. A column of 1357 British soldiers, of all ranks, started on 28 January, 1945, toward Spremberg.

THE PRESIDENT: Possibly this is the first document in your document book which has been handed up to us.

M. DUBOST: That is right, Mr. President. I shall now read to you the document on the evacuation of the Sagan camp from 4- 6 February, 1945, since the Tribunal has not the copy before it. I pass to Document U.K. 170, Exhibit RF 355.

THE PRESIDENT: I am just telling you that I rather think this may be the document, if it begins with "1,357 English prisoners of war... " Does it begin in that way?

M. DUBOST: The document which you have before you, Mr. President, deals with the transfer of British prisoners of war. The one about which I wished to speak and from which I wanted to read to you deals with the transfer of French prisoners. I think that it is not necessary for me to lengthen the proceedings by showing the Tribunal that the British and the French prisoners were treated in the same way. I shall, therefore, restrict myself to your document.

> "1,357 British war prisoners of all ranks were marched out of Stalag 3 in three columns on 28 January, 1945, and were thereafter marched for distances varying from 17 to 31 kilometres per day to Spremberg, where they were entrained for Luckenwalde. Food, water, medical supplies were more or less non-existent throughout the trip. At least three prisoners had to be left at Muskau." - on the bottom of page, three lines before the end:
>
> "On the 31st they covered the distance of thirty-one kilometres to Muskau. It is small wonder that at this stage three men, first lieutenants Kelly and Wise, and W.O Burton collapsed and had to be left in the hospital in Muskau."

Page 2, at the end of the document: "On the March," -the last paragraph -

> "apart from the Red Cross parcels already referred to, the only rations issued were one loaf of bread and one issue of barley soup per man. The supply of water is described as 'haphazard.'"

There were fifteen who escaped.

The camp conditions of the Franco-Belgian column were even more rigorous. The camps were organised in a manner which was contrary to all the rules of hygiene. The prisoners were crammed into a very narrow space. They had no heating or water. There were thirty to forty men in a room. (Boudot's statement).

M. Boudot's statement is to be found in the report on prisoners and deportees which was also handed to you the other day by M. Herzog. I suppose that the Tribunal has kept its documents of last Thursday -

THE PRESIDENT: We have kept these documents, but if we had them on the Bench before us you would not be able to see us.

M. DUBOST: Similar statements are found in the Red Cross report. Berger, who was in charge, under Himmler, from 1 October, 1944, of prisoner-of-war camps, has admitted, in the course of his interrogation, that the food supply of prisoners of war was entirely insufficient. The Tribunal will find on Page 3 of the document book, which is before it, an extract from Berger's interrogation. The original is submitted as Exhibit RF 355.

Second paragraph: "I visited a camp south of Berlin, the name of which I cannot remember at the moment. I shall perhaps remember later. At that time it was obvious to me that the food conditions were absolutely inadequate, and a violent argument between Himmler and myself arose. Himmler was violently opposed to continuing the distribution of Red Cross parcels in the prisoner-of-war camps at the same rate as before. As for me, I thought that in this case we should be faced with serious problems regarding the men's health."

We present Document 826-PS, as Exhibit RF 356. This document was issued by the Fuehrer's Headquarters. This is a report on a visit to Norway and Denmark. It is on Page 7 of your document book. Paragraph 3:

> "All the prisoners of war in Norway receive an amount of food which enables them just to live without working. However, the cutting down of trees demands such hard work on the part of these prisoners of war that, if the food remains the same, a considerable lessening of production must soon be expected."

This note applies to the situation of the 82,000 prisoners of war who were held in Norway, 30,000 of whom were employed on very hard construction work which was being carried out by the Todt organisation. This is found in the first paragraph of Page 7.

I now present to the Tribunal Document 820-PS, Page 9 in the document book. It deals with the establishment of prisoner-of-war camps in the regions exposed to aerial bombardment. It was issued by Headquarters. It is dated 18.8.1943. It is addressed by the Commander-in-Chief of the Air Force to the Supreme Commander of the Wehrmacht. We submit it as Exhibit RF 358, and we shall read to the Tribunal paragraph 3:

> "The Chief of the General Staff of the Air Force, proposes to set up prisoner of war camps in the residential quarters of the cities in order to obtain a certain protection."

I omit a paragraph.

> "In view of the above considerations, there is a question of setting up such camps immediately in a large number of towns where there is danger of air attacks. As the discussions with the City of Frankfurt ... have shown, these towns will support and hasten the construction of the camps by all means at their disposal."

The last paragraph:

> "So far, there are in Germany about 8,000 prisoners-of-war who are British and American airmen (without counting those in hospital). By evacuating the camps actually in existence, which might be used to house bombed-out people, we should immediately have at our disposal prisoners of war for a fairly large number of such camps."

This refers to the camps set up in bombed areas and areas which were particularly exposed.

On Page 10 the Tribunal will find a document issued by the Fuehrer's Headquarters, dated 3-9-1943, still dealing with the establishment of these new prisoner of war camps for British and American airmen. We submit this document as Exhibit RF 359.

> "(1) The Chief of the General Staff of the Air Force, is planning the establishment of other camps for Air Force prisoners, for these are

coming in at the rate of more than 1,000 per month, and the space provided at the moment is becoming insufficient. The C in C Air Force proposes the establishment of these camps within residential quarters of the towns - as this will constitute at the same time a protection for the populations - and to transfer all the existing camps, where there are about 8,000 British and American Air Force prisoners, into larger towns threatened by enemy aircraft.

(2) The Supreme Commander of the Wehrmacht, Chief of War Prisoners Department has approved this project in principle."

Page 12 of the document book which the Tribunal has before it, is Document F-551, which we shall submit as Exhibit RF 360. It deals with the condemnation of prisoners of war in violation of Article 60 and the following articles of the Geneva Convention. The Geneva Convention provides that the protecting power shall be advised of judicial prosecutions that are made against prisoners of war, and will have the right to be represented at the trial.

THE PRESIDENT: Where are you? We are on Page 12 but we have lost the place.

M. DUBOST: In the middle of Page 12 - the practical application of Articles 60-66. I am now about to read, or rather, I am commenting on this order.

I have explained to the Tribunal that Article 60 and the following articles of the Geneva Convention provide that the protecting power shall be advised of judicial prosecutions against war prisoners. The document which we submit as Exhibit RF 360 shows that these provisions were violated. We read on the first line "In practice, the application of Articles 60 and 66, particularly paragraph 2 of Article 66, of the Convention of 1929, concerning the treatment or prisoners of war, meets with serious difficulties. For the application of a severe penal jurisdiction it is intolerable that actually for the most serious offences - as for instance, attacking the guards - the death sentence cannot be executed until three months after its notification to the protecting power. The discipline of prisoners of war is bound to suffer from this."

I pass over the rest of the paragraph. (Page 12.)

"The following regulation is proposed: (a) The French should be made to feel confident that the trials of prisoners of war in German hands, will, as formerly, be carried out thoroughly and conscientiously. (b) Germany will designate a defence counsel and an interpreter. (c) In the case of a death sentence" (bottom of page 12) "a certain period of time shall elapse after notification has been be given to this effect."

On top of Page 13

"In this respect Germany must in any case reserve the right, even if this is not explicitly stipulated, to carry out the sentence immediately in periods of crises...."

Third paragraph:

"There is no question of authorising France, who might perhaps refer to Article 62, paragraph 3 (P.O.W.) of the Geneva Convention, to send a representative to the sessions of the German Military Tribunals."

We possess an example of the violation of Article 60 and those following of the Geneva Convention in the report of the Netherlands Government, which the Tribunal will find on Page 14 of the document book.

THE PRESIDENT: I think we better break off now.

(A recess was taken until 1400 hours)

MARSHAL OF THE COURT: May it please the Court, I desire to announce that the defendants Kaltenbrunner and Seyss-Inquart will be absent from this afternoon's session due to illness.

THE PRESIDENT: I have an announcement to make.

When the attention of the Tribunal was called by the defendant Hess to the absence of his counsel, the Tribunal directed that the presentation of the individual case against Hess be postponed, so that counsel could be present when it was presented. So far as the cross-examination of witnesses who testified to matters affecting the general case and not against Hess specifically is concerned, it is the view of the Tribunal that the cross-examination conducted by counsel representing the defendants equally interested with Hess in this feature of the case, was sufficient to protect his interests, and the witnesses will therefore not be recalled.

The Tribunal has received a letter from the defendant Hess dated 30 of January, 1946, to the effect that he is dissatisfied with the services of counsel who has been appearing for him, and does not wish to be represented by him further, but wishes to represent himself.

The Tribunal is of the opinion that, having elected, in conformity with Article 16 of the Charter, to be represented by counsel, the defendant Hess ought not to be allowed at this stage of the Trial to dispense with the services of counsel and defend himself. The matter is of importance to the Tribunal, as well as to the defendant, and the Tribunal is of the opinion that it is not in the interests of the defendant that he should be unrepresented by counsel.

The Tribunal has therefore appointed Dr. Stahmer to represent the defendant Hess, in place of Dr. Rohrscheidt.

Yes, M. Dubost.

M. DUBOST: I beg the Tribunal to excuse me; I was completing the work which they had requested me to do in relation to concentration camps. I shall present to the Tribunal in a few moments, when I have completed the presentation of the question of prisoners of war, the end of the French presentation concerning concentration camps, which consists of very few matters; for we shall only have a few documents to cite since, subject to such counter-evidence as the defence may bring, the systematic repetition of the same methods seems, so far, sufficiently established.

We were at the point of reading a document of the Dutch Government, which has already been presented to the Tribunal under the number 324, and which establishes that a protest was lodged, following the execution and the secret condemnation to death of three officers: Lieutenants H. J. B. Ten Bosch, Braat and Thibo.

I think that the document to which I alluded this morning, which is the official report of the French Government concerning prisoners, is now in the hands of the Tribunal. It is the document submitted by M. Herzog under the number 46.

I ask the Tribunal to excuse me, as I cannot present this document again. I have no more copies.

It is evident from this document that the Nazis had a systematic policy of intimidation. They strove to keep the greatest possible number of prisoners of war in order to be able, if necessary, to exercise effective pressure on the countries from which these prisoners came. This policy was exercised by the illegal capture of prisoners, and also by the refusal, which was systematically upheld, to repatriate the prisoners whose state of health would have justified this measure.

Concerning the illegal capture of prisoners of war, we can cite the example of French prisoners.

The report of the Ministry of Prisoners of War and Deportees, to which we refer, indicates, on Page 4, that in 1940 certain French military formations laid down their arms at the time of the armistice, under an assurance given by the German Army that troops who had thus surrendered would not be taken into captivity. These troops were, nevertheless, captured. The Alpine Army had crossed the Rhone in order to be demobilised, and was West of the region of Vienne. They were taken prisoner and were sent to Germany until the end of July, 1940.

Moreover, non-combatant formations of special civilians were led into captivity and imprisoned in accordance with Himmler's orders, which directed that all Frenchmen of military age were to be seized indiscriminately. In short, it was only through special reports, and the private initiative of Unit Commanders, that not all Frenchmen were transferred to Germany.

Because of the enormous number of prisoners, and the difficulties that faced the German Army in taking all those men to Germany, the German Army decided, in 1940, to create what they called 'Front Stalags.'

The promise had been made to the de facto French Government, which was established after the armistice, that soldiers who were kept in these "Front Stalags" would be kept in France. Yet they began to be sent to Germany in October 1940.

In an additional report appended to the document book which is before you, the Ministry of Prisoners of War and Deportees points out the irregular capture of the troops of the fortified sector of Haguenau, the 22nd RIF, the 81st BCF, the 51st and 58th Infantry Regiments and a North African division. It is Document 668-F, Exhibit RF 361, the pages of which are not numbered. It is appended to the document book. I quote the document:

> "Troops of the fortified sector of Haguenau - the 22nd RIF and the 81st BCF - fought until 25 June, 1.30, and only ceased firing after an agreement between the Colonel in charge of the sector and the German Generals, an agreement which guaranteed the troops the honours of war, and notably that they would not be made prisoners. The 51st and 58th Infantry Divisions, as well as a North African Division, withdrew towards Toul only after an agreement, signed on 22 June, between the French General Dubuisson and the German General Andreas, at Thuille aux Groseilles, (Meurthe et Moselle); an agreement guaranteeing military honours and confirming that the troops would not be imprisoned."

THE PRESIDENT: What official document does this document come from?

M. DUBOST: From the Ministry of Prisoners of War and Deportees. It is an additional report which was made by the French Government.

THE PRESIDENT: Have you got any number for that report?

M. DUBOST: The French number is 668-F. A copy of the document is included in the file which is appended to the document book submitted to the Tribunal this morning. We submit it under the number -

THE PRESIDENT: Have you got the report on the captivity?

M. DUBOST: This report will be submitted to you, Mr. President.

THE PRESIDENT: It appears to be Appendix No. 2 to the report on the captivity, for the attention of the French Delegation to the Court of Justice at Nuremberg.

M. DUBOST: That is correct, sir. The information which I have just read to the Tribunal consists of extracts from a note from Darlan to Ambassador Scapini on 22 April, 1941.

THE PRESIDENT: But M. Dubost, is there anything to show that it is an official document, such as this book?

M. DUBOST: This document, Mr. President, bears no relation to the one which I am quoting.

THE PRESIDENT: No, I know it does not, but this is an official document produced by the Republic of France, is it not?

M. DUBOST: Yes.

THE PRESIDENT: How do you show that this Appendix No. 2 to the report on captivity is equally an official document with this one? That is what we want to know.

M. DUBOST: Mr. President, it is a report which was submitted in the name of the French Government by the delegation which I represent.

THE PRESIDENT: Well, you see, this one here is headed "Service of Information of War Crimes, Official French Edition." Now, that seems to us to be different from this mere typewritten copy, which has on it "Appendix Number 2 to the Report on the Captivity." We do not know whose report on the captivity.

M. DUBOST: Mr. President, you have before you the official note of transmission from our government. I requested that it should be handed to you.

THE PRESIDENT: In this document?

M. DUBOST: From this distance I think that is it.

THE PRESIDENT: We have this document, which appears to be an official document, but this Appendix has no such seal upon it as this has.

M. DUBOST: There is mention of an appendix to this document.

THE PRESIDENT: The other is marked: Appendix. It must be identified by a seal.

M. DUBOST: The covering letter has a seal, and the fact that it alludes to the document is sufficient, in my opinion, to authenticate the document transmitted.

THE PRESIDENT: This one?

M. DUBOST: The covering letter is officially sealed and the appended document is attached to it.

THE PRESIDENT: Is the explanation that you have torn off the appendix from this document and have put in the appendix separately?

M. DUBOST: I did not tear any document, Mr. President. I received an official document, whose authentic character is attested by the covering letter.

THE PRESIDENT: Where is this letter?

M. DUBOST: The letter is at the top of the sheaf of papers which you are holding in your right hand, Mr. President, if I am not mistaken.

THE PRESIDENT: I see the letter now, yes.

M. DUBOST: May I continue?

THE PRESIDENT: No.

This document here has a letter attached to it. This document here is not referred to in that letter specifically. Therefore, there is nothing to connect the two documents together.

M. DUBOST: I think there is a note in the margin in manuscript. I have not the document before me here, and cannot be positive about it, but I think there is a note in the margin in manuscript.

THE PRESIDENT: The Tribunal wishes you to put this in as one document. I see there is a manuscript note here at the side, which refers to the Appendix. If you will put the whole thing in together—

M. DUBOST: It is all submitted in one file: I wish to read to the Tribunal, extracts from two letters addressed to the German Armistice Commission at Wiesbaden by the ex- ambassador Scapini, both dated 4 April, 1941. The Tribunal will find them reproduced in the document book before them, Pages 16, 17, 18, 19, 20, 21, and 22.

Top right-hand corner, Page 16:

"4 April, 1941:

M. Scapini, Ambassador of France, to his Excellency Monsieur Abetz, German Ambassador in Paris. Subject: Men captured after the coming into force of the Armistice Convention and treated as prisoners of war."

At the bottom of this page:

"1. The Geneva Convention

The Geneva Convention applies only during a state of war as far as captures are concerned. Now, armistice suspends war operations. Hence, any man captured after the Armistice Convention came into force, and treated as a prisoner of war, is wrongfully retained in captivity."

Page 17, third paragraph-concerns the Armistice Convention in its second section. It states only that the French Armed Forces stationed in regions to be occupied by Germany are to be brought back quickly into unoccupied territory and be demobilised, but does not say that they are to be taken into captivity, which would be contrary to the Geneva Convention.

Fifth paragraph of the same page: "1. Civilians: If it is admitted that civilians captured before the Armistice cannot be treated as prisoners of war as discussed in my previous letter, surely there is all the more reason not to consider as such those captured after the Armistice. I note in this respect that captures, some of which were collective, were carried out several months after the end of hostilities."

Then on Page 18, the top of the page: "To the categories of civilians defined in my first letter, I wish to add one more: that of demobilised men who were going back to their homes in the occupied zone after the Armistice and who, more often than not, were captured on their way home and sent in to captivity as a result of the initiative of local military authorities.

2. Soldiers: That is how I would define, by convention, men who, though freed after the Armistice, could not for some reason - due to the difficult circumstances of that period - be provided with the regular demobilisation papers. Many of them were captured and taken into captivity under the same conditions as those mentioned above."

I think the Tribunal will not require the reading of that example, but if the President wishes, I shall read it.

THE PRESIDENT: No.

M. DUBOST: Let us turn to Page 19, second half of the page, the last paragraph :

"A. Civilians not subject to military requirements: It is obvious that these men could not be considered soldiers according to French law. They can be classified, according to age, into three groups :

(a) Men under twenty-one not yet mobilised. Example: Flanquart, Alexandre, eighteen years old, captured by the German troops at Courrieres, in the Department Pas-de-Calais, at the time of the arrival of these troops, in that region. His address in captivity was No. 65/388, Stalag 11-B. (b) Men between twenty-one and forty-eight who were not mobilised, or who were demobilised, or who were considered unfit for service."

There follows a rather lengthy list which the Tribunal will perhaps accept without my reading it. It consists merely of names. In the middle of the page:

"Men specially assigned to the army: I will classify them into two groups:

1. Men mobilised into special corps which are military formations, established at the time of the mobilisation by different ministerial departments, according to the following chart."

At the top of Page 21:

"Men specially assigned, who on mobilisation were kept in the positions which they held, in peace time, in military services or establishments. Example: Workers in artillery depots.

Civilians specially assigned: Contrary to those mentioned above, the civilians who were specially assigned did not belong to military formations and were not subject to military authority. Nevertheless they were arrested. Example: (I omit several lines) Mouisset, Henri, specially assigned to the Marret-Bonin factory. (I omit a few more lines) Address in captivity: No. 102 Stalag II-A."

Those people were not all freed, far from it. Some remained prisoners until the end of the war.

Arrest of Dutch Army officers. We shall cite now a document submitted under No. 324 RF, the text of which is in your document book, on Page 15 his. This text may be summarised in a few words. It is the story of Dutch officers who were freed after the capitulation of the Dutch Army, and recaptured shortly afterwards to be sent to captivity in Germany. Paragraph 3 of this document:

"On 9 May, 1942, a summons addressed to all regular officers of the former Dutch Army who were on active service on 10 May, 1940, was published in the Dutch newspapers, according to which they were to be present on 15 May, 1942, at the Chassee Barracks in Breda."

Paragraph 5:

"More than one thousand regular officers reported to the Chassee Barracks on 15 May. The doors were closed after them."

Paragraph 7:

"A German officer of high rank came into the barracks and declared that the officers had not kept their word to undertake no action against the Fuehrer and, as a result of this, they were to be kept in captivity."

The following paragraph states that they were taken from the station at Breda to Nuremberg, in Germany.

Numerous obstacles were placed in the way of the release of French prisoners of war who, for reasons of health, should have been sent back to their families. I shall quote a document already submitted as Exhibit RF 297, Page 23 of your document book:

"The question of releasing French generals, prisoners of war in German hands, for reasons of health or age, was taken up on several occasions by the French authorities."

This reproduction of the stencil is not quite clear.

I continue with paragraph 2:

"So far as this question is concerned, the Fuehrer has always refused to consider either to release them, or to allow them to be put in hospitals in foreign or neutral countries."

Paragraph 3:

"Today there is less question than ever of release or of putting in hospitals"

— and a written note reads: "No reply to be given to the French note."

This note, in fact, was addressed by the C in C of the German Army to the German Armistice Commission, who had discussed with the General Staff whether or not to reply to the request concerning the release of French generals who were ill, a request made by the de facto government ruling France at that time.

Much more serious measures were taken against our prisoners of war by the German authorities when, for reasons of a patriotic nature, some of our compatriots who were prisoners gave the Germans to understand that they were not willing to collaborate with Germany. The German authorities considered those of our compatriots who acted in this way as incapable of being assimilated, and as dangerous, because of their courage and their determination. The measures formulated concerning them amounted to nothing less than murder. We know of numerous examples of murders perpetrated on prisoners of war, either because they took part in commando actions or because the Nazis charged them with having committed terroristic acts from the air, or with escaping or attempting to escape; or they even simply accused them of active resistance or merely ethical resistance against the Nazi regime. These murders were carried out by means of deportation and the internment of these prisoners in concentration camps. While interned in these camps, they were subjected to the regime about which you know, and which was bound to cause their death, or else they killed them quite simply with a bullet in the back of the neck, according to the method which has been described by our American colleagues and on which I will not dwell at length.

In other cases they were lynched on the spot by the population in accordance with direct orders, and with the tacit consent of the German Government.

In still other cases, they were handed over to the Gestapo and the SD who, as I will prove to you at the end of my statement, during the last years of the occupation had the right to carry out executions.

With the authorisation of the Tribunal we shall study two cases of extermination of combat troops captured after military operations; commandos and airmen.

As the Tribunal knows, men who were in commandos were nearly always volunteers. In any case, they were selected from the most courageous fighters and those who showed the greatest physical aptitude for combat. We can consider them, therefore, as the elite, and the order to exterminate them as an attempt to annihilate the elite by spreading terror through the ranks of the Allied Armies. From a legal point of view the execution of the commandos cannot be justified. The Germans themselves, moreover, used commandos quite extensively, but whereas, in the case of their own men being taken prisoner, they always insisted that they be recognised as belligerents, they denied that right to our men or to those of the Allied Armies.

The major order concerning these exterminations was signed by Hitler on 18 October, 1942, and it was extensively carried out. Moreover, this order was preceded by other orders of the OKW, which show that the question had been carefully studied before becoming the object of a final order by the Chief of the German Government.

Under Number 553-PS, the Tribunal will find, on Page 24 of the document book, an order signed by Keitel, which we submit as Exhibit RF 363. This order demands that all isolated parachutists or small groups of parachutists shall be executed. It is dated 4 August, 1942, and is on Page 25. The Tribunal will see it is signed by Keitel; it has already been quoted. Paragraph 3 says:

THE PRESIDENT: Do not read it.

M. DUBOST: I thank the Tribunal for sparing me the reading of it.

On 7 October, 1942, a communique of the OKW, circulated by Press and radio, announced the decision taken by the High Command to execute saboteurs. On Page 26, the Tribunal will find in the document book extracts from the "Volkischer Beobachter" of 8 October 1942, stating:

"In future all terrorist and sabotage troops of the British and their allies, who do not behave as soldiers but as bandits, will be treated as such by the German troops and shot on the spot without any consideration, wherever it may be." (Exhibit RF 364).

As Exhibit RF 365 we submit minutes of meetings of the General Staff of the Wehrmacht, dated 14 October 1942.

Paragraph 3: "During the era of total warfare sabotage has become one of the most important elements in the conduct of war. It is sufficient to state our attitude to this question. The enemy will find evidence of it in the reports of our own propaganda departments."

Page 29, paragraph 3, the end of the paragraph, still from the notes of this meeting, dated 14 October 1942, of the General Staff of the Army:

"Sabotage is an essential element, and we have developed it ourselves as a means of combat."

THE PRESIDENT: What paragraph?

M. DUBOST: The third paragraph, Mr. President, then the sixth paragraph.

"We have already by radio announced our intention of liquidating, in future, all groups of terrorists and saboteurs conducting themselves like bandits. Consequently we are of opinion that the task of the OKW is only to give certain practical directives concerning what the troops should do with these groups."

Page thirty. The Tribunal will see what were the orders which were given as to the treatment of what the German General Staff called "Groups of terrorists and British saboteurs," since they were commandos of the other side, commandos of the enemy. It is certain that the German General Staff never called their own commandos "groups of terrorists and saboteurs."

Paragraph one, fourth line, refers to groups of the British Army in British uniform or not in British uniform. I cite: "We must exterminate them in the course of combat or when they are fleeing."

Sub-paragraph (B). "Member of terrorist groups and sabotage groups of the British Army who, in uniform, have fought our troops in dishonourable fashion, contrary to International Law, must be kept in separate custody."

I omit two lines and I read: "The instructions on their treatment will be given by the OKW in agreement with the juridical service and the Counter Intelligence Department - Foreign Section."

Finally, Page thirty-one, paragraph two: "In future every group of terrorists or saboteurs will be considered as acting contrary to the laws of war in cases where terrorists, saboteurs, agents, etc. are found to be carrying out acts considered by the troops to constitute acts of terrorism or barbarism. This applies equally to soldiers and civilians, whether in uniform or not."

Paragraph three. "In that event the groups will be annihilated to the last man, during combat or when they try to flee."

Paragraph four: "It is forbidden to intern them in war prison camps."

Thus in carrying out these orders, if British soldiers, even in uniform, were captured during a commando operation, the German troops were to judge whether they had acted according to the laws of war or not, and, without any appeal, subordinates could annihilate them to the last man, even when they were not engaged in active fighting. These orders were applied to British commandos.

We shall now quote Document 498-PS, which was submitted by our American colleagues and which confirms the information which we have just brought to the Tribunal by reading the preceding documents. It seems useless to read this document.

THE PRESIDENT: M. Dubost, had the document on Page 31 been received before? - the one you just read?

M. DUBOST: Document on Page 31, which I have just read, was not read before Mr. President, but it was submitted. I thought you were speaking -

THE PRESIDENT: The next one has been read, has it not, 498?

M. DUBOST: Document 498, which I told the Tribunal I was not going to read, was read by our American colleagues. The Tribunal will find it, nevertheless, in the document book on Pages 32 and 33.

THE PRESIDENT: There are two points to which I wish to draw your attention. In the first place, it is said that you are not offering these documents in evidence, you are simply reading them, and they must be offered in evidence so that the document itself may be put in evidence. You have not offered in evidence any of these documents; you have just been reading from them or have given them numbers.

M. DUBOST: Mr. President, they were all filed, absolutely all of them except those which were already filed by our colleagues, and all were filed with a number, and can be handed to you immediately. I shall ask the French secretary to hand them to you with the exhibit numbers which I read out.

THE PRESIDENT: They have all been put in evidence already?

M. DUBOST: Mr. President, some have been put into evidence; I quoted them with their exhibit numbers, but some have not been submitted. I will submit these and give them French numbers.

THE PRESIDENT: You are saying, "have been put in evidence by some other member of the prosecution;" is that right?

M. DUBOST: That is correct, Mr. President. When I quote them I give the number under which they were filed by my American colleagues.

THE PRESIDENT: That was filed by the American Prosecution, was it not 498, on Page 32?

M. DUBOST: 498, on Page 32 has already been filed as exhibit U.S.A. 501, as I said before, Sir.

THE PRESIDENT: I am speaking of 498, Page 32.

M. DUBOST: That is correct. It is the American number 501 filed by my American colleagues as Exhibit U.S.A. 501.

THE PRESIDENT: Very well.

M. DUBOST: No. 498-PS, Mr. President, Page 32 in your document book has already been submitted, as I said, by my American colleagues and has been read by them. I shall not read it. I shall merely comment on it briefly.

THE PRESIDENT: Very well, with reference to the document which preceded it on Pages 27 29, 30 and 31 -

M. DUBOST: I will ask the French secretary to give them to you with the numbers under which they were filed, which correspond to the ones I began to read.

THE PRESIDENT: Have they been filed by the American prosecutor too?

M. DUBOST: Not all, Mr. President. Some were filed by the American Prosecution and others were filed by me.

THE PRESIDENT: All I am pointing out - I think, M. Dubost, that what the

Tribunal wants you to do is - when you put in a document -

M. DUBOST: Will you excuse me, Mr. President. I do not understand.

THE PRESIDENT: I have not finished the sentence. What I was saying was, what the Tribunal wants you to do is, when you put in a document, if it has not already been put in, give it a number and announce the exhibit number so that the record may be complete.

Is that clear?

M. DUBOST: It is clear, Mr. President, but I believe that I have done so from the beginning, since the French secretary has just given you the file.

THE PRESIDENT: You may have put numbers on the documents, but you have not announced them in some cases.

There is another matter which I wish to state and it is this. When I spoke before, what I asked you to do was to confine yourself to any new points, and you are now giving us evidence about commandos and about British commandos, all of which has been already gone into in previous stages of the trial, and that appears to us to be unnecessary.

M. DUBOST: The Tribunal will pardon me, but I have not read any of the documents already mentioned. The documents from which I have read were documents not cited before. I had just reached a document which had been mentioned before, and I asked the Tribunal to excuse me from even commenting on it, since I thought the document was already well known to the Tribunal.

THE PRESIDENT: Well, we have had a good deal of evidence already about the treatment of commandos and sabotage groups, evidence, if I remember rightly, which attempted to draw some distinction between troops which were dropped from the air, for instance, close up to the battle zone, and troops that were dropped at a distance behind the battle zone. We had quite a lot of evidence upon that subject. If there is anything which is of special interest to the case of France we would be most willing to hear it, but we do not desire to hear cumulative evidence upon subjects which we have already heard.

M. DUBOST: I did not think that I had brought cumulative proof to the Tribunal in reading documents which had not previously been read, but since that is so, I will continue, but not without emphasising that, in our view, the responsibility of Keitel is seriously involved by the orders which were given and by the execution of these orders.

Document 510-PS, Page 48, has not been read. We submit it as Exhibit RF 367, and we ask the Tribunal to take judicial notice of it: it concerns the carrying out of the orders which were given concerning the landing of British detachments at Patmos.

A memorandum from the General Staff to the commander of the different units, Document 532-PS, which is the appendix to the document book repeats and specifies the instructions which the Tribunal knows and does not bring anything new into the case. We submit this document as Exhibit RF 368, and we ask the Tribunal to take judicial notice of it.

We shall now deal with the execution of Allied airmen who were captured.

From the presentation which was made of this question, the Tribunal has learned that a certain number of air operations were considered as criminal acts by the German Government, who indirectly encouraged the lynching of the airmen by the population or their immediate extermination by the action "Sonderbehandlung" (special treatment), which need not be discussed again. This was the subject of Exhibit USA 333, which has already been cited, and USA 334.

Within the scope of these instructions, orders were given by the letter of 4 June 1944 to the Minister of Justice to forbid any prosecution against German civilians in connection with the murder of Allied airmen. This is the subject of Document 635-PS, which you will find in the appendix of the document book, same paragraph.

"Reich Ministry of Justice." This document will become as Exhibit RF 370.

"The Reich Minister and Head of the Reich Chancellery, 4 June 1944, to the Reich Minister of Justice, Doctor Thierack:

Subject: The justice of the people against Anglo-American murderers. The Chief of the Party Chancellery has informed me of his secret memorandum, a copy of which is enclosed, and has asked me to make it known to you also. I am complying with this in asking you to examine to what extent you wish to inform the tribunals and the public prosecutors."

On 6 June, two important conferences were held, notably between Kaltenbrunner, Ribbentrop, Goering (all three defendants), Himmler, and Von Brauchitsch, at which officers from the Luftwaffe and the SS were present, also. They decided to draw up a final list of air operations which would be considered acts of terrorism.

The original record made by Warlimont and bearing written notes by Jodl and Keitel is Document 735-PS, which I submit as Exhibit RF 371. It was decided at this conference that lynching would be the ideal punishment to stop certain types of air operations directed against the civilian population.

Kaltenbrunner, on his part, promised the active collaboration of the SD (Page 68 at the end of the first paragraph and the second paragraph.).

THE PRESIDENT: Was it already read?

M. DUBOST: This document, so far as I know, was never read.

DR. EXNER (Counsel for defendant Jodl): I am protesting against the presentation of Document 532-PS dated 24.6.44. (NB. See Tribunal's ruling on page 293.) That is a draft of an order which was submitted to Jodl, but which was crossed out by him, and so annulled.

At this juncture I would also like to call the attention of the Court to the fact that we defence counsel did not receive a document book like the one presented to the Tribunal, and it is therefore very hard for us to check and to follow the presentations of the prosecution. Every morning we receive a pile of documents, some of which partially refer to future and some to past proceedings. But I have not seen document book in chronological order for weeks. Furthermore, it would be desirable for us to receive the documents the day before. In that case, when testimony is given, we could be of assistance to both sides.

THE PRESIDENT: Dr. Exner, are you saying that you have not received the document book, or that you have not received the dossier? Are you saying that you have not received the document book, or this thing which is the dossier of the speech.

DR. EXNER: I did not receive the document book. I would like to add something. Some of the documents which have just been presented were quoted without signatures, and without date, and it is questionable whether these so-called documents are to be considered as documents at all.

THE PRESIDENT: Well, I imagine that you have just heard - I have told M. Dubost that he must announce the exhibit number which the French prosecutor is giving to any document which he puts in evidence. As I understand it, he has been putting numbers upon the documents, but in certain cases he has not announced the number in open court. The document, as you have seen, has been presented, and, as I understand, it has a number upon it, but he has not in every case announced the number, and the Tribunal has told M. Dubost that it wishes and it orders that every document put in by the French prosecutor should have an exhibit number announced in Court. That meets one of the points that you raised.

As to your not having the document book, that is, of course, a breach of the order which the Tribunal has made that a certain number of copies of the documents should be deposited in the defendants' Information Centre, or otherwise furnished to defendants' counsel.

As to Document 532-PS -

(Off the record discussion by the Court.)

THE PRESIDENT: Dr. Exner, is there anything further you wish to say upon these points, because we are just about to have a recess for a few moments. We would like to hear what you have to say before we have the recess.

DR. EXNER: I have nothing further to add, but if I may be permitted to make a further remark, we were advised that it was your Honours wish that we should hear every day what is to be the subject of the proceedings on the following day, which would, of course, be a great help to our preparations. So far, that has never been the case. I myself have never heard what was to be dealt with the following day.

THE PRESIDENT: Thank you. M. Dubost, the Tribunal would like to hear what you have to say upon the points raised by Dr. Exner: first of all, upon Document 532-PS; secondly, why he did not receive a document book; and lastly, why he has not received any programme as to what is to be gone into on the following day.

M. DUBOST: As to the question of programme, as Dr. Exner pointed out, the custom of providing it has not been established by the prosecution. No one has ever given it, neither the French prosecution nor its predecessors. Perhaps I did not attend the session the day the Tribunal requested that the programme should be given. In any case I do not remember that the prosecution was ever requested to do that.

As far as the document book is concerned, it is possible that this book was not handed to the defence in the form which is before the Tribunal, that is to say, with the pages numbered in a certain order. However, I am certain that yesterday I sent the defence the text in German and several texts in French of all the documents which I was to submit to-day. I cannot assure the Tribunal that they were handed over in the order in which you have them before you, but I am sure that that was done.

THE PRESIDENT: As to Document 532?

M. DUBOST: Document 532 was not read in the hearing, Mr. President. I could not hide the fact that there was a manuscript note in the margin, but I did not read this document.

THE PRESIDENT: Is it a document that had been put in before?

M. DUBOST: I do not believe so, Mr. President. In my dossier there are a certain number of documents which I have not read, as I knew the Tribunal's wish that I should shorten my presentation, and Document 532 is one of those.

THE PRESIDENT: I know you did not read it, but did you put it in evidence? Did you give it a number?

M. DUBOST: No, Mr. President. It is part of this series of documents which I shall not read, in order to finish more quickly, since that is the wish of the Tribunal.

THE PRESIDENT: Well, M. Dubost, I have said that I knew that you did not read it, and I have asked you - I think twice - whether you intended to put it in evidence. Did you give it a number?

M. DUBOST: Perhaps, Mr. President .... Yes, that is correct, Exhibit RF 368, I remember.

THE PRESIDENT: The document, according to Dr. Exner, is a draft of a order which was submitted to Jodl but was not approved by him. Those were his words, as they came through in the translation, and, therefore, he submits that it is not to be considered, and there is nothing to show that the document was ever anything more than a draft. If so, is it not clear that it ought not to be received in evidence?

M. DUBOST: This is a question which the Tribunal will decide after having heard the explanation of Dr. Exner. This document did not seem to me of major importance in my presentation, since I did not read from it. In any case, I could not hide from the Tribunal, since I did not read it, that there was a manuscript note in the margin. It is certain that this manuscript note is an element to be taken into consideration, and on which the Tribunal will base its decision whether the Exhibit RF 368 should be accepted or rejected, after having heard the explanation of the defence.

(A recess was taken)

DR. NELTE (Defence counsel for Keitel): Mr. President, I had occasion during the recess to talk to my client, Keitel. Before the recess, the French prosecutor had submitted as evidence Document F-668, and an extract from a note from Admiral Darlan, addressed to the French Ambassador Scapini.

The French prosecutor believes I presume from his words, that he has proved by these documents that the agreements between German generals and French troops who had laid down their arms had not been kept. In view of the gravity of these accusations I would be obliged to the French prosecution if they would declare, with respect to this document, first, whether these serious accusations of the French Government had also been brought to the attention of the German Government -

THE PRESIDENT: Document 668, is it?

DR. NELTE: Yes, 668.

THE PRESIDENT: Are you referring to Document F-668?

DR. NELTE: Yes, appendix 2.

THE PRESIDENT: It would be more convenient if you could refer to the document by the usual document number. The document I have is Document F-668, at the top of the document.

DR. NELTE: On my document it has been inserted in pencil.

THE PRESIDENT: Is it dated 4 April, 1941?

DR. NELTE: It has no date.

THE PRESIDENT: Will you hand it up?

(The paper was handed to the President.)

Yes, I follow now, What do you say about it?

DR. NELTE: The French prosecutor had concluded from this document that the information contained in the document was also proved. I would like to point out that it is an excerpt from a note of Admiral Darlan, addressed to the French Ambassador Scapini. In other words, it is not clear from this document whether Ambassador Scapini had taken the necessary steps with the German Government or, furthermore, what reply was made by the German Government to this note. For this reason I would like to ask the French prosecutor to declare whether he can establish from his documents whether these serious accusations were brought to the attention of the German Government, and secondly, if so, what reply was made by the German Government. Since these documents of the Armistice Commission are in possession of the victorious powers, neither the defendant nor the defence can themselves produce them.

(M. Dubost stepped before the microphone.)

THE PRESIDENT: Perhaps the most convenient course would be, if you wish to say anything about the objection which Dr. Nelte has just made, for you to say it now. As I understand it, that objection is that this Document, 668, is a note by Admiral Darlan complaining that certain French troops were surrendered on the terms that they were not to be made prisoners-of-war, but were afterwards sent to Germany as prisoners-of-war. What Dr. Nelte asks is, was that matter taken up with the German Government, and if so, what answer did the German Government give? That seems to the Tribunal to be a reasonable request for Dr. Nelte to make.

M. DUBOST: The reply was given, Mr. President, through the reading of Ambassador Scapini's letter addressed to Ambassador Abetz.

THE PRESIDENT: My attention is drawn to the fact that the two documents to which you refer are dated 4 April. The document to which Dr. Nelte refers is a subsequent document, namely, 22 April. Therefore it does not appear from documents which were anterior to the document of 22 April as to what happened afterwards.

M. DUBOST: Mr. President, I myself am not aware of this. These documents were forwarded to me by the Prisoners-of-War agency. They are fragmentary archives forwarded by an official French agency, which I will inform of the Tribunal's wish.

THE PRESIDENT: Perhaps it should be investigated and found out whether the matter was taken up with the German Government and, if so, what answer the German Government gave.

M. DUBOST: I shall do so, Mr. President.

THE PRESIDENT: Not at the moment but in the course of time.

M. DUBOST: I shall have to apply to the French Government in order to find out whether in our archives there is any trace of a communication dated later than 26 April from the French Government to the German Government.

THE PRESIDENT: In the event of your not being able to get any satisfactory explanation, the Tribunal will take notice of Dr. Nelte's objection, or criticism, rather than of the document.

It is pointed out to me, too, that the two earlier documents to which you are referring are documents addressed by the Ambassador of France to M. Abetz, the Ambassador of Germany, and it may be, therefore, that there is a similar correspondence in reference to Document 668 here in the same file, which is the file of which the French Government presumably has, or might have copies.

M. DUBOST: It is possible but that is only a hypothesis, which I do not want to expound before the Tribunal. I prefer to produce the documents.

THE PRESIDENT: I quite follow; you cannot deal with it for the moment. As to the other matter which is raised by Dr. Exner; the Tribunal consider that Document 532-PS should be struck out of the record in so far as it is therein. If the United States and French prosecutors wish the document to be put in evidence at a future date, they may apply to do so. Similarly the defendant's counsel, Dr. Exner, for instance, if he wishes to make any use of the document, is of course at liberty to do so.

In reference to the other matters which Dr. Exner raised, it is the wish of the Tribunal to assist defendants' counsel in any way possible in their work, and they are, therefore, most anxious that the rules which they have laid down as to documents should be strictly complied with, and they think that copies of the original documents certainly should contain anything the original documents themselves contain.

This particular Document - 532-PS - as a copy, I think I am right in saying, does not contain the marginal note in the script which the original contains. At any rate it is important that copies should contain everything which is on the originals.

Then there is another matter to which I wish to refer. I have already said that it is very important that documents, when they are put in evidence, should not only be numbered as exhibits, but that the exhibit number should be stated at the time, and also even more important, or as important, that the certificate certifying where the document comes from should also be produced for the Tribunal. Every document put in by the United States bore upon it a certificate stating where it had been found, or what was its origin, and it is important that this practice should be adopted in every case.

The only other thing I want to say is that it would be very convenient, both to defendant's counsel and to the Tribunal too, that they should be informed at least the night before of the programme which counsel proposes to adopt for the following day. It is true, as was said, that perhaps that has not been absolutely regularly carried out by the prosecutor on all occasions, but it has been done on quite a number of occasions within my recollection, and it is at any rate a most convenient practice and one which the Tribunal desires should be carried out. They would also be glad to know, above all, what you, M. Dubost, propose to address yourself to tomorrow, and would be very grateful to know how long the French prosecutors anticipate their case will take. They would like you before you finish, or at the conclusion of your address this afternoon, to indicate to the Tribunal, and to the defendants' counsel, what the programme for tomorrow is to be.

SIR DAVID MAXWELL FYFE: If your Honour please, I wonder if I could say one word in regard to the position as to documents, because I had an opportunity during recess of consulting with my friend Mr. Dodd, and also with my friend M. Dubost; all PS documents form a series of captured documents, whose origin, and the process taken subsequent to the article, was verified on 22 November by Major Coogan, and was put in by my friend Colonel Storey.

Yes, it is the submission of the prosecution, which, of course, it is delighted to elaborate at any time convenient to the Tribunal, that all such documents being captured and verified in that way are admissible. I stress the word admissible, but the weight which the Tribunal will attach to any respective document is, of course, a matter which the Tribunal would decide from the contents of the document and the circumstances under which it came into being. That I, fear, is the only reason I ventured to intervene at the moment; that there might be some confusion between the general verification of the document as a captured document, which is done by Major Coogan's affidavit, and the individual certificate of translation, that is, of the correctness of the translation of the different documents, which appear at the end of each individual American document. The fact is that my friend, Mr. Dodd, and I were very anxious that this matter should be before the Tribunal, and we should be only too delighted to give to the Tribunal any further information which it desires.

THE PRESIDENT: Does that affidavit of Major Coogan apply to all the other series of documents put in by the United States.

SIR DAVID MAXWELL FYFE: It applies to PS and I think to D, C, L, R and EC.

THE PRESIDENT: What about the L?

SIR DAVID MAXWELL FYFE: I think it is L and not D.

THE PRESIDENT: Does that certificate then cover this particular sheet of paper which is marked 532-PS, and has it no other identifying mark?

SIR DAVID MAXWELL FYFE: Yes. The affidavit proves that that was a document captured from German sources; it gives the whole process as to what happens after that. I have not troubled the Tribunal by reading it, because as such we submit that it is admissible as a submission; of course, the matter of weight may vary.

THE PRESIDENT: Yes.

SIR DAVID MAXWELL FYFE: I do not want the Tribunal to be under the misapprehension that every document is certified individually. If a document comes from any of the sources mentioned in Article 21, then some one with authority from his Government certifies it as coming from one of these sources, and that we do individually. But concerning captured documents, we do not make an individual certification; we depend on Major Coogan's affidavit.

THE PRESIDENT: Yes, but just a moment. Sir David, it is perhaps right to say in reference to this particular Document, 532-PS, or the portion of it which has been produced, first of all, that the copy which was put before us did not contain the marginal note, and that it is, therefore, wrong. We are in agreement with your submission that it has been certified, as you say, by Major Coogan's affidavit, which is admissible; but, of course, that has nothing to do with its weight. That is the point on which Dr. Exner was addressing us.

SIR DAVID MAXWELL FYFE: So I appreciated it, your Honour.

THE PRESIDENT: It is a document, being a private document and not a document of which we can take judicial notice, which has not been read in court by the United States or other prosecutors, and it is not in evidence now because it has not been read by M. Dubost.

SIR DAVID MAXWELL FYFE: Your Honour, on that, of course, I do not desire to say anything further. That is the ruling of the Tribunal. The only part that I did want to stress was that the PS series of documents as such is being verified and, of course, subject to reading it in Court it could be put in.

THE PRESIDENT: Thank you. We quite understand that.

I ought to say, on behalf of the Tribunal, that we owe an apology to the French prosecutor and his staff because it has just been pointed out to me that this marginal note does appear upon the translation and, therefore, M. Dubost, I tender to you my apology.

M. DUBOST: Mr. President, the Tribunal will certainly remember that this morning Document 1553-PS was set aside. It contains bills for gas destined for Oranienburg and Auschwitz. I believe that, after the explanation given by Sir David, this Document 1553-PS may now be admitted by the Tribunal since it has already been certified.

THE PRESIDENT: Was it read, M. Dubost?

M. DUBOST: Yes, Mr. President. I was about to read it this morning.

It is the 27th document in the second document book, but the Tribunal rejected it, with the demand that I furnish an affidavit. The intervention of Sir David settled this affidavit question. I beg the Tribunal to forgive my making the following request, I should be grateful if it would accept the document which was refused this morning?

THE PRESIDENT: M. Dubost, it was a question of gas, was it not?

M. DUBOST: That is right.

THE PRESIDENT: There was one bill of lading and then there were a number of other bills of lading which were referred to.

M. DUBOST: Yes. And the whole constituted Document 1553-PS. This document is included in the series covered by the affidavit of which Sir David has spoken to you.

THE PRESIDENT: Mr. Dubost, if you attach importance to it, would it not be possible for you to give us the figures from these other bills of lading? I mean the amount of the gas.

M. DUBOST: Certainly, Mr. President.

THE PRESIDENT: Just in order that it may be upon the shorthand note.

M. DUBOST :

> 14 February 1944...Gross weight: 832 kilos...Net weight: 555 kilos
> 16 February 1944...Gross weight: 832 kilos...Net weight: 555 kilos
> The first is addressed to Auschwitz and the second to Oranienburg.
> 13 March 1944...Gross weight: 896 kilos...Net weight: 598 kilos (addressed to Auschwitz)
> 13 March 1944...Gross weight: 896 kilos...Net weight: 598 kilos (addressed to Oranienburg)
> 30 April 1944...Gross weight: 832 kilos...Net weight: 555 kilos (addressed to Auschwitz)
> 30 April 1944...Gross weight: 832 kilos...Net weight: 555 kilos (addressed to Oranienburg)
> 18 May 1944...Gross weight: 832 kilos... Net weight: 555 kilos (addressed to Oranienburg)
> 31 May 1944...Gross weight: 832 kilos... Net weight: 555 kilos (addressed to Auschwitz)

This appears to me to be all.

To Document 1553-PS is added the statement by Gessner and also the statement by the Chief of the American Service who collected this document.

With the permission of the Tribunal, I shall proceed with the presentation of the crimes of which we accuse the defendants against allied prisoners of war who were interned in Germany. Document 735-PS, Page 68 of the document book, which we submitted a short time ago as Exhibit RF 371, is a report on important meetings which brought together Kaltenbrunner, Ribbentrop and Goering, and in the course of which was drawn up the list of air operations which constituted acts of terrorism.

It was decided at these meetings that lynching would be the ideal punishment for all actions directed against civilian populations which the German Government claimed to be terroristic.

On Page 68 Ribbentrop is involved. We read in one of the three copies notes of the meetings that were held that day - in the first paragraph, 11th line "Contrary to the proposals of the Minister of Foreign Affairs, who wanted to include all terroristic attacks against the civilian population and consequently air attacks against cities" -

The proposals made by Ribbentrop were far in excess of what was accepted at the time of this meeting. The three lines which follow deserve the attention of the Tribunal:

> "Lynch law would be the means of settlement. There was, on the other hand, no question of a judgement to be passed by a tribunal or handing over to the police."

Then, at the bottom of the page

> "One had to distinguish between enemy airmen who were suspected of criminal acts of this kind, and prepare for their admission to the airmen's camp at Oberursel, and if the suspicions were confirmed, they were to be

turned over for special treatment by the SD."

The Tribunal will certainly remember the description which was given of this "special treatment" by the American prosecution. What is involved is purely and simply the extermination of allied airmen who had fallen into the hands of the German Army.

On Page 69, the Tribunal may read, under No. 3, the description and the enumeration of the acts which are to be considered as terroristic acts and as justifying lynching.

> "(a) Attacks with weapons against the civilian population, either against individuals or against gatherings of civilians.
>
> (b) Attacks against German airmen, who have baled out of their aircraft.
>
> (c) Attacks against civilian passenger trains.
>
> (d) Attacks against hospitals or hospital trains that are clearly marked with a red cross."

Three lines below:

> "Should such acts be committed and should it be established in the course of interrogation, the prisoners must be handed over to the SD."

This document originates from the Fuehrer's Headquarters. It was drawn up there on 6 June 1944, and it bears the stamp of the Assistant Chief of Staff of the Wehrmacht.

THE PRESIDENT: I think that has all been read, M. Dubost. I think that document was all read before.

M. DUBOST: Mr. President, I had been told that it had not been read.

THE PRESIDENT: I have not verified it.

M. DUBOST: We submit Document 729-PS, as Exhibit RF 372. This document confirms the preceding one. It originates from the Fuehrer's Headquarters, is dated 15 June 1944, and it reiterates the orders I have read.

But this document is signed by Marshal Keitel, whereas the preceding one was signed "J." We have not been able to identify the author of this initial. Document 730-PS, which we next submit as Exhibit RF 373, is likewise from the Fuehrer's Headquarters, still dated 15 June 1944. It is addressed to the Ministry of Foreign Affairs for the attention of Ambassador Ritter. The Tribunal will find it on Page 71 in the document book. This document reproduces the instructions signed "Keitel" in the preceding document, and it is likewise signed by Keitel.

We shall submit as Exhibit RF 374, Document 733-PS, which concerns the treatment which is to be meted out to airmen falling into the hands of the German Army. It is a telephone message. The call is from the Adjutant of the Marshal of the Reich (Captain Breuer).

DR. NELTE (Counsel for Keitel): I assume, Mr. Prosecutor, that you have finished with the question of lynching. In the presentation of this case the words "Orders of Keitel" have been used repeatedly. The prosecutor has not read these documents. I would be obliged if the prosecutor would produce a document which contains an order which raises lynch-law to the level of an order, as it had been claimed by the prosecution. The defendants Keitel and Jodl maintain that such an order was never given, that these conferences concerning which documents have been produced-that these documents never became orders because the authorities concerned prevented this.

THE PRESIDENT: The documents speak for themselves.

M. DUBOST: Does the Tribunal wish to listen to the complete reading of these documents which are signed by Keitel? They are not orders, they are projects. Moreover, I emphasised that when I announced them to the Tribunal. On Page 80 of our document book, you will find dated 30 June 1944, with Keitel's initials, a Note of a Meeting.

"Subject: the treatment of enemy terror flyers

(1) Enclosed the draft of a reply by the Reich Minister of Foreign Affairs to the Chief of the OKW forwarded by Ambassador Ritter to the Operational Staff of the Wehrmacht."

I am omitting a paragraph:

(2) The Marshal of the Reich approves the definition of terror flyers communicated by the OKW, as well as the procedure which is proposed.

This document is submitted as Exhibit RF 375. I did not submit to the Tribunal a regular formal order, but I brought three documents which, in my opinion, are equivalent to a formal order because, with the initials of Keitel, we have this note signed by Warlimont which states: "The Marshal of the Reich approves the definition of terror flyers communicated by the OKW, as well as the procedure which is proposed." This document bears the initials of Keitel.

We shall now submit Document L-154, which has already been submitted by our American colleagues as Exhibit USA 335. My colleague has read this text in extenso. I will refer to only three lines, in order not to delay the proceedings: "As a matter of principle, no fighter-bomber pilots brought down are to be saved from the anger of the people," This comes from the office of the Gauleiter and Commissar for the Defence of the Reich, Gau South Westphalia.

As Exhibit RF 376 we shall submit Document F-686, on Page 82 of our document book. This is the minutes of an interrogation of Hugo Gruener on 29 December 1945; he was subordinate to Robert Wagner, Gauleiter of Baden and Alsace. In the last lines of this document, Page 82, Gruener states:

"Wagner gave the formal order to beat up and kill all airmen we could capture. In this connection Gauleiter Wagner explained to us that Allied airmen caused great havoc on German territory; that they considered it was an inhuman war, and that therefore, under the circumstances, any airmen captured should not be considered as prisoners of war, and deserved no mercy."

Page 83, at the top of the page: "He stated that Kreisleiter, if the occasion offered, should not fail to capture and shoot the Allied airmen themselves. As I have told you, Roehn was assistant to Wagner, but Wagner himself did not speak. I can affirm that SS-General Hoffmann, who was the SS leader of the police for the Southwest Region, was present when the order was given to us by Wagner to assassinate allied airmen."

This witness, Hugo Gruener, confesses that he participated in the execution of Allied airmen. "Going through Rheinweiler, - this took place in October or November 1944 - he (Gruener) noticed that some English or American airmen had been pulled out of the Rhine by soldiers. The four airmen were wearing khaki uniforms, were bareheaded and were of average height. He could not speak to them because he did not know the English language. The Wehrmacht refused to take charge of them.

That is the third paragraph at the bottom of the page and the witness declares: "I told the gendarmes that I had received from Wagner the order to execute any Allied airmen taken prisoner. The gendarmes replied that it was the only thing to be done. I then decided to execute the four Allied prisoners and one of the gendarmes present advised me to do this on the banks of the Rhine."

On Page 84, paragraph 1, Gruener describes how he proceeded to assassinate these airmen. In the second paragraph he confesses that he killed them with machine gun shots in the back. In the third paragraph he gives the name of one of his accomplices, Erich Meissner, who was a Gestapo agent from Lorrach, and in the fifth paragraph he denounces Meissner for having himself assassinated an airman as he was getting out of a car and was on his way toward the Rhine. I read:

> "I murdered them by firing a machine gun salvo at each of them in the back, after which each airman was dragged by the feet and thrown into the Rhine."

This affidavit was received by the Police Magistrate of Strasbourg. The document which we shall submit was signed by his clerk as a certified copy.

This is how the orders given by the leaders of the German Government were carried out by the German people.

THE PRESIDENT: M. Dubost, I see that it is five o'clock now, and perhaps you would be able to tell us what your programme would be for tomorrow.

M. DUBOST: Tomorrow we shall complete the presentation of the question of prisoners-of-war. We shall present to you in an abridged form, documents which seem to us to be indispensable, in spite of the hearing of witnesses, in regard to the camps. There are only a few documents, but they all directly inculpate one or another of the defendants. Then we shall show how the orders given by the leaders of the German Army led the subordinates to commit acts of terrorism and banditry in France against the innocent population, and against patriots who were not treated as franc-tireurs but as common law bandits.

We expect to finish tomorrow morning. In the afternoon, my colleague, M. Faure, could begin the presentation of this last part of the French charges concerning Crimes against Humanity.

THE PRESIDENT: Are you not able to give us any estimate of the length of the whole of the French prosecution?

M. DUBOST: I believe that three days will be sufficient for M. Faure. The individual charges will be summarised in one half day by our colleague M. Mounier, and that will be the end.

THE PRESIDENT: The Tribunal will adjourn now.

(The Tribunal adjourned until 31st January at 1000 hours)

Forty-seventh day:
Thursday, 31st January, 1946

THE MARSHAL OF THE COURT: May it please the Court, I desire to announce that the defendants Kaltenbrunner and Seyss-Inquart will be absent from this morning's session on account of illness.

M. DUBOST: Before finishing, Gentlemen, I must read a few more documents concerning war prisoners.

First of all, it will be Document L-166, which we present as Exhibit RF-377, Page 65 in your document book. It concerns a note regarding pursuit planes, and summarises an interview with the Reich Marshal on 15 and 16 May 1944. Page 8, paragraph 20:

> "The Reich Marshal will propose to the Fuehrer that American and British crews who fire on towns indiscriminately, on civilian trains in motion, or on soldiers dropping by parachute, shall be immediately shot on the spot."

The importance of this document need not be emphasised. It shows the guilt of the defendant Goering in reprisals against Allied military aviators brought down in Germany.

We shall now read Document R-1 17, which we submit as Exhibit RF 378.

THE PRESIDENT: What page?

M. DUBOST: Page 88.

Two Liberators brought down on 21 June 1944 in the district of Mecklenburg landed with their crews intact, fifteen men all told. All were shot on the pretext of attempting to escape. The documents which we present to you on Page 88 and which we submit as Exhibit RF 378 relate to this murder. They were found in the files of the headquarters of the Eleventh Luftgaukommando, and state that nine members of the crew were handed over to the local police.

The penultimate paragraph, third line:

> "They were taken prisoner and handed over to the municipal police in Waren. Lieutenants Helton and Ludka were handed over on 21 June by the municipal police to the SS Understurmfuehrer and Commissar of the Criminal Police. Stamp of the Security Police in Furstenberg (Mecklenburg)."

Last paragraph:

> "These seven prisoners were shot en route while attempting to escape."

Last line of the page:

> "Lieutenants Helton and Ludka were also shot on the same day while attempting to escape."

Regarding the second Liberator, Page 91:

> "Subject, Crash-landing of a Liberator on 21 June 1944, at 11.30 a.m." - this is the third paragraph - "six of crew shot while attempting to escape, one seriously wounded, was brought to the station hospital at Schuwrin."

Now, as Exhibit RF 379, we submit Document F-553, which the Tribunal will find on Page 101 of the document book. This document concerns the internment of war prisoners in concentration camps and extermination camps. Among the escaped prisoners a discrimination was made. If they were privates, or non-commissioned officers who had agreed to work, they were generally sent to the camp and punished in conformity with Article 47 and the following of the Geneva Convention. If they were officers or non-commissioned officers - this is a comment I am making on the document which I shall read to the Tribunal - if it was a question of officers or non-commissioned officers who refused to work they were handed over to the police and, in general, murdered without trial.

One understands the aim of this discrimination. Those French commissioned officers who, in spite of the pressure of the German authorities, refused to work in German war industry, had a very high conception of their patriotic duty. Their attempt to escape, therefore, created against them a kind of presumption of inadaptability to the Nazi Order, and they had to be eliminated. Extermination of these patriots assumed a systematic character from the beginning of 1944; and the responsibility of Keitel is unquestionably involved in this extermination, as he approved it if he did not specifically order it.

The document which the Tribunal has before it is a letter of protest by General Berard, Head of the French Delegation, to the German Armistice Commission, addressed to the German General Vogl, the chief of the said commission. It deals specifically with information reaching France concerning the extermination of escaped prisoners.

First paragraph, fourth line: "This note takes notice of a German organisation independent of the Wehrmacht, under whose authority fall escaped prisoners."

This note was addressed on 29 April 1944 by the commandant of OFLAG X-C. Page 102:

> "Captain Lussus of OFLAG X-C," declares General Berard to the German Armistice Commission, "and Lieutenant Girot, also of OFLAG X-C, who had made an attempt to escape on 27 April 1944, were recaptured in the immediate vicinity by the camp guard.
>
> "On 23 June 1944 the French PW liaison officer of OFLAG X-C received two funeral urns containing the ashes of these two officers. The commandant of the camp declared that no information could be given, and the French authorities remain ignorant of the date, place or circumstances of the deaths of Captain Lussus and Lieutenant Girot."

General Berard pointed out at the same time to the German Armistice Commission that the note - which the Tribunal will find on Page 104 - had been communicated by the commandant of OFLAG X-C to the French PW liaison officer responsible for his comrades at that camp.

> "You will bring to the attention of your comrades the fact that there exists, for the control of people moving about illicitly, a German organisation which extends its activity over all zones of war from Poland to the Spanish frontier. Every escaped prisoner who is recaptured and found to be in possession of civilian goods, false papers, and identity cards and photographs, falls under the authority of this organisation. What becomes of him, I cannot tell you.
>
> Warn your comrades that this matter is particularly serious."

The significance of the last two lines becomes only too clear in the case of the two urns of the escaped officers, handed to the French liaison officer of the camp.

Our colleagues of the Soviet prosecution will present the methods by which the escapes of the officers from the Sagan camp were dealt with.

THE PRESIDENT: Was there any answer to this complaint? What have you just been reading, as I understand it, is a complaint made by the French General, Berard, to the German head of the Armistice Commission, is that right?

M. DUBOST: Mr. President, I do not know if there was an answer. What I know is that the archives in Vichy at the time of the Liberation were in part looted and in part destroyed through military action. If we had an answer it would have been found in the Vichy archives, for the documents we present now are the documents of the German archives of the German Armistice Commission. As to the French archives, I don't know what has become of them. In any case it is possible they may have disappeared as a result of military action.

Will the Tribunal pardon me? I was about to inform it that my Soviet colleagues would present the repressive measures employed at Sagan camp against attempts to escape.

We submit as Exhibit RF 320, Document F-672, which the Tribunal will find on Page 115 of the document book. This is a report from the Service for War Prisoners and Deportees, dated 9 January 1946, which relates to the deportation to Buchenwald of twenty French war prisoners. This report must be considered as an authentic document, as well as the reports of war prisoners which are annexed thereto. On Page 116, the Tribunal may read the report of Claude Petit, former chief spokesman in Stalag 6-G.

> "In September 1943" - and I am quoting the first paragraph -"as French civilian workers in Germany and France, transformed war prisoners" - transformed into workers is to be understood - "were deprived of all spiritual help, having not one priest among them, Lieutenant Piard, head chaplain of Stalag 6-G, after having spoken with the chaplain of the war prisoners, Abbe Rodhain, decided to transform into workers six war-prisoner priests, so that they could carry out their religious duties, among the French civilians."

I quote only three lines of the following paragraph; the first:

> "This transformation of priests, which was difficult to accomplish, since the Gestapo did not authorise the presence of chaplains among civilian workers ... these priests and a few scouts organised a group of Catholic Action and a Scout group."

On Page 157, paragraph 3:

> "From the beginning of 1944 the priests felt they were being watched by the Gestapo in their various activities."

The following paragraph:

> "At the end of July 1944, the six priests were arrested almost simultaneously and taken to the prison of Brauweiler, near Cologne."

Page 116, first and second paragraphs:

> "The same happened to the scouts."

I quote:

> "Against this flagrant violation of the Geneva Convention I took numerous steps and made numerous protests, in order that the prisoners of war arrested by the Gestapo might be handed over to the military authorities. I likewise asked to be told the reason for their arrest."

Fifth paragraph:

> "By reason of the rapid advance of the Allies who were approaching Aachen, all prisoners of Brauweiler were taken to Cologne ... "

(Dr. Stahmer, Counsel for defendant Goering, approached the lectern.)

M. DUBOST: Mr. President, before allowing the defence counsel to interrupt me, allow me to finish reading this document.

THE PRESIDENT: Continue.

M. DUBOST: Thank you, Mr. President. From the last sentences of this, paragraph the Tribunal will learn that the German military authorities themselves took steps in order to learn the fate of these prisoners.

> "The military authorities having no knowledge thereof, immediately wrote to Buchenwald, but received no answer. At the beginning of March, Major Bramkamp, Chief of the Abwehr was to go personally to Buchenwald."

On Pages 120-121 the Tribunal will find the list of the prisoners who thus disappeared.

Finally - Page 122 - a confirmation of this testimony by M. Souche, confidential agent of Kommando 624, who in paragraph 3 writes:

> "Certain war prisoners transformed into workers, and French civilian workers, had organised in Cologne a group of 'Catholic Action' under the direction of the transformed war-prisoner priests, Pannier and Cleton."

Finally, Page 123 - and this is the end of my quotation:

> "The arrests began with members of the 'Catholic Action'" and the accusations were "anti-German manoeuvres."

THE PRESIDENT: I do not know what Dr. Stahmer's objection is.

DR. STAHMER (Counsel for Goering): We are not in a position to follow the expose of the French prosecutor. First of all, the translation is not very good. Some sentences are left out. Especially, wrong numbers are mentioned. For instance, 612 has been mentioned. I have it here. It is quite a different document. We have not the document books and therefore we cannot follow the page citations. My colleagues also complain that they are not in a position to follow the proceedings with this manner of presentation.

THE PRESIDENT: May I see your document?

(It is handed up to the Bench.)

DR. STAHMER: This number was just mentioned and is confirmed by the other gentlemen.

THE PRESIDENT: The document which M. Dubost was reading was 672. The document you have got there is a different number.

DR. STAHMER: But this number was given us over the microphone, and not only I but the other counsel heard the same number. And not only this number, but all the numbers have been mentioned incorrectly.

Another difficulty is that we have not the document book. Page 118 has been referred to, but the number of the page does not mean anything to us. We cannot follow at this rate.

THE PRESIDENT: M. Dubost, I think the trouble really arises from the fact that you give the numbers too fast and the numbers are very often wrongly translated, not only into German but sometimes into English. It is very difficult for the interpreters to pick up all these numbers. First of all, you give the number of the document, then the number of the exhibit, then the page of the document book - and that means that the interpreters have got to translate many numbers spoken very quickly.

It is essential that the defendants should be able to follow the document, and as I understand it, they have not got the document books in the same shape we have. It is only the way we can follow But we have them now in this particular document book by page, and therefore it is absolutely essential to go slowly.

M. DUBOST: Mr. President, the document books have all been handed to the defence. All the documents have been presented to the defence.

THE PRESIDENT: Are you telling us that document books have been handed to the defence in the same shape they are handed to us, let us say, with page numbers on them? Speaking for myself, that is the only way I am able to follow the document. You mentioned Page 115 and that does show me where the document is. If I had not that page, I shouldn't be able to find the document.

M. DUBOST: Mr. President, I announced at the same time RF- 380, which is the number of the exhibit; F-672 is the classification number. All our documents bear a classification number. On the other hand, it was not possible to hand to the defence a document book with the pages numbered, like the one the Tribunal has, for it is not submitted in the same language. It is submitted in German and the pages are not in the same place. There is not an absolute identity of page numbering between the German document book and yours.

THE PRESIDENT: I am telling you the difficulties under which the defendants' counsel are working, and if we had simply a number of documents without the page numbering, we should be under a similar difficulty. And it is a very great difficulty. Therefore you must go very slowly in giving the identification of the document.

M. DUBOST: I will conform to the wishes of the Tribunal, Mr. President.

THE PRESIDENT: Dr. Stahmer, the document being read was Document 672.

DR. STAHMER: We cannot find Document 672. We have 673. We have nothing but loose sheets, and we have to hunt through them first to find the number. We have number 673 but we have not yet found number 672 among our documents. It is very difficult for us to follow a citation, because it takes us so much time to find the numbers even if they have been mentioned correctly.

THE PRESIDENT: I can understand the difficulty. Will you continue, M. Dubost, and do as I say, going very slowly so as to give the defendants' counsel as far as possible, the opportunity to find the document. And I think that you ought to do something satisfactory, if you can, to make it possible for them to find that document. An index, for instance, giving the order in which the documents are set out.

M. DUBOST: Three days ago, two document books in French, with pages numbered like the books which the Tribunal has before it, were handed to the defence. We were only able to hand two to them, for reasons of a technical nature. But at the same time we handed to the defence a sufficient number of documents in German to enable each defence counsel to have his file in German. Does the Tribunal ask me to collate the pages of the French document which we submit to the defence with the pages of a document book which we set up, seeing that the defence can do it and has the time to do it? Three days ago the two French document books were handed to the defence. They had the possibility of comparing the French texts with the German texts to make sure that our translations were correct and to prepare themselves for the sessions.

THE PRESIDENT: Go on, M. Dubost. As I say, do it slowly.

DR. STAHMER: It is not correct that we received it three days ago. We found this pile in our room yesterday evening. We really have not had the time to number these pages. As I say, this was in our room only yesterday evening or this morning.

THE PRESIDENT: Let us go on, now, M. Dubost, and go slowly in describing the identification of the document.

M. DUBOST: We shall pass to Document F-357, which will be submitted as Exhibit RF 381, which is on Page 120 in the French document book. This document deals with the carrying out of general orders concerning the execution of prisoners of war. It contains the testimony of a German police officer who was made prisoner on 25 May 1945 and who (on Page 127, paragraph before the last, underscored lines in the French text) declares:

"All war prisoners whom we might have in our possession, however that might have happened, were to be killed by us instead of being handed over to the nearest Wehrmacht post as had been done until then."

This has to do with an order which was given in the middle of August 1944.

The witness continues:

"This execution was to be carried out in a deserted spot."

On Page 128, the same witness gives, paragraph 3, the names of the Germans who had executed war prisoners.

We shall now submit Document 1634-PS, which will become Exhibit RF 382. The Tribunal will find it on Page 129 in their document book. It is a document which has not yet been read, which relates to the murder of 129 American war prisoners, carried out by the German Army in a field South west and West of Baignes, in Belgium, on 17 December 1944 during the German offensive.

Page 129, bottom of the page. The author of this report summarised the facts.

"The American prisoners are brought together near the cross-roads. A few soldiers, whose names are indicated, rush across the field toward the West, hide among the trees in the high grass and thickets and ditches, and thus escape the massacre of their companions. A few others who, at the moment when this massacre began, were in the proximity of a barn, were able to hide in it. They are also survivors."

Third paragraph:

"The artillery and machine-gun fire on the column of American vehicles continued for about ten to fifteen minutes, and then two German tanks and some half-track vehicles came down the road from the direction of Weismes. Upon reaching the intersection, these vehicles turned South on the road toward St. Vith. The tanks directed machine gun fire into the ditch along the side of the road in which the American soldiers were crouching, and upon seeing this, the other American soldiers dropped their weapons and raised their arms over their heads. The surrendering American soldiers were then required to march back to the road intersection, and while doing this, and as they passed by some of the German vehicles then on Highway N-23, German soldiers on these vehicles took from the American prisoners of war such items as wrist watches, rings and gloves. The American soldiers were then assembled on the St. Vith road in front of a house standing on the Southwest corner of the intersection. Other German soldiers who had arrived at the road intersection in tanks and half-track vehicles, further searched some of the captured Americans at this place and also took valuables from them."

Top of Page 131, before the end of the paragraph:

"An American prisoner was questioned and led with his other comrades to the crossroads just referred to."

Third paragraph:

"At about this time some German light tank or half-track vehicles attempted to manoeuvre into position on the road so that their cannon would be directed at the group of American PW's gathered in the field approximately twenty to twenty-five yards from the road. I again omit four lines. "Some of these stopped when they came opposite the field in which the unarmed American PW's were standing in a group, with their hands up in the air or clasped behind their heads. A German soldier, believed to be a non-commissioned officer, in one of these vehicles which stopped, raised and pointed a pistol and took deliberate aim and fired into the group of American PW's. One of the American soldiers fell. This was repeated a second time and another American soldier in the group fell to the ground. At about this time, machine guns on two of the vehicles on the road started to fire into the group of American PW's in the field. All, or most of the American soldiers dropped to the ground and stayed there while the firing continued for two or three minutes. Most of the individuals in the field were hit by this machine gun fire. The German vehicles on the road then moved on toward the South and were followed by more vehicles which also came from the direction of Weismes and as these latter vehicles came opposite the field in which the American soldiers were lying, they also fired with small arms from the moving vehicles at the prostrate bodies in the field."

Page 132, first paragraph:

"Some German soldiers, evidently from the group of those who were on guard at the intersection, then walked among the group of American PW's who were still in the original position in the field, and also among those who had run away for a short distance, and shot with pistol or rifle, or clubbed with a rifle butt or other heavy object, any of the individual American soldiers who still showed any sign of life. In some instances, it is evident that American PW's were shot at close range squarely between the eyes, in the temple, or the back of the head."

This act constitutes an act of pure terrorism, the shame of which will remain with the German Army, for nothing justified it. These prisoners were un-armed and had surrendered.

The Tribunal authorised me yesterday to present the documents on which the French accusation is based for establishing the guilt of Goering, Keitel, Jodl, Bormann, Frank, Rosenberg, Streicher, Schirach, Hess, Frick, the OKW, OKH, OKL, the Reich Cabinet, and the Nazi Leadership Corps, as well as the SS and the Gestapo, in the atrocities committed in the camps. I shall be very brief. I have very few documents to present in addition to those which have already been presented.

The first places Kaltenbrunner under accusation. It is the American Document L-35 which the Tribunal will find on Page 266 of the document book concerning concentration camps, i.e., the second book. This document has not been submitted. Paragraph 3, Page 246, is the testimony of Rudolf Mildner, Doctor of Law, Colonel of the Police, who declares, paragraph 2 of his declaration:

"The internment orders were signed by the Chief of the Sipo and SD, Dr. Kaltenbrunner, or, as deputy, the Chief of Amt IV, SS Gruppenfuehrer Muller."

I submit this as Exhibit RF 383. Concerning Goering we submit American Document 343-PS, Page 203 of document book 11. This is a letter from Field Marshal Milch to Wolff. On Page 204, this letter concludes with the phrase:

"I express to the SS the special thanks of the Commander-in-Chief of the Luftwaffe for the considerable aid they have rendered."

Now, from the preceding one can conclude that these thanks refer to the biological experiments of Dr. Rascher. Thus, Goering is involved in these.

The German SS Medical Corps is implicated also. This one can gather from Document 1635-PS, which has not yet been handed to the Tribunal, which becomes Exhibit RF-385, which the Tribunal will find in the annex of the second document book. These are extracts from reviews on microscopic and anatomical research. They deal with experiments made on persons who died suddenly, although in good health.

The circumstances of their death are described by the experimenters in such a way that no reader can be in any doubt as to what they were.

With the authorisation of the Tribunal, I shall read a few brief extracts. Page 132, at the top of the document which we submit to the Tribunal:

> "The thyroid glands. 21 persons between 20 and 40 years of age were examined. They had been in supposedly good health, but suddenly died."

The following paragraph

> "The persons in question, 19 men and 2 women, until their death had all lived for several months under the same conditions both of housing and food. At the end the food they were given consisted chiefly of hydrocarbons."

"Replacement Products and Examination Methods": (this is the title) "In the course of a rather long period, substance for the experiment was taken from the liver of 24 adults in good health, who suddenly died between 5 and 6 o'clock in the morning."

In examining these documents, the Tribunal will see that German medical literature is very rich in experiments carried out on "adults in good health who died suddenly between five and six o'clock in the morning." No one in Germany could be fooled, since the accounts of the SS doctors' experiments in the camps were published in this way.

A last document is F-185, A and B, which refers to an experiment with poisoned bullets, carried out on 11 August 1944, in the presence of SS Sturmbannfuehrer Dr. Ding, and Dr. Widmann; Page 187 of the second document book concerning concentration camps. These two documents are submitted as Exhibits RF 386 and 387. The Tribunal will find on Page 187 the description of this experiment, in which the victims are persons sentenced to death, where, in fact . . .

THE PRESIDENT: The document has been read already, I think.

M. DUBOST: F-185 is a French document.

THE PRESIDENT: But I cannot help that. It has been read already, I think.

M. DUBOST: I beg the Tribunal's pardon. I did not realise that. It is a document from the French archives. However, Mr. President, I doubt if the Tribunal has heard Document 185 B, which is by the French Professor, May, a surgeon. This document will become Exhibit RF 386, and, on Page 222, second paragraph, Professor May, Fellow of Surgery, to whom the pseudo-scientific documents to which I alluded a while ago were submitted - the reports from scientific reviews on experiments - wrote :

> "The wickedness and the stupidity of the experimenters amazed me. The symptoms of aconite poisoning have been known from time immemorial. This poison is sometimes employed by certain savage tribes to poison their war arrows. It is unheard of that observations on the anticipated result of experiments should be presented in such a pretentious style, observations, by the way, which are completely inadequate and childish or that these could be signed by a 'Doz,', that is to say, a professor."

We now submit Document F-278A, as Exhibit RF 388. The Tribunal will find it on Page 75. It involves Keitel. It is a letter signed: " By order of the High Command of the Wehrmacht, Dr. Lehmann." It is addressed on 10 February 1942 to the Ministry of Foreign Affairs, and it incriminates him. I quote paragraphs 2 and 3 on Page 75, which concern the regime in the internment camps:

> "The delinquents brought to Germany in application of the decree of the Fuehrer are to have no communication of any kind with the outside world. They must, therefore, neither write themselves, nor receive letters, parcels or visits. The letters, parcels and visits are to be refused, with the remark that all

communications with the outside world is forbidden."

The High Command shares the point of view of the recipient of this letter, expressed in his letter of 31 January 1942, according to which access of Belgian lawyers to Belgian prisoners shall not be permitted.

We now submit Document 682-PS, Page 134 of the second document book, which becomes Exhibit RF 389. This document involves the German Government and the Reich Cabinet. It is a record of a conversation between Dr. Goebbels and Thierack, Minister of Justice, on 15 September 1942, from 13.00 hours to 14.15 hours.

> "With regard to the destruction of asocial elements Dr. Goebbels is of the opinion that the following groups should be exterminated: Jews and Gypsies unconditionally, Poles who have to serve 3-4 years of penal servitude, and Czechs and Germans who are sentenced to death or penal servitude for life or to protective custody (Sicherungsverwahrung) for life. The idea of extermination through work is the best..."

We stress this last phrase which shows, in the German Government itself, the will to "extermination through work."

THE PRESIDENT: Has that document been read before?

M. DUBOST: This document does not seem to have been read before. We made enquiries of the American Delegation.

THE PRESIDENT: Read the last two lines.

M. DUBOST: "The idea of extermination through work is the best."

The last document that we shall submit in regard to the concentration camps is F-662, which becomes Exhibit RF 390. Pages 77 and 78, second document book. This document is the testimony of M. Poutiers, living in Paris, Place de Breteuil, who points out that the prisoners in the commandos of Mauthausen Ebens worked under the direct control of civilians, the SS dealing only with the supervision of the prisoners. This witness, who was in numerous work commandos, testifies that all were controlled by civilians, and only supervised by the SS, and that, thus, the inhabitants of the country, during the movement of the labourers to and from work, could observe their misery, which confirms the testimony which has already been given before the Tribunal.

We shall summarise the progress of the German criminal policy in the West: At the beginning of the occupation: Violation of Article 50: execution of hostages, but creation of a pseudo "law of hostages" to justify these executions in the eyes of the populace of the occupied countries.

In the years that follow; contempt for the rights of the human being increases. It becomes complete in the last months of the occupation. At that time arbitrary imprisonment, parodies of trials, or executions without trials were a daily practice.

The sentences, the Tribunal will remember, are no longer put into effect in cases of acquittal or reprieve; those acquitted by German tribunals, who should be released are deported and die in concentration camps.

At the same time there develops and grows in strength the organisation of Frenchmen who remain on the soil of France and refuse to let their country die. At this stage German terrorism intensifies against them, increasing from month to month. What follows is the description of the terroristic repression by the Germans against the patriots of the West of Europe, against what was called the "Resistance," without giving this word any other meaning than its generic sense.

From the time when Germany understands that its policy of collaboration is doomed to failure, that its policy of hostages only exasperates the fury of the people whom it is trying to subdue, instead of modifying its policy with regard to the citizens of the occupied countries, it intensifies the terror which already reigns over them, and tries to justify itself by saying it is an anti-Communist campaign.

The Tribunal recalls Keitel's order; The tribunal understands what one must think of this pretext. All the French, all the citizens of Europe, without any distinction of party, profession, religion, or race who were involved in resistance against Germany, were mingled in the graves, in the collective charnel houses into which the Germans threw them after their extermination.

But this confusion is deliberate, it is calculated, it justifies to a certain degree this arbitrariness of repressive measures, this arbitrariness of which we have already had evidence in Document F-278, Page 4 of the document book, which we submit as Exhibit RF 391, dated 12 January 1943, signed "Falkenhausen"

THE PRESIDENT: Which document book is it?

M. DUBOST: "Terrorist action against Patriots," Document F- 278, Page 4, second paragraph:

> "In the future, persons who are found in possession of explosives and fire arms without valid authorisation, may be immediately shot without trial."

This order and others analogous to it continue to be executed even after the Allied landing in Western Europe. These orders are even executed against organised forces in Belgium as well as in France, although the Germans themselves to a certain extent considered these forces as troops. This can be verified by reference to Document F-673, Page 167, third paragraph.

THE PRESIDENT: That is in a different book, I am afraid, is it not?

M. DUBOST: We are now dealing with the terrorist actions against patriots, and it is in the document book entitled "Terrorist Action Against Patriots."

THE PRESIDENT: The number of the page came through to me as one hundred and sixty something, and my pages end at 155.

M. DUBOST: Excuse me ; I made the mistake. It is Page 6 of the document book, paragraph 3, third line. "The action of the German troops, if we acknowledge the truth of the facts presented by the French, exceeds by far in scope any purely police action against isolated outlaws .... "

THE PRESIDENT: Is this from 673? Are you reading from 673?

M. DUBOST: Excuse me, Mr. President, this document is not before the Tribunal, and I shall not quote it.

THE PRESIDENT: Perhaps this would be a convenient time to break off.

(A recess was taken).

THE PRESIDENT: Yes, M. Dubost.

M. DUBOST: The few minutes recess has afforded me the opportunity now to submit a passage from Document F-673 (Exhibit RF 392) which I cited to you, and I am thankful to the Tribunal. This document is now before you. It has just been given to you. In paragraph three of this document, which is a note of presentation to the Wiesbaden Commission, we read the following:

> "The action of the German troops, if we acknowledge the truth of the facts presented by the French exceeds by far in scope any purely police action against isolated outlaws. On the enemy side we have organisations which absolutely refuse to accept the sovereignty of the Vichy Government, and which also, from the point of view of numbers as well as of armament and command, can almost be considered to be troops. It has been reiterated that these revolutionary units consider themselves as being a part of the forces fighting against Germany.

General Eisenhower has designated the terrorists who are fighting in France as 'Troops under my orders.' It is against such troops" (on the original is written in red pencil "unfortunately not only") "that preventive measures are directed."

This document shows us that when in action the French Forces of the Interior, as well as all French forces in the Western occupied countries, were considered as troops by the German Army.

THE PRESIDENT: I see that it may be useful for the record. It is in the document book on the extermination of innocent populations, on Page 167.

M. DUBOST: I thank you, Mr. President.

The patriots who were consequently considered by the German Army as constituting regular troops, were they then treated as soldiers? No.

The order of Falkenhausen is proof thereof. They were either to be killed on the spot and, after all, that is the fate of a combatant, or else delivered to the Sipo, or to the SD, and tortured to death by units free of any legal constraint, in the manner demonstrated by Document 835-PS, which has already been submitted as Exhibit USA 527. and by F-673, Page 6 in your document book, which is now before you as Exhibit RF-392.

THE PRESIDENT: What page?

M. DUBOST: Six of your document book.

THE PRESIDENT: Of the same document book?

M. DUBOST: This is the only document book that we are referring to now Mr. President, "Terrorist Action against Patriots", F-673, on Page 6 of the book which is now before you. The whole of that document has already been submitted as Exhibit RF-392. F-673 is a considerable bundle of papers which comes from the archives of the German Commission at Wiesbaden, and we are placing it in its entirety as Exhibit RF 392 after classifying it in the French archive as number 673. Whenever we refer to Document 673 it will be one of the documents in this big German book.

"Letter from the Fuehrer's headquarters, 18 August 1944, thirty copies, copy number twenty-six. Top secret. Subject.

(1) Action against terrorists and saboteurs in occupied territories.

(2) Jurisdiction over non-German civilians in occupied territories."

"(1) In the enclosure," says the writer of this letter, " we are transmitting a copy of the order of the Fuehrer of 30 July 1944 ". This order of the Fuehrer of 30 July 1944 will be found on Page 9 of your document book. Here is the order, Page 9, paragraph three.

"I therefore order the troops and every individual member of the Wehrmacht, the SS and the police, immediately to shoot on the spot terrorists and saboteurs who are caught red-handed. (2) Whoever is captured later is to be transferred to the nearest local office of the Security Police and SD. Sympathisers, particularly women, who are not taking direct part in these hostile acts are to be put to work."

We know what that means. We know the working conditions in concentration camps. But I shall proceed to read the text of the letter covering this order, paragraph four. This paragraph is a comment on the order itself.

THE PRESIDENT: Has this not been read before?

M. DUBOST: It has never been read, Mr. President.

This is F-673 of the Wiesbaden Armistice Commission.

"Pending judicial proceedings against any act of terror or sabotage, or any other crime committed by non-German civilians in the occupied territories which endangers the security or the state of tactical readiness of the occupying power, are suspended. Indictments are to be withdrawn. The carrying out of sentences is not to be ordered. The accused and the records are to be turned over to the nearest office of the Security Police and SD."

This order, which is to be transmitted to all commanding generals, as indicated on Page 7, is accompanied by one last comment on Page 8, the penultimate paragraph.

"Non-German civilians in the occupied territories who endanger the security or state of tactical readiness of the occupying power in a manner other than through acts of terrorism and sabotage are to be turned over to the SD." This order is signed by Keitel.

By this comment, which we have just read to you, Keitel has associated himself in spirit with the order of his Fuehrer. He has brought about the execution of numerous innocent individuals, for the uncontrolled killing of any one suspected of being a terrorist affects not only the terrorists but the innocent, and affects the innocent more than the terrorists. Moreover, Keitel's comment goes even beyond even Hitler's own order. Keitel applied Hitler's stipulation, - on Page 9 of your document book - to a hypothetical case which had not been foreseen, to wit:

"Acts committed by non-German civilians in occupied territories which endanger the security of state of tactical readiness of the occupying power."

This is from the General himself. It is a political act which has nothing to do with the conduct of war. It is a political act which compromises and involves him. It makes him participate in the development and extension of the Hitlerian policy; for it is the interpretation of an order from Hitler, within the spirit of the order, perhaps, but beyond its scope.

Instructions were given to the Sipo and the SD to execute without sentence. These instructions were carried out. Document F-574 on Page 10 of your document book, which is placed before you as Exhibit RF 393, is testimony by a certain Goldberg, an adjutant to the Security Service in Chalon sur Saone before the liberation of that city. He was captured by the patriots and interrogated by the divisional commissar who was Chief of the Regional Office of Criminal Investigation (Police Judiciaire) at Dijon. The defence will certainly not reproach us for having had him examined by a junior police officer. It was the same chief of the Regional Office of Criminal Investigation for the Dijon region who had interrogated this very witness. The witness declared, Page 12, at the bottom of the page:

"At the end of May 1944, without my having seen any written order on this subject, the Security Police of Chalon had the right to pronounce capital punishment, and to have the sentence carried out without those concerned having appeared before a Tribunal, and without the case having been submitted for approval to the commander in Dijon. It is the Chief of the SD in Chalon, that is, Kruger, who had all necessary authority to make such a decision. There was no opposition so far as I know on the part of the SD of Dijon, which allows me to conclude that this procedure was regular and was the result of instructions which were not officially communicated to me but which emanated from higher authorities."

The execution was carried out by members of the SD. The names are given by the witness, but they are not of particular interest to this Tribunal, which is only concerned with the punishment of the major criminals, those who gave orders and from whom orders emanated.

How were these orders applied in the various countries of the West?

In the case of Holland, we have the following testimony in a report given by the Dutch Government. I read from Page 15 of that report:

> "Three days after the attempt against Rauter, I witnessed the execution of several Dutch patriots by the German green (political) police."

This Dutch document is classified in the French file as F- 224, and it has been submitted to you, but the specific passage to which I refer has not been read.

The witness continues, on Page 16 of your document book:

> "I spoke to a master sergeant of the green (political) police, whose name is unknown to me, and he told me that this execution was revenge for the attempt against Rauter. He told me also that hundreds of Dutch terrorists had been executed in accordance with the order."

In the penultimate paragraph of Page 17, another witness stated:

> "About 6 o'clock in the evening" - this is the German who gave the orders to execute the Dutch patriots - "when I went to my office, I received the order to have 40 prisoners shot."

On Page 19, at the very bottom of the page, the investigators, who were Canadian officers, state the circumstances under which the corpses were discovered. I do not think that the Tribunal will wish me to read this passage.

On Page 21 the Tribunal will find the report of Munt, completing and correcting his report of 4 June on the execution of Dutchmen after the attempt against Rauter.

The execution was carried out upon order from Kolitz; 198 prisoners were involved. Munt denies having sanctioned the execution of the Dutch patriots, but says that it was nevertheless impossible for him to prevent it, in view of the orders from higher sources which he had received.

On Page 22, penultimate paragraph, the same Munt states:

> "After an attack against two members of the Wehrmacht on two days in succession in which both were wounded and robbed of their rifles, my chief insisted that 15 Dutch citizens be shot; 12 were shot."

An important document is to be found on Page 30 in your document book. It is included in Document F-224, which comprises the documents relative to inquiries made by the Dutch Government. This is a decree concerning the proclamation of summary justice for the Occupied Netherlands. It is signed by the defendant Seyss-Inquart. Therefore one must go to him when one seeks the chief responsibility for these summary executions of patriots in Holland.

From this decree we stress paragraph 1:

> "I proclaim summary police justice for the whole of the Occupied Netherlands, and this will take effect immediately.
>
> At the same time I order that all must abstain from any kind of agitation which might disturb public order and the security of public life."

I omit a paragraph.

> "The senior officer of the SS and of the police will take every step deemed necessary by him for the maintenance or restoration of public order or the security of public life."

The following paragraph:

> "In the execution of his task he can deviate from the existing law."

Summary police justice! These words do not deceive us. This is purely and simply a matter of murder, in that the police is authorised, in executing its functions, to deviate from the existing law. This decree which Seyss-Inquart signed, and which, gave impunity to his subordinates, who murdered Dutch patriots, is his very condemnation.

In accordance with this decree the Tribunal will see that on 2 May - this is Page 32 of your document book - a summary police court pronounced the death sentence against ten Dutch patriots.

Another summary police court pronounced the death sentence on ten other Dutch patriots. All of them were executed - this is on Page 34 of your document book.

On the next page, still in application of the same decree, you will see that a summary police court pronounced the death sentence on a patriot, and he was executed.

This Document, F-224, comprises a very long list of similar acts, which seem to me superfluous to cite. The Tribunal may refer to the last only, which is especially interesting. We may consider it for a moment; it is on Page 46 of your document book. This is the report of the Identification and Investigation Service of the Netherlands, according to which, while it was not possible to make known at that time the number of ordinary citizens who were shot by the military units of the occupying power, we can state now that a total of more than 4,000 of them were executed. The details of the executions, with the places where the corpses were discovered, follow.

This constitutes only a very fragmentary aspect of the sufferings endured by Holland and the sacrifices in human life which she made in our common cause. That needs to be stated because it is the consequence of the criminal orders of the defendant Seyss-Inquart.

In the case of Belgium, the basic document is the French Document F-685, submitted as Exhibit RF 394, and you will find it on Page 48 of your document book. It is a report drawn up by the Belgian War Crimes Commission, which deals only with the crimes committed by the German troops at the time of the liberation of Belgian territory, September 1944. These crimes were all committed against Belgian patriots who were fighting against the German Army.

It is not merely a question of executions, but of ill- treatment and tortures as well.

> Page 50: "At Graide a camp of the secret army was attacked. 15 corpses were discovered to have been frightfully mutilated." That is the first paragraph at the top of Page 50. "The Germans employed bullets with sawn off tips. Some of the bodies had been pierced with bayonets. Two of the prisoners had been beaten with cudgels before being finished off with a pistol shot."

The prisoners were soldiers taken with weapons in hand and in battle, belonging to those units which officially, according to documents formerly cited to you, were considered by the German General Staff as from that time on as being combatants.

> The sixth paragraph: "At Foret, on 6 September, several hundred men of the Resistance were billeted in the Chateau de Foret. The Germans, having been warned that they were going into action, decided to carry out a repressive operation. A certain number of unarmed members of the Resistance tried to flee. Some were shot down; others succeeded in getting back to the castle, not having been able to break through the cordon of German troops; others were finally made prisoners. The Germans advanced with the Resistance prisoners in front of them. After two hours the fighting stopped for lack of ammunition. The Germans promised to spare the lives of those who surrendered. Some of the prisoners were loaded on a lorry; others, in spite of the promise, were massacred after having been tortured. The castle, and the corpses, sprinkled with petrol, were set on fire. Twenty men perished in this massacre; fifteen others had been killed during the fight."

The examples are numerous. This tribute to heroic Belgium was necessary. It was necessary that there should be recalled here what we owe to these combatants of the secret army, and the price paid by it.

With regard to Luxembourg, we have a document given to us by the Ministry of Justice of the Grand Duchy of Luxembourg, which is UK-77, already submitted as Exhibit RF 325, which the Tribunal will find on page 53 of the document book.

In paragraph 4, the Tribunal will note that a special court of summary jurisdiction, similar to those which functioned in Holland, was set up in Luxembourg; that it functioned in that country and pronounced a certain number of death sentences, twenty-one-all of them equally arbitrary, in view of the arbitrary character of the court which pronounced such sentences.

On Page 54 is contained the official accusation made by the Grand Duchy of Luxembourg against all members of the Reich Cabinet, specifically against the Ministers of the Interior, of Justice, and the Party Chancellery, against the leaders of the SS and Police, and particularly against those of the Reich Commission for the Strengthening of Germanism (Reichskommissariat fur die Festigung des Deutschen Volkstums).

In the case of Norway, Document UK-19, already submitted as Exhibit RF 326, shows, in the third paragraph, at the middle of Page 55 of the document book, that a tribunal similar to that special tribunal in Holland, composed of police, was in operation in Norway. It was called the SS Court. More than 150 Norwegians were condemned to death. That is the penultimate paragraph on that page.

Besides, the Tribunal will remember the testimony of M. Cappelen, who came before you to relate what his country and his compatriots had endured.

In the case of Denmark, on Page 57 of your document book, Document F-666, already submitted as RF-278, Page 57, the Tribunal will note that, according to this official report submitted by the Danish Government, police courts-martial similar to those which functioned in Luxembourg, in Norway and in Holland, also functioned in Denmark. These summary police courts composed of SS or police officers, in reality cloaked the arbitrariness of the police and of the SS, the arbitrariness not only tolerated but even intended by the Government, as can be shown by documents which we have placed before you at the beginning of this presentation.

We, therefore, can assert that the victims of those courts were murdered without having been able to justify or defend themselves.

In France the question should be carefully examined. The Tribunal knows that from the very moment of landing, answering the call of the General Staff, the French Secret Army rose and began to fight. Undoubtedly, in spite of the warning given by the Allied General Staff, these combatants, at the beginning, found themselves in a rather irregular situation. We do not contest that in many instances they were francs-tireurs, we admitted that they could be condemned to death; but we protest that they were not condemned to death, but were assassinated after having been brutally tortured. We are going to give you proof thereof.

Document F-577, which is submitted as Exhibit RF 395, is to be found on Page 62 of your document book. It states that on 17th August, on the eve of the liberation of Rodez, the Germans shot 30 patriots with a submachine gun. Then, to finish them off, they detached large stones from the wall of the trench in which they were and hurled them on the bodies, with a little earth. Their chests and skulls were crushed.

Document F-580, Page 79 of your document book, which was submitted to you as Exhibit RF 396, shows that five oblates from the order of Marie - to my knowledge these lay brothers were not communists - were assassinated after having been tortured, because they belonged to a group of the Secret Army. Thirty-six corpses in all were discovered after this execution, a punitive measure carried out by the German Army.

On Page 85 the Tribunal will read the result of the inquiry and will see how these five oblates, after having been tortured, were killed, and how the Staff of the Resistance group, which had been betrayed, was arrested and deported together with a few members of the same religious order.

In the fourth paragraph, starting from the bottom of the page, the proof is before you that the Maquis from the forest of Acheres were arrested and tortured after having been incarcerated in the prison of Fontainebleau. We even know the name of the German member of the Gestapo who tortured those patriots. His name is unimportant. Korf carried out the orders that were given by Keitel, and by others whose names were mentioned a while ago.

Document F-584, Page 87 - which becomes Exhibit RF 397, and the Tribunal will find it on Page 87-88 - shows the Tribunal that, when the bodies were found, it was discovered that ten of these men had been blindfolded before being shot, that eight had had their arms broken, by blows or torture, and many had wounds in the lower parts of their legs as a result of the tightness with which they had been bound. That was the report of the Police Commissar, drawn up on 28 August 1944, on the day following the liberation of Pau.

We now present Document F-585, which will be Exhibit RF 398, the Tribunal will find it on Page 96 of the document book. I summarise:

The day following the liberation, 38 corpses were found in two graves near Signes in the mountain of Var. One of the leaders of the Resistance of the Cote d'Azur, Valmy, and with him two parachutists, Pageout and Manuel, were identified. There was witness of this massacre - his name is Quirot - whose statements are transcribed on Pages 11 and 12 of Document 505, Pages 105, 106 and 107 of your document book.

Quirot was tortured, together with his comrades, without having been given the opportunity of having counsel or chaplain. The thirty-eight men were taken to the woods. They appeared before a parody of a court made up of SS, were condemned to death, and executed.

We place now before the Tribunal Document F-586 as Exhibit RF 399. The Tribunal will find it on Page 110 of the document book. It deals with the execution at Saint Nazaire and Royans of thirty-seven patriots, members of the French Secret Army, who were tortured before being executed. The Tribunal will read on Page 110, at the beginning of paragraph 2, the statement of facts by one of the eye- witnesses

> "I came through the ruins and I arrived at the Chateau of Mme. Laurent, a widow. There a frightful spectacle confronted me. The castle, which the Gestapo had used as a place of torture of the young Maquis, had been set on fire. In a cellar there was a calcined skeleton of a man who, prior to death, had had his forearms and a foot pulled off and who had perhaps been burned while still alive."

But I proceed. Wherever the Gestapo was in operation the same horrors are encountered.

Now we place before the Tribunal Document F-699, which relates to the assassination at Grenoble of forty-eight members of the Secret Army, all of whom were tortured. It is submitted as Exhibit RF 400. It begins on Page 112 of your document book.

I now come to Document F-587, which we place before you as Exhibit RF 401. The Tribunal will find this document on Page 115 of the document book. It concerns the execution at Nimes, by hanging, of twelve patriots, two of whom were dragged from the hospital where they were under care for battle wounds. All these young men had been captured in combat at St. Hippolyte-du-Fort (paragraph 4 of Page 115). The corpses of these wretched men were profaned. On their chests had been written: "Thus are French terrorists punished." When the French sought to give the last honours to these unfortunate men the corpses had disappeared. The German Army had removed them. They have never yet been discovered. It is a fact that two of these victims were dragged from the hospital. Document F-587 contains the report of a witness who saw the men taken from the hospital where they were being cared for.

I place before you now Document F-561 as Exhibit RF 402. It is found on Page 118 of your book. It deals with the execution in Lyons of one hundred arid nine patriots who were shot under inhuman conditions. They were killed at the end of a day's toil. On 14 August Allied planes had bombed the Brou airfield and from 16 to 22 August the German authorities had compelled civilians and internees at the Fort of Montluc at Lyons to fill the bomb craters. At the end of the day, when the work was finished (this is at the end of paragraph 2) the civilian labourers went away, but the internees were shot on the spot, after having been more or less ill-treated.

Their bodies were stacked in craters which had not yet been filled in.

Document F-591, which we submit as Exhibit RF 403 and which appears on Page 199 of the document book before the Tribunal, is a report of atrocities committed by the German Army on 30 August 1944 at Tavaux in Aisne.

"During the afternoon of that day soldiers of the Adolf Hitler Division arrived at Tavaux. They appeared at the home of M. Maujean, who was the leader of the Resistance. His wife opened the door. Without explanation they shot at her, wounding her in the thigh and also in the lower jaw. They dragged her to the kitchen; they broke one arm and one leg. In the presence of her children, aged nine, eight, seven, six years and eight months, they poured an inflammable liquid over her and set fire to her. The elder child held his little sister, eight-months old, in his arms. Then they told the children that they were going to shoot them if they did not tell where their father was. The children said nothing, although they knew the whereabouts of their father. They were led down into the cellar. They were locked in. Then the Germans poured gasoline on the house and set it on fire. The fire was put out and the children were saved. These facts were stated to M. Maujean by the eldest child. No other person was a witness to these facts because the inhabitants, frightened by the first houses set on fire, had sought refuge either in trenches or in the neighbouring fields and woods."

During the same evening twenty-one persons were killed at Tavaux and eighty-three houses were set on fire."

On the following page there is a report transmitted by the gendarme, Carlier, on the day following the events.

On Page 121 the Tribunal will find French Document F-589, which we submit as Exhibit RF 404. This document shows the provisional figures of murders of patriots committed in the region of Lyons, under date of 25 September 1944:

"713 victims have been found in eight departments, 217 only have been identified.

This figure is approximate; it is definitely less than the number of people who are missing in the eight departments of Ain, Areche, Drome, Isere, Loire, Rhone, Savoie, Haute Savoie."

A German general, General von Brodowski, has confessed in his diary, which fell into our hands, that he had caused the assassination of numerous patriots and that the Wehrmacht, Police and SS, operating simultaneously, were equally responsible for these murders. These troops murdered wounded men in hospital camps of the French Forces of the Interior. This document, which is Number F-257, is submitted as Exhibit RF 405, and is to be found on Page 123 of your document book.

On Page 125 the police and the army are combined. Paragraph 2 (fourth from the bottom):

> "I have been charged with the restoration of the authority of the Army of Occupation in the department of Cantal." Dated 6 June 1944.

Paragraph 5: - "General Jesser has been charged with the tactical direction of the undertaking. All troops. available for the operation will be subordinate to him, as well as all other forces."

Paragraph 6: - " The Commander of the Sipo and of the SD, Hauptsturmfuehrer Geissler, remains at my immediate disposal. He will submit proposals for the possible intervention ... " and so forth.

The last paragraph: - "The staff and two battalions of a regiment of SS Panzer Division 'Das Reich' are, in addition, to remain available for the operation in Cantal."

Then - on Page 127 - this general turned over some wounded prisoners to the SD which was equivalent to their execution without sentence. These prisoners were wounded on 15 June 1944. The Prefect of Le Puy asked the liaison staff whether the men wounded in the battle of Montmouchet and taken into safety by the Red Cross of Puy could be delivered to Puy as prisoners of war. . . The German general executing the orders of the German High Command, particularly of Keitel and Jodl, said: "These men are to be treated as ' francs-tireurs ' and are to be delivered to the SD or to the Abwehr."

These wounded men were turned over to the German Police and tortured and killed without trial.

Page 129: Execution without trial according to the statement of Colbert, of which we have just spoken. Any man turned over to the SD is to be executed without trial.

On 21 June 1944, events took place as indicated by Colbert. Paragraph 4, at the end -

> "Twelve suspects were arrested and turned over to the SD."

Under the date of 16 August 1944, Page 133, this general of the German Army calls for the assassination of 40 men after combat at Bourg-Lashe and at Cosnat. This is the second paragraph of Page 11 of the document.

> "In the course of operation Jesser on 15 July in the Bourg-Lashe region twenty-three persons were executed (martial law). Attack on Cosnat, three kilometres east of St. Hilaire, during the night of 17 July, forty terrorists were shot down."

On Page 136: - This German general admits in his own journal that our comrades were fighting as soldiers and not as assassins.

Paragraph 5: This general of the German Army acknowledges that the French Forces of the Interior took prisoners.

> "South-east of d'Argenton, thirty kilometres South-west of Chateauroux, the 'Jako' discovered a centre of terrorists. Sixteen German soldiers were liberated; arms and ammunition were captured. Seven terrorists were killed, two of them captains. One German soldier was seriously wounded."

Another similar incident is related on Page 137, at the very top of the page.

> "Discovery of two camps of terrorists in the region of d'Argenton. Nine of the enemy were killed, two of whom were officers. Sixteen German soldiers

were liberated." At the bottom of the page is stated:

"We liberated two SS men."

The soldiers were entitled to the respect of their adversaries. They conducted themselves as soldiers; they were assassinated.

I shall conclude, Mr. President, if the Tribunal will give me five minutes. I will only need one hour to present the remainder of my case this afternoon.

THE PRESIDENT: We will adjourn now until 1400 hours.

(A recess was taken)

MARSHAL OF THE COURT: May it please the Court, I desire to announce that the defendants Kaltenbrunner and Seyss-Inquart will be absent from this afternoon's session on account of illness.

M. DUBOST: We had arrived, gentlemen, at the presentation of the terrorist policy carried out by the German Army, Police and SS, indistinguishably united in their evil task against the French patriots.

Not only the militant patriots were to be the victims of this terrorist policy. There were threats of reprisals against their relatives, and these threats were carried out in deeds.

We place before you Document 719 PS, as Exhibit RF 406, which your Tribunal will find on Page 147 of the document book. It is a pencilled note from the German Embassy in Paris, to the Ministry of Foreign Affairs in Berlin. The German Ambassador reports a conversation which the Vichy echelon had with Laval.

In the fourth paragraph, the last three lines, the author of this note, who is probably Abetz, explains that Bousquet, who was with Laval at the time of this conversation, stated that he was completely ignorant of the recent flight of Giraud's brother.

> "Madame Giraud, three of her daughters, her mother and another brother of the general, and his daughter-in-law are reported to be at the camp of Valse-les-Bains. I replied that such measures were insufficient and that it would not be surprising if the German police some day took these matters into its own hands, in view of the obvious incompetence of the French police in numerous cases."

The threat was put into execution. We have already stated before you that the family of General Giraud had been deported.

We place before you Document 717, as Exhibit RF 407, Page 149 of your document book.

> "Paris, 1030 hours, Official State Telegram, Paris, to the French Delegation of IMT, Nuremberg."

From this telegram it is evident that 17 persons, members of the family of General Giraud, were deported to Germany: Madame Granger, daughter of General Giraud, aged 32, was arrested without cause in Tunis in April 1943, as well as her four children, aged two to eleven years, with their young nurse, and her brother-in-law, M. Granger. They were first deported to Berlin, then to Thuringia. General Giraud's family, too, was arrested on 9 October 1943.

May I ask the forbearance of the Tribunal ; the telegraphic style is not easy to interpret.

> "First to Berlin and then to Thuringia, the women and children of M. Granger to Dachau."

I suppose that we must understand this to mean the wife of M. Granger and the nurse who accompanied her.

THE PRESIDENT: What is the document?

M. DUBOST: This is a French official telegram. You have the original before you, Mr. President. "Official Paris. State Telegram 101, State, Paris," typed on the text of the telegram itself.

THE PRESIDENT: Can we receive a telegram from anybody addressed to the Tribunal?

M. DUBOST: Mr. President, it is not addressed to the Tribunal; it is addressed to the French Delegation. It is an official telegram from the French Government in Paris, and it was transmitted as an official telegram to the French Delegation.

THE PRESIDENT: What is the Delegation Francais, IMT, Paris?

M. DUBOST: This is the Delegation in Paris of the International Military Tribunal in the French Ministry of Justice. It is one of the sections of the French Ministry of Justice, Place Vendome. The telegram begins, "By General Giraud." This is a statement of testimony by telegram. The letters "OFF" at the beginning of the telegram mean "Official."

Forgive me for not insisting that the three letters "OFF" at the beginning of the telegram means "Official" or "Government Telegram." No French Telegraph Office could transmit an official telegram which did not come from an official authority. This official authority is the French Delegation of the IMT in Paris, which received the statement made by General Giraud and transmitted it to us, "By General Giraud, care of the French Delegation at the IMT."

THE PRESIDENT: Very well, the Tribunal will receive the document under Article 21 of the Charter.

M. DUBOST: I am grateful to the Tribunal.

On Page 2 of the document - that is Page 150 of your own document book, in the middle of the page, we read:

> "On the other hand the death of Madame Granger on 24 September 1943 is undoubtedly due to lack of care and medicine, in spite of her reiterated requests for both. After an autopsy of her body, which took place in the presence of French doctors who had been specially summoned from Paris after her death, authorisation was given to Dr. Claque to bring the three children back to France and then to Spain, where they would be turned over to their father. This was refused by the Gestapo in Paris, and the children were sent back to Germany as hostages, where their grandmother found them only six months later."

In the last four lines is stated:

> "The health of Madame Giraud, her daughter, Marie Theresa, and two of her grandchildren has been gravely impaired by the physical, and particularly by the moral hardships of their deportation."

Seventeen persons, all of them innocent of the escape of General Giraud, were therefore arrested as punishment therefore.

I have frequently shown that, in their determination to impose their reign of terror, the Germans resorted to means which revolt the human conscience. Of these one of the most repugnant is inducement to become informers.

Document F-278, Page 152, which we place before you as Exhibit RF 408, is a reproduction of an ordinance of 20 September 1941, which is so obviously contrary to International Law that the Foreign Ministry of the Reich itself took cognisance of it. On Page 152, paragraph 2, the ordinance of 27 December 1941 prescribes as follows:

"Whosoever may have knowledge that arms are in the possession of an unauthorised person or persons is obliged to declare this at the nearest police headquarters."

On Page 153, the Ministry of Foreign Affairs in Berlin, on 29 June 1942, objected to the draft of the reply to the French note, which we have not here, but which must have been a protest against this ordinance of 27 December 1941. The Tribunal knows that in the military operations which accompanied the liberation of our land, many archives disappeared, and therefore we cannot give the Tribunal knowledge of the protest of the de facto government to which the note of 29 June of the German Foreign Ministry relates.

Paragraph 2 summarises the arguments of the French protest.

The French evidently had replied as follows: "Assuming that German territory were occupied by the French, we surely would consider as a man without honour any German who denounced -to the occupying power an infraction of the laws."

This was taken up and adopted by the German Foreign Ministry.

The note continues:

"On consideration of this matter, the Foreign Office considers it subject to question whether a punishment, applicable without any instructions whatever, should be prescribed for anyone who fails to denounce a person possessing or known to possess arms. Such a prescription of penalty under a general form is, in the opinion of the Foreign Office, the more impracticable in that it would offer the French the possibility of calling attention to the fact that the German Army is demanding of them acts which it would consider criminal if committed by German citizens."

This German note, I repeat, comes from the Reich Ministry of Foreign Affairs and is signed "Strack." There is no more severe condemnation of the German Army than that by the Reich Ministry of Foreign Affairs itself. The reply of the German Army will be found by the Tribunal on Page 155:

"Berlin. 8 December 1942. High Command of the Wehrmacht."

The High Command of the Wehrmacht concludes in the fourth paragraph:

"Since it does not seem desirable to undertake any discussion with the French Government on the questions of law evoked by them, we also consider it appropriate not to reply to the French note."

This note begins by asserting that amelioration of the given orders would be considered a sign of weakness in France and in Belgium. (These are the last two lines of paragraph 1.)

These are not the signs of weakness that the German Army gave in our occupied countries of the West. The weakness manifested itself in terror, it brought terror to reign throughout our countries so as to permit the development of the policy of extermination of the vanquished nations, which, in the minds of all German leaders, has remained the principal purpose, if not the single purpose, of this war.

This terrorist policy, of which the Tribunal has just seen examples in the repression of attacks of our French Forces of the Interior, developed without any military necessity in all of the countries of the West. The devastations committed by the enemy are extremely numerous. We shall limit our presentation to the destruction of Rotterdam at a time when the city had already capitulated, and when only the question of the form of capitulation was to be settled; and secondly, to a description of the inundations which the German Army caused, without any military necessity of any sort, in 1945, on the eve of its destruction, when that Army already knew that the game was lost.

We have chosen the example of Rotterdam because it is the first act of terrorism of the German Army in the West. We have taken the inundations because, without her dykes, without fresh water, Holland ceases to be. When her dykes are destroyed Holland disappears.

One sees here the fulfilment of the enemy's project of destruction formulated long ago by Germany, as already shown by the citation from Hitler with which I opened my presentation, and which was carried on to the very last minute of Nazi Germany's existence, as proved by the inundation of Holland.

We place before the Tribunal Document F-719 as Exhibit RF 409, which will be found on Page 38 of the second document book, which comprises a Dutch report on the bombing of Rotterdam and the capitulation of the Dutch Army.

On Pages 38 and 39 are copies of the translations of documents exchanged between the commander of the German troops before Rotterdam and the colonel who was in command of the Dutch troops defending the city.

On Page 40 Engineer Captain Backer relates the incidents of that evening which ended with the bombing: At 1030 hours a German representative appeared with an ultimatum, unsigned and without any indication of the sender, demanding that the Dutch capitulate before 1230 hours. This document was returned by the Dutch colonel, who asked to be told the name and the military rank of the officer who had called upon him to surrender.

At 1215 Captain Backer appeared before the German lines and was received by a German officer. At 1235 hours he had a conversation with the German officers in a creamery. A German general wrote his terms for capitulation on the letter of reply, which the representative of the Dutch General Staff had just brought to him.

At 1320 hours Captain Backer left the place where the negotiations had taken place with the new terms, to which a reply was to be given. Two German officers escorted him. These escorting officers were protected by the flight of German aircraft, and red rockets were fired by the Germans, at 1322 and 1325 hours.

At 1330 hours the first bomb fell upon Rotterdam, which was completely set on fire.

On Page 41 - the entry of the German troops was to take place at 1850 hours, but it was put forward to 1820 hours.

Paragraph 4 - later the Germans said to Captain Backer that the purpose of the red rockets was to avoid being bombed. However, there had been excellent wireless communication from the ground to the aircraft. Captain Backer expressed his surprise that this should have been done by means of fuses.

The inundation of the polder "Wieringermeer" took place on 9 and 10 April 1945. The Tribunal will find the document on Page 7 of the document book.

"Today German soldiers appeared on the polder, gave orders, and set up a guard for the dyke."

Paragraph 2 of Page 7:

"On 17 April 1945, at 1215, the dyke was dynamited so that two parts of it were destroyed up to a height somewhat above the surface of the water of the Ijesselmeer."

Paragraph 2, the last paragraph of Page 7:

"As for the population, they had an alert during the night of 16 to 17 April; that is, at the time when the water was about to flood the polder.

In Wieringerwerf the news received at the City Hall was transmitted from house to house that at noon the dyke would be destroyed. In general, for the great polder, with an area of 20,000 hectares, not more than 8 1/2-9 hours were granted for its evacuation. Telephone communications had been completely interrupted, and it was impossible to use automobiles, which meant that some individuals did not receive any warning until eight o'clock in the morning."

Page 8, paragraph 2:

"The time given to the population was, therefore, too short to permit them to evacuate the polder."

The next to the last paragraph:

"The looting in the flooded polder has already been mentioned. During the morning of 17 April, on the day of the disaster, groups of German soldiers began to loot. These soldiers came from Wieringen. Moreover, they broke everything that they did not want to take."

On Page 10, Paragraph 1:

"The polder by itself covers half of all the flooded lands in Northern Holland. It was flooded on 17 April, when defeat was already a fact as far as the German Army was concerned."

The Dutch people are seeking to recover the land which they have lost. Their courage, industry and energy arouse our admiration, but it is an immense loss which the German Army imposed upon those people on 17 April.

Terrorism and extermination are intimately interwoven in all countries in the West.

Document C-45, 10 February 1944, which we submit as Exhibit RF 410 and is the first in the Tribunal's document book, in paragraph 1, shows that repression, in the minds of the leaders of the German Army, is to be carried out without consideration of any kind.

"One must immediately shoot back. If, as a result, innocents are struck, this is to be regretted, but it is entirely the fault of the terrorists."

These lines were written over the signature of an officer of the General Staff of the German Military Command in Belgium and Northern France. This officer was never condemned by his superiors.

Document F-665 is submitted as Exhibit RF-411. Page 2 of your document book, the last paragraph:

"The search of suspected villages requires experience. SD or GFP (Secret Field Police) personnel should be called upon. The real accomplices of the guerrillas must be unmasked, and apprehended with all severity. Collective measures against the inhabitants of entire villages (this includes the burning of villages) are to be taken only in exceptional cases and may be ordered exclusively by divisional commanders or by chiefs of the SS and Police."

This document is dated 6 May 1944. It comes from the High Command of the Wehrmacht, and it, or at least the covering letter, is signed by Jodl.

This document involves not only the Army General Staff, but the Labour Service, that is to say, Sauckel, and the Todt Organisation, that is to say, defendant Speer.

In the next to the last paragraph we can read:

"The directive is applicable to all branches of the Wehrmacht and to all organisations which exercise their activities in occupied territories (the Reich Labour Service, the Todt Organisation, etc.)."

These orders, which in their spirit tend to the extermination of civilian populations, will be carried out vigorously, but at the price of constant collusion of the German Army, the SS, the SD and Sipo, which the people of all countries of the West mass together in the same horror and in the same reprobation.

We submitted to the Tribunal the war diary of General Brodowski as Exhibit

RF-405, an excerpt of which is to be found on Pages 3, 4 and 5 of the document book. It states - Page 3, the penultimate paragraph-(Page nine ,of the German text), second paragraph starting from the top,-that repressive operations were carried out.

> "An action was undertaken in the South-western area of the department of Dordogne near Lalinde, in which a company of Georgians, a detachment of Field Police, and members of the SD took part ..."

On Page 4 - Page 10 of the German text - 14 June 1944, is a statement of the destruction of Oradour Sur Glane. I shall come back to the destruction ,of this village. "Six hundred persons were killed," writes General Brodowski. It is underscored in the text.

> "The whole male population of Oradour has been shot. Women and children took refuge in the church. The church caught fire. Explosives had been placed in the church. All the women and children perished as well."

We shall let you know the results of the French inquiry on the destruction of Oradour. The Tribunal will see to what degree General Brodowski lied when he described the annihilation of Oradour in these terms.

Page 5, paragraph 2:

> "Tulle, 11 July 1944: The barracks occupied by the 13th Company 95th Security Regiment was attacked by terrorists. The struggle was terminated by the arrival of the Panzer Division, " Das Reich ". One hundred and twenty male inhabitants of Tulle were shot, and 1,000 turned over to the SD of Limoges for inquiries."

In reality, those 120 patriots were not shot, but hanged, as we shall show presently.

THE PRESIDENT: M. Dubost, could we see the original of this document?

M. DUBOST: I showed it to you this morning, Mr. President. I placed it before you this morning. It is rather a large document, if you will remember, Sir.

THE PRESIDENT: Yes. We would like to see it.

DR. SERVATUS (Counsel for defendant Sauckel): I should like briefly to rectify an error now, before it is carried any further.

The French prosecutor pointed out that certain people were put at the disposal of the Arbeitsdienst. I should like to point out that Arbeitsdienst is not to be confused with Arbeitseinsatz. The Arbeitsiensatz was ultimately directed Sauckel, whereas the Arbeitsdienst had nothing whatsoever to do with Sauckel. I should like to ask the Tribunal to take judicial notice of that distinction. That is what I wished to state.

THE PRESIDENT: It is not coming through correctly to the Russian members. The Tribunal will adjourn for five minutes.

(A recess was taken)

THE PRESIDENT: Counsel for Sauckel, I think, was addressing the Tribunal.

DR. SERVATUS: I had pointed out the difference between the Arbeitsdienst and the Arbeitseinsatz. The French prosecuting attorney apparently confused the two, for he said that the Arbeitsdienst was connected with Sauckel. That is not so. The former was an organisation for pre-military training, in which young people had to render a labour service. These young people were to some extent used for military purposes. The Arbeitseinsatz was concerned solely with the recruiting of labour to be used in factories or other places of work. It follows, therefore, that Sauckel cannot be associated with the accusations that were made in this connection. That is what I wanted to say.

M. DUBOST: The two German words were translated in an identical manner in French. A verification having been made, the remarks of the defence are correct and

Sauckel is not involved, only the Army is.

THE PRESIDENT: Very well.

M. DUBOST: When we were interrupted by this technical difficulty we were about to present a few examples of terrorist exterminations in Holland, in Belgium, and in other countries of the West.

In Holland, as one example out of a thousand, there were the massacres of Putten of 30 September 1944. They are included in Document F-719, which we submitted as Exhibit RF 409, and which is to be found on Page 46 of the, document book before the Tribunal. On 30 September 1944 an attack was attempted by members of the Dutch resistance against a German automobile. The Germans concluded that the village was a refuge for partisans. They searched the houses of the inhabitants; they gathered the population together.

A wounded German officer had been taken prisoner by the Dutch resistance. The Germans declared that if the officer was released within twenty-four hours there would be no reprisal exercised. The officer was released, after having received medical care from the soldiers of the Dutch resistance who had captured him. However, in spite of the pledge given, reprisals were inflicted upon the village of Putten, whose inhabitants were all innocent.

Paragraph 2 of the Dutch report which I now cite:

"The population, which had gathered together in the church, was informed that the men would be taken away; that the women had to leave the village and that the village would be destroyed. One hundred and five houses were burned. It is estimated that the centre of the village comprised 2000 houses. Eight persons, among whom was one woman, who sought to escape were shot and killed.

In the third paragraph:

"The men were transported to the concentration camp of Amersfoort.

There they found many people who, in passing through had entered the penned-in village and could not leave it again. At Amersfoort they released about fifty men. About twelve had jumped from the train during the convoy. Finally, 622 men were transported to Auschwitz. The greater part of them had died at the end of the first two months. Of the 622 men who were taken away only 32 inhabitants of Putten and ten from other towns returned after the liberation."

In Belgium, we will cite only a few facts which are related in Document F-685, already submitted to the Tribunal as Exhibit RF 394. This document is to be found on Page 48 in your document book. The penultimate paragraph describes the murder of a young man who had sought refuge in a dug-out. He was killed by the Germans, who were looking for soldiers of the Belgian Secret Army.

At Herve - the last paragraph of that page - the Germans fired on a lorry filled with young people and killed them. The same day some civilians were killed by a tank.

On Page 49, paragraph 1 and 2 are described the summary executions of members of the secret army. Paragraph 3; I quote :

"At Anhee, shots having been fired upon them, the Germans crossed the Meuse River. They set fire to fifty- eight houses and killed thirteen men. At Annevoie, on the 4th, the Germans came across the river and burned fifty-eight houses."

The five paragraphs which follow report useless destruction from the military point of view. Let us now proceed to the last paragraph.

"At Arendonck, on the 3rd, eighty men were killed; five houses were burned. At St. Hubert, on the 6th, three men killed and four houses burned. At Hody, on the 6th, systematic destruction of the village; forty houses destroyed ; sixteen people killed. At Marcourt, ten people were shot; thirty-five houses were burned. At Nerosteren, on the 9th, nine people were killed. At Oost-Ham, on the 10th, five persons were killed. At Balen-Neet, on the 11th, ten persons were shot."

Page 50 contains the description of German exactions at the time of the temporary stabilisation of the front. Next to the last paragraph:

"At Hechtel, the Germans having withdrawn before the British vanguard, the inhabitants hung out our flags. Then fresh German troops came to hold back the British vanguard and reprisals were exercised. Thirty-one people were shot; 80 houses were burned, and general looting took place. At Helchteren under similar circumstances, thirty-four houses were set on fire and ten people were killed." The same events at Herenthout.

Paragraph 2 of Page 50;

"The circumstances in which these men were executed are always identical. The Germans search the cellars, bring the men out, line them along the highway and shoot them, after having given them the order to run. In the meantime grenades are thrown into the cellars, wounding the women and the children."

Last paragraph:

"At Lommel, the unexpected return of the German soldiers found the village with flags out. Seventeen persons who had sought refuge in a shelter were noticed by a German. He motioned to a tank which ran over the shelter backwards and forwards until it crushed it, killing twelve people."

In the case of Norway we shall read an excerpt from a document already placed before you as Exhibit RF 325, page 51 and 52 of your book:

"On 13 April, 1940, two women aged thirty were shot at Reingeke.

On 15 April, four civilians, among them two boys aged fifteen and sixteen, were shot at Aadal. One of the victims received a shot in the head and was wounded in the abdomen. On 19th April, four civilians, among whom were two women and a little boy thirteen years old, were shot at Ringsaker."

The last paragraph on that Page - Page 51:

"To avenge the death of two German policemen killed on 26 April 1942 at Televaag, the entire town was destroyed; that is to say, more than eighty premises with 334 buildings, causing damage to the value of 4,200,000 crowns."

On Page 52 the Tribunal will find the continuation of the descriptions of German atrocities committed in Norway without any military character, simply to maintain the reign of terror.

In France, massacres, destruction without military purpose, were extremely numerous, and all of them were closely associated. We place before you F-243 as Exhibit RF 412. The Tribunal will find this document on Page 178 of the document book. It is a long list drawn up by the French Service for Inquiry into War Crimes on the towns that were destroyed and looted without any military necessity. These enumerations go from Page 179 to Page 193 of the document book placed before the Tribunal. The Tribunal will undoubtedly be enlightened by the reading of this document. We shall give but a few examples. Document F-909, Exhibit RF-413, shows the conditions under which a whole section of Marseilles was destroyed - Pages 56, 57, and 58 of the document book which the Tribunal has in hand.

Page 57, if you please, eighth line of the paragraph before the last. It is estimated that around 20,000 people were evacuated. This evacuation was ordered on the 23rd of January. It was carried out without warning during the night of the 23rd to the 24th. I quote:

> "It is estimated that 20,000 persons were evacuated. From Frejus some of them were shipped by the Germans to the concentration camp of Compiegne."

On Page 58, paragraph 2:

> "The demolition operations began on the 1st of February at about 9 o'clock in the morning. They were carried out by troops of the German Engineer Corps."

The last three lines of this paragraph:

> "The area destroyed is equivalent to fourteen hectares that is to say, approximately twelve hundred buildings."

Inquiry was made to find those who were responsible for this destruction. After the liberation of Marseilles the German consul in Marseilles, von Spiegel, was interrogated. His testimony is incorporated in Document F-908, which we place before you as Exhibit RF 414, Page 53 of your document book. We will read only the last paragraph on Page 54; Spiegel stated:

> "I know that a very short time after the evacuation of the old port, the rumour was prevalent that this measure had been brought about by financial interests. I am in a position to affirm that such a hypothesis is erroneous. The order came from the higher echelons of the Reich Government which pointed out only two motives: Security of troops, dangers of epidemics."

We do not intend to give you a complete description of the attacks committed by the Germans, but merely a few examples. Document F-600, Page 59, which we submit as Exhibit RF 415.

> "At Ohis (Aisne) a civilian sought to give something to drink to an American soldier. The Germans returned. The American soldier was taken prisoner and M. Hennebert was also taken away by the Germans to a spot designated as the "black mountain" in the village of Origny en Thierarche where his body was later discovered partly hidden under a stack of wood. The body bore the trace of two bayonet wounds in the back."

At Lagnieu - Document F-604, submitted as Exhibit RF 416, Page 61 of the document book.

> "A civilian was killed in his vineyard. Young people, young women were killed on the highway."

At the bottom of Page 61, before the certification formula, the motive is given as "Presence of Maquis in the Region."

All these victims were completely innocent.

At Culoz, Document F-904, which I submit as Exhibit RF 417, Page 62 of your document book :

> "Young boys were arrested because they had run away at the sight of the Germans. They were deported."

This is three paragraphs before the end of the page. I am quoting the next to the last paragraph:

> "Not one of them belonged to the Resistance."

At St. Jean Maurienne, Document F-906, submitted as Exhibit RF 418, Page 63 of your book of documents, paragraph 3:

On 23 July the Gendarmes - I am now quoting - "Chavanne and Empereur, dressed in civilian clothes, were arrested by German soldiers without reasonable motives. The lieutenant who was in charge of the Kommandantur promised the officer of the Gendarmes to liberate these three men. This German later surreptitiously ordered his men to shoot these prisoners."

Page 64, paragraph 4, the 1st of September:

"Mademoiselle Perraud, twenty-one years of age, who was a maid at the Cafi Dentroux, was raped by a German soldier under threat of a pistol."

I merely mention all the atrocities described in the document, up to Page 68 of your book.

I come to the Vercors. This region was undeniably an important assembly centre for French Forces of the Interior. Document F-611, which we submit as Exhibit RF 419 describes the atrocities committed against the innocent population of this region as reprisals because of the presence of the Maquis men. This document appears in your book under Page 69, et seq.

Paragraph 3 of Page 69 is an enumeration of police operations in this area on 15 June, carried out in the region of St. Donat, first: rapes and looting; second: execution at Portes-Les-Valence on 8 July of thirty hostages taken from the political prisoners interned at Fort Montluc at Lyons; third: police raids carried out against the Maquis of the Vercors Region from 21 July to 5 August 1944, rape and looting in the region of Crest, Soillant, and St. Die; fourth: Aerial bombing by aircraft of numerous villages in the Vercors and in particular Chapelle and Vassieux in Vercors; fifth: summary execution of inhabitants of these towns; sixth: looting, execution after summary judgement of about a hundred young men at St. Nazaire-en-Rayons; Seventh deportation to Germany of three hundred others from this region; and lastly murder of fifty gravely wounded persons in the Grotto of La Luire.

Page 70, paragraph 1, on 15 June 1944; Attack by German troops at St. Donat - I am quoting - "Which the Maquis had evacuated several days earlier."

Paragraph 5, Page 54: I am quoting:

"Fifty-four young women from thirteen to fifteen years of age were raped by the maddened soldiers."

The Tribunal will forgive me if I avoid citing the atrocious details which follow.

Page 71, the last paragraph: Bombing of the villages of Combovin, La Baume-Cornillanne, Durches, et cetera - I am now quoting:

"The losses caused by these bombings among the civilian population were rather high, for in most cases the inhabitants, caught by surprise, had no time to seek shelter."

Page 72, third paragraph: "Two women were raped at Crest." This in paragraph 3, and in the same connection, three women in Saillans. Page 73, Paragraph 4, I am quoting:

"A young girl of twelve, who was wounded, and pinned down between beams, awaited death for six long days without being able either to sit down or sleep and without receiving any food, and that under the eyes of the Germans who were occupying the village."

I proceed: F-612, submitted as Exhibit RF 420, Page 77:

Page 76: medical certificate from Doctor Nicolaides, who examined the women who were raped in this region.

"To terrorise the inhabitants at Trebeurden in Brittany they hanged innocent people, and slashed the corpses to make the blood flow."

I proceed: F-912, submitted as Exhibit RF 421, Page 82 of your book: It is the recital of the massacre of thirty-five Jews at St. Amand-Montrond. These men were arrested, and killed with pistol shots in the back by members of the Gestapo and of the German Army. They were innocent of any crime.

I proceed: Document F-913, submitted as Exhibit RF 422, Page 96, at the bottom of the page. I am quoting:

"On 6 of April 1944 German soldiers of the Gestapo arrested young Bezillon, eighteen years of age, dwelling at Oyonnaxain, whose brother is in the Maquis."

On Page 97:

"The body of this young man was discovered on 11 April 1944 at Sieges (Jura) frightfully mutilated. His nose and tongue had been cut off. There were traces of blows over his whole body and of slashes on his legs. Four other young men were also found at Sieges at the same time as Bezillon. All of them had been mutilated in such a manner that they could not be identified. They bore no trace of bullets, which clearly indicates that they died from the consequences of ill-treatment."

I proceed: F-615, which I submit as Exhibit RF 423, Page 98 of your document book. "Destruction of the village of Cerisay, Page 100 of your document book, next to the last paragraph:

"The fire did not cause any accident to persons, but the bodies of the two persons killed by German convoys and those of two victims of the bombardment were burned."

This village was destroyed by artillery fire. One hundred and seventy-two buildings were destroyed and five hundred and fifty-nine people were left homeless. That is from the last line on Page 100 of your document book.

We place before you Document F-919 as Exhibit RF 424 and we shall quote only Page 103, paragraph 5: This is the murder of a young man of Tourch in the Finistere Dept. The murderers compelled the mother to prepare a meal for them. I am quoting:

"Having been fed, they disinterred the victim. They searched and found that the body bore a card of identity bearing the same name and address as his mother, brothers, and sisters, who were present and who were in tears. One of the soldiers, finding no excuse to explain this crime, said dryly before going away, "It is too bad," and the body was again buried.

Document F-616, submitted as Exhibit RF 425, Page 104: This concerns the report of the operations of the German Army in the region of Nice around 20 July 1944, Page 105 of your document book, second paragraph: I quote:

"Having been attacked at Presle by several groups of Maquis in the region, by way of reprisals, a Mongolian detachment, still under the SS, went to a farm where two French members of the Resistance had been hidden. Being unable to take them prisoner, these soldiers then took the proprietors of that farm, (the husband and wife), and after subjecting them to numerous atrocities (knifing, rape, et cetera) they shot them down with sub-machine guns. Then they took the son of these victims who was only three years of age, and, after having frightfully tortured him, they crucified him on the gate of the farmhouse."

We present Document 914 as Exhibit RF 426, Page 107 of your document book. This was a long recital of the murders committed without any cause whatever by the German Army in Rus Tronchet at Lyons. Page 109 at the end of the last paragraph. I now read:

"Without preliminary warning, without any effort having been made to verify the exact character of the situation and, if necessary, to seize those responsible for the act, the soldiers opened fire. A certain number of civilians, men and women and children, fell. Others who were untouched or only slightly wounded fled in haste."

On Page 110 or 111 the Tribunal will find the official testimony that was drawn up on the occasion of this murder. We submit without quoting, which we ask you to take judicial notice of, only the minutes relating to the crimes of the German Army committed in the region of Loches (Indre-et- Loire), Document F-617, placed before you as Exhibit RF 427 and on Page 115 of your document book.

Document F-607, submitted as Exhibit RF 428, which is on Page 119 of your document book, describes the looting, rape, and burnings at Saillan during the months of July and of August 1944. I quote the third paragraph:

"During their sojourn in the region - I mean the German soldiers - three rapes were committed against three women in that area."

I pass on to F-608, Page 120 of your document book, submitted as Exhibit RF 429: A person was burned alive at Puisots by a punitive expedition. This person was innocent. I present Document F-610 as Exhibit RF 430, Page 122 of your document book. The whole region of Vassieux in the Vercors is devastated. This Document, F-610, is a report by the Red Cross prepared prior to the liberation. Page 123 of your document book. I am quoting:

"We find in a farm a man wounded. He was struck by eight bullets under the following circumstances. The Germans forced him to set fire to his own house, and tried to prevent him from emerging by shooting at him with their pistols. In spite of his wounds he was miraculously able to escape."

We present Document F-618 as Exhibit RF 431, Page 124 of the document book, also Page 125, the next to the last line. I quote, concerning people who were executed:

"Before being shot these people were tortured. One of them, M. Francis Duperrier, had his arm broken and his face completely mutilated, and M. Perroud Plattet, had been completely disembowelled with a piece of sharp wood. His jaw bone was also crushed."

We present Document 605 as Exhibit RF 432, Page 126. This document relates and describes the burning of the hamlet, Des Plaines near Moutiers, in the Department of Savoy. I read at the beginning of the eighth line, and end of the second paragraph: "Two women, Mine. Romanet, 72 years old and her daughter, age 41, were burned in a small room of their dwelling, where they had sought refuge. In the same place a man, M. Charvaz, who had had his thigh shattered by a bullet, was found burnt to a cinder.

We now present as Exhibit RF 433, French Document F-298, Page 127, and the following, in your document book, which describes the destruction of Naille in the department of Indre-et-Loire. That area was entirely destroyed on 25 August 1944, and a large number of its inhabitants were killed or seriously wounded. This destruction and these crimes were motivated by no terrorist action, by no action of the French Forces of the Interior. We place before you Document F-907 as Exhibit RF-434, Page 132 and the following, in your document book. This document related to the crimes committed by the German Army at Montpezat-de- Quercy. This is a letter written to the French Delegation by the Bishop of Montauban, Monseigneur Theas, on 2 May. I quote the second paragraph of Page 132, " On 2 May 1944 under the pretext of combating the Maquis. . .

THE PRESIDENT: Can I see your document?

M. DUBOST: Yes.

THE PRESIDENT: M. Dubost, how do you make out this exhibit? It is not an official document, is it, in any shape or form?

M. DUBOST: Document F 673, Page 129 of your document book, refers to the events.

THE PRESIDENT: There is some other document, you mean?

M. DUBOST: Document F-907 really explains Document F-673, which is on Page 139 of the document book, and this document authenticates the letter by Monseigneur Theas, who is Bishop of Montauban. I wish to present that by referring to Document F-673 if the Tribunal is not disposed to grant sufficient credit to Document F-907.

THE PRESIDENT: I think that would be better.

M. DUBOST: F-673, submitted as Exhibit RF 392, Page 139 of your document book, related to the incident leading to crimes by the Germans at Montprezat-de-Quercy. . . Paragraph 1, Page 139, is a letter by the French Armistice Commission, and is extracted from the archives of the Armistice Commission in Wiesbaden.

"On the night of 6 or 7 June last, at the time of an operation in the region of Montpezat-de-Quercy, German troops set fire to four farmhouses which formed the hamlet called Perches. Three men, two women and two children, 14 and 4 years old, were burned alive. Two women and a child of ten disappeared, having suffered the same fate.

On Saturday, 10 June, having been shot at by two refractories in the village of Marsoulas, German troops killed these two men. Moreover, they massacred, without any explanation, all the other inhabitants of the village that they could lay their hands on.

Thus seven men, six women, and 14 children were killed, most of them still in their beds at the early hour when this happened.

On 10 June, at about 1900 hours, five Luftwaffe fliers attacked the town of Tarbes for half-an-hour with bombs and machine guns. Several buildings were destroyed, among them the Hotel des Ponts et Chaussdes, and the Academic Inspectorate. There were seven dead and about ten wounded who were naturally hit by chance among the population of the city.

On this occasion the general in command of the VS 659 at Tarbes immediately announced to the Prefect of the Department of Basses-Pyrenees that the operation had been neither provoked nor ordered by him.

Following each of these events the Prefect of the Region of Toulouse addressed to the General commanding the HVS. 564, letters in which, in dignified and measured terms he protested against the acts in question through which innocent women and children were deliberately put to death. He formulated quite accurately the opinion that under no circumstances could children in the cradle be considered as accomplices of the terror raids. He requested finally that instructions be given to avoid the recurrence of such painful scenes.

Answering in toto on 19 June, to the three letters of the Regional Prefect of Toulouse, the chief of staff of the general commanding the Principal General Staff Liaison 564 announced the principal position taken by his chief. This justified the acts of reprisal cited because of the following : The French population has the duty not only of fleeing from terrorists but also of rendering their operations impossible, which will avoid any reprisals against innocents.

In the struggle against terrorism the German Army must employ and will employ all means at its disposal, even methods of combat new in Western Europe.

The terroristic raids of the Anglo-Americans are now causing the massacre of thousands and thousands of innocent women and children in Germany. That their innocent blood has been shed is the guilt of the enemy, wherefore the German soldier is obliged to use his arms in the South of France.

I have the honour to ask you," concluded General Bridoux, who was with the German Commission "whether the French Government is to consider the arguments cited above as reflecting accurately the position taken by the German High Command, in view of the facts disclosed in the first part of the present letter."

We now place before you Document F-190, Exhibit RF-435, Page 141 of the document book, which describes the crimes committed at Aseq by a German unit, which, in reprisal for the destruction of the railway, massacred 77 men of all categories and all ages, among whom were 22 railway workers, employees, industrialists, business men and workmen. I quote the last part of the penultimate paragraph of Page 145:

"The oldest of these victims, M. Briet, retired, was 74 years old, born on 3 October, 1869, at Ascq. The youngest, Jean Roques, a student, son of the postmaster, was 15 years old, born on 4 January, 1929, at Saint Quentin. Father Gilleron, a priest of Ascq, and his two protegees, M. Averlon and sons, who had fled from the coastal area, were shot."

This massacre was the cause of a protest made by the French Government at that time, to which Commander-in-Chief von Rundstedt replied on 2 May 1944, Document F-673, which we have already placed before you. That is on Page 154; it was submitted as Exhibit RF 392. The reply of this superior officer of the German Army is the last paragraph of 154:

"The population of Aseq bears the responsibility for the consequences of its treacherous conduct, which I can only severely condemn."

General Berard, president of the French delegation attached to the German Armistice Commission, was not satisfied with the reply given by Rundstedt, and on 21 June, 1944 he reiterated the French protest, addressing it this time to General Vogl, president of the German Armistice Commission. This is F-673, Page 155, of your document book. I now quote the second paragraph of Page 155:

"In all, from 10 October 1943 to May 1944, more than 1200 persons were thus made victims of those measures of repression."

The last two lines of Page 155:

"These measures of repression strike innocents and cause terror to reign against the French population."

Page 157, next to the last paragraph:

"A great number of the acts that have been mentioned took place in the course of repressive operations directed against populations accused of having had relations with the Resistance. In such operations there was never any concern about discovering whether the people suspected of having rendered service to the Maquis were really guilty; and still less in this case, to ascertain whether these people had acted voluntarily or under duress. The number of innocent people executed is therefore considerable."

The last paragraph:

"The repressive operation in Dordogne of 26 March to 3 April 1944, and particularly the tragic incident of Ascq, which have already brought about the intervention of the French Government, are grievous examples: At Ascq specifically, 86 innocents paid with their lives for one attempt, which, according to my information, did not cause the death of a single German soldier."

End of paragraph 3, Page 158:

"Such acts can only stimulate the spirit of revolt in the adversaries of Germany, who after all are the only beneficiaries."

The reply of the Armistice Commission, Document F-707, submitted as Exhibit RF 436, is the rejection of General Berard's request. The document is before you. I do not think it is necessary for me to quote it.

General Berard, on 3 August, 1944, reiterated this protest. This is Document 673, already deposited before you, Page 160 and Page 162 in your document book. At the end of his protest he writes:

"An enemy who surrenders must not be killed even though he is a franc-tireur or a spy. The latter is to receive just punishment through legal procedure." But this is only the text of the German stipulations applying to domestic matters.

We place Document F-706, which becomes Exhibit RF 437, before the Tribunal; it is a note from the French State Secretary for Defence to the German general, a protest against measures of destruction taken by the German troops in Chaudebonne and Chavroches. We shall not read this document. The Tribunal may take judicial notice of it if it deems it necessary.

We now come to the statement of the events of Tulle in which 120 Frenchmen were killed, Page 169, paragraph 2. I am now quoting:

"On 7 June an important group of franc-tireurs attacked the French Forces for the maintenance of order and succeeded in seizing the greater part of the town of Tulle after a struggle which lasted until dawn."

On Page 170, first paragraph:

"The same day at about 2000 hours, important German armoured forces came to the assistance of the garrison and penetrated into the city from which the terrorists withdrew in haste."

Next to the last paragraph:

"These troops decided to exercise reprisals. The French Forces of the Interior that had taken the town had withdrawn. The Germans had taken no prisoners. The reprisals were exercised upon civilians. Without discrimination they were arrested." And I am now reading the next to last paragraph of Page 170.

"The victims were selected without any inquiry, without even any questioning, haphazardly; workmen, students, professors, industrialists. There were even among them some militia sympathisers and candidates for the Waffen SS. The 120 corpses which were hanged from the balconies and lamp-posts of the avenue of the station, along a distance of 500 metres, were a horrible spectacle and will remain in the memory of the unfortunate population of Tulle for a long time."

And the crowning event in these German atrocities - we now come to it will be the destruction of Orandour sur Glane, in the month of June 1944. The Tribunal will accept, we hope, the presentation of Document F-236, which now becomes Exhibit RF 438. This is a book, an official book, edited by the French Government, which gives a full description of the events. I shall give you a brief analysis of the report of the "de facto " government of the time, sent to the German general who was Commander-in-Chief for the Regions of the West.

"On Saturday, 10 June, beginning in the afternoon, a detachment of SS, belonging very likely to the "Das Reich " Division which was present in the area, burst into the village after having surrounded it entirely, and ordered the population to gather in the central square. It was then announced that a denunciation had indicated that explosives had been hidden in the village and that searches and verifications of identity were about to take place. The men were invited to group together in four or five units, each of which was locked into a barn. The women and children were led into and locked in the church. It was about 1400 hours. A little later machine-gunning began and the whole village was set on fire, as well as the surrounding farms. The houses were set on fire one by one. The operation lasted undoubtedly several hours, in view of the extent of the locality and the town.

In the meantime the women and the children were in anguish as they heard the echoes of the fire and of the shootings. At 1700 hours, German soldiers penetrated into the church and placed upon the communion table an asphyxiating apparatus which comprised a sort of box from which lighted fuses emerged: A little time shortly thereafter the atmosphere became unbreathable. Someone was able to break the door which brought the women and children back to consciousness. The German soldiers then started to shoot through the windows of the church, and they came in to finish off the survivors with machine guns. Then they spread upon the soil inflammable material. One woman was able to escape; she reached the window when the cries of a mother who tried to give her child to her, drew the attention of one of the guards, who fired on the would-be fugitive and wounded her seriously. She saved her life by simulating death and she was later cared for in a hospital of Limoges.

At about 1800 hours the German soldiers stopped the Departmental train which was passing in the vicinity. They told the passengers going to Oradour to get off, and, having machine-gunned them, threw their bodies in the furnace. At the end of the evening as well as the following Sunday morning, the inhabitants of the surrounding hamlets, alarmed by the fire and anguished because of the absence of their children who had been going to school at Oradour, attempted to approach, but they were either machine-gunned or driven away by force by German guards who were guarding the exits of the village. However, on the afternoon of Sunday some were able to come into the ruins, and they stated that the church was filled with the remains of women and children, all shrivelled up and calcinated.

An absolutely reliable witness was able to see the body of a woman holding her child in her arms at the entrance of the church and in front of the alter the body of a little child kneeling, and near the confessional the bodies of two children arm-in-arm.

During the night from Sunday to Monday the German troops returned and attempted to remove the traces by proceeding with the summary burial of the women and children outside the church.

The news of this tragedy spread through Limoges during the day of

Sunday, 11 June.

The general commanding the Verbindungsstab refused to grant any passes which were personally requested by the regional prefect, so that he himself and a delegate of the prefect could move about in the area. Only the sub-prefect of Rochechouart was able to go to Oradour and report to his chief on the following day that the village, which comprised 85 houses, was only a mass of ruins and that the greater part of the population, women and children included, had perished.

On Tuesday, 13 June, the regional prefect finally obtained authorisation to go there, and was able to proceed to the town, accompanied by the delegate prefect and the Bishop of Limoges. In the church, which was partly in ruins, there were still calcinated remains of children. Bones were mixed with the ashes of the woodwork. The ground was strewn with shells having the 'S.T.K.A.M.' brand upon them and there were numerous traces of bullets at a man's height.

Outside the church the soil was freshly disturbed, children's garments were piled up, half burned. Where the barns had stood could be seen completely calcinated human skeletons, heaped one on the other, partially covered with various clothes. They constituted a horrible sight."

The paragraph before the last :

"Although it is impossible to give the exact number of these victims, one can state that there were 800 to 1000 dead, among them many children who had been evacuated from regions threatened by bombardment. There do not seem to be more than ten survivors among the persons who were present in the village at the beginning of the afternoon of 10 June."

Such are the facts:

"I have the honour, General, of asking you," - General Bridoux speaking to his enemy - "to be good enough to communicate these facts to the German High Command in France. I strongly hope that he will bring them to the knowledge of the Government of the Reich, because of the political importance which they will have from their repercussion on the mind of the French population."

Since that time an inquiry was conducted, and you will find it in the book which has been placed before you. This inquiry has shown that no member of the French Forces of the Interior was in the village. There was none within several kilometres. It is even proved that the causes of the massacre of Oradour sur Glane were distant and remote. The unit which perpetrated this crime apparently did so as an act of vengeance, because of an attempt against it about 50 kilometres further away.

The German Army ordered a judicial inquiry. The Document F- 673, Page 175 and 176, so indicates. This document is dated 4 January, 1945. There were no Germans in France at that time, at least not in Oradour sur Glane. The version given by the German authority is that:

"The reprisals appear to be absolutely justified for military reasons.

The German military commander who was responsible for it fell in combat in Normandy."

These are the last four lines of paragraph 1 of Page 176: We recall the phrase "The reprisals appear to be justified for military reasons." Therefore, in the eyes of the German Army, the crime of Oradour sur Glane which I have described to you plainly, is a crime which is fully justified.

The guilt of Keitel in all these matters is certain.

In Document F-673, and this will be the end of my explanations, is a strange document which is signed by him. It was drafted on 5 March 1945. It concerns alleged executions, without trial, of French citizens. You will find it on Page 177. It will show the Tribunal the manner in which these criminal inquiries were conducted, on orders by the German Army, following incidents as grave as that of Oradour Sur Glane which had to be justified at any price. In this document, Page 177, which I should cite in its entirety, I wish only to look at the next to the last paragraph. It was in the interest of the Germans to answer these condemnations as promptly as possible.

THE PRESIDENT: This is not a document of which we can take judicial notice and therefore if you want to put the whole document in you must read it in.

M. DUBOST: You have already accepted it. This is F-673. It was placed before you as Exhibit RF 392, and this is the whole bundle of documents of the German Armistice Commission.

THE PRESIDENT: Yes, but is it a public document? It is not a public document, is it?

M. DUBOST: Am I to understand that the Tribunal wants me to read it in its entirety?

THE PRESIDENT: Well, F-673, seems to be a very large bundle of documents. That is right, is it not?

M. DUBOST: Yes, Sir.

THE PRESIDENT: This particular part of it, this document signed by Keitel, is a private document.

M. DUBOST: It is a document which comes from the German Armistice Commission in Wiesbaden, which was presented several hours ago and you did accept its being deposited before you.

THE PRESIDENT: I know we accepted its being deposited, but that does not mean that the whole of the document is in evidence. I mean, we have ruled over and over again that documents of which we do not take judicial notice must be read so that they will go through the interpreting system and will be interpreted into German to the German Counsel.

M. DUBOST: I am therefore going to give you the reading of the whole document.

THE PRESIDENT: Very well.

M. DUBOST: " The High Command of the Wehrmacht, Headquarters of the Fuehrer, 5 March 1945, No. 01487/45-g; by Captain Cartellieri.

Subject: Alleged executions without trial of French citizens.

1. German Armistice Commission.
2. High Command West.

In August 1944, the French Commission attached to the German Armistice Commission addressed a note to the latter, giving an exact statement of incidents concerning alleged arbitrary executions of Frenchmen from 9 to 20 January 1944.

The information given in the French note was for the most part so detailed that verification from the German side was undoubtedly possible.

On 26-9-1944, the High Command of the Wehrmacht entrusted the German Armistice Commission with the study of this affair. The said commission later requested High Command West for an inquiry on the incidents and an opinion on the facts submitted in the French note.

On 12 February 1945, the German Armistice Commission received from the Army

Group B (from the President of the Military Tribunal of Army Group B) a note stating that the documents referring to this affair were, since November 1944, with the Army Judge of Pz, AOK 6, and that Pz, AOK 6 and the Second SS Panzer Division "Das Reich" had in the meanwhile been detached from Army Group B.

The manner in which this affair was inquired into causes the following remarks to be made:

The French, and specifically the Vichy Government Delegation, have addressed to the German Wehrmacht the grave reproach of having carried out executions, unjustified by the laws of war, and therefore, murders, against citizens of France. It was in the interest of Germany to reply as promptly as possible to such charges. In the long period which has elapsed since the French note was prepared it should have been possible, even considering the evolution of military events and the movement of troops in relation to such events, to take at least part of these charges and to refute them by examination of the facts. If merely one fraction of the condemnation had been refuted," - this sentence is important - " if merely one fraction of these condemnations had been refuted, it would have been possible to show the French that all of their claims rested upon doubtful data. By the fact that in this matter nothing was done as far as the Germans were concerned, the enemy must have the impression that we are not in a position to answer these condemnations.

The study of this matter shows that very frequently there exists an utter lack of awareness of the importance of refuting all reproaches against the Wehrmacht and of acting against enemy propaganda and refuting alleged atrocities immediately.

The German Armistice Commission is hereby entrusted to continue the study of this matter with all energy. We ask that every assistance be given, especially at this time with respect to expediting this work within one's own jurisdiction. The fact that Pz. AOK 6 is no longer under High Command West is not an obstacle to obtaining the necessary information for the explanation and the refutation of the French charges."

THE PRESIDENT: M. Dubost, you stated, I think, that this document implicated Keitel.

M. DUBOST: It is signed by Keitel, sir.

THE PRESIDENT: Signed by him, yes, but how does it implicate him in the affair of Oradour?

M. DUBOST: Mr. President, the French Commission, together with the Vichy Government, frequently brought to the attention of the German Government not only the atrocities of Oradour but numerous other atrocities. Orders were given so that these facts, which constitute absolute reality, not merely in the eyes of the French, but in the eyes of all those who have objectively inquired into the problem, should be examined for the purpose of refuting part of the reproaches. This letter refers to the protest lodged earlier by the French, and we read part of it before you in the course of this examination of the problem, to be exact, the facts noted in the letter of General Bridoux which mentions the assassinations of Frenchmen at Marsoulas in the department of Haute-Garonne, among them fourteen children.

THE PRESIDENT: I think you said that that was the last document you were going to refer to?

M. DUBOST: It is the last document.

THE PRESIDENT: Ten minutes past five. Shall we adjourn? M. Dubost, could you let us know what subject is to be gone into tomorrow?

M. DUBOST: Crimes Against Humanity, by my colleague M. Faure. If you will allow me to present my conclusion this evening - I will not take long. Our work has been delayed somewhat this afternoon.

THE PRESIDENT: How long do you think you will take, M. Dubost, to make your concluding statement?

M. DUBOST: I think by five-thirty I shall be through.

THE PRESIDENT: I think perhaps, if it is as convenient to you, we had better hear you in the morning. Is it equally convenient to you?

M. DUBOST: I am at the orders of the Tribunal.

(The Tribunal adjourned until 1000 hours, 1st February 1946)

Forty-eighth day: Friday, 1st February, 1946

MARSHAL OF THE COURT: May it please the Court, I desire to announce that defendants Kaltenbrunner and Seyss-Inquart will be absent from this morning's session on account of illness.

M. DUBOST: I have now completed my presentation of facts. This presentation has consisted of a dry enumeration of crimes, atrocities, extortions of all sorts, which I deliberately presented to you without any embellishments of oratory, for the facts alone have a profound and sufficient eloquence. They are, so it seems to me, definitely established and I do not believe that either the defence or history, even German history, will be able to set aside their essential aspects, though they will, no doubt, be exposed to criticism.

Our evidence was hastily collected, in a ruined country, whose every means of communication had been destroyed by an enemy in flight, in a country where each individual was more concerned with preparation for the future than looking back upon the past, even to exact vengeance, for the future is the life of our children, and the past is but death and destruction.

For the whole of France, for each country in the West, the demands of daily life, the difficulty of preparing for a better future once again give full meaning to the words of the Scriptures, "Sinite mortuos sepelire mortuos" ("Let the dead bury their dead"); and that is why in spite of all our efforts, all our endeavours, to prepare the work of justice which France and universal conscience demand, we were not able to be more thorough. That is why errors of detail may have slipped into our work, but the corrections which time and the defence will effect can be but mere accessories. They will not eliminate the fact that millions of men have been deported, starved, exhausted through labour and privations before being butchered.

Corrections may affect circumstances of time, and sometimes of place - they will not change the essential facts even if a few details are modified.

But these facts having been established in their general aspect, it remains for us to complete our task by giving them juridical significance, by analysing them with reference to the law of which they constitute a violation, and by making clear the inculpations, - in other words, by fixing the responsibilities of each defendant in respect to that law.

What law shall we apply? Taken one by one and separated from the systematic policy which conceived, willed, and ordered them as a means of achieving domination through terror, and beyond that as a means of extermination pure and simple, these facts constitute crimes against common law as much as violations of the laws and usages of war and of International Law. All of them could therefore be defined separately as a violation of an International Convention and of a penal provision of one or another of our established domestic laws. All, rather, could be qualified as a violation of a rule of common law which has emerged from each of our own domestic laws, as shown by M. de Menthon in his address; of that common law which, in the last analysis, was designated by him as being the foundation, the root of international customs, and which, beyond the Charter itself, is and remains the one and only guide of your decisions.

But it is right to know that this common law springs from our elementary laws and, like them punishes in principle actual misdeeds. Now, all the defendants remained physically divorced from each of the criminal acts which in the ubiquity of their power they multiplied throughout the world. It was their will which commanded; but, as Mr. Justice Jackson recalled, they never reddened their own hands with blood of their victims. Therefore, if we refer exclusively to our positive jurisprudence, and specifically to French domestic laws the defendants could not, in any case, be considered as principal authors, but merely as accomplices who have provoked the act through abuse of authority or of power. All of that is indeed, a contradiction of the conception which each person in our countries holds of the guilt of the major war criminals. To solve the problem thus would be to narrow singularly the field of responsibility of each of the defendants. This responsibility would appear merely accessory, where, in fact it is the principal responsibility; it would appear fragmentary, whereas to be truly fixed it must be presented at one single time, in the whole of their thoughts, intentions and acts as chiefs of the Nazi government which conceived, willed, ordered or tolerated the development of that systematic policy of terror and extermination, of which each fact, taken separately is but a single aspect; merely a constituent element. Thus a simple reference to common law does not bring us close enough to reality. If it does not omit as such, any of the facts to which guilt attaches, it, does leave aside the psychological factor and does not give us a complete conception of the guilt of the accused in a single formula embracing all the reality. That is because common law expresses a certain status of common morality, which is accepted by civilised nations as law for the relations of citizens, between them. Profoundly imbued with the concept of individualism this common law is not adequate to meet the exigencies of collective life which international morality must govern. Furthermore, this common jurisprudence which is the foundation of our tradition, has become static in a Cartesian sense, whereas our custom remains enriched by all the dynamism of International Penal Law. The Charter has not fixed the manner in which we are to qualify in a juridical sense the facts which I have presented before you. In creating your Tribunal the authors of the Charter limited themselves to establishing the limits of your jurisdiction: War Crimes, Crimes against Humanity, Crimes against Peace; and even then they did not give an exhaustive definition of each of these crimes. Will the Tribunal refer on this point to Article 6, paragraphs B and C of the Charter of the Tribunal. This article merely gives an indicative enumeration. That is because the authors of the Charter bore in mind that Penal International Law is still only in the first phase of the birth of a custom, in which law is developed by reaction to the deed, and where the judge intervenes only to save the criminals from individual vengeance, or where law is applied by the judge alone and the penalty pronounced according to his sole judgement. Thus, the authors of the Charter abstained from giving us a fixed method of qualification, by reference to common law, or, on the contrary, to custom. They did not say to you:

"You will take one by one the criminal facts submitted to you, and each fact taken separately shall be isolated from the others to be defined by reference to a stipulation of any one domestic law or to a synthesis of internal law, yielding thus a common law."

Nor did they say to you:

"You will take these scattered criminal facts, you will group them together to make of them one single crime of which the definition respecting in a general sense the rules of common law, will be essentially determined by the sole intention or purpose sought, without attempting to seek, by analogy, any precedents in the different domestic laws which only apply, moreover, to an entirely different subject."

The authors of the Charter have left you free, entirely free within the limits of custom, and consequently we ourselves within the same limitations, are free to propose to you such qualification as appear to us to come closest to the reality of facts in their relation to the general principles of law, and the broad rules of morality which may seem to us to be such as to meet best the demands of human conscience expressed by international public opinion duly enlightened on Hitlerian atrocities, which will, in fact, remain within the limits of international penal custom. This custom is indeed still in a formulative stage, but if this trial is without precedent, the problems that are being examined in this court have arisen before, and the jurists who preceded us have already given them solutions. These solutions constitute precedents, and, as such, they constitute the first elements of your custom. In their memorandum to the Commission on the Responsibility of the Authors of the War and on Sanctions at the Peace Conference of 1919-20 the French jurists headed by M. Larnaude and M. Lapradelle wrote:

"Criminal law could not foresee that through a singular defiance of the essential laws of humanity, of civilisation, and of honour, an army, by virtue of the instructions of its sovereign, could systematically lend itself to the perpetration of acts, such as the enemy has not shrunk from, in order to achieve success and victory. Therefore, domestic criminal law has never before been able to make provisions for the repression of such acts. And still one must, in the interpretation of every law, cling to the intention of the law maker. If, in certain cases considered particularly propitious, one might succeed in apprehending individuals bearing responsibility of whom the Emperor could be considered an accomplice, one would only succeed, and not without difficulty, in narrowing the field of his responsibility by limiting it to a few precise cases. It is a very restricted approach to the problem of William II, to diminish it and reduce it to the proportions of a criminal or a court-martial case. The justice which an anxious world awaits would not be satisfied if the German Emperor were judged only as an accomplice or even as the author of a common law crime. His actions as Chief of State must be considered in conformity with their true juridical character."

But except for minor details all of this is indeed implicitly contained in the last paragraph of Article 6 of the Tribunal: 'Leaders, organisers, instigators and accomplices participating in the formulation or execution of a common plan or conspiracy to commit any of the foregoing crimes "Crimes against Peace, War Crimes, Crimes against Humanity -" are responsible for all acts performed by any persons in execution of such plan.

Fundamentally, all this is in strict conformity with the primordial German concept of "Fuehrertum", which places all responsibility on the leader and those who are with the leader, from the very start. Thus we can, by coming as close as possible to reality, by applying the Charter of 8 August and Article 6 of the Charter of your Tribunal, by respecting the rules of common law defined by the chief of our delegation, M. de Menthon, and by following international custom, which is sketched in the field of penal law, require of your Tribunal to declare that: all the defendants are guilty of having, in their role as the Chief Hitlerian leaders of the German people, conceived, willed, ordained or merely tolerated by their silence that assassinations or other inhuman acts should be systematically committed; that violent treatment should be systematically imposed on prisoners of war or civilians; and that devastations without justification should be systematically employed as a deliberate instrument for the accomplishment of their purpose of dominating Europe and the world through terrorism, and exterminating entire populations, in order to enlarge the living-space of the German people.

More specifically, we ask you to declare Goering, Keitel and Jodl guilty of having taken part in the execution of this plan by ordering the seizure and the execution of hostages in violation of Article 50 of the Hague Convention which prohibits collective sanctions and reprisals.

We ask you to find Keitel, Jodl, Kaltenbrunner, Seyss-Inquart, Bormann and Ribbentrop guilty of having taken part in the execution of this plan.

1. By ordering the assassination by terrorists of innocent civilians.

2. By ordering execution without trial and torture to death of members of the Resistance.

3. By ordering devastations without justification.

To declare Goering, Keitel, Jodl, Speer and Sauckel guilty of having taken part in the execution of this plan by jeopardising the health and the lives of prisoners of war, notably by submitting them to privations and harsh treatment, and by exposing them, or by attempting to expose them without necessity, to bombings or other risks of war.

To declare Goering, Keitel, Jodl, Kaltenbrunner and Bormann guilty of having taken part in the execution of this plan, by personally ordering or by provoking the formulation of orders leading to assassinations of terrorists or the lynching by the population of certain combatants; more specifically of airmen and members of commando groups as well as the terroristic assassination or slow extermination of certain categories of prisoners of war.

To declare Keitel guilty of having taken part in the execution of this plan by prescribing the deportation of innocent civilians and by applying to some of them the "N.N." (Nacht und Nebel) regime which marked them for extermination.

To declare Jodl guilty of having taken part in the execution of this plan by ordering the arrest, with a view to deportation, of the Jews of Denmark.

To declare Frank, Rosenberg, Streicher, von Schirach, Sauckel, Frick and Hess guilty of having taken part in the execution of this plan, by justifying the extermination of Jews or by working out a statute with a view to their extermination.

To declare Goering guilty of having taken part in the execution of this plan:

1. By creating concentration camps and by placing them under the control of the State Police for the purpose of ridding National Socialism of any opposition.

2. By tolerating and then by approving fatal physiological experiments on the effect of cold, and increasing or decreasing pressure; which experiments were carried out with material provided by the Luftwaffe and controlled by Prof. Rascher, medical officer of the Luftwaffe, detailed to the concentration camp of Dachau for that purpose, on healthy deportees who were involuntary subjects for the said experiments with which he (Goering) as chief associated himself.

3. By utilising a large number of internees in exhausting work under inhuman conditions in the armament factories of the Luftwaffe.

To find Speer guilty of having taken part in the execution of this plan by employing a large number of internees in exhausting work under inhuman conditions in the armament factories.

To find Bormann guilty of having taken part in the execution of this plan by participating in the extermination of internees in concentration camps.

With regard to Donitz, Raeder, von Papen, Neurath, Fritsche, Schacht and Funk, we associate ourselves with the conclusions of our British and American colleagues. And in connection with the acts above defined, we ask you further, in accordance with the stipulation of Article 9 of the Charter of your Tribunal, to find the OKW and the

OKH guilty of the execution of this plan by having ordered and participated in the deportation of innocent civilians from the occupied countries in the West.

To find the OKW, the OKH and the OKL guilty of the execution of this plan by participating in the setting-up of the doctrine of hostages as a means to terrorise, and by prescribing the seizure and execution of hostages in the countries of the West, by reducing to a degrading level the material living conditions of prisoners of war, by depriving the latter of the guarantees granted them by international custom and by positive International Law, by ordering or by tolerating the employment of prisoners of war in dangerous work or in work directly connected with military operations, by ordering the execution of escaped prisoners or prisoners attempting to escape, and numerous groups of commandos, and by giving the SS and SD directives for the extermination of airmen.

To find the OKL guilty of having participated in the execution of this plan:

1. By employing a large number of internees in concentration camps for exhaustive labour under inhuman conditions in the armament factories of the Luftwaffe.

2. By participating in fatal physiological experiments on the effect of cold, and increasing or decreasing pressure, which experiments were carried out for the benefit of the Luftwaffe and conducted by Dr. Rascher, medical officer of the Luftwaffe, attached to the concentration camp at Dachau.

To find the SS and SD guilty of the execution of this plan by having deported and participated in the deportation of innocent civilians from the occupied countries in the West and by having tortured them and exterminated them by every means in concentration camps.

To find the SA, the SS, the SD, and the Gestapo guilty of the execution of this plan by having given direct orders for the execution or the deportation, with a view to their slow extermination, of members of commando groups, airmen, escaped prisoners, those who refused to accept forced labour, or those who were rebellious to the Nazi order ; by forbidding any repression of acts of lynching committed by the German population on airmen brought down.

To find the SS, the SD and the Gestapo guilty of having tortured, and of having executed without trial members of the Resistance.

To find the same organisations, and, in addition, the OKW, and the OKH, in collusion with the SS, the SD, and the Gestapo, guilty of having committed or ordered massacres and devastations without justification.

To find the Gestapo guilty of having participated in the execution of this plan by the deportation of innocent civilians from the countries of the West and by the tortures and assassinations which were inflicted on them.

To find the government of the Reich (Reichsregierung) and the Leadership Corps of the National Socialist Party guilty of having, for the purpose of dominating Europe and the world, conceived, prepared and participated in the systematic extermination of innocent civilians from the occupied countries of the West through their deportation and their assassination in concentration camps.

To find the Leadership Corps of the National Socialist Party and the government of the Reich guilty of having, for the purpose of dominating Europe and the world through terrorism, systematically conceived and provoked tortures, summary executions, massacres and devastation without cause, as described above.

To find the Government of the Reich and the Leadership Corps of the Nazi Party guilty of having for the purpose of dominating Europe and the World, conceived, prepared and participated in the extermination of combatants who had surrendered, and in the demoralisation, extensive exploitation and extermination, of prisoners of war.

Such are the juridical qualifications of the facts which I have the honour of submitting to you. But a few lessons emerge from these facts. May the Tribunal permit me to state them in conclusion.

For hundreds of years, humanity has renounced the deportation of the vanquished, their enslavement and their annihilation through misery, through hunger, steel and fire. It is because a message of brotherhood had been given to the world, and the world could not entirely forget this message even in the midst of the horrors of war. From generation to generation we observed an upward effort ever since this message of peace had been given. We were confident that it was without any thought of going back that man had taken the road to moral progress which formed a part of the common heritage of civilised nations. All nations equally revered good faith in relations among individuals. All of them had come to accept good faith as the law of their mutual relationship. International morality was little by little emerging and international relationship, like that between individuals, was more and more falling in line with the three precepts of the classical Roman jurists, "honeste vivere, alterurn non lacdere, sum ouique tribuere." (Live honourably, inflict no harm on another, give each his due).

Every civilised nation had been impregnated with a common humanism, the growth of a long tradition, Christian and liberal. Based on this common heritage and achieved at the price of hard experience, each nation, enlightened by the well conceived interests of man, had understood, or was coming to understand, that in public as in private affairs, loyalty, moderation and mutual aid were golden rules which none could transgress indefinitely and with impunity.

The defeat, the catastrophe which has fallen upon Germany, confirm us in this thought and give only more meaning and more clarity to the solemn warning addressed to the American people by President Roosevelt in his address of 27 May 1940:

> "Although our Navy, our guns and our planes are the first line of defence, it is certain that at the back of all that there is the spirit and the morality of a free people which give to their material defence power, support and efficiency... "

And in this struggle, the echoes of which are still rumbling in our ears, it was indeed those who could rest their strength upon law, nourish their force with justice, who succeeded. But because we have followed step by step the development of the criminal madness of the defendants and the consequences of that madness throughout these last years, we must conclude that the patrimony of man, of which we are the heirs, is frail indeed; that all kinds of regressions are possible and that we must with care watch over this heritage. There is not a nation which, ill educated, badly led by evil masters, would not in the long run revert to the barbarity of the early ages.

This German people, whose military virtue we recognise, whose poets and musicians we love, whose concentration on work we admire, and who has given examples of probity in the most noble works of the spirit; this German people, which came rather late to civilisation, beginning only with the seventh century, had slowly raised itself to the ranks of nations possessing the oldest culture. The contributions to modern or contemporary thought seemed to prove that this conquest of the spirit was final - Kant, Goethe, and Johann Sebastian Bach belong to humanity just as much as Calvin, Dante or Shakespeare; nevertheless, we behold the fact that millions of innocent men have been exterminated on the very soil of this people, by men of this people, in execution of a common plan conceived by their leaders, and that this people made not a single effort to revolt.

This is what this people has come to because it had scorned the virtues of political freedom, of civic equality, of human fraternity. This is what it has come to, because it forgot that all men are born free and equal before the law; that the essential action of a State has for its purpose the deeper and deeper penetration of a respect for spiritual liberty and fraternal solidarity in social relations and in international institutions.

It allows itself to be robbed of its conscience and its very soul. Evil masters came who awakened its primitive passions and made possible the atrocities which I have described to you. In truth, the crime of these men is that they caused the German people to retrogress twelve centuries. Their crime is that they conceived and achieved, as an instrument of government, a policy of terrorism toward the whole of the subjugated nations and toward their own people; their crime is that they pursued as an end in itself a policy of extermination of entire categories of innocent citizens. That alone would suffice to determine capital punishment. Still, the French prosecution, represented by M. Faure, intends to present proof of a still greater crime, the crime of attempting to obliterate from the world certain ideas which are called liberty, independence, security of nations, which are also called faith in the given word and respect for the human person, the crime of having attempted to kill the very soul, the spirit of France and other occupied nations in the West. We consider that to be the gravest crime committed by these men, the gravest because it is written in the Scriptures, Matthew, XII, 31-32:

> "All manner of sin and blasphemy shall be forgiven unto men, but the blasphemy unto the Spirit shall not be forgiven unto men. Whosoever speakest against the Spirit shall not be forgiven, neither in this world, nor in the world to come. For the tree is known by its fruit. Race of vipers, how could ye speak good words when ye are evil ...."

THE PRESIDENT: Yes. M. Faure:

M. EDGAR FAURE: Mr. President, Honourable Judges: I have the honour of delivering to the Tribunal the concluding address of the French prosecution. This presentation relates more particularly to the sections lettered I and J of Count No. 3 of the Indictment: "Oath of Allegiance, and Germanisation:" and on the other hand to section B of Count No. 4, "Persecutions on Political, Racial and Religious Grounds."

First of all I should like to present in a brief introduction the general ideas which govern the plan of my final pleading. The concept of Germanisation has been stated in the presentation of M. de Menthon. It consists essentially in imposing upon the inhabitants of occupied territories forms for their political and social life such as the Nazis have determined according to their own doctrine and for their own profit. The combined activities which carried out Germanisation or which have Germanisation for their purpose, and which are illegal, have been defined as a criminal undertaking against humanity. The complete process of Germanisation was employed in certain territories, to annex them to the Reich. The Germans intended even before the end of the war to incorporate these territories within their own country. These territories, annexed and then Germanised in an absolute manner, are the Grand Duchy of Luxembourg, the Belgian cantons of Eupen, Malmedy and Moresnet, and the three French Departments of Haut-Rhin, Bas- Rhin and the Moselle.

These territories can be considered relatively small in comparison with the total area of territories occupied by the Germans.

This, in no wise, mitigates the reprehensible character of these annexations moreover, we should note at this point two essential aspects of our subject in the shape of two propositions.

The first proposition: The Germans had conceived and prepared more extensive annexations than those actually carried out in an official manner. For reasons of expediency, they did not proceed with these planned annexations during the time at their disposal.

The second proposition: Annexation, on the other hand, was not the unique or obligatory procedure of Germanisation. The Germans discovered that they could employ different and varied means to achieve their purpose of universal domination. The selection of means which vary according to circumstances, to attain and to camouflage an identical result, was characteristic of what has been called Nazi Machiavellism. Their conception is technically much more pliable, more clever and more dangerous than the classical conception of territorial conquest. In this respect, the most brutal competitor has over them the advantage of candour.

To begin with I say that the Germans had formulated the plan to annex more extensive territory. Numerous indications point to this. I would like to give you only two citations.

The first of these is taken from the documentation collected by our colleagues of the American prosecution, American documents which have not yet been submitted to the Tribunal. I should say in addition that in my final pleading I shall refer only twice to these very remarkable American documents. All the other documents which I shall submit will be new ones belonging to the French prosecution.

The document of which I speak now is 1155-PS of the American documents, and it appears in the file of documents submitted to you as Exhibit RF 601, which will become, may it please the Tribunal, that number in French documentation.

This document is dated Berlin, 20 June 1940. It bears the notation: "Secret General Staff Document." Its title is: "Note for the Dossier on the Conference of 19 June 1940. At Headquarters of General Field Marshal Goering."

The notes which are included in this document reflect, therefore, the views of the leaders, and not individual interpretations. I would like to read to the Tribunal only paragraph 6 of the document, which is to be found on Page 3. It is the first document:

> "General plans in regard to political development."
>
> "Luxembourg is to be annexed to the Reich. Norway is to become German. Alsace-Lorraine is to be re-incorporated into the Reich. An autonomous Breton State is to be created. Furthermore, considerations are pending concerning Belgium, the special treatment of the Flemish in that country, and the creation of a State of Burgundy."

The second citation which I shall submit to the Tribunal on this point refers to a French document which I submit as Exhibit RF 602. This document comprises the minutes of the interrogation of Dr. Globke, for some time assistant of the Secretary of State in the Ministry of the Interior, Dr. Stuckart. It is dated 25 September 1945. This interrogation was taken by Commandant Graf of the French Judiciary Service.

To the minutes has been added a memorandum which was delivered following the questioning by Dr. Globke. I read a passage from this interrogation, at the beginning of the document, paragraph 1.

"Questions: Have you any knowledge of plans which envisage the annexation of other French territories at the time of the conclusion of peace (Belfort, Nancy Bassin de Briey, the coal fields of the North, the so-called "Red Zone," territories attached to the Government General of Belgium)?

Answer: Yes, these plans did exist. They were worked out by Dr. Stuckart, upon the personal instruction of the Fuehrer, and I have seen them. They were communicated to the Ministry of Foreign Affairs, to the OKW and to the Armistice Commission in Wiesbaden. All these documents have been destroyed," (at least so said Dr. Globke). "The State Secretary Stuckart brought a preliminary project to the headquarters of the Fuehrer" (before the launching of the Russian campaign. End of 1940!)

After examination the Fuehrer thought that this project was too moderate, and he gave instructions that it should extend to other territories, specifically those along the Channel.

Dr. Stuckart then prepared a second draft, with a map attached, on which the approximate borders were indicated. I have seen it, and I can show it to you roughly on a large-scale map of France. I do not know whether this second plan was approved by Hitler."

I now read a passage from the memorandum, appended to the minutes just cited.

THE PRESIDENT: Did you tell us who Dr. Globke was?

M. FAURE: Yes, Mr. President, he was the assistant of Dr. Stuckart who was Secretary of State in the Ministry of the Interior. He styled himself in his interrogation "Officer in charge of matters. concerning Alsace-Lorraine and Luxembourg, in the Ministry of the Interior, since 1940."

I now read a passage from the attached memorandum. This appears in your document book immediately after the passage I have just read. Still under RF 602, I am now reading paragraph 6 of the memorandum in question; it is the beginning of the document before you.

> "The project of moving the Franco-German border was elaborated upon in the Ministry of Interior by the State Secretary von Stuckart, upon an order given him personally by Hitler. This plan envisaged that the territories in the North and the East of France which, for so-called historical or political, racial, geographical reasons or any other reason whatsoever, could be considered as not belonging to Western, but to Central Europe, were to be given back to Germany. A first draft was submitted to Hitler at his Headquarters and it was approved by him in full. Hitler nevertheless wanted an enlargement ..."

THE PRESIDENT: The typing of these documents has got mixed, because our copy of this part of the document after translation into English reads, "After examination, the Fuehrer found this project too moderate and ordered it to extend to other territories, notably to the length of the Channel." I think there must be a miscopying there, if what you read is right.

M. FAURE: I ask the Tribunal to excuse me. There is indeed a paragraph which has been, omitted. In the file which is entitled "Presentation," and which is before you the citation is reproduced in its entirety. If the Tribunal is willing -

THE PRESIDENT: Perhaps you could give us a corrected copy afterwards. If you continue your reading now, perhaps you could let the Tribunal have the corrected copy afterwards.

M. FAURE: I shall not fail to do that, Mr. President.

DR. STAHMER (Counsel for defendant Goering): The defence has not received these documents at all! Consequently, even today we are not in a position to follow the presentation. Above all, we are not in a position to check individually whether the formal suppositions for the validity of those documents really exist.

THE PRESIDENT: M. Faure, is that correct, that none of these documents have been deposited in the Defence Information Centre.

M. FAURE: They have been deposited, Mr. President. They were deposited with two photostat copies in the document centre of the defendants' counsel. Moreover, before I complete my statement, I am sure that the defence counsel will have all opportunity to study this very brief document and to make any observations which they may desire, but I can give you formal assurance that those documents were delivered.

THE PRESIDENT: What assurance can you give me that the orders which the Tribunal has given have been carried out?

M. FAURE: The documents have been delivered to the defence counsel in accordance with instructions and two photostat copies have been delivered in the document room of the defence. These documents are, moreover, in the German language, which should greatly facilitate the task of the defence counsel, as the interrogation was taken in the German language by an officer of the French Judiciary Services.

THE PRESIDENT: You have heard what M. Faure has said.

DR. STAHMER: I should certainly not raise any objections if these documents really were in our document room and at our disposal. This morning I and several others looked into the matter and made an effort to determine whether the documents were really there. We could not find out. Dr. Steinhauer and I went there; we could not find the documents. I shall go there again to see whether they may not have come in the meantime.

THE PRESIDENT: The Tribunal has stated on a variety of occasions that they attach a great importance to the documents being deposited in the defendants' Information Centre and copies supplied in accordance with the regulations which they have laid down. Whether that has been done on this occasion, is disputed by Dr. Stahmer. The Tribunal proposes therefore to have the matter investigated as soon as possible and to see exactly whether the rules have been carried out or not. And in future they hope that they will be carried out with the greatest strictness. In the meantime, I think it will be most convenient for you to continue.

M. FAURE: The defendants' counsel tells me that the documents are in the defence counsel room, but they have not yet been distributed. It can be seen, therefore, that the orders were fully respected, but because of the burden of work it may be that the defence may not individually have received these documents. In any event, I am prepared to submit immediately to the defence counsel mainly concerned with this, photostat copies which will enable them to follow my reading of the documents, which, incidentally, are quite brief.

THE PRESIDENT: Well, the Tribunal will have the facts investigated. And in the meantime, you can continue. The Marshal of the Court will immediately find out and report to the Tribunal what the facts are, about the deposition of the documents and the time at which they were deposited. In the meantime you can continue, and we shall be glad if you will assist the defendants' counsel by giving them any copies you may have available.

M. FAURE: I was referring, then, to Exhibit RF 602, the attached memorandum. - If the Tribunal wishes to follow the reading of this document will it kindly take the book entitled "Expose" or "Presentation," and turn to Page 6 thereof. The passage which I am now coming to is the last paragraph of Page 6.

THE PRESIDENT: Is this expose entitled "Luxembourg" or "Alsace-Lorraine"?

M. FAURE: It is entitled "Introduction."

THE PRESIDENT: Oh yes, the document entitled "Introduction" on the last page.

M. FAURE: Mr. President, you indicated to me a while ago that in the document book a sentence had been skipped. I was therefore asking you to take the file called "Expose" where this sentence is included, the same citation being reproduced in the two files in order to avoid the consequences of similar errors.

"Introduction-Espose," Page 6, third and last paragraph, I am continuing;

> "A first draft was submitted to Hitler at his headquarters and it was approved by him as a whole. Hitler, however, expressed his desire to see allocated to Germany parts of more extensive areas of territory, in particular along the Channel coast. The final draft was to serve as the basis for future discussions with the administrative departments of the Governments concerned. These discussions did not take place. The approximate outline of the frontier which was considered then started from the mouth of the Somme, went Eastward along the Northern edge of the Parisian Basin and Champagne, up to the Argonne, then curved to the South, crossing Burgundy, next Franche Comte, and finally reaching the Lake of Geneva. Various solutions were suggested for a few districts."

These German plans were indicated on several occasions by specific measures having to do with the territories in question, measures which might be designated pre-annexation measures.

I come now to the second proposition which I referred to a while ago. With or without annexation, the Germans had in mind to take and maintain under their domination all the occupied countries. As a matter of fact, their determination was to Germanise and to Nazify all of Western Europe and even the African Continent. This intention appears from the very fact of the conspiracy which has been laid bare so completely before the Tribunal by my colleagues of the American prosecution. It will also be shown by its applications the most important of which will be retraced in this concluding address.

I merely want to recall to the Tribunal this general point: that the plan for Germanic predominance is defined according to the German interpretation itself in a public diplomatic document, which is the Tripartite Pact of 27 September 1940 between Germany, Italy and Japan. In this connection I would like to quote before the Tribunal a few sentences of a comment made upon this treaty by an official German author, von Freytagh-Loringhoven, a member of the Reichstag, who wrote a book on German foreign policy from 1933 to 1941. This book was published in a French translation in Paris at the editing house of Sorlot, during the occupation.

I do not intend to submit this as a document, but merely as a quotation from a published work, a book, which is here in your hands. I am reading from Page 311:

> "This treaty granted to Germany and Italy a dominant position in the new European order, and it accorded Japan a similar role in the area of Eastern Asia."

I am now omitting a sentence that has no significance.

> "At first glance, one could realise that the Tripartite Pact had in mind a double purpose."

I shall omit the following sentence which is without interest, and I go to the sentence dealing with the second purpose:

> "Moreover, it entrusted the signatory parties with a mission for the future, that is to say, the establishment of a new order in Europe and in Eastern Asia."

> "Without seeking to lessen the importance of the first purpose, there can be no doubt that this second purpose, dealing with the future, involved vaster

projects and was, in fact, the principal one. For the first time in an international treaty, in the Tripartite Pact, the terms of "Space" and "Orientation" were used, linking one with the other."

I now go to Page 314 where the author makes a remark which appears to me to be significant:

"Now, the Tripartite Pact places a clear delimitation of the wider spaces created by nature on our globe. The concept of space, it is true, is employed explicitly only for the Far East, but it is clear that it is equally applicable to Europe and that within this conception Africa is comprised.

The latter - that is Africa - is certainly politically and economically a complement, or, if you like, an annex of Europe. Moreover, it is obvious that the Tripartite Pact fixes the limits of the two great regions or spaces reserved for the partners, that the Pact tacitly recognises the third area, that is Eurasia, properly speaking, and that it omits the fourth, the American Continent, thus leaving the latter to its own destiny. In this way the whole surface of the globe is included, and an idea which as yet had not been considered except in theory, is given the significance of a political principle derived from International Law."

I have felt that this text was of interest because, on the one hand, it clarifies the fact that the African Continent is itself included in the space reserved to the German claimants and, on the other, it states that the government of such an immense space by Germany constitutes International Law. This pretence of acting juridically is one of the characteristics of the undertaking to Germanise the world from 1940 to 1945. It is undoubtedly one of the reasons which inspired Nazi Germany to proceed only on rare occasions by the annexation of territories.

Annexation is not indispensable for the domination of a great area. It can be replaced by other methods which correspond rather accurately to the usual term of "vassalisation."

(A recess was taken)

M. FAURE: Mr. President: Before resuming my brief, I should like to ask the Tribunal if they could agree to hear, during the afternoon session, a witness M. Reuter, President of the Chamber of Luxembourg.

THE PRESIDENT: Certainly, M. Faure, if that is convenient to you, the Tribunal is quite willing to hear the witness you name.

M. FAURE: I propose then to have him heard at the beginning of the second part of the afternoon session.

Further I should like to point out in connection with Exhibit RF 602, that where a part of the text was missing in the document book, this is due to the fact that the page was affixed elsewhere, that is to say before the first page - I beg your pardon, but I must say the text was complete. However, it was not in its proper order. I shall subsequently put it in the dossier in its proper place.

I pointed out a moment ago that the different methods of disguised annexation can correspond to the term "vassalisation." From a German author I will borrow a formula which is eloquent. It is Dr. Sperl, in an article in the "Krakauer Zeitung," who used this expression: "A differentiation in methods of German domination." In using, thus, indirect and differentiated methods of domination, the Germans acted in political matters, as we have seen before, in the same way as they acted in economic matters. I had the opportunity to point out to the Tribunal, in my first brief, that the Germans immediately seized the keys of economic life. If you will permit me to use this Latin expression, I shall say as far as sovereignty in the occupied countries is concerned they insured for themselves the power of the keys, "potestas clavium"; they seized the keys of sovereignty in each country. In that fashion, without being obliged to abolish officially national sovereignty as in the case of annexation, they were able to control and direct the exercise of this sovereignty.

Beginning with these principle ideas, the plan of my brief was conceived as follows:

In the first chapter I shall examine the regime in annexed territories where national sovereignty was abolished. In a second chapter I shall examine the mechanism of the seizure of sovereignty for the benefit of the occupying power in the regions which were not annexed. Then it will be suitable to scrutinise the results of these usurpations of sovereignty and the violation of the rights of the population which resulted from them. I thought it necessary that I should group these results by dealing only with the principal ones in a third and fourth chapter.

The third chapter will be devoted to spiritual Germanisation, that is to the propaganda in the very extensive sense that the German concept gives to this term.

Chapter four and the last, will bear the heading, "The Administrative Organisation of Criminal Action."

I would now like to point out, as far as the documentation of my brief is concerned, I have forced myself to limit the number of texts which will be presented to the Tribunal and I shall attempt to make my quotations as short as possible. For the fourth chapter, for example, I might point out that the French Delegation examined more than two thousand documents, counting only the original German documents, and of these I have kept only about fifty.

I should like also to point out to the Tribunal how the documents will be presented in the document books which you have before you. The documents are numbered at the top of the page to the right; they are numbered in pencil and correspond to the order in which I will quote them. Each dossier has the pages numbered from one hundred onwards.

I would ask the Tribunal to now take up the document book entitled: "The Annexed Territories of Eupen, Malmedy and Moresnet."

In carrying out, without any attempt or cloak of legality, the annexation of occupied territories, Germany did something much more serious than violating the rules of war. It is the negation of the very idea of International Law. The lawyer, Bustamante Y Sirven, in his treaties on International Law expresses himself in the following terms regarding this subject:

"It can be observed that never have we alluded at any moment to the hypothesis that an occupation terminates because the occupying power takes possession of the occupied territory through his military forces and without any convention. The motive for this omission is very simple and very clear. Since conquest cannot be considered as a legitimate mode of acquisition, these results are uniquely the result of force and cannot be either determined or measured by the rules of law."

On the other hand, I have said just now that Germanisation did not necessarily imply annexation. Inversely, we might conceive that annexation did not necessarily mean Germanisation. We shall prove to the Tribunal that annexation was only a means, the most brutal one of Germanisation, that is to say, Nazification.

The annexation of the Belgian Cantons of Eupen, Malmedy and Moresnet, was made possible by a German law of 18 May 1940, and was the subject of an executive decree of 23 May 1940. These are public regulations which were published in the Reichsgesetzblatt, Pages 777 and 804. I should like to ask the Tribunal to take judicial notice of this.

As a result of this decree the three Belgian districts were attached to the province of the Rhineland district of Aachen.

A decree dated 24 September 1940 installed local German government and German municipal laws. A decree of 28 July 1940 introduced the German judicial system in these territories. Local courts were established in Malmedy, in Eupen and St. Vith and district courts at Aachen which could promulgate statutes for the local courts.

The Court of Appeal of Cologne replaced the Belgian Court of Cassation for cases where the latter would have been competent. German law was introduced in these territories by the decree of 23 May 1940, signed by Hitler, Goering, Frick and Lammers, and was effective as from September 1940.

A decree of 3 September 1940, regulates the details of the transition of Belgian law into German law, in the domains of private law, commercial law and law of procedure.

By the decree of annexation German nationality was conferred upon the inhabitants of German racial origin in Belgian territory. The details of this measure were specified and stipulated by the decree of 23 September 1941. All persons who had acquired Belgian nationality as a result of the ceding of these territories could, according to the terms of the decree, resume their German nationality, with the exception, however, of Jews and Gypsies.

All other inhabitants, on condition that they were racially German, could acquire German nationality, which might be revoked after ten years.

I shall not take up, at great length, the situation which resulted from the annexation of these Belgian territories, for the developments of the situation are analogous to those which we shall examine in the other countries. I simply would like to point out a special detail of this subject: A law of 4 February 1941, signed by Hitler, Goering, Frick and Lammers, granted the citizens of Eupen, Malmedy and Moresnet, representation in the Reichstag, that is to say, the benefits of the German parliamentary regime, the democratic character of which is known.

I shall ask the Tribunal now to take up the file entitled "Alsace and Lorraine." There is a file "Expose" and a file "Documents."

Contrary to what took place in the Belgian cantons the Germans did not officially proclaim by law the annexation of the three French departments which constitute Alsace and Lorraine. The very fact of this annexation, however, is in no way doubtful. I should like to remind the Tribunal here of extracts from a document which has already been submitted to it, which is Number 3 of the French documentation. It concerns a deposition made before the French High Court of Justice by the French Ambassador, Leon Noel, who was a member of the Armistice Delegation. I did not put this document in your book again because I will only cite one sentence from it. The document has already been submitted to the Tribunal, as I have just said.

Ambassador Noel, in this document, pointed out the conversations which he had at the time of the signing of the Armistice Convention with the German representatives, notably with the accused Keitel and Jodl. The sentence which I would like to remind the Tribunal of is as follows:

> " ... and likewise, in thinking of Alsace and Lorraine, I required them to say that the administrative and judicial authorities of the occupied territories would keep their positions and functions and would be able. to correspond freely with the government."

The affirmations are dated 22 June 1940.

I am now going to submit to the Tribunal a document of 3 September 1940, which is a note of protest of the French Delegation, addressed to the Armistice Commission. I submit this to the Tribunal in order that the Tribunal may see that during the period which elapsed between these two dates, a period which covers barely two months, the Nazis had already applied a series of measures which created, in an incontestable manner, a state of annexation.

This document which I submit bears the number 701 of the French documentation. It is the first document of the document book which the Tribunal has before it. All the documents in this chapter will bear numbers beginning with the number 7, that is to say, beginning with 701.

This document comes from the file of the French High Court of Justice and the copy submitted to the Tribunal has been certified by the clerk of this jurisdiction, I should like to quote from this document, beginning with the fourth paragraph on Page 1 of the Exhibit RF 701:

"1. Prefects, sub-prefects and mayors, as well as a number of local officials whose tendencies were considered suspicious, have been evicted from their respective offices.

2. Monseigneur Heintz, Bishop appointed under the Concordat to Metz, was driven from his diocese. Several members of the clergy, secular as well as regular, were also expelled, under the pretext that they were French in tongue and mentality.

3. Monsiegneur Ruch, the Bishop appointed under the Concordat to Strasbourg, was forbidden to enter his diocese and; consequently, to resume his ministry.

4. M. Joseph Burckel was appointed on 7 August, Gauleiter of Alsace. The first of these provinces." -

I ask the Tribunal's pardon: "M. Joseph Burckel, Gauleiter of Lorraine and M. Robert Wagner, Gauleiter of Alsace." I omit a line.

"the first of these provinces was attached to the Gau of Saar-Palatinate the second to the Gau of Baden.

5. Alsace and Lorraine were incorporated in the civil administration of Germany. The frontier and custom police were then placed on the Western limits of these territories.

6. The railroads were incorporated in the German network.

7. The post offices, telegraph and telephone administration was taken over by the German postal authorities, who gradually substituted for the Alsatian personnel their own personnel.

8. The French language was eliminated, not only in administrative life, but also from public use.

9. Names of localities were Germanised.

10. The racial legislation of Germany was introduced into the country and, as a result of this measure, the Jews were expelled, as well as nationals which the German authorities considered to be intruders.

11. Only those Alsatians and Lothringians, who agreed to consider themselves as being of German stock, were permitted to return to their homes.

12. The property of associations of a political character and of Jews was confiscated, as well as property acquired after 11 November 1918, by French

persons.

Nothing illustrates better the spirit which animates these measures, in themselves arbitrary, than the words pronounced publicly July 16, at Strasbourg, by M. Robert Wagner. Stressing the elimination which was taking place of all elements of foreign stock or nationality, this high official affirmed that the purpose of Germany was to settle once and for all the Alsatian question.

> "Such a policy, which could not be the function of subordinate occupational authorities, was equivalent to disguised annexation, and is strictly contrary to agreements subscribed to by Germany at Rethondes."

Numerous protests were subsequently addressed or lodged by the French delegation. We have attached to our file a list of these protests; there are 62 of them. This list is found in the book as Exhibit RF 702.

The development of the German policy may now be studied through three series of measures which were carried out.

(a) A group or body of measures destined to ensure the elimination of what can be called the French complex, that is to say, of everything which can bind an inhabitant of an annexed country to his way of life and to his national tradition.

(b) A body of measures destined to impose German standards in all domains of life of the population.

(c) The measures of transplantation and of colonisation. We use here the German terminology.

(a) Elimination of the French complex.

The elimination of French nationality and of French law automatically resulted from the measures which we shall study relative to the imposition of German standards.

I should like to point out particularly, that the Germans tried to fight against all elements of French organisation which might have survived the suppression of their national juridical conditions.

At first they prescribed, in an extraordinarily brutal way, the use of the French language. Several regulations were formulated relative to this. I shall cite only the third regulation, bearing the date of 16 August 1940, entitled, "Concerning the Reintroduction of the Mother Tongue." This document is published in the Journal of German Ordinances or Decrees of 1940, (Verordnungsblatt) at Page 2. It will become Exhibit RF 703. The Tribunal will find it in the document book after 702, which is the list of French protests. I should like to read a large part of this document, which is interesting, and I shall begin at the beginning.

> "Following the measures undertaken to reintroduce the mother tongue of the Alsatian people, I decree as follows:
>
> 1. Official Language.
>
> All public services or departments in Alsace, including administration of communities, of corporations within the meaning of civil law, public establishments, churches, and foundations, as well as tribunals, will exclusively use the German language, orally and in writing. The Alsatian population will exclusively use its German mother tongue in both oral and written applications to the above establishments."
>
> 2. Christian and Family Names.
>
> Christian names will be exclusively used in their German form orally and in writing, even when they have been inscribed in the French language on the birth register. As soon as this present decree comes into force, only German Christian names may be inscribed upon the birth register. Alsatians who bear

French Christian names, which do not exist in German form, are asked to apply for a change of their Christian names in order to show their attachment to Germanism. The same holds good for French family names." I omit the following page. "3. Social Reasons.

The enterprises and establishments having their seat in Alsace, trading, under a name which is entirely or partly French, must replace this trade name by a corresponding German designation by 15 September 1940, at the latest."

I shall omit the following sentence and go to paragraph 4:

"It is forbidden to draw up, in the French language, contracts and accounts under private seal, of whatever nature they may be. Anything printed on business paper and on forms must be drawn up in the German language. Books and 'accounts of all business firms, establishments and companies must be kept in the German language.

5. Inscriptions in Cemeteries.

In the future, inscriptions on crosses and on tombstones can only be written in the German language. This provision applies to new inscriptions as well as to the renewal of old ones."

These measures were accompanied by a Press campaign. Because of the resistance of the population, this campaign was carried on throughout the occupation.

I should like to make one citation of an article which is particularly significant, published in the "Dernieres Nouvelles de Strasbourg" on the 30 March 1943. This is not introduced as a document; it is merely a quotation of a published article. When we read this article, we think it at first a joke, but we see, subsequently, that it is quite serious, because actual reprisals are there extolled against people who sabotaged the German language.

I cite:

"Germans greet one another with ' Heil Hitler.' We do not want any more French greetings, which we still hear constantly in a thousand different forms. The elegant salutation 'Bonjour' is not made for the rough Alsatian throats, accustomed to the German tongue since the distant epoch of Osfried von Weissenburg. The Alsation hurts our ears when he says 'beschurr!' When he says 'Au Revoir', the French think they are listening to an Arabic word, which sounds like 'arwar.' Sometimes they say 'Adje ' (Adieu).

These phonetic monstrosities which disfigure our beautiful Alsatian Germanic dialect resemble a thistle in a flower bed. Let us weed them out! They are not worthy of Alsace. Do you believe feminine susceptibility is wounded by saying 'Frau' instead of 'Madame'? We are sure that Alsatians will drop the habit of linguistic whims so that the authorities will not have to use rigorous measures against saboteurs of the German language."

After this attack on the language, the National Socialists attack music. This is the purpose of a decree of 1st March 1941, signed by Dressler, the Chief of Administration for Alsace, Department of Public Enlightenment and Propaganda.

This is Exhibit RF 704, published in the German Official Journal (Verordnungsblatt) Page 170, of the year 1941. I shall cite only the title of this decree: "Concerning Undesirable and Unwholesome Music." The first lines are:

"Musical works contrary to the cultural will of National Socialists will be placed on a list of undesirable and unwholesome music, by the Department for Public Enlightenment and Propaganda."

After music, now, we have the question of headgear. In this regulation the ridiculous constantly disputes supremacy with the odious. I would almost like to ask the Tribunal to pardon me, but, truly, nothing in this is invented by us.

Here is Exhibit RF 705. It is a decree of December 13, 1941, published in the Official Bulletin of 1941, Page 744. It concerns the wearing of French berets (Basque: berets in Alsace).

I read only the first paragraph:

> "The wearing of French berets (Basque berets) is forbidden in Alsace. Under this prohibition are included all berets which by form or appearance resemble French berets."

I may add that any violation of this decree was punishable by fine or prison.

The leaders also undertook a long struggle against French flags which the inhabitants kept in their homes. I cite as an example Exhibit RF 706, a German administrative document which we found in the archives of the Gau Administration of Strasbourg. It is dated 19 February 1941. I read three paragraphs of this document.

> "The Gauleiter desires that through the organisation of Block and Zellenleiter (Section Heads) it be recommended to the Alsatian population that they unstitch French flags which they still have in their possession and use them in an adequate way for household needs.
>
> By the 1st of May next no French flag should be in private hands. This operation must be carried out in the following way. The Blockleiter (Section heads) will visit the houses one by one and recommend that the families use flags for household needs.
>
> It must also be pointed out that after the 1st of May next we will draw the proper conclusion concerning the attitude of proprietors or householders in whose homes we still find French flags in private hands."

The following document, submitted as Exhibit RF 707, is also an administrative memorandum on the same subject, dated Strasbourg, April 26, 1941, of which I should like to read only the last sentence:

> "If, after 1st June 1941, Alsatians still are found to have French flags in their possession, they will have to spend one year in a concentration camp."

The Nazis feared French influence to such a degree that they even took a special measure to prevent the coming to Alsace of French workers among the labourers brought into this territory for compulsory labour service. This is the purpose of a memorandum of the 7 September 1942 of the civil administration in Alsace, submitted as Exhibit RF 708, which was also found in the archives of the Gauleiteung of Strasbourg. I read the first few lines:

> "Given the general situation of the labour market, the Chief of the Civil Administration has decided that foreign labour from all European countries could, in the future, be used in Alsace. There is an exception, however, for French and Belgians, who cannot be employed in Alsace."

The German undertaking against the French sentiment of Alsatians.

THE PRESIDENT: The translation which came through to me was "must." It came through that the foreign workers of all countries of Europe must in the future, be used. The word is "pouvait." That does not mean "must," does it? It is "pouvait." Does that not mean "could?"

M. FAURE: "Could," according to necessity; the interesting aspect is that those who are French may not work there, even if labour is needed in Alsace.

The German undertaking against the French sentiments of the Alsatians found its complementary aspect in the attempt also to destroy anything which might be an indication of Alsace belonging to the Motherland, France. I shall cite one example in relation to this point. This is our Document RF 709.

It is a letter of the German Ambassador in Paris, May 7, 1941, which is reproduced in a memorandum of the General Delegation of the French Government, found in the archives of the government. I read this Document 709, which is short:

"The German Embassy has the honour to point out the following to the General Delegation of the French Government in occupied territory.

The German Embassy has been informed that in a series of reports on a theme concerning the Fatherland, a French radio station in the nonoccupied territory, on 16 or 17 April 1941, about 21 hours, is said to have made a broadcast about the village of Brumath."

As Brumath, near Strasbourg, is in a German language territory, the German Ambassador requests that they inform him if such a broadcast was actually made."

There exist numerous protests of this kind, which fortunately have often had an anecdotic character. We must now cite two especially serious cases, for they included assault, flagrant violations of sovereignty, and even crimes.

The first case concerns the seizure and profanation of the treasure of the cathedral of Strasbourg. I shall submit, concerning this subject, Exhibit RF 710, which is a letter of protest of 14 August 1943, written by General Berard, President of the French delegation of the Armistice Commission. I read the beginning of the letter and repeat that the date is 14 August 1943:

"Dear General,

From the beginning of the war, the treasure of Strasbourg Cathedral and the property of certain parishes of this diocese had been entrusted by Monseigneur Ruch, Bishop of Strasbourg, to the Beaux-Arts Department. This Department had put them in a safe place in the castles of Hautefort and of Bourdeilles in Dordogne, where they still were on the date of 20 May 1943.

The treasures and this property included in particular, the pontificalia reserved for the exclusive use of the Bishop, several of which were his personal property; the relics of saints; and vessels or objects for the performance of ceremonies.

After having sought on several occasions, but in vain, to obtain the consent of Monseigneur Ruch, the Ministerial Counsellor Kraft on the 20th of May, requested not only the prefect of Dordogne, but also the director of religious matters, for authority to remove the objects deposited. Faced with the refusal of these high officials, he declared that the repatriation to Alsace of the property of the Catholic Church would be entrusted to the Sicherheitspolizei.

As a result, at dawn on 21 May, the castles of Hautefort and Bourdeilles were entered and occupied by troops, despite the protests of the guardian. The sacred objects were placed in trucks and taken to an unknown destination.

This seizure, moreover, was extended to consecrated vases, vessels and ceremonial objects, and the relics of saints worshipped by the faithful. The seizure of these sacred objects by laymen not legally authorised, and the conditions under which the operation was carried out, aroused the emotion and unanimous reprobation of the faithful"

Relative to this document I would like to emphasise to the Tribunal one fact which we shall find frequently hereafter, and which is, in our opinion, very important in this trial. It is the constant collaboration of different or diverse German administrations. Thus, the Tribunal must through this document, see that Ministerial Counsellor Kraft, belonging to the civilian service dealing with national education, appeals to the police of the SS to obtain objects which he cannot obtain through his own efforts.

The second case which I would like to cite concerns the University of Strasbourg.

From the beginning of the war, the University of Strasbourg, which was one of the finest in France, had withdrawn to Clermont-Ferrand to continue its teaching there. After the occupation of Alsace, and since this occupation really meant annexation, it was not reinstated in Strasbourg but remained in its city of refuge. The Nazis expressed their great disapproval of this in numerous, threatening memoranda.

We would like to submit Exhibit RF 711 relative to this. In this we shall again come across the Ministerial Counsellor, Herbert Kraft, about whom I spoke in the preceding document. The document which is an original memorandum signed by Kraft, was found in the archives of the German Embassy.

In this memorandum, which is dated 4 July 1941, Counsellor Kraft expresses his disappointment at the result of steps which he had undertaken with the rector of the University of Strasbourg, M. Danjon.

I believe that it is adequate if I read a very short passage of this memorandum in order to show the insolence and the threatening methods which the Germans used, even in that part of France which was not yet occupied. The passage which I am going to read will be the last paragraph on page 2. Mr. Kraft relates the end of his conversation with the rector. I cite:

"I cut the conversation short, arose, and asked him if, by chance, the decisions of Admiral Darlan did not represent for him an order from his government. As I went out I added, 'I hope that they will arrest you.' He ran after me, made me repeat my remark, and as I went off he said to me, ironically, that it would be for him a great honour."

This document gives an amusing impression, but the matter as a whole was very serious.

The 15 June 1943, the German Embassy wrote a note which I submit as Exhibit RF 712. This is an extract from the archives of the High Court and has been certified by the clerk of that jurisdiction. Here is the text. I shall not read the beginning of it.

"The German Embassy feels that it is extremely desirable to find a solution of the affair of the University of Strasbourg at Clermont-Ferrand.

We would be happy to learn that no further publication would appear under the heading 'University of Strasbourg' so that new disagreements may not result from publications of that kind.

The German Embassy has taken note of the fact that the Ministry of National Education can no longer fill vacant professorial chairs.

We request that in the future no examination certificate mentioning 'University of Strasbourg' be awarded."

I must, in concluding this subject of the University of Strasbourg, point out to the Tribunal a fact which is notorious. On Thursday, 25 November 1943, the German police took possession of the buildings of the University of Strasbourg in Clermont-Ferrand, arrested the professors and students, screened them, and deported a great number of persons. During this operation, they even shot at two professors; one was killed and the other seriously wounded.

I will be able to produce a document relative to this, but I think that is not indispensable since there is not any proof for the prosecution that these murders were committed under orders which definitely show governmental responsibility.

THE PRESIDENT: M. Faure, did you say that you had or had not got proof of the facts that you have just stated about the seizure of the property of the university?

M. FAURE: I said just this, Mr. President: We consider that these facts are facts of public knowledge, because of the interpretation which was given by the Tribunal. I have considered that it would be better to prove it by a document. As this document was not added to my file at that time, it will be submitted as an appendix. I am going to read a passage of this document, but I should like to explain that it is not found in its proper place as I added it to the brief after the statement of the Tribunal the other day on the interpretation of facts of "public knowledge."

THE PRESIDENT: The Court will adjourn now.

Tomorrow being Saturday, the Tribunal will sit from 1000 o'clock in the morning until 0100 o'clock. We will then adjourn.

DR. KAUFFMANN (Counsel for the defendant Kaltenbrunner): It was said that this afternoon there will be a witness. I would like to ask that this testimony be postponed to another day. I believe that we have reached a so-called silent agreement that we will be notified in advance as to whether there will be witnesses and what the subject of their evidence will be.

I do not know whether there will be cross-examination, but the possibility exists, of course, and pertinent questions can only be put when we know, first of all, who the witness is to be, and secondly, what the subject will be on which the witness is to be cross-examined, just a clue perhaps.

THE PRESIDENT: The Tribunal does not think it is necessary to postpone the evidence of this witness. As a matter of courtesy on the part of the prosecution, it would be well, perhaps, that the subject matter - not necessarily the name, but the subject matter upon which the witness is to give evidence - should be communicated to the defence so that they may prepare themselves upon that subject matter for any cross-examination.

I understand that this afternoon you propose to call a witness who will deal with the circumstances in respect to the German occupation of Luxembourg. That is right, is it not?

M. FAURE: Yes, Mr. President.

THE PRESIDENT: Perhaps you will give the defendant's counsel the subject matter upon which they can prepare themselves for cross-examination. I am told that this subject matter has already been communicated to the defendants and is on their bulletin board at the present moment.

(A recess was taken)

MARSHAL OF THE COURT: May it please the Court, I desire to announce that the defendants Kaltenbrunner, Seyss-Inquart and Streicher will be absent from this afternoon's session on account of illness.

THE PRESIDENT: The question which was raised this morning about certain documents has been investigated, and the Tribunal understands that the documents were placed in the defence counsel's Information Centre yesterday, but it may be that the misunderstanding arose owing to those documents not having been in any way indexed, and it would, I think, be very helpful to the defence counsel if prosecuting counsel could, with the documents, deposit also some sort of index which would enable the defence counsel to find them.

M. FAURE: It is understood that we shall present a table of contents of the documents to the German defence.

THE PRESIDENT: I think if you could, yes.

M. FAURE: Your Honours, I was speaking this morning of the incident which occurred at the Strasbourg faculty in Clermont-Ferrand, on 25 November 1943. I pointed out to the Tribunal that I would produce to this a relevant document. This document has not been classified in the document book, and I shall ask the Tribunal to accept it as an annex number or as the last document of this book, if that is agreeable.

This is a report of M. Hoeppfher, Dean of the Faculty of Letters, established on the 8 January 1946, and transmitted from Lorraine to the French prosecution. I should like to read to the Tribunal, in order not to take up too much of its time, only the two passages which constitute the texts which were submitted to it as an appendix.

THE PRESIDENT: Have you the original document here?

M. FAURE: Yes.

"It is the 25 of November 1943, a Thursday. The 1000 o'clock class is drawing to an end. As I come out of the room, a student posted at a window in the hall makes a signal to me to approach and shows me in the inner court in front of the Department of Physics, a Wehrmacht soldier with helmet, boots, a submachine gun in his arm, mounting guard. 'Let us try to flee!' - Too late. At the same moment, wild cries arise from all directions - the corridors, the stairways are filled with the sound of heavy boots, the clanking of weapons, fierce cries, a frantic shuffling. A soldier rushes down the hall shouting 'Everybody to courtyard - tell the others.' Naturally, everyone understood."

Second passage:

"One of our people, Paul Collomp, was cold-bloodedly murdered with a shot in the chest, and an eye-witness confirms the fact. Alas, it is only too true. Asked to leave the Secretariat where he was alone, he was, no doubt, obeying too slowly to suit the policeman, for the latter gave him a violent blow on the back ; instinctively, our colleague turned around, and the other then fired a shot directly into his chest. Death was almost immediate, but the body was left there alone for some time. Another sound reached us. We did not know from where. A colleague in Protestant Theology, M. Eppel, was apparently also shot down, in his own house, where they had gone to look for him. He received, as was later learned, several bullet shots in the abdomen, but miraculously recovered and even survived the horrors of Buchenwald Camp."

As I indicated to the Tribunal this morning, I wish to say that the prosecution has no proof that such crimes were due to a German governmental order, but I believe that it is nevertheless interesting to advise the Tribunal of this last episode in the German undertakings against the University of Strasbourg, for the episode constitutes the sequel, and in a sense, the climax of the preceding incidents. We have seen, in fact, that German procedure began at first regularly, and that after these regular procedures, it reached the stage of recourse to the police. Brutality and violation accompanied this recourse.

I wish to advise you that this document which I have just read will be Exhibit RF 712b.

(b) A body of measures destined to impose German standards in all domains of life of the population.

The leaders of the Reich began by organising specifically German administration. I already indicated a while ago the appointment of Gauleiter as Heads of the civil administration. I continue on this point by submitting as Exhibit RF 713 the Ordinance of 28 August, 1940, German Official Journal 1940, Page 22. The Ordinance is entitled: "Concerning the Introduction of the German Regime in Alsace." I shall not read this Ordinance. I simply indicate that its object is put into effect, from 1st October 1940 on, the German municipal regime of 30 January 1935.

The text and the organisation show that the territories annexed were reorganised on the basis of German administrative concepts. At the head of each district (arrondisement) we no longer have a French sub-prefect but a Landkommissar, who has under his orders the different offices of Finance, Labour, School Inspection, Commerce, and Health. The large towns, the chief towns of arrondissements and even of cantons, were endowed with a Stadtkommissar instead of, and replacing, the mayors and elected counsellors, who had been got rid of.

The judiciary offices were attached to the court of appeals in Karlsruhe. The economic departments, and in particular the chambers of commerce, were run by the representatives of chambers of commerce of Karlsruhe for Alsace and of Saarbrucken for Moselle.

After having Germanised the forms of administrative activity, the Germans undertook to Germanise the staffs. They nominated numerous German officials to posts of authority. They attempted, moreover, on a number of occasions, to make the officials who had remained in office sign declarations of loyalty to the Germans. These attempts, however, met with a refusal from the officials. They were therefore renewed on a number of occasions in different forms. We have recovered from the archives of the Gauleiter of Strasbourg eight or ten different formulas for these declarations of loyalty. I shall produce one of these for the Tribunal, by way of example.

This will be Exhibit RF 714. It is the formula for the new declaration which the officials are obliged to sign if they wish to retain their position:

> "Name and first name, grade and service, residence. I have been employed from ..... 1940 to this date in the public service of the German administration in Alsace. During this period I have had, from my own observation as well as from the Party and the authorities, verbally and in writing, occasion to learn the obligations of a German official and the requirements which are exacted of him from a political and ideological point of view. I approve these obligations and these requirements without reservation and am resolved to be ruled by them in my personal and professional life. I affirm my adherence to the German people and to the National Socialist ideals of Adolf Hitler."

Together with the administration proper, the Nazis set up in Alsace the parallel administration of the National Socialist Party, as well as that of the Arbeitsfront, which was the sole labour organisation.

German currency legislation was introduced in Alsace on 19 October and in Lorraine on 25 October 1940. The Reichsmark became thenceforth the legal means of payment in the annexed territory. The German judiciary organisation was introduced by a series of successive measures leading up to the decree of 30 September 1941 concerning the simplification of the judiciary organisation in Alsace. I produce this ordinance as Exhibit RF 715, without reading it.

In regard to the teaching system, the German authorities established a series of regulations and ordinances which were aimed at assuring the unification of the Alsatian school system with the German teaching system. I shall merely mention the dates of the principal texts, which we produce as documents, and which are of a public nature, since they were all published in the Official Journal in Germany.

Here are the main texts:

Exhibit RF 717, regulation of 2 October, 1940.

Exhibit RF 718, ordinance of 24 March, 1941 on elementary teaching in Alsace.

Exhibit RF 719, ordinance of 21 April, 1941, concerning the allocation of subsidies in Alsace.

Exhibit RF 720, ordinance of 11 June, 1941, on obligatory education in Alsace.

I now quote a series of measures regarding the introduction in Alsace and Lorraine of German civil law, German criminal law, and even, procedure. I shall quote as the most important, as Exhibit RF 721, the ordinance of 19 June 1941 concerning the application of the provisions of German legislation to Alsatians. I should like to read the first paragraph of Article I because it contains an interesting item

"Para. 1.

The law in force in pre-1938 Germany shall be deemed to be the domiciliary law (Heimatrecht) governing the legal relationships of persons who acquired French citizenship under the Appendix to Articles 51-79 of the Versailles Dictate (or those who derive their nationality from such person), in particular in the domain of personal and family law, and in so far as the law of pre-1938 Germany declares the statutes of the country of domicile (Heimatstaat) to be applicable."

A similar ordinance was drawn up for Lorraine - Exhibit RF 722, ordinance of 15 September, 1941 concerning the application of German legislation to personal and family status in Lorraine. German Official Bulletin, Page 817.

I should like to quote, indicating the titles and the references, the principal measures which have been introduced in penal matters.

Exhibit RF 723, notice of 14 February 1941, relative to the penal dispositions declared applicable in Lorraine by virtue of Section I of the second ordinance concerning certain transitory measures in the domain of justice.

Exhibit RF 724, ordinance of 29 October 1941 relative to the introduction into Alsace of the German legislation of penal procedure and of other penal laws.

Exhibit RF 725, ordinance of 30 January 1942 relative to the introduction into Alsace of the German penal code and other penal laws.

I do not wish to read the long text, but I should like to draw the attention of the Tribunal to two features which show that the Germans introduced into Alsace the most extraordinary provisions of their penal law, conceived from the point of view of the National Socialist regime. The Tribunal will thus see in this Exhibit RF 725, Page 1 under No. 6 of the enumeration, that the law of 20 December 1934, repressing perfidious attacks directed against the State and the Party and protecting Party uniforms and insignia, was introduced into Alsace, as well as the ordinance of 25 November 1939-under No. 11 of the enumeration - completing, the penal provisions relating to the protection of the military power of the German people.

As concerns public freedom, the Germans eliminated from the beginning the right of association, and they dissolved all existing associations. They intended to leave free room for the Nazi system, which was to be the only and obligatory association.

I shall quote in the same way a number of documents, with the titles of these public texts. I give them their exhibit numbers:

Exhibit RF 726, regulation of 16 August 1940, dissolving the youth organisations in Alsace.

Exhibit RF 727, regulation of 22 August 1940, setting up a supervising commissariat for associations in Lorraine.

Exhibit RF 728, regulation of 3 September 1940, providing for the dissolution of teachers' unions. I point out in regard to this document 728, that the last article provides an exception in favour of the organisation called "Union of National Socialist Teachers."

Exhibit RF 729, regulation of 3 September 1940, providing for the dissolution of gymnastic societies and of sports associations in Alsace.

I should like to read Article 4 of 729:

"My commissar of Physical Culture will take, in regard to other gymnastic societies and sports associations in Alsace, all necessary provisions in view of their integration into the Reich's National Socialist Union for Physical Culture."

Following up these measures of Germanisation, we now encounter two texts which are very characteristic, and which I produce as Exhibits RF 730 and 731. Of 730 I read only the title, which is significant:

"Ordinance of 7 February 1942 relative to the creation of an Office of Genealogical Research of the Upper Rhine."

I shall likewise read the title of Exhibit RF 731: "Regulation of 17 February 1942 concerning the creation of the Department of the Reichskommissar for the Strengthening of Germanism."

I indicated a moment ago to the Tribunal that the Party had been established in Alsace and in Lorraine in a way that was parallel with the administration in Germany. I shall produce in this connection Exhibit RF 732, which is a confidential note of the National Socialist Workers Party of the province of Baden, dated Strasbourg, 5 March 1942. This document belongs likewise to the series found in the files of the Gauleiter of Strasbourg. It bears as a heading, "Gaudirektion - Auxiliary Bureau of Strasbourg."

If it pleases the Tribunal, I shall read the beginning of it:

"Evaluation of possible adherence to the Party, to its subdivisions and related groups in Alsace.

In the framework of the drive of '19 June,' organised for the recruiting of Party members, the Kreisleiter, in collaboration with the Ortsgruppen-leiter, is to establish which Alsatians over the age of 18, even if their membership has not yet been effected within the framework of the drive, are to be considered as future members of the Party, its subdivisions, and affiliated groups; and also the men between the ages of 17 and 48 who may be actively employed in the Party or in its subdivisions. These evaluations are equally to include, in order that we may soon obtain a numerical estimate, persons already enrolled in the Party, in the Opferring - this is the collecting organisation for the Party - its subdivisions and affiliated groups.

The Kreisleiter may call upon the collaboration of the Kreisorganisationsleiter" - these are the organising directors of the sections- "and of the Kreispersonalamtsleiter" - the personnel information offices of the sections - "The '19th June' drive, organised with a view to recruiting members, must not because of this become a secondary matter, but must be carried on, by all possible means, toward the purpose indicated by the Director of the Gau, and must be concluded at the date specified.

The results of the investigation of the population are to be compiled in five lists, namely:

List 1a

List 1b

List 2a
List 2b
Control list."

I shall omit the following paragraphs, which are a bit long and purely administrative, and I shall continue on Page 2 of the document, paragraph 9:

"The objective of the National Socialist movement being that of putting all Germans into a National Socialist organisation in order to be able to influence and to lead them according to the design of the movement, it will be necessary to feature on List I (a) and (b) 2 (a) and (b), ninety per cent of the population, and on the control list solely those who shall have been considered unworthy of belonging to an organisation led or supported by the Party; namely, persons of inferior race or Germanophobes."

I shall now enter upon two most serious questions which are directly interconnected, questions which, on the one hand, concern nationality, and, on the other hand, military recruiting.

The German policy in the matter of nationality reveals a certain hesitation, which is related to the German policy in regard to military recruiting. Indeed the German leaders seem to have been swayed by two contradictory trends. One of these trends was that of bestowing the German nationality on a large number of people, in order to impose the corresponding obligation for military service. The other trend was that of conferring nationality only with discrimination. According to this viewpoint, it was considered, first of all, that the possession of nationality was an honour and should to some extent constitute a reward when conferred on those who had not previously possessed it. On the other hand, nationality confers on its possessor a certain special quality. In spite of the abolition of all democracy, it gives that person a certain influence in the German community. It should, therefore, be granted only to persons who give guarantees in certain regards: notably that of loyalty (and we know that from the German point of view, loyalty is not only a matter of mental attitude and choice, but that it also applies to certain well-known physical elements, such as those of blood, race and origin).

These are the two opposed trends in the German policy of conferring nationality. This is how they develop:

At first - and up to the month of August 1942 - the Reich, not yet requiring soldiers as urgently as it did later, deferred the introduction of compulsory recruiting. Along with this, they also deferred any action to impose German nationality on the population generally. During this earlier period, the Nazis did not resort to compulsory recruiting, but relied simply on voluntary recruiting, which, however, they tried to render more effective by offering all kinds of inducements and exercising pressure in various ways.

I shall not go into details regarding these German procedures for voluntary recruitment. I should like simply to give, by way of example, the subject matter of Exhibit RF 733. It is an appeal posted in Alsace on the 15 of January 1942 and constitutes one of the appendices of the governmental report, which was submitted under Document UK 72. In this document, I shall read only the first sentence of the second paragraph:

"Alsatians: Since the beginning of the campaign in the East, hundreds of Alsatians have freely decided to march as volunteers, side by side with the men of the other German regions against the enemy of civilisation and European culture," etc.

For anyone who knows German propaganda and its technique of exaggeration, the term "Hundreds" which is used in this document immediately betrays the failure of the Nazi recruiters. "Hundreds " may obviously be translated by "tens," and it must be admitted that this was a very poor supply for the Wehrmacht.

During the period that I am speaking of, the Nazis practised, in regard to nationality, a policy similar to their policy in recruiting military forces, i.e. a policy of nationalisation by choice. They appealed for volunteers for German nationality. It is desirable to quote in this regard an ordinance of 20 January 1942, a general ordinance of the Reich, not a special one for the annexed territories.

This ordinance, in its first article, increases the possibilities of naturalisation which until then had been extremely limited, in accordance with the Reich statute book. In Article 3 it gives the following provision: (This ordinance is not produced in the document book, for it is an ordinance of the German Reich, and, therefore, a public document.)

> "The Reich Minister of the Interior may, by means of a general regulation, grant German nationality to categories of foreigners established on a territory placed under the sovereign power of Germany or having their origin in such territory."

In connection with this earlier period, it is necessary to stress that natives of Alsace-Lorraine who did not become German citizens did not retain their French nationality either. They are all considered as German subjects. They are qualified in the documents of the period as "members of the German community (Volksdeutsch)" and are consequently liable for German labour service. I submit Exhibit RF 734 in this connection, "Regulation of 27 August 1932, on compulsory military service and on labour service in Alsace." I shall return to this document presently with regard to military service, but I would like to quote now the passage relating to service in the Hitler Youth - one of which bears an earlier date - the ordinance of 2 January 1942 for Alsace, and ordinance of 4 August 1942 for Lorraine.

The German policy regarding nationality and military recruiting reaches its turning point in the month of August 1942. At this moment, on account of military difficulties and the need for extensive recruiting, the Germans instituted compulsory military service in Lorraine by an ordinance of 19 August, 1942, and in Alsace by an ordinance of 25 August 1942. These two ordinances, relative to the introduction of compulsory military service, constitute Exhibit RF 735, ordinance for Lorraine, and Exhibit RF 736, ordinance for Alsace. At the same time, the Germans promulgated an ordinance of 23 August 1942 on German nationality in Alsace, Lorraine and Luxembourg. This text is the subject of a circular issued by the Reich Minister of the Interior, which constitutes Exhibit RF 737. I should like simply to summarise for the Tribunal the provisions of the various texts, which it would take too long to read. These provisions are the following:

Full rights of nationality are acquired by natives of Alsace and Lorraine and Luxembourgers in the following cases:

Firstly, when they have been or will be called upon to serve in the armed forces of the Reich or in SS armed formations; secondly, when they are recognised as having acted as good Germans.

As concerns the expression "of German origin," which is used in these texts, this concerns Alsatians and Lorrainians who have become French either through the Treaty of Versailles or subsequently, on condition of having previously been German nationals, or having transferred their domicile from Alsace or Lorraine to the territory of the Reich after 1st September 1939; and finally, children, grandchildren, and wives of the preceding categories of persons are likewise considered as of German origin.

Lastly, it was anticipated that the Alsatians, Lorrainians and Luxembourgers who did not acquire German nationality absolutely could obtain it provisionally.

I should like to mention, to complete this question of nationality, that an ordinance of the 2 February 1943 gave details as to the German nationality laws applicable in Alsace, and that an ordinance of the 2 November 1943 likewise conferred German nationality upon persons who had been in concentration camps during the war.

The German texts indicate that, on the one hand, German nationality was imposed upon a great number of persons; and, on the other hand, that Alsatian and Lothringians who were French were forced to comply with the exorbitant and truly criminal requirements of military service in the German Army against their own country. These military obligations were constantly extended by the calling-up of successive classes, as far as the 1908 class.

These German exigencies provoked a solemn protest on the part of the French National Committee, which in London represented the Free French government authority. I should like to read to the Tribunal the text of this protest, which is dated 16 September 1942, and which I submit as Exhibit RF 739. I shall merely read the three paragraphs of the official protest, which constitute the beginning of this document of the Information Agency in London.

> "After having proclaimed, in the course of the war, the annexation of Alsace and Lorraine, banished and robbed a great number of the inhabitants and enforced the most rigorous measures of Germanisation, the Reich now constrains Alsatians and Lothringians, declared German by the Reich, to serve in the German Armies against their own compatriots and against the allies of France.
>
> The National Committee, defender of the integrity and of the unity of France, and trustee of the principle of the rights of peoples, protests, in the face of the civilised world, against these new crimes committed in contempt of international conventions against the will of populations ardently attached to France. It proclaims as inviolable the right of Alsatians and of Lorrainians to remain members of the French family."

This protest could not have been unknown to the Germans, for it was read and commented on over the radio by the French National Commissioner of Justice, Professor Fene Cassin, on a number of occasions.

In regard to this solemn protest on the part of France, I shall allow myself to quote the "justification," if one may use this term, which was furnished in a speech by Gauleiter Wagner delivered in Colmar on 20 June, 1943.

This quotation is drawn from the Muehlhaeuser Tageblatt of 21 June 1943. In view of its importance I shall not deal with it simply as a quotation, but I produce it as a document and submit it as Exhibit RF 740. The clerk has been given this paper. I read the "explanations" of Gauleiter Wagner, as they are reproduced in this newspaper under the title " Alsace will not Stand Aloof":

> "The decisive event for Alsace in 1942 was thus the introduction of compulsory military service. It cannot be my intention to justify from the juridical point of view, a measure which strikes so deeply at the life of Alsace. There is no need for such a justification. Every decision which here touches the Greater German Reich has a motive and cannot be attacked as to its juridical and its *defacto* form."

Naturally, the Alsatians and Lorrainians refused to accept the criminal orders of the German authorities, and they undertook to avoid these by every means. The Nazis then decided to compel them by means of merciless measures. The frontiers were strictly guarded, and the guards had orders to fire on the numerous recalcitrants who attempted to escape across the border. I should like to quote in this connection a sentence from a newspaper article which appeared in the Dernieres Nouvelles de Strasbourg of 28 August 1942. This will become Exhibit RF 741. This article deals with the death of one of these men who refused to serve in the German Army, and it concludes with the following sentence: "We insist most particularly on the fact that it is suicidal to attempt to cross the frontier illegally."

Naturally, judicial penalties were applied with great severity in a large number of cases. I do not consider that I should bring to the Tribunal instances of all these cases, for that would take too long, but I should like just to insist on the principle that governed this form of repression.

I shall quote first of all a document which is entirely characteristic of the conception which the German administration had of justice and of the independence of judicial power. This is submitted as Exhibit RF 742. It is a part of a series of documents discovered in the files of the Gauleitung, It is a teletype message dated Strasbourg, June 1944, addressed by Gauleiter Wagner to the Chief of the Court of Appeals in Karlsruhe. I shall read paragraph 2, Page 1:

"It is particularly necessary in Alsace that the penalties pronounced against those who refuse to do military service shall produce the effect of intimidation, but the effect of intimidation upon those who are recalcitrant through the fear of personal danger can only be achieved by the death penalty. All the more so, as an Alsatian who emigrates with the intention of escaping military service generally counts on an early coming victory for the enemy powers and, in the case of conviction and consequent loss of freedom, on the very early cancellation of the penalty. Consequently, in the case of all attempts at illegal emigration to escape military service after 6 June 1944, apart from any other judicial proceeding in force in the old Reich, the death penalty must be applied as the only penalty provided."

But I wish to indicate that the consideration of personal risk, however great, even that of being killed at the frontier or condemned to death, was not sufficient to make the people of Alsace and Lorraine acknowledge the obligation for military service. Thus the Nazis decided to have recourse to the only threat which could be effective - the threat of reprisals against families. On 4 September 1942, there appeared in the Dernieres Nouvelles de Strasbourg a notice entitled "Severe Sanctions against those who fail to Appear before the Revision Council" An extract from this notice will be submitted as Exhibit RF 743. I shall read from it:

"In the cases mentioned above it has been shown that parents have not given proof of authority in this regard. They have thus proved that they do not yet understand the requirements of the present time, which can tolerate in Alsace only reliable persons. The parents of the above named young men will therefore shortly be deported to the Altreich in order to re-acquire in a National Socialist atmosphere an attitude in conformity with the German spirit."

Thus the deportation of families was decreed, not to punish a definite insubordination, but to punish failure to appear before the recruiting board.

In order to avoid repeated readings, I shall now present to the Tribunal as Exhibit RF 744, the ordinance of 1st October 1943, to check failure to perform military service (Official Bulletin for 1943, Page 152). I shall read the first two articles:

"Article 1: The chief of the civil administration in Alsace may refuse the right of residence in Alsace to deserters and to persons who fail to fulfil their military obligations or those of the compulsory labour service, as well as to members of their families. This prohibition entails, for persons of German origin whom it may effect, transplantation to Reich territory by the delegate of the Reichsfuehrer of the SS, Reich commissioner for the strengthening of Germanism. Measures to be taken in regard to property, seizure, indemnity, etc. are prescribed in the ordinance of 2 February 1943, concerning property measures to be applied in the case of persons of German origin transferred from Alsace to Reich territory.

Article 2. Independently of the preceding measures, proceedings may be instituted under the penal code for violation of the provisions of the penal laws."

THE PRESIDENT: Exactly what did "German origin" mean? How far did it go?

M. FAURE: The term "Souche Allemande", German origin, applies, as indicated in connection with the preceding text, to the following categories of persons: In the first place, persons who were in Alsace and Lorraine before the Treaty of Versailles and who became French through the Treaty. In the second place, persons whose nationality before 1919 was German, are considered as of German origin, as well as their children, their grandchildren, and their spouses. This affects the great majority of the population of the three departments.

I continue reading paragraph 2 of Article 1:

"Independently of the foregoing measures, penal prosecutions may be brought for violation of the provisions of the penal laws."

According to Article 52, paragraph 2, of the Reich Penal Code, members of the family who bring proof of their genuine efforts to prevent or dissuade the fugitive from committing his act, or avoiding the necessity of flight, shall not be punishable.

These abominable measures - compulsory denunciation, punishment inflicted upon families - permitted the German authorities to carry out the enlistment of Alsatians and Lorrainians, which for many of them had fatal consequences, and which was for all of them a particularly tragic ordeal.

I must finally indicate, to conclude this part, that the Germans proceeded to the mobilisation of women for war work. I produce as Exhibit RF 745 the ordinance of the 26 January 1942, completing the war organisation of labour service for the young women of Lorraine.

Then we find an ordinance of the 2 February 1943 - which will become Exhibit RF 746 concerning the declaration of men and women for the accomplishment of tasks pertaining to national defence. This is taken from the German official bulletin, 1943, Page 26. This ordinance concerns Alsace.

The following Exhibit RF 747, deals with Lorraine. This is an ordinance of 8 February 1943, concerning the enrolment of men and women for tasks relating to the organisation of labour. The Tribunal will note that the ordinance concerning Alsace used the expression " tasks of interest to national defence", whereas the ordinance relative to Lorraine specifies simply "tasks concerning the organisation of labour", but in principle these are the same. Article 1 of this second ordinance, refers to the ordinance of the General Delegate for the Organisation of Labour, relative to the declaration of men and women for tasks of interest to national defence, etc. It is thus a case of making not only men, but also women, work for the German war effort. I shall read for the Tribunal an extract from a newspaper article which comments on this legislation and likewise on the measures which Gauleiter Wagner proposed to undertake in this connection. This constitutes Exhibit RF 748, taken from the newspaper Dernieres Nouvelles de Strasbourg, dated 23rd February 1943.

"In his Karlsruhe speech Gauleiter Robert Wagner stressed that measures of total mobilisation would be applied to Alsace, and that the authorities would abstain from any bureaucratic working method. The Alsatian labour offices have already invited the first category of mobilisable young women to fill out the enlistment."

Here is the second passage of the same article.

"In principle, all women who until the present have worked only at home, who have had to care only for their husbands and who have no other relatives, shall work a full day, Many married men who until now had never offered to help their wives with the household work will be obliged to put their shoulder to the wheel. They will work in the household and do errands. With a little goodwill, everything will work out. Women who have received a professional education will be put, if possible, to tasks related to their professions, on condition that they have an important bearing on the war effort. This prescription applies only to all feminine professions which imply care given to other persons."

Here again a rather comical or clumsily worded presentation should not prevent one from perceiving the odious character of these measures, which obliged French women to work for the German war effort.

THE PRESIDENT: We will adjourn now for ten minutes.

(A recess was taken)

M. FAURE: Mr. Dodd would like to speak to the Tribunal concerning a question he wishes to put.

MR. DODD: Mr. President, I ask to be heard briefly to inform this Tribunal that the affiant Andreas Pfaffenberger, whom the Tribunal directed the prosecution for the United States to locate, if possible, was located yesterday and he is here in Nuremberg today. He is available for the cross-examination which, if I remember correctly, was requested by Counsel for the defendant Kaltenbrunner.

THE PRESIDENT: Was his affidavit read?

MR. DODD: Yes, your Honour, it was.

THE PRESIDENT: And on the condition that he should be brought here for cross-examination?

MR. DODD: Yes, Sir. He asked for him to be brought, if I recall it.

THE PRESIDENT: Does counsel for Kaltenbrunner wish to cross-examine him now - I mean, not this moment - does he still wish to cross-examine him?

DR. KAUFFMANN (counsel for defendant Kaltenbrunner): I believe that the defendant Kaltenbrunner does not need the testimony of this witness. However, I would have to take this question up with him once more, for up till today it was not certain that Pfaffenberger would be in court, and if he is to be cross-examined and to testify, I believe Kaltenbrunner would have to be present at the hearing.

THE PRESIDENT: It seems somewhat unfortunate that this witness should be brought here for cross-examination and that then you should be saying that you do not want to cross-examine him, after reading the affidavit. It seems to me that the reasonable thing to do would be to make up your mind whether you do, or do not, want to cross-examine him, and I should have thought that would have been done and he would have been brought here, if you wanted to cross-examine, and not brought here if you did not want to cross-examine. Anyway, as he has been brought here now, it seems to me that if you want to cross-examine him you must do so. Mr. Dodd, can he be kept here for some time?

MR. DODD: He can, your Honour, except that he was in a concentration camp, for six years, and we have to keep him here under certain security, and it is somewhat of a hardship on him to be kept too long. We would like not to keep him any longer than necessary. We located him with some difficulty with the help of the United States Forces.

DR. KAUFFMANN: In perhaps two or three days we might wish to cross-examine; perhaps two or three days.

THE PRESIDENT: I imagine that after the affidavit had been read, you demanded to cross-examine him and that he has therefore been produced - well, in those circumstances it seems to me unreasonable that you should ask that he should now be kept for two or three days when he is produced. Mr. Dodd, would it be possible to keep him here until Monday?

MR. DODD: Yes, he can be kept here until Monday.

THE PRESIDENT: We will keep him here until Monday, and you can cross-examine as you wish. You understand what I mean; when an affidavit has been put in and one of the defence counsel said that he wants to cross-examine him, he ought to inform the prosecution if, after reading and considering the affidavit, they find that they do not want to cross-examine him; they ought to inform the prosecution so as to avoid all the cost and trouble of bringing a witness from some distance off. Do you follow?

DR. KAUFFMANN: I will proceed with the cross-examination on Monday.

THE PRESIDENT: Yes.

M. FAURE: Mr. President, I would ask the Tribunal whether they would agree to hear the witness Emil Reuter at this point?

(EMIL REUTER, a witness on behalf of the French prosecution takes the stand.)

THE PRESIDENT: What is your name?

THE WITNESS: Reuter, Emil.

THE PRESIDENT: Emil Reuter, do you swear to speak without hate nor fear, to speak the truth, all the truth, only the truth? Raise the right hand and say, "I swear."

(The witness repeated the oath in French.)

THE PRESIDENT: You may sit down.

DIRECT EXAMINATION BY M. FAURE:

Q. M. Reuter, you are a lawyer of the Luxembourg Bar?

A. Yes.

Q. You are President of the Chamber of Deputies in Luxembourg?

A. Yes.

Q. You had been exercising these functions at the time of the invasion of the Grand Duchy of Luxembourg by the German troops?

A. Yes.

Q. Can you give us any indication on the fact that the Government of the Reich had, a few days before the invasion of Luxembourg, given to the Government of the Grand Duchy assurances of its peaceful intentions?

A. In August 1939 the German Minister for Luxembourg gave to the Minister of Foreign Affairs of the country a statement according to which the German Reich, in the event of a European war, would respect the independence and neutrality of the country, provided that the Luxembourg Grand Duchy should not violate its own neutrality. A few days before the invasion, in May, 1940, the Germans constructed pontoon bridges over half of the Moselle River which separates the two countries. An explanation from the German Minister in Luxembourg tried to represent such construction of pontoon bridges as landing stages in the interest of navigation. In the general public opinion, these installations were really of a military character.

Q. Can you tell us about the situation of public authorities in Luxembourg, following the departure of Her Royal Highness, the Grand Duchess, and of her Government?

A. The further administration of the country was ensured by a government commission which possessed the necessary powers bestowed upon it by the competent constitutional authorities. There was, therefore, no lack of authority in the administration.

Q. Is it not true that the Germans claimed, upon their arrival in that country, that the Government had failed to carry out its functions, and that following the departure of the Government there was no regular authority in the Grand Duchy of Luxembourg?

A. Yes, indeed. Such a declaration was made by the Ministers of the Reich in Luxembourg before a Parliamentary Commission.

Q. Do I understand correctly that these statements on the part of the German authorities did not in fact correspond to the truth inasmuch as you have told us that there did exist a higher organism for the administration of the country?

A. This statement did not correspond to the reality. It was evidently aimed at usurping authority.

Q. M. Reuter, the Germans never proclaimed by law the annexation of Luxembourg. Do you consider that the measures adopted by the Germans in that country were equivalent to annexation?

A. The measures that were taken by the Germans in the Grand Duchy of Luxembourg were obviously equivalent to an annexation of that country. A few days after the invasion the leaders of the Reich in Luxembourg stated in public and official speeches that the annexation by law would occur at a time which would be freely selected by the Fuehrer. The proof of this de facto annexation is shown in a clear manner by the whole series of ordinances which the Germans published in the Grand Duchy.

Q. The Germans organised a census in Luxembourg. In the form that was given the inhabitants of Luxembourg to effect the census, there was one question concerning the native or usual language, and also another question as to the racial background of the individual. Are you prepared to assert that in view of these two questions this census was considered as having the character of a plebiscite?

A. From the comminatory instructions published by the German authorities in connection with this census, the political purpose was obvious; therefore public opinion never envisaged this census except as a sort of attempt to achieve a plebiscite camouflaged as a census, a political operation destined to give a certain justification to the annexation which was to follow.

Q. The report of the Luxembourg Government does not give any indication of the statistical results of this census, specifically with regard to the political question of which I spoke a moment ago. Would you be kind enough to tell us why these statistical data are not to be found in any document?

A. The complete statistical data have never been collected, because after a partial examination of the first results the German authorities noted that only an infinitesimal fraction of the population had answered the two tricky questions in the German sense. The German authorities then preferred to stop the process, and the forms distributed in the country for obtaining the answers were never collected.

Q. Do you remember the date of the census?

A. This census must have taken place in 1942.

Q. After the census the Germans realised that there was no majority, and not even any considerable part of the population which was desirous of being incorporated into the German Reich. However, did they continue to apply their measures of annexation?

A. Measures tending to Germanisation, and later to the annexation of the country, were continued, and later on they were even reinforced by further new measures.

Q. Am I to understand, therefore, that during the application of these measures the Germans could not be ignorant of the fact that the Luxembourg population was opposed to them?

A. There can be no doubt at all on this question.

Q. Can you tell us whether it is correct that the German authorities obliged members of the constabulary force and the police to take an oath of allegiance to the Chancellor of the Reich?

A. Yes. This was forced upon the constabulary corps and the police with very serious threats and punishments. Recalcitrants were usually deported, if I remember rightly, to Sachsenhausen, and on the approach of the Russian Army all or a part of the recalcitrants who were in the camp were shot (about 150).

Q. Can you tell us anything concerning the transfer - I believe the Germans call it "Umsiedlung" - of a certain number of inhabitants and families living in your country?

A. The transplanting was ordered by the German authority of Luxembourg for elements which appeared to be unfit for assimilation or unworthy of or undesirable for residence on the frontiers of the Reich.

Q. Can you indicate the approximate number of people who were victims of this transplanting?

A. There must have been about 7000 people who were transplanted in this manner, because we found in Luxembourg a list mentioning between 2800 and 2900 homes or families.

Q. These indications are based on knowledge you received as President of the Chamber of Deputies?

A. Not exactly, the list was found in Luxembourg; it is still deposited there and the office of War Criminals took cognisance of it, like all the judiciary authorities in Luxembourg.

Q. Can you state, M. Reuter, how the people who were transplanted were informed of this measure concerning them, and how much time they had to get ready?

A. The families to be transplanted were never given notice in advance, officially at least. About six o'clock in the morning, the Gestapo rang at the door, and they notified those who were selected to be ready for departure within one or two hours with a minimum of luggage. Then they were taken to the station and put on a train for the camp to which they were at first to be sent.

Q. Can you tell us whether these measures were applied to people whom you know personally?

A. I know personally a large number of people who were transplanted among them members of my own family, a great number of colleagues of the Chamber of Deputies, many members of the Bar, many magistrates and so forth.

Q. In addition to these transplantations, were there deportations to concentration camps? This is another question.

A. Yes, there were deportations to concentration camps which everyone knew about. The number of such deportations in the Grand Duchy may be approximately four thousand.

Q. M. Reuter, it has been established, through their ordinances, that the German authorities prescribed compulsory military service, - I will not ask you, therefore, any question on this particular point. However, I would like to ask you whether you are able to state, approximately, the number of Luxembourg citizens who were enrolled in the Germany Army.

A. The young people who were incorporated into the German Army by force belonged to five classes, beginning with the class of 1920. The number is about eleven thousand to twelve thousand, at least. A certain number of them, I think about one-third, succeeded in avoiding conscription, and became refractory. Others later deserted the German Army and fled to other countries.

Q. Can you indicate the approximate number of Luxembourgers who died as a result of their forced enlistment?

A. At the end of September 1944 we had about two thousand five hundred dead. Searches have continued and at present, I think, we have established the names of at least three thousand.

Q. The sanctions that had been provided to force the enlistment of the Luxembourgers, were they very severe?

A. These sanctions were extremely severe. First of all, the young people who were refractory were pursued and hunted by the police and by the Gestapo. Then they were brought before various types of Tribunals, in Luxembourg, France, Belgium, or Germany. Their families were deported; the family fortune was generally confiscated. The penalties pronounced by the Tribunals against these young people were likewise very severe. The death penalty was general, or else imprisonment, forced labour, deportation to concentration camps. Some of them were released later on, but there were some who were shot as hostages after having been released.

Q. I would like to ask one last question. Do you think it is possible that these measures, which constituted a de facto annexation of Luxembourg, could have been unknown to the persons who belonged to the Reich Government, or to the German High Command?

A. I believe that it is hardly possible that such a situation could have been unknown to the members of the Reich and the Supreme Military Authority. My opinion is based on the following facts: First of all, our young people, when mobilised by force, frequently protested, at the time of their arrival in Germany, by invoking the fact that they were all of Luxembourg nationality, and that they were the victims of force, so that the military authorities must have been informed of the situation in the Grand Duchy.

In the second place, several Ministers of the Reich, among them Thierack, Rust and Ley, visited the Grand Duchy of Luxembourg, and could see for themselves the situation of the country and the reaction of the population: other high political personalities of the Reich, such as Bormann and Sauckel, also paid visits.

Finally there were German decrees and ordinances, concerning the denationalisation of certain categories of Luxembourg citizens. These ordinances bore the signature of the Minister of the Reich. The executive measures implementing these ordinances were published in the Official Gazette of the Reich Ministry of the Interior, under the signature of the Minister of Interior Frick, with the indication that these instructions were to be communicated to all the superior

Reich authorities.

M. FAURE: I thank you. Those are all the questions I have to put to you.

THE PRESIDENT: Is there any member of the defendants' counsel who wishes to ask the witness any questions? (No response). Then the witness can retire.

M. FAURE: Mr. President, am I to understand that the witness will not have to remain any longer at the disposal of the Tribunal and he may return to his home?

THE PRESIDENT: Certainly.

M. FAURE: I had stopped my presentation at the end of the second part. That is to say, I have examined so far, in the first place, the elimination of the French formation or culture and, secondly, the imposition of German rules.

(c) Measures for transplantation and colonisation

The German authorities applied, in these annexed departments, characteristic methods for the transport of populations. It so happens that, as the witness from Luxembourg was heard sooner than I had anticipated, the Tribunal is already informed of the aspect which these measures of transplantation assumed in the annexed territories.

The situation which I am about to describe with respect to Alsace-Lorraine is, indeed, analogous to the situation which existed with regard to the Grand Duchy of Luxembourg. The principal purpose of the application of such methods by the Germans was to enable them to colonise by bringing German subjects into the country, who then seized the lands and property of the inhabitants who had been expelled.

A second advantage was the elimination of groups considered especially difficult to assimilate. I should like to quote in this connection - this will be Exhibit RF 749 - what Gauleiter Wagner stated in a speech given at Saverne, according to the Dernieres Nouvelles de Strasbourg, of 15 December 1941.

> "Today we must make up our mind. In the moment of our nation's supreme struggle - a struggle in which you, too, must participate - I can only say to anyone who says: 'I am a Frenchman.' 'Get the hell out of here! In Germany there is only room for Germans'."

From the very beginning the Germans proceeded, firstly, to the expulsion of individuals or small groups, especially Jews and members of the teaching profession. Moreover, as is shown by a document which I have already cited this morning as Exhibit RF 701, and which was the first general protest made by the French delegation, under date of 3 September 1940, the Germans authorised the people of Alsace-Lorraine to return to their homes only if they acknowledged themselves to be of German origin. Now, the Tribunal will understand that these restrictions upon the return of refugees were in themselves equivalent to expulsion. Mass expulsions began in September 1940. I now submit in this connection Exhibit RF 750; it is again a note from the French armistice delegation taken from the files of the Court of Justice. I am now reading this document, paragraph 2.

> "Since then it has been brought to the knowledge of the French Government that the German authorities are proceeding to mass expulsions of families in the three Eastern departments. Every day French citizens, forced to abandon all of their belongings on the spot, are driven into unoccupied France in groups of 800 to 1,000 persons."

It is only the 19th of September. On the 3rd of November the Germans undertook the systematic expulsion of the populations of the Moselle region. This operation was accomplished with extreme perfidy. The Germans, as a matter of fact, gave the Lorrainers of certain localities the choice of either going to Eastern Germany or to

France. They gave them only a few hours to make up their minds. Moreover, they sought to promote the belief that such a choice was imposed upon the Lorrainers as a result of an agreement reached with the French authorities.

From the physical point of view, the transport of these people was effected under very difficult conditions. The Lorrainers were allowed to take away only a very small part of their personal belongings and a sum of 2,000 francs, plus 1,000 francs for the children. On 18th November, four trains filled with Lorrainers who had been torn away from their homes were headed for Lyons. The arrival in unoccupied France of these people who had been so sorely tried was for them nevertheless, an opportunity for nobly manifesting their patriotic sentiments. With regard to the facts which I have presented I submit to the Tribunal Exhibit RF 751, which is a note of protest on the part of the French delegation signed by General Doyen, dated 18th November 1940. I shall read excerpts of this Document RF 751, beginning with paragraph 3 of Page 1.

"France is faced with an act of force which is in formal contradiction to the armistice convention as well as the assurances, recently given, of a desire for collaboration between the two countries. On the contrary, in Article 16, which the German commission had frequently invoked, with specific regard to the departments of the East, the armistice convention stipulates the reinstallation of refugees in the regions in which they were domiciled. The creation of new refugees constitutes, therefore, a violation of the armistice convention. France is faced with an unjust act affecting peaceful populations against whom the Reich has no grievance, and who, settled for centuries on these territories, have made of them a particularly prosperous region.

The unexpected decision of the German authorities is likewise an inhuman act. In the very middle of winter, without warning, families have to leave their homes, taking with them only a strict minimum of personal property and a sum of money absolutely insufficient to enable them to live for even a few weeks. Thousands of Frenchmen were thus suddenly hurled into misery without their country, already so heavily tried, and surprised by the suddenness and amplitude of the measures adopted without its knowledge, being in a position to assure them, from one day to the next, a normal livelihood. This exodus and the conditions under which it is taking place causes most painful and sorrowful impressions throughout the French nation. The French people are particularly disturbed by the explanations given to the Lorrainers, according to which the French Government was reputed to be the source of their misfortune.

It is that impression in fact, which the poster in certain villages, where the populations had to choose between leaving for eastern Germany or for unoccupied France, was intended to convey.

The poster is appended hereto, but we are not in possession of it's text.

That also encouraged the belief that these populations had themselves requested permission to leave, following the appeal broadcast by the Bordeaux radio. Even if we admit that such appeals had been made by radio it should be noted that the Bordeaux radio station is under German control. The good faith of the Lorrainers has been deceived as was shown by their reaction on arrival in the free zone."

In spite of these protests, the expulsions continued. They reached a total of about 70,000 people, augmented by the deportation of Alsatians and Lorrainers to Eastern Germany and to Poland. These deportations were meant to create terror; and they particularly affected the families of men who had rightfully decided to refuse the

German demand for forced labour and military service. I am presenting, regarding the whole question, a French protest dated 3 September 1942; it is Exhibit RF 752.

Since I do not wish to read to the Tribunal texts dealing with an identical subject I submit this document solely to show that this protest was made, and I believe that I can refrain from reading its content.

I shall refer, desiring to give only a short citation, to a document belonging to the American prosecution. This document bears the number R-114. It is a memorandum of the minutes of a meeting which took place between several officials of the SS concerning general directions in regard to the treatment of deported Alsatians.

It will be observed that this document has already been submitted by my American colleagues as Exhibit USA 314, the French Exhibit No. is RF 753. I merely wish to read one paragraph of that document, which may be interpreted as a supplement to this problem of deportation. I must say that these sentences have not been formally read in Court. The passage that I cite is on Page 2 of the document. At the end of that page there is a paragraph which begins with the letter "D":

"The following persons, members of patois-speaking communities, are to be listed for future deportation - The Gauleiter wishes to keep in these zones only the people who adhere to Germanism in their customs, their language and their general attitude, according to the cases provided for in paragraphs A to D above, mentioned. It should be noted that we shall first examine the problem of race and that we shall do so in such a manner that people of racial value will be deported to Germany proper, and people of inferior racial value will be deported to France."

Finally, I should like to read to the Tribunal a few sentences from a newspaper article, which appeared in "Dernieres Nouvelles de Strasbourg," August 31 1942 - We are here dealing with a citation and not a document.

"On the 28th of August the families designated hereafter, of the Arrondissements of Mulhouse and Guebwiller, were deported to the Reich in order that they might recover a trustworthy German ' outlook in National Socialist surroundings. In several cases the persons involved did not conceal their hostility, in that they stirred up sentiments of opposition, spoke French in public in a provocative manner, did not obey the ordinances concerning the education of youth, or, in other ways showed a lack of loyalty."

I would now like to indicate to the Tribunal that deportation or transportation entails also the spoliation of property. This is not merely a fact; for the Germans it is a law. Indeed, there is an ordinance, of 28 January, 1943, which appeared in the Official Bulletin for 1943, Page 40, bearing the title, "Ordinance concerning the Safeguarding of Property in Lorraine as a Result of Transplantation Measures." I have placed this ordinance before you as Exhibit RF 754. I would like to read Article One and the first paragraph of Article Two. I believe that the title itself is a sufficient indication of the contents.

"Article One. The safeguarding of property of people transplanted from Lorraine to the Greater German Reich or to territory placed under the sovereign power of Germany has been entrusted to the Transfer Services for Lorraine under the Chief of the Administration.

Article Two. These services are authorised to put in effective safekeeping the property of the Lothringians who have been transplanted, in order that such property may be administered, and - in so far as orders may have been given for this - exploited."

This ordinance, therefore, still manifests some scruples of form. The intention is to "safeguard," but we now know what the word "safeguard" means in Nazi terminology. We have already seen what safeguarding meant in the case of works of art and Jewish property. Even here, we have been specifically warned that the term "safeguard" carries with it the right of disposal or exploitation.

Other texts are even more specific or clear.

Here is Exhibit RF 755. This is the ordinance of 6 November 1940, pertaining to the declaration of property in Lorraine belonging to the enemies of the people and of the Reich. And on the same subject I shall also submit to you Exhibit RF 756, which is the regulation of 13 July 1940, applying to property in Alsace belonging to the enemies of the people and of the Reich. These two texts, one of which applies to Alsace and the other to Lorraine, permit the seizure and confiscation of properties designated as "enemy property." Now, to realise the extent of the property covered by this term, I will read this exhibit: -

> "Any objects and rights of any nature whatsoever, without regard to conditions of title, which are used for, or intended for use in, activities hostile to the people of Germany or the Reich will be considered as property belonging to the German people and to the Reich.
>
> Such stipulation shall apply to the entire patrimony:-
>
> (a) of all political parties, as well as of secondary or complementary organisations depending thereon;
>
> (b) of lodges and similar associations
>
> (c) of Jews;
>
> (d) of Frenchmen who have acquired property in Alsace since 11 November 1918;
>
> The Chief of the Administration Department and the Police will decide what patrimony in addition to the property mentioned above is likewise to be considered as property belonging to the enemies of the German people and of the Reich. He will likewise decide on doubtful cases."

We see, therefore, that in spite of the title, we are not dealing here with the measures of sequestration of enemy property taken in all countries within the scope of the laws of war. First of all, these are measures of definite confiscation, and in addition, they are applied to the property of numerous individuals who are in no wise subjects of enemy countries. We also see at this point the absolutely arbitrary power placed in the hands of the administration.

These texts are accompanied by many regulations; although the spoliations are particularly important in Alsace and in Lorraine, I shall not speak of them here in more detail, as the prosecution has already dealt with the subject. I shall merely limit myself to the mentioning of two institutions special to Alsace and to Lorraine, - that is, agricultural colonisation, and industrial colonisation.

In the first place, agricultural colonisation is not a term that has been invented by the prosecution; it is an expression which the Germans used. I submit in this connection, Exhibit RF 757, which is the ordinance of 7 December 1940, "pertaining to the new regime of settlement or colonisation in Lorraine." I shall read the beginning of this Document No. 757.

> "Real estate which has been vacated in Lorraine as a result of deportations will serve principally for the reconstitution of a German peasant class and for the requirements of internal colonisation. In this connection, and specifically in order to set up the required programmes, I order, by virtue of the powers which have been conferred upon me by the Fuehrer the following:
>
> Article One. Real estate property of individuals deported from Lorraine shall be

seized and confiscated for the benefit of the Chief of the Civil Administration."

I will not cite the second paragraph of Article One, but I will cite Article Two:

"Agricultural properties or forest properties which are seized in consequence of the ordinance concerning enemy property of the people and the Reich in Lorraine are confiscated. In so far as they are needed, they are included in the methodical organisation of the region."

Article Three:

"In addition to the cases provided for in Articles One and Two, and according to the needs, other real estate property may be included in the programmes for methodical reorganisation if appropriate compensation is provided for.

The Chief of the Civilian Administration and the Services designated by him will decide upon the amount and nature of the compensation. Any recourse to the law on the part of the person involved is forbidden."

Thus the Tribunal can see in a striking manner the processes and the methods pursued by the German authorities.

The first ordinance, cited earlier, spoke only of safeguarding the property of people who had been deported or displaced. A second ordinance now speaks of confiscations. It still refers only to the notion of enemies of the people and of the Reich.

The third ordinance is more complete, since it comprises confiscation prescriptions which are quite formal in their character, and which are no longer qualified as "safeguarding property which has become vacant as the result of deportations."

This agricultural colonisation of which I have spoken assumed a special importance in Lorraine. On the other hand, it is in Alsace that we find the greatest number of measures involving a veritable industrial colonisation. These measures consisted in stripping the French industrial enterprises for the benefit of German firms. On this subject there are protests of the French delegation to the Armistice Commission.

I submit three of these protests as Exhibits RF 758, 759 and 760, which are notes under date of - respectively - 27 April 1941, 9 May 1941 and 8 April 1943. I believe that it is preferable for me not to read these to the Tribunal and that I merely ask the Tribunal to take judicial notice of them, as proof of the existence of these protests, because I fear that such a reading would be a mere repetition to the Tribunal, to whom the matter of economic spoliation has already been explained in sufficient detail.

I shall say, finally, that the Germans carried their audacity to the point of demanding the seizure in unoccupied France and the transportation to Alsace of assets belonging to French companies which were by this means stripped of their property and actually "colonised." I am speaking of assets belonging to companies in the other zone of France, under the control of the regular shareholders of such companies.

I think it is worth while considering just one example of such procedure, contained in a very short document, which I submit to you as Exhibit RF 761. This document appears in the Archives of the French Agencies of the Armistice Commission, to which it had been sent by the director of the company mentioned in the document. It is a paper which is partly written in German and partly translated into French - in the same document - and it is signed by the German Commissioner for a French enterprise called the Societe Alsacienne et Lorraine d'Electricite. In Alsace this enterprise had been placed illegally under the administration of this Commissioner; and the Commissioner - as the document will show - had come to Paris to seize the remainder of the Company's assets. He drafted this document, which he signed, and which he also made the President of the French company sign. This document is of interest as revealing the insolence of German procedure and also the German's odd conception of law. I quote now:

> "Today the undersigned has instructed me that in future I am strictly forbidden to take legal action with regard to the property of the former Societe Alsacienne et Lorraine d'Electricite. If I should transgress this order in any way, I know that I shall be punished.
>
> Paris, 10 March 1941.
> Signed: Kucka.
> F. B. Kommissar.
> Signed: Garnier."

Now, this German economic colonisation in the areas annexed was to serve as an experiment for the application of similar methods on a broader scale.

There will be submitted to the Tribunal, in this connection, a document concerning a colonisation attempt in the French Department Ardennes. On this procedure of annexation by the Germans of Alsace and of Lorraine, many other items could be cited, and I could submit many more documents - even if I were to deal only with the circumstances and the documents which are useful from the point of view of our own Prosecution.

I want to limit myself in order to save the time of the Tribunal and to comply with the necessities of this trial where so many items have to be discussed. Therefore I have limited myself to the submission of documents, or to examples, which are particularly characteristic. I believe that this documentation will enable the Tribunal to appraise the criminality of the German undertakings which I have brought to its attention - criminality which is particularly characteristic in the matter of military conscription, which is a criminal offence, since it entails death. At the same time I believe the Tribunal can evaluate the grave sufferings that were imposed for five years on the populace of these French provinces, already so sorely tried in the course of history.

I have submitted a few details which may have seemed ridiculous, or facetious, but I did so because I thought it desirable that one should visualise the oppression exercised by the German Administration in all circumstances of life, even in private life, that general oppression characterised by its attempt to destroy and annihilate, and extended in a most complete manner over the departments and regions which were annexed.

I believe that the Tribunal will possibly prefer me to leave until tomorrow my comments with respect to the Grand Duchy of Luxembourg.

I would like, moreover, to have the Tribunal's assent concerning a question of testimony.

I should like to put a witness on the stand, but it is only a little while ago that I gave the Tribunal a letter concerning this request. May I ask to be excused for not having done so earlier because there has been some uncertainty on this point.

If the Tribunal finds it convenient, I should like to have this witness here at tomorrow, Saturday morning's, session. I state that this witness would be M. Koos Vorink, who is of Dutch nationality. I also wish to say for the benefit of the defence, that the question I would like to submit to the witness will deal with certain items concerning Germanisation in the Netherlands.

THE PRESIDENT: Do you wish to call him tomorrow?

M. FAURE: If that is convenient to the Tribunal.

THE PRESIDENT: Yes, certainly, call him tomorrow.

M. FAURE: If it pleases the Tribunal, his testimony could be taken after the recess tomorrow morning.

DR. STEINBAUER (Counsel for defendant Seyss-Inquart): Mr. President, I do not wish to prolong the proceedings, but I believe it will be to the interest of justice if I ask that the Dutch witness be heard, not tomorrow, but Monday, on the assumption that Seyss-Inquart who is now ill may be expected back on that date.

THE PRESIDENT: Monsieur Faure, would it be equally convenient to you to call him on Monday?

M. FAURE: Mr. President, I do not desire to vex the defence, but the witness might like to leave Nuremberg fairly promptly. Perhaps I might suggest that he be heard tomorrow and that after he has been heard, if counsel for the defendant Seyss-Inquart expresses his desire to cross- examine him, the witness could remain until Monday's session.

If, on the other hand, after having heard the questions involved the counsel considers that there is no need for any cross-examination, then Seyss-Inquart's absence would not matter. But I will naturally accept the decision of the Tribunal.

THE PRESIDENT: That seems a very reasonable suggestion.

DR. STEINBAUER: I am agreeable to the suggestion of the French prosecutor.

THE PRESIDENT: We will adjourn now.

(The Tribunal adjourned until 1000 hours on 2nd February, 1946.)

About Coda Books

Most Coda books are edited and endorsed by Emmy Award winning film maker and military historian Bob Carruthers, producer of Discovery Channel's Line of Fire and Weapons of War and BBC's Both Sides of the Line. Long experience and strong editorial control gives the history enthusiast the ability to buy with confidence. Where possible the books draw on rare primary sources to give new insights into a fascinating subject.

All 22 volumes of the Nuremberg Trials are now available.
Visit www.codabooks.com for more information

www.ingramcontent.com/pod-product-compliance
Lightning Source LLC
Chambersburg PA
CBHW020326240426
43665CB00044B/649